A People & A Nation

A HISTORY OF THE UNITED STATES

VOLUME I: TO 1877

Ninth Edition

Mary Beth Norton
Cornell University

Carol Sheriff
College of William and Mary

David W. Blight
Yale University

Howard P. Chudacoff
Brown University

Fredrik Logevall
Cornell University

Beth Bailey
Temple University

 WADSWORTH
CENGAGE Learning

Australia • Brazil • Japan • Korea • Mexico • Singapore • Spain • United Kingdom • United States

A People and A Nation, Volume I: To 1877,
Ninth Edition
Mary Beth Norton, Carol Sheriff, David W.
Blight, Howard P. Chudacoff, Fredrik Logevall,
Beth Bailey

Senior Publisher: Suzanne Jeans

Senior Sponsoring Editor: Ann West

Senior Development Editor: Julia Giannotti

Assistant Editor: Megan Chrisman

Senior Marketing Manager: Katherine Bates

Marketing Coordinator: Lorreen Pelletier

Marketing Communications Manager:
  Caitlin Green

Senior Content Project Manager: Jane Lee

Senior Art Director: Cate Rickard Barr

Senior Print Buyer: Rebecca Cross

Senior Rights Acquisition Specialist: Katie Huha

Production Service: Elm Street Publishing
  Services

Text Designer: Debby Dutton

Senior Photo Manager: Jennifer Meyer Dare

Cover Image: Catlin, George (1796–1872).
  Bod-a-sin, Chief of the Tribe, 1830. Oil on
  canvas 29 × 24 in. Smithsonian American
  Art Museum, Washington, DC/Art
  Resource, NY.

Compositor: Integra Software Services Pvt. Ltd.

For product information and technology assistance, contact us at
Cengage Learning Customer & Sales Support, 1-800-354-9706

For permission to use material from this text or product,
submit all requests online at **www.cengage.com/permissions**.

Further permissions questions can be emailed to
permissionrequest@cengage.com.

Library of Congress Control Number: 2010932778

Student Edition:

ISBN-13: 978-0-495-91589-8

ISBN-10: 0-495-91589-0

Wadsworth
20 Channel Center Street
Boston, MA 02210
USA

Cengage Learning is a leading provider of customized learning solutions with office locations around the globe, including Singapore, the United Kingdom, Australia, Mexico, Brazil and Japan. Locate your local office at **international. cengage.com/region**

Cengage Learning products are represented in Canada by Nelson Education, Ltd.

For your course and learning solutions, visit **www.cengage.com**.

Purchase any of our products at your local college store or at our preferred online store **www.cengagebrain.com**.

Printed in the United States of America
1 2 3 4 5 6 7 14 13 12 11 10

Brief Contents

Contents

1 Three Old Worlds Create a New, 1492–1600 2

2 Europeans Colonize North America, 1600–1650 32

3   North America in the Atlantic World, 1650–1720   58

4   American Society Transformed, 1720–1770   86

5 Severing the Bonds of Empire, 1754–1774   114

6 A Revolution, Indeed, 1774–1783   140

7 Forging a National Republic, 1776–1789   164

8 The Early Republic: Conflicts at Home and Abroad, 1789–1800   192

11   The Restless North, 1815–1860   276

12   Reform and Politics, 1824–1845   304

13 The Contested West, 1815–1860   330

14 Slavery and America's Future: The Road to War, 1845–1861   360

15 Transforming Fire: The Civil War, 1861–1865   388

16 Reconstruction: An Unfinished Revolution, 1865–1877   426

Special Features

Maps

Figures

Tables

Links to the World

Legacy for A People and A Nation

Visualizing the Past

Preface

In this ninth edition, *A People and A Nation* has undergone significant revisions, while still retaining the narrative strength and focus that have made it so popular with students and teachers alike. In the years since the publication of the eighth edition, new material has been uncovered, novel interpretations advanced, and new themes have come to the forefront of American historical scholarship. All of the authors have incorporated those findings into this text.

Like other teachers and students, we are always re-creating our past, restructuring our memory, and rediscovering the personalities and events that have influenced us, injured us, and bedeviled us. This book represents our continuing rediscovery of America's history—its diverse people and the nation they created and nurtured. As this book demonstrates, there are many different Americans and many different memories. We have sought to present as many of them as possible, in both triumph and tragedy, in both division and unity.

About *A People and A Nation*

A People and A Nation, first published in 1982, was the first major textbook in the United States to fully integrate social and political history. From the outset, the authors have been determined to tell the story of *all* the people of the United States. This book's hallmarks have been its melding of social and political history and its movement beyond history's common focus on public figures and events to examine the daily life of America's people. All editions of the book have stressed the interaction of public policy and personal experience, the relationship between domestic concerns and foreign affairs, the various manifestations of popular culture, and the multiple origins of America and Americans. We have consistently built our narrative on a firm foundation in primary sources—on both well-known and obscure letters, diaries, public documents, oral histories, and artifacts of material culture. We have long challenged readers to think about the meaning of American history—not just to memorize facts. Both students and instructors have repeatedly told us how much they appreciate and enjoy our approach to the past.

As has been true since the first edition, each chapter opens with a dramatic vignette focusing on an individual or a group of people. These vignettes introduce key themes, which then frame the chapters in succinct introductions and summaries. Numerous maps, tables, graphs, and charts provide readers with the necessary geographical and statistical context for observations in the text. Carefully selected illustrations—many of them unique to this book—offer readers visual insight into the topics under discussion, especially because the authors have written the captions. In this edition, as in all previous ones, we have sought to incorporate up-to-date scholarship, readability, a clear structure, critical thinking, and instructive illustrative material on every page.

Themes in This Book

Several themes and questions stand out in our continuing effort to integrate political, social, and cultural history. We study the many ways that Americans have defined themselves—gender, race, class, region, ethnicity, religion, sexual orientation—and the many subjects that have reflected their multidimensional experiences. We highlight the remarkably diverse everyday lives of the American people—in cities and on farms and ranches, in factories and in corporate headquarters, in neighborhoods and in legislatures, in love relationships and in hate groups, in recreation and in work, in the classroom and in military uniform, in secret national security conferences and in public foreign relations debates, in church and in voluntary associations, in polluted environments and in conservation areas. We pay particular attention to lifestyles, diet and dress, family life and structure, labor conditions, gender roles, migration and mobility, childbearing, and child rearing. We explore how Americans have entertained and informed themselves by discussing their music, sports, theater, print media, film, radio, television, graphic arts, and literature, in both "high" culture and popular culture. We study how technology— such as the internal combustion engine and the computer—has influenced Americans' lives.

Americans' personal lives have always interacted with the public realm of politics and government. To understand how Americans have sought to protect their different ways of life and to work out solutions to thorny problems, we emphasize their expectations of governments at the local, state, and federal levels; governments' role in providing answers; the lobbying of interest groups; the campaigns and outcomes of elections; and the hierarchy of power in any period. Because the United States has long been a major participant in world affairs, we explore America's participation in wars, interventions in other nations, empire-building, immigration patterns, images of foreign peoples, cross-national cultural ties, and international economic trends.

What's New in This Edition

Planning for the ninth edition began at a two-day authors' meeting at the Cengage offices in Boston. There we discussed the most recent scholarship in the field, the reviews of the eighth edition solicited from instructors, and the findings of our own continuing research. Our author meetings, which we greatly enjoy, are always characterized by intellectual exhilaration and vigorous discussion as we exchange views and ideas.

This edition builds on its predecessors in continuing to enhance the global perspective on American history that has characterized the book since its first edition. From the "Atlantic world" context of European colonies in North and South America to the discussion of international terrorism, the authors have incorporated the most recent globally oriented scholarship throughout the volume. As in the eighth edition, we have worked to strengthen our treatment of the diversity of America's people by examining differences within the broad ethnic categories commonly employed and by paying attention to immigration, cultural, and intellectual infusions from around the world and America's growing religious diversity. We have also stressed the incorporation of different peoples into the United States through territorial acquisition as well as through immigration. At the same time, we have integrated the discussion of such diversity into our narrative so as not to artificially isolate any group from the mainstream. We have continued the practice of placing three probing questions at the end of each chapter's introduction to guide students' reading of the pages that follow.

Primary Sources

We believe that students need lots of opportunities to engage in historical thinking around primary sources, and we have provided more opportunities for this type of work in the ninth edition. The new "Visualizing the Past" feature described below helps students engage with visual sources with guided captions and questions. In addition, the authors have identified for each chapter a set of primary sources that would add useful context for students; these are noted (with a feather icon) in the margins of the text. Students will be able to access each of these sources through links on the student CourseMate web site. Instructors who want a fully integrated online primary source reader to use in conjunction with *A People and A Nation* will find it available as an "Editor's Choice" option inside the new CourseReader for U.S. History (described in the supplements section).

As always, the authors reexamined every sentence, interpretation, map, chart, illustration, and caption, refining the narrative, presenting new examples, and bringing to the text the latest findings of scholars in many areas of history, anthropology, sociology, and political science.

Some chapter-opening vignettes are new to this edition. The maps have been completely redesigned and revised in this edition to be more dynamic, engaging, and relevant.

"Legacies," "Links to the World," and "Visualizing the Past"

Each chapter contains two brief feature essays: "Legacies for A People and A Nation" (introduced in the sixth edition) and "Links to the World" (introduced in the seventh edition). Legacies appear toward the end of each chapter and offer compelling and timely answers to students who question the relevance of historical study by exploring the historical roots of contemporary topics. New subjects of Legacies include P. T. Barnum's publicity stunts, abstinence campaigns by moral reformers, Lincoln's second inaugural address, national parks, and mass-produced toys for children. Numerous other Legacies have been updated.

"Links to the World" examine both inward and outward ties between America (and Americans) and the rest of the world. The Links appear at appropriate places in each chapter to explore specific topics at considerable length. Tightly constructed essays detail the often-little-known connections between developments here and abroad. The topics range broadly over economic, political, social, technological, medical, and cultural history, vividly demonstrating that the geographical region that is now the United States has never lived in isolation from other peoples and countries. New to this edition are Links on turkeys, writing and stationery supplies, internal improvements, filibustering, the "back to Africa" movement, study abroad programs, Tokyo Rose, and swine flu. Each Link highlights global interconnections with unusual and lively examples that will both intrigue and inform students.

We have a brand-new feature in this edition, "Visualizing the Past," which aims to give students the chance to examine primary source material and engage in critical thinking about it. For each chapter, the authors have selected one or two visual sources (including cartoons, photographic images, artwork, and magazine covers) that tell a story about the era with captions that help students understand how the careful examination of primary source content can reveal deeper insights into the period under discussion. We have chosen to focus on visual sources for this feature because these are often the hardest for instructors to find and prepare good pedagogy around—and because we have always given visual material a strong role in the text. An example from Chapter 25 includes a photograph of the women's "emergency brigade" demonstration during the 1937 sit-down strike by automobile workers in Flint, Michigan. The caption describes the scene and then asks questions that guide students toward a deeper analysis of the image—and of its historical significance.

Section-by-Section Changes in This Edition

Mary Beth Norton, who had primary responsibility for Chapters 1 through 8 and served as coordinating author, augmented the treatment of early European explorations of the Americas (including the publicist Richard Hakluyt) and now explores the use of the calumet (the so-called peace pipe) by Indian nations and Europeans alike. She expanded the discussion of religious diversity in England and its colonies and the religious impulse for colonization and revised the section on the middle passage to give more attention to the experience of enslaved captives on shipboard. To clarify chronology, she moved some material on the French and Spanish colonies in North America from Chapter 3 to Chapter 4 and in the latter greatly increased coverage of the residents of the west in the eighteenth century—Native Americans, Spaniards, and French people alike. A new opening vignette is featured in Chapter 4 about Marie-Joseph Angélique, a slave convicted of starting a fire that destroyed the merchant quarter of Montreal. New scholarship on the Seven Years' War, the American Revolution, and the Constitutional Convention has been incorporated into Chapters 5 through 7. A table now conveniently summarizes state conventions' ratification votes. More information on women's political roles and aims has been added, in conjunction with a considerably expanded treatment of partisanship in the early republic.

Carol Sheriff, responsible for Chapters 9 and 11 through 13, enhanced coverage of the nationalistic culture of the early republic and early New Orleans and revised the discussion of the War of 1812 and Aaron Burr. She has added discussions of the penny press, Henry David Thoreau, science and engineering, women's activities, and penitentiaries. The treatment of politics in general has been reworked, with special attention to political violence, and a new chart detailing the era's presidents has been included. Chapter 13 now contains considerably more information on the southwestern borderlands, includes more quotations from residents of the American West, and deals with anti-expansionism and the abuse of Indians in Catholic missions.

David W. Blight, who had primary responsibility for Chapter 10 and Chapters 14 through 16, has enhanced the discussion of the economic causes of secession and the Civil War and the economic history of the war itself, drawing on extensive new scholarship. Chapter 10 features a new chapter-opening vignette on the 1827 slave auction held at Monticello and Jefferson and Sally Hemings. He now considers the Union soldiers' ideology and has added material on the effects of the cultural impact of the large numbers of war dead in both North and South. Chapters 15 and 16 both include new treatments of judicial topics, and the latter also discusses scalawags and carpetbaggers at greater length than before.

Howard P. Chudacoff, responsible for Chapters 17 through 21 and Chapter 24, has extensively revised and updated the treatment of technological change in the late nineteenth century and of women's suffrage. He has added discussions of Native peoples in the Southwest, western folk heroes, government and water rights, labor violence in the west, female entertainers (and opposition to them from moralists like Anthony Comstock), Woodrow Wilson's racism, Marcus Garvey, and the Great Migration of African Americans to the North in the twenties. The new Chapter 20 opening vignette features the life of Frances Willard, the president of the Women's Christian Temperance Union. He has also consolidated the analysis of settlement houses in Chapter 21 to avoid repetition.

Fredrik Logevall, with primary responsibility for Chapters 22, 23, 26, and 28, updated the discussions of late nineteenth-century American imperialism and the origins of the Cold War and added new material on nurses and African American soldiers in World War I.

Beth Bailey, primarily responsible for Chapters 25, 27, and 29, incorporated new scholarship on popular culture, the institutional history of the New Deal, the ecological crisis of the thirties, the internment of Japanese citizens and Japanese Americans during World War II, the liberation of Europe, the GI Bill, and the return of veterans in the postwar period. She enhanced the discussion of wartime propaganda and censorship. The new Chapter 29 opening vignette on downwinders ties more closely to the Cold War coverage through the chapter. Parts of Chapter 29 underwent extensive revision and reorganization as well.

Logevall and Bailey shared responsibility for Chapters 30 through 33. These chapters now include expanded consideration of the struggle for civil rights and social justice in the North and the opposition to that struggle in the form of protests against school busing. Chapter 31 has a new section on the freedom and responsibilities of youth and enhanced discussions of popular culture, women in the military, and religious cults. New material has been added on foreign policy and changes in American living patterns. As is always the case, Chapter 33, which covers the recent past, underwent thorough revision and reorganization. It covers the second term of George W. Bush, the election of Barack Obama, the Great Recession, and the Iraq and Afghanistan wars.

Teaching and Learning Aids

The supplements listed here accompany the ninth edition of *A People and A Nation*. They have been created with the diverse needs of today's students and instructors in mind.

For the Instructor

- *Aplia.* Aplia™ is an online learning solution that helps students take responsibility for their learning by engaging them with course material, honing their critical thinking skills, and preparing them for class. Created by an instructor for other instructors, Aplia prompts history students to read carefully and think critically. For every chapter, text-specific exercises ask students to consider individual details that support larger historical concepts and draw conclusions rather than reciting historical facts. Every chapter includes at least one set of questions based on a map from the text. The assignments also give students experience reading and interpreting primary source documents, images, and other media. The automatically graded assignments include detailed, immediate explanations that ensure students put forth effort on a regular basis. Gradebook analytics help instructors monitor and address student performance on an individual or group basis. For more information, please visit www.aplia.com/cengage.

■ *Instructor Companion Site.* Instructors will find here all the tools they need to teach a rich and successful U.S. history survey course. The protected teaching materials include the *Instructor's Resource Manual*, written by George C. Warren of Central Piedmont Community College; a set of customizable Microsoft® PowerPoint® lecture slides, created by Barney Rickman of Valdosta State University; and a set of customizable Microsoft® PowerPoint® slides, including all the images (photos, art, and maps) from the text. The companion web site also provides instructors with access to HistoryFinder and to the Wadsworth American History Resource Center (see descriptions below). Go to www.Cengage .com/history to access this site.

■ *PowerLecture CD-ROM with ExamView® and JoinIn®.* This dual-platform, all-in-one multimedia resource includes the *Instructor's Resource Manual*; Test Bank in Word® and PDF formats; customizable Microsoft® PowerPoint® slides of both lecture outlines and images from the text; and *JoinIn®* PowerPoint slides with clicker content. Also included is ExamView®, an easy-to-use assessment and tutorial system that allows instructors to create, deliver, and customize tests in minutes. The test items, written by George C. Warren of Central Piedmont Community College, include multiple-choice, identification, geography, and essay questions.

■ *HistoryFinder.* This searchable online database allows instructors to quickly and easily search and download selections from among thousands of assets, including art, photographs, maps, primary sources, and audio/video clips. Each asset downloads directly into a Microsoft® PowerPoint® slide, allowing instructors to easily create exciting PowerPoint presentations for their classrooms.

■ *eInstructor's Resource Manual.* Written by George C. Warren of Central Piedmont Community College, this manual contains for each chapter a set of learning objectives, a comprehensive chapter outline, ideas for classroom activities, discussion questions, suggested

paper topics, and a lecture supplement. It is available on the instructor's companion web site and in the PowerLecture CD-ROM.

■ *WebTutor™ on Blackboard® and WebCT®.* With WebTutor's text-specific, preformatted content and total flexibility, instructors can easily create and manage their own custom course web site. WebTutor's course management tool gives instructors the ability to provide virtual office hours, post syllabi, set up threaded discussions, track student progress with quiz material, and much more. For students, WebTutor offers real-time access to a full array of study tools, including audio chapter summaries, practice quizzes, glossary flashcards, and web links.

■ *CourseMate.* Cengage Learning's CourseMate brings course concepts to life with interactive learning, study, and exam preparation tools that support the printed textbook. Watch student comprehension soar as your class works with the printed textbook and the *A People and A Nation* CourseMate web site, with interactive teaching and learning tools, and EngagementTracker, a first-of-its-kind tool that monitors student engagement in the course. Learn more at www.cengagebrain.com.

Student Resources

■ *CourseMate.* For students, the CourseMate web site provides an additional source of interactive learning, study, and exam preparation outside the classroom. Students will find outlines and objectives, focus questions, flashcards, quizzes, primary source links (including those noted in the text and marked with the feather icon), and video clips. The CourseMate site also includes an integrated *A People and A Nation* eBook. Students taking quizzes will be linked directly to relevant sections in the ebook for additional information. The ebook is fully searchable and students can even take notes and save them for later review. In addition, the ebook links to rich media assets such as video and MP3 chapter summaries, primary source documents with critical-thinking questions, and interactive (zoomable) maps. Students can use the ebook as their primary text or as a companion multimedia support. It is available at www .cengagebrain.com.

■ *Wadsworth American History Resource Center.* The resource center gives your students access to a "virtual reader" with hundreds of primary sources, including speeches, letters, legal documents and transcripts, poems, maps, simulations, timelines, and additional images that bring history to life, along with interactive assignable exercises. A map feature including Google Earth™ coordinates and exercises will aid in student comprehension of geography and use of maps. Students can compare the traditional textbook map with an aerial view of the location today. It's an ideal resource for study, review, and research. In addition to this map feature, the resource center also provides blank maps for student review and testing. Ask your sales representative for more information on how to bundle access to the HRC with your text.

- *cengagebrain.com.* Save your students time and money. Direct them to www.cengagebrain.com for choice in formats and savings and a better chance to succeed in class. Students have the freedom to purchase à la carte exactly what they need when they need it. There, students can purchase a downloadable ebook or electronic access to the American History Resource Center, the premium study tools and interactive ebook in the *A People and A Nation* CourseMate, or eAudio modules from *The History Handbook*. Students can save 50 percent on the electronic textbook and can pay as little as $1.99 for an individual eChapter.

- *Reader Program.* Cengage Learning publishes a number of readers, some containing exclusively primary sources, others a combination of primary and secondary sources, and many designed to guide students through the process of historical inquiry. Visit Cengage.com/history for a complete list of readers or ask your sales representative to recommend a reader that would work well for your specific needs.

Custom Options

Nobody knows your students like you, so why not give them a text tailor-fit to their needs? Cengage Learning offers custom solutions for your course—whether it's making a small modification to *A People and A Nation* to match your syllabus or combining multiple sources to create something truly unique. You can pick and choose chapters, include your own material, and add additional map exercises along with the Rand McNally Atlas (including questions developed around the maps in the atlas) to create a text that fits the way you teach. Ensure that your students get the most out of their textbook dollar by giving them exactly what they need. Contact your Cengage Learning representative to explore custom solutions for your course.

- *Rand McNally Atlas of American History, 2e.* This comprehensive atlas features more than 80 maps, with new content covering global perspectives, including events in the Middle East from 1945 to 2005, as well as population trends in the United States and around the world. Additional maps document voyages of discovery; the settling of the colonies; major U.S. military engagements, including the American Revolution and World Wars I and II; and sources of immigrations, ethnic populations, and patterns of economic change.

- *CourseReader.* Cengage Learning's new CourseReader lets instructors create a customized electronic reader in minutes. Instructors can choose exactly what their students will be assigned by searching or browsing Cengage Learning's extensive document database. Sources include hundreds of historical documents, images, and media, plus literary essays that can add additional interest and insight to a primary source assignment. Or instructors can start with the "Editor's Choice" collection created for *A People and A Nation*—and then update it to suit their particular needs. Each source comes with all the pedagogical tools needed to provide a full learning experience, including a descriptive headnote that puts the reading into context as well as critical-thinking and multiple-choice questions designed to reinforce key points. Contact your local Cengage Learning sales representative for more information and packaging options.

Acknowledgments

The authors would like to thank the following people for their assistance with the preparation of this edition: Philip Daileader, David Farber, Danyel Logevall, Jon Parmenter, Anna Daileader Sheriff, Benjamin Daileader Sheriff, and Selene Sheriff.

At each stage of this revision, a sizable panel of historian reviewers read drafts of our chapters. Their suggestions, corrections, and pleas helped guide us through this momentous revision. We could not include all of their recommendations, but the book is better for our having heeded most of their advice. We heartily thank:

Sara Alpern, *Texas A&M University*

Friederike Baer, *Temple University*

Troy Bickham, *Texas A&M University*

Robert Bionaz, *Chicago State University*

Victoria Bynum, *Texas State University, San Marcos*

Mario Fenyo, *Bowie State University*

Walter Hixson, *University of Akron*

Allison McNeese, *Mount Mercy College*

Steve O'Brien, *Bridgewater State College*

Paul O'Hara, *Xavier University*

John Putman, *San Diego State University*

Thomas Roy, *University of Oklahoma*

Manfred Silva, *El Paso Community College*

Michael Vollbach, *Oakland Community College*

The authors thank the helpful Cengage people who designed, edited, produced, and nourished this book. Many thanks to Ann West, senior sponsoring editor; Julia Giannotti, senior development editor; Jane Lee, content product manager; Debbie Meyer, project editor; Pembroke Herbert, photo researcher; and Charlotte Miller, art editor.

M. B. N.

C. S.

D. B.

H. C.

F. L.

B. B.

About the Authors

Mary Beth Norton

Born in Ann Arbor, Michigan, Mary Beth Norton received her B.A. from the University of Michigan (1964) and her Ph.D. from Harvard University (1969). She is the Mary Donlon Alger Professor of American History at Cornell University. Her dissertation won the Allan Nevins Prize. She has written *The British-Americans* (1972); *Liberty's Daughters* (1980, 1996); *Founding Mothers & Fathers* (1996), which was one of three finalists for the 1997 Pulitzer Prize in History; and *In the Devil's Snare* (2002), which was one of five finalists for the 2003 *LA Times* Book Prize in History and which won the English-Speaking Union's Ambassador Book Award in American Studies for 2003. She has co-edited three volumes on American women's history. She was also general editor of the *American Historical Association's Guide to Historical Literature* (1995). Her articles have appeared in such journals as the *American Historical Review, William and Mary Quarterly*, and *Journal of Women's History*. Mary Beth has served as president of the Berkshire Conference of Women Historians, as vice president for research of the American Historical Association, and as a presidential appointee to the National Council on the Humanities. She has appeared on Book TV, the History and Discovery Channels, PBS, and NBC as a commentator on Early American history, and she lectures frequently to high school teachers through the Teaching American History program. She has received four honorary degrees and in 1999 was elected a fellow of the American Academy of Arts and Sciences. She has held fellowships from the National Endowment for the Humanities; the Guggenheim, Rockefeller, and Starr Foundations; and the Henry E. Huntington Library. In 2005–2006, she was the Pitt Professor of American History and Institutions at the University of Cambridge and Newnham College.

Carol Sheriff

Born in Washington, D.C., and raised in Bethesda, Maryland, Carol Sheriff received her B.A. from Wesleyan University (1985) and her Ph.D. from Yale University (1993). Since 1993, she has taught history at the College of William and Mary, where she has won the Thomas Jefferson Teaching Award, the Alumni Teaching Fellowship Award, and the University Professorship for Teaching Excellence. Her publications include *The Artificial River: The Erie Canal and the Paradox of Progress* (1996), which won the Dixon Ryan Fox Award from the New York State Historical Association and the Award for Excellence in Research

from the New York State Archives, and *A People at War: Civilians and Soldiers in America's Civil War, 1854–1877* (with Scott Reynolds Nelson, 2007). Carol has written sections of a teaching manual for the New York State history curriculum, given presentations at Teaching American History grant projects, consulted on an exhibit for the Rochester Museum and Science Center, and appeared in the History Channel's Modern Marvels show on the Erie Canal, and she is engaged in several public-history projects marking the sesquicentennial of the Civil War. At William and Mary, she teaches the U.S. history survey as well as upper-level classes on the Early Republic, the Civil War Era, and the American West. Most recently, Carol has been named Class of 2013 term distinguished professor in recognition of her teaching, scholarship, and service.

David W. Blight

Born in Flint, Michigan, David W. Blight received his B.A. from Michigan State University (1971) and his Ph.D. from the University of Wisconsin (1985). He is now Class of 1954 Professor of American History and director of the Gilder Lehrman Center for the Study of Slavery, Resistance, and Abolition at Yale University. For the first seven years of his career, David was a public high school teacher in Flint. He has written *Frederick Douglass's Civil War* (1989) and *Race and Reunion: The Civil War in American Memory, 1863–1915* (2001), which received eight awards, including the Bancroft Prize, the Frederick Douglass Prize, and the Abraham Lincoln Prize, as well as four prizes awarded by the Organization of American Historians. His most recent book is *A Slave No More: The Emancipation of John Washington and Wallace Turnage* (2007), which won three prizes. He has edited or co-edited six other books, including editions of W. E. B. DuBois, *The Souls of Black Folk*, and *Narrative of the Life of Frederick Douglass*. David's essays have appeared in the *Journal of American History, Civil War History*, and Gabor Boritt, ed., *Why the Civil War Came* (1996), among others. In 1992–1993, he was senior Fulbright Professor in American Studies at the University of Munich, Germany, and in 2006–2007 he held a fellowship at the Dorothy and Lewis B. Cullman Center, New York Public Library. A consultant to several documentary films, David appeared in the 1998 PBS series, *Africans in America*. He has served on the Council of the American Historical Association. David also teaches summer seminars for secondary school teachers as well as for park rangers and historians of the National Park Service.

Howard P. Chudacoff

Howard P. Chudacoff, the George L. Littlefield Professor of American History and Professor of Urban Studies at Brown University, was born in Omaha, Nebraska. He earned his A.B. (1965) and Ph.D. (1969) from the University of Chicago. He has written *Mobile Americans* (1972), *How Old Are You?* (1989), *The Age of the Bachelor* (1999), *The Evolution of American Urban Society* (with Judith Smith, 2004), and *Children at Play: An American History* (2007). He has also co-edited with Peter Baldwin *Major Problems in American Urban History* (2004). His articles have appeared in such journals as the *Journal of Family History, Reviews in American History*, and *Journal of American History*. At Brown University, Howard has co-chaired the American Civilization Program and chaired the Department of History, and serves as Brown's faculty representative to the NCAA. He has also served on the board of directors of the Urban History Association. The National Endowment for the Humanities, Ford Foundation, and Rockefeller Foundation have given him awards to advance his scholarship.

Fredrik Logevall

A native of Stockholm, Sweden, Fredrik Logevall is John S. Knight Professor of International Studies and Professor of History at Cornell University, where he serves as director of the Mario Einaudi Center for International Studies. He received his B.A. from Simon Fraser University (1986) and his Ph.D. from Yale University (1993). His most recent book is *America's Cold War: The Politics of Insecurity* (with Campbell Craig, 2009). His other publications include *Choosing War* (1999), which won three prizes, including the Warren F. Kuehl Book Prize from the Society for Historians of American Foreign Relations (SHAFR); *The Origins of the Vietnam War* (2001); *Terrorism and 9/11: A Reader* (2002); as coeditor, the *Encyclopedia of American Foreign Policy* (2002); and, as co-editor, *The First Vietnam War: Colonial Conflict and Cold War Crisis* (2007). Fred is a past recipient of the Stuart L. Bernath article, book, and lecture prizes from SHAFR and is a member of the SHAFR Council, the Cornell University Press faculty board, and the editorial advisory board of the Presidential Recordings Project at the Miller Center of Public Affairs at the University of Virginia. In 2006–2007, he was Leverhulme Visiting Professor at the University of Nottingham and Mellon Senior Fellow at the University of Cambridge.

Beth Bailey

Born in Atlanta, Georgia, Beth Bailey received her B.A. from Northwestern University (1979) and her Ph.D. from the University of Chicago (1986). She is now a professor of history at Temple University. Her research and teaching fields include war and society and the U.S. military, American cultural history (nineteenth and twentieth centuries), popular culture, and gender and sexuality. She is the author, most recently, of *America's Army: Making the All-Volunteer Force* (2009). Her other publications include *From Front Porch to Back Seat: Courtship in 20th Century America* (1988), *The First Strange Place: The Alchemy of Race and Sex in WWII Hawaii* (with David Farber, 1992), *Sex in the Heartland* (1999), and *The Columbia Companion to America in the 1960s* (with David Farber, 2001). She is co-editor of *A History of Our Time* (with William Chafe and Harvard Sitkoff, 7th ed., 2007). Beth has served as a consultant and/or on-screen expert for numerous television documentaries developed for PBS and the History Channel. She has received grants or fellowships from the American Council of Learned Societies, the National Endowment for the Humanities, and the Woodrow Wilson International Center for Scholars, and she was named the Ann Whitney Olin scholar at Barnard College, Columbia University, where she was the director of the American Studies Program and Regents Lecturer at the University of New Mexico. She has been a visiting scholar at Saitama University, Japan; at Trinity College at the University of Melbourne; and a senior Fulbright lecturer in Indonesia. She teaches courses on sexuality and gender and war and American culture.

A People & A Nation

Chapter 1

Three Old Worlds Create a New 1492–1600

Detail of "Carancahusese" by Lino Sanchez y Tapia. Gilcrease Museum, Tulsa, Oklahoma

Lino Sanchez y Tapia

Carancahueses

ive years later, Alvar Nuñez Cabeza de Vaca still recalled the amazement he had encountered. "I reached four Christians on horseback who registered great surprise at seeing me so strangely dressed and in the company of Indians. They remained looking at me for a long time, so astonished that they neither spoke to me nor dared to ask anything."

The man whom the "four Christians" encountered in northern Mexico in mid-February 1536 was indeed astonishing. Cabeza de Vaca and three other men, one an enslaved North African named Estevan, had just walked across North America. They, along with about six hundred others, had left Spain in June 1527 on an ill-fated expedition under the command of Pánfilo de Narváez. After exploring the west coast of Florida, eighty of the men, including Cabeza de Vaca, were shipwrecked in late 1528 on the coast of modern Texas (probably near Galveston), at a place they named Isla de Malhado, or Island of Misfortune. Most of the survivors— alternately abused, aided, or enslaved by different Indian nations—died one by one. Cabeza de Vaca got to the mainland, where he survived as a traveling trader, exchanging seashells for hides and flint.

In January 1533, he stumbled on the other three. The Spaniards and Estevan plotted to leave but could not find the opportunity to do so until September 1534. They walked south, then turned inland and headed north, exploring the upper reaches of the Rio Grande. They continued west, almost reaching the Pacific before turning south once more, all the while guided from village to village by Indians. They convinced the people they encountered that they could heal the sick, earning food in exchange for their ministrations. Vaca described the diets, living arrangements, and customs of many of the villages they saw, thus providing modern historians and anthropologists with an invaluable record of native cultures as they first met Europeans. Little is known about Estevan's role en route, but that Vaca's account largely ignored him suggests that the Spaniards viewed him as a subordinate.

◄ Cabeza de Vaca and his walk across North America in the 1530–1540s. Cabeza de Vaca lived with the Karankawas of the Texas Gulf coast for several years after the shipwreck of 1528. This is the only known depiction by an artist who actually saw them, the Spaniard Lino Sanchez y Tapia.

Chronology

12,000–10,000 B.C.E.	■ Paleo-Indians migrate from Asia to North America across the Beringia land bridge
7000 B.C.E.	■ Cultivation of food crops begins in America
ca. 2000 B.C.E.	■ Olmec civilization appears
ca. 300–600 C.E.	■ Height of influence of Teotihuacán
ca. 600–900 C.E.	■ Classic Mayan civilization
1000 C.E.	■ Ancient Pueblos build settlements in modern states of Arizona and New Mexico
1001	■ Norse establish settlement in "Vinland"
1050–1250	■ Height of influence of Cahokia ■ Prevalence of Mississippian culture in modern midwestern and southeastern United States
14th century	■ Aztec rise to power
1450s–80s	■ Portuguese explore and colonize islands in the Mediterranean Atlantic
1477	■ Marco Polo's *Travels* describes China
1492	■ Columbus reaches Bahamas

1494	■ Treaty of Tordesillas divides land claims between Spain and Portugal in Africa, India, and South America
1496	■ Last Canary Island falls to Spain
1497	■ Cabot reaches North America
1513	■ Ponce de León explores Florida
1518–30	■ Smallpox epidemic devastates Indian population of West Indies and Central and South America
1519	■ Cortés invades Mexico
1521	■ Aztec Empire falls to Spaniards
1524	■ Verrazzano sails along Atlantic coast of United States
1534–35	■ Cartier explores St. Lawrence River
1534–36	■ Vaca, Estevan, and two companions walk across North America
1539–42	■ Soto explores southeastern United States
1540–42	■ Coronado explores southwestern United States
1587–90	■ Raleigh's Roanoke colony vanishes
1588	■ Harriot publishes *A Briefe and True Report of the New Found Land of Virginia*

When the four travelers finally arrived in Mexico City in July 1536, their extraordinary feat won them unanimous praise. The other two Spaniards settled permanently in Mexico. Estevan was killed while guiding an expedition north into the modern United States. And Cabeza de Vaca himself was appointed governor of Paraguay, his fame forever established by the 1555 publication of his account of the remarkable journey.

For thousands of years before 1492, human societies in the Americas had developed in isolation from the rest of the world. The era that began in the Christian fifteenth century brought that long-standing isolation to an end. As Europeans sought treasure and trade, peoples from different cultures came into regular contact for the first time. All were profoundly changed. Their interactions involved cruelty and kindness, greed and deception, trade and theft, surprise and sickness, captivity and enslavement. By the time the three Spaniards and the African crossed North America, the age of European expansion and colonization was already well under way. Over the next 350 years, Europeans would spread their influence across the globe. The history of the tiny colonies that would become the United States must be seen in this broad context of European exploration and exploitation.

The continents that European sailors reached in the late fifteenth century had their own histories, which the intruders largely ignored. The residents of the Americas were the world's most skillful plant breeders; they developed vegetable crops more nutritious and productive than those grown in Europe, Asia, or Africa. They had invented systems of writing and mathematics, and created more accurate calendars than those used on the other side of the Atlantic. In the Americas, as in Europe, societies rose and fell as leaders succeeded or failed in expanding their political and economic power. But the arrival of Europeans immeasurably altered the Americans' struggles with one another.

After 1400, European nations not only warred on their own continent but also tried to acquire valuable colonies and trading posts elsewhere in the world. Initially interested primarily in Asia and Africa, Europeans eventually focused mostly on the Americas. Their contests for trade and conquest changed the course of history on four continents. Even as Europeans slowly achieved dominance, their fates were shaped by the strategies of Americans and Africans. In the Americas of the fifteenth and sixteenth centuries, three old worlds came together to produce a new.

 Link to Cabeza de Vaca's original narrative in English.

- What were the key characteristics of the three worlds that met in the Americas?

- What impact did their encounter have on each of them?

- What were the crucial initial developments in that encounter?

American Societies

Human beings originated on the continent of Africa, where humanlike remains about 3 million years old have been found in what is now Ethiopia. Over many millennia, the growing population slowly dispersed to the other continents. Because the climate was then far colder than it is now, much of the earth's water was concentrated in huge rivers of ice called glaciers. Sea levels were accordingly lower, and land masses covered a larger proportion of the earth's surface than they do today. Scholars long believed the earliest inhabitants of the Americas crossed a land bridge known as Beringia (at the site of the Bering Strait) approximately twelve thousand to fourteen thousand years ago. Yet striking new archaeological discoveries in both North and South America suggest that parts of the Americas may have been settled much earlier, perhaps by seafarers.

Some geneticists now theorize that three successive waves of migrants began at least thirty thousand years ago. About 12,500 years ago, when the climate warmed and sea levels rose, Americans were separated from the peoples living on the connected continents of Asia, Africa, and Europe.

The first Americans are called Paleo-Indians. Nomadic hunters of game and gatherers of wild plants, they spread throughout North and South America, probably moving as bands composed of extended families. By about 11,500 years ago, the Paleo-Indians were making fine stone projectile points, which they attached to wooden spears and used to kill and butcher bison (buffalo), woolly mammoths, and other large mammals then living in the Americas. But as the Ice Age ended and the human population increased, all the large American mammals except the bison disappeared. Scholars disagree about whether overhunting or the change in climate caused their demise. In either case, deprived of their primary source of meat, Paleo-Indians found new ways to survive.

Ancient America

By approximately nine thousand years ago, the residents of what is now central Mexico began to cultivate food crops, especially maize (corn), squash, beans, avocados, and peppers. In the Andes Mountains of South America, people started to grow potatoes. As knowledge of agricultural techniques improved and spread through the Americas, vegetables and maize proved a more reliable source of food than hunting and gathering. Except for those living in the harshest climates, most Americans started to adopt a more sedentary style of life so that they could tend fields regularly. Some established permanent settlements; others moved several times a year among fixed sites. They cleared forests through the use of controlled burning. The fires not only created cultivable lands by killing trees and fertilizing the soil with ashes but also opened meadows that attracted deer and other wildlife. All the American cultures emphasized producing sufficient food. Although they traded such items as shells, flint, salt, and copper, no society ever became dependent on another group for items vital to its survival.

Wherever agriculture dominated the economy, complex civilizations flourished. Such societies, assured of steady supplies of grains and vegetables, no longer had to devote all their energies to subsistence. Instead, they were able to accumulate wealth, produce ornamental objects, trade with other groups, and create elaborate rituals and ceremonies. In North America, the successful cultivation of nutritious crops, such as maize, beans, and squash, seems to have led to the growth and development of all the major civilizations: first the large city-states of Mesoamerica (modern Mexico and Guatemala) and then the urban clusters known collectively as the Mississippian culture and located in the present-day United States. Each of these societies, historians and archaeologists now believe, reached its height of population and influence only after achieving success in agriculture. Each later declined and collapsed after reaching the limits of its food supply, with dire political and military consequences.

Archaeologists and historians still know little about the first major Mesoamerican civilization, the Olmecs, who about four thousand

Mesoamerican Civilizations

years ago lived near the Gulf of Mexico in cities dominated by temple pyramids. The Mayas and Teotihuacán, which developed approximately two thousand years later, are better recorded. Teotihuacán, founded in the Valley of Mexico about 300 B.C.E. (Before the Common Era), eventually became one of the largest urban areas in the world, housing perhaps 100,000 people in the fifth century C.E. (Common Era). Teotihuacán's commercial network extended hundreds of miles in all directions; many peoples prized its obsidian (a green glass), used to make fine knives and mirrors. Pilgrims traveled long distances to visit Teotihuacan's impressive pyramids and the great temple of Quetzalcoatl—the feathered serpent, primary god of central Mexico.

On the Yucatan Peninsula, in today's eastern Mexico, the Mayas built urban centers containing tall pyramids and temples. They studied astronomy and created an elaborate writing system. Their city-states, though, engaged in near-constant warfare with one another. Warfare and an inadequate food supply caused the collapse of the most powerful cities by 900 C.E., thus ending the classic era of Mayan civilization. By the time Spaniards arrived 600 years later, only a few remnants of the once-mighty society remained.

Ancient native societies in what is now the United States learned to grow maize, squash, and beans from

Pueblos and Mississippians

Mesoamericans, but the exact nature of the relationship of the various cultures is unknown. (No Mesoamerican artifacts have been found north of the Rio Grande, but some items resembling Mississippian objects have been excavated in northern Mexico.) The Hohokam, Mogollon, and ancient Pueblo peoples of the modern states of Arizona and New Mexico subsisted by combining hunting and gathering with agriculture in an arid region of unpredictable rainfall. Hohokam villagers constructed extensive irrigation systems, but even so, they occasionally had to relocate their settlements when water supplies failed. Between 900 and 1150 C.E. in Chaco Canyon, the Pueblos built fourteen "Great Houses," multistory stone structures averaging two hundred rooms. The canyon, at the juncture of perhaps four hundred miles of roads, served as a major regional trading and processing center for turquoise, used then as now to create beautiful ornamental objects. Yet the aridity eventually caused the Chacoans to migrate to other sites.

At almost the same time, the unrelated Mississippian culture flourished in what is now the midwestern and southeastern United States. Relying largely on maize, squash, nuts, pumpkins, and venison for food, the Mississippians lived in substantial settlements organized hierarchically. The largest of their urban centers was the City of the Sun (now called Cahokia), near modern St. Louis. Located on rich farmland close to the confluence of the Illinois, Missouri, and Mississippi Rivers, Cahokia, like Teotihuacán and Chaco Canyon, served as a focal point for both religion and trade. At its peak (in the eleventh and twelfth centuries C.E.), the City of the Sun covered more than 5 square miles and had a population of about twenty thousand—small by Mesoamerican standards but larger than any other northern community, and larger than London in the same era.

Although the Cahokians never invented a writing system, these sun-worshippers developed an accurate calendar, evidenced by their creation of a woodhenge—a large circle of tall timber posts aligned with the solstices and the equinox. The city's main pyramid (one of 120 of varying sizes), today called Monks Mound, was at the time of its construction the third largest structure of any description in the Western Hemisphere; it remains the largest earthwork ever built anywhere in the Americas. It sat at the northern end of the Grand Plaza, surrounded by seventeen other mounds, some used for burials. Yet following 1250 C.E., the city was abandoned, several decades after a disastrous earthquake. Archaeologists believe that climate change and the degradation of the environment, caused by overpopulation and the destruction of nearby forests, contributed to the city's collapse. Afterwards, warfare increased as large-scale population movements destabilized the region.

Far to the South, the Aztecs (also called Mexicas) migrated into the Valley of Mexico during the twelfth century. The uninhabited

Aztecs

ruins of Teotihuacán, which by then had been deserted for at least two hundred years, awed and mystified the migrants. Their chronicles record that their primary deity, Huitzilopochtli—a war god represented by an eagle—directed them to establish their capital on an island where they saw an eagle eating a serpent, the symbol of Quetzalcoatl. That island city became Tenochtitlán, the center of a rigidly stratified society composed of hereditary classes of warriors, merchants, priests, common folk, and slaves.

The Aztecs conquered their neighbors, forcing them to pay tribute in textiles, gold, foodstuffs, and human beings who could be sacrificed to Huitzilopochtli. They also engaged in ritual combat, known as flowery wars, to obtain further sacrificial victims. The war god's taste for blood was not easily quenched. In the Aztec year Ten Rabbit (1502), at the coronation of Motecuhzoma II

Visualizing THE PAST

City of the Sun

Today the remains of the City of the Sun (Cahokia) are preserved in a state park in southern Illinois. The mounds are now either largely gone or greatly reduced in size, but archaeologists have been able to visualize the site. Few of their finds were more important than the two shown here: the woodhenge and the Birger figurine. Archaeologists discovered the post holes where the woodhenge once stood, showing how the sun-worshipping Cahokians monitored the sun's annual movements through shadows cast by poles they erected in a precise formation. The red clay Birger figurine, found near Cahokia, depicts a woman with a vine winding around her body sitting on a cat-faced serpent (symbol of the earth) and holding a hoe. Why would the woodhenge have been important for Cahokia's farmers? What is the significance of the squash vine and the other attributes of the Birger figurine?

Cahokia Mounds Historic Site

An artist's conception of the construction of Cahokia's woodhenge. Monks Mound is in the background.

Courtesy of the Illinois State Archaeological Survey, University of Illinois

Front view of the Birger figurine.

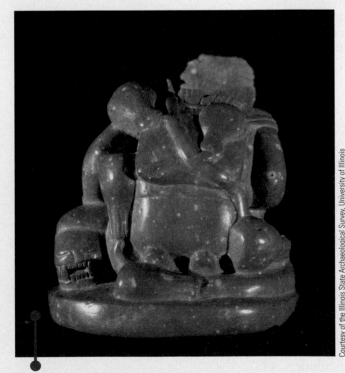

Courtesy of the Illinois State Archaeological Survey, University of Illinois

Back view of the Birger figurine.

Map 1.1 Native Cultures of North America

The Natives of the North American continent effectively used the resources of the regions in which they lived. As this map shows, coastal groups relied on fishing, residents of fertile areas engaged in agriculture, and other peoples employed hunting (often combined with gathering) as a primary mode of subsitence.

Source: Copyright © Cengage Learning

(the Spaniards could not pronounce his name correctly, so they called him Montezuma), thousands of people were sacrificed by having their still-beating hearts torn from their bodies.

The Aztecs believed they lived in the age of the Fifth Sun. Four times previously, they wrote, the earth and all the people who lived on it had been destroyed. They predicted their own world would end in earthquakes and hunger. In the Aztec year Thirteen Flint, volcanoes erupted, sickness and hunger spread, wild beasts attacked children, and an eclipse of the sun darkened the sky. Did some priest wonder whether the Fifth Sun was approaching its end? In time, the Aztecs learned that Thirteen Flint was called, by Europeans, 1492.

North America in 1492

Over the centuries, the Americans who lived north of Mexico adapted their once-similar ways of life to very different climates and terrains, thus creating the diverse culture areas (ways of subsistence) that the Europeans encountered when they arrived (see Map 1.1). Scholars often refer to such culture areas by language group (such as Algonquian or Iroquoian) because neighboring Indian nations commonly spoke related languages. Bands that lived in environments not well suited to agriculture—because of inadequate rainfall or poor soil, for example—followed a nomadic lifestyle. Within the area of the present-day United States, these groups included the

Paiutes and Shoshones, who inhabited the Great Basin (now Nevada and Utah). Because of the difficulty of finding sufficient food for more than a few people, such hunter-gatherer bands were small, usually composed of one or more related families. The men hunted small animals, and women gathered seeds and berries. Where large game was more plentiful and food supplies therefore more certain, as in present-day central and western Canada and the Great Plains, bands of hunters were somewhat larger.

In more favorable environments, larger groups combined agriculture with gathering, hunting, and fishing. Those who lived near the seacoasts, like the Chinooks of present-day Washington and Oregon, consumed fish and shellfish in addition to growing crops and gathering seeds and berries. Residents of the interior (for example, the Arikaras of the Missouri River valley) hunted large animals while also cultivating maize, squash, and beans. The peoples of what is now eastern Canada and the northeastern United States also combined hunting, fishing, and agriculture. They regularly used controlled fires both to open land for cultivation and to assist in hunting.

Extensive trade routes linked distant peoples. For instance, hoe and spade blades manufactured from stone mined in modern southern Illinois have been found as far northeast as Lake Erie and as far west as the Plains. Commercial and other interactions among disparate groups speaking different languages were aided by the universally understood symbol of friendship—the calumet, a feathered tobacco pipe offered to strangers at initial encounters.

Societies that relied primarily on hunting large animals, such as deer and buffalo, assigned that task to

Gendered Division of Labor

men, allotting food preparation and clothing production to women. Before such nomadic bands acquired horses from the Spaniards, women—occasionally assisted by dogs—also carried the family's belongings whenever the band relocated. Such a

Collection of Mary Beth Norton

▲ Jacques Le Moyne, an artist accompanying the French settlement in Florida in the 1560s (see page 35), produced some of the first European images of North American peoples. His depiction of native agricultural practices shows the gendered division of labor: men breaking up the ground with fishbone hoes before women drop seeds into the holes. But Le Moyne's version of the scene cannot be accepted uncritically: unable to abandon a European view of proper farming methods, he erroneously drew plowed furrows in the soil.

sexual division of labor was universal among hunting peoples, regardless of their location. So, too, among seacoast peoples women gathered shellfish along the shore while men fished from boats. Yet agricultural societies assigned work in divergent ways. The Pueblo peoples, who lived in sixty or seventy autonomous villages and spoke five different languages, defined agricultural labor as men's work. In the east, large clusters of peoples speaking Algonquian, Iroquoian, and Muskogean languages allocated most agricultural chores to women, although men cleared the land. In all the farming societies, women gathered wild foods and prepared food for consumption or storage, whereas men were responsible for hunting.

Everywhere in North America, women cared for young children, while older youths learned adult skills from their same-sex parent. Children generally had a great deal of freedom. Young people commonly chose their own marital partners, and in most societies couples could easily divorce if they no longer wished to live together. In contrast to the earlier Mississippian cultures, populations in these societies remained at a level sustainable by existing food supplies, largely because of low birth rates. Infants and toddlers were nursed until the age of two or even longer, and taboos prevented couples from having sexual intercourse during that period.

The southwestern and eastern agricultural peoples had similar social organizations. They lived in villages,

Social Organization

sometimes with a thousand or more inhabitants. The Pueblos resided in multistory buildings constructed on terraces along the sides of cliffs or other easily defended sites. Northern Iroquois villages (in modern New York State) were composed of large, rectangular, bark-covered structures, or long houses; the name Haudenosaunee, which the Iroquois called themselves, means "People of the Long House." In the present-day southeastern United States, Muskogeans and southern Algonquians lived in large houses made of thatch. Most of the eastern villages were surrounded by wooden palisades and ditches to aid in fending off attackers.

In all the agricultural societies, each dwelling housed an extended family defined matrilineally (through a female line of descent). Mothers, their married daughters, and their daughters' husbands and children all lived together. Matrilineal descent did not imply matriarchy, or the wielding of power by women, but rather served as a means of reckoning kinship. Matrilineal ties also linked extended families into clans. The nomadic bands of the Prairies and Great Plains, by contrast, were most often related patrilineally (through the male line). They lacked settled villages and defended themselves from attack primarily through their ability to move to safer locations when necessary.

The defensive design of native villages discloses the significance of warfare in pre-Columbian America.

War and Politics

Long before Europeans arrived, residents of the continent fought one another for control of the best hunting and fishing territories, the most fertile agricultural lands, or the sources of essential items, such as salt (for preserving meat) and flint (for making knives and arrowheads). Bands of Americans protected by wooden armor battled while standing in ranks facing each other, the better to employ their clubs and throwing spears, which were effective only at close quarters. They began to shoot arrows from behind trees only when they confronted European guns, which rendered their armor useless. People captured by the enemy in such wars were sometimes enslaved and dishonored by losing their previous names and identities, but slavery was never an important source of labor in pre-Columbian America.

American political structures varied considerably. Among Pueblos, the village council, composed of ten to thirty men, was the highest political authority; no government structure connected the villages. Nomadic hunters also lacked formal links among separate bands. The Iroquois, by contrast, had an elaborate political hierarchy incorporating villages into nations and nations into a confederation. A council comprising representatives from each nation made crucial decisions of war and peace for the entire confederacy. In all the North American cultures, civil and war leaders divided political power and wielded authority only so long as they retained the confidence of the people. Autocratic rulers held sway only in southeastern chiefdoms descended from the Mississippians. Women more often assumed leadership roles among agricultural peoples, especially those in which females were the primary cultivators, than among nomadic hunters. Female sachems (rulers) led Algonquian villages in what is now Massachusetts, but women never became heads of hunting bands. Iroquois women did not become chiefs, yet clan matrons exercised political power. The older women of each village chose its chief and could both start wars (by calling for the capture of prisoners to replace dead relatives) and stop them (by refusing to supply warriors with necessary foodstuffs).

All the American peoples were polytheistic, worshiping a multitude of gods. Each group's most important beliefs

Religion

and rituals were closely tied to its means of subsistence. The major deities of agricultural peoples like the Pueblos and Muskogeans were associated with cultivation, and their chief festivals centered on planting and harvest. The most important gods of hunters like those living on the Great Plains were associated with animals, and their major festivals were related to hunting. A band's economy and women's role in it helped to determine women's potential as religious leaders. Women held the most prominent positions in those agricultural societies in which they were also the chief food producers, whereas in hunting societies men took the lead in religious as well as political affairs.

A wide variety of cultures, comprising more than 10 million people, thus inhabited America north of Mexico when Europeans arrived. The hierarchical kingdoms of Mesoamerica bore little resemblance to the nomadic hunting societies of the Great Plains or to the agriculturalists of the Northeast or Southwest. The diverse inhabitants of North America spoke well over one thousand different languages. For obvious reasons, they did not consider themselves one people, nor did they think of uniting to repel the European invaders.

African Societies

Fifteenth-century Africa, like fifteenth-century America, housed a variety of cultures adapted to different terrains and climates (see Map 1.2). Many of these cultures were of great antiquity. In the north, along the Mediterranean Sea, lived the Berbers, who were Muslims, or followers of the Islamic religion founded by the prophet Mohammed in the seventh century C.E. On the east coast of Africa, Muslim city-states engaged in extensive trade with India, the Moluccas (part of modern Indonesia), and China. In these ports, sustained contact and intermarriage among Arabs and Africans created the Swahili language and culture. Through the East African city-states passed the Spice Route, water-borne commerce between the eastern Mediterranean and East Asia; the rest followed the long land route across Central Asia known as the Silk Road.

South of the Mediterranean coast in the African interior lie the great Saharan and Libyan Deserts, vast expanses of nearly waterless terrain crisscrossed by trade routes passing through oases. The introduction of the camel in the fifth century C.E. made long-distance travel possible, and as Islam expanded after the ninth century, commerce controlled by Muslim merchants helped to spread similar religious and cultural ideas throughout the region. Below the deserts, much of the continent is divided between tropical rain forests (along the coasts) and grassy plains (in the interior). People speaking a variety of languages and pursuing different subsistence strategies lived in a wide belt south of the deserts. South of the Gulf of Guinea, the grassy landscape came to be dominated by Bantu-speaking peoples, who left their homeland in modern Nigeria about two thousand years ago and slowly migrated south and east across the continent.

West Africa was a land of tropical forests and savanna grasslands where fishing, cattle herding, and agriculture had supported the inhabitants for at least ten thousand years before Europeans set foot there in the fifteenth century. The northern region of West Africa, or Upper Guinea, was heavily influenced by the Islamic culture of the Mediterranean. By the eleventh century C.E., many of the region's inhabitants had become Muslims. Trade via camel caravans between Upper Guinea and the Muslim Mediterranean was sub-Saharan Africa's major connection to Europe and West Asia. Africans sold ivory, gold, and slaves to northern merchants to obtain salt, dates, silk, and cotton cloth.

West Africa (Guinea)

Upper Guinea runs northeast-southwest from Cape Verde to Cape Palmas. The people of its northernmost region, the so-called Rice Coast (present-day Gambia, Senegal, and Guinea), fished and cultivated rice in coastal swamplands. The Grain Coast, to the south, was thinly populated and not readily accessible from the sea because it had only one good harbor (modern Freetown, Sierra Leone). Its people concentrated on farming and raising livestock.

In Lower Guinea, south and east of Cape Palmas, most Africans were farmers who practiced traditional religions, rather than Islam. Believing that spirits inhabited particular places, they invested those places with special significance. Like the agricultural peoples of the Americas, they developed rituals intended to ensure good harvests. Throughout the region, individual villages composed of kin groups were linked into hierarchical kingdoms. At the time of initial European contact, decentralized political and social authority characterized the region.

▲ This brass depiction of a hunting scene with a man and animals was employed by the Akan peoples of the modern Ivory Coast to weigh gold. An otherwise mundane object required for domestic and foreign trade thus was decorative as well as useful, providing for today's viewers a sense of ancient African life.

Major climatic zones of Africa

- Wet equatorial
- Woodland savannah
- Dry savannah with long dry season (6–9 months)
- Sahel or subdesert
- Desert
- Mediterranean
- Highland (climate moderated by altitude)
- → Trans-Saharan trade routes
- → Traditional Arab spice routes
- ⇒ Spread of Bantu-speakers, by ca. 1000
- **TEDA** Major language
- **BERBERS** Selected peoples

Map 1.2 Africa and Its Peoples, ca. 1400

On the African continent resided many different peoples in a variety of ecological settings and political units. Even before Europeans began to explore Africa's coastlines, its northern regions were linked to the Mediterranean (and thus to Europe) by a network of trade routes.

Source: Copyright © Cengage Learning

The societies of West Africa, like those of the Americas, assigned different tasks to men and women. In general, the sexes shared agricultural duties. Men also hunted, managed livestock, and did most of the fishing. Women were responsible for childcare, food preparation, manufacture, and trade. They managed the extensive local and regional networks through which families, villages, and small kingdoms exchanged goods.

Complementary Gender Roles

Despite their different economies and the rivalries among states, the peoples of Lower Guinea had similar social systems organized on the basis of what anthropologists have called the dual-sex principle. In Lower Guinea, each sex handled its own affairs: just as male political and religious leaders governed men, so females ruled women. In the Dahomean kingdom, for example, every male official had his female counterpart; in the thirty little Akan states on the Gold Coast, chiefs inherited their status through the female line, and each male chief had a female assistant who supervised other women. Many West African societies practiced polygyny (one man's having several wives, each of whom lived separately with her children). Thus, few adults lived permanently in marital households, but the dual-sex system ensured that their actions were subject to scrutiny by members of their own sex.

Throughout Guinea, religious beliefs stressed complementary male and female roles. Both women and men served as heads of the cults and secret societies that directed the spiritual life of the villages. Young women were initiated into the Sandé cult, young men into Poro. Neither cult was allowed to reveal its secrets to the opposite sex. Although West African women (unlike some of their Native American contemporaries) rarely held formal power over men, female religious leaders did govern other members of their sex within the Sandé cult, enforcing conformity to accepted norms of behavior and overseeing their spiritual well-being.

West African law recognized both individual and communal land ownership, but men seeking to accumulate wealth needed access to labor—wives, children, or slaves—who could work the land. West Africans enslaved for life therefore composed essential elements of the economy. Africans could be enslaved as punishment for crimes, but more often such slaves were enemy captives or people who voluntarily enslaved themselves or their children to pay debts. An African who possessed bondspeople had a right to the products of their labor, although the degree to which slaves were exploited varied greatly, and slave status did not always descend to the next generation. Some slaves were held as chattel; others

Slavery in Guinea

could engage in trade, retaining a portion of their profits; and still others achieved prominent political or military positions. All, however, found it difficult to overcome the social stigma of enslavement, and they could be traded or sold at the will of their owners.

West Africans, then, were agricultural peoples, skilled at tending livestock, hunting, fishing, and manufacturing cloth from plant fibers and animal skins. Both men and women worked communally, in family groups or alongside others of their own sex. They were accustomed to a relatively egalitarian relationship between the sexes, especially within the context of religion. Carried as captives to the Americas, they became essential to transplanted European societies that used their labor but had little respect for their cultural traditions.

European Societies

In the fifteenth century, Europeans, too, were agricultural peoples. The daily lives of Europe's rural people had changed little for several hundred years. Split into numerous small, warring countries, Europe was divided linguistically, politically, and economically, yet in social terms Europeans' lives exhibited many similarities. In the hierarchical European societies, a few families wielded autocratic power over the majority of the people. English society in particular was organized as a series of interlocking hierarchies; that is, each person (except those at the very top or bottom) was superior to some, inferior to others. At the base of such hierarchies were people held in various forms of bondage. Although Europeans were not subjected to perpetual slavery, Christian doctrine permitted the enslavement of "heathens" (non-Christians), and some Europeans' freedom was restricted by such conditions as serfdom, which tied them to the land if not to specific owners. In short, Europe's kingdoms resembled those of Africa or Mesoamerica but differed greatly from the more egalitarian societies found in America north of Mexico (see Map 1.3).

Most Europeans, like most Africans and Americans, lived in small villages. Only a few cities dotted the landscape, most of them seaports or political capitals. European farmers, called peasants, owned or leased separate landholdings, but they worked the fields communally. Because fields had to lie fallow (unplanted) every second or third year to regain fertility, a family could not ensure itself a regular food supply unless all villagers shared annually the work and the crops. Men did most of the fieldwork; women helped out chiefly at planting and harvest. In some regions men concentrated on herding livestock. Women's duties consisted primarily of childcare

Gender, Work, Politics, and Religion

Map 1.3 Europe in 1453

The Europeans who ventured out into the Atlantic came from countries on the northwestern edge of the continent, which was divided into numerous competing nations.

Source: Copyright © Cengage Learning

Spread of Roman Christendom

- In 1000 C.E.
- Added 1000–1200
- Lost 1000–1200 (Regained 1200–1500)
- Added 1200–1500
- Lost 1200–1500
- English holdings, 1360
- Boundary of the Holy Roman Empire

ATLANTIC OCEAN

North Sea

Baltic Sea

Mediterranean Sea

Black Sea

Adriatic Sea

IRELAND
Dublin

SCOTLAND

WALES

ENGLAND
London

FRANCE
Paris
Orléans

BRITTANY

FLANDERS
LUXEMBOURG
CHAMPAGNE
FRANCHE-COMTÉ
BURGUNDY
Lyons
Avignon
Marseilles

AQUITAINE

NAVARRE

KINGDOM OF CASTILE AND LEÓN
Toledo

PORTUGAL
Lisbon

KINGDOM OF ARAGON
Barcelona

GRANADA
Granada

Ebro R.

MOROCCO

ALGIERS

TUNIS

Corsica
Sardinia
Sicily
Malta

NORWAY
Oslo

SWEDEN
Stockholm

DENMARK
Copenhagen

Hamburg

Frankfurt
HOLY ROMAN EMPIRE

Elbe R.
Rhine R.

SWITZERLAND
ALPS
SAVOY
Po R.
MILAN
GENOA
Venice
VENETIAN REPUBLIC
FLORENCE
Genoa
PAPAL STATES
Rome
Naples
KINGDOM OF NAPLES

TYROL
AUSTRIA
STYRIA
Vienna
BOHEMIA

ESTONIA
Riga
PRUSSIA
Königsberg
Danzig

POLAND
Warsaw
PRUSSIA

Budapest
HUNGARY

BOSNIA
SERBIA
MONTENEGRO
ALBANIA

MOLDAVIA
WALLACHIA
Danube R.

NOVGOROD

GRAND PRINCIPALITY OF LITHUANIA
Kiev
Dnieper R.

GRAND PRINCIPALITY OF MOSCOW
Moscow
Don R.
Volga R.

KHANATE OF THE KAZAN

KHANATE OF THE GOLDEN HORDE

KHANATE OF THE ASTRAKHAN

KHANATE OF THE CRIMEA

OTTOMAN EMPIRE
Constantinople
Athens
Rhodes
Crete
Cyprus

Tigris R.
Euphrates R.

10°W
10°E
20°E
30°E
40°E
50°E

50°N

0   150   300 Mi.
0   150   300 Km.

and household tasks, including preserving food, milking cows, and caring for poultry. If a woman's husband was a city artisan or storekeeper, she might assist him in business. Because Europeans kept domesticated animals (pigs, goats, sheep, and cattle) for meat, hunting had little economic importance in their cultures. Instead, hunting was primarily a sport for male aristocrats.

Unlike in Africa or America, where women often played prominent roles in politics and religion, men dominated all areas of life in Europe. A few women—notably Queen Elizabeth I of England—achieved status or power by right of birth, but the vast majority were excluded from positions of political authority. European women also generally held inferior social, religious, and economic positions, yet they wielded power in their own households over children and servants. In contrast to the freedom children enjoyed in American families, European children were tightly controlled and subjected to harsh discipline.

Christianity was the dominant European religion. In the West, authority rested in the Catholic Church, based in Rome and led by the pope, who directed a wholly male clergy. Although Europeans were nominally Catholic, many adhered to local belief systems the church deemed heretical and proved unable to extinguish. Kings would ally themselves with the church when it suited their needs but often acted independently. Yet even so, the Christian nations of Europe from the twelfth century on publicly united in a goal of driving nonbelievers (especially Muslims) not only from their own domains but also from the holy city of Jerusalem, which caused the series of wars known as the Crusades. Nevertheless, in the fifteenth century, Muslims dominated the commerce and geography of the Mediterranean world, especially after they conquered Constantinople (capital of the Christian Byzantine empire) in 1453. Few would have predicted that Christian Europeans would ever be able to challenge that dominance.

When the fifteenth century began, European nations were slowly recovering from the devastating epidemic of plague known as the Black Death, which first struck them in 1346. The Black Death seems to have arrived in Europe from China, traveling with long-distance traders along the Silk Road to the eastern Mediterranean. The disease then recurred with particular severity in the 1360s and 1370s. Although no precise figures are available and the impact of the Black Death varied from region to region, the best estimate is that fully one-third of Europe's people died during those terrible years. A precipitous economic decline followed—in some regions more than half of the workers had died—as did severe social, political, and religious disruption because of the deaths of clergymen and other leading figures.

Effects of Plague and Warfare

▲ Daily life in early sixteenth-century Portugal, as illustrated in a manuscript prayer book. At top a prosperous family shares a meal being served by an African slave. Other scenes show male laborers clearing land and hunting birds (left) and chopping wood (right), while at bottom a woman plants seeds in a prepared bed and in the top background female servants work in the kitchen.

As plague ravaged the population, England and France waged the Hundred Years' War (1337–1453), initiated because English monarchs had claimed the French throne. The war interrupted overland trade routes connecting England and Antwerp (in modern Belgium) to Venice, a Christian trading center, and thence to India and China. England, on the periphery of the Mediterranean commercial core, exported wool and cloth to Antwerp in exchange for spices and silks from the East. Needing a new way to reach their northern trading partners, eastern Mediterranean merchants forged a maritime route to Antwerp. Using a triangular, or lateen, sail (rather than the then-standard square rigging) improved the maneuverability of ships, enabling vessels to sail out of the Mediterranean and north around the European coast. Other developments of key importance were the acquisition of a Chinese invention, the compass, and the perfection of navigational instruments like the astrolabe and the quadrant, which allowed oceangoing sailors to estimate their position (latitude) by measuring the relationship of the sun, moon, or certain stars to the horizon.

After the Hundred Years' War, European monarchs forcefully consolidated their previously diffuse political

Political and Technological Change

power and raised new revenues through increased taxation of an already hard-pressed peasantry. The long military struggle led to new pride in national identity, which eclipsed the prevailing regional and dynastic loyalties. In England, Henry VII in 1485 founded the Tudor dynasty and began uniting a previously divided land. In France, the successors of Charles VII unified the kingdom. Most successful of all were Ferdinand of Aragón and Isabella of Castile, who married in 1469, founding a strongly Catholic Spain. In 1492, they defeated the Muslims who had lived in Spain and Portugal for centuries, thereafter expelling all Jews and Muslims from their domain.

The fifteenth century also brought technological change to Europe. Movable type and the printing press, invented in Germany in the 1450s, made information more accessible than ever before. Printing stimulated the Europeans' curiosity about fabled lands across the seas, lands they could now read about in books. The most important such works were Ptolemy's *Geography*, a description of the known world written in ancient times, first published in 1475 and later updated with new finds; and Marco Polo's *Travels*, published in 1477. The *Travels* recounted a Venetian merchant's adventures in thirteenth-century China and intriguingly described that nation as bordered on the east by an ocean. Polo's account circulated widely among Europe's educated elites, first in manuscript and later in print. The book led many Europeans to believe they could trade directly with China in oceangoing vessels instead of relying on the Silk Road or the Spice Route through East Africa. A transoceanic route, if it existed, would allow northern Europeans to circumvent the Muslim and Venetian merchants who hitherto had controlled their access to Asian goods.

Technological advances and the growing strength of newly powerful national rulers made possible the Euro-

Motives for Exploration

pean explorations of the fifteenth and sixteenth centuries. Each country craved easy access to African and Asian goods—silk, dyes, perfumes, jewels, sugar, gold, and especially spices such as pepper, cloves, cinnamon, and nutmeg. Spices were desirable not only for seasoning food but also because they were believed to have medicinal and magical properties. Their allure stemmed largely from their rarity, their extraordinary cost, and their mysterious origins. They passed through so many hands en route to London or Seville that no European knew exactly where they came from. (Nutmeg, for example, grew only on nine tiny

islands in the Moluccas, now eastern Indonesia.) Avoiding intermediaries in Venice and Constantinople, and acquiring such valuable products directly, would improve a nation's income and its standing relative to other countries, in addition to supplying its wealthy leaders with coveted luxury items.

A concern for spreading Christianity around the world supplemented the economic motive. The linking of materialistic and spiritual goals seems contradictory today, but fifteenth-century Europeans saw no necessary conflict between the two. Explorers and colonizers—especially Roman Catholics—honestly sought to convert "heathen" peoples to Christianity. At the same time, they hoped to increase their nation's wealth by establishing direct trade with Africa, China, India, and the Moluccas.

Early European Explorations

To establish that trade, European mariners first had to explore the oceans. Seafarers needed not just the maneuverable vessels and navigational aids increasingly used in the fourteenth century but also knowledge of the sea, its currents, and especially its winds. Wind would power their ships. But how did the winds run? Where would Atlantic breezes carry their square-rigged ships, which, even with the addition of a triangular sail, needed to run before the wind (that is, to have the wind directly behind the vessel)?

Europeans learned the answers to these questions in the region called the Mediterranean Atlantic, the expanse

Sailing the Mediterranean Atlantic

of ocean located south and west of Spain and bounded by the islands of the Azores (on the west) and the Canaries (on the south), with the Madeiras in their midst

(see Map 1.4). Europeans reached all three sets of islands during the fourteenth century—first the Canaries in the 1330s, then the Madeiras and the Azores. The Canaries proved a popular destination for mariners from Iberia, the peninsula that includes Spain and Portugal. Sailing to the Canaries from Europe was easy because strong winds known as the Northeast Trades blow southward along the Iberian and African coastlines. The voyage took about a week, and the volcanic peaks on the islands made them difficult to miss even with imprecise navigational instruments.

The problem was getting back. The Iberian sailor attempting to return home faced a major obstacle: the very winds that had brought him so quickly to the Canaries now blew directly at him. Rowing and tacking back and forth against the wind were similarly tedious and ineffectual. Confronted by contrary winds, mariners had traditionally waited for the wind to change, but the Northeast Trades blew steadily. So they developed a new

Map 1.4 Atlantic Winds and Islands

European mariners had to explore the oceans before they could find new lands. The first realm they discovered was that of Atlantic winds and islands.

Source: Copyright © Cengage Learning

technique: sailing "around the wind." That meant sailing as directly against the wind as was possible without being forced to change course. In the Mediterranean Atlantic, a mariner would head northwest into the open ocean, until—weeks later—he reached the winds that would carry him home, the so-called Westerlies. Those winds blow (we now know, although the seafarers at first did not) northward along the coast of North America before heading east toward Europe.

This solution must at first have seemed to defy common sense, but it became the key to successful exploration of both the Atlantic and the Pacific Oceans. Once a sailor understood the winds and their allied currents, he no longer feared leaving Europe without being able to return. Faced with a contrary wind, he simply had to sail around it until he found a wind to carry him in the proper direction.

During the fifteenth century, armed with knowledge of the winds and currents of the Mediterranean Atlantic,

Islands of the Mediterranean Atlantic

Iberian seamen regularly visited the three island groups, all of which they could reach in two weeks or less. The uninhabited Azores were soon settled by Portuguese migrants who raised wheat for sale in Europe and sold livestock to passing sailors. The Madeiras also had no native peoples, and by the 1450s Portuguese colonists were employing slaves (probably Jews and Muslims brought from Iberia) to grow large quantities of sugar for export to the mainland. By the 1470s, Madeira had developed a colonial plantation economy. For the first time in world history, a region was settled explicitly to cultivate a valuable crop—sugar—to be sold elsewhere. Moreover, because the work involved in large-scale plantation agriculture was so backbreaking, only a supply of enslaved laborers (who could not opt to quit) could ensure the system's continued success.

The Canaries did have indigenous residents—the Guanche people, who began trading animal skins and dyes with their European visitors. After 1402, the French, Portuguese, and Spanish began sporadically attacking the islands. The Guanches resisted vigorously, even though they were weakened by their susceptibility to alien European diseases. One by one, the seven islands fell to Europeans who then carried off Guanches as slaves to the Madeiras or Iberia. Spain conquered the last island in 1496 and subsequently devoted the land to sugar plantations. Collectively, the Canaries and Madeira became known as the Wine Islands because much of their sugar production was directed to making sweet wines.

While some Europeans concentrated on exploiting the islands of the Mediterranean Atlantic, others used them as steppingstones to Africa. In 1415, Portugal seized control of Ceuta, a Muslim city in North Africa (see Map 1.2). Prince Henry the Navigator, son of King John I of Portugal, knew that vast wealth awaited the first European nation to tap the riches of Africa and Asia directly. Repeatedly, he dispatched ships southward along the African coast, attempting to discover an oceanic route to Asia. But not until after Prince Henry's death did Bartholomew Dias round the southern tip of Africa (1488) and Vasco da Gama finally reach India (1498), where at Malabar he located the richest source of peppercorns in the world.

Portuguese Trading Posts in Africa

Long before that, Portugal reaped the benefits of its seafarers' voyages. Although West African states successfully resisted European penetration of the interior, they allowed the Portuguese to establish trading posts along their coasts. Charging the traders rent and levying duties on goods they imported, the African kingdoms benefited considerably from their new, easier access to European manufactures. The Portuguese gained, too, for they no longer had to rely on trans-Saharan camel caravans. Their vessels earned immense profits by swiftly transporting African gold, ivory, and slaves to Europe. By bargaining with African masters to purchase their slaves and then carrying those bondspeople to Iberia, the Portuguese introduced black slavery into Europe.

An island off the African coast, previously uninhabited, proved critical to Portuguese success. In the 1480s, they colonized São Tomé, located in the Gulf of Guinea (see Map 1.2). By that time, Madeira had already reached the limit of its capacity to produce sugar. The soil of São Tomé proved ideal for raising that valuable crop, and plantation agriculture there expanded rapidly. Planters imported large numbers of slaves from the mainland to work in the cane fields, thus creating the first economy based primarily on the bondage of black Africans.

Lessons of Early Colonization

By the 1490s, even before Christopher Columbus set sail to the west, Europeans had learned three key lessons of colonization in the Mediterranean Atlantic. First, they had learned how to transplant their crops and livestock successfully to exotic locations. Second, they had discovered that the native peoples of those lands could be either conquered (like the Guanches) or exploited (like the Africans). Third, they had developed a viable model of plantation slavery and a system for supplying nearly unlimited quantities of such workers. The stage was set for a pivotal moment in world history.

Collection of Mary Beth Norton

◀ A relief carving of a square-rigged vessel, with a lateen sail at the rear for maneuverability. Fittingly, it is found on Vasco da Gama's tomb in the Jéronimos monastery in Belém, Portugal, which is located on the very spot whence he set sail in just such a ship on his voyage to India.

Voyages of Columbus, Cabot, and Their Successors

Christopher Columbus was well schooled in the lessons of the Mediterranean Atlantic. Born in 1451 in the Italian city-state of Genoa, this largely self-educated son of a wool merchant was by the 1490s an experienced sailor and mapmaker. Like many mariners of the day, he was drawn to Portugal and its islands, especially Madeira, where he commanded a merchant vessel. At least once he voyaged to the Portuguese outpost on the Gold Coast. There he became obsessed with gold, and there he came to understand the economic potential of the slave trade.

Like all accomplished seafarers, Columbus knew the world was round. But he differed from other cartographers in his estimate of the earth's size: he thought that China lay only three thousand miles from the southern European coast. Thus, he argued, it would be easier to reach Asia by sailing west than by making the difficult voyage around the southern tip of Africa. Experts scoffed at this crackpot notion, accurately predicting that the two continents lay twelve thousand miles apart. When Columbus in 1484 asked the Portuguese rulers to back his plan to sail west to Asia, they rejected what appeared to be a crazy scheme.

Ferdinand and Isabella of Spain, jealous of Portugal's successes in Africa, were more receptive to Columbus's ideas. Urged on by some Spanish noblemen and a group of Italian merchants residing in Castile, the monarchs agreed

Columbus's Voyage

to finance the risky voyage, in part because they hoped the profits would pay for a new expedition to conquer Muslim-held Jerusalem. And so, on August 3, 1492, in command of three ships—the *Pinta*, the *Niña*, and the *Santa Maria*—Columbus set sail from the Spanish port of Palos.

The first part of the journey was familiar, for the ships steered down the Northeast Trades to the Canary Islands. There Columbus refitted his square-rigged ships, adding triangular sails to make them more maneuverable. On September 6, the ships weighed anchor and headed out into the unknown ocean.

Just over a month later, pushed by favorable trade winds, the vessels found land approximately where Columbus thought Cipangu (Japan) was located (see Map 1.5). On October 12, he and his men landed on an island in the Bahamas, which its inhabitants called Guanahaní but which he renamed San Salvador. (Because Columbus's description of his landfall can be variously interpreted, several different places today claim to be his landing site.) Later, he went on to explore the islands now known as Cuba and Hispaniola, which their residents, the Taíno people, called Colba and Bohío. Because he thought he had reached the East Indies (the Spice Islands), Columbus referred to the inhabitants of the region as "Indians." The Taínos thought the Europeans had come from the sky, and wherever Columbus went crowds of curious Taínos gathered to meet and exchange gifts with him.

Three themes predominate in Columbus's log, the major source of information on this first encounter. First,

Columbus's Observations

he insistently asked the Taínos where he could find gold, pearls, and spices. Each time, his informants replied (via signs) that such products could be obtained on other islands or on the mainland. Eventually, he came to mistrust such answers, noting, "I am beginning to believe . . . they will tell me anything I want to hear."

Second, Columbus wrote repeatedly of the strange and beautiful plants and animals. "Here the fishes are so unlike ours that it is amazing. . . . The colors are so bright that anyone would marvel," he

> Link to the logbook of Columbus's first voyage.

noted, and again, "The song of the little birds might make a man wish never to leave here. I never tire from looking at such luxurious vegetation." Yet Columbus's interest was not only aesthetic. "I believe that there are many plants and trees here that could be worth a lot in Spain for use as dyes, spices, and medicines," he observed, adding that he was carrying home to Europe "a sample of everything I can," so that experts could examine them.

Third, Columbus also described the islands' human residents, and he seized some to take back to Spain. The Taínos were, he said, very handsome, gentle, and friendly, though they told him of the fierce Caniba (today called Caribs) who lived on other islands, raided their villages, and ate some captives (hence today's word *cannibal*). Although Columbus feared and distrusted the Caribs, he believed the Taínos to be likely converts to Catholicism, remarking that "if devout religious persons knew the Indian language well, all these people would soon become Christians." But he had more in mind than conversion. The islanders "ought to make good and skilled servants," Columbus declared. It would be easy to "subject everyone and make them do what you wished."

Thus, the records of the first encounter between Europeans and Americans revealed themes that would be of enormous significance for centuries to come. Europeans wanted to extract

> Link to Columbus's letter to Ferdinand and Isabella announcing his discoveries.

profits by exploiting American resources, including plants, animals, and peoples alike, and like Columbus others later divided the native peoples into "good" (Taínos) and "bad" (Caribs). Columbus made three more voyages to the west, exploring most of the major Caribbean islands and sailing along the coasts of Central and South America. Until the day he died in 1506 at the age of fifty-five, he

Map 1.5 European Explorations in America

In the century following Columbus's voyages, European adventurers explored the coasts and parts of the interior of North and South America.

Source: Copyright © Cengage Learning

believed he had reached Asia. Even before his death, others knew better. Because the Florentine Amerigo Vespucci, who explored the South American coast in 1499, was the first to publish the idea that a new continent had been discovered, Martin Waldseemüller in 1507 labeled the land "America," as is evident in his map. By then, Spain, Portugal, and Pope Alexander VI had signed the Treaty of Tordesillas (1494), confirming Portugal's dominance in Africa— and later Brazil—in exchange for Spanish pre-eminence in the rest of the Americas.

Five hundred years before Columbus, about the year 1001, a Norse expedition under Leif Ericsson had sailed

Norse and Other Northern Voyagers

to North America across the Davis Strait, which separated their villages in Greenland from Baffin Island (located

northeast of Hudson Bay; see Map 1.1) by just 200 nautical miles, settling at a site they named "Vinland." Attacks by local residents forced them to depart hurriedly from Vinland after just a few years. In the 1960s, archaeologists determined that the Norse had established an outpost at what is now L'Anse aux Meadows, Newfoundland, but Vinland itself was probably located farther south.

Later Europeans did not know of the Norse explorers, but some historians argue that during the fifteenth century Basque whalers and fishermen (from modern northern France and Spain) located rich fishing grounds off Newfoundland but kept the information secret. Whether or not fishermen crossed the entire Atlantic, they thoroughly explored its northern reaches. Fifteenth-century seafarers voyaged regularly between the

▲ This map, produced in 1489 by Henricus Marcellus, represents the world as Christopher Columbus knew it, for it incorporates information obtained after Bartholomew Dias, a Portuguese sailor, rounded the Cape of Good Hope at the southern tip of Africa in 1488. Marcellus did not try to estimate the extent of the ocean separating the west coast of Europe from the east coast of Asia.

▲ In 1507, German mapmaker Martin Waldseemüller was the first person to designate the newly discovered southern continent as "America." He named the continent after Amerigo Vespucci, the Italian explorer who realized he had reached a "new world" rather than islands off the coast of Asia.

European continent, England, Ireland, and Iceland. The mariners who explored the region of North America that was to become the United States and Canada built on their knowledge.

The winds that the northern sailors confronted posed problems on their outbound rather than on their homeward journeys. The same Westerlies that carried Columbus back to Europe blew in the faces of northerners looking west. But mariners soon learned that the strongest winds shifted southward during the winter and that, by departing from northern ports in the spring, they could make adequate headway if they steered northward. Thus, whereas the first landfall of most sailors to the south was somewhere in the Caribbean, those taking the northern route usually reached America along the coast of today's Maine or Canada.

The European generally credited with "discovering" North America is Zuan Cabboto, known today as

John Cabot's Explorations

John Cabot. More precisely, Cabot brought to Europe the first formal knowledge of the northern continental coastline and claimed the land for England. Like Columbus, Cabot was a master mariner from the Italian city-state of Genoa; the two men probably knew each other well. Calculating that England—which traded with Asia only through a long series of intermediaries stretching from Antwerp to Venice to the Muslim world—would be eager to sponsor exploratory voyages, he gained financial backing from King Henry VII. He set sail from Bristol in late May 1497 in the *Mathew*, reaching North America about a month later. After exploring the coast of modern Newfoundland for a month, Cabot rode the Westerlies back to England, arriving just fifteen days after he left North America.

The voyages of Columbus, Cabot, and their successors finally brought the Eastern and Western Hemi-

spheres together. Portuguese explorer Pedro Álvares Cabral reached Brazil in 1500; John Cabot's son Sebastian followed his father to North America in 1507; France financed Giovanni da Verrazzano in 1524 and Jacques Cartier in 1534; and in 1609 and 1610, Henry Hudson explored the North American coast for the Dutch West India Company (see Map 1.5). All were searching primarily for the legendary, nonexistent "Northwest Passage" through the Americas, hoping to find an easy route to the riches of Asia. But in a sign of what was to come, Verrazzano observed that "the [American] countryside is, in fact, full of promise and deserves to be developed for itself. The flora is rich and the fauna abundant."

Spanish Exploration and Conquest

Only in the areas that Spain explored and claimed did colonization begin immediately. On his second voyage in 1493, Columbus brought to Hispaniola seventeen ships loaded with twelve hundred men, seeds, plants, livestock, chickens, and dogs—along with microbes, rats, and weeds. The settlement named Isabela (in the modern Dominican Republic) and its successors became the staging area for the Spanish invasion of America. On the islands of Cuba and Hispaniola, the Europeans learned to adapt to the new environment as did the horses, cattle, and hogs they imported. When the Spaniards moved on to explore the mainland, they rode island-bred horses and ate island-bred cattle and hogs.

At first, Spanish explorers fanned out around the Caribbean basin. In 1513, Juan Ponce de León reached

Cortés and Other Explorers

Florida, and Vasco Núñez de Balboa crossed the Isthmus of Panama to the Pacific Ocean, followed by Pánfilo de Narváez and others who traced the coast of the Gulf of Mexico. In the 1530s and 1540s, conquistadors traveled farther, exploring many regions claimed by the Spanish monarchs: Francisco Vásquez de Coronado journeyed through the southwestern portion of what is now the United States at approximately the same time Hernán de Soto explored the Southeast. Juan Rodríguez Cabrillo sailed along the California coast. Francisco Pizarro, who ventured into western South America, acquired the richest silver mines in the world by conquering the Incas. But the most important conquistador was Hernán Cortés, who in 1521 seized control of the Aztec Empire.

Cortés, an adventurer who first arrived in the Caribbean in 1506, landed a force on the Mexican mainland in 1519 to search for rumored wealthy cities. Near the coast, local Mayas presented him with a group of young enslaved women. One of them, Malinche (whom

▲ Artifacts from L'Anse aux Meadows, Newfoundland, a site the Norse called Straumond. These inconspicuous items reveal a great deal to archaeologists investigating the Norse settlements in North America. The small circular object, a spindle whorl for use in spinning yarn, discloses women's presence at Straumond; the nut comes from a tree that grows only south of the St. Lawrence River, thus indicating the extent of Norse travel along the coast.

L'Anse aux Meadows, Canada   L'Anse aux Meadows, Canada

the Spaniards baptized as a Christian and renamed Doña Marina), had been sold into slavery by the Aztecs and raised by the Mayas. Because she became Cortés's translator, some modern Mexicans regard her as a traitor, but others suggest that she owed no loyalty to people who had enslaved her. In her own day, both Europeans and Aztecs accorded her great respect. Malinche bore Cortés a son, Martín—one of the first *mestizos*, or mixed-blood children—and eventually married one of his officers.

As he traveled toward the Aztec capital, Cortés, with Malinche's help, cleverly recruited peoples whom the Aztecs had long subjugated. The Spaniards' strange beasts (horses, livestock) and noisy weapons (guns, cannon) awed their new allies.

Capture of Tenochtitlán

Yet the Spaniards, too, were awed. Years later, Bernal Díaz del Castillo recalled his first sight of Tenochtitlán, situated in the midst of Lake Texcoco: "We were amazed and said that it was like the enchantments . . . on account of the great towers and cues [temples] and buildings rising from the water, and all built of masonry." Some soldiers asked, he remembered, "whether the things that we saw were not a dream."

The Spaniards came to Tenochtitlán not only with horses and steel weapons but also with smallpox, bringing an epidemic that had begun on Hispaniola. The disease peaked in 1520, fatally weakening Tenochtitlán's defenders. "It spread over the people as great destruction," an Aztec later remembered. "Some it quite covered [with pustules] on all parts—their faces, their heads, their breasts. . . There was great havoc. Very many died of

it." Largely as a consequence, Tenochtitlán surrendered in 1521, and the Spaniards built Mexico City on its site. Cortes and his men seized a fabulous treasure of gold and silver. Thus, less than three decades after Columbus's first voyage, the Spanish monarchs—who treated the American territories as their personal possessions—controlled the richest, most extensive empire Europe had known since ancient Rome.

Spain established the model of colonization that other countries later attempted to imitate, a model with three major elements. First, the Crown tried to maintain tight control over the colonies, imposing a hierarchical government that allowed little autonomy to American jurisdictions. That control included, for example, carefully vetting prospective emigrants and limiting their number and insisting that the colonies import all their manufactured goods from Spain. In order to encourage social stability, those settlers were then required to live in towns under the authorities' watchful eyes. Roman Catholic priests attempted to ensure the colonists' conformity with orthodox religious views.

Spanish Colonization

Second, men constituted most of the first colonists. Although some Spanish women later immigrated to America, the men took primarily Indian—and, later, African—women as their wives or concubines, a development more often than not encouraged by colonial administrators. They thereby began creating the racially mixed population that characterizes much of Latin America to the present day.

◄ An image from the Codex Azcatitlan, an account of the Aztec (Mexica) people's history from their arrival in the Valley of Mexico through the conquest by Cortez. Printed European-style in the late sixteenth century—that is, about seven decades after the conquest—the codex nonetheless presents a Native viewpoint on the cataclysmic events. Here Cortez and his men are preceded by Malinche, his interpreter and mistress, and followed by their Native allies bearing food supplies. Also in the crowd is Cortez's black slave.

Third, the colonies' wealth was based on the exploitation of both the native population and slaves imported from Africa. The Mesoamerican peoples were accustomed to autocratic rule. Spaniards simply took over the role once assumed by native leaders who had exacted labor and tribute from their subjects. Cortés established the *encomienda* system, which granted Indian villages to individual conquistadors as a reward for their services, thus legalizing slavery in all but name.

In 1542, after cogent criticism from a colonial priest, Bartolomé de las Casas, the monarch formulated a new code of laws to reform the system, forbidding the conquerors from enslaving Indians while still allowing them to collect money and goods from tributary villages. In response to the restrictions and to the declining Indian population, the *encomenderos*, familiar with slavery in Spain, began to import Africans in order to increase the labor force under their direct control. They employed Indians and Africans primarily in gold and silver mines, on sugar plantations, and on huge horse, cattle, and sheep ranches. African slavery was far more common on the larger Caribbean islands than on the mainland.

Many demoralized residents of Mesoamerica accepted the Christian religion brought to New Spain by Franciscan and Dominican friars—men who had joined religious orders bound by vows of poverty and celibacy. The friars devoted their energies to persuading Mesoamerican people to move into towns and to build Roman Catholic churches. Spaniards leveled existing cities, constructing cathedrals and monasteries on sites once occupied by Aztec, Incan, and Mayan temples. In such towns, Indians were exposed to European customs and religious rituals designed to assimilate Catholic and pagan beliefs. Friars deliberately juxtaposed the cult of the Virgin Mary with that of the corn goddess, and the Indians adeptly melded aspects of their traditional worldview with Christianity, in a process called *syncretism*. Thousands of Indians residing in Spanish territory embraced Catholicism, at least partly because it was the religion of their new rulers and they were accustomed to obedience.

The New World's gold and silver, initially a boon, ultimately brought about the decline of Spain as a major power. China, a huge country with silver coinage, insatiably demanded Spanish silver, gobbling up an estimated half of the total output of New World mines while paying twice the price current in Europe. Especially after the Spanish began in the 1570s to dispatch silver-laden galleons annually from Acapulco (on Mexico's west coast) to trade at their new settlement at Manila, in the Philippines, Spaniards acquired easy access to luxury Chinese goods such as silk and Asian spices.

Gold, Silver, and Spain's Decline

The influx of unprecedented wealth led to rapid inflation, which (among other adverse effects) caused Spanish products to be overpriced in international markets and imported goods to become cheaper in Spain. The once-profitable Spanish textile-manufacturing industry collapsed as did scores of other businesses. The seemingly endless income from American colonies emboldened successive Spanish monarchs to spend lavishly on wars against the Dutch and the English. Several times in the late sixteenth and early seventeenth centuries, the monarchs repudiated the state debt, wreaking havoc on the nation's finances. When the South American gold and silver mines started to give out in the mid-seventeenth century, Spain's economy crumbled, and the nation lost its international importance.

The Columbian Exchange

A broad mutual transfer of diseases, plants, and animals (called the Columbian Exchange by historian Alfred Crosby; see Map 1.6) resulted directly from the European voyages of the fifteenth and sixteenth centuries and from Spanish colonization. The Eastern and Western Hemispheres had evolved separately for thousands of years, developing widely different forms of life. Many large mammals, such as cattle and horses, were native to the connected continents of Europe, Asia, and Africa, but the Americas contained no domesticated beasts larger than dogs and llamas. The vegetable crops of the Americas—particularly maize, beans, squash, cassava, and potatoes—were more nutritious and produced higher yields than those of Europe and Africa, such as wheat, millet, and rye. In time, native peoples learned to raise and consume European livestock, and Europeans and Africans became accustomed to planting and eating American crops. The diets of all three peoples were consequently vastly enriched. Partly as a result, the world's population doubled over the next three hundred years. About three-fifths of all crops cultivated in the world today were first grown in the Americas.

Diseases carried from Europe and Africa, though, had a devastating impact on the Americas. Indians fell victim to microbes that had long infested the other continents and had repeatedly killed hundreds of thousands but had also often left survivors with some measure of immunity. The statistics are staggering. When Columbus landed on Hispaniola in 1492, approximately half a million people resided there. Fifty years later, that island had fewer than two thousand native inhabitants. Within thirty years of the first landfall at Guanahaní, not one Taíno survived in the Bahamas.

Smallpox and Other Diseases

Although measles, typhus, influenza, malaria, and other illnesses severely afflicted the native peoples, as at Tenochtitlán the greatest killer was smallpox, spread primarily by direct human contact. Overall,

Map 1.6 Major Items in the Columbian Exchange

As European adventurers traversed the world in the fifteenth and sixteenth centuries, they initiated the "Columbian Exchange" of plants, animals, and diseases. These events changed the lives of the peoples of the world forever, bringing new foods and new pestilence to both sides of the Atlantic.

Source: Copyright © Cengage Learning

historians estimate that the long-term effects of the alien microorganisms could have reduced the precontact American population by as much as 90 percent. The epidemics recurred at twenty- to thirty-year intervals, frequently appearing either in tandem or in quick succession, so that weakened survivors of one would be felled by a second or third. Large numbers of deaths also disrupted societies already undergoing severe strains caused by colonization, thus rendering native peoples more vulnerable to droughts, crop failures, or other challenging circumstances.

Even far to the north, where smaller American populations encountered only a few Europeans, disease also ravaged the countryside. A great epidemic, probably viral hepatitis, swept through the villages along the coast north of Cape Cod from 1616 to 1618. Again, the mortality rate may have been as high as 90 percent. An English traveler several years later commented that the people had "died on heaps, as they lay in their houses," and that bones and skulls covered the ruins of villages. Because of this dramatic depopulation of the area, just a few years later English colonists were able to establish settlements virtually unopposed.

The Americans, though, seem to have taken a revenge of sorts. They probably gave the Europeans syphilis, a virulent venereal disease. The first recorded European case of the new ailment occurred in 1493 in Barcelona, Spain, shortly after Columbus's return from the Caribbean.

▲ A male effigy dating from 200–800 C.E., found in a burial site in Nayarit, Mexico. The lesions covering the figurine suggest that the person it represents is suffering from syphilis, which, untreated, produces these characteristic markings on the body in its later stages. Such evidence as this pre-Columbian effigy has now convinced most scholars that syphilis originated in the Americas—a hypothesis in dispute for many years.

Although less likely than smallpox to cause immediate death, syphilis was dangerous and debilitating. Carried by soldiers, sailors, and prostitutes, it spread quickly through Europe and Asia, reaching China by 1505.

The exchange of three commodities had significant impacts on Europe and the Americas. Sugar, first domes

Sugar, Horses, and Tobacco

ticated in the East Indies, was being grown on the islands of the Mediterranean Atlantic by 1450. The ravenous European demand for sugar—which, after initially regarded as a medicine, became a desirable luxury foodstuff—led Columbus to take Canary Island sugar canes to Hispaniola on his 1493 voyage. By the 1520s, plantations in the Greater Antilles worked by African slaves regularly shipped cargoes of sugar to Spain. Half a century later, the Portuguese colony in Brazil (founded 1532) was producing sugar for the European market on an even larger scale, and after 1640 (see pages 39–40), sugar cultivation became the crucial component of English and French colonization in the Caribbean.

Horses—which, like sugar, were brought to America by Columbus in 1493—fell into the hands of North American Indians during the seventeenth century. Through trade and theft, horses spread among the peoples of the Great Plains, reaching most areas by 1750. Lakotas, Comanches, and Crows, among others, came to use horses for transportation and hunting, calculated their wealth in number of horses owned, and waged war primarily on horseback. Women no longer had to carry the band's belongings on their backs. Some groups that previously had cultivated crops abandoned agriculture. Because of the acquisition of horses, a mode of subsistence that had been based on hunting several different animals, in combination with gathering and agriculture, became one focused almost wholly on hunting buffalo.

In America, Europeans encountered tobacco, which at first they believed to have beneficial medicinal effects. Smoking and chewing the "Indian weed" became a fad in Europe after it was planted in Turkey in the sixteenth century. Despite the efforts of such skeptics as King James I of England, who in 1604 pronounced smoking "loathsome to the eye, hatefull to the Nose, harmfull to the brain, [and] dangerous to the Lungs," tobacco's popularity climbed. Its addictive nicotine and its connection to lung cancer were discovered only in the twentieth century.

The Pierpont Morgan Library/Art Resource, NY

▲ The mysterious illustrated text known as the Drake Manuscript and formally titled *Histoire Naturelle des Indies* (Natural History of the Indies) contains many paintings of the life of the indigenous people of Spanish America in the 1580s. This delightful scene shows the end of a successful courtship: the woman's father sits under a tree while giving his blessing to the young couple. The future husband has proved his prowess as a hunter (note the rabbit in his hand) and the future wife her ability as a cook (she is grinding corn). Both are well dressed, and the pot boiling in the house in the background suggests a prosperous future for the happy pair.

Maize

Maize, to Mesoamericans, was a gift from Quetzalcoatl, the plumed serpent god. Cherokees told of an old woman whose blood produced the prized stalks after her grandson buried her body in a cleared, sunny field. For the Abenakis, the crop began when a beautiful maiden ordered a youth to drag her by the hair through a burned-over field. The long hair of the Cherokee grandmother and the Abenaki maiden turned into silk, the flower on the stalks that Europeans called Indian corn. Both tales' symbolic association of corn and women intriguingly supports archaeologists' recent suggestion that—in eastern North America at least—female plant breeders were responsible for substantial improvements in the productivity of maize.

Sacred to all the Indian peoples who grew it, maize was a major part of their diet. They dried the kernels; ground into meal, maize was cooked as a mush or shaped into baked flat cakes, the forerunners of modern tortillas. Indians also heated the dried kernels of some varieties until they popped open, just as is done today. Although the European invaders of North and South America initially disdained maize, they soon learned it could be cultivated in a wide variety of conditions—from sea level to twelve thousand feet, from regions with abundant rainfall to dry lands with as little as twelve inches of rain a year. Corn was also highly productive, yielding almost twice as many calories per acre as wheat. So Europeans, too, came to rely on corn, growing it not only in their American settlements but also in their homelands.

Maize cultivation spread to Asia and Africa. Today, China is second only to the United States in total corn production, and corn is more widely grown in Africa than any other crop. Still, the United States produces 45 percent of the world's corn—almost half of it in the three states of Illinois, Iowa, and Nebraska—and corn is the nation's single largest crop. More than half of American corn is consumed by livestock. Much of the rest is processed into syrup, which sweetens carbonated beverages and candies, or into ethanol, a gasoline additive that reduces both pollution and dependence on fossil fuels. Corn is an ingredient in light beer and toothpaste. It is used in the manufacture of tires, wallpaper, cat litter, and aspirin. Remarkably, of the ten thousand products in a modern American grocery store, about one-fourth rely to some extent on corn.

Today, this crop bequeathed to the world by ancient American plant breeders provides one-fifth of all the calories consumed by the earth's peoples. The gift of Quetzalcoatl has linked the globe.

The LuEsther T. Mertz Library, NYBG/Art Resource, NY

◄ The earliest known European drawing of maize, the American plant that was to have such an extraordinary impact on the entire world.

The European and African invasion of the Americas therefore had a significant biological component, for the invaders carried plants and animals with them. Some creatures, such as livestock, they brought deliberately. Others, including rats (which infested their ships), weeds, and diseases, arrived unexpectedly. And the same process occurred in reverse. When the Europeans returned home, they deliberately took back such crops as maize, potatoes, and tobacco, along with that unanticipated stowaway, syphilis.

Europeans in North America

Europeans were initially more interested in exploiting North America's natural resources than in the difficult task of establishing colonies there. John Cabot had reported that fish were extraordinarily plentiful near Newfoundland, so Europeans rushed to take advantage of abundant codfish, which were in great demand in their homelands as an inexpensive source of protein. The French, Spanish, Basques, and Portuguese regularly fished North American waters throughout the sixteenth century; Verrazzano and Cartier, in 1524 and 1534, respectively, both encountered anonymous vessels already fishing along the American coast. In the early 1570s, after Spain opened its markets to English shipping, the English (who previously had fished near Iceland for home consumption only) eagerly joined the Newfoundland fishery, thereafter selling salt cod to the Spanish in exchange for valuable Asian goods. The English soon became dominant in the region, which by the end of the century was the focal point of a European commerce more valuable than that with the Gulf of Mexico.

Fishermen quickly realized they could increase their profits by exchanging cloth and metal goods, such as pots

Trade Among Indians and Europeans

and knives, for native trappers' beaver pelts, used to make fashionable hats in Europe. Initially, Europeans traded from ships sailing along the coast, but later they set up outposts on the mainland to centralize and control the traffic in furs. Such outposts were inhabited chiefly by male adventurers, whose major aim was to send as many pelts as possible home to Europe.

The Europeans' demand for furs, especially beaver, was matched by the Indians' desire for European goods that could make their lives easier and establish their superiority over their neighbors. Some bands began to concentrate so completely on trapping for the European market that they abandoned their traditional economies and became partially dependent on others for food. The intensive trade in pelts also had serious ecological consequences. In some regions, beavers were wiped out. The disappearance of their dams led to soil erosion, which

increased when European settlers cleared forests for farmland in later decades.

English merchants and political leaders watched enviously as Spain was enriched by its valuable American pos-

Contest Between Spain and England

sessions. In the mid-sixteenth century, English "sea dogs" like John Hawkins and Sir Francis Drake began to raid Spanish treasure fleets sailing home from the Caribbean. Their actions caused friction between the two countries and helped foment a war that in 1588 culminated in the defeat of a huge invasion force—the Spanish Armada—off the English coast. As part of the contest with Spain, English leaders started to think about planting colonies in the Western Hemisphere, thereby gaining better access to valuable trade goods while simultaneously preventing their enemy from dominating the Americas.

Encouraging the queen and her courtiers in that aim was Richard Hakluyt, a clergyman who became fascinated by tales of exploratory voyages while he was a student in the 1560s. He prepared and published English translations of numerous accounts of discoveries around the globe, repeatedly insisting on England's preeminent claim to the North American continent. In *Divers Voyages* (1582) and especially *Principall Navigations* (1589), he argued unreservedly for the benefits of English colonization in such "fertill and temperate places," contending that "there is none, that of right may be more bolde in this enterprice than the Englishmen."

The first English colonial planners saw Spain's possessions as a model and a challenge. They hoped to reproduce Spanish successes by dispatching to America men who would exploit the native peoples for their own and their nation's benefit. A group that included Sir Walter Raleigh began to promote a scheme to establish outposts that could trade with the Indians and provide bases for attacks on New Spain. Approving the idea, Queen Elizabeth I authorized Raleigh to colonize North America.

After two preliminary expeditions, in 1587 Sir Walter Raleigh sent 117 colonists to the territory he named

Roanoke

Virginia, after Elizabeth, the "Virgin Queen." They established a settlement on Roanoke Island, in what is now North Carolina, but in 1590 a resupply ship—delayed in leaving England because of the Spanish Armada—could not find them. The colonists had vanished, leaving only the word *Croatoan* (the name of a nearby island) carved on a tree. Recent tree-ring studies have shown that the North Carolina coast experienced a severe drought between 1587 and 1589, which would have created a subsistence crisis for the settlers and could well have led them to abandon the Roanoke site.

▲ A watercolor by John White, an artist with Raleigh's second preliminary expedition (and who later was governor of the ill-fated 1587 colony). He identified his subjects as the wife and daughter of the chief of Pomeioc, a village near Roanoke. Note the woman's elaborate tattoos and the fact that the daughter carries an Elizabethan doll, obviously given to her by one of the Englishmen.

The explanation for such failings becomes clear in Thomas Harriot's *A Briefe and True Report of the New Found Land of Virginia*, published in 1588 to publicize Raleigh's colony. Harriot, a noted scientist who sailed with the second of the preliminary voyages to Roanoke, described the animals, plants, and people of the region for an English readership. His account revealed that, although the explorers depended on nearby villagers for most of their food, they needlessly antagonized their neighbors by killing some of them for what Harriot admitted were unjustifiable reasons.

Harriot's *Briefe and True Report*

The scientist advised later colonizers to deal with the native peoples of America more humanely than his comrades had. But the content of his book suggested why that advice would rarely be followed. *A Briefe and True Report* examined the possibilities for economic development in America. Harriot stressed three points: the availability of commodities familiar to Europeans,

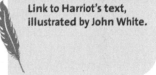

Link to Harriot's text, illustrated by John White.

such as grapes, iron, copper, and fur-bearing animals; the potential profitability of exotic American products, such as maize, cassava, and tobacco; and the relative ease of manipulating the native population to the Europeans' advantage. Should the Americans attempt to resist the English by force, Harriot asserted, the latter's advantages of disciplined soldiers and superior weaponry would quickly deliver victory.

Harriot's *Briefe and True Report* depicted for his English readers a bountiful land full of opportunities for quick profit. The people residing there would, he thought, "in a short time be brought to civilitie" through conversion to Christianity, admiration for European superiority, or conquest—if they did not die from disease, the ravages of which he witnessed. Thomas Harriot understood the key elements of the story, but his prediction was far off the mark. European dominance of North America would be difficult to achieve. Indeed, it never was fully achieved, in the sense Harriot and his compatriots intended.

SUMMARY

The process of initial contact among Europeans, Africans, and Americans that ended with Thomas Harriot near the close of the sixteenth century began approximately 250 years earlier when Portuguese sailors first set out to explore the Mediterranean Atlantic and the West African coast. Those seamen established commercial ties that brought African slaves first to Iberia and then to the islands the Europeans conquered and settled. The Mediterranean Atlantic and its island sugar plantations nurtured the mariners who, like Christopher Columbus,

Thus, England's first attempt to plant a permanent settlement on the North American coast failed, as had earlier efforts by Portugal on Cape Breton Island (early 1520s), Spain in modern Georgia (mid-1520s), and France in South Carolina and northern Florida (1560s). All three enterprises collapsed because of the hostility of neighboring peoples and colonists' inability to be self-sustaining in foodstuffs. The Portuguese, the Spanish, the first French settlers, and the English could not maintain friendly relations with local Indians, and Spanish soldiers destroyed the Florida French colony in 1565 (see page 35).

Legacy FOR A PEOPLE AND A NATION

Kennewick Man/Ancient One

On July 28, 1996, Will Thomas, a college student wading in the Columbia River near Kennewick, Washington, felt something round underfoot. Shocked when he realized it was a skull, Thomas initially believed he had found a recent murder victim. Yet soon the antiquity of Thomas's find had been determined: it was about 9,200 years old. During the next decade, the skeleton dubbed "Kennewick Man" (by the press) or "Ancient One" (by local Indian tribes) was featured on CBS television's *60 Minutes* (October 1998), in *National Geographic* (December 2000), in a *Time* cover story (March 2006), and in several documentary films. The oldest nearly complete skeleton found in the United States, the remains became the subject of a major federal court case and numerous books and articles.

At issue in the lawsuit was the interpretation of the Native American Graves Protection and Repatriation Act (NAGPRA), adopted by Congress in 1990 to prevent the desecration of Indian gravesites and to provide for the return of bones and sacred objects to native peoples. It defined the term *Native American* as "of, or relating to, a tribe, people, or culture that is indigenous to the United States." Tribes in the area, led by the Umatillas, prepared to reclaim and rebury the remains with appropriate rituals.

But then eight anthropologists filed suit in federal court, contending that bones of such antiquity were unlikely to be linked to modern tribes and requesting access to them for scientific study.

Although the U.S. government supported the tribes' claims, in late August 2002 a federal judge ruled in favor of the anthropologists, in a decision upheld on appeal two years later. He declared that the Interior Department had erred in concluding that all pre-1492 remains found in the United States should automatically be considered Native American under the NAGPRA definition. The Umatillas protested his decision, contending that it clearly contradicted Congress's intent in enacting NAGPRA and that "this treatment of Native American remains as scientific specimens deprives native people of the basic right to properly bury or care for these ancestors." In June 2006, Umatilla leaders visited the bones at a Seattle museum, where they were under study, to honor and pray for them.

The debate over the skeleton known alternately as Kennewick Man and Ancient One reveals one facet of the continuing legacy to the nation of the often-contentious relationship between its indigenous inhabitants and later immigrants.

---

ventured into previously unknown waters—those who sailed to India and Brazil as well as to the Caribbean and the North American coast. When Columbus first reached the Americas, he thought he had found Asia, his intended destination. Later explorers knew better but, except for the Spanish, regarded the Americas primarily as a barrier that prevented them from reaching their long-sought goal of an oceanic route to the riches of China and the Moluccas. Ordinary European fishermen were the first to realize that the northern coasts had valuable products to offer: fish and furs, both much in demand in their homelands.

The Aztecs had predicted that their Fifth Sun would end in earthquakes and hunger. Hunger they surely experienced after Cortés's invasion, and even if there were no earthquakes, their great temples tumbled to the ground nevertheless, as the Spaniards used their

stones (and Indian laborers) to construct cathedrals honoring their God and his son, Jesus, rather than Huitzilopochtli. The conquerors employed, first, American and, later, enslaved African workers to till the fields, mine the precious metals, and herd the livestock that earned immense profits for themselves and their mother country.

The initial impact of Europeans on the Americas proved devastating. Flourishing civilizations were markedly altered in just a few short decades. Europeans' diseases killed millions of the Western Hemisphere's inhabitants; their livestock, along with a wide range of other imported animals and plants, irrevocably modified the American environment. Europe, too, was changed: American foodstuffs like corn and potatoes improved nutrition throughout the continent, and American gold and silver first enriched, then ruined, the Spanish economy.

By the end of the sixteenth century, fewer people resided in North America than had lived there before Columbus's arrival. And the people who did live there—Indian, African, and European—resided in a world that was indeed new—a world engaged in the unprecedented process of combining foods, religions, economies, ways of life, and political systems that had developed separately for millennia. Understandably, conflict and dissension permeated that process.

SUGGESTIONS FOR FURTHER READING

David Abulafia, *The Discovery of Mankind: Atlantic Encounters in the Age of Columbus* (2008)

Alfred W. Crosby, *The Columbian Exchange: Biological and Cultural Consequences of 1492* (1972)

John H. Elliott, *Empires of the Atlantic World: Britain and Spain in America, 1492–1830* (2006)

Alvin Josephy, Jr., ed., *America in 1492* (1992)

Peter C. Mancall, *Hakluyt's Promise: An Elizabethan's Obsession for an English America* (2007)

Charles C. Mann, *1491: New Revelations of the Americas Before Columbus* (2005)

D. W. Meinig, *Atlantic America, 1492–1800* (1986)

Samuel Eliot Morison, *The European Discovery of America: The Southern Voyages, A.D. 1492–1616* (1974); *The Northern Voyages, A.D. 1500–1600* (1971)

John K. Thornton, *Africa and Africans in the Making of the Atlantic World, 1400–1680* (1992)

Go to the CourseMate website for primary source links, study tools, and review materials for this chapter. www.cengagebrain.com

Chapter 2

Europeans Colonize North America 1600–1650

Detail of Providence Island: Map of North America by George Willdey, 1710. Colonial Williamsburg Foundation

Captain William Rudyerd seemed like the sort of man any Puritan colony in the Americas would prize, so when his older brother urged the planners of the new settlement to appoint him muster master general, they readily agreed. Rudyerd, a veteran of wars on the European continent, followed the new dissenting English faith, as did the planners and many of the settlers. In the first years of the colony, Rudyerd proved to be a vigorous soldier who worked hard to train the settlers to defend themselves from attack. But he also proved to be a vigorous defender of his own status, and his actions wreaked havoc in the fragile community. The captain beat to death a servant suffering from scurvy (Rudyerd thought the servant was merely lazy) and quarreled continually with other settlers whom he believed failed to show the proper respect to a gentleman of noble birth.

One of Rudyerd's antagonists was the Reverend Lewis Morgan, with whom the captain argued about religious books and the conduct of church services. Rudyerd, traditional minded despite his Puritan beliefs, found Morgan's encouragement of congregational psalm singing scandalously radical. Their disagreements quickly escalated into exchanges of insults. "Your foul mouthed answer deserves rather sharp retribution than any equal respect from A gentleman," the captain once haughtily told the clergyman. "I have given you too Much respect; which has begot so much incivility."

Similar conflicts occurred in all the Anglo-American settlements, as gentlemen accustomed to unquestioning deference learned to their dismay that in a colonial setting their inherited social standing could be challenged by various upstarts. But in Rudyerd and Morgan's colony the disputes were especially dangerous because the two lived on Providence Island, an isolated Puritan outpost off the coast of modern Nicaragua.

◀ This early-eighteenth-century British map of the Caribbean and Central America vividly illustrates the precarious position of the seventeenth-century Providence Island settlers, on their tiny island surrounded by Spanish territory on the mainland to the east, south, and west, and the Spanish-dominated Greater Antilles to the north.

Chronology

1558	■ Elizabeth I becomes queen
1565	■ Founding of St. Augustine (Florida), oldest permanent European settlement in present-day United States
1598	■ Oñate conquers Pueblos in New Mexico for Spain
1603	■ James I becomes king
1607	■ Jamestown founded, first permanent English settlement in North America
1608	■ Quebec founded by the French
1610	■ Founding of Santa Fe, New Mexico
1614	■ Fort Orange (Albany) founded by the Dutch
1619	■ Virginia House of Burgesses established, first representative assembly in the English colonies
1620	■ Plymouth colony founded, first permanent English settlement in New England
1622	■ Powhatan Confederacy attacks Virginia
1624	■ Dutch settle on Manhattan Island (New Amsterdam)
	■ English colonize St. Kitts, first island in Lesser Antilles settled by Europeans
	■ James I revokes Virginia Company's charter
1625	■ Charles I becomes king
1630	■ Massachusetts Bay colony founded
1634	■ Maryland founded
1636	■ Williams expelled from Massachusetts Bay, founds Providence, Rhode Island
	■ Connecticut founded
1637	■ Pequot War in New England
1638	■ Hutchinson expelled from Massachusetts Bay, goes to Rhode Island
1642	■ Montreal founded by the French
1646	■ Treaty ends hostilities between Virginia and Powhatan Confederacy

*P*rovidence Island, founded by a company of Puritan adventurers in 1630—the same year as Massachusetts Bay—sought to establish an English beachhead in the fertile tropics, which could lead to successful colonization of the Central American mainland. Yet the outpost's perilous location amid Spanish settlements, its failure to establish a viable local economy, and, ultimately, its desperate attempts to stay afloat financially by serving as a base for English privateers caused its downfall. That decision led the Spaniards to conclude that the Puritans *had* to be removed. Twice, in 1635 and 1640, Providence Island fended off Spanish attacks. But in May 1641, a large Spanish fleet of seven ships carrying two thousand soldiers and sailors captured the island, and the survivors scattered to other Caribbean settlements, to English colonies on the mainland, or back to England.

By this time, though, Spain no longer predominated in the Americas. France, the Netherlands, and England all had permanent colonies in North America by the 1640s. The French and Dutch colonies, like the Spanish outposts, were settled largely by European men who interacted regularly with indigenous peoples, using their labor or seeking to convert them to Christianity. Like the conquistadors, French and Dutch merchants (on the mainland) and planters (in the Caribbean) hoped to make a quick profit and then perhaps return to their homelands. The English, as Thomas Harriot had made clear in the 1580s, were just as interested in profiting from North America. But they pursued those profits in a different way.

In contrast to other Europeans, most of the English settlers—including those of the failed Providence Island colony—came to America intending to stay. Along the northeast Atlantic coast of the continent, in the area that came to be known as New England, they arrived in family groups, sometimes accompanied by friends and relatives from neighboring villages back home. They re-created the European agricultural economy and family life to an extent impossible in the other colonies, where single men predominated. English colonies in the Chesapeake region and on the Caribbean islands, though, came to be based on large-scale agricultural production for the international market by a labor force composed of bonded servants and slaves.

Wherever they settled, the English, like other Europeans, prospered only after they learned to adapt to the alien environment, something the Providence Islanders never achieved. The first permanent English colonies survived because of contacts with nearby Indians. The settlers had to learn to grow such unfamiliar American crops as maize and squash. They also had to develop extensive trading relationships with native peoples and with colonies established by other European countries. Needing laborers for their fields, they first used English indentured servants, then later began to import African slaves. Thus the early history of the region that became the United States and the English Caribbean is best understood not as an isolated story of English colonization but rather as a series of complex interactions among a variety of European, African, and American peoples and environments.

- Why did different groups of Europeans choose to migrate to the Americas?

- How did different native peoples react to their presence?

- In what ways did the English colonies in the Chesapeake and New England differ, and in what ways were they alike?

Spanish, French, and Dutch North America

Spaniards established the first permanent European settlement within the boundaries of the modern United States, but others had initially attempted that feat. Twice in the 1560s Huguenots (French Protestants), who were seeking to escape persecution, planted colonies on the south Atlantic coast. A passing ship rescued the starving survivors of the first colony, located in present-day South Carolina. The second colony, near modern Jacksonville, Florida, was destroyed in 1565 by a Spanish expedition under the command of Pedro Menéndez de Avilés. To ensure Spanish domination of the strategically important region (located near sea-lanes used by Spanish treasure ships bound for Europe), Menéndez set up a small fortified outpost, which he named St. Augustine—now the oldest continuously inhabited European settlement in the United States.

The local Guale and Timucua nations initially allied themselves with the powerful newcomers and welcomed Franciscan friars into their villages. The relationship did not remain peaceful for long, though, because the natives resisted the imposition of Spanish authority. Still, the Franciscans offered the Indians spiritual solace for the diseases and troubles besetting them after the Europeans' invasion, and eventually they gained numerous converts at missions that stretched westward across Florida and northward into the islands along the Atlantic coast.

More than thirty years passed after the founding of St. Augustine before conquistadors ventured anew into the present-day United States.

New Mexico

In 1598, drawn northward by rumors of rich cities, Juan de Oñate, a Mexican-born adventurer whose wife descended from both Cortés and Moctezuma, led a group of about five hundred soldiers and settlers to New Mexico. At first, the Pueblo peoples greeted the newcomers cordially. But when the Spaniards began to use torture, murder, and rape to extort food and clothing from the villagers, the residents of Acoma killed several soldiers, among them Oñate's nephew. The invaders responded ferociously, killing more than eight hundred people and capturing the remainder. All the captives above the age of twelve were ordered enslaved for twenty years, and men older than twenty-five had one foot amputated. Not surprisingly, the other Pueblo villages surrendered.

Yet Oñate's bloody victory proved illusory, for New Mexico held little wealth. It also was too far from the Pacific coast to assist in protecting Spanish sea-lanes, which had been one of Oñate's aims (he, like others, initially believed the continent to be much narrower than it actually is). Many of the Spaniards returned to Mexico, but horses remained, transforming the lives of the indigenous inhabitants. Officials considered abandoning the isolated colony, which lay 800 miles north of the nearest Spanish settlement. Still, for defensive purposes, the authorities decided to maintain a small military outpost and a few Christian missions in the area, with the capital at Santa Fe (founded 1610) (see Map 4.1). As in regions to the south, Spanish leaders were granted *encomiendas,* guaranteeing them control over the labor of Pueblo villagers. But in the absence of mines or fertile agricultural lands, such grants yielded small profit.

On the Atlantic coast, the French turned their attention northward, to the area that Jacques Cartier had explored in the 1530s. Several

Quebec and Montreal

times they tried to establish permanent bases along the Canadian coast but failed until 1605, when they founded Port Royal. Then in 1608, Samuel de Champlain set up a trading post at an interior site that the local Iroquois had called Stadacona when Cartier spent the winter there seventy-five years earlier. Champlain renamed it Quebec. He had chosen well: Quebec was the most defensible spot in the entire St. Lawrence River valley, a stronghold that controlled access to the heartland of the continent. In 1642, the French established a second post, Montreal, at the falls of the St. Lawrence (and thus at the end of navigation by oceangoing vessels), a place the Indians called Hochelaga.

Visualizing THE PAST

Acoma Pueblo

Today, as in the late sixteenth century when it was besieged and eventually captured by the Spanish conquistador Juan de Oñate, the Acoma Pueblo sits high atop an isolated mesa. Long before the Spaniards arrived in modern New Mexico, the location was selected because it was easily defensible; some structures that date back to the eleventh century are still standing in the middle of the village. Building on a mesa 365 feet high was safer than living on the plains below, but it caused other problems—most notably, with the water supply. To this day there is no source of water in the village. Acoma's residents had to carry water up a steep set of stairs cut into the mesa's side (today there is an almost equally steep road). The women of Acoma were and are accomplished potters. Some pots, like the one shown here, were designed with a low center of gravity. How would that design help women to reach the top of the mesa with much-needed water? How would they carry such pots?

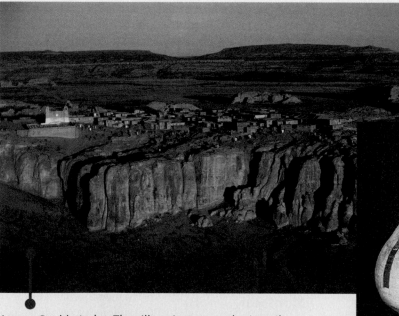

© Kevin Fleming/CORBIS

Acoma Pueblo today. The village is now used primarily for ritual purposes; few people reside there permanently, because all water must be trucked in.

Field Museum of Natural History FMNH Neg # A109998c

A pot designed for carrying water to the top of the mesa.

Table 2.1 The Founding of Permanent European Colonies in North America, 1565–1640

Colony	Founder(s)	Date	Basis of Economy
Florida	Pedro Menéndez de Avilés	1565	Farming
New Mexico	Juan de Oñate	1598	Livestock
Virginia	Virginia Co.	1607	Tobacco
New France	France	1608	Fur trading
New Netherland	Dutch West India Co.	1614	Fur trading
Plymouth	Separatists	1620	Farming, fishing
Maine	Sir Ferdinando Gorges	1622	Fishing
St. Kitts, Barbados, et al.	European immigrants	1624	Sugar
Massachusetts Bay	Massachusetts Bay	1630	Farming, fishing, fur trading
Maryland	Cecilius Calvert	1634	Tobacco
Rhode Island	Roger Williams	1636	Farming
Connecticut	Thomas Hooker	1636	Farming, fur trading
New Haven	Massachusetts migrants	1638	Farming
New Hampshire	Massachusetts migrants	1638	Farming, fishing

Before the founding of these settlements, fishermen served as the major transporters of North American beaver pelts to France, but the new posts quickly took over control of the lucrative trade in furs (see Table 2.1). Only a few Europeans resided in New France; most were men, some of whom married Indian women. The colony's leaders gave land grants along the river to wealthy seigneurs (nobles), who then imported tenants to work their farms. A small number of Frenchmen brought their wives and took up agriculture; even so, more than twenty-five years after Quebec's founding, it had just sixty-four resident families, along with traders and soldiers. With respect to territory occupied and farmed, northern New France never grew much beyond the confines of the river valley between Quebec and Montreal (see Map 2.1). Thus, it differed significantly from New Spain, characterized by scattered cities and direct supervision of Indian laborers.

French missionaries of the Society of Jesus (Jesuits), a Roman Catholic order dedicated to converting nonbelievers to Christianity, also came

Jesuit Missions in New France

to New France. First arriving in Quebec in 1625, the Jesuits, whom the Indians called Black Robes, tried to persuade indigenous peoples to live near French settlements and to adopt European agricultural methods. When that effort failed, the Jesuits concluded that they could introduce Catholicism to their new charges without insisting that they fundamentally alter their traditional ways of life. Accordingly, the Black Robes learned Indian languages and traveled to remote regions of the interior, where they lived in twos and threes among hundreds of potential converts.

Using a variety of strategies, Jesuits sought to gain the confidence of influential men and to undermine the authority of village shamans, the traditional religious leaders. Trained in rhetoric, Jesuits won admirers with their eloquence. Immune to smallpox (for all had survived the disease already), they explained epidemics among the Indians as God's punishment for sin, their arguments aided by the ineffectiveness of the shamans' traditional remedies against the new pestilence. Drawing on European science, Jesuits predicted solar and lunar eclipses. Perhaps most important, they amazed villagers by communicating with each other over long distances through marks on paper. The Indians' desire to learn how to harness the extraordinary power of literacy was one of the critical factors that made them receptive to the missionaries' spiritual message.

Although the process took many years, Jesuits slowly gained thousands of converts, some of whom moved to reserves set aside for Christian Indians. Catholicism offered women in particular the inspiring role model of the Virgin Mary, personified in Montreal and Quebec by communities of nuns who taught Indian women and children, and ministered to their needs. Many male and female converts followed Catholic teachings with fervor and piety, altering traditional

Link to excerpts about Indian and Jesuit relations.

Map 2.1 European Settlements and Indian Tribes in Eastern North America, 1650

The few European settlements established in the East before 1650 were widely scattered, hugging the shores of the Atlantic Ocean and the banks of its major rivers. By contrast, America's native inhabitants controlled the vast interior expanse of the continent, and Spaniards had begun to move into the West.

Source: Copyright © Cengage Learning

native customs of allowing premarital sexual relationships and easy divorce, because Catholic doctrine prohibited both. Yet they resisted Jesuits' attempts to have them adopt strict European child-rearing methods, instead retaining their more relaxed practices. Jesuits, unlike Franciscans in New Mexico, recognized that such aspects of native culture could be compatible with Christian beliefs. Their efforts to attract converts were further aided by their lack of interest in labor tribute or land acquisition.

Jesuit missionaries faced little competition from other Europeans for native peoples' souls, but French fur traders had to confront a direct challenge. In 1614, only five years after Henry Hudson explored the river that now bears his name, his sponsor, the Dutch West India Company, established an outpost (Fort Orange) on that river at the site of present-day Albany, New York. Like the French, the Dutch sought beaver pelts, and their presence so close to Quebec threatened French domination of the region. The Netherlands, at the time the world's dominant commercial power, aimed primarily at trade rather than at colonization. Thus New Netherland, like New France, remained small, confined largely to a river valley that offered easy access to its settlements. The colony's southern anchor was New Amsterdam, founded in 1624 on Manhattan Island, at the mouth of the Hudson River.

New Netherland

As the Dutch West India Company's colony in North America, New Netherland was a small outpost of a vast commercial empire that extended to Africa, Brazil, the Caribbean, and modern-day Indonesia. Autocratic directors-general ruled the colony for the company; with no elected assembly, settlers felt little loyalty to their nominal leaders. Few migrants arrived. Even an offer in 1629 of large land grants, or patroonships, to people who would bring fifty settlers to the province failed to attract takers. (Only one such tract—Rensselaerswyck, near Albany—was ever fully developed.) As late as the mid-1660s, New Netherland had only about five thousand inhabitants. Some were Swedes and Finns who resided in the former colony of New Sweden (founded in 1638 on the Delaware River; see Map 2.1), which was seized by the Dutch in 1655. New Sweden's chief legacy to North American settlement was log cabin construction.

The Indian allies of New France and New Netherland clashed in part because of fur-trade rivalries. In the 1640s the Iroquois, who traded chiefly with the Dutch and lived in modern upstate New York, went to war against the Hurons, who traded primarily with the French and lived in present-day Ontario. The Iroquois wanted to become the major supplier of pelts to Europeans and they wanted to ensure the security of their hunting territories. They achieved both goals by using guns supplied by the Dutch to virtually exterminate the Hurons, whose population had already been decimated by a smallpox epidemic. The Iroquois thus established themselves as a major force in the region, one that in the future Europeans could ignore only at their peril.

The Caribbean

In the Caribbean, France, the Netherlands, and England collided repeatedly in the first half of the seventeenth century. The Spanish concentrated their colonization efforts on the Greater Antilles—Cuba, Hispaniola, Jamaica, and Puerto Rico. They ignored many smaller islands, partly because of resistance by their Carib inhabitants and partly because the mainland offered greater wealth for less effort. But the tiny islands attracted other European powers: they could provide bases from which to attack Spanish vessels loaded with American gold and silver, and they could serve as sources of valuable tropical products such as dyes and fruits.

England was the first northern European nation to establish a permanent foothold in the smaller Caribbean islands (the Lesser Antilles), settling on St. Christopher (St. Kitts) in 1624, then later on other islands, such as Barbados (1627) and Providence (1630). France was able to colonize Guadeloupe and Martinique only by defeating the Caribs, whereas the Dutch more easily gained control of tiny St. Eustatius (strategically located near St. Christopher). In addition to indigenous inhabitants, Europeans had to worry about conflicts with Spaniards and with one another. Like Providence Island, many colonies changed hands during the seventeenth century. For example, the English drove the Spanish out of Jamaica in 1655, and the French soon thereafter took over half of Hispaniola, creating the colony of St. Domingue (modern Haiti).

Warfare and Hurricanes

Another danger, too, confronted the new settlers: the great windstorms called by the Taíno people *hurakán*, or, in English, hurricanes. Just nine months after the establishment of the first English outpost on St. Christopher, wrote one colonist, "came a Hericano and blew it away." Two years later, a second storm again devastated the infant colony, leaving the settlers "very miserable," without housing or adequate provisions. Almost every year in the late summer months, one or two islands suffered significant damage from hurricanes. Survivors expressed awe at the destructive force of the storms, which repeatedly forced them to rebuild and replant. To withstand the winds, they designed one- or two-story brick and stone houses with low roofs and heavy wooden shutters over the windows.

Why did Europeans try to gain and retain control of such imperiled islands? The primary answer is sugar. Europeans loved sugar, which provided a sweet taste and a quick energy boost and greatly enriched those who grew and processed it for international markets. Entering Europe in substantial quantities at approximately the same time as coffee and tea—the stimulating, addictive, and bitter Asian drinks improved by sweetening—sugar quickly became a crucial element of the European diet.

Sugar Cultivation

English residents of Barbados, after first experimenting with tobacco, cotton, and indigo, discovered in the early 1640s that the island's soil and climate were ideal for cultivating sugar cane. At the time, the world's supply of sugar came primarily from the Madeiras, the Canaries, São Tomé, and especially Brazil, where farmers, each with a few servants or slaves, grew much of the crop. Sugar

▲ In the 1660s, a French book illustrated the various phases of sugar processing for curious European readers. Teams of oxen (A) turned the mill, the rollers of which crushed the canes (C), producing the sap (D), which was collected in a vat (E), then boiled down into molasses (K). African slaves, with minimal supervision by a few Europeans (foreground), managed all phases of the process.

cane needed to be processed within two days of being harvested, or the juice would dry, so Brazilian producers quickly took their cane to central mills where it was crushed, boiled down, and finally refined into brown and white sugars.

Barbadians, several of whom visited northeastern Brazil while it was briefly ruled by the Dutch in the 1630s and 1640s, initially copied both the Brazilians' machinery and their small-scale methods of production, which used an existing work force of servants and slaves. By the mid-1650s, funded by wealthy English merchants and their own profits from raising tobacco and cotton, the more substantial planters expanded their enterprises dramatically. They increased the size of their landholdings, built their own sugar mills, and purchased growing numbers of laborers—first English and Irish servants, then African slaves.

As other Caribbean planters embraced sugar-cane cultivation, Barbadians' profit margins were reduced. Even so, sugar remained the most valuable American commodity for more than one hundred years. In the eighteenth century, sugar grown by large gangs of slaves in British Jamaica and French St. Domingue dominated the world market. Yet, in the long run, the future economic importance of the Europeans' American colonies lay on the mainland rather than in the Caribbean.

> Link to an excerpt from Richard Ligon's book on slavery in Barbados.

English Interest in Colonization

The failure of Raleigh's Roanoke colony ended English efforts to settle in North America for nearly two decades. When the English decided in 1606 to try once more, they again planned colonies that imitated the Spanish model. Yet greater success came when they abandoned that model and founded settlements very different from those of other European powers. Unlike Spain, France, or the Netherlands, England eventually sent large numbers of men and women to set up agriculturally based colonies on the mainland. Two major developments prompted approximately 200,000 ordinary English men and women to move to North America in the seventeenth century and led their government to encourage their emigration.

The first development was the onset of dramatic social and economic change. In the 150-year period after

Social and Economic Change

1530, largely as a result of the introduction of nutritious American crops, England's population doubled. All those additional people needed food, clothing, and other goods. The competition for goods led to inflation, coupled with a fall in real wages as the number of workers increased. In these new economic and demographic circumstances, some English people—especially those with sizable landholdings that could produce food and clothing fibers for the growing population—substantially improved their lot. Others, particularly landless laborers and those with small amounts of land, fell into poverty. When landowners raised rents, took control of lands that peasants had long been allowed to use in common (enclosure), or decided to combine small holdings into large units, they forced tenants off the land. Consequently, geographical as well as social mobility increased, and the population of the cities swelled. London, for example, more than tripled in size by 1650, when 375,000 residents lived in its crowded buildings.

Wealthy English people reacted with alarm to what they saw as the disappearance of traditional ways of life. Steady streams of the landless and homeless filled the streets and highways. Obsessed with the problem of maintaining order, officials came to believe England was overcrowded. They concluded that colonies established in North America could siphon off England's "surplus population," thus easing social strains at home. For similar reasons, many English people decided they could improve their circumstances by migrating from a small, land-scarce, apparently overpopulated island to a large, land-rich, apparently empty continent and its nearby islands. Among those attracted by prospects for emigration were such younger sons of gentlemen as William Rudyerd, who were excluded from inheriting land by wealthy families' practice of primogeniture, which reserved all real estate for the eldest son. Such economic considerations were rendered even more significant in light of the second development: a major change in English religious practice.

The sixteenth century witnessed a religious transformation that eventually led large numbers of English dis-

English Reformation

senters to leave their homeland. In 1533 Henry VIII, wanting a male heir and infatuated with Anne Boleyn, asked the pope to annul his marriage to his Spanish-born queen, Catherine of Aragón, despite nearly twenty years of marriage and the birth of a daughter. When the pope refused, Henry left the Roman Catholic Church. He founded the Church of England and—with Parliament's concurrence—proclaimed himself its head. At first, the reformed Church of England differed little from Catholicism in its

practices. Under Henry's daughter, Elizabeth I (child of his later marriage to Anne Boleyn), though, new currents of religious belief, which had originated on the European continent early in the sixteenth century, dramatically affected that established church, termed thus because it had the official imprimatur of the government and was supported by tax revenues.

These currents constituted the Protestant Reformation, led by Martin Luther, a German monk, and John Calvin, a French cleric and lawyer. Challenging the Catholic doctrine that priests were intermediaries between laypeople and God, Luther and Calvin insisted that people could interpret the Bible for themselves. That notion stimulated the spread of literacy: to understand and interpret the Bible, people had to learn how to read. Both Luther and Calvin rejected Catholic rituals, denying the need for an elaborate church hierarchy. They also asserted that the key to salvation was faith in God, rather than—as Catholic teaching had it—a combination of faith and good works. Calvin went further than Luther, stressing God's omnipotence and emphasizing the need for people to submit totally to God's will.

Elizabeth I tolerated diverse forms of Christianity as long as her subjects acknowledged her authority as head

Puritans, Separatists, and Presbyterians

of the Church of England. During her long reign (1558–1603), Calvin's ideas gained influence in England, Wales, and especially Scotland. (In Ireland, also part of her realm, Catholicism remained dominant.) The Scottish church eventually adopted Presbyterianism, an organizational system that dispensed with bishops and placed religious authority in bodies of clerics and laymen called presbyteries. By the late sixteenth century, though, many Calvinists—including those who came to be called Puritans, because they wanted to purify the church, or Separatists, because they wanted to leave it entirely—believed that reformers in England and Scotland had not gone far enough. Henry had simplified the church hierarchy, and the Scots had altered it; they wanted to abolish it altogether. Henry and the Scots had subordinated the church to the interests of the state; they wanted a church free from political interference. The established churches of England and Scotland, like the Catholic Church or the official Protestant churches of continental European countries, continued to nominally encompass all residents of the realm. Calvinists in England and Scotland preferred a more restricted definition; they wanted to confine church membership to persons they believed "saved"—those God had selected for salvation before birth.

Paradoxically, though, a key article of their faith insisted that people could not know for certain if they were "saved" because mere mortals could not comprehend or affect their predestination to heaven or hell. Thus, pious Calvinists daily confronted serious dilemmas: if the saved (or "elect") could not be identified with certainty, how could proper churches be constituted? If one was predestined and could not alter one's fate, why should one attend church or do good works? Calvinists dealt with the first dilemma by admitting that their judgments as to eligibility for church membership only approximated God's unknowable decisions. They resolved the second by reasoning that God gave the elect the ability to accept salvation and to lead a good life. Therefore, even though one could not earn a place in heaven by piety and good works, such practices could indicate one's place in the ranks of the saved.

Elizabeth I's Stuart successors, her cousin James I (1603–1625) and his son Charles I (1625–1649), exhibited less tolerance for Calvinists. As Scots, they also had little respect for the traditions of representative government that had developed in England under the Tudors and their predecessors (see Table 2.2). The wealthy landowners who sat in Parliament had grown accustomed to having considerable influence on government policies, especially taxation. But James I, taking a position later endorsed by his son, publicly declared his belief in the divine right of kings. The Stuarts insisted that a monarch's power came directly from God and that his subjects had a duty to obey him. They likened the king's absolute authority to a father's authority over his children.

Stuart Monarchs

Both James I and Charles I believed their authority included the power to enforce religious conformity. Because Calvinists—and remaining Catholics in England and Scotland—challenged many of the most important precepts of the established churches, the Stuart monarchs authorized the removal of dissenting clergymen from their pulpits. In the 1620s and 1630s, some Puritans, Separatists, Presbyterians, and Catholics decided to move to America where they hoped to put their diverse religious beliefs into practice unhindered by the Stuarts or the church hierarchy. Some fled hurriedly to avoid arrest and imprisonment.

Table 2.2 Tudor and Stuart Monarchs of England, 1509–1649

Monarch	Reign	Relation to Predecessor
Henry VIII	1509–1547	Son
Edward VI	1547–1553	Son
Mary I	1553–1558	Half-sister
Elizabeth I	1558–1603	Half-sister
James I	1603–1625	Cousin
Charles I	1625–1649	Son

The Founding of Virginia

The impetus for England's first permanent colony in the Western Hemisphere was both religious and economic. The newly militant English Protestants were eager to combat "popery" both at home and in the Americas. They concurred with Richard Hakluyt, who remarked that if Spaniards, "in their superstition," had "don so great thinges in so shorte space," surely the adherents of "our true and syncere Religion" could achieve even more remarkable results.

Accordingly, in 1606, a group of merchants and wealthy gentry—some of them aligned with religious reformers—obtained a royal charter for the Virginia Company, organized as a joint-stock company. Such forerunners of modern corporations, initially created for trading voyages and often very profitable, pooled the resources of many small investors through stock sales and spread the risks. Yet the joint-stock company, then as later, proved to be a poor vehicle for establishing colonies because colonies required significant continuing investments of capital. The lack of immediate returns thus generated tension between stockholders and colonists. Although at the outset investors in the Virginia Company anticipated great profits, and neither settlement established by the Virginia Company—one in Maine that collapsed within a year and Jamestown—ever earned much.

In 1607, the company dispatched 104 men and boys to a region near Chesapeake Bay called Tsenacommacah by its native inhabitants. There in May they established the palisaded settlement called Jamestown on a swampy peninsula in a river they also named for their monarch. They quickly constructed small houses and a chapel. Ill-equipped for survival in the unfamiliar environment, the colonists fell victim to dissension and disease as they attempted to maintain traditional English social and political hierarchies. Familiar with Spanish experience, the gentlemen and soldiers at Jamestown expected to rely on local Indians for food and tribute, yet the residents of Tsenacommacah refused to cooperate. Moreover, through sheer bad luck, the settlers arrived in the midst of a severe drought (now known to be the worst in the region for 1,700 years) that persisted until 1612. The lack of rainfall not only made it difficult to cultivate crops but also polluted their drinking water.

Jamestown and Tsenacommacah

The weroance (chief) of Tsenacommacah, Powhatan, had inherited rule over six Algonquian villages and later gained control of some twenty-five others (see Map 2.1). In late 1607 negotiations with Captain John Smith, one of the colony's leaders, the weroance tentatively agreed to an alliance with the Englishmen. In exchange for foodstuffs, Powhatan hoped to acquire guns, hatchets, and swords, which would give him a technological advantage over the enemies of his people. Each side in the alliance wanted to subordinate the other, but neither succeeded.

The fragile relationship soon foundered on mutual mistrust. The wereoance relocated his primary village in early 1609 to a place the newcomers could not access easily. Without Powhatan's assistance, the settlement experienced a "starving time" (winter 1609–1610) when many died and at least one colonist resorted to cannibalism. In spring 1610, the survivors packed up to leave on a newly arrived ship but en route out of the James River encountered a new governor, male and female settlers, and added supplies, so they returned to Jamestown. Sporadic skirmishes ensued as the standoff with the Powhatans continued. To gain the upper hand, the settlers in 1613 kidnapped Powhatan's daughter, Pocahontas, and held her hostage. In captivity, she agreed to convert to Christianity and to marry a colonist, John Rolfe. He had fallen in love with her, but she probably married him for diplomatic reasons; their union initiated a period of peace between the English and her people. Funded by the Virginia Company, she and Rolfe sailed to England to promote interest in the colony. Pocahontas died at Gravesend in 1616, probably of dysentery, leaving an infant son who returned to Virginia as a young adult.

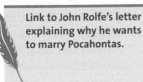

Link to John Rolfe's letter explaining why he wants to marry Pocahontas.

Although their royal charter nominally laid claim to a much wider territory, the Jamestown settlers saw their "Virginia" as essentially corresponding to Tsenacommacah. Powhatan's dominion was bounded on the north by the Potomac, on the south by the Great Dismal Swamp, and on the west by the fall line—the beginning of the upland Piedmont. Beyond those boundaries lay the Powhatans' enemies and (especially in the west) lands the Powhatans feared to enter. English people relied on the Powhatans as guides and interpreters, traveling along rivers and precontact paths in order to trade with the Powhatans' partners. For more than half a century, settlement in "Virginia" was confined to Tsenacommacah.

Algonquian and English Cultural Differences

In Tsenacommacah and elsewhere on the North American coast, English settlers and local Algonquians focused on their cultural differences—not their similarities—although both groups held deep religious beliefs, subsisted primarily through agriculture, accepted social and political hierarchy, and observed well-defined gender roles. From the outset, English men regarded Indian men as lazy because they did not cultivate crops and spent much of their time hunting (a sport, not work, in English eyes). Indian men thought English men effeminate because they did the "woman's work" of cultivation. In the same vein, the English believed Algonquian women were oppressed because they did heavy field labor.

The nature of Algonquian and English hierarchies differed. Among Algonquians like the Powhatans, political power and social status did not necessarily pass directly through the male line, instead commonly flowing through sisters' sons. By contrast, English gentlemen inherited their position from their father. English political and military leaders tended to rule autocratically, whereas Algonquian leaders (even Powhatan) had limited authority over their people. Accustomed to the powerful kings of Europe, the English overestimated the ability of chiefs to make treaties that would bind their people.

Furthermore, Algonquian and English concepts of property differed. Most Algonquian villages held their land communally. Land could not be bought or sold absolutely, although certain rights to use it (for example, for hunting or fishing) could be transferred. Once, most English villagers, too, had used land in common, but because of enclosures in the previous century they had become accustomed to individual farms and to buying and selling land. The English also refused to accept the validity of Indians'

National Portrait Gallery, Smithsonian Institution/Art Resource, NY

Ætatis suæ 21. A.º 1616.

◄ During her visit to London, the Powhatan princess—called "Pocahontas" in her childhood but Matoaka or Rebecca as an adult—sat for her portrait by Simon Van de Passe, a young Dutch-German engraver. Her upright stance suggests her pride in her background. He depicted her wearing pearl earrings and an elaborate outfit topped by a gorgeous lace ruff. The ostrich fan she holds symbolizes royalty, but her hat is one worn more commonly by a Puritan man. Her features are clearly those of an indigenous Indian woman; Van de Passe did not "Europeanize" her looks. The portrait was originally reproduced in John Smith's *General Historie of Virginia* (1624).

claims to traditional hunting territories, insisting that only land intensively cultivated could be regarded as owned or occupied. As one colonist put it, "salvadge peoples" who "rambled" over a region without farming it could claim no "title or propertye" in the land. Ownership of such "unclaimed" property, the English believed, lay with the English monarchy, in whose name John Cabot had laid claim to North America in 1497.

Above all, the English settlers believed unwaveringly in the superiority of their civilization. Although in the early years of colonization they often anticipated living peacefully alongside indigenous peoples, they always assumed that they would dictate the terms of such coexistence. Like Thomas Harriot at Roanoke, they expected native peoples to adopt English customs and to convert to Christianity. They showed little respect for the Indians when they believed English interests were at stake, as was demonstrated by developments in Virginia once the settlers found the salable commodity they sought.

That commodity was tobacco, the American crop previously introduced to Europe by the Spanish and subsequently cultivated in Turkey. In 1611, John Rolfe

Tobacco Cultivation

planted seeds of a variety from the Spanish Caribbean, which was superior to the strain grown by Virginia Indians. Nine years later, Virginians exported forty thousand pounds of cured leaves; by the late 1620s, shipments had jumped dramatically to 1.5 million pounds. The great tobacco boom had begun, fueled by high prices and substantial profits for planters as they responded to escalating demand from Europe and Africa. The price later fell almost as sharply as it had risen, fluctuating wildly from year to year in response to increasing supply and international competition. Nevertheless, tobacco made Virginia prosper.

The spread of tobacco cultivation altered life for everyone. Successful tobacco cultivation required abundant land because the crop quickly drained soil of nutrients. Farmers soon learned that a field could produce only about three satisfactory crops before it had to lie fallow for several years to regain its fertility. Thus, the once-small English settlements began to expand rapidly: eager applicants asked the Virginia Company for land grants on both sides

▲ A comparison of the portrait of Sir Walter Raleigh and his son (left), with that of an Algonquian Indian drawn by John White, from Raleigh's Roanoke expedition (right), shows a dramatic difference in standard dress styles that, for many, must have symbolized the apparent cultural gap between Europeans and Americans. Yet the fact that both men (and the young boy) were portrayed in similar stances, with "arms akimbo," demonstrated that all were high-status individuals. In Europe, only aristocrats were represented in such a domineering pose.

of the James River and its tributary streams. Lulled into a false sense of security by years of peace, Virginians established farms at some distance from one another along the riverbanks—a settlement pattern convenient for tobacco cultivation but dangerous for defense.

Opechancanough, Powhatan's brother and successor, watched the English colonists' expansion and witnessed their attempts to convert natives to Christianity. Recognizing the danger, the war leader launched coordinated attacks along the James River on March 22, 1622. By the end of the day, 347 colonists (about one-quarter of the total) lay dead, and only a timely warning from two Christian converts saved Jamestown itself from destruction.

Indian Assaults

Virginia reeled from the blow but did not collapse. Reinforced by new shipments of men and arms from England, the settlers repeatedly attacked Opechancanough's villages. A peace treaty was signed in 1632, but in April 1644 the elderly Opechancanough assaulted the invaders one last time, though he must have known he could not prevail. In 1646, survivors of the Powhatan Confederacy formally subordinated themselves to England. Although they continued to live in the region, their efforts to resist the spread of European settlement ended.

The 1622 assault that failed to destroy the colony did succeed in killing its parent. The Virginia Company never made any profits from the enterprise, for internal corruption and the heavy cost of supporting the settlers offset all its earnings. But before its demise, the company developed two policies that set key precedents. First, to attract settlers, the company in 1617 established the "headright" system. Every new arrival paying his or her own way was promised a land grant of fifty acres; those who financed the passage of others received similar headrights for each person. To ordinary English farmers, many of whom owned little or no land, the headright system offered a powerful incentive to move to Virginia. To wealthy gentry, it promised even more: the possibility of establishing vast agricultural enterprises worked by large numbers of laborers. Two years later, the company introduced a second reform, authorizing the landowning men of the major Virginia settlements to elect representatives to an assembly called the House of Burgesses. English landholders had long been accustomed to electing members of Parliament and controlling their own local governments; therefore, they expected the same privilege in the nation's colonies.

End of Virginia Company

When James I revoked the charter in 1624, transforming Virginia into a royal colony, he continued the company's headright policy. Because he distrusted legislative bodies, though, James abolished the assembly.

But Virginians protested so vigorously that by 1629 the House of Burgesses was functioning once again. Only two decades after the first permanent English settlement was planted in North America, the colonists successfully insisted on governing themselves at the local level. Thus, the political structure of England's American possessions came to differ from those of the Spanish, Dutch, and French colonies—all of which were ruled autocratically.

Life in the Chesapeake

By the 1630s, tobacco was firmly established as the staple crop and chief source of revenue in Virginia. It quickly became just as important in the second English colony planted on Chesapeake Bay: Maryland, given by Charles I to George Calvert, first Lord Baltimore, as a personal possession (proprietorship), which was settled in 1634. (Because Virginia and Maryland both border Chesapeake Bay—see Map 2.1—they often are referred to collectively as "the Chesapeake.") Members of the Calvert family intended the colony to serve as a haven for their persecuted fellow Catholics. Cecilius Calvert, second Lord Baltimore, became the first colonizer to offer freedom of religion to all Christian settlers; he understood that protecting the Protestant majority could also ensure Catholics' rights. Maryland's Act of Religious Toleration codified his policy in 1649.

In everything but religion, the two Chesapeake colonies resembled each other. In Maryland as in Virginia, tobacco planters spread out along the riverbanks, establishing isolated farms instead of towns. The region's deep, wide rivers offered dependable water transportation in an age of few and inadequate roads. Each farm or group of farms had its own wharf, where oceangoing vessels could take on or discharge cargo. Consequently, Virginia and Maryland had few towns, for their residents did not need commercial centers in order to buy and sell goods.

The planting, cultivation, harvesting, and curing of tobacco were repetitious, time-consuming, and labor-intensive tasks. Clearing land for new fields, necessary every few years, also demanded heavy labor.

Demand for Laborers

Above all else, then, successful Chesapeake farms required workers. But where and how could they be found? Nearby Indians, their numbers reduced by war and disease, could not supply such needs. Nor were enslaved Africans available: traders could more easily and profitably sell slaves to Caribbean sugar planters. Only a few people of African descent, some of them free, initially trickled into the Chesapeake. By 1650, about three hundred blacks lived in Virginia—a tiny fraction of the population.

Chesapeake tobacco farmers thus looked primarily to England to supply their labor needs. Because of the headright system (which Maryland also adopted in 1640), a tobacco farmer anywhere in the Chesapeake could simultaneously obtain both land and labor by importing workers from England. Good management would make the process self-perpetuating: a farmer could use his profits to pay for the passage of more workers and thereby gain title to more land. Success could even bring movement into the ranks of the planter gentry that began to develop in the region.

Because men did the agricultural work in European societies, colonists assumed that field laborers should be men. Such laborers, along with a few women, immigrated to America as indentured servants—that is, in return for their passage they contracted to work for periods ranging from four to seven years. Indentured servants accounted for 75 to 85 percent of the approximately 130,000 English immigrants to Virginia and Maryland during the seventeenth century. The rest tended to be young couples with one or two children.

Males between the ages of fifteen and twenty-four composed roughly three-quarters of the servants; only one immigrant in five or six was female. Most of these young men came from farming or laboring families, and many originated in regions of England experiencing severe social disruption. Some had already moved several times within England before relocating to America. Often they came from the middling ranks of society—what their contemporaries called the "common sort." Their youth indicated that most probably had not yet established themselves in their homeland.

For such people, the Chesapeake appeared to offer good prospects. Servants who fulfilled the terms of their indenture earned "freedom dues" consisting of clothes, tools, livestock, casks of corn and tobacco, and sometimes even land. From a distance at least, America seemed to offer chances for advancement unavailable in England. Yet immigrants' lives were difficult. Servants typically worked six days a week, ten to fourteen hours a day, in a climate much warmer than England's. Their masters could discipline or sell them, and they faced severe penalties for running away. Even so, the laws did give them some protection. For example, their masters were supposed to supply them with sufficient food, clothing, and shelter, and they were not to be beaten excessively. Cruelly treated servants could turn to the courts for assistance, sometimes winning verdicts directing that they be transferred to more humane masters or released from their indenture.

Conditions of Servitude

Servants and their owners alike contended with epidemic disease. Immigrants first had to survive the process the colonists called "seasoning," a bout with disease (probably malaria) that usually occurred during their first Chesapeake summer. They then often endured recurrences of malaria, along with dysentery, typhoid fever, and other illnesses. Consequently, about 40 percent of male servants did not survive long enough to become freedmen. Even young men of twenty-two who successfully weathered their seasoning could expect to live only another twenty years.

For those who survived, though, the opportunities for advancement were real. Until the last decades of the seventeenth century, former servants often became independent farmers ("freeholders"), thereafter living a modest but comfortable existence. Some even assumed positions of political prominence, such as justice of the peace or militia officer. But in the 1670s, tobacco prices entered a fifty-year period of stagnation and decline. Simultaneously, good land grew increasingly scarce and expensive. In 1681, Maryland dropped its legal requirement that servants receive land as part of their freedom dues, forcing large numbers of freed servants to live for years as wage laborers or tenant farmers. By 1700, the Chesapeake was no longer the land of opportunity it once had been.

Life in the early Chesapeake was hard for everyone, regardless of sex or status. Farmers (and sometimes their wives) toiled in the fields alongside servants, laboriously clearing land, then planting and harvesting tobacco and corn. Because hogs could forage for themselves in the forests and needed little tending, Chesapeake households subsisted mainly on pork and corn, a filling diet but not sufficiently nutritious. Families supplemented this monotonous fare by eating fish, shellfish, and wildfowl, in addition to vegetables such as lettuce and peas, which they grew in small gardens. The near impossibility of preserving food for safe winter consumption magnified the health problems caused by epidemic disease. Salting, drying, and smoking, the only methods the colonists knew, did not always prevent spoilage.

Standard of Living

Few households had many material possessions other than farm implements, bedding, and basic cooking and eating utensils. Chairs, tables, candles, and knives and forks were luxury items. Most people rose and went to bed with the sun, sat on crude benches or storage chests, and held plates or bowls in their hands while eating meat and vegetable stews with spoons. The ramshackle houses commonly had just one or two rooms. Colonists devoted their income to improving their farms, buying livestock, and purchasing more laborers instead of improving their standard of living. Rather than making such items as clothing or tools, families imported necessary manufactured goods from England.

The predominance of males (see Figure 2.1), the incidence of servitude, and the high mortality rates combined to produce unusual patterns of family life. Female servants normally could not marry during their term of indenture

Chesapeake Families

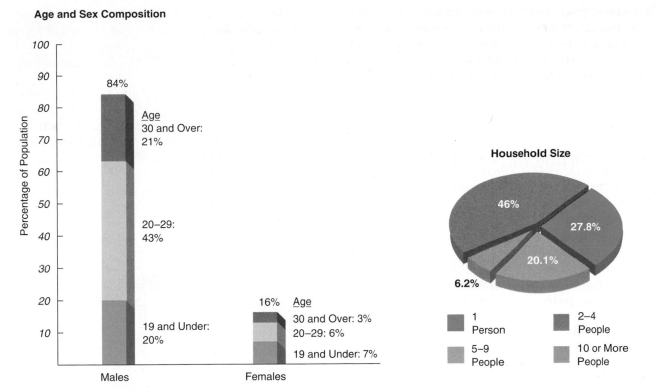

Figure 2-1 Population of Virginia, 1625

The only detailed census taken in the English mainland North American colonies during the seventeenth century was prepared in Virginia in 1625. It listed a total of 1,218 people, constituting 309 "households" and living in 278 dwellings—so some houses contained more than one family. The chart shows, on the left, the proportionate age and gender distribution of the 765 individuals for whom full information was recorded, and, on the right, the percentage variation in the sizes of the 309 households. The approximately 42 percent of the residents of the colony who were servants were concentrated in 30 percent of the households. Nearly 70 percent of the households had no servants at all.

Source: Wells, Peter S., *The Population of the British Colonies in America Before 1776.* © 1975 Princeton University Press, 2003 renewed PUP. Reprinted by permission of Princeton University Press.

because masters did not want pregnancies to deprive them of workers. Many male ex-servants could not marry at all because of the scarcity of women; such men lived alone, in pairs, or as the third member of a household containing a married couple. In contrast, nearly every adult free woman in the Chesapeake married, and widows usually remarried within a few months of a husband's death. Yet because of high infant mortality and because almost all marriages were delayed by servitude or broken by death, Chesapeake women commonly reared only one to three healthy children, in contrast to English women who normally had at least five.

Thus, Chesapeake families were few, small, and short-lived. Youthful immigrants came to America as individuals free of familial control; they commonly died while their children were still young. In one Virginia county, for example, more than three-quarters of the children had lost at least one parent by the time they either married or reached age twenty-one. Those children were put to work as soon as possible on the farms of parents, stepparents, or guardians. Their schooling, if any, was haphaz-

ard; whether Chesapeake-born children learned to read or write depended largely on whether their parents were literate and took the time to teach them.

Throughout the seventeenth century, immigrants composed a majority of the Chesapeake population, with important implications for regional political patterns. Most of the members of Virginia's House of Burgesses and Maryland's House of Delegates (established in 1635) were immigrants; they also dominated the governor's council, which simultaneously served as each colony's highest court, part of the legislature, and executive adviser to the governor. A cohesive, native-born ruling elite emerged only in the early eighteenth century.

Chesapeake Politics

Representative institutions based on the consent of the governed usually function as a major source of political stability. In the seventeenth-century Chesapeake, most property-owning white males could vote, and such freeholders chose as their legislators (burgesses) the local elites who seemed to be the natural leaders of their respective areas. But because most such men were immigrants lacking strong ties to one another or to the colonies, the assemblies' existence did not create political stability. Unusual demographic patterns thus contributed to the region's contentious politics.

The Founding of New England

The economic and religious motives that prompted English people to move to the Chesapeake also drew men and women to New England, the region known as North Virginia before Captain John Smith renamed it in 1616 after exploring its coast (see Map 2.2). But because Puritans organized the New England colonies and because of environmental factors, the northern settlements developed very differently from their southern counterparts. The divergence became apparent even as the would-be colonists left England.

Hoping to exert control over a migration that appeared disorderly (and which included dissenters seeking to flee

Contrasting Regional Demographic Patterns

the authority of the Church of England), royal bureaucrats in late 1634 ordered port officials in London to collect information on all travelers departing for the colonies. The resulting records for the year 1635 are a treasure trove for historians. They document the departure of fifty-three vessels in that year alone—twenty to Virginia, seventeen to New England, eight to Barbados, five to St. Christopher, two to Bermuda, and one to Providence Island. Almost five thousand people sailed on those ships, with two thousand departing for Virginia, about twelve hundred for New England, and the rest for island destinations. Nearly three-fifths of all the passengers were between fifteen and twenty-four years old, reflecting the predominance of young male servants among migrants to America.

But among those bound for New England, such youths constituted less than one-third of the total; nearly 40 percent were older, and another third were younger. Whereas women made up just 14 percent of those going to Virginia, they composed almost 40 percent of the passengers to New England. Such composite figures show that New England migrants often traveled in family groups. They also brought more goods and livestock with them and tended to travel with other people from the same region. For example, aboard one vessel, more than half came from York; on another, nearly half came from Buckinghamshire. In short, people migrated to New England together with their close associates. Their lives in North America must have been more comfortable and less lonely than those of their southern counterparts.

Map 2.2 New England Colonies, 1650

The most densely settled region of the mainland was New England, where English settlements and Indian villages existed side by side.

Source: Copyright © Cengage Learning

Puritan congregations quickly became key institutions in colonial New England, whereas no church had much

Contrasting Regional Religious Patterns

impact on the early development of the Chesapeake colonies. Spread-out settlement patterns brought great difficulty to anyone who wanted to organize a church. Catholic and Anglican bishops in England paid little attention to their coreligionists in America, and all Chesapeake congregations languished in the absence of sufficient numbers of ordained clergymen. (For example, in 1665, an observer noted that only ten of the fifty Virginia Church of England parishes had resident clerics.) Not until the 1690s did the Church of England begin to take firmer root in Virginia; by then, it had also replaced Catholicism as the established church in Maryland, and Calvinists were in the minority in both colonies.

In both New England and the Chesapeake, religion affected the lives of pious Calvinists who were expected to reassess the state of their souls regularly. Many devoted themselves to self-examination and Bible study, and families often prayed together each day under the guidance of the husband and father. Yet because even the most pious could never be certain they were numbered among the elect, anxiety about their spiritual state troubled devout Calvinists. This anxiety lent a special intensity to their religious beliefs and to their concern with proper behavior—their own and that of others. During brief periods when they governed Maryland and Virginia, Calvinists attempted to enforce rules of morality Catholics and Anglicans tended to ignore.

Separatists

Separatists who thought the Church of England too corrupt to be salvaged became the first religious dissenters to move to New England. In 1609, a Separatist congregation relocated to Leiden, in the Netherlands, where they found the freedom of worship denied them in Stuart England. But eventually the Netherlands worried them, for the nation that tolerated them also tolerated religions and behaviors they abhorred. Hoping to isolate themselves and their children from the corrupting influence of worldly temptations, these people, known today as Pilgrims, received permission from the Virginia Company to colonize the northern part of its territory.

In September 1620, more than one hundred people, only thirty of them Separatists, set sail from England on the old and crowded *Mayflower*. Like a few English families that had settled permanently along the coast of Newfoundland during the previous decade, the Pilgrims expected to support their colony through profits from codfishery. In November, they landed on Cape Cod, farther north than they had intended. Still, given the lateness of the season, they decided to stay in the region. They moved across Massachusetts Bay to a fine harbor (named Plymouth by John Smith, who had visited it in 1614) and into the empty dwellings of a Pautuxet village whose inhabitants had died in the epidemic of 1616–1618.

Pilgrims and Pokanokets

Even before they landed, the Pilgrims had to surmount their first challenge—from the "strangers," or non-Separatists, who sailed with them to America. Because they landed outside the jurisdiction of the Virginia Company, some of the strangers questioned the authority of the colony's leaders. In response, the Mayflower Compact, signed in November 1620 on shipboard, established a "Civil Body Politic" as a temporary substitute for a charter. The male settlers elected a governor and initially made all decisions for the colony at town meetings. Later, after more towns had been founded and the population increased, Plymouth, like Virginia and Maryland, created an assembly to which the landowning male settlers elected representatives.

Link to the Mayflower Compact

Like the Jamestown settlers before them, the residents of Plymouth were poorly prepared to subsist in the new environment. Only half of the *Mayflower*'s passengers lived to see the spring. That the others survived owed much to the Pokanokets (a branch of the Wampanoags), who controlled the area in which they had settled. Pokanoket villages had suffered terrible losses in the recent epidemic, so to protect themselves from the powerful Narragansetts of the southern New England coast (who had been spared the ravages of the disease), the Pokanokets allied themselves with the newcomers. In the spring of 1621, their leader, Massasoit, agreed to a treaty, and during the colony's first difficult years the Pokanokets supplied the settlers with essential foodstuffs. The colonists also relied on Squanto, a Pautuxet who, like Malinche, served as a conduit between native peoples and Europeans. Captured by fishermen in the early 1610s and taken to Europe, Squanto had learned to speak English. On his return, he discovered that the epidemic had wiped out his village. Squanto became the settlers' interpreter and a major source of information about the environment.

Massachusetts Bay Company

Before the 1620s ended, another group of Puritans (Congregationalists, who hoped to reform the Church of England from within) launched the colonial enterprise that would come to dominate New England and would absorb Plymouth in 1691. Charles I, who became king in 1625, was more hostile to Puritans than his father had been. Under his leadership, the Church of England attempted to suppress Puritan practices, driving clergymen from their pulpits and forcing congregations to worship secretly. Some Congregationalist merchants, concerned about their long-term prospects in England, sent out a body of colonists to Cape Ann (north of Cape Cod) in 1628. The following year, the merchants obtained a royal charter, constituting themselves as the Massachusetts Bay Company.

The new joint-stock company quickly attracted the attention of Puritans who were becoming increasingly convinced that they no longer would be able to practice their religion freely in their homeland. They remained committed to the goal of reforming the Church of England but concluded that they should pursue that aim in America. In a dramatic move, the Congregationalist merchants decided to transfer the Massachusetts Bay Company's headquarters to New England. The settlers would then be answerable to no one in the mother country and would be able to handle their affairs—secular and religious—as they pleased. Like the Plymouth settlers, they expected to profit from the codfishery; they also planned to export timber products.

Turkeys

As they neared the end of their first year in North America, the Plymouth colonists held a traditional English feast to celebrate the harvest. Famously, they invited Massasoit's Pokanokets to join them, and just as famously, they probably together consumed the bird known even then as the turkey. But why was this bird, originally from America and still commonly eaten by Americans at Thanksgiving, given the name of a region of the then-Ottoman Empire? The native peoples of the Americas had named the fowl in their own languages; Aztecs, for example, called a male bird *huexoloti* and a female *totolin*, while some northeastern Indians termed both *nehm*.

When Columbus returned to Spain from his first voyage, the birds were among the items he carried to Europe. The Iberian Peninsula had long served as a major focal point for Mediterranean commerce, and Spanish mariners sailed frequently to ports in the Middle East.

Before long, one of those Spanish vessels took some *huexoloti* and *totolin* to the Ottoman Empire. There, farmers already familiar with such distant Asian relatives of the bird as the pheasant began to work to improve the breed. Within a few decades, they succeeded in producing a plumper and tamer version of the American fowl. By the 1540s, that bird had arrived in England, and by the end of the century "turkeys" were widely consumed for food throughout the British Isles.

Accordingly, when Thomas Harriot in his 1588 *Briefe and True Report* mentioned the wild North American version of the birds, he termed them "Turkie cockes and Turkie hennes." He failed to give the names local native peoples used because—unlike the many other new plants and animals he encountered—these birds were already familiar to him and his reading audience.

The settlers at Jamestown and Plymouth also recognized the birds they saw in their new homelands as relatives of the fowls they had consumed in England. But they regarded the North American birds as inferior to English ones; the wild American turkeys seemingly could not be tamed. Swift and hungry foragers, they ravaged young crops and were viewed primarily as pests. (Of course, any colonist fortunate enough to shoot one of them could then have a tasty meal.) So the settlers in both Virginia and New England soon imported English turkeys, which they raised for meat along with chickens and pigs.

The origin of the "turkeys" most likely consumed at the so-called First Thanksgiving remains a mystery. Were they the wild American birds or the tame Ottoman-English variety? No matter; that they were termed "turkeys" linked these fowls of American origin to the Mediterranean, Europe, and the Middle East as a prime example of animals in the Columbian Exchange.

Victoria & Albert Museum; London; UK/ The Bridgeman Art Library

◀ Turkeys from the Americas quickly traveled around the world, as is illustrated by this Mughal painting from the Islamic empire in India. The local artist Ustad Mansur painted a "turkey-cock" brought to the emperor Jahangir in 1612 from Goa—a Portuguese enclave on the west coast of the Indian subcontinent. Presumably the turkey had been transported from the Iberian peninsula to that European outpost, whence the fowl made its way to Jahangir's court—where it was immortalized by an artist to whom it was an unusual sight.

▲ Some scholars now believe that this 1638 painting by Dutch artist Adam Willaerts depicts the Plymouth colony about fifteen years after its founding. The shape of the harbor, the wooden gate, and the houses straggling up the hill all coincide with contemporary accounts of the settlement. No one believes that Willaerts himself visited Plymouth, but people returning from the colony to the Netherlands, where the Pilgrims had lived for years before emigrating, could well have described Plymouth to him.

The most important recruit to the new venture was John Winthrop, a member of the lesser English gentry. In October 1629, the Massachusetts Bay Company elected Winthrop as its governor, and until his death twenty years later, he served the colony continuously in one leadership post or another. Winthrop organized the initial segment of the great Puritan migration to America. In 1630, more than one thousand English men and women moved to Massachusetts—most of them to Boston. By 1643, nearly twenty thousand more had followed.

Governor John Winthrop

On board the *Arbella*, en route to New England in 1630, John Winthrop preached a sermon, "A Model of Christian Charity," laying out his expectations for the new colony. Above all, he stressed the communal nature of the endeavor on which he and his fellow settlers had embarked. God, he explained, "hath so disposed of the condition of mankind as in all times some must be rich, some poor, some high and eminent in power and dignity, others mean and in subjection." But differences in status did not imply differences in worth. On the contrary, God had planned the world so that "every man might have need of other, and from hence they might be all knit more nearly together in the bond of brotherly affection." In

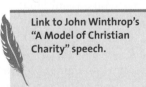

Link to John Winthrop's "A Model of Christian Charity" speech.

America, Winthrop asserted, "we shall be as a city upon a hill, the eyes of all people are upon us." If the Puritans failed to carry out their "special commission" from God, "the Lord will surely break out in wrath against us."

Winthrop's was a transcendent vision. He foresaw in Puritan America a true commonwealth, a community in which each person put the good of the whole ahead of his or her private concerns. Although, as in seventeenth-century England, that society would be characterized by social inequality and clear hierarchies of status and power, Winthrop hoped its members would live according to the precepts of Christian love. Of course, such an ideal was beyond human reach. Early Massachusetts and its Caribbean counterpart, Providence Island, had their share of bitter quarrels and unchristian behavior. Remarkably, though, in New England the ideal persisted well into the third and fourth generations of the immigrants' descendants.

The Puritans expressed their communal ideal chiefly in the doctrine of the covenant. They believed God had made a covenant—that is, an agreement or contract—with them when they were chosen for the special mission to America. In turn, they covenanted with one another, promising to work together toward their goals. The founders of churches, towns, and even colonies in Anglo-America often drafted formal documents setting forth the principles on which their institutions would be based. The Pilgrims' Mayflower Compact was a covenant; so, too, was the

Covenant Ideal

Fundamental Orders of Connecticut (1639), which laid down the basic law for the settlements established along the Connecticut River valley in 1636 and thereafter.

The leaders of Massachusetts Bay likewise transformed their original joint-stock company charter into the basis for a covenanted community based on mutual consent. Under pressure from landowning male settlers, they gradually changed the General Court—officially the company's small governing body—into a colonial legislature. They also granted the status of freeman, or voting member of the company, to all property-owning adult male church members. Like the Virginians who won the reestablishment of the House of Burgesses after the king had abolished it, the male residents of Massachusetts insisted that their reluctant leaders allow them a greater voice in their government. Less than two decades after the first large group of Puritans arrived in Massachusetts Bay, the colony had a functioning system of self-government composed of a governor and a two-house legislature. The General Court also established a judicial system modeled on England's, although the laws they adopted differed from those of their homeland.

The colony's method of distributing land helped to further the communal ideal. Unlike Virginia and Maryland,

New England Towns

where individual applicants acquired headrights and sited their farms separately, in Massachusetts groups of men—often from the same English village—applied together to the General Court for grants of land on which to establish towns (novel governance units that did not exist in England). The men receiving such grants determined how the land would be distributed. Understandably, the grantees copied the villages whence they had come. First, they laid out lots for houses and a church. Then they gave each family parcels of land scattered around the town center: a pasture here, a woodlot there, an arable field elsewhere. They reserved the best and largest plots for the most distinguished residents, including the minister. People who had low status in England received smaller and less desirable allotments. Still, every man and even a few single women obtained land, thus sharply differentiating these villages from their English counterparts. When migrants began to move beyond the territorial limits of Massachusetts Bay into Connecticut (1636), New Haven (1638), and New Hampshire (1638), the same pattern of land grants and town formation persisted. (Only Maine, with coastal regions thinly populated by fishermen and their families, deviated from the standard practice.)

Town centers developed quickly, evolving in three distinctly different ways. Some, chiefly isolated agricultural settlements in the interior, tried to sustain Winthrop's vision of harmonious community life based on diversified family farms. A second group, the coastal towns like Boston and Salem, became bustling seaports, serving as focal points for trade and places of entry for thousands of new immigrants. The third category, commercialized agricultural towns, grew up in the Connecticut River valley, where easy water transportation made it possible for farmers to sell surplus goods readily. In Springfield, Massachusetts, for example, the merchant-entrepreneur William Pynchon and his son John began as fur traders and ended as large landowners with thousands of acres. Even in New England, then, the entrepreneurial spirit characteristic of the Chesapeake found expression. Yet the plans to profit from timber and fish exports did not materialize quickly or easily; the new settlements lacked the infrastructure necessary to support such enterprises.

Migration into the Connecticut valley ended the Puritans' relative freedom from clashes with nearby

Pequot War and Its Aftermath

Indians. The first English people in the valley moved there from Massachusetts Bay under the direction of their minister, Thomas Hooker. Although their new settlements were remote from other English towns, the wide river promised ready access to the ocean. The site had just one problem: it fell within the territory controlled by the powerful Pequots.

The Pequots' dominance stemmed from their role as primary intermediaries in the trade between New England Algonquians and the Dutch in New Netherland. The arrival of English settlers signaled the end of the Pequots' power over such regional trading networks, for previously subordinate bands could now trade directly with Europeans. Clashes between Pequots and English colonists began even before the establishment of settlements in the Connecticut valley, but their founding tipped the balance toward war. The Pequots tried unsuccessfully to enlist other Indians in resisting English expansion. After two English traders were killed (not by Pequots), the English raided a Pequot village. In return, Pequots attacked Wethersfield, Connecticut, in April 1637, killing nine and capturing two. To retaliate, an expedition the following month surrounded and burned the main Pequot town on the Mystic River. The Englishmen and their Narragansett allies slaughtered at least four hundred Pequots, mostly women and children, capturing and enslaving the survivors.

For the next four decades, New England Indians accommodated themselves to the European invasion. They traded with the newcomers and sometimes worked for them, but for the most part they resisted acculturation or incorporation into English society. Native Americans persisted in using traditional farming methods, which did not employ plows or fences, and women rather than men continued to be the chief cultivators. When Indian men learned "European" trades in order to survive, they chose those—like broom making, basket weaving, and shingle splitting—that most nearly accorded with their customary occupations and ensured both independence and income. The one European practice they adopted

Photograph by Jeffrey Howe

▲ The Fairbanks house, in Dedham, Massachusetts, is one of the oldest surviving homes in New England. But only the central core (with the large chimney) was constructed in 1636; the other wings were added later. Early Massachusetts towns were filled with similar dwellings.

was keeping livestock, for domesticated animals provided excellent sources of meat once earlier hunting territories had been turned into English farms and wild game had consequently disappeared.

Although the official seal of the Massachusetts Bay colony showed an Indian crying, "Come over and help us," most colonists showed little interest in converting the Algonquians to Christianity. Only a few Massachusetts clerics, most notably John Eliot and Thomas Mayhew, seriously undertook missionary work. Eliot insisted that converts reside in towns, farm the land in English fashion, assume English names, wear European-style clothing and shoes, cut their hair, and stop observing a wide range of their own customs. Because Eliot demanded a cultural transformation from his adherents—on the theory that Indians could not be properly Christianized unless they were also "civilized"—he understandably met with little success. At the peak of Eliot's efforts, only eleven hundred Indians (out of many thousands) lived in the fourteen "Praying Towns" he established, and just 10 percent of those town residents had been formally baptized.

Eliot's failure to win many converts contrasted sharply with the successful missions in New France. Puritan services lacked Catholicism's beautiful ceremonies and special

Missionary Activities

appeal for women, and the Calvinist Puritans could not offer pious believers assurances of a heavenly afterlife. Yet on the island of Martha's Vineyard, Thomas Mayhew showed that it was possible to convert substantial numbers of Indians to Calvinist Christianity. He allowed Wampanoag Christians there to lead traditional lives, and he trained men of their own community to minister to them.

What attracted Indians to such religious ideas? Conversion often alienated new Christians (both Catholic and Puritan) from their relatives and traditions—a likely outcome that must have caused many potential converts to hesitate. But surely many hoped to use the Europeans' religion as a means of coping with the dramatic changes the intruders had wrought. The combination of disease, alcohol, new trading patterns, and loss of territory disrupted customary ways of life to an unprecedented extent. Shamans had little success in restoring traditional ways. Many Indians must have concluded that the Europeans' own ideas could provide the key to survival in the new circumstances.

John Winthrop's description of a great smallpox epidemic that swept through southern New England in the early 1630s reveals the relationship among smallpox, conversion to Christianity, and English land claims. "A great mortality among the Indians," he noted in his diary in 1633. "Divers of them, in their sickness, confessed that the Englishmen's God was a good God; and that if they recovered, they would serve him." But most did not

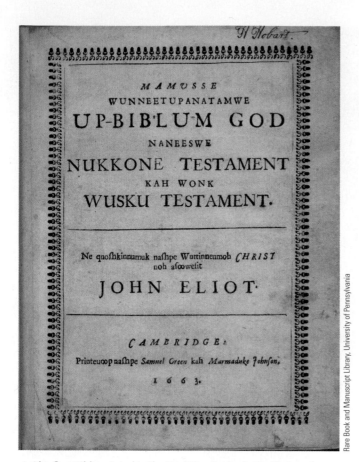

▲ The first Bible printed in the English colonies in North America was this translation into the Algonquian dialect spoken by the Indians of Massachusetts. The Puritan minister John Eliot arranged for its translation and publication as part of his efforts to convert the Natives to Christianity. He did not succeed in gaining many adherents, but today this Bible is serving as a vocabulary source for Native Americans in New England trying to revive their spoken language, knowledge of which had been lost by the nineteenth century.

recover: in January 1634, an English scout reported that smallpox had spread "as far as any Indian plantation was known to the west." By July, Winthrop observed that most of the Indians within a 300-mile radius of Boston had died of the disease. Therefore, he declared with satisfaction, "the Lord hath cleared our title to what we possess."

Life in New England

New England's colonizers adopted modes of life that differed from those of both their Algonquian neighbors and their Chesapeake counterparts. Algonquian bands usually moved four or five times each year to take full advantage of their environment. In spring, women planted the fields, but once crops were established, the plants did not need regular attention for several months. Villages then divided into small groups, women gathering wild foods and men hunting and fishing. The villagers returned to their fields for harvest, then separated again for fall hunt-

ing. Finally, the people wintered together in a sheltered spot before returning to the fields to start the cycle anew the following spring. Women probably determined the timing of these moves because their activities (gathering wild foods, including shellfish along the shore, and cultivating plants) used the nearby environment more intensively than did men's.

Unlike the mobile Algonquians, English people lived year-round in the same location. And unlike residents of the Chesapeake, New Englanders constructed sturdy dwellings intended to last. (Some survive to this day.) Household furnishings and house sizes resembled those in the Chesapeake, but New Englanders' diets were somewhat more varied. They replowed the same fields, believing it was less arduous to employ manure as fertilizer than to clear new fields every few years. Furthermore, they fenced their croplands to prevent them from being overrun by the cattle, sheep, and hogs that were their chief sources of meat. Animal crowding more than human crowding caused New Englanders to spread out across the countryside; all their livestock constantly needed more pasturage.

Because Puritans commonly moved to America in family groups, the age range in early New England was wide; and because many more women migrated to New England than to the tobacco colonies, the population could immediately begin to reproduce itself. Lacking such tropical diseases as malaria, New England was also healthier than the Chesapeake and even the mother country, once settlements had survived the difficult first few years. Adult male migrants to the Chesapeake lost about a decade from their English life expectancy of fifty to fifty-five years; their Massachusetts counterparts gained five or more years.

New England Families

Consequently, whereas Chesapeake population patterns gave rise to families that were few in number, small in size, and transitory, the demographic characteristics of New England made families there numerous, large, and long-lived. In New England, most men married; immigrant women married young (at age twenty, on the average); and marriages lasted longer and produced more children, who were more likely to live to maturity. If seventeenth-century Chesapeake women could expect to rear one to three healthy children, New England women could anticipate raising five to seven.

The nature of the population had other major implications for family life. The presence of many children combined with Puritans' stress on the importance of reading the Bible led to widespread concern for the education of youth. That people lived in towns meant small schools could be established; girls and boys were taught basic reading by their parents or a school "dame," and boys could then proceed to learn writing and eventually arithmetic and Latin. Further, New England in effect created grandparents because in England people rarely

Wadsworth Atheneum Museum of Art, Hartford, CT. Gift of Mrs. Walter H. Clark. Endowed by her daughter, Mrs. Thomas L. Archibald/Art Resource, NY

▲ In 1664, an eight-year-old girl, Elizabeth Eggington, became the subject of the earliest known dated New England painting. Her mother died shortly after her birth, perhaps because of childbirth complications; the girl's rich clothing, elaborate jewelry, and feather fan not only reveal her family's wealth but also suggest that she was much loved by her father, a merchant and ship captain. Unfortunately, Elizabeth died about the time this portrait was painted; perhaps it—like some other colonial portraits of young children—was actually painted after her death to memorialize her.

and New Haven, church membership was a prerequisite for voting in colony elections. All the early colonies, north and south, taxed residents to build churches and pay ministers' salaries, but only New England based provisions of criminal codes on the Old Testament. Massachusetts's first bodies of law (1641 and 1648) incorporated regulations drawn from scriptures; New Haven, Plymouth, New Hampshire, and Connecticut later copied them. All New Englanders were required to attend religious services, whether or not they were church members, and people who expressed contempt for ministers could be punished with fines or whippings.

The Puritan colonies attempted to enforce strict codes of moral conduct. Colonists there could be tried for drunkenness, card playing, dancing, or even idleness—although the frequent prosecutions for such offenses suggest that New Englanders often disobeyed the laws and thoroughly enjoyed such activities. Couples who had sex during their engagement (as revealed by the birth of a baby less than nine months after their wedding) were fined and publicly humiliated. Men, and a handful of women, who engaged in behaviors that today would be called homosexual were seen as especially sinful and reprehensible, and some were executed.

In New England, church and state were thus intertwined to a greater extent than in the Chesapeake, where few such prosecutions occurred. Puritans objected to secular interference in religious affairs but at the same time expected the church to influence the conduct of politics and the affairs of society. They also believed the state was obliged to support and protect the one true church—theirs. Consequently, although they came to America seeking freedom to worship as they pleased, they saw no contradiction in refusing to grant that freedom to those who held different religious beliefs.

Roger Williams, a Separatist who migrated to Massachusetts Bay in 1631, quickly ran afoul of Puritan orthodoxy. He told his fellow settlers that the king of England had no right to grant them land already occupied by Indians, that church and state should be kept entirely separate, and that Puritans should not impose their ideas on others. Because Puritan leaders placed a heavy emphasis on achieving consensus in both religion and politics, they could not tolerate significant dissent. In October 1635, Massachusetts tried Williams for challenging the validity of the colony's charter and for maintaining that New England Congregationalists had not separated themselves, their churches, or their polity sufficiently from England's corrupt institutions and practices.

Roger Williams

Convicted and banished, Williams journeyed in early 1636 to the head of Narragansett Bay, where he founded the town of Providence on land he obtained from the Narragansetts and Wampanoags. Because Williams believed government should not interfere with religion

lived long enough to know their children's children. And whereas early Chesapeake parents commonly died before their children married, New England parents exercised a good deal of control over their adult offspring. Young men could not marry without acreage to cultivate, and because of the communal land-grant system, they had to depend on their fathers for that land. Daughters, too, needed a dowry of household goods supplied by their parents. Parents relied on their children's labor and often seemed reluctant to see them marry and start their own households. These needs sometimes led to conflict between the generations. On the whole, though, children seem to have obeyed their parents' wishes, for they had few alternatives.

Puritans controlled the governments of Massachusetts Bay, Plymouth, Connecticut, and the other early northern colonies. Congregationalism was the only officially recognized religion; except in Rhode Island members of other sects had no freedom of worship. Some non-Puritans voted in town meetings, but in Massachusetts Bay

Impact of Religion

Legacy FOR A PEOPLE AND A NATION

Blue Laws

The seventeenth-century New England colonies enacted statutes, now generally called *blue laws*, preventing their residents from working or engaging in recreation on Sundays, when they were supposed to attend church. Although the laws were inconsistently enforced, over the years various colonists found themselves fined for such forbidden Sabbath activities as plowing their fields, pursuing wandering livestock, drinking in taverns, or playing such games as shuffleboard. More harshly treated were those thieves who took advantage of others' attendance at church services to break into their houses to steal food, clothing, and other items.

The term appears to have been coined by the Reverend Samuel Peters, a loyalist, in his *General History of Connecticut*, published in London in 1781. Peters—hardly an unbiased observer of the state that had forced him into exile—used *blue laws* to refer to Connecticut's early legal code in general, defining it as "bloody Laws; for they were all sanctified with whippings, cutting off the ears, burning the tongue, and death." Eventually, though, *blue laws* acquired its current primary meaning, that is, legislation regulating behavior on Sundays. States continued to enact such statutes after independence, especially in the nineteenth century, but just as in the colonial period, many of the laws were rarely enforced.

Still, they remained on the books, and some were rigorously applied. A 1961 Supreme Court decision, *McGowan v. Maryland*, upheld that state's law restricting what could be sold on Sundays because of its secular purpose—promoting the "health, safety, recreation, and general well-being" of the populace. Whereas colonial legislators were attempting to prevent Sunday work, modern Americans (like the Maryland legislature) seem more concerned about halting Sunday shopping. Not until 1991 did the last state (North Dakota) repeal a law requiring all stores to be closed on Sundays, and only in 2003 did New York State remove its ban on Sunday liquor sales. Bergen County, New Jersey, still forbids the many shopping malls within its borders from opening on Sundays. Advocates of the ban cite the benefits of traffic reduction on that one day a week.

During the recession beginning in 2008, remaining blue laws came under new attack by people hoping to stimulate commercial activity in their communities, and a onetime Internet campaign to "Keep Sunday Special" collapsed. Even so, persistent pleas to "restore the observance of the Lord's Day in our nation" show the continuing legacy of the seventeenth century for the American people.

---

in any way, Providence and other towns in what became Rhode Island adopted a policy of tolerating all religions, including Judaism. Along with Maryland, the tiny colony founded by Williams thus presaged the religious freedom that eventually became one of the hallmarks of the United States.

A dissenter who presented a more sustained challenge to Massachusetts' leaders was Mistress Anne Hutchinson. (The title *Mistress* revealed her high status.) A skilled medical practitioner popular with the women of Boston, she greatly admired John Cotton, a minister who stressed the covenant of grace, or God's free gift of salvation to unworthy human beings. By contrast, most Massachusetts clerics emphasized the need for Puritans to engage in good works, study, and reflection in preparation for receiving God's grace. (In its most extreme form, such a doctrine could verge on the covenant of works, or the idea that people could earn their salvation.) After spreading her ideas for months in the context of gatherings at

Anne Hutchinson

childbirths—when no men were present—Mistress Hutchinson began holding women's meetings in her home to discuss Cotton's sermons. Stressing the covenant of grace, she even asserted that the elect could be assured of salvation and communicate directly with God. Such ideas had an immense appeal for Puritans. Anne Hutchinson offered them certainty of salvation instead of a state of constant anxiety. Her approach also lessened the importance of the institutional church and its ministers.

Thus, Mistress Hutchinson's ideas posed a dangerous threat to Puritan orthodoxy. So in November 1637, officials charged her with having maligned the colony's ministers by accusing them of preaching the covenant of works. For two days, she defended herself cleverly, matching scriptural references and wits with John Winthrop himself. But then Anne Hutchinson triumphantly and boldly declared that God had spoken to her directly, explaining that he would curse the Puritans' descendants for generations if they harmed her. That assertion assured her banishment, for what member of the court could acknowledge the legitimacy of such a revelation? After she had also been excommunicated from the church, she and her family, along with some faithful followers, were exiled to Rhode Island in 1638. Several years later, after she moved to New Netherland, she and most of her children were killed by Indians.

The authorities in Massachusetts perceived Anne Hutchinson as doubly dangerous to the existing order: she threatened not only religious orthodoxy but also traditional gender roles. Puritans believed in the equality before God of all souls, but they considered actual women (as distinct from their spiritual selves) inferior to men. Christians had long followed Saint Paul's dictum that women should keep silent in church and submit to their husbands. Mistress Hutchinson did neither. The magistrates' comments during her trial reveal that they were almost as outraged by her "masculine" behavior as by her religious beliefs. Winthrop charged her with having set wife against husband because so many of her followers were women. A clergyman later told her bluntly, "You have stepped out of your place, you have rather been a Husband than a Wife and a preacher than a Hearer; and a Magistrate than a Subject."

The New England authorities' reaction to Anne Hutchinson reveals the depth of their adherence to European gender-role concepts. To them, an orderly society required the obedience of wives to husbands, subjects to rulers, and ordinary folk to gentry. English people intended to change many aspects of their lives by colonizing North America, but not the gendered division of labor, the assumption of male superiority, or the maintenance of social hierarchies.

SUMMARY

By the middle of the seventeenth century, Europeans had come to North America and the Caribbean to stay, a fact that signaled major changes for the peoples of both hemispheres. These newcomers had indelibly altered not only their own lives but also those of native peoples. Europeans killed Indians with their weapons and diseases and had varying success in converting them to Christianity. Contacts with indigenous peoples taught Europeans to eat new foods, speak new languages, and recognize—however reluctantly—the persistence of other cultural patterns. The prosperity and even survival of many of the European colonies depended heavily on the cultivation of American crops (maize and tobacco) and an Asian crop (sugar), thus attesting to the importance of post-Columbian ecological exchange.

Political rivalries once confined to Europe spread around the globe, as England, Spain, Portugal, France, and the Netherlands vied for control of the peoples and resources of Asia, Africa, and the Americas. In South America, Spaniards reaped the benefits of their gold and silver mines, while French people earned their primary profits from the fur trade (in Canada) and cultivating sugar (in the Caribbean). Sugar also enriched the Portuguese in Brazil. The Dutch concentrated on commerce, trading in furs and sugar in North America and the Caribbean.

Although the English colonies, too, at first sought to rely on trade, they quickly took another form altogether when so many English people of the "middling sort" decided to migrate to North America. To a greater extent than their European counterparts, the English transferred the society and politics of their homeland to a new environment. Their sheer numbers, coupled with their need for vast quantities of land on which to grow their crops and raise their livestock, inevitably brought them into conflict with their Indian neighbors. New England and the Chesapeake differed in the sex ratio and age range of their immigrant populations, the nature of their developing economies, their settlement patterns, and the impact of religion. Yet they resembled each other in the internal and external conflicts their expansion engendered. In years to come, both regions would become embroiled in increasingly fierce rivalries besetting the European powers. Those rivalries would continue to affect Americans of all races until after the mid-eighteenth century, when France and England fought the greatest war yet known, and the Anglo-American colonies won their independence.

SUGGESTIONS FOR FURTHER READING

Virginia DeJohn Anderson, *Creatures of Empire: How Domestic Animals Transformed Early America* (2004)

Richard S. Dunn, *Sugar and Slaves: The Rise of the Planter Class in the English West Indies, 1624–1713* (1972)

David Hackett Fischer, *Champlain's Dream: The European Founding of North America* (2008)

Alison Games, *Migration and the Origins of the English Atlantic World* (1999)

David D. Hall, *Worlds of Wonder, Days of Judgment: Popular Religious Belief in Early New England* (1989)

Karen O. Kupperman, *The Jamestown Project* (2007)

Mary Beth Norton, *Founding Mothers & Fathers: Gendered Power and the Forming of American Society* (1996)

Carla Gardina Pestana, *Protestant Empire: Religion and the Making of the British Atlantic World* (2009)

Helen C. Rountree, *Pocahontas, Powhatan, Opechancanough: Three Indian Lives Changed by Jamestown* (2005)

David J. Weber, *The Spanish Frontier in North America* (1992)

North America in the Atlantic World 1650–1720

NARRATIVE

OF THE

CAPTIVITY, SUFFERINGS AND REMOVES

OF

Mrs. *Mary Rowlandson,*

She was starving. Offered a piece of boiled horse's foot by a compassionate neighbor, the slave gulped it down. Desperate, she seized another piece from a small child, who "could not bite it . . . but lay sucking, gnawing, chewing and slobbering of it in the mouth and hand." Later, she recalled that "savoury it was to my taste. . . . Thus the Lord made that pleasant refreshing, which another time would have been an abomination." But Mary Rowlandson recorded that her mistress then threatened to kill her, telling her that she had "disgraced" the household by begging for food. The captive retorted, "they had as good knock me in the head as starve me to death."

What had brought the wife of the Reverend Joseph Rowlandson of Lancaster, Massachusetts, to such distress? On February 10, 1676, a force of Wampanoags, Narragansetts, and Nipmucks had killed fourteen towns-people (including her daughter) and captured twenty-three others, in the midst of the conflict that New Englanders called King Philip's War. Carried away by the attackers to be held for ransom, she endured their hardships as they fled through the wintry countryside of western Massachusetts and southern New Hampshire. She became the slave of Quinnapin, a Narragansett sachem, and his three wives, one of whom, Weetamoo, herself a Wampanoag sachem, was her mistress. Both were eventually killed by the colonists after the death of their leader, the Wampanoag known as King Philip, in August 1676. But months before that, in May, Mary Rowlandson had been ransomed from her captors for £20—roughly equivalent to $500 today. Her experience, the Puritan woman later wrote, had taught her an important religious lesson: "to look beyond present and smaller troubles, and to be quieted under them."

◄ Mary White Rowlandson's account of her experiences during King Philip's War, first published in 1682, became the colonial equivalent of a bestseller. Republished many times, it established an entire genre of popular literature: the captivity narrative. Generations of colonial readers were enthralled by tales of English settlers who spent months or years living with their native captors.

Chronology

1642–46	■ English Civil War
1649	■ Charles I executed
1651	■ First Navigation Act passed to regulate colonial trade
1660	■ Stuarts (Charles II) restored to throne
1663	■ Carolina chartered
1664	■ English conquer New Netherland
	■ New York founded
	■ New Jersey established
1670s	■ Marquette, Jolliet, and La Salle explore the Great Lakes and Mississippi valley for France
1675–76	■ Bacon's Rebellion disrupts Virginia government; Jamestown destroyed
1675–78	■ King Philip's War devastates New England
1680–1700	■ Pueblo revolt temporarily drives Spaniards from New Mexico
1681	■ Pennsylvania chartered
1685	■ James II becomes king
1686–88	■ Dominion of New England established, superseding all charters of colonies from Maine to New Jersey
1688–89	■ James II deposed in Glorious Revolution
	■ William and Mary ascend throne
1689	■ Glorious Revolution in America; Massachusetts, New York, and Maryland overthrow colonial governors
1688–99	■ King William's War fought on northern New England frontier
1691	■ New Massachusetts charter issued
1692	■ Witchcraft crisis in Salem; nineteen people hanged
1696	■ Board of Trade and Plantations established to coordinate English colonial administration
	■ Vice-admiralty courts established in America
1701	■ Iroquois adopt neutrality policy toward France and England
1702–13	■ Queen Anne's War fought by French and English
1711–13	■ Tuscarora War (North Carolina) leads to capture or migration of most Tuscaroras
1715	■ Yamasee War nearly destroys South Carolina

*M*ary Rowlandson's famous narrative, *The Sovereignty and Goodness of God*, published in 1682, exposes more than the sufferings she shared with her captors; it also reveals that she had little understanding of, or sympathy for, their circumstances. When Weetamoo's baby died, she remarked coldly that "there was one benefit in it, that there was more room" in the wigwam. Even though Christian Indians served as go-betweens when her ransom was arranged, she distrusted them. Her narrative illustrates not only her own experiences as a captive but also the contentious relationships of Anglo New Englanders and their native neighbors. Much had changed since King Philip's father, Massasoit, had allied himself with the first settlers of Plymouth.

Many of those changes were directly related to the mainland colonies' involvement in a growing international network. Few developments demonstrated that fact more clearly than the postwar fate of many of King Philip's captured followers: they were sold into slavery in the Caribbean and elsewhere, some transported as far away as Tangier, in modern Morocco. North America, like England itself, was becoming embedded in a worldwide matrix of trade and warfare. The web woven by oceangoing vessels—once composed of only a few strands spun by Columbus and his successors—now crisscrossed the globe, carrying European goods to America and Africa, Caribbean sugar to New England and Europe, Africans to the Americas, and New England fish and wood products—and occasionally Indian slaves—to the Caribbean. Formerly tiny outposts, the North American colonies expanded their territorial claims and diversified their economies after the mid-seventeenth century.

Three developments shaped life in the mainland English colonies between 1640 and 1720: escalating conflicts with Indians and other European colonies in North America; the expansion of slavery, especially in the southern coastal regions; and changes in the colonies' political and economic relationships with England.

The explosive growth of the slave trade significantly altered the Anglo-American economy. Carrying human cargoes paid off handsomely, as many mariners and ship owners learned. Planters who could afford to buy slaves also reaped huge profits. At first involving primarily Indians and already enslaved Africans from the Caribbean, the trade soon came to focus on cargoes brought to the Americas directly from Africa. The arrival of large numbers of West African peoples thus pressed into labor expanded agricultural productivity, fueled the international trading system, and dramatically reshaped colonial society.

The burgeoning North American economy attracted new attention from colonial administrators. Especially after the Stuarts had been restored to the throne in 1660 (having lost it for a time because of the English Civil War), London bureaucrats attempted to supervise the American settlements more effectively and ensure that the mother country benefited from their economic growth. By the early eighteenth century, following three decades of upheaval, a new stability characterized colonial political institutions.

Neither English colonists nor London administrators could ignore other peoples living on the North American continent. As English settlements expanded, they came into violent conflict not only with powerful Indian nations but also with the Dutch, the Spanish, and especially the French. Moreover, all the European colonies confronted significant crises during the decade of the 1670s. By 1720, war—between Europeans and Indians, among Europeans, and among Indians allied with different colonial powers— had become an all-too-familiar feature of American life. No longer isolated from one another or from Europe, the people and products of the North American colonies had become integral to the world trading system and inextricably enmeshed in its conflicts.

- What were the consequences of the transatlantic slave trade in North America and Africa?

- How did English policy toward the colonies change from 1650 to 1720?

- What were the causes and results of new friction between Europeans and native peoples?

The Growth of Anglo-American Settlements

Between 1642 and 1646, civil war between supporters of King Charles I and the Puritan-dominated Parliament engulfed the colonists' English homeland. Parliament triumphed, leading to the execution of the king in 1649 and interim rule by the parliamentary army's leader, Oliver Cromwell, during the so-called Commonwealth period. But after Cromwell's death, Parliament decided to restore the monarchy if Charles I's son and heir agreed to restrictions on his authority. Charles II did so, and the Stuarts were returned to the throne in 1660 (see Table 3.1). The new king subsequently rewarded nobles and others who had supported him during the Civil War with huge tracts of land on the North American mainland. The colonies thereby established made up six of the thirteen polities that eventually would form the American nation: New York, New Jersey, Pennsylvania (including Delaware), and North and South Carolina (see Map 3.1). Collectively, these became known as the Restoration colonies because they were created by the restored Stuart monarchy. All were proprietorships; in each of them one man or several men held title to the soil and controlled the government.

Charles's younger brother James, the duke of York, benefited quickly. In 1664, Charles II gave James the region between the Connecticut and Delaware Rivers, including the Hudson valley and Long Island. That the Dutch had settled there mattered little; the English and the Dutch were at the time engaged in sporadic warfare, and the English were also attacking other Dutch colonies. In August, James's warships anchored off Manhattan Island, demanding New Netherland's surrender. The colony complied without resistance. Although in 1672 the Netherlands briefly retook the colony, the Dutch permanently ceded it in 1674.

New York

Table 3.1 Restored Stuart Monarchs of England, 1660–1714

Monarch	Reign	Relation to Predecessor
Charles II	1660–1685	Son
James II	1685–1688	Brother
Mary	1688–1694	Daughter
William	1688–1702	Son-in-law
Anne	1702–1714	Sister, Sister-in-law

Map 3.1 The Anglo-American Colonies in the Early Eighteenth Century

By the early eighteenth century, the English colonies nominally dominated the Atlantic coastline of North America. But the colonies' formal boundary lines are deceiving because the western reaches of each colony were still largely unfamiliar to Europeans and because much of the land was still inhabited by Native Americans.

Source: Copyright © Cengage Learning

Thus, James acquired a heterogeneous possession, which he renamed New York (see Table 3.2). In 1664, a significant minority of English people (mostly Puritan New Englanders on Long Island) already lived there, along with the Dutch and sizable numbers of Indians, Africans, Germans, Scandinavians, and a smattering of other European peoples. The Dutch West India Company had imported slaves into the colony, intending some for resale in the Chesapeake. Many, though, remained in New Netherland as laborers; at the time of the English conquest, almost one-fifth of Manhattan's approximately fifteen hundred free and enslaved inhabitants were of African descent. Slaves then made up a higher proportion of New York's urban population than of the Chesapeake's rural people.

Table 3.2 The Founding of English Colonies in North America, 1664–1681

Colony	Founder(s)	Date	Basis of Economy
New York (formerly New Netherland)	James, duke of York	1664	Farming, fur trading
New Jersey	Sir George Carteret, John Lord Berkeley	1664	Farming
North Carolina	Carlina proprietors	1665	Tobacco, forest products
South Carolina	Carolina proprietors	1670	Rice, indigo
Pennsylvania (incl. Delaware)	William Penn	1681	Farming

Recognizing the population's diversity, James's representatives moved cautiously in their efforts to establish English authority. The Duke's Laws, a legal code proclaimed in 1665, applied solely to the English settlements on Long Island, only later extended to the rest of the colony. James's policies initially maintained Dutch forms of local government, confirmed Dutch land titles, and allowed Dutch residents to maintain customary legal practices. Each town was permitted to decide which church (Dutch Reformed, Congregational, or Church of England) to support with its tax revenues. Much to the dismay of English residents, the Duke's Laws made no provision for a representative assembly. Like other Stuarts, James distrusted legislative bodies, and not until 1683 did he agree to the colonists' requests for an elected legislature. Before then, an autocratic governor ruled New York.

The English takeover thus had little immediate effect on the colony. The duke did not promote migration, so its population grew slowly, barely reaching eighteen thousand by the time of the first English census in 1698. Until the second decade of the eighteenth century, Manhattan remained a commercial backwater within the orbit of Boston.

The English conquest brought so little change to New York primarily because the duke of York in 1664 regranted the land between the Hudson and Delaware Rivers—East and West Jersey—to his friends Sir George Carteret and John Lord Berkeley. That grant left the duke's own colony hemmed in between Connecticut to the east and the Jerseys to the west and south, depriving it of much fertile land and hindering its economic growth. Meanwhile, the Jersey proprietors acted rapidly to attract settlers, promising generous land grants, limited freedom of religion, and—without authorization from the Crown—a representative assembly. In response, large numbers of Puritan New Englanders migrated southward to the Jerseys, along with some Barbadians, Dutch New Yorkers, and eventually Scots. New Jersey grew quickly; in 1726, at the time of its first census as a united colony, it had 32,500 inhabitants, only eight thousand fewer than New York.

New Jersey

NIEUW AMSTERDAM OFTE NUE NIEUW IORX OPT TEYLANT MAN

National Archives of the Netherlands

◄ The Dutch artist Johannes Vingboons painted this view of New Amersterdam/New York in 1665, shortly after the English takeover. Note the windmill, the tall government buildings, and the small row houses—which made the settlement resemble European villages of its day. The contrast to Plymouth (page 51) is striking.

Within twenty years, Berkeley and Carteret sold their interests in the Jerseys to separate groups of investors. The purchasers of all of Carteret's share (West Jersey) and portions of Berkeley's (East Jersey) were members of the Society of Friends, also called Quakers. That small radical sect rejected earthly and religious hierarchies. Quakers believed anyone could directly receive God's "inner light" and all people were equal in God's sight. With no formally trained clergy, Quakers allowed both men and women to speak in meetings and become "public Friends" who traveled to spread God's word. Quakers proselytized throughout the Atlantic world in the 1650s, recruiting followers in all of England's colonies from a base in Barbados. The authorities did not welcome the Quakers' radical egalitarianism, and they encountered persecution everywhere. Mary Dyer—previously a follower of Anne Hutchinson—became a Quaker, returned to Boston as a missionary, and was hanged in 1660 (along with several men) for preaching Quaker doctrines.

The Quakers obtained their own colony in 1681, when Charles II granted the region between Maryland and New York to his close

Pennsylvania

friend William Penn, a prominent member of the sect. Penn was then thirty-seven years old; he held the colony as a personal proprietorship, one that earned profits for his descendants until the American Revolution. Even so, Penn, like the Roman Catholic Calverts of Maryland before him, saw his province not merely as a source of revenue but also as a haven for persecuted coreligionists. Penn offered land to all comers on liberal terms, promising toleration of all religions, although only Christian men could vote; guaranteeing English liberties, such as the right to bail and trial by jury; and pledging to establish a representative assembly. He also publicized the ready availability of land in Pennsylvania through widely distributed promotional tracts printed in German, French, and Dutch.

Penn's activities and the Quakers' attraction to his lands gave rise to a migration whose magnitude equaled the Puritan exodus to New England in the 1630s. By mid-1683, more than three thousand people—among them Welsh, Irish, Dutch, and Germans—had already moved to Pennsylvania, and within five years the population reached twelve thousand. (By contrast, it had taken Virginia more than thirty years to achieve a comparable population.) Philadelphia, carefully sited on the easily navigable Delaware River and planned to be the major city in the province, drew merchants and artisans from throughout the English-speaking world. From mainland

▲ ▶ William Penn, later the proprietor of Pennsylvania, as he looked during his youth in Ireland. In such pamphlets as the one shown here, Penn spread the word about his new colony to thousands of readers in England and its other colonial possessions.

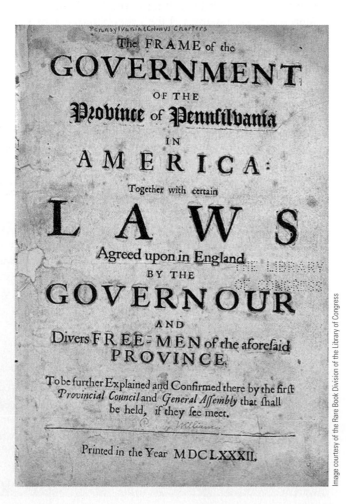

and Caribbean colonies alike came Quakers who brought with them years of experience on American soil and well-established trading connections. Pennsylvania's plentiful and fertile lands soon enabled its residents to begin exporting surplus flour and other foodstuffs to the West Indies. Practically overnight Philadelphia acquired more than two thousand citizens and started to challenge Boston's commercial dominance.

A pacifist with egalitarian principles, Penn attempted to treat native peoples fairly. He learned to speak the language of the Delawares (or Lenapes), from whom he purchased tracts of land to sell to European settlers. Penn also established strict regulations for trade and forbade the sale of alcohol to Indians. His policies attracted native peoples who moved to Pennsylvania near the end of the seventeenth century to escape repeated clashes with English colonists in Maryland, Virginia, and North Carolina. Most important were the Tuscaroras, whose experiences are described later in this chapter. Likewise, Shawnees and Miamis moved eastward from the Ohio valley. Ironically, however, the same toleration that attracted Native Americans also brought non-Quaker Europeans who showed little respect for Indian claims to the soil. In effect, Penn's policy was so successful that it caused its own downfall. The Scots-Irish, Germans, and Swiss who settled in Pennsylvania in the first half of the eighteenth century clashed repeatedly over land with Indians who had also recently migrated to the colony.

The southernmost proprietary colony, granted by Charles II in 1663, encompassed a huge tract stretching from the southern boundary of Virginia to Spanish Florida. The area had great strategic importance: a successful English settlement there would prevent Spaniards from pushing farther north. The fertile, semitropical land also held forth the promise of producing such exotic and valuable commodities as figs, olives, wines, and silk. The proprietors named their new province Carolina in honor of Charles, whose Latin name was Carolus. The "Fundamental Constitutions of Carolina," which they asked the political philosopher John Locke to draft for them, set forth an elaborate plan for a colony governed by a hierarchy of landholding aristocrats and characterized by a carefully structured distribution of political and economic power.

Carolina

But Carolina failed to follow the course the proprietors had laid out. Instead, it quickly developed two distinct population centers, which in 1729 split into separate colonies under direct royal rule. Virginia planters settled the Albemarle region that became North Carolina. They established a society much like their own, with an economy based on cultivating tobacco and exporting such forest products as pitch, tar, and timber. Because North Carolina lacked a satisfactory harbor, its planters relied on Virginia's ports and merchants to conduct their trade.

The other population center, which eventually formed the core of South Carolina, developed at Charles Town, founded in 1670 near the juncture of the Ashley and Cooper Rivers. Many of its early residents migrated from overcrowded Barbados. These sugar planters expected to reestablish plantation agriculture and hoped to escape hurricanes. They were disappointed in both respects: they soon learned that sugar would not grow successfully in Carolina, and they experienced a "wonderfully horrid and destructive" hurricane in 1686.

The settlers began to raise corn and herds of cattle, which they sold to Caribbean planters. Like other colonists before them, they also depended on trade with nearby Indians to supply commodities they could sell elsewhere. In Carolina, those items were deerskins, sent to Europe, and enslaved Indians, who were shipped to Caribbean islands and northern colonies. Nearby Indian nations hunted deer with increasing intensity and readily sold captured enemies to the English settlers. During the first decade of the eighteenth century, South Carolina exported an average of 54,000 skins annually, and overseas shipments later peaked at 160,000 a year. Before 1715, Carolinians additionally exported an estimated thirty thousand to fifty thousand Indian slaves.

The English Civil War retarded the development of the earlier English settlements. In the Chesapeake, struggles between supporters of the king and Parliament caused military clashes in Maryland and political upheavals in Virginia. But once the war ended and immigration resumed, the colonies expanded once again. Some settlers, especially those on Virginia's eastern shore and along that colony's southern border, raised grain, livestock, and flax, which they sold to English and Dutch merchants. Tobacco growers began importing increasing numbers of English indentured servants to work on their farms, which had by then begun to develop into plantations. Freed from concerns about Indian attacks by the final defeat of the Powhatan Confederacy in 1646, they—especially recent immigrants—eagerly sought to enlarge their landholdings.

Chesapeake

Although they still depended primarily on English laborers, Chesapeake tobacco planters also started to acquire small numbers of enslaved workers. Almost all came from a population that historian Ira Berlin has termed "Atlantic creoles"—that is, people (perhaps of mixed race) who came from other European settlements in the Atlantic world, primarily from Iberian outposts. Not all the Atlantic creoles who came to the Chesapeake were bondspeople; some were free or indentured. With their arrival, the Chesapeake became what Berlin calls a "society with slaves," or one in which slavery does not dominate the economy but is one of a number of coexisting labor systems.

▲ Map from A *New Description of Carolina*, by John Ogilby, 1671 (with south at the top). Ogilby's tract, illustrated by a map drawn from information supplied by John Lederer, a German Indian trader, was intended to attract settlers to the new Carolina colony. He filled his text with information supplied by the Lords Proprietors, stressing the colony's pleasant climate, abundant resources, and friendly Native peoples, a message underscored by the peaceful scenes in the corner cartouches.

In New England, migration essentially ceased after the Civil War began in 1642. While Puritans were first challenging the king and then governing England as a commonwealth, they had little incentive to leave their homeland, and few migrated after the Restoration. Yet the Puritan colonies' population continued to grow dramatically because of natural increase. By the 1670s, New England's population had more than tripled to reach approximately seventy thousand. Such a rapid expansion placed great pressure on available land. Colonial settlement spread far into the interior of Massachusetts and Connecticut, and many members of the third and fourth generations migrated—north to New Hampshire or Maine, southwest to New York or New Jersey—to find sufficient farmland for themselves and their children. Others abandoned agriculture and learned such skills as blacksmithing or carpentry to support themselves in the growing towns.

New England

The people who remained behind in the small, yet densely populated older New England communities experienced a new phenomenon after approximately 1650: witchcraft accusations and trials. Other regions largely escaped such incidents, even though most seventeenth-century people believed witches existed. These allies of the Devil were thought to harness invisible spirits for good or evil purposes. For example, a witch might engage in fortunetelling, prepare healing potions or charms, or harm others by causing the death of a child or valuable animals. Yet only New England witnessed many trials of accused witches (about one hundred in all before 1690). Most, though not all, of the accused were middle-aged women who had angered their neighbors. Historians have accordingly concluded that the dynamics of daily interactions in the close-knit communities, where the same families lived nearby for decades, fostered longstanding quarrels that led some colonists to believe others had diabolically caused certain misfortunes. Even so, only a few of the accused were convicted, and fewer still were executed, because judges and juries remained skeptical of such charges.

That New England courts halted questionable prosecutions suggests the maturity of colonial institutions. By the last quarter of the seventeenth century, almost all the Anglo-American colonies had well-established political and judicial structures. In New England, property-holding men or the legislature elected the governors; in other regions, the king or the proprietor appointed such leaders. A council, either elected or appointed, advised the governor on matters of policy and served as the upper house of the legislature. Each colony had a judiciary with local justices of the peace, county courts, and, usually, an appeals court composed of the councilors.

Colonial Political Structures

Local political institutions also developed. In New England, elected selectmen initially governed the towns, but by the end of the seventeenth century, town meetings—held at least annually and attended by most free adult male residents—handled matters of local concern. In the Chesapeake colonies and in both of the Carolinas, appointed magistrates ran local governments. At first, the same was true in Pennsylvania, but by the early eighteenth century, elected county officials began to take over some government functions. And in New York, local elections were the rule even before the establishment of the colonial assembly in 1683.

A Decade of Imperial Crises: The 1670s

As the Restoration colonies were extending the range of English settlement, the first English colonies and French and Spanish settlements in North America faced crises caused primarily by their changing relationships with America's indigenous peoples. Between 1670 and 1680, New France, New Mexico, New England, and Virginia experienced bitter conflicts as their interests collided with those of America's original inhabitants. All the early colonies changed irrevocably as a result.

In the mid-1670s Louis de Buade de Frontenac, the governor-general of Canada, decided to expand New France's reach into the south and west, hoping to establish a trade route to Mexico and to gain direct control of the valuable fur trade on which the prosperity of the colony rested. Accordingly, he encouraged the explorations of Father Jacques Marquette, Louis Jolliet, and René-Robert Cavelier de La Salle in the Great Lakes and Mississippi valley regions. His goal, however, brought

New France and the Iroquois

Palace of the Governors, New Mexico History Museum

▲ Don Diego de Vargas, leader of the expedition to reconquer the Pueblo peoples in 1692. This is the only known portrait of him; today it hangs in the Palace of the Governors in the New Mexico History Museum.

him into conflict with the powerful Iroquois Confederacy, composed of five Indian nations—the Mohawks, Oneidas, Onondagas, Cayugas, and Senecas. (In 1722, the Tuscaroras became the sixth.)

Under the terms of a unique defensive alliance forged in the sixteenth century, a representative council

Link to Marquette's account of his exploration of the Mississippi.

made decisions of war and peace for the entire Iroquois Confederacy, although each nation still retained some autonomy and could not be forced to comply with a council directive against its will. Before the arrival of Europeans, the Iroquois waged wars primarily to acquire captives to replenish their population. Contact with foreign traders brought ravaging disease as early as 1633, intensifying the need for captives. Simultaneously, the Europeans' presence created an economic motive for warfare: the desire to dominate the fur trade and to gain unimpeded access to European goods. The war with the Hurons in the 1640s initiated a series of conflicts with other Indians known as the Beaver Wars, in which the Iroquois fought to achieve control of the lucrative peltry trade. Iroquois warriors did not themselves trap beaver; instead, they raided other villages in search of caches of pelts or attacked Indians from the interior as they carried furs to European outposts. Then the Iroquois traded that booty for European-made blankets, knives, guns, alcohol, and other desirable items.

In the mid-1670s, as Iroquois dominance grew, the French intervened, for an Iroquois triumph would have destroyed France's plans to trade directly with western Indians. Over the next twenty years, the French launched repeated attacks on Iroquois villages. Although in 1677 New Yorkers and the Iroquois established a formal alliance known as the Covenant Chain, the English offered little assistance other than weapons to their trading partners. Without much aid, the confederacy held its own and even expanded its reach, enabling it in 1701 to negotiate neutrality treaties with France and other Indians. For the next half-century, the Iroquois nations maintained their power through trade and skillful diplomacy rather than warfare, forming or abandoning alliances with Indian or European nations to best achieve their goals.

In New Mexico, too, events of the 1670s led to a crisis with long-term consequences. Over the years under

Pueblo Peoples and Spaniards

Spanish domination, the Pueblo peoples had added Christianity to their religious beliefs while still retaining traditional rituals, engaging in syncretic practices as had Mesoamericans. But as decades passed, Franciscans adopted increasingly brutal and violent tactics in order to erase all traces of the native religion. Priests and secular colonists who held *encomiendas* placed heavy labor demands on the people who were also suffering from Apache raids and food shortages caused by a serious drought. In 1680, the Pueblos revolted under the leadership of Popé, a respected shaman, successfully driving the Spaniards out of New Mexico (see Map 3.2). Even though Spain managed to restore its authority by 1700, imperial officials had learned their lesson. Afterward, Spanish governors stressed cooperation with the Pueblos, relying on their labor but no longer attempting to violate their cultural

integrity. The Pueblo revolt constituted the most successful and longest-sustained Indian resistance movement in colonial North America.

Other native peoples, including those with homelands many miles away from New Mexico, felt the Spanish presence as well. Spanish military outposts (presidios) and Franciscan missions offered some protection to Pueblos, but other Indians' desire to obtain horses and guns led to endemic violence throughout the region. Navajos, Apaches, and Utes attacked each other and the Pueblos in order to obtain captives and hides to trade to the Spanish. Captured Indian men might be sent to Mexican silver mines, whereas Spaniards often retained women and children as domestic laborers. When Comanches migrated west from the Great Plains in the late seventeenth century, Utes allied with them, and after the Pueblo revolt that alliance dominated New Mexico's northern borderlands for several decades.

In the more densely settled English colonies, hostilities developed in the decade of the 1670s, not over religion (as in New Mexico) or trade (as in New France), but over land. Put simply, the rapidly expanding Anglo-American population wanted more of it. In both New England and Virginia—though for different reasons—settlers began to encroach on territories that until then had remained in the hands of Native Americans.

By the early 1670s, the growing settlements in southern New England surrounded Wampanoag ancestral lands on Narragansett Bay.

King Philip's War

The local chief, Metacom, or King Philip, was troubled by the loss of territory and concerned about the impact of European culture and Christianity on his people. Philip led his warriors in attacks on nearby communities in June 1675. Other Algonquian peoples, among them Nipmucks and Narragansetts, soon joined King Philip's forces. In the fall, the Indian nations jointly attacked settlements in the northern Connecticut River valley, and the war spread to Maine, too, when the Abenakis entered the conflict. In early 1676, the Indian allies devastated villages like Lancaster, where they captured Mary Rowlandson and others, and even attacked Plymouth and Providence; later that year, Abenaki assaults forced the abandonment of most settlements in Maine. Altogether, the alliance wholly or partially destroyed twenty-seven of ninety-two towns and attacked forty others, pushing the line of English settlement back toward the east and south.

The tide turned in the south in the summer of 1676. The Indian coalition ran short of food and ammunition, and colonists began to use Christian Indians as guides and scouts. On June 12, the Mohawks—ancient Iroquois enemies of New England Algonquians— devastated a major Wampanoag encampment while most

Map 3.2 New Mexico, ca. 1680

In 1680, the lone Spanish settlement at Santa Fe was surrounded and vastly outnumbered by the many Pueblo villages nearby.

Source: Adapted from *Apache, Navaho, and Spaniard,* by Jack D. Forbes. Copyright 1960 by the University of Oklahoma Press. Reprinted by permission of the University of Oklahoma Press.

of the warriors were away attacking an English town. After King Philip was killed that August, the southern alliance crumbled. Fighting, though, continued on the Maine frontier for another two years. There the English colonists never defeated the Abenakis; both sides, their resources depleted, simply agreed to end the conflict in 1678.

In addition to the Wampanoags, Nipmucks, Narragansetts, and Abenakis who were captured and sold into slavery, still more died of starvation and disease. New Englanders had broken the power of the southern coastal tribes. Thereafter the southern Indians lived in small clusters, subordinated to the colonists and often working as servants or sailors. Only on the island of Martha's Vineyard did Christian Wampanoags (who had not participated in the war) preserve their cultural identity intact.

The settlers paid a terrible price for their victory: an estimated one-tenth of the able-bodied adult male population was killed or wounded. Proportional to popula-

tion, it was the most costly conflict in American history. The heavy losses in the war also caused many Puritan colonists to question their earlier confidence that God supported their endeavors; they now wondered if God had turned against them. New Englanders did not fully rebuild abandoned interior towns for another three decades, and not until the American Revolution did the region's per capita income again reach pre-1675 levels.

Not coincidentally, conflict simultaneously wracked Virginia. In the early 1670s, ex-servants unable to acquire land greedily eyed the territory reserved by treaty for Virginia's Indians. Governor William Berkeley, the leader of an entrenched coterie of large landowners, resisted starting a war to further the aims of settlers who were challenging his authority. Dissatisfied colonists then rallied behind the leadership of a recent immigrant, the gentleman Nathaniel Bacon, who like other new arrivals

Bacon's Rebellion

◄ This Virginia mansion, one of only three surviving Jacobean-style great houses in North America or the Caribbean, is known as "Bacon's Castle." Built in 1665, it was captured and fortified by Nathaniel Bacon's men during the rebellion, but Bacon is not known to have visited it. In early 1677, it was one of the last rebel outposts to fall to Sir William Berkeley's forces.

had found that all the desirable land in settled areas had already been claimed. Using as a pretext the July 1675 killing of an indentured servant by some Doeg Indians, settlers attacked not only the Doegs but also the Susquehannocks, a more powerful nation. In retaliation, Susquehannock bands raided outlying farms early in 1676.

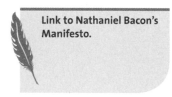

Link to Nathaniel Bacon's Manifesto.

Berkeley and Bacon soon clashed. The governor outlawed Bacon and his men; the rebels then held Berkeley hostage, forcing him to authorize them to attack the Indians. During the chaotic summer of 1676, Bacon alternately pursued Indians and battled the governor. In September, Bacon's forces attacked Jamestown, burning the capital to the ground. But when Bacon died of dysentery the following month, the rebellion began to collapse. Even so, the rebels had made their point. Berkeley was recalled to England, and a new treaty signed in 1677 opened much of the disputed territory to settlement. The end of Bacon's Rebellion thus pushed most of Virginia's Indians farther west, beyond the Appalachians.

The Atlantic Trading System

In the 1670s and 1680s, the prosperity of the Chesapeake rested on tobacco, and successful tobacco cultivation depended, as it always had, on an ample labor supply. But fewer and fewer English men and women proved willing to indenture themselves for long terms of service in Maryland and Virginia. Population pressures had eased in England, and the founding of the Restoration colonies meant that migrants could choose other American destinations. Furthermore, fluctuating tobacco prices in Europe and the growing scarcity of land made the Chesapeake less appealing to potential settlers. That posed a problem for wealthy Chesapeake tobacco growers. Where could they obtain the workers they needed? They found the answer in the Caribbean sugar islands where Dutch, French, English, and Spanish planters were accustomed to purchasing African slaves.

Slavery had been practiced in Europe and Islamic lands for centuries. European Christians—both Catholics and Protestants—believed enslaving heathen peoples, especially those of exotic origin, was justifiable in religious terms. Muslims, too, thought infidels could be enslaved, and they imported tens of thousands of black African bondspeople into North Africa and the Middle East. Some Christians argued that holding heathens in bondage would lead to their conversion. Others believed any heathen taken prisoner in wartime could be enslaved. Consequently, when Portuguese mariners reached the sub-Saharan coast and encountered African societies holding slaves, they purchased bondspeople along with gold and other items. Indeed, they initially bought enslaved people in one African nation and sold them in another. From the 1440s on, Portugal imported large numbers of slaves into the Iberian Peninsula; by 1500, enslaved Africans composed about one-tenth of the population of Lisbon and Seville, the chief cities of Portugal and Spain. In 1555, a few of them were taken to

Why African Slavery?

England, where—when others followed—residents of London and Bristol in particular became accustomed to seeing black slaves on the streets.

Iberians exported African slavery to their American possessions, New Spain and Brazil. Because the Catholic Church prevented the formal enslavement of Indians in those domains and free laborers saw no reason to work voluntarily in mines or on sugar plantations when they could earn better wages under easier conditions elsewhere, African bondspeople (who had no choice) became mainstays of the Caribbean and Brazilian economies. European planters on all the sugar islands began purchasing slaves—often from the Iberians—soon after they settled in the Caribbean. Accordingly, the first enslaved Africans in the Americas were imported from Angola, Portugal's major early trading partner, and the Portuguese word *Negro* came into use as a common descriptor.

English people had few moral qualms about enslaving other humans. Slavery, after all, was sanctioned in the Bible, and it was widely practiced by their contemporaries. Few at the time questioned the decision to hold Africans and their descendants—or captive Indians from New England or Carolina—in perpetual bondage. Yet their convoluted early attempts to define slave status nevertheless indicate that seventeenth-century English colonists initially lacked clear conceptual categories defining both "race" and "slave." For example, the 1670 Virginia law that first tried to define which people were enslaveable notably failed to employ the racial terminology that would later become commonplace. Instead, awkwardly seeking to single out imported Africans, it declared that "all servants not being christians imported into this colony by shipping shalbe slaves for their lives." Such nonracial phrasing reveals that Anglo-American settlers had not yet fully developed the meaning of *race* and *slave* and that they did so in tandem over time through their experience with the institution of slavery itself.

The planters of the North American mainland could not have obtained the bondspeople they wanted had it

Atlantic Slave Trade

not been for the rapid development of an Atlantic trading system, the linchpin of which was the traffic in enslaved human beings. Although this elaborate Atlantic economic system has been called the triangular trade,

TRADING ON Y COAST OF AFRICA — THE SOUTHWELL FRIGATE — TRADING ON Y COAST OF AFRICA

▲ Nicholas Pocock made this engraving of the Southwell frigate, a former privateer from Bristol, England, turned into a slave-trading vessel, about 1760. The images at the bottom show the ship's company trading for slaves on the coast of West Africa.

Bristol City Museum and Art Gallery, UK/The Bridgeman Art Library Nationality people and products did not move across the ocean in easily diagrammed patterns. Instead, their movements created a complicated web of exchange that inextricably tied the peoples of the Atlantic world together (see Map 3.3).

The oceanic slave trade was entirely new, though enslavement was not. The expanding network of commerce between Europe and its colonies was fueled by the sale and transport of slaves, the exchange of commodities produced by slave labor, and the need to feed and clothe so many bound laborers. The European economy, previously oriented toward the Mediterranean and Asia, shifted its emphasis to the Atlantic. By the late seventeenth century, commerce in slaves and the products of slave labor constituted the basis of the European economic system. The irony of Columbus's discoveries thus became complete: seeking the wealth of Asia, Columbus instead found the lands that—along with Africa—ultimately replaced Asia as the source of European prosperity.

The various elements of the trade had different relationships to one another and to the wider web of exchange. Chesapeake tobacco and Caribbean and Brazilian sugar were in great demand in Europe, so planters shipped those products directly to their home countries. The profits paid for both the African laborers who grew their crops and European manufactured goods. The African coastal rulers who ran the entrepôts where European slavers acquired their human cargoes received their payment in European manufactures and East Indian textiles; they had little need for most American products. Europeans purchased slaves from Africa for resale in their colonies and acquired sugar and tobacco from America, in exchange dispatching their manufactures everywhere.

European nations fought bitterly to control the lucrative trade. The Portuguese, who at first dominated the trade, were supplanted by the Dutch in the 1630s. In the Anglo-Dutch wars, the Dutch lost out to the English, who controlled the trade through the Royal African Company, a joint-stock company chartered by Charles II in 1672. Holding a monopoly on all English trade with sub-Saharan Africa, the company built and maintained seventeen forts and trading posts, dispatched to

Map 3.3 Atlantic Trade Routes

By the late seventeenth century, an elaborate trade network linked the countries and colonies bordering the Atlantic Ocean. The most valuable commodities exchanged were enslaved people and the products of slave labor.

Source: Copyright © Cengage Learning

▲ By the middle of the eighteenth century, American tobacco had become closely associated with African slavery. An English woodcut advertising tobacco from the York River in Virginia accordingly depicted not a Chesapeake planter but rather an African, shown with a hoe in one hand and a pipe in the other. Usually, of course, slaves would not have smoked the high-quality tobacco produced for export, although they were allowed to cultivate small crops for their own use.

regularly at coastal forts. Such rulers controlled Europeans' access to bound laborers and simultaneously controlled inland peoples' access to desirable trade goods, such as textiles, iron bars, alcohol, tobacco, guns, and cowry shells from the Maldive Islands (in the Indian Ocean), which were widely used as currency. Through Whydah, Dahomey's major slave-trading port, passed at least 10 percent of all slaves exported to the Americas, and Whydah's merchants earned substantial annual profits from the trade. Portugal, England, and France established forts there; Europeans had to pay fees to Whydah's rulers before they could begin to acquire cargoes.

The slave trade had varying consequences for the nations of West Africa. The trade's centralizing tendencies helped to create such powerful eighteenth-century kingdoms as Dahomey and Asante (formed from the Akan States). Traffic in slaves destroyed smaller polities and disrupted traditional economic patterns, as goods once sent north toward the Mediterranean were redirected to the Atlantic and as local manufactures declined in the face of European competition. Agricultural production intensified, especially in rice-growing areas, because of the need to supply hundreds of slave ships with foodstuffs for transatlantic voyages. Because prisoners of war constituted the bulk of the exported slaves, the most active traders were also the most successful in battle. Some nations even initiated conflicts specifically to acquire valuable captives. For example, the state of Benin sold captive enemies to the Portuguese in the late fifteenth century, did not do so at the height of its power in the sixteenth and seventeenth centuries, and renewed the sale of prisoners in the eighteenth century when its waning power led to conflicts with neighboring states.

The trade therefore affected African regions unevenly. Rulers in parts of Upper Guinea, especially modern Gambia and Senegal, largely resisted involvement with the trade; the few slave vessels that departed from that area were much more likely than others to experience onboard rebellions. Despite planters' preference for male slaves, women predominated in cargoes originating in the Bight of Biafra. In such regions as the Gold Coast, the trade had a significant impact on the sex ratio of the remaining population. There a relative shortage of men increased work demands on women, encouraged polygyny, and opened new opportunities to women and their children.

New England had the most complex relationship to the trading system. The region produced only one item

West Africa hundreds of ships carrying English manufactured goods, and transported about 100,000 slaves to England's Caribbean colonies. It paid regular dividends averaging 10 percent yearly, and some of its agents made fortunes. Yet even before the company's monopoly expired in 1712, many individual English and North American traders had illegally entered the market for slaves. By the early eighteenth century, such independent traders carried most of the Africans imported into the colonies, earning huge profits from successful voyages.

Most of the enslaved people carried to North America originated in West Africa. Some came from the Rice and Grain Coasts, especially the former, but even more had resided in the Gold and Slave Coasts and the Bight of Biafra (modern Nigeria) and Angola (see Map 1.2). Certain coastal rulers—for instance, the Adja kings of the Slave Coast—served as intermediaries, allowing the establishment of permanent slave-trading posts in their territories and supplying resident Europeans with slaves to fill ships that stopped

West Africa and the Slave Trade

New England and the Caribbean

England wanted: tall trees to serve as masts for sailing vessels. To buy English manufactures, New Englanders therefore needed profits earned elsewhere, especially in the Caribbean. Those islands lacked precisely the items that New England

Exotic Beverages

The seventeenth-century colonists developed a taste not only for tea (from China) but also for coffee (from Arabia), chocolate (from Mesoamerica), and rum (distilled from sugar, which also sweetened the bitter taste of the other three). The American and European demand for these once-exotic beverages helped reshape the world economy after the mid-seventeenth century. Indeed, one historian has estimated that approximately two-thirds of the people who migrated across the Atlantic before 1776 were involved in one way or another, primarily as slaves, in the production of tobacco, calico, and these four drinks for the world market. The exotic beverages had a profound impact, too, on custom and culture as they moved swiftly from luxury to necessity.

Each beverage had its own pattern of consumption. Chocolate, brought to Spain from Mexico and enjoyed there for a century before spreading more widely throughout Europe, became the preferred drink of aristocrats, consumed hot at intimate gatherings in palaces and mansions. Coffee, by contrast, became the preeminent morning beverage of English and colonial businessmen, who praised its caffeine for keeping drinkers sober and focused. Coffee was served in new public coffeehouses, patronized only by men, where politics and business were the topics of conversation. The first coffeehouse opened in London in the late 1660s; Boston had several by the 1690s. By the mid-eighteenth century, though, tea had supplanted coffee as the preferred hot, caffeinated beverage in England and America. It was consumed in the afternoon in private homes at tea tables presided over by women. Tea embodied genteel status and polite conversation. In contrast, rum was the drink of the masses. This inexpensive, potent distilled spirit, made possible by new technology and the increasing production of sugar, was enthusiastically imbibed by free working people everywhere in the Atlantic world.

The American colonies played a vital role in the production, distribution, and consumption of each of these beverages. Chocolate, most obviously, originated in America, and cacao plantations in the South American tropics multiplied in size and number to meet the rising demand. Coffee and tea (particularly the latter) were as avidly consumed in the colonies as in England. And rum involved Americans in every phase of its production and consumption. The sugar grown on French and English Caribbean plantations was transported to the mainland in barrels and ships made from North American wood.

There the syrup was turned into rum at 140 distilleries. The Americans themselves drank a substantial share of the distilleries' output—an estimated four gallons per person annually—but exported much of it to Africa. There the rum purchased more slaves to produce more sugar to make still more rum, and the cycle began again.

Thus, new tastes and customs connected to four different beverages linked the colonies to the rest of the world and altered their economic and social development.

▲ The frontispiece of Peter Muguet, *Tractatus De Poto Caphe, Chinesium The et de Chocolata*, 1685. Muguet's treatise visually linked the three hot, exotic beverages recently introduced to Europeans. The drinks are consumed by representatives of the cultures in which they originated: a turbaned Turk (with coffeepot in the foreground), a Chinese man (with teapot on the table), and an Indian drinking from a hollowed, handled gourd (with a chocolate pot and ladle on the floor in front of him).

De Stadt
BENIN.

BENIN,
Ville de la Guinée, en Afrique.

▲ A Procession in Benin, 1668. A contemporary European engraving shows a royal procession leaving the city of Benin, capital of the prosperous West African kingdom. During the seventeenth century, the power of Benin's rulers scared off would-be challengers, and so the kingdom did not engage in frequent warfare. In the fifteenth and eighteenth centuries, by contrast, when the kingdom was weaker, it did capture and sell its enemies.

could produce in abundance: cheap food (primarily corn and salt fish) to feed the burgeoning slave population and wood for barrels to hold sugar and molasses. By the late 1640s, decades before the Chesapeake economy became dependent on *production* by slaves, New England's already rested on *consumption* by slaves and their owners. The sale of foodstuffs and wood products to Caribbean sugar planters provided New England farmers and merchants with a major source of income. After the founding of Pennsylvania, New York, and New Jersey, those colonies, too, participated in the lucrative West Indian trade.

Shopkeepers in the interior of New England and the middle colonies bartered with local farmers for grains, livestock, and barrel staves, then traded those items to merchants located in port towns. Such merchants dispatched ships to the Caribbean, where they sailed from island to island, exchanging their cargoes for molasses, sugar, fruit, dyestuffs, and slaves. The system's sole constant was uncertainty, due to the weather, rapid shifts in supply and demand in the small island markets, and the delicate system of credit on which the entire structure depended. Once they had a full load, the ships returned to Boston, Newport, New York, or Philadelphia to dispose of their cargoes (often including enslaved people). Americans began to distill molasses into rum, a crucial aspect of the only part of the trade that could accurately be termed triangular. Rhode Islanders took rum to Africa and traded it for slaves, whom they carried to Caribbean islands to exchange for more molasses to produce still more rum.

Tying the system together was the voyage (commonly called the middle passage) that brought Africans to the Americas, where they cultivated the profitable crops and—on Caribbean islands—consumed foods produced in North America. On shipboard, men were shackled in pairs in the hold except for periods of exercise on deck, whereas during the day women and children were usually free to move around, and to work at such assigned tasks as food preparation and cleaning. At night, men and women were confined to separate quarters. The best evidence of the captives' reaction to their plight comes from accounts of their behavior, since few ever had the chance to record their experiences.

Slaving Voyages

Many resisted enslavement by refusing to eat, jumping overboard, or joining in revolts, which rarely succeeded. Their communal singing and drumming, reported by numerous observers, must have simultaneously lifted their spirits and forged a sense of solidarity. But conditions on board were hellish, as captains often packed as many people as possible into holds that were hot, crowded, and reeking with smells from vomit and the "necessary tubs."

The traumatic voyage unsurprisingly brought heavy fatalities to captives and crew alike. An average of 10 to 20 percent of the newly enslaved died en route; on long or disease-ridden voyages, mortality rates could be much higher. In addition, another 20 percent or so died either before the ships left Africa or shortly after their arrival in the Americas. Sailors also died at high rates, chiefly through exposure to such diseases as yellow fever and malaria, which were endemic to Africa. One in every four or five died on voyages, and just 10 percent of the men sent to run the Royal African Company's forts in Lower Guinea lived to return home to England. Sailors signed on to slaving voyages reluctantly; indeed, many had to be coerced or tricked, because conditions on shipboard were difficult for the crew as well as the human cargo. Slave merchants were notoriously greedy and captains notoriously brutal—to sailors as well as to the captives in the hold. Some crew members were themselves slaves or freedmen. Unfortunately, the sailors, often the subject of abuse, in turn frequently abused the bondspeople in their charge. Yet at the same time, through intimate contact with the enslaved, they learned the value of freedom, and sailors became well known throughout the Atlantic world for their fierce attachment to personal independence.

Slavery in North America and the Caribbean

Barbados, America's first "slave society" (an economy wholly dependent on enslavement, as opposed to a "society with slaves"), spawned many others. As the island's population expanded and large planters consolidated their landholdings, about 40 percent of the early English residents dispersed to other colonies. The migrants carried their laws, commercial contacts, and slaveholding practices with them; the Barbados slave code of 1661, for example, served as the model for later codes in Jamaica, Antigua, Virginia, and South Carolina. Moreover, a large proportion of the first Africans imported into North America came via Barbados. In addition to the many Barbadians who settled in Carolina, others moved to the southern regions of Virginia (where they specialized in selling foodstuffs and livestock to their

former island home), New Jersey, and New England, where they already had slave-trading partners.

Newly arrived Africans in the Chesapeake tended to be assigned to outlying parts of plantations (called quarters), at least until they learned some English and the routines of American tobacco cultivation. The crop that originated in the Americas was also grown in various locations in West Africa, so Chesapeake planters, who in the late seventeenth century were still experimenting with curing and processing techniques, could well have drawn on their laborers' expertise. Such Africans—the vast majority of them men—lived in quarters composed of ten to fifteen workers housed together in one or two buildings and supervised by an Anglo-American overseer. Each man was expected to cultivate about two acres of tobacco a year. Their lives must have been filled with toil and loneliness, for few spoke the same language, and all were expected to work for their owners six days a week. On Sundays, planters allowed them a day off. Many used that time to cultivate their own gardens or to hunt or fish to supplement their meager diet. Only rarely could they form families because of the scarcity of women.

African Enslavement in the Chesapeake

Slaves usually cost about two and a half times as much as indentured servants, but they could repay the greater investment with a lifetime of service, assuming they survived—which large numbers did not, having been weakened by the voyage and sickened by exposure to new diseases. Those with enough money could take the chance and acquire slaves, accumulate greater wealth, and establish large plantations worked by tens, if not hundreds, of bondspeople, whereas the less affluent could not even afford to purchase indentured servants, whose price rose because of scarcity. As time passed, Anglo-American society in the Chesapeake thus became increasingly stratified—that is, the gap between rich and poor planters steadily widened. The introduction of large numbers of Africans into the Chesapeake accordingly had a significant impact on the shape of Anglo-American society, in addition to reshaping the population as a whole.

So many Africans were imported into Virginia and Maryland so rapidly that, as early as 1690, those colonies contained more slaves than English indentured servants. By 1710, people of African descent composed one-fifth of the region's population. Even so, and despite sizable continuing imports, a decade later American-born slaves already outnumbered their African-born counterparts in the Chesapeake, and the native-born proportion of the slave population continued to increase thereafter.

Link to Colonial Virginia and Maryland slave laws.

Joseph Regenstein Library

▲ In 1726, William Smith, an employee of the Royal African Company, sketched this musician playing a traditional marimba-like instrument called a *balafo*. Later in the eighteenth century, Virginians described slaves playing the same instrument, thus showing that African music came to North America with the enslaved multitudes.

African Enslavement in South Carolina

Africans who had lived in the Caribbean came with their masters to South Carolina from Barbados in 1670, composing one-quarter to one-third of the early population. The Barbadian slaveowners quickly discovered that African-born slaves had a variety of skills well suited to the semitropical environment of South Carolina. African-style dugout canoes became the chief means of transportation in the colony, which was crossed by rivers and included large islands just off shore. Fishing nets copied from African models proved more efficient than those of English origin. Baskets that enslaved laborers wove and gourds they hollowed out came into general use as containers for food and drink. Africans' skill at killing crocodiles equipped them to handle alligators. And, finally, Africans adapted their traditional techniques of cattle herding for use in America. Because meat and hides numbered among the colony's chief exports in its earliest years, Africans contributed significantly to South Carolina's prosperity.

In 1693, as slavery was taking firm root in South Carolina, officials in Spanish Florida began offering freedom to runaways who would convert to Catholicism. Over the years, hundreds of South Carolina fugitives took advantage of the offer, although not all won their liberty. Many settled in a town founded for them near St. Augustine, Gracia Real de Santa Teresa de Mose, headed by a former slave, Francisco Menendez.

After 1700, South Carolinians started to import slaves directly from Africa. From about 1710 until mid-century, the African-born constituted a majority of the enslaved population in the colony, and, bondspeople by 1750 composed a majority of its residents. The similarity of the South Carolinian and West African environments, coupled with the substantial African-born population, ensured the survival of more aspects of West African culture than elsewhere on the North American mainland. Only in South Carolina did enslaved parents continue to give their children African names; only there did a dialect develop that combined English words with African terms. (Known as Gullah, it has survived to the present day in isolated areas.) African skills remained useful, so techniques lost in other regions when the migrant generation died were instead passed down to the migrants' children. And in South Carolina, African women became the primary petty traders, dominating the markets of Charles Town as they did those of Guinea.

The importation of Africans coincided with the successful introduction of rice in South Carolina.

Rice and Indigo

English people knew nothing about the techniques of growing and processing rice, but people from Africa's Rice Coast had spent their lives working with the crop. Although the evidence is circumstantial, the Africans' expertise may well have assisted their English masters in cultivating rice profitably. Productive rice-growing techniques known in West Africa, especially cultivation in inland swamps and tidal rivers, both of which involved substantial water-control projects, were widely adopted and combined with European technologies. In West Africa, women played a crucial role in cultivating and processing rice, and they did so in South Carolina as well. Enslaved men dug the ditches and prepared the fields for planting, but women were responsible for sowing and weeding the crop as well as for pounding harvested rice with a mortar and pestle to remove the hulls and bran, then winnowing to separate the grains from the chaff. Because English grindstones damaged rice kernels (not until the late eighteenth century were new processes developed), South Carolinians continued to utilize the West African system of pounding rice by hand; planters assigned men as well as women to that task.

Every field worker on rice plantations, which were far larger than Chesapeake tobacco quarters, was expected to cultivate three to four acres of rice a year. Most of those field workers were female because many enslaved men were assigned to jobs like blacksmithing or carpentry, which were not given to women. To cut expenses, planters also expected slaves to grow part of their own food. A universally adopted "task" system of predefined work

Courtesy of The Rice Museum, Georgetown, South Carolina

▲ Although this rice basket dates from nineteenth-century South Carolina, it is woven in traditional West African style. Enslaved women winnowed rice in such baskets, tossing the grains into the air after they had been pounded, so that the lighter pieces of hull would be blown away by the wind.

assignments provided that, after bondspeople had finished their set tasks for the day, they could then rest or work in their own garden plots or on other projects. Experienced laborers could often complete their tasks by early afternoon; after that, as on Sundays, their masters had no legitimate claim on their time. One scholar has suggested that the unique task system, which gave bondspeople more freedom than gang labor, and which was used in South Carolina by the early eighteenth century, resulted from negotiations between slaves familiar with rice cultivation and masters who needed their expertise.

Developers of South Carolina's second cash crop also used the task system and drew on slaves' specialized skills. Indigo, the only source of blue dye for the growing English textile industry, was much prized. Eliza Lucas, a young woman managing her father's plantations, began to experiment with indigo cultivation during the early 1740s. Drawing on the knowledge of slaves and overseers from the Caribbean, she developed the planting and processing techniques later adopted throughout the colony. Indigo grew on high ground, and rice was planted in low-lying regions; rice and indigo also had different growing seasons. Thus, the two crops complemented each other. South Carolina indigo never matched the quality of that from the Caribbean, but indigo plantations flourished because the crop was so valuable that Parliament offered Carolinians a bounty on every pound exported to Great Britain.

Among the enslaved people in both Carolinas were Indian captives who had been retained rather than exported. In 1708, such Indians composed as much as 14 percent of the South Carolina population. The widespread and lucrative traffic in Indian slaves significantly affected South Carolina's relationship with its indigenous neighbors. Native Americans knew they could always find a ready market for captive enemies in Charles Town, so they took that means of ridding themselves of real or potential rivals. Yet Indian nations soon learned that Carolinians could not be trusted. As settlers and traders shifted their priorities, first one set of former allies, then another, found themselves the enslaved rather than the enslavers.

Indian Enslavement in North and South Carolina

The trade in Indian slaves began when the Westos (originally known as the Eries), migrated south from the Great Lakes region in the mid-1650s, fleeing their Iroquois enemies after the Beaver Wars. Expert in the use of European firearms, the Westos began raiding Spain's lightly defended Florida missions and selling the resulting Indian captives to Virginians. With the establishment of Carolina, the proprietors took for themselves a monopoly of trade with the Westos, which infuriated local settlers shut out of the profitable commerce in slaves and deerskins. The planters secretly financed attacks on the Westos, essentially wiping them out by 1682. Southeastern Indians reacted to such slave raids—continued by other native peoples after the defeat of the Westos—by trying to protect themselves either through subordination to the English or Spanish, or by coalescing into new, larger political units, such as those known later as Creeks, Chickasaws, or Cherokees.

At first, the Carolinians did not engage directly in conflicts with neighboring Indians. But in 1711 the Tuscaroras, an Iroquoian people, attacked a Swiss-German settlement at New Bern, North Carolina, which had expropriated their lands. South Carolinians and their Indian allies then combined to defeat the Tuscaroras in a bloody war. Afterward, more than a thousand Tuscaroras were enslaved, and the remainder drifted northward, where they joined the Iroquois Confederacy but were not allotted a seat on the council, instead being represented by the Oneidas.

Four years later, the Yamasees, who had helped to overcome the Tuscaroras, turned on their one-time English allies. In what seems to have been long-planned retaliation for multiple abuses by traders as well as threats to their own lands, the Yamasees enlisted the Creeks and other Muskogean peoples in coordinated attacks on outlying English settlements. In the spring and summer of 1715, English and African refugees by the hundreds streamed into Charles Town. The Yamasee-Creek offensive was eventually thwarted when reinforcements arrived from the north, colonists hastily armed their African slaves, and Cherokees joined the fight against the Creeks. After the war, Carolinian involvement in the Indian slave trade ceased, because all their native neighbors moved away for self-protection: Creeks migrated west, Yamasees went south, and other groups moved north. The abuses of the Carolina slave trade thus in effect caused its own destruction. And in the war's aftermath, the native peoples of the Carolinas were able to regroup and rebuild their strength, for they were no longer subjected to slavers' raids.

Atlantic creoles from the Caribbean and native peoples from the Carolinas and Florida, along with local Indians

Enslavement in the North

sentenced to slavery for crime or debt, composed the diverse group of bound laborers in the northern mainland colonies. The intricate involvement of northerners in the web of commerce surrounding the slave trade ensured that many people of African descent lived in America north of Virginia and that "Spanish Indians" became an identifiable component of the New England population. Some bondspeople resided in urban areas, especially New York, which in 1700 had a larger black population than any other mainland city. Women tended to work as domestic servants, men as unskilled laborers on the docks. At the end of the seventeenth century, three-quarters of wealthy Philadelphia households included one or two slaves.

Yet even in the North most bondspeople worked in the countryside, the majority at agricultural tasks. Dutch farmers in the Hudson valley and northern New Jersey were especially likely to rely on enslaved Africans, as were the owners of large landholdings in the Narragansett region of Rhode Island. Some bondsmen toiled in new rural enterprises, such as ironworks, working alongside hired laborers and indentured servants at forges and foundries. Although relatively few northern colonists owned slaves, those who did relied heavily on their labor. Therefore, even though slavery overall did not make a substantial contribution to the northern economy, certain individual slaveholders benefited greatly from the institution and had good reason to want to preserve it.

As slavery became an integral part of the North American and Caribbean landscapes, so too did slaves'

Slave Resistance

resistance to their masters. Most commonly, that resistance took the form of malingering or running away, but occasionally bondspeople planned rebellions. Seven times before 1713, the English Caribbean experienced major revolts involving at least fifty slaves and causing the deaths of both whites and blacks. Twice, in 1675 and 1692, Barbados authorities thwarted plots shortly before they were to be implemented, afterward executing more than sixty convicted conspirators.

▲ An advertisement for a sale of slaves of African descent that appeared in the *New York Journal* in 1768. The expertise of two would have appealed to urban buyers: a cooper would have been useful to a barrelmaker or shipper, and the seamstress might have attracted attention from dressmakers. The other bondspeople mentioned could have been purchased by people who wanted house servants or laborers.

The first slave revolt in the mainland colonies took place in New York in 1712, at a time when enslaved people constituted about 15 percent of the population. The rebels, primarily recent arrivals from the Akan States of the Gold Coast, set a fire and then ambushed those who tried to put it out, killing eight and wounding another twelve. Some rebels committed suicide to avoid capture; of those caught and tried, eighteen were executed. Their decapitated bodies were left to rot outdoors as a warning to others.

Imperial Reorganization and the Witchcraft Crisis

English officials seeking new sources of revenue decided to tap into the profits of the expanding Atlantic trading system in slaves and the products of slave labor. Chesapeake tobacco and Caribbean sugar had obvious value, but other colonial products also had considerable potential.

Parliament and the Stuart monarchs accordingly drafted laws designed to harness the proceeds of the trade for the primary benefit of the mother country.

Like other European nations, England based its commercial policy on a series of assumptions about the operations of the world's economic

Colonial Autonomy Challenged

system, collectively called *mercantilism*. The theory viewed the economic world as a collection of national states whose governments competed for shares of a finite amount of wealth. What one nation gained, another nation lost. Each nation sought to become as economically self-sufficient as possible while maintaining a favorable balance of trade with other countries by exporting more than it imported. Colonies played an important role, supplying the mother country with valuable raw materials to be consumed at home or sent abroad and serving as a market for the mother country's manufactured goods.

Parliament's Navigation Acts—passed between 1651 and 1673—established three main principles that accorded with mercantilist theory. First, only English or colonial merchants and ships could legally trade in the colonies. Second, certain valuable American products could be sold only in the mother country or in other English colonies. At first, these "enumerated" goods included wool, sugar, tobacco, indigo, ginger, and dyes; later acts added rice, naval stores (masts, spars, pitch, tar, and turpentine), copper, and furs to the list. Third, all foreign goods destined for sale in the colonies had to be shipped through England, paying English import duties. Some years later, new laws established a fourth principle: the colonies could not export items (such as wool clothing, hats, or iron) that competed with English products.

These laws adversely affected some colonies, like those in the Chesapeake, because planters there could not seek foreign markets for their staple crops. The statutes initially helped the sugar producers of the English Caribbean by driving Brazilian sugar out of the home market, but later prevented those English planters from selling their sugar elsewhere. In some places, the impact was minimal or even positive. Builders and owners of ships benefited from the monopoly on American trade given to English and colonial merchants; the laws stimulated the creation of a lucrative colonial shipbuilding industry, especially in New England. And the northern and middle colonies produced many unenumerated goods—for example, fish, flour, meat and livestock, and barrel staves. Such products could be traded directly to the French, Spanish, or Dutch Caribbean islands as long as they were carried in English or American ships.

The English authorities soon learned that writing mercantilist legislation was far easier than enforcing it. The many harbors of the American coast provided ready havens for smugglers, and colonial officials often looked the other way when illegally imported goods were offered for sale. In Dutch Caribbean ports like St. Eustatius, American merchants could easily dispose of enumerated goods and purchase foreign items on which duty had not been paid. Because American juries tended to favor

Mercantilism and Navigation Acts

local smugglers over customs officers (a colonial customs service was instituted in 1671), Parliament in 1696 established several American vice-admiralty courts, which operated without juries and adjudicated violations of the Navigation Acts.

The Navigation Acts imposed regulations on Americans' international trade, but by the early 1680s mainland governments and their residents had become accustomed to a considerable degree of political autonomy. The tradition of local rule was especially firmly established in New England, where Massachusetts, Plymouth, Connecticut, and Rhode Island operated essentially as independent entities, subject neither to the direct authority of the king nor to a proprietor. Whereas Virginia was a royal colony and New Hampshire (1679) and New York (1685) gained that status, all other mainland settlements were proprietorships, over which the nation exercised little control. Everywhere in the English colonies, free adult men who owned more than a minimum amount of property expected to have an influential voice in their governments, especially in decisions concerning taxation.

After James II became king in 1685, such expectations clashed with those of the monarch. The new king and his successors sought to bring order to the apparently chaotic state of colonial administration by tightening the reins of government and by reducing the colonies' political autonomy. Most significantly, colonial administrators targeted New England. Reports from America convinced English officials that New England was a hotbed of smuggling. Moreover, Puritans refused to allow freedom of religion to non-Congregationalists and insisted on maintaining laws incompatible with English practice. New England thus seemed an appropriate place to exert English authority with greater vigor. The charters of all the colonies from New Jersey to Maine were revoked, and a Dominion of New England was established in 1686. (For the boundaries of the Dominion, see Map 3.1.) Sir Edmund Andros, the governor, had immense power: Parliament dissolved all the assemblies, and Andros needed only the consent of an appointed council to make laws and levy taxes.

New Englanders endured Andros's autocratic rule for more than two years. Then they learned that James II's hold

Glorious Revolution in America

on power was crumbling. James had angered his subjects by levying taxes without parliamentary approval and by announcing his conversion to Catholicism. In April 1689, Boston's leaders jailed Andros and his associates. The following month, they received definite news of the bloodless coup known as the Glorious Revolution, in which James was replaced on the throne in late 1688 by his daughter Mary and her husband, the Dutch prince William of Orange. When Parliament offered the throne to the Protestants William and Mary, the Glorious Revolution affirmed the supremacy of both Parliament and Protestantism.

In other colonies, too, the Glorious Revolution emboldened people for revolt. In Maryland, the Protestant Association overturned the government of the Catholic proprietor, and in New York a militia officer of German origin, Jacob Leisler, assumed control of the government. Bostonians, Marylanders, and New Yorkers alike allied themselves with the supporters of William and Mary. They saw themselves as carrying out the colonial phase of the English revolt against Stuart absolutism.

But like James II, William and Mary believed England should exercise tighter control over its unruly American possessions. Consequently, only the Maryland rebellion received royal sanction, primarily because of its anti-Catholic thrust. In New York, Leisler was hanged for treason, and Massachusetts (incorporating the formerly independent Plymouth) became a royal colony with an appointed governor. The province retained its town meeting system of local government and continued to

elect its council, but the new 1691 charter eliminated the traditional religious test for voting and office holding. A parish of the Church of England appeared in the heart of Boston. The "city upon a hill," as John Winthrop had envisioned it, had ended.

A war with the French and their Algonquian allies compounded New England's difficulties. King Louis XIV

King William's War

of France allied himself with the deposed James II, and England declared war on France in 1689. (This war is today known as the Nine Years' War, but the colonists called it King William's War.) Even before war broke out in Europe, Anglo-Americans and Abenakis clashed over the English settlements in Maine that had been reoccupied after the 1678 truce and were once again expanding. Attacks wholly or partially destroyed a number of towns, including Schenectady, New York, and such Maine communities as Falmouth (now Portland) and York. Expeditions organized by the colonies against Montreal and Quebec in 1690 failed miserably, and throughout the rest of the conflict New England found itself on the defensive. Even the Peace of Ryswick (1697), which formally ended the war in Europe, failed to bring much respite from warfare to the northern frontiers. Maine could not be resettled for several decades because of the continuing conflict.

During the hostilities, New Englanders understandably feared a repetition of the devastation of King Philip's War.

The 1692 Witchcraft Crisis

For eight months in 1692, witchcraft accusations spread like wildfire through the rural communities of Essex County, Massachusetts—a heavily populated area directly threatened by the Indian attacks in neighboring southern Maine and New Hampshire. Earlier incidents in which personal disputes occasionally led to isolated witchcraft charges bore little relationship to the witch fears that convulsed the region in 1692 while the war raged just to the north. Before the crisis ended, fourteen women and five men were hanged, one man was pressed to death with heavy stones, fifty-four people confessed to being witches, and more than 140 people were jailed, some for many months.

The crisis began in late February when several children and young women in Salem Village (an outlying precinct of the bustling port of Salem) formally charged some older female

> Link to excerpts from the Salem Witchcraft Papers.

neighbors with having tortured them in spectral form. Soon, other accusers and confessors chimed in, some of them female domestic servants who had been orphaned in the Maine war. One had lost her grandparents in King Philip's War and other relatives in King William's

▲ Sir Edmund Andros (1637–1714), the much-detested autocratic governor of the Dominion of New England. In April 1689, he was overthrown by a coalition including some of the foremost leaders of the Bay Colony. He was imprisoned and eventually shipped back to England.

Massachusetts State Archives

Visualizing THE PAST

Debating the Witchcraft Trials

By late September 1692, disagreements over the Salem witchcraft trials (which had begun in June) sharply divided the intellectual leaders of Massachusetts Bay. Key among them were the colony's ministers, and especially a father and son: the Reverend Increase Mather and his son Cotton. Both were prolific authors, and both chose to present their views in print. The twenty-nine-year-old Cotton Mather strongly supported the trials, and at the request of the governor wrote *The Wonders of the Invisible World* to defend the procedures and verdicts. Through its typeface, the title page of his book revealed its subject: DEVILS. On the title page of the

related book by his father, *Cases of Conscience*, the less-prominent words were instead "evil Spirits," and rather than language affirming the "Grievous Molestations by Daemons and Witchcrafts" it included the caution that "infallible proofs" would be required to find the accused guilty. Even though Increase inserted an addendum at the end of his text insisting that he agreed with his son, anyone simply comparing the title pages could recognize that he was attempting to conceal competing opinions about the trials within his own family. What other contrasts between the two books are evident in the contents of the title pages?

Massachusetts Historical Society

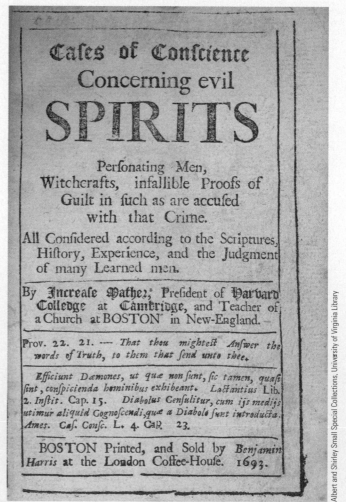

Albert and Shirley Small Special Collections, University of Virginia Library

War. These young women, perhaps the most powerless people in a region apparently powerless to affect its fate, offered their fellow New Englanders a compelling explanation for the seemingly endless chain of troubles afflicting them: their province was under direct assault not only by the Indians and their French allies but also by the Devil and his allied witches.

The so-called afflicted girls accused not just the older women commonly suspected of such offenses but also prominent men from the Maine frontier who had traded with or failed to defeat the Indians. The leader of the witch conspiracy, accusers and confessors alike declared, was the Reverend George Burroughs, a Harvard graduate who had ministered in both Maine and Salem Village and was charged with bewitching the soldiers sent to combat the Abenakis. The colony's magistrates, who were also its political and military leaders, were all too willing to believe such accusations, because, if the Devil had caused New England's current troubles, they personally bore no responsibility for the terrible losses on the frontier.

In October, the worst phase of the crisis ended when the governor dissolved the special court established to try the suspects. He and several prominent clergymen began to regard the descriptions of spectral torturers as "the Devil's testimony"—and everyone knew the Devil could not be trusted. Most critics of the trials did not think the afflicted were faking, nor did they conclude that witches did not exist or that confessions were false. Rather, they questioned whether the guilt of the accused could be legally established by the evidence presented in court. Accordingly, during the final trials (ending in May 1693) in regular courts, almost all the defendants were acquitted, and the governor quickly reprieved the few found guilty.

In 1696, England took a major step in colonial administration by creating the fifteen-member Board

New Imperial Measures

of Trade and Plantations, which thereafter served as the chief organ of government concerned with the

Legacy FOR A PEOPLE AND A NATION

Americans of African Descent

Before 1650, people of African descent composed only a tiny proportion of the population of the mainland North American colonies. After the 1670s, the rise of southern economies based largely on the enslavement of Africans, coupled with the widespread employment of enslaved Africans in northern colonies, dramatically altered the composition of the American population. By 1775, more than a quarter-million Africans had been imported into the territory that later became the United States; they and their descendants constituted about 20 percent of the population at that time.

According to the 2000 census, 12.5 percent of the American people now claim descent from African ancestors. Because the legal importation of African slaves ended in 1808 and because the United States attracted relatively few voluntary migrants of African descent until late in the twentieth century, most of today's native-born African Americans have colonial ancestors—a claim few Americans of European descent can make. Most European Americans are descended at least in part from the massive European migrations of the nineteenth and early twentieth centuries.

The modern African American population includes people with many different skin colors, reflecting the large number of interracial sexual relationships (both coerced and voluntary) that have developed during the long African

residence in mainland North America. African Americans, both free and enslaved, have had children with both Europeans and Indians since the colonial period; more recently, they have intermarried with Asian immigrants. In large part, the mingling of different peoples of color resulted from state laws, which from the early years of the American republic until 1967—when they were struck down by the Supreme Court—forbade legal marriages between people of European descent and those of other races. Thus, if people of color wanted to wed legally, they had to marry other people of color.

Recently, increasing numbers of interracial unions have produced multiracial children. The 2000 census for the first time allowed Americans to define themselves simultaneously as members of more than one race. Opposition to this change came largely from leaders of the African American community, who feared a diminution of political clout. For years, state and federal laws defined people with any appreciable African ancestry as "black"; on census forms, people of African descent have now proved less willing to define themselves as multiracial than do others. The racial self-definition of this large component of the American people thus continues to be influenced by a legacy of discrimination.

American colonies. The board gathered information, reviewed Crown appointments in America, scrutinized legislation passed by colonial assemblies, supervised trade policies, and advised successive ministries on colonial issues. Still, the Board of Trade did not have any direct powers of enforcement. It also shared jurisdiction over American affairs not only with the customs service and the navy but also with a member of the ministry. Although this reform improved the quality of colonial administration, supervision of the American provinces remained decentralized and haphazard.

That surely made it easier for Massachusetts and the rest of the English colonies in America to accommodate themselves to the new imperial order. Most colonists resented alien officials who arrived in America determined to implement the policies of king and Parliament, but they adjusted to their demands and to the trade restrictions imposed by the Navigation Acts. They fought another of Europe's wars—the War of the Spanish Succession, called Queen Anne's War in the colonies—from 1702 to 1713, without enduring the stresses of the first war, despite the heavy economic burdens the conflict imposed. Colonists who allied themselves with the royal government received patronage in the form of offices and land grants, and composed "court parties" that supported English officials. Others, who were either less fortunate in their friends or more principled in defense of colonial autonomy, made up the opposition, or "country" interest. By the end of the first quarter of the eighteenth century, most men in both groups had been born in America. They were members of elite families whose wealth derived in the South from staple-crop production and in the North from commerce.

SUMMARY

The seventy years from 1650 to 1720 established the basic economic and political patterns that were to structure subsequent changes in mainland colonial society. In 1650, just two isolated centers of English population, New England and the Chesapeake, existed along the seaboard, along with the tiny Dutch colony of New Netherland. In 1720, nearly the entire East Coast of North America was in English hands, and Indian control east of the Appalachian Mountains had largely been broken by the outcomes of King Philip's War, Bacon's Rebellion, the Yamasee and Tuscarora wars, and Queen Anne's War. To the west of the mountains, though, Iroquois power reigned supreme. What had been an immigrant population was now mostly American-born, except for the many African-born people in South Carolina and the Chesapeake; economies originally based on trade in fur and skins had become far more complex and more closely linked with the mother country; and a wide variety of political structures had been reshaped into a more uniform pattern. Yet at the same time the adoption of large-scale slavery in the Chesapeake and the Carolinas differentiated their societies from those of the colonies to the north. The production of tobacco, rice, and indigo for international markets distinguished the southern regional economies. They had become true slave societies, heavily reliant on a system of perpetual servitude, not societies with slaves, in which a few bondspeople mingled with indentured servants and free wage laborers.

Even the economies of the northern colonies, though, rested on profits derived from the Atlantic trading system, the key element of which was traffic in enslaved humans, primarily Africans but also including Indians. New England sold corn, salt fish, and wood products to the West Indies, where slaves consumed the foodstuffs and whence planters shipped sugar and molasses in barrels made from staves crafted by northern farmers. Pennsylvania and New York, too, found in the Caribbean islands a ready market for their livestock, grains, and wheat flour. The rapid growth of enslavement drove all the English colonial economies in these years.

Meanwhile, in America north of Mexico Spanish settlements remained largely centered on Florida missions and on New Mexican presidios and missions. The French had explored the Mississippi valley from their base on the St. Lawrence between Montreal and Quebec, but had not yet planted many settlements in the Great Lakes or the west. Both nations' colonists depended on indigenous people's labor and goodwill. The Spanish could not fully control their Indian allies, and the French did not even try. Yet the extensive Spanish and French presence to the south and west of the English settlements meant that future conflicts among the European powers in North America were nearly inevitable.

By 1720, the essential elements of the imperial administrative structure that would govern the English colonies until 1775 had been put firmly in place. The regional economic systems originating in the late seventeenth and early eighteenth centuries also continued to dominate North American life for another century—until after independence had been won. And Anglo-Americans had developed the commitment to autonomous local government that later would lead them into conflict with Parliament and the king.

SUGGESTIONS FOR FURTHER READING

Ned Blackhawk, *Violence over the Land: Indians and Empires in the Early American West* (2006)

David Eltis, *The Rise of African Slavery in the Americas* (1998)

Alan Gallay, *The Indian Slave Trade: The Rise of the English Empire in the American South, 1670–1717* (2002)

Andrew Knaut, *The Pueblo Revolt of 1680* (1995)

Jill Lepore, *The Name of War: King Philip's War and the Origins of American Identity* (1998)

Edmund S. Morgan, *American Slavery, American Freedom: The Ordeal of Colonial Virginia* (1975)

Jennifer L. Morgan, *Laboring Women: Reproduction and Gender in New World Slavery* (2004)

Mary Beth Norton, *In the Devil's Snare: The Salem Witchcraft Crisis of 1692* (2002)

Marcus Rediker, *The Slave Ship: A Human History* (2007)

Betty Wood, *The Origins of American Slavery* (1997)

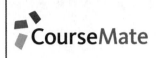

Go to the CourseMate website for primary source links, study tools, and review materials for this chapter. www.cengagebrain.com

Chapter 4

American Society Transformed 1720–1770

Quebec, 1722 (Detail) North Wind Picture Archives

QUEBEC

A. Le Fort
B. les Recollets
C. La plate forme
D. Les Jesuittes
E. La Cathedralle
F. Le Seminaire
G. l'Hostel Dieu
H. L'évêché
I. La Redoute
K. Le magaoin apoudre

The crime was devastating, the punishment terrible. Marie-Joseph Angélique, a Portuguese-born slave of African descent, was hanged for arson in Montréal on June 21, 1734. Judges had convicted Angélique of setting a fire that destroyed the merchant quarter of the town, and the Hotel-Dieu, a convent and hospital. Under torture before her execution, she confessed to the crime and insisted she had acted alone. "Hang me!" she cried out. "I did it. I did it by myself." Afterwards, her body was left hanging from the gibbet for several hours as a sign to all of her infamy, then it was burned and her ashes scattered.

Angélique had arrived in Montréal nine years earlier, purchased by a wealthy merchant, the Sieur de Francheville, and his wife. She worked in their large household under her mistress's direction, along with several free laborers and an enslaved Indian boy. In 1734, the twenty-nine-year-old Angélique was one of 150 or so bondspeople living among the approximately three thousand residents of Montréal. Questioned by the authorities about her origins, she revealed that she had been held for a time as a slave in an English colony, most likely New York, before being sold to Francheville.

Angélique was immediately suspected of setting the destructive fire that began in the Francheville home on April 10. After her master's sudden death in late 1733, she asked her mistress for her freedom, presumably so she could leave Montréal with her lover, Claude Thibault, a former French soldier who was also a servant in the house. When the request was refused, she became insolent and uncontrollable, and she defiantly threatened to "roast" her mistress, who retaliated by preparing to sell her to a French Caribbean island. She and Claude had already set fire to another house in January, before they made a futile attempt to run away together. Witnesses testified that prior to the fire she had made statements implying that she was planning to burn down the Francheville house. Yet until Angélique was tortured, she protested her innocence, and she never implicated Claude Thibault, who vanished from New France, not to be seen again.

◀ A view of Quebec in 1722, just over a decade before the devastating fire for which Marie-Joseph Angélique was executed. The merchant quarter destroyed in the fire stretches along the river, and the Hotel-Dieu is at letter G in the far-right hand corner of the engraving.

Chronology

1690	■ Locke's *Essay Concerning Human Understanding* published, a key example of Enlightenment thought
1718	■ New Orleans founded in French Louisiana
1721–22	■ Smallpox epidemic in Boston leads to first widespread adoption of inoculation in America
1732	■ Founding of Georgia
1733	■ John Peter Zenger is tried for and acquitted of "seditious libel" in New York
1739	■ Stono Rebellion (South Carolina) leads to increased white fears of slave revolts
	■ George Whitefield arrives in America; Great Awakening broadens
1739–48	■ King George's War affects American economies
1740s	■ Black population of the Chesapeake begins to grow by natural increase, contributing to rise of large plantations
1741	■ New York City "conspiracy" reflects whites' continuing fears of slave revolts
1751	■ Franklin's *Experiments and Observations on Electricity* published, important American contribution to Enlightenment science
1760–75	■ Peak of eighteenth-century European and African migration to English colonies
1765–66	■ Hudson River land riots pit tenants and squatters against large landlords
1767–69	■ Regulator movement (South Carolina) tries to establish order in backcountry
1771	■ North Carolina Regulators defeated by eastern militia at Battle of Alamance

*a*ngélique's tragic story reveals the extensive reach of African slavery in North America during the eighteenth century. Her personal experience—as a woman of African descent born in Portugal who had spent time in the English colonies—points up the swirling movement of peoples around the Atlantic world, movements that after 1720 brought many new groups to the British colonies in particular. A massive eighteenth-century migration of European and African peoples changed the nature of the North American population and the look of the North American landscape. Ethnic diversity was especially pronounced in the small cities of Anglo America. The British colonies south of New England drew by far the largest number of newcomers, many to the fertile countryside. Their arrival not only swelled the population but also altered political balances and affected the religious climate by introducing new sects. Unwilling immigrants (slaves and transported convicts), too, clustered primarily in the middle and southern colonies.

Several key themes marked the development of Europe's North American colonies in the mid-eighteenth century: not only population growth (through natural increase as well as immigration) and the new ethnic diversity, but also the increasing importance of colonial urban centers, the creation of a prosperous urban elite including merchant families like the Franchevilles, rising levels of consumption for all social ranks, and the new significance of internal markets. In the French and British mainland colonies, exports dominated the economy. Settlers along the Atlantic and Gulf coasts were tied to an international commercial system that fluctuated wildly for reasons having little to do with the colonies but inescapable in their effects. Yet expanding local populations demanded greater quantities and types of goods, and Europe could not supply all those needs. Therefore, in English and French America, as well as in the northern portions of New Spain known as the Borderlands (where exports were never an important element of the economy), colonists increasingly depended on exploiting and consuming their own resources (see Map 5.2). Sieur de Francheville, for example, made his fortune as a fur trader but by the time of his death had invested considerable sums in a new ironworks.

Intermarried networks of wealthy families developed in each of Europe's American possessions by the 1760s. These well-off, educated colonists participated in transatlantic intellectual life, such as the movement known as the Enlightenment, whereas some colonists of the "lesser sort" could neither read nor write. The elites lived in comfortable houses and enjoyed leisure-time activities. Most colonists, whether free or enslaved, worked with their hands daily from dawn to dark. Such divisions were most pronounced in British America, the largest and most prosperous settlements on the continent. By the last half of the century, the social and economic distance among different ranks of Anglo-Americans had widened noticeably. As such stratification increased, so did conflicts—political, economic, and even religious—among people of diverse origins and social ranks.

In 1720, much of North America was under Indian control. Fifty years later, indigenous peoples still dominated the interior of the continent, yet even so their lives had been indelibly altered by the geographic expansion of European settlements. As France extended its reach from the St. Lawrence to the Gulf of Mexico and Spanish outposts expanded both east and west from a New Mexican heartland, and as British colonies filled in the territory between the Appalachian Mountains and the Atlantic, North America was transformed.

- **What were the effects of demographic, geographic, and economic changes on Europeans, Africans, and Indian nations alike?**

- **What were the key elements of eighteenth-century colonial cultures?**

- **What developments at midcentury began the process of political and religious change in British North America?**

Geographic Expansion and Ethnic Diversity

Europe's North American possessions expanded both geographically and demographically during the middle decades of the eighteenth century. The most striking development was the dramatic population growth of the British mainland colonies. Only about 250,000 European-Americans and African Americans resided in the colonies in 1700. Thirty years later, that number had more than doubled; by 1775, it had become 2.5 million.

Although migration from Africa, Scotland, Ireland, England, and Germany accounted for a considerable share of the growth, most of the gain resulted from natural increase. Once the difficult early decades of settlement had passed, the American population doubled approximately every twenty-five years. Such a rate of growth, unparalleled in human history until very recent times, had a variety of causes, chief among them women's youthful age at the onset of childbearing (early twenties for European-Americans, late teens for African Americans). Because married women became pregnant every two or three years, women normally bore five to ten children. Since the colonies, especially those north of

Virginia, were relatively healthful places to live, a large proportion of children who survived infancy reached maturity and began families of their own. Consequently, about half of the population of Anglo America was under sixteen years old in 1775. (By contrast, less than one-quarter of the United States population is currently under sixteen.)

That rapidly expanding population of British North America was largely sandwiched between the Appalachian Mountains (on the west) and the Atlantic coast (on the east). By contrast, Spanish and French territories expanded across much of North America while their populations increased only modestly. At the end of the eighteenth century, Texas had only about three thousand Spanish residents and California less than one thousand; the largest Spanish colony, New Mexico, included twenty thousand or so. The total European population of the mainland French colonies increased from approximately fifteen thousand in 1700 to about seventy thousand in the 1760s, but those colonists clustered in only a few widely scattered locations. That geographic expansion of French and Spanish settlements had far-reaching effects on native peoples.

Spanish and French Territorial Expansion

The French by water and the Spanish by land ventured separately into the Mississippi valley in the early eighteenth century. There they encountered powerful Indian nations like the Quapaws, Osages, and Caddos. A few Europeans—priests, soldiers, farmers, traders, ranchers—found themselves surrounded by native peoples who wanted access to manufactured goods, and who accordingly sought friendly relations with the newcomers. The Spanish and French invaders of these territories had to accommodate themselves to Indian diplomatic and cultural practices in order to achieve their objectives. French officials, for example, often complained of being forced to endure lengthy calumet ceremonies; Spaniards, unaccustomed to involving women in diplomacy, had to accede to Texas Indians' use of female representatives. The European nations established neighboring outposts in the lower Mississippi region in 1716—the French at Natchitoches (west of the Mississippi), the Spaniards at Los Adaes, 12 miles further southwest (see Map 4.1). France had already founded a settlement on Biloxi Bay (in the modern state of Mississippi) in 1699 and later strengthened its presence near the Gulf of Mexico by establishing New Orleans in 1718, a move the Spanish could not counter because of the overland distance from Santa Fe.

Instead, Spaniards focused their attention first on Texas (for instance, establishing San Antonio in 1718), then later on the region they called Alta (upper) California. After learning that Russians who hunted

Link to Eulalia Perez's account of her work in a California Spanish mission.

sea otters along the coast of northwestern North America were planning to colonize the region, they sent expeditions north from their missions in Baja California. From a base at San Diego where the Franciscan Junipero Serra set up the first mission in Alta California in July 1769, they traveled north by land and sea to Monterey Bay. Here, in April 1770, they formally claimed Alta California for Spain. Over the next decades, they established presidios and missions along the coast from modern San Francisco south to San Diego. In those centers, Franciscan friars from Spain and a few settlers from Mexico lived amid thousands of Indians who had converted to Christianity.

Along the Mississippi, French posts north of New Orleans served as the glue of empire. *Coureurs de bois* (literally, "forest runners")

France and the Mississippi

used the rivers and lakes of the American interior to carry goods between Quebec and the new Louisiana territory. At such sites as Michilimackinac (at the junction of Lakes Michigan and Huron) and Kaskaskia (in present-day Illinois), Indians traded furs and hides for guns, ammunition, and other valuable items. The Osages were so eager to acquire firearms that they became, in effect, commercial hunters; witnesses reported that their women were sometimes so fully occupied processing hides that older men prepared the communities' meals. The largest French settlements in the region, known collectively as *le pays de Illinois* ("the Illinois country"), never totaled much above three thousand in population. Located along the Mississippi south of

modern St. Louis, the settlements produced wheat for export to New Orleans. In such French outposts, the shortage of European women led to interracial unions between French men and Indian women, and to the creation of mixed-race people known as *metís*. French expansion contributed to the reshaping of native alliances far from the Mississippi. For example, the equestrian Comanches of the Plains, who were now able to trade with the French through Indian intermediaries, no longer needed Spanish goods—or their previous allies, the Utes. Deprived of such powerful partners, the Utes negotiated peace with New Mexico in 1752 and began to attend annual Spanish trade fairs. Once commonly enslaved by Spaniards, Utes instead became the enslavers of Paiutes and other nonequestrian peoples who lived to the north and west of the colony. They exchanged hides and slaves—mostly young women—for horses and metal goods. That commercial relationship endured until the end of Spanish rule in the region.

In French officials' minds, Louisiana's chief function was supportive and defensive: its paramount goals were protection of the valuable Caribbean islands and prevention of Spanish and British expansion. They accordingly did not focus their attention on Louisiana's economic development, but the profit-seeking farmers and Indian traders from Canada who settled there soon demanded that the French government supply them with slaves. In 1719 officials acquiesced, dispatching more than six thousand Africans, mostly from Senegal, over the next decade. But residents failed to develop a successful plantation economy. They did raise some tobacco and indigo, which, along with skins and hides obtained from the Indians, composed Louisiana's major exports for most of the eighteenth century. Some enslaved Africans were

◄ A Russian artist in 1816 painted this view of California mission Indians dancing in front of Mission Delores and Spanish spectators. Today the building shown at the left still stands in the middle of the city of San Francisco. The scene conveys a sense of the religious syncretism characteristic of the missions, as Native customs combined with the friars' Catholicism to create a fertile blend of spiritual beliefs.

University of California at Berkeley, Bancroft Library

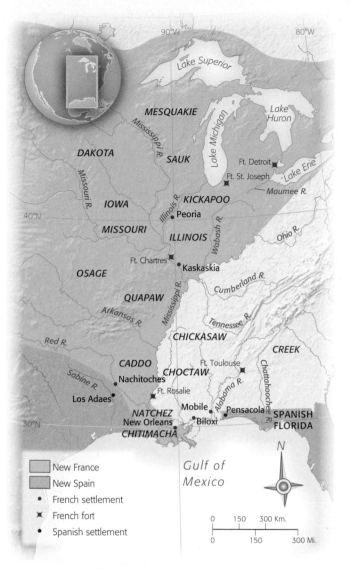

Map 4.1 Louisiana, ca. 1720

By 1720, French forts and settlements dotted the Mississippi River and its tributaries in the interior of North America. Two isolated Spanish outposts were situated near the Gulf of Mexico.

Source: Copyright © Cengage Learning

Elsewhere in the Americas, slavery took hold more firmly during the eighteenth century. In all, more Africans than Europeans came to the Americas, the overwhelming majority of them as slaves and about half between 1700 and 1800. Most were transported to Brazil or the Caribbean, primarily in British or Portuguese vessels. Of at least 11 million enslaved people brought to the Americas during the existence of slavery, only about 260,000 were imported by 1775 into the region that became the United States. Rice, indigo, tobacco, and sugar plantations all expanded rapidly in these years, steadily increasing the demand for bondspeople. In the slaveholding societies of South America and the Caribbean, a surplus of males over females and appallingly high mortality rates meant that only a large, continuing influx of slaves could maintain the work force at constant levels. On the mainland of North America, only South Carolina, where rice cultivation was difficult and unhealthful (chiefly because malaria-carrying mosquitoes bred in the rice swamps), similarly required an inflow of Africans to sustain as well as expand its labor force.

The involuntary migrants came from many different ethnic groups and regions of Africa (see Map 4.2). More than 40 percent embarked from West Central Africa (modern Congo and Angola), nearly 20 percent from the Bight of Benin (modern Togo, Benin, and southwestern Nigeria), about 13 percent from the Bight of Biafra (today's Cameroon, Gabon, and southeastern Nigeria), and approximately 9 percent from the Gold Coast (modern Ghana and neighboring countries). Smaller proportions came from East Africa and the Windward and Rice Coasts (modern Senegal, Gambia, and Sierra Leone).

Standard slave-trading practice, in which a vessel loaded an entire cargo at one port and likewise sold them in one place, meant that people from the same area (enemies as well as allies) tended to be taken to the Americas together. That tendency was heightened by planter partiality for slaves of particular ethnic groups. Virginians, for example, purchased primarily Igbos from the Bight of Biafra, whereas South Carolinians and Georgians selected Senegambians and people from West Central Africa. Louisiana planters first chose slaves from the Bight of Benin but later bought many from West Central Africa. Rice planters' desire to purchase Senegambians, who had cultivated rice in their homeland, is easily explained, but historians disagree about the reasons for the other preferences.

Thousands, possibly tens of thousands, of these enslaved Africans were Muslims. Some were literate in Arabic, and several came from aristocratic families. The discovery of noble birth could lead to slaves' being freed to return home. Job Ben Solomon, for example, arrived in Maryland in 1732. A slave trader from Senegal, he had been captured by raiders while selling bondspeople in Gambia.

carried north to the Illinois country, where as farm laborers and domestic servants they made up nearly 40 percent of the population in the 1730s.

Louisiana's expansion angered the Natchez Indians, whose lands it had usurped. In 1729, the Natchez, assisted by newly arrived slaves, attacked northern reaches of the colony, killing more than 10 percent of its European people. The French struck back, slaughtering the Natchez and their enslaved allies, but Louisiana remained a fragile and neglected colony as long as French rule continued.

Involuntary Migrants from Africa

Map 4.2 Major Origins and Destinations of Africans Enslaved in the Americas

As this schematic map shows, enslaved Africans were drawn from many regions of western Africa (with some coming from the interior of the continent) and were shipped to areas throughout the Americas.

Source: Copyright © Cengage Learning

A letter he wrote in Arabic so impressed his owners that he was liberated the next year. Abd al-Rahman, brought to Louisiana in 1788, was less fortunate. Known to his master as "Prince" because of his aristocratic origins, he was not freed until 1829 through the assistance of a European he had befriended in West Africa.

Despite the approximately 260,000 slaves brought to the mainland, American-born people of African descent came to dominate the enslaved population numerically because of high levels of natural increase, especially after 1740. Although about 40 percent of the Africans were male, women and children together composed a majority of slave imports; the girls and women were valued for their reproductive as well as productive capacities. A planter who owned adult female slaves could watch the size of his labor force expand steadily—through the births of their children, designated as slaves in all the colonies—without making additional major purchases of workers. The slaveholder Thomas Jefferson later pointed up the connections when he observed, "I consider a woman who brings a child every two years more profitable than the best man of the farm. What she produces is an addition to the capital, while his labors disappear in mere consumption."

In the Chesapeake, the number of bondspeople grew rapidly because the imports were added to an enslaved population that had begun to sustain itself through natural increase. The work routines involved in cultivating tobacco, coupled with a roughly equal sex ratio, reduced slave mortality and increased fertility. Even in unhealthful South Carolina, where substantial imports continued, American-born slaves outnumbered the African-born as early as 1750.

In addition to the new Africans, about 500,000 Europeans moved to British North America during the eighteenth century, most of them after 1730. Late in the seventeenth century, English officials decided to recruit German and French Protestants to prevent further large-scale emigration from England itself. Influenced by mercantilist thought, they had come to regard a large, industrious population at home as an asset rather than a liability. Thus, they ordered the deportation to the colonies of such

Newcomers from Europe

Visualizing THE PAST

Slaves' Symbolic Resistance

Although revolts and running away have been the focus of many studies of enslaved Africans' resistance to bondage in North America, archaeological finds from the mid-eighteenth-century such as those illustrated here have revealed important aspects of slaves' personal lives and other forms of resistance. The set of objects found in Annapolis constitutes a *minkisi,* or West African spiritual bundle. Africans and African Americans placed such bundles of objects, each with a symbolic meaning (for example, bent nails reflected the power of fire), under hearths or sills to direct the spirits, who entered and left houses through doors or chimneys. Their primary purpose was to protect bondspeople from the power of their masters— for example, by preventing the breakup of a family. The statue of a man was uncovered in an enslaved blacksmith's quarters. It too reflects resistance, but of a different sort: the quiet rebellion of a talented craftsman who used his master's iron and his own time and skill to secretly create a remarkable object. Can students today derive insights about enslaved people's lives from such artifacts as these, even though the illiterate bondspeople left no written records? If so, what?

Private Collection/Picture Research Consultants & Archives

Artifact found in an excavation in Alexandria, Virginia.

Photograph courtesy of Archaeology in Annapolis, University of Maryland, College Park

A minkisi from the eighteenth century found under the floor of the Charles Carroll house in Annapolis, Maryland.

Table 4.1 Who Moved to America from England and Scotland in the Early 1770s, and Why?

	English Emigrants	Scottish Emigrants	Free American Population
Destination			
13 British colonies	81.1%	92.7%	—
Canada	12.1	4.2	—
West Indies	6.8	3.1	—
Age Distribution			
Under 21	26.8	45.3	56.8%
21–25	37.1	19.9	9.7
26–44	33.3	29.5	20.4
45 and over	2.7	5.3	13.1
Sex Distribution			
Male	83.8	59.9	—
Female	16.2	40.1	—
Unknown	4.2	13.5	—
Traveling Alone or with Families			
In families	20.0	48.0	—
Alone	80.0	52.0	—
Known Occupation or Status			
Gentry	2.5	1.2	—
Merchandising	5.2	5.2	—
Agriculture	17.8	24.0	—
Artisanry	54.2	37.7	—
Laborer	20.3	31.9	—
Why They Left			
Positive reasons (e.g., desire to better one's position)	90.0	36.0	—
Negative reasons (e.g., poverty, unemployment)	10.0	64.0	—

Note: Between December 1773 and March 1776, the British government questioned individuals and families leaving ports in Scotland and England for the American colonies to learn who they were, where they were going, and why they were leaving. This table summarizes just a few of the findings of the official inquiries, which revealed a number of significant differences between the Scottish and English emigrants.

Source: Bernard Bailyn, *Voyagers to the West* (New York: Knopf, 1986), Tables 4.1, 5.2, 5.4, 5.7, 5.23, and 6.1.

"undesirables" as vagabonds and Jacobite rebels (supporters of the deposed Stuart monarchs) but otherwise discouraged emigration. They offered foreign Protestants free lands and religious toleration, even financing the passage of some groups. After 1740, they relaxed citizenship (naturalization) requirements, insisting on only the payment of a small fee, seven years' residence, Protestantism, and an oath of allegiance to the king. Such policies created an ethnic diversity found only in Britain's American colonies.

▲ In December 1729, probably in New York's Hudson Valley, an unknown artist portrayed J. M. Stolle, son of a Palatine immigrant who came to North America from Germany in 1709. The young man's fancy clothing and the column and balustrade in the background suggest that the artist wanted to convey an image of the family's economic success, though whether that image was accurate is unknown.

Early arrivals wrote home, urging others to come; those contacts created chains of migration from particular regions. The most successful migrants came well prepared, having learned from their American correspondents that land and resources were abundant, especially in the inland areas known as the backcountry, but that they would need capital to take full advantage of the new opportunities. People who arrived penniless did less well; approximately 40 percent of the newcomers fell into that category, for they immigrated as bound laborers of some sort.

Worst off were the fifty thousand or so migrants who came as criminals convicted of such offenses as theft and murder and sentenced to transportation for two to fourteen years instead of execution. Many unskilled and perhaps one-third female, they were dispatched most often to Maryland, where they were employed in the tobacco fields, or as ironworkers or household servants. Little is known about the ultimate fate of most, but some who committed further crimes in the colonies became notorious on both sides of the Atlantic, thanks to newspaper accounts of their exploits.

One of the largest groups of immigrants—over 150,000—came from Ireland or Scotland, largely in family units. About seventy thousand Scots-Irish descendants of Presbyterian Scots who had settled in the north of Ireland during the seventeenth century joined some 35,000 people who came directly to America from Scotland (see Table 4.1). Another 45,000, both Protestants and Catholics, migrated from southern Ireland (often as individuals). High rents, poor harvests, and religious discrimination (in Ireland) combined to push people from lands their families had long occupied. Many of the Irish migrants had supported themselves in Ireland by weaving linen cloth, but linen prices declined significantly in the late 1710s. Because the flax used for weaving was imported from Pennsylvania and flaxseed was exported to the same place, vessels with plenty of room for passengers regularly sailed from Ireland to Pennsylvania. By the 1720s, the migration route was well established, fueled by positive reports of prospects for advancement in North America.

Scots-Irish, Scots, and Germans

Such immigrants usually landed in Philadelphia or New Castle, Delaware. They moved into the backcountry of western Pennsylvania along the Susquehanna River where the colonial government created a county named Donegal for them. Later migrants moved farther west and south to the backcountry of Maryland, Virginia, and the Carolinas. Frequently unable to afford any acreage, they lived illegally on land belonging to Indians, land speculators, or colonial governments. In the frontier setting, they gained a reputation for lawlessness, hard drinking, and ferocious fighting among themselves and with neighboring Indians.

Migrants from Germany and German-speaking areas of Switzerland numbered about 85,000, most of them emigrating from the Rhineland between 1730 and 1755. They, too, usually came in family groups and landed in Philadelphia. Many, like the English indentured servants of the previous century, contracted to work as servants for a specified period of years to pay for their passage. When free to do so, Germans tended to settle together; they composed up to half of the population of some counties. Many Germans moved west into Pennsylvania and then south into the backcountry of Maryland and Virginia. Others landed in Charles Town and settled in the southern interior. The Germans belonged to a wide variety of Protestant sects—primarily Lutheran, German Reformed, and Moravian—and therefore added to the already substantial religious diversity of Pennsylvania. Late in the century, they and their descendants accounted

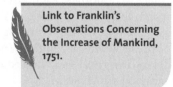

Link to Franklin's Observations Concerning the Increase of Mankind, 1751.

for one-third of Pennsylvania's residents. Benjamin Franklin, for one, feared as early as 1751 that they would "Germanize" Pennsylvania. They "will never adopt our Language or Customs," he predicted inaccurately.

The most concentrated period of immigration to the colonies fell between 1760 and 1775. Tough economic times in Germany and the British Isles led many to decide to seek a better life in America; simultaneously, the slave trade burgeoned. In those fifteen years alone, more than 220,000 free and enslaved people arrived— nearly 10 percent of the entire population of British North America in 1775. Late-arriving free immigrants had little choice but to remain in the cities or move to the edges of settlement; land elsewhere was fully occupied (see Map 4.3). In the peripheries they became the tenants of, or bought property from, land speculators who had purchased giant tracts in the (usually vain) hope of making a fortune.

Because of these migration patterns and the concentration of slaveholding in the South, half of the colonial

Maintaining Ethnic and Religious Identities

population south of New England had non-English origins by 1775. Whether the migrants assimilated readily into Anglo-American culture depended on patterns of settlement, the size of the group, and the strength of the migrants' ties to their common culture. For example, in the late seventeenth century, the French Protestants (Huguenots) who migrated to Charles Town or New York City were unable to sustain either their language or their religious practices for more than two generations. Yet the Huguenots who created the rural communities of New Paltz and New Rochelle in the Hudson Valley remained recognizably French and Calvinist for a century. By contrast, the equally small group of colonial Jews maintained a distinct identity regardless of where they settled. Most were Sephardic descended from persecuted Spanish and Portuguese Jews who had first fled to the Netherlands or its American colonies, then later migrated into English territory. In places like New York and Newport, Rhode Island, they established synagogues and worked actively to preserve their religion (for instance, by observing dietary laws and by trying to prevent their children from marrying Christians).

Members of the larger groups of migrants (Germans, Irish, and Scots) found it easier to sustain European ways. Some ethnic groups dominated certain localities. Near Frederick, Maryland, a visitor would have heard more German than English; in Anson and Cumberland Counties, North Carolina, the same visitor might have thought she was in Scotland. Where migrants from different countries settled in the same region, ethnic antagonisms often surfaced. One German clergyman in Pennsylvania, for example, claimed that Scots-Irish migrants were "lazy,

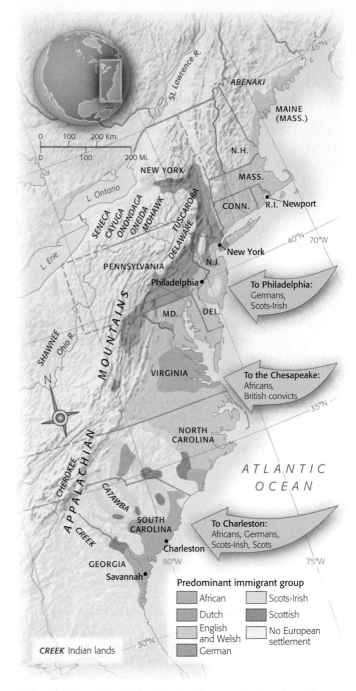

Map 4.3 Non-English Ethnic Groups in the British Colonies, ca. 1775

Non-African immigrants arriving in the years after 1720 were pushed to the peripheries of settlement, as is shown by these maps. Scottish, Scots-Irish, French, and German newcomers had to move to the frontiers. The Dutch remained where they had originally settled in the seventeenth century. Africans were concentrated in coastal plantation regions.

Source: Copyright © Cengage Learning

dissipated and poor" and that "it is very seldom that German and English blood is happily united in wedlock." Anglo-American elites fostered such antagonisms in order to fracture opposition and maintain their political and economic power, and they frequently subverted the colonies' generous naturalization laws, thus depriving even long-resident immigrants of a voice in government.

The elites probably would have preferred to ignore the British colonies' growing racial and ethnic diversity, but ultimately they could not do so. When they moved toward revolution in the 1770s, they recognized that they needed the support of non-English Americans. Quite deliberately, they began to speak of "the rights of man," rather than "English liberties," when they sought recruits for their cause.

Economic Growth and Development in British America

The dramatic increase in the population of Anglo America caused colonial economies to grow, despite the vagaries of international markets. A comparison with French and Spanish America reveals significant differences. The population and economy of New Spain's northern Borderlands stagnated, for the isolated settlements produced few items for export. French Canada exported large quantities of furs and fish, but the government's monopoly of trade ensured that most of the profits ended up in the home country instead of the colony. The Louisiana colony required substantial government subsidies to survive, and so—of France's American possessions—only the Caribbean islands flourished economically.

In British North America, by contrast, each year the rising population generated ever-greater demands for

Commerce and Manufacturing

goods and services, leading to the development of small-scale colonial manufacturing and a complex network of internal trade. Roads, bridges, mills, and stores were built to serve the many new settlements. A lively coastal trade developed; by the late 1760s, more than half of the vessels leaving Boston harbor sailed to other mainland colonies. Such ships not only collected goods for export and distributed imports but also sold items made in America. The colonies no longer wholly depended on European manufactured goods. For the first time, the American population generated sufficient demand to support local manufacturing.

Iron making became the largest industry. Ironworks in the Chesapeake and middle colonies required sizable investments and the coordination of substantial workforces—usually indentured servants, convicts, and slaves—who dug the ore, chopped trees for charcoal production, and finally smelted and refined the ore into iron bars using that charcoal. Because the work was dirty, dangerous, and difficult, convicts and servants often tried to flee, but it offered enslaved men new avenues to learn valuable skills and accumulate property when they were compensated for doing more than their assigned tasks. By 1775, Anglo America's iron production surpassed England's.

Foreign trade nevertheless constituted the major influence on the economy. Colonial prosperity depended heavily on overseas demand for American products like tobacco, rice, indigo, fish, and timber products. The sale of such items earned the colonists the credit they needed to purchase English and European imports. If demand for American exports slowed, the colonists' income dropped, as did their ability to buy imported goods. Merchants were particularly vulnerable to economic downswings, and bankruptcies were common.

Despite fluctuations, the American economy slowly grew during the eighteenth century. That growth, which

Wealth and Poverty

resulted partly from higher earnings from exports, in turn produced better standards of living for all property-owning Americans. Early in the century, as the price of British manufactures fell in relation to Americans' incomes, households began to acquire amenities such as chairs and earthenware dishes. Diet also improved as trading networks brought access to more varied foodstuffs. After 1750, luxury items could be found in the homes of the wealthy, and the "middling sort" started to purchase imported English ceramics and teapots. Even the poorest property owners had more and better household goods. The differences lay not so much in *what* items people owned, but rather in the quality and quantity of those possessions.

Yet the benefits of economic growth were unevenly distributed: wealthy Americans improved their position relative to other colonists. The native-born elite families who dominated American political, economic, and social life by 1750 had begun the century with sufficient capital to take advantage of the changes caused by population growth. They were the urban merchants who exported staples and imported luxury goods, the large landowners who rented small farms to immigrant tenants, the slave traders who supplied wealthy planters with their bondspeople, and the owners of rum distilleries. The rise of this group of moneyed families helped to make the social and economic structure of mid-eighteenth-century America more stratified than before.

New arrivals did not have the opportunities for advancement that had greeted their predecessors. Even so, few free settlers in rural areas (where about 95 percent of the colonists lived) appear to have been truly poor; at least two-thirds of rural householders owned their own land by 1750. But in the cities, families of urban laborers lived on the edge of destitution, and everywhere landless workers were available for hire. By the 1760s, applicants for assistance overwhelmed public urban poor-relief systems, and some cities began to build workhouses or almshouses to shelter growing numbers of elderly and infirm people along with widows and their children.

Within this overall picture, varying regional patterns emerged, in part because of King George's War, also called the War of the Austrian Succession (1739–1748).

Regional Economies

New England's export economy rested on trade with the Caribbean: northern forests supplied the timber for building the ships that carried salt fish to feed the slaves on island sugar plantations. The outbreak of war created strong demand for New England's ships and sailors, thus invigorating the economy, but New Englanders suffered major losses of men and materiel in Caribbean battles and in their successful attack on the fortress of Louisbourg (in modern Nova Scotia), which guarded the sea-lanes leading to New France. When the shipbuilding boom ended with the war, the economy stagnated, and widows and orphans crowded relief rolls. Britain even returned Louisbourg to France in the Treaty of Aix-la-Chapelle (1748).

By contrast, King George's War and its aftermath brought prosperity to the middle colonies and the Chesapeake because the fertile soil and longer growing season in both regions readily produced an abundance of grain. After 1748, when a series of poor harvests in Europe caused flour prices to rise rapidly, Philadelphia and New York took the lead in the foodstuffs trade. Some Chesapeake planters began to convert tobacco fields to wheat and corn. Tobacco remained the largest single export from the mainland colonies, yet the beginnings of grain cultivation caused a significant change in Chesapeake settlement patterns by encouraging the development of port towns (like Baltimore) where merchants and shipbuilders established businesses to handle the new trade.

That South Carolina's staple crop was rice determined its distinctive economic pattern as did its location in the path of Atlantic hurricanes. The colony's rice and indigo

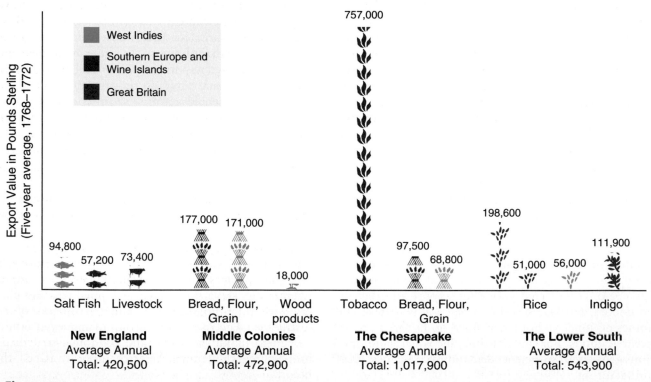

Figure 4.1

As this figure shows, the different regions of the British mainland colonies had distinct trading patterns: they exported diverse products to different markets. By far the most valuable export was the tobacco grown by Chesapeake slaves.

Source: Adapted from James F. Shepherd and Gary M. Walton, *Shipping, Maritime Trade, and the Economic Development of Colonial North America* (Cambridge University press, 1972).

crops—like sugar cane in the Caribbean—were periodically devastated by violent storms, causing hardship and bankruptcies. Yet after Parliament in 1730 removed rice from the list of enumerated products, South Carolinians prospered by trading directly with continental Europe. The outbreak of war disrupted that trade, and the colony entered a depression that did not end until the 1760s brought renewed European demand. Overall, though, South Carolina experienced more rapid economic growth than did other British colonies, and it had the highest average wealth per freeholder in mainland Anglo America by the time of the American Revolution.

Closely linked to South Carolina was the newest British settlement, Georgia, chartered in 1732 as a haven for English debtors released from prison so they could emigrate. Its founder, James Oglethorpe, envisioned Georgia as a garrison province peopled by sturdy farmers who would defend the southern flank of English settlement against Spanish Florida. Accordingly, its charter prohibited slavery to ensure that all adult men in the colony could be its protectors. But Carolina rice planters won the removal of the restriction in 1751. Thereafter, they essentially invaded Georgia, which—despite remaining politically independent and becoming a royal colony in 1752—developed into a rice-planting slave society resembling South Carolina.

King George's War initially helped New England and hurt South Carolina and Georgia, but in the long run those effects were reversed. In the Chesapeake and the middle colonies, the war ushered in a long period of prosperity. Such variations highlight the British mainland colonies' disparate experiences within the empire. Despite increasing coastal trade, the colonies' economic fortunes depended not on their North American neighbors but rather on the shifting markets of Europe and the Caribbean. Had it not been for an unprecedented crisis in the British imperial system (discussed in Chapter 5), it is hard to see how they could have been persuaded to join in a common endeavor. Even with that impetus, they found unity difficult to maintain.

Colonial Cultures

By 1750, the population of Britain's American possessions was not only denser and more diverse than it had been a half-century earlier but also marked by new extremes of wealth and poverty, especially visible in the growing cities. Native-born colonial elites sought to distinguish themselves from ordinary folk in a variety of ways as they consolidated their hold on the local economy and political power.

One historian has termed these processes "the refinement of America." Colonists who acquired wealth through trade, agriculture, or manufacturing spent their

Genteel Culture

money ostentatiously, dressing fashionably, traveling in horse-drawn carriages driven by uniformed servants, and entertaining one another at lavish parties. Most notably, they built large houses containing rooms designed for such forms of socializing as dancing, card-playing, or drinking tea. Sufficiently well-off to enjoy "leisure" time (a first for North America), they attended concerts and the theater, gambled at horse races, and played billiards and other games. They also cultivated polite manners, adopting stylized forms of address and paying attention to "proper" ways of behaving. Although the effects of accumulated wealth were most pronounced in Anglo America, elite families in New Mexico, Louisiana, and Quebec set themselves off from the "lesser sort." Together, these wealthy families deliberately constructed a genteel culture quite different from ordinary colonists.

Men from such families prided themselves not only on their possessions and on their positions in the colonial political, social, and economic hierarchy, but also on their level of education and their intellectual connections to Europe. Many had been tutored by private teachers hired by their families; some even attended college in Europe or America. (Harvard, the first colonial college, founded in 1636, was joined by William and Mary in 1693, Yale in 1701, and later by several others, including Princeton in 1747.) In the seventeenth century, only aspiring clergymen attended college, studying a curriculum based on ancient languages and theology. But by the mid-eighteenth century, colleges broadened their curricula to include mathematics, the natural sciences, law, and medicine. Accordingly, a minuscule number of young men from elite or upwardly mobile families enrolled in college to study for careers other than the ministry. American women were mostly excluded from advanced education, with the exception of some who joined nunneries in Canada or Louisiana and could engage in sustained study within convent walls.

The intellectual current known as the Enlightenment deeply affected the learned clergymen who headed colonial colleges and their students. Around 1650, some European thinkers began to analyze nature in order to determine the laws governing the universe. They employed experimentation and abstract reasoning to discover general principles behind phenomena like the motions of planets and stars, the behavior of falling objects, and the characteristics of light and sound. Above all, Enlightenment philosophers emphasized acquiring knowledge through reason, taking particular delight in challenging previously unquestioned assumptions. John Locke's *Essay Concerning Human Understanding* (1690), for example, disputed the notion that human beings are born already imprinted with innate ideas. All knowledge, Locke asserted, derives from one's observations

The Enlightenment

▲ Elizabeth Murray, the subject of this 1769 painting by John Singleton Copley, was the wife of James Smith, a wealthy rum distiller. Her fashionable dress and pose would seem to mark her as a lady of leisure, yet both before and during her marriage this Scottish immigrant ran a successful dry goods shop in Boston. She thus simultaneously catered to and participated in the new culture of consumption.

experimentation and public service. His *Experiments and Observations on Electricity* (1751) established the terminology and basic theory of electricity still used today.

Enlightenment rationalism affected politics as well as science. Locke's *Two Treatises of Government* (1691) and other works by French and Scottish philosophers challenged previous concepts of a divinely sanctioned, hierarchical political order originating in the power of fathers over families. Men created governments and so could alter them, Locke declared. A ruler who broke the social contract and failed to protect people's rights could legitimately be ousted from power by peaceful— or even violent—means. Government should aim at the good of the people, Enlightenment theorists proclaimed. A proper political order could prevent the rise of tyrants; God's natural laws governed even the power of monarchs.

The world in which such ideas were discussed was that of the few, not the many. Most residents of North America were illiterate. Even those who could read—a small proportion in French or Spanish America, about two-thirds of Anglo-Americans—often could not write. Books were scarce until the 1750s, and colonial newspapers did not begin publication until the 1720s. Parents, older siblings, or local widows who needed extra income usually taught youngsters to read; several years later, the more fortunate boys (and genteel girls after the 1750s) might learn to write in private schools. Few Americans other than some Church of England missionaries in the South tried to instruct enslaved children. And only the most zealous Indian converts learned Europeans' literacy skills.

Oral Cultures

Thus, the cultures of colonial North America were primarily oral, communal, and—at least through the first half of the eighteenth century—intensely local. Face-to-face conversation served as the major means of communication. Information tended to travel slowly and within relatively confined regions. Different locales developed divergent cultural traditions, and racial and ethnic variations heightened those differences. Public rituals served as the chief means through which the colonists forged their cultural identities.

Attendance at church was perhaps the most important such ritual. In Congregational (Puritan) churches, church leaders assigned seating to reflect standing in the community. In early New England, men and women sat on opposite sides of a central aisle, arranged in ranks according to age, wealth, and whether or not they had formally become church members. By the mid-eighteenth century, wealthy men and their wives sat in privately owned pews; their children,

Religious and Civic Rituals

of the external world. Belief in witchcraft and astrology, among other similar phenomena, thus came under attack.

The Enlightenment had an enormous impact on educated, well-to-do people in Europe and America. It supplied them with a common vocabulary and a unified view of the world, one that insisted the enlightened eighteenth century was better, and wiser, than all previous ages. It joined them in a common endeavor, the effort to make sense of God's orderly creation. Thus, American naturalists like John and William Bartram supplied European scientists with information about New World plants and animals for newly formulated universal classification systems. So, too, Americans interested in astronomy took part in an international effort to learn about the solar system by studying a rare occurrence, the transit of Venus across the face of the sun in 1769. A prime example of America's participation in the Enlightenment was Benjamin Franklin, who retired from a successful printing business in 1748 when he was just forty-two, thereafter devoting himself to scientific

Smallpox Inoculation

Smallpox, the world's greatest killer of human beings, repeatedly ravaged the population of North America, colonists and Indians alike. Thus, when the vessel *Seahorse* arrived in Boston from the Caribbean in April 1721 with smallpox-infected people on board, New Englanders feared the worst. The authorities ordered the ship and its passengers quarantined, but it was too late: smallpox escaped into the city, and by June several dozen people had caught the dread disease.

Yet there was perhaps some hope. The Reverend Cotton Mather, a member of London's Royal Society (an organization promoting Enlightenment approaches to science), had read in its journal several years earlier two accounts by physicians—one in Constantinople and one in Smyrna—of a medical technique previously unknown to Europeans but widely employed in North Africa and the Middle East. Called inoculation, it involved taking pus from the pustules (or poxes) of an infected person and inserting it into a small cut on the arm of a healthy individual. With luck, that person would experience a mild case of smallpox, thereafter gaining lifetime immunity from the disease. Mather's interest in inoculation was further piqued by his slave, Onesimus, a North African who had been inoculated as a youth and who described the procedure in detail to his master.

With the disease coursing through the city, Mather circulated a manuscript among the local medical community, promoting inoculation as a solution to the current epidemic. But nearly all the city's doctors ridiculed his ideas, challenging his sources—and especially denigrating his reliance on information from Onesimus. Mather won only one major convert, Zabdiel Boylston, a physician and apothecary. The two men inoculated their own children and about two hundred others, despite bitter opposition, which included an attempt to bomb Mather's house. Yet after the epidemic ended, Bostonians could clearly see the results: of those inoculated, just 3 percent had died; among the thousands who took the disease "in the natural way," mortality was 15 percent. Even Mather's most vocal opponents were convinced, thereafter supporting inoculation as a remedy for the disease. Mather wrote reports for the Royal Society, and

following their publication even Britain's royal family was inoculated.

Thus, through transatlantic links forged by the Enlightenment and enslavement, American colonists learned how to combat the deadliest disease of all. Today, thanks to a successful campaign by the World Health Organization, smallpox has been wholly eradicated.

An Historical

ACCOUNT

OF THE

SMALL-POX
INOCULATED

IN

NEW ENGLAND,

Upon all Sorts of Persons, *Whites, Blacks,* and of all Ages and Constitutions.

With some Account of the Nature of the Infection in the NATURAL and INOCULATED Way, and their different Effects on HUMAN BODIES.

With some short DIRECTIONS to the UNEXPERIENCED in this Method of Practice.

Humbly dedicated to her Royal Highness the Princess of WALES, by *Zabdiel Boylston,* Physician.

LONDON:

Printed for S. CHANDLER, *at the* Cross-Keys *in the* Poultry. M.DCC.XXVI.

Private Collection/Picture Research Consultants & Archives

▲ Several years after he and Cotton Mather combated a Boston smallpox epidemic by employing inoculation, Zabdiel Boylston published this pamphlet in London to spread the news of their success. The dedication to the Princess of Wales was designed to indicate the royal family's support of the procedure.

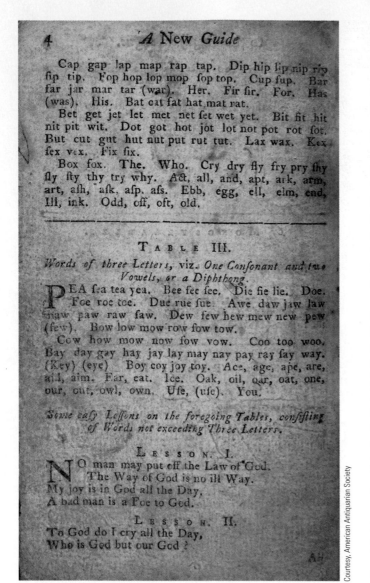

▲ Thomas Dilworth's A *New Guide to the English Tongue*, first published in London in 1740 and reprinted by Benjamin Franklin in Philadelphia seven years later, was one of the most popular texts used to instruct colonial children in reading and spelling. It used what its author called a "step by step" approach, introducing words of two, then three, then four, and more letters, taking care to exclude any words that might "excite loose and disorderly Thoughts."

servants, slaves, and the less fortunate still sat in sex-segregated fashion at the rear, sides, or balcony of the church. In eighteenth-century Virginia, seating in Church of England parishes also conformed to the local status hierarchy. Planter families purchased their own pews, and in some parishes landed gentlemen customarily strode into church as a group just before the service, deliberately drawing attention to their exalted position. In Quebec City, formal processions of men into the parish church celebrated Catholic feast days; each participant's rank determined his place in the procession. By contrast, Quaker meetinghouses in Pennsylvania and elsewhere used an egalitarian but sex-segregated seating system. The varying rituals surrounding people's entrance into and seating in colonial churches thus symbolized their place in society and the values of the local community.

Communal culture also centered on the civic sphere. In New England, governments proclaimed official days of thanksgiving (for good harvests, military victories, and so forth) and days of fasting and prayer (when the colony was experiencing such difficulties as droughts or epidemics). Everyone was expected to participate in the public rituals held in churches on such occasions. Because all able-bodied men between the ages of sixteen and sixty were required to serve in local militias—the only military forces in the colonies—monthly musters also brought the community together.

In the Chesapeake, important rituals occurred on court and election days. When the county court met, men came to file lawsuits, appear as witnesses, or serve as jurors. Attendance at court functioned as a method of civic education; from watching the proceedings, men learned what behavior their neighbors expected of them. Elections served the same purpose, for property-holding men voted in public. An election official, often flanked by the candidates for office, would call each man forward to declare his preference. The voter would then be thanked politely by the gentleman for whom he had cast his oral ballot. Traditionally, the candidates afterward treated their supporters to rum at nearby taverns.

Everywhere in colonial North America, the public punishment of criminals served not just to humiliate the offender but also to remind the community of proper behavioral standards. Public hangings and whippings, along with orders to sit in the stocks, expressed the community's outrage about crimes and restored harmony to its ranks. Judges often assigned penalties that shamed miscreants in especially appropriate ways. In San Antonio, Texas, for example, one cattle thief was sentenced to be led through the town's streets "with the entrails hanging from his neck"; and when a New Mexico man assaulted his father-in-law, he was directed not merely to pay medical expenses but also to kneel before him and beg his forgiveness publicly. New Englanders reprieved after being convicted of capital offenses did not thereby escape public humiliation: frequently, they were ordered to wear a noose around their neck for years, as a constant reminder to themselves, their families, and their neighbors of their heinous violation of community norms.

By 1770, Anglo-American households on average allocated one-quarter of their spending to purchasing

Rituals of Consumption

consumer goods, which fostered new rituals centered on consumption. Such purchases established novel links among the various residents

◀ Convicted criminals were publicly punished and shamed in front of their friends, relatives, and neighbors. A man might be put in the stocks for offenses such as contempt of authority, drunken and disorderly conduct, or theft. The intent was not simply to deter him from future misbehavior but to let his fate serve as a warning to all who saw his humiliating posture.

Library of Congress

of North America, creating what historians have termed "an empire of goods." First came the acquisition of desirable items. In the seventeenth century, settlers acquired necessities by bartering with neighbors or ordering products from a home-country merchant. By the middle of the eighteenth century, specialized shops selling nonessentials had proliferated in cities like Philadelphia and New Orleans. In 1770, Boston alone had more than five hundred stores, which offered consumers a vast selection of millinery, sewing supplies, tobacco, gloves, tableware, and the like. Even small towns had one or two retail establishments. Colonists would set aside time to "go shopping," a novel and pleasurable leisure activity. The purchase of an object—for example, a ceramic bowl, a mirror, or a length of beautiful fabric—initiated the consumption rituals.

Consumers would deploy their purchases in an appropriate manner: hanging the mirror prominently on a wall, displaying the bowl on a table or sideboard, turning the fabric into a special piece of clothing. Colonists took pleasure in owning lovely objects, but they also proudly displayed their acquisitions (and thus their wealth and good taste) publicly to kin and neighbors. A rich man might hire an artist to paint his family using the objects and wearing the clothing, thereby creating a pictorial record that also would be displayed for admiration.

Poor, rural people also participated in the new trends, taking obvious pleasure even in inexpensive purchases. The accounts kept by a backcountry storekeeper in eighteenth-century Virginia, for instance, show that he accepted bartered goods from customers who lacked cash. One woman traded hens and chickens for a pewter dish; another, yards of hand-woven cloth for fancy fabric, ribbons, and a necklace. Local slaves exchanged cotton they had grown in their free time for colorful ribbons and and hats they must have worn with pride. Some also purchased mirrors so they could see themselves bedecked in their acquisitions.

Tea drinking, a consumption ritual dominated and controlled by women, played an important role throughout rural and urban Anglo America alike. Households with aspirations to genteel status sought to acquire the items necessary for the proper consumption of tea: not just pots and cups but also strainers, sugar tongs, bowls, and even special tables. Tea provided a focal point for socializing and, because of its cost, served as a crucial marker of status. Wealthy women regularly entertained their male and female friends at afternoon tea parties. A hot and mildly stimulating drink, tea also appeared healthful. Thus, even poor households consumed tea, although they could not afford the fancy equipment used by their better-off neighbors. Some Mohawk Indians adopted the custom, much to the surprise of a traveler from Sweden, who observed them drinking tea in the late 1740s.

Tea and Madeira

Another drink with connotations of gentility was Madeira wine, imported from the Portuguese islands by merchants with extensive transatlantic familial connections. By 1770, Madeira had become the favored drink of the elite, expensive to purchase and consume properly. Opening the bottle, letting it breathe, decanting and serving it with appropriate glassware were all accomplished with elaborate ceremony. Colonial consumers in different regions had varying tastes to which producers and merchants responded; mainlanders tended to like their Madeira liberally laced with brandy, whereas residents of the Caribbean preferred sweeter and darker wines without added spirits. From the 1750s on, urban dwellers could buy such wines at specialized stores. And much of what they drank must

▲ This trade card (advertisement) issued by a Philadelphia tobacco dealer in 1770 shows a convivial group of wealthy men at a tavern. Both the leisurely activity depicted here and the advertisement itself were signs of the new rituals of consumption. Merchants began to advertise only when their customers could choose among different ways of spending money.

have been smuggled because more wines were advertised for sale than were recorded in customs records.

Other sorts of rituals allowed the disparate cultures of colonial North America to interact with one another. Particularly important rituals developed on what the historian Richard White has termed the "middle ground"—that is, the psychological and geographical space in which Indians and Europeans encountered each other. Most of those cultural encounters occurred in the context of trade or warfare.

Rituals on the "Middle Ground"

When Europeans sought to trade with Indians, they encountered an indigenous system of exchange that stressed gift giving rather than formalized buying and selling. Successful bargaining required French and English traders to present Indians with gifts (cloth, rum, gunpowder, and other items) before negotiating with them for pelts and skins. Eventually, those gifts would be reciprocated, after which formal trading could take place. And that commerce often responded to the native peoples' preferences. For example, Indians in northeastern North America wanted heavy cloths called strouds. Because British manufacturers produced such material in response to natives' demands, British traders acquired an important advantage over their French competitors. To the detriment of Indian societies, rum became a crucial component of many trading rituals. Traders concluded that drunken Indians would sell their furs more cheaply, and some Indians refused to hunt or trade unless they first received rum. Alcohol abuse hastened the deterioration of villages already devastated by disease and dislocation.

Intercultural rituals also developed to deal with murders. Indians and Europeans both believed that murders required a compensatory act but differed over what that act should be. Europeans sought primarily to identify and punish the murderer. To Indians, such "eye for an eye" revenge was just one of many possible responses to murder. Compensation could also be accomplished by capturing another Indian or a colonist who could take the dead person's place, or by "covering the dead"—that is, by providing the family of the deceased with compensatory goods, a crucial strategy for maintaining peace on the frontiers. Eventually, the French and the Algonquians evolved an elaborate ritual for handling frontier murders that encompassed elements of both societies' traditions: murders were investigated and murderers identified, but by mutual agreement deaths were usually "covered" by trade goods rather than by blood revenge.

Colonial Families

Families (rather than individuals) constituted the basic units of colonial society; never-married adults were rare. People living together as families, commonly under the direction of a marital pair, everywhere constituted the chief mechanisms for both production and consumption. Yet family forms and structures varied widely in the mainland colonies.

As Europeans consolidated their hold on North America, Indians had to adapt to novel circumstances.

Indian and Mixed-Race Families

Bands reduced in numbers by disease and warfare recombined into new units; for example, the Catawbas emerged in the 1730s in the western Carolinas from the coalescence of several earlier peoples, including Yamasees and Guales. Likewise, European secular and religious authorities reshaped Indian family forms. Whereas many Indian societies had permitted easy divorce, European missionaries frowned on such practices; societies that had allowed polygynous marriages (including New England Algonquians) redefined such relationships, designating one wife as "legitimate" and others as "concubines."

Continued high mortality rates created Indian societies in which extended kin took on new importance, for when parents died, other relatives—even occasionally nonkin—assumed child-rearing responsibilities. Furthermore, once Europeans established dominance in any region, Indians there could no longer pursue traditional modes of subsistence. That led to unusual family structures as well as to a variety of economic strategies. In New England, for instance, Algonquian husbands and wives often could not live together for adults supported themselves by working separately (perhaps wives as domestic servants, husbands as sailors). Some native women married African American men, unions encouraged by sexual imbalances in both populations. And in New Mexico, detribalized Navajos, Pueblos, Paiutes, and Apaches employed as servants by Spanish settlers clustered in the small towns of the Borderlands. Known collectively as *genizaros,* they lost contact with Indian cultures, instead living on the fringes of Latino society.

Wherever the population contained relatively few European women, sexual liaisons (both inside and outside marriage) occurred between European men and Indian women. The resulting mixed-race population of *mestizos* and *métis* worked as a familial "middle ground" to ease other cultural interactions. In New France and the Anglo-American backcountry, such families frequently resided in Indian villages and were enmeshed in trading networks. Often, children of these unions became prominent leaders of Native American societies. For example, Peter Chartier, son of a Shawnee mother and a French father, led a pro-French Shawnee band in western Pennsylvania in the 1740s. By contrast, in the Spanish Borderlands, the offspring of Europeans and *genizaros* were treated as degraded individuals. Largely denied the privilege of legal marriage, they bore generations of

▲ In eighteenth-century Spain, the existence of mixed-race North American families aroused great curiosity, creating a market for so-called casta paintings, which illustrated different sorts of multiracial households. In 1763, Mexican artist Miguel Cabrera depicted a Spanish father and an Indian mother, who have produced a mestiza daughter. Real families resembling this idealized picture would have been seen in New Mexico.

"illegitimate" children of various racial mixtures, giving rise in Latino society to a wide range of labels describing degrees of skin color with a precision unknown in English or French America.

Eighteenth-century Anglo-Americans used the word *family* to mean all the people who occupied one household (including any resident

European American Families

servants or slaves). The many European migrants to North America had more stable family lives than did Indian

and *mestizo* peoples. European men or their widows headed households considerably larger than American families today. In 1790, the average home in the United States contained 5.7 free people; few such households included extended kin, such as grandparents. Family members—bound by ties of blood or servitude—worked together to produce goods for consumption or sale. The head of the household represented it to the outside world, voting in elections, managing the finances, and holding legal authority over the rest of the family—his wife, his children, and his servants or slaves.

In English, French, and Spanish America, the vast majority of European families supported themselves through agriculture by cultivating crops and raising livestock. The scale and nature of the work varied: the production of indigo in Louisiana or tobacco in the Chesapeake required different sorts of labor from subsistence farming in New England or cattle ranching in New Mexico and Texas. Still, just as in the European, African, and Indian societies discussed in Chapter 1, household tasks were allocated by sex. The master, his sons, and his male servants or slaves performed one set of chores; the mistress, her daughters, and her female servants or slaves, a different set.

The mistress took responsibility for what Anglo-Americans called "indoor affairs." She and her female helpers prepared food, cleaned the house, did laundry, and often made clothing. Preparing food involved planting and cultivating a garden, harvesting and preserving vegetables, salting and smoking meat, drying apples and pressing cider, milking cows and making butter and cheese, not to mention cooking and baking. The head of the household and his male helpers, responsible for "outdoor affairs," also had heavy workloads. They planted and cultivated the fields, built fences, chopped wood for the fireplace, harvested and marketed crops, cared for livestock, and butchered cattle and hogs to provide the household with meat. So extensive was the work involved in maintaining a farm household that a married couple could not do it alone. If they had no children to help them, they turned to servants or slaves.

Most African American families lived as components of European American households—sometimes on plantations that masters perceived as one large family. More than 95 percent of colonial African Americans were held in perpetual bondage. Although many lived on farms with only one or two other slaves, others had the experience of living and working in a largely black setting. In South Carolina, a majority of the population was of African origin; in Georgia, about half; and in the Chesapeake, 40 percent. Portions of the Carolina low country were nearly 90 percent African American by 1790.

African American Families

The setting in which African Americans lived determined the shape of their families, yet wherever possible slaves established family structures in which youngsters carried relatives' names or—in South Carolina—followed African naming patterns. In the North, the scarcity of other blacks often made it difficult for bondspeople to form stable households.

▲ William L. Breton's watercolor of "The Old London Coffee House" in eighteenth-century Philadelphia shows a slave auction taking place on its porch. That such a scene could have occurred in front of such a prominent and popular meeting place serves as a reminder of the ubiquity of slavery in the colonies, north as well as south.

Historical Society of Pennsylvania

In the Chesapeake, men and women who regarded themselves as married (slaves could not legally wed) frequently lived on different quarters or even on different plantations. Children generally resided with their mother, seeing their father only on Sundays. Simultaneously, the natural increase of the population created wide American-born kinship networks among Chesapeake slaves. On large Carolina and Georgia rice plantations, enslaved couples not only usually lived together with their children but also accumulated property through working for themselves after they had completed their daily "tasks." Some Georgia slaves sold their surplus produce at the market in Savannah, thereby earning money to buy nice clothing or such luxuries as tobacco or jewelry, but rarely enough to purchase their freedom.

Because all the British colonies legally permitted slavery, bondspeople had few options for escaping servitude other than fleeing to Florida, where the Spanish offered protection. Some recently arrived Africans stole boats to try to return home or ran off in groups to frontier regions, to join the Indians or establish independent communities. Among American-born slaves, family ties strongly affected such decisions. South Carolina planters soon learned, as one wrote, that slaves "love their families dearly and none runs away from the other," so many owners sought to keep families together for practical reasons. In the Chesapeake, where family members often lived separately, affectionate ties could cause slaves to run away, especially if a family member had been sold or moved to a distant quarter.

Forms of Resistance

Although colonial slaves rarely rebelled collectively, they often resisted enslavement in other ways. Bondspeople uniformly rejected attempts by their owners to commandeer their labor on Sundays without compensation. Extended-kin groups protested excessive punishment of relatives and sought to live near one another. The links that developed among African American families who had lived on the same plantation for several generations served as insurance against the uncertainties of existence under slavery. If parents and children were separated by sale, other relatives could help with child rearing. Among African Americans, just as among Indians, the extended family thus served a more important function than it did among European-Americans.

Most slave families managed to carve out a small measure of autonomy, especially in their working and spiritual lives, and particularly in the Lower South. Enslaved Muslims often clung to their Islamic faith, a pattern especially evident in Louisiana and Georgia. Some African Americans preserved traditional beliefs, and others converted to Christianity (often retaining some African elements), finding comfort in the assurances of their new religion that all people would be free and equal in heaven. Slaves in South Carolina and Georgia jealously guarded their customary ability to control their own time after completing their "tasks." Even on Chesapeake tobacco plantations, slaves planted their own gardens, trapped, or fished to supplement the minimal diet their masters supplied. Late in the century, some Chesapeake planters with a surplus of laborers began to hire slaves out to others, often allowing the workers to keep a small part of their earnings. Such accumulated property could buy desired goods or serve as a legacy for children.

Just as African Americans and European Americans resided together on plantations, so too they lived side by side in urban neighborhoods. (In 1760s Philadelphia, one-fifth of the work force was enslaved, and by 1775 blacks composed nearly 15 percent of the population of New York City.) Such cities were nothing but medium-sized towns by today's standards. In 1750, the largest, Boston and Philadelphia, had just seventeen thousand and thirteen thousand inhabitants, respectively. Life in the cities nonetheless differed considerably from that on northern farms, southern plantations, or southwestern ranches. City dwellers everywhere purchased food and wood in the markets. Urban residents lived by the clock rather than the sun, and men's jobs frequently took them away from their household. City people also had much more contact with the world beyond their own homes than did their rural counterparts.

City Life

By the 1750s, most major cities had at least one weekly newspaper, and some had two or three. Anglo-American newspapers printed the latest "advices from London" (usually two to three months old) and news from other colonies, as well as local reports. Newspapers were available (and often read aloud) at taverns and coffeehouses, so people who could not afford them, even illiterates, could learn the news. Contact with the outside world, however, had its drawbacks. Sailors sometimes brought deadly diseases into port. Boston, New York, Philadelphia, and New Orleans endured terrible epidemics of smallpox and yellow fever, which Europeans and Africans in the countryside largely escaped.

Politics: Stability and Crisis in British America

Early in the eighteenth century, Anglo-American political life exhibited a new stability. Despite substantial migration from overseas, most residents of the mainland had been born in America. Men from genteel families

◄ Fire posed a major hazard to colonial cities; several suffered considerable damage in the seventeenth and eighteenth centuries from fires that raged out of control for hours. In the mid-eighteenth-century, cities like New York organized volunteer companies, such as the Hand-in-Hand company pictured here on an unidentified city street about 1750. The firemen are passing buckets of water from the well on the left to the engine on the right, where men on each side operate the pump that directs a stream of water on the fire. The chief is shouting orders through his trumpet at the right of the engine, and the people on the far right are carrying items from the burning building.

Stokes Collection, The New York Public Library

dominated the political structures in each province, for voters (free male property holders) tended to defer to their well-educated "betters" on election days.

Throughout the Anglo-American colonies, political leaders sought to increase the powers of elected assemblies

Colonial Assemblies

relative to the powers of the governors and other appointed officials. Assemblies began to claim privileges associated with the British House of Commons, such as the rights to initiate all tax legislation and to control the militia. The assemblies also developed effective ways of influencing British appointees, especially by threatening to withhold their salaries. In some colonies (Virginia and South Carolina, for example), elite members of the assemblies usually presented a united front to royal officials, but in others (such as New York), they fought among themselves long and bitterly. To win hotly contested elections, New York's genteel leaders began to appeal to "the people," competing openly

for votes. Yet in 1735, the New York government imprisoned a newspaper editor, John Peter Zenger, who had too vigorously criticized its actions. Defending Zenger against the charge of "seditious libel," his lawyer argued that the truth could not be defamatory, thus helping to establish a free-press principle now found in American law.

Assemblymen saw themselves as acting defensively to prevent encroachments on colonists' liberties—for example, by preventing governors from imposing oppressive taxes. By midcentury, they were comparing the structure of their governments to Britain's balanced polity, reputedly a combination of monarchy, aristocracy, and democracy of the sort admired since the days of ancient Greece and Rome. Drawing rough analogies, political leaders equated their governors with the monarch, their councils with the aristocracy, and their assemblies with the House of Commons. All three were believed essential to good government, but Anglo-Americans did not regard them with the same degree of approval. They viewed governors and appointed councils as representatives of Britain who posed potential threats to customary colonial ways of life. Many colonists saw the assemblies, however, as the people's protectors. And in turn, the assemblies regarded themselves as representatives of the people.

Yet such beliefs should not be equated with modern practice. The assemblies, many controlled by dominant families whose members were reelected year after year, rarely responded to the concerns of their poorer constituents. Although settlements continually expanded, assemblies failed to reapportion themselves, which led to serious grievances among backcountry dwellers, especially those from non-English ethnic groups. The colonial ideal of the assembly as the representative defender of liberty must therefore be distinguished from the colonial reality: the most dearly defended and ably represented were wealthy male colonists, particularly the assembly members themselves.

At midcentury, the political structures that had stabilized in a period of relative calm confronted a series of crises. None affected all the mainland colonies, but no colony escaped untouched. The crises of various descriptions—ethnic, racial, economic, regional—exposed internal tensions building in the pluralistic American society, foreshadowing the greater disorder of the revolutionary era. Significantly, they demonstrated that the political accommodations arrived at in the aftermath of the Glorious Revolution were no longer adequate to govern Britain's American empire. Once again, changes appeared necessary, and imminent.

One of the first crises occurred in South Carolina. Early on Sunday, September 9, 1739, about twenty

Slave Rebellions in South Carolina and New York

enslaved men, most likely Catholics from Kongo, gathered near the Stono River south of Charles Town. September fell in the midst of the rice harvest (and thus at a time of great pressure for male Africans, less accustomed than women to rice cultivation), and September 8 was, to Catholics, the birthday of the Virgin Mary, venerated in Kongo with special fervor. Seizing guns and ammunition, the slaves killed storekeepers and nearby planter families. Then, joined by other local bondsmen, they headed toward Florida in hopes of finding refuge. By midday, however, the alarm had been sounded among slaveowners in the district. That afternoon a troop of militia attacked the fugitives, who then numbered about a hundred, killing some and dispersing the rest. More than a week later, most of the remaining conspirators were captured. The colony quickly executed the survivors, but for over two years rumors about escaped renegades haunted the colony.

The Stono Rebellion shocked slaveholding Carolinians as well as residents of other colonies. Throughout British America, laws governing the behavior of African

Americans were stiffened. The most striking response came in New York City, the site of the first mainland slave revolt in 1712. There, the news from the South, coupled with fears of Spain generated by the outbreak of King George's War, set off a reign of terror in the summer of 1741. Colonial authorities suspected a biracial gang of thieves and arsonists of conspiring to foment a slave uprising under the guidance of a European thought to be a priest in the pay of Spain. By summer's end, thirty-one blacks and four whites had been executed for participating in the alleged plot. The Stono Rebellion and the New York "conspiracy" not only exposed and confirmed Anglo-Americans' deepest fears about the dangers of slaveholding but also revealed the assemblies' inability to prevent serious internal disorder. Events of the next two decades confirmed that pattern.

By midcentury, most of the fertile land east of the Appalachians had been purchased or occupied.

Rioters and Regulators

Consequently, conflicts over land titles and conditions of landholding grew in number and frequency. In 1746, for example, some New Jersey farmers clashed violently with agents of the East Jersey proprietors. The proprietors claimed the farmers' land and demanded annual payments, called quit-rents, for the use of the property. Similar violence occurred in the 1760s in the region that later became Vermont. There, farmers holding land grants issued by New Hampshire battled with speculators claiming title to the area through New York grants.

The most serious land riots took place along the Hudson River in 1765–1766. Late in the seventeenth century, the governor of New York had granted huge tracts in the lower Hudson Valley to prominent families. The proprietors in turn divided these estates into small farms, which they rented chiefly to poor Dutch and German migrants who regarded tenancy as a step on the road to independent freeholder status. By the 1750s, some proprietors had earned large sums annually from quit-rents and other fees.

After 1740, though, increasing migration from New England and Europe brought conflict to the great New York estates. Newcomers resisted the tenancy system. Many squatted on vacant portions of the manors, rejecting all attempts at eviction. In the mid-1760s, the Philipse family sued farmers who had lived on Philipse land for two decades. New York courts upheld the Philipse claim, ordering squatters to make way for tenants with valid leases. Instead of complying, a diverse group of farmers rebelled, terrorizing proprietors and loyal tenants, freeing their friends from jail, and on one occasion battling a county sheriff and his posse. The rebellion lasted nearly a year, ending only when British troops finally captured its leaders.

Violent conflicts of a different sort soon erupted in the Carolinas as well. The Regulator movements of the late

1760s (South Carolina) and early 1770s (North Carolina) pitted backcountry farmers against wealthy eastern planters who controlled the colonial governments. In South Carolina, Scots-Irish settlers protested their lack of an adequate voice in colonial political affairs. For months, they policed the countryside in vigilante bands known as Regulators, complaining of lax and biased law enforcement. North Carolina Regulators who objected primarily to heavy taxation fought and lost a battle with eastern militiamen at Alamance in 1771. Regional, ethnic, and economic tensions thus combined to create these disturbances, which ultimately arose from frontier people's dissatisfaction with the Carolina governments.

A Crisis in Anglo-American Religion

The most widespread crisis, though, was religious. From the mid-1730s through the 1760s, waves of religious revivalism—today known collectively as the First Great Awakening—swept over various colonies, primarily New England (1735–1745) and Virginia (1750s–1760s). Orthodox Calvinists sought to combat Enlightenment rationalism, which denied innate human depravity. Simultaneously, the economic and political uncertainty accompanying King George's War made colonists receptive to evangelists' spiritual messages. Moreover, many recent immigrants and residents of the backcountry had no prior religious affiliation, thus presenting evangelists with many potential converts.

The Great Awakening began in New England, where descendants of the Puritan founding generation composed the membership of Congregational churches. Whether in full or "halfway" communion—the latter, a category established in 1662 to ensure that people who had not experienced saving faith would still be subject to church discipline—such members were predominantly female. From the beginnings of the Awakening, though, men and women responded with equal fervor. In the mid-1730s, the Reverend Jonathan Edwards, a noted preacher and theologian, noticed a remarkable reaction among the youthful members of his church in Northampton, Massachusetts, to a message based squarely on Calvinist principles. Individuals could attain salvation, Edwards contended, only through recognition of their own depraved nature and the need to surrender completely to God's will. Such surrender brought to Congregationalists of both sexes an intensely emotional release from sin, coming to be seen as a single identifiable moment of conversion.

The effects of such conversions remained isolated until 1739, when George Whitefield, a Church of England

George Whitefield

clergyman already celebrated for leading revivals in England, arrived in America. For fifteen months, he toured the British colonies, preaching to large audiences from Georgia to New England and concentrating his efforts in the major cities: Boston, New York, Philadelphia, Charles Town, and Savannah. A gripping orator, Whitefield in effect generated the Great Awakening. One historian has termed him "the first modern celebrity" because of his skillful self-promotion and clever manipulation of both his listeners and the newspapers. Everywhere he traveled, his fame preceded him. Readers snapped up books by and about him, the first colonial bestsellers. Thousands of free and enslaved folk turned out to listen—and to experience conversion. Whitefield's journey, the first such ever undertaken, created new interconnections among the previously distinct colonies.

Regular clerics initially welcomed Whitefield and the American-born itinerant evangelist preachers who imitated him. Soon, however, many clergymen began to realize that, although "revived" religion filled their churches, it ran counter to their own approach to doctrine and matters of faith. They disliked the emotional style of the

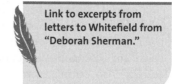

Link to excerpts from letters to Whitefield from "Deborah Sherman."

revivalists, whose itinerancy also disrupted normal patterns of church attendance because it took churchgoers away from the services they usually attended. Particularly troublesome to the orthodox were the dozens of female exhorters who took to streets and pulpits, proclaiming their right (even duty) to expound God's word.

Opposition to the Awakening heightened rapidly, causing congregations to splinter. "Old Lights"—tradi-

Impact of the Awakening

tional clerics and their followers—engaged in bitter disputes with the "New Light" evangelicals. Already characterized by numerous sects, American Protestantism fragmented even further as Congregationalists and Presbyterians split into Old Light and New Light factions and as new evangelical sects—Methodists and Baptists—gained adherents. After 1771, Methodists sent "circuit riders" (preachers on horseback) to the far reaches of settlement where they achieved widespread success in converting frontier dwellers. Paradoxically, the angry fights and the rapid rise in the number of distinct denominations eventually led to an American willingness to tolerate religious diversity. No single sect could make an unequivocal claim to orthodoxy, so they had to coexist if they were to exist at all.

Most significantly, the Awakening challenged traditional modes of thought, for the revivalists' message directly contested the colonial tradition of deference. Itinerant preachers, only a few of whom were ordained clergymen, claimed they understood the will of God

Private Collection/The Bridgeman Art Library

▲ This painting by John Collet shows the charismatic evangelist George Whitefield preaching out of doors in Britain, but the same scene would have been repeated many times in the colonies, especially after the clergy of established churches denied him access to their pulpits, deeming him too radical for their liking. Note the swooning woman in the foreground; women were reputed to be especially susceptible to Whitefield's message. Is the worker offering him a mug of ale derisively or devotedly? The answer is not clear, except that the gesture underscores the diversity of Whitefield's audience—not all were genteel or middling folk.

better than did elite college-educated clerics. Moreover, they and their followers divided the world into two groups—the saved and the damned—without respect to gender, age, or status, the previously dominant social categories. The revivalists' emphasis on emotion rather than learning undermined the validity of received wisdom, and New Lights questioned not only religious but also social and political orthodoxy. For example, New Lights began to defend the rights of groups and individuals to dissent from a community consensus, thereby challenging one of the fundamental tenets of colonial political life. The egalitarian themes of the Awakening simultaneously attracted ordinary folk and repelled the elite.

Nowhere was this trend more evident than in Virginia, where tax money supported the established Church of England, and the plantation gentry and their ostentatious lifestyle dominated society.

Virginia Baptists

By the 1760s, Baptists had gained a secure foothold in Virginia; inevitably, their beliefs and behavior clashed with the way most genteel families lived. They rejected as sinful the horseracing, gambling, and dancing that occupied much of the gentry's leisure time. They dressed plainly, in contrast to the gentry's fashionable opulence. They addressed one another as "Brother" and "Sister" regardless of social status, and they elected the leaders of their congregations—more than ninety of them by 1776. Their monthly "great meetings," which attracted hundreds of people, introduced new public rituals that rivaled the weekly Anglican services.

Strikingly, almost all the Virginia Baptist congregations included both free and enslaved members. At the founding of the Dan River Baptist Church in 1760, for example, eleven of seventy-four members were African Americans, and some congregations had African American majorities. Church rules applied equally to all members; interracial sexual relationships, divorce, and

Legacy FOR A PEOPLE AND A NATION

"Self-Made Men"

One of the most common American themes celebrates the "self-made man" (always someone explicitly *male*) of humble origins who gains wealth or prominence through extraordinary effort and talent. Those most commonly cited are such successful nineteenth-century businessmen as Andrew Carnegie (once a poor immigrant from Scotland) and John D. Rockefeller (born on a hardscrabble farm in upstate New York).

The initial exemplars of this tradition, though, lived in the eighteenth century. Benjamin Franklin's *Autobiography* chronicled his method for achieving success after beginning life as the seventeenth child of a Boston candle maker. From such humble origins Franklin became a wealthy, influential man active in science, politics, education, and diplomacy. Yet Franklin's tale is rivaled by that of a man apparently born a slave in South Carolina who subsequently worked as a sailor. He acquired literacy, purchased his freedom, became an influential abolitionist, married a wealthy Englishwoman, and published a popular autobiography that predated Franklin's in print. His first master called him Gustavus Vassa, the name he primarily used. But when publishing his *Interesting Narrative* in 1789, he called himself Olaudah Equiano.

In that *Narrative*, Equiano said he was born in Africa in 1745, kidnapped at the age of eleven, and transported to Barbados and then to Virginia, where a British naval officer purchased him. For years, scholars and students have relied on that account for its insights into the experience of the middle passage. But evidence recently uncovered by Vincent Carretta, although confirming the accuracy of much of Equiano's autobiography, shows that Equiano twice identified his birthplace as Carolina and was three to five years younger than he claimed. Why would Equiano conceal his origins and alter his age? Carretta speculates that the *Narrative* gained part of its credibility from Equiano's African birth and that admitting his real age would have raised questions about the account of his early life by revealing his youth at the time of the reputed kidnapping.

Equiano, or Vassa, thus truly "made himself," just as Benjamin Franklin and many others have done. (Franklin tended to omit, rather than alter, inconvenient parts of his personal history—for example, his having fathered an illegitimate son.) Equiano used information undoubtedly gleaned from acquaintances who *had* experienced the middle passage to craft an accurate depiction of the horrors of the slave trade. In the process, he became one of the first Americans to explicitly reinvent himself.

---

adultery were forbidden to all. In addition, congregations forbade masters' breaking up slave couples through sale. Biracial committees investigated complaints about church members' misbehavior. Churches excommunicated slaves for stealing from their masters, but they also excommunicated masters for physically abusing their slaves. One such slaveowner so dismissed in 1772 experienced a true conversion. Penalized for "burning" one of his slaves, Charles Cook apologized to the congregation and became a preacher in a largely African American church.

By injecting an egalitarian strain into Anglo-American life at midcentury, the Great Awakening had important social and political consequences, calling into question habitual modes of behavior in the secular as well as the religious realm.

SUMMARY

Over the half-century before 1770, North America was transformed. French and Spanish settlements expanded their geographic reach dramatically, and in the British colonies newcomers from Germany, Scotland, Ireland, and Africa brought their languages, customs, and religions with them. European immigrants settled throughout the English colonies but were concentrated in the growing cities and the backcountry. By contrast, enslaved migrants from Africa lived and worked primarily within one hundred miles of the Atlantic coast. In many areas of the colonial South, 50 to 90 percent of the population was of African origin.

The economic life of Europe's North American colonies proceeded simultaneously on two levels. On the farms, plantations, and ranches on which most colonists resided, the daily, weekly, monthly, and yearly rounds of chores for men, women, and children dominated people's lives while providing the goods consumed by households and sold in markets. Simultaneously, an intricate international trade network affected the economies of the British, French, and Spanish colonies. The bitter wars fought by European nations during the eighteenth century inevitably involved the colonists by creating new opportunities for overseas sales or by disrupting their traditional markets. The volatile colonial economy fluctuated for reasons beyond Americans' control. Those fortunate few who—through skill, control of essential resources, or luck—reaped the profits of international commerce made up the wealthy class of merchants and landowners who dominated colonial political, intellectual, and social life. At the other end of the economic scale, poor colonists, especially city dwellers, struggled to make ends meet.

A century and a half after European peoples first settled in North America, the colonies mixed diverse European, American, and African traditions into a novel cultural blend that owed much to Europe but just as much, if not more, to North America itself. Europeans who interacted regularly with peoples of African and American origin—and with Europeans who came from nations other than their own—had to develop new methods of accommodating intercultural differences in addition to creating ties within their own potentially fragmenting communities. Yet at the same time, the dominant colonists continued to identify themselves as French, Spanish, or British rather than as Americans.

That did not change in Canada, Louisiana, or Spanish territory, but in the 1760s some Anglo-Americans began to realize that their interests did not necessarily coincide with those of Great Britain or its monarch. For the first time, they offered a direct challenge to British authority.

SUGGESTIONS FOR FURTHER READING

Marilyn Baseler, *"Asylum for Mankind": America 1607–1800* (1998)

Richard R. Beeman, *The Varieties of Political Experience in Eighteenth-Century America* (2004)

James F. Brooks, *Captives and Cousins: Slavery, Kinship, and Community in the Southwest Borderlands* (2002)

William E. Burns, *Science and Technology in Colonial America* (2005)

Richard Bushman, *The Refinement of America: Persons, Houses, Cities* (1992)

Kathleen DuVal, *The Native Ground: Indians and Colonists in the Heart of the Continent* (2006)

Rhys Isaac, *The Transformation of Virginia, 1740–1790* (1982)

Jill Lepore, *New York Burning: Liberty, Slavery, and Conspiracy in Eighteenth-Century Manhattan* (2005)

Harry S. Stout, *The Divine Dramatist: George Whitefield and the Rise of Modern Evangelicalism* (1991)

Stephanie G. Wolf, *As Various as Their Land: The Everyday Lives of 18th Century Americans* (1992)

Chapter 5

Severing the Bonds of Empire 1754–1774

We the Ladys of Edenton do hereby Solemnly Engage not to Conform to that Pernicious Custom of Drinking Tea, or that we the aforesaid Ladys will not promote y.e wear of any Manufacture from England untill such time that all Acts which tend to Enslave this our Native Country shall be Repealed

The well-born Scotswoman Janet Schaw chose an inopportune time to visit her older brother, who had moved to North America many years earlier. She and her companions set sail from Edinburgh in October 1774, arriving in the West Indies in January 1775 after a voyage plagued by storms. She enjoyed pleasant visits with the planter families of Antigua and St. Christopher, a number of whom were Scots like herself, and she did some shopping at the international free port of St. Eustatius, purchasing "excellent French gloves" and some "English thread-stockings" cheaper than at home. Then she sailed on to meet her brother in North Carolina. There she encountered indolent and unhealthy looking "rusticks" who had, in her opinion, a "rooted hatred" for the mother country and who were forming "schemes" detrimental to both Britain and America.

Janet Schaw soon learned that an American congress had forbidden "every kind of diversion, even card-playing." When Wilmington residents held a final ball before the ban went into effect, she found the event "laughable," comparing it to seventeenth-century Dutch paintings of comic, carousing peasants. She also reported that "the Ladies have burnt their tea in a solemn procession," but, she sniffed, "they had delayed however till the sacrifice was not very considerable, as I do not think any one offered above a quarter of a pound." All the "genteel" merchants, she observed, "disapprove of the present proceedings," and they were planning to leave as soon as they could. She pronounced the people "infatuated." Although insisting that "I am no politician," she concluded that the trouble in the colonies had been caused by "mistaken notions of moderation" in parliamentary policy. Schaw herself returned to Scotland within the year. Her brother's property was later confiscated by the state because he refused to take an oath of allegiance, but he remained in his new homeland until his death.

◀ In 1775, an English cartoonist satirized American women's involvement in the resistance movement by depicting the women of Edenton, North Carolina, as grotesque, flirtatious figures. In his view, they neglected their responsibilities as mothers when they dared to enter the political arena by signing a statement in October 1774 pledging to do "every thing as far as lies in our power" to support the "publick good." In the background, he showed them discarding their tea, an action similar to that Janet Schaw described in the nearby town of Wilmington.

Chronology

1754	■ Albany Congress meets to try to forge colonial unity
	■ Washington defeated at Fort Necessity, Great Meadows, Pennsylvania
1755	■ Braddock's army defeated in Pennsylvania
1756	■ Britain declares war on France; Seven Years' War officially begins
1759	■ British forces take Quebec
1760	■ American phase of war ends with fall of Montreal to British troops
	■ George III becomes king
1763	■ Treaty of Paris ends Seven Years' War
	■ Pontiac's allies attack forts and settlements in West
	■ Proclamation of 1763 attempts to close land west of Appalachians to settlement
1764	■ Sugar Act lays new duties on molasses, tightens customs regulations
	■ Currency Act outlaws paper money issued by the colonies
1765	■ Stamp Act requires stamps on all printed materials in colonies
	■ Sons of Liberty formed
1766	■ Stamp Act repealed
	■ Declaratory Act insists that Parliament can tax the colonies
1767	■ Townshend Acts lay duties on trade within the empire, send new officials to America
1768	■ Fort Stanwix treaty opens Kentucky to Anglo-American settlement
1768–70	■ Townshend duties resisted; boycotts and public demonstrations divide merchants and urban artisans
1770	■ Lord North becomes prime minister
	■ Townshend duties repealed, except for tea tax
	■ Boston Massacre kills five colonial rioters
1772	■ Boston Committee of Correspondence formed
1773	■ Tea Act aids East India Company
	■ Bostonians protest the Tea Act
1774	■ Coercive Acts punish Boston and Massachusetts as a whole
	■ Quebec Act reforms government of Quebec
	■ First Continental Congress called

*I*n retrospect, John Adams identified the period between 1760 and 1775 as the era of the true American Revolution. The Revolution, Adams declared, ended before the fighting started, for it was "in the Minds of the people," involving not the actual winning of independence but a fundamental shift of allegiance from Britain to America. Today, not all historians would concur with Adams that the shift he identified, and which Janet Schaw witnessed, constituted the Revolution. But none would deny the importance of the events of those crucial years in which the mainland colonies began to unite to resist British policies.

The story of the 1760s and early 1770s describes an ever-widening split between Great Britain and Anglo America. In the long history of British settlement in the Western Hemisphere, considerable tension had occasionally marred the relationship between individual provinces and the mother country. Still, that tension had rarely persisted for long, nor had it been widespread, except during the crisis following the Glorious Revolution in 1689. The primary divisions affecting the colonies had been internal rather than external. In the 1750s, however, a series of events began to draw the colonists' attention from domestic matters to their relations with Great Britain. It started with the Seven Years' War.

Britain's overwhelming victory in that war, confirmed by treaty in 1763, forever altered the balance of power in North America. France was ousted from the continent and Spain from Florida, events with major consequences for both the indigenous peoples of the interior and the residents of the British colonies. Indians, who had become expert at playing European powers off against one another, lost one of their major diplomatic tools. Anglo-Americans no longer had to fear the French threat on their northern and western borders or the Spanish in the Southeast. The British colonies along the coast would never have dared to break with their mother country, some historians contend, had France controlled the Mississippi River and the Great Lakes in 1776.

The British victory in 1763, then, dramatically affected all the residents of North America. That victory also had a significant impact on Great Britain, one that involved the colonies. Britain's massive war-related debt needed to be paid, so Parliament for the first time imposed revenue-raising taxes on the colonies in addition to the customs duties that had long regulated trade. That decision exposed differences in the political thinking of Americans and Britons—differences that until then had been obscured by a shared political vocabulary.

During the 1760s and early 1770s, a broad coalition of the residents of Anglo America, men and women alike, resisted new tax levies and attempts by British officials to tighten controls over provincial governments. The colonies' elected leaders became ever more suspicious of Britain's motives as the years passed. They laid aside old antagonisms to coordinate their responses to the new measures, and they slowly began to reorient their political thinking. As late as the summer of 1774, though, most were still seeking a solution within the framework of the empire; few harbored thoughts of independence.

- What were the causes and consequences of the Seven Years' War?

- What British policies did Americans protest, and what theories and strategies did they develop to support those protests?

- Why did the Tea Act of 1773 cause such a major escalation in tensions between the mainland colonies and Great Britain?

Renewed Warfare Among Europeans and Indians

In the mid-eighteenth century, the British colonies along the Atlantic seaboard were surrounded by hostile, or potentially hostile, neighbors: Indians everywhere, the Spanish in Florida and along the coast of the Gulf of Mexico, the French along the great inland system of rivers and lakes that stretched from the St. Lawrence to the Mississippi. The Spanish outposts posed little direct threat, for Spain's days as a major power had passed. The French were another matter. Their long chain of forts and settlements dominated the North American interior, facilitating trading partnerships and alliances with the Indians. In none of the three Anglo-French wars fought between 1689 and 1748 was Britain able to shake France's hold on the American frontier. Under the Peace of Utrecht, which ended Queen Anne's War in 1713, the English won control of such peripheral northern areas as Newfoundland, Hudson's Bay, and Acadia (Nova Scotia) and gained access to the Great Lakes region, previously dominated by France. But Britain made no territorial gains in King George's War (see Table 5.1 and Map 5.2).

During both Queen Anne's War and King George's War, the Iroquois Confederacy maintained the policy of neutrality that it first developed in 1701. While British and French forces vied for nominal control of the North American continent, the confederacy skillfully manipulated the Europeans, refusing to commit warriors fully to either side despite being showered with gifts by both. The Iroquois continued a long-standing conflict with Cherokees and Catawbas in the South, thus giving their young warriors combat experience and allowing the replacement of population losses by acquiring new captives. They also cultivated peaceful relationships with Pennsylvania and Virginia, in part to obtain the colonists' imprimatur for their domination of the Shawnees and Delawares. And they forged friendly ties with Algonquians of the Great Lakes region, thereby thwarting potential assaults from those allies of the French and simultaneously making themselves indispensable go-betweens for commerce and communication between the Atlantic coast and the West. Thus, the Iroquois consolidated their control over the entire American interior north of Virginia and south of the Great Lakes.

Iroquois Neutrality

But even the Iroquois could not prevent the region inhabited by the Shawnees and Delawares (now western Pennsylvania and Virginia, and eastern Ohio) from providing the spark that set off a major war. In a significant reversal of previous patterns, that conflict spread from

Table 5.1 The Colonial Wars, 1689–1763

American Name	European Name	Dates	Participants	American Sites	Dispute
King William's War	Nine Years' War	1689–97	England, Holland versus France, Spain	New England, New York, Canada	French power
Queen Anne's War	War of Spanish Succession	1702–13	England, Holland, Austria versus France, Spain	Florida, New England	Throne of Spain
King George's War	War of Austrian Succession	1739–48	England, Holland, Austria versus France, Spain, Prussia	West Indies, New England, Canada	Throne of Austria
French and Indian War	Seven Years' War	1756–63	England versus France, Spain	Ohio country, Canada	Possession of Ohio country

▲ An eighteenth-century Iroquois warrior as depicted by a European artist. Such men of the Six Nations confederacy dominated the North American interior before the Seven Years' War. Lines drawn on maps by colonizing powers and the incursions of traders made little impact on their power.

America to Europe, decisively resolving the contest for North America.

As early as the late 1730s, trouble began brewing east of the Mississippi as British traders pushed west from the Carolinas and Virginia, challenging French power beyond the Appalachians. The French had difficulty supplying their settlements and native allies during a successful British naval blockade of the St. Lawrence during King George's War, which heightened French colonial officials' fear of British incursions, especially when in the 1740s Iroquois negotiators, claiming to speak for the Delawares and Shawnees, ceded large tracts of land to Pennsylvania officials. Squatters (mainly Scots-Irish and Germans) had already moved into parts of the region and had negotiated agreements with the Delawares for rights to settle there; some even paid rent to native "landlords." All resided on isolated farms in Delaware territory, coexisting peacefully with their native neighbors. But the agreements reached by the Penn family's agents and the Iroquois ignored both the local Indians and the squatters, all of whom were told to move. Disgruntled Delawares and Shawnees migrated west, where they joined other displaced eastern Indians and nursed their grievances.

The region to which they moved, claimed by both Virginia and Pennsylvania, was coveted by wealthy Virginians, who, organized as the Ohio Company, received a huge land grant in 1749. The company's agents established trading posts that aimed to dominate the crucial area where the Allegheny and Monongahela Rivers join to form the Ohio (see Map 5.1). But that "Ohio country" was also vital to the French. Because the Ohio River offered direct access by water to French posts on the Mississippi, permanent British presence in the Ohio country would further challenge France's prominence along the western rivers. Thus, in the early 1750s, Pennsylvania fur traders, Ohio Company representatives, the French military, squatters, Iroquois, Delawares, and Shawnees all jostled for position in the region. A 1752 raid by the French and their native allies on a trading outpost sited at modern Cleveland rid the region of Pennsylvanians, but the Virginians posed a more serious challenge. Accordingly, in 1753, the French pushed southward from Lake Erie, building fortified outposts at strategic points.

In response to the French threat, delegates from seven northern and middle colonies gathered in Albany, New York, in June 1754. With the backing of London officials, they sought two goals: to persuade the Iroquois to abandon their traditional neutrality and to coordinate plans for defense. They succeeded in neither. The Iroquois listened politely to the colonists' arguments but saw no reason to change a policy that had served them well for half a century. And, although the Albany Congress delegates adopted a Plan of Union (which would have established an elected intercolonial legislature with the power to tax), their provincial governments uniformly rejected the plan because those governments feared a loss of autonomy.

Albany Congress

While the Albany Congress delegates deliberated, the war for which they sought to prepare was already beginning. Governor Robert Dinwiddie of Virginia sent a small militia troop to build a palisade at the forks of the Ohio, then dispatched reinforcements. When a substantial French force arrived at the forks, the first contingent of Virginia militia surrendered, peacefully abandoning the strategic site. The French began to construct the larger and more elaborate Fort Duquesne. Upon learning of the confrontation, the inexperienced young officer who commanded the Virginia reinforcements pressed onward instead of awaiting further instructions. He encountered a French detachment, and Tanaghrisson, the leader of his Ohio Indian scouts, viciously killed the French commander, leading the Indians to slaughter other wounded French soldiers. Tanaghrisson hoped to start a war that would force the British to defend the Ohio Country against the French, and he succeeded. The Virginians were trapped by pursuing French troops in a crudely built Fort Necessity at Great Meadows, Pennsylvania. After a day-long battle

Map 5.1 European Settlements and Indians, 1754

By 1754, Europeans had expanded the limits of the English colonies to the eastern slopes of the Appalachian Mountains. Few independent Indian nations still existed in the East, but beyond the mountains they controlled the countryside. Only a few widely scattered English and French forts maintained the Europeans' presence there.

Source: Copyright © Cengage Learning

(on July 3, 1754), during which more than one-third of his men were killed or wounded, twenty-two-year-old George Washington surrendered. He and his men were allowed to return to Virginia.

Washington's blunder and Tanaghrisson's aggression helped ignite a war that eventually encompassed nearly the entire world. In July 1755, a few miles south of Fort Duquesne, a combined force of French and Indians attacked British and colonial troops readying a renewed assault on the fort. In the devastating defeat, General Edward Braddock was killed, and his surviving soldiers were demoralized. Many Ohio Indians subsequently joined the French, believing that the British could not protect them. The Pennsylvania frontier bore the brunt of repeated attacks by Delawares for two more years; over a thousand residents were killed. Settlers felt betrayed because the Indians attacking them had once been (an observer noted) "allmost dayly familiars at their houses eat drank cursed and swore together were even intimate play mates."

After news of the debacle reached London, Britain declared war on France in 1756, thus formally beginning

Seven Years' War

the Seven Years' War. Even before then, Britain, poised for renewed conflict with old enemies, took a fateful step. Britons and New Englanders feared that France would try to retake Nova Scotia, where most of the population was descended from seventeenth-century French settlers who had intermarried with local M'ikmaqs. Afraid that in the event of an attack the approximately twelve thousand French Nova Scotians would abandon the policy of neutrality they had followed since the early years of the century, British commanders in 1755 forced about seven thousand of them from their homeland—the first large-scale modern deportation, now called ethnic cleansing. Ships crammed with Acadians sailed to each of the mainland colonies, where the exiles encountered hostility and discrimination as they were dispersed into widely scattered communities. Many families were separated, some forever. After 1763, the survivors relocated: some returned to Canada, others traveled to France or its Caribbean islands, and many eventually settled in Louisiana, where they became known as Cajuns (derived from *Acadian*).

For three years, one disaster followed another. British officers tried without much success to coerce the colonies into supplying men and materiel to the army. Then, led

▲ A 1769 Dutch atlas charted the successful British attack on Quebec ten years earlier. Ships of the British fleet fill the St. Lawrence River. Cannon on the southern shore bombard the fortified town (indicated by the lines across the river). And to the left of the city, on the Plains of Abraham, the string of small red blocks represents the British troops who had stealthily climbed the heights at night to confront Quebec's French defenders (the blue blocks).

The First Worldwide War

Today, we call two twentieth-century conflicts world wars, but the first worldwide war predated them by more than a century. The contest that historians term the "Great War for the Empire" began in spring 1754 in southwestern Pennsylvania, over a seemingly local quarrel—whether Britain or France would build a fort at the forks of the Ohio. That it eventually involved combatants around the world attests not only to the growing importance of European nations' overseas empires but also to the increasing centrality of North America to their struggles for dominance.

Previous wars among Europeans had taken place mostly in Europe, though overseas colonies occasionally got involved. But the contest at the forks of the Ohio helped to reinvigorate a conflict between Austria and Prussia that sent European nations scrambling for allies. Eventually England, Hanover, and Prussia lined up against France, Austria, and Russia, joined by Sweden, Saxony, and, later, Spain. The war in Europe would last seven years. In 1763, these nations signed a peace treaty that returned the continent to the prewar status quo, but in the rest of the world Britain had decisively vanquished both France and Spain.

In the Caribbean, Britain seized the French islands of Guadeloupe and Martinique, and took Havana from Spain. In North America, the British recaptured the French fortress of Louisbourg and at last conquered Quebec. In Africa, Britain overwhelmed France's slave-trading posts in Senegambia. In India, British forces won control of Bengal. Three years later, the British beat a French army at Pondicherry, so four months after France lost Canada, its influence in India was also extinguished. Late in the war, a British expedition took Manila in the Philippines from Spain. The commander did not know that his nation had declared war on Britain, so the assault caught him unaware.

Thus the war that started in the American backcountry revealed the steadily growing links between North America and the rest of the world. And the aftermath exposed an unexpected additional link. Both winners and losers had to pay for this first worldwide war. Financial struggles in Britain and France, though separate, ultimately produced similar outcomes: revolutions abroad (for Britain, in America) and at home (for France).

National Maritime Museum, London

▲ In 1771, artist Dominic Serres, the Elder, depicted British naval vessels attacking the French fortress at Chandernagore in India in 1757 (at left in background). Cannon fire from the warships was critical to the British victory, one of the keys to the conquest of India during the Seven Years' War.

by William Pitt, the civilian official placed in charge of the war effort in 1757, Britain finally pursued a successful military strategy. Pitt agreed to reimburse the colonies for their wartime expenditures and placed recruitment in local hands, thereby gaining greater American support for the war. (Even so, Virginia burgesses appropriated more funds to defend against possible slave insurrections than to fight the French and Indians.) Large numbers of colonial militiamen served alongside equally large numbers of red-coated regulars sent to North America from Britain; the two groups nevertheless had an antagonistic relationship, lacking mutual respect.

Adding to the tensions were the actions of Anglo-American merchants. During the war, firms in Boston, Philadelphia, and New York continued trading with the French West Indies. Seeking markets for their fish, flour, timber, and other products, they bribed customs officers to look the other way while cargoes nominally bound for such neutral ports as Dutch St. Eustatius or Spanish Monte Cristi (on Hispaniola) actually ended up in the French Caribbean, and they acquired valuable French sugar in return. British officials tried but failed to stop the illicit commerce, some of which was conducted under the guise of exchanging prisoners of war using flags of truce. North American merchants in fact supplied not only the

French Caribbean but also France itself with vital materiel during the war.

Nevertheless, in July 1758, British forces recaptured the fortress at Louisbourg, winning control of the entrance to the St. Lawrence River and cutting the major French supply route. In the fall, the Delawares and Shawnees accepted British peace overtures, and the French abandoned Fort Duquesne. Then, in a stunning attack in September 1759, General James Wolfe's regulars defeated the French on the Plains of Abraham and took Quebec. Sensing a British victory, the Iroquois abandoned their traditional neutrality, hoping to gain a postwar advantage by allying themselves with Britain. A year later, the British captured Montreal, the last French stronghold on the continent, and the American phase of the war ended.

In the Treaty of Paris (1763), France ceded its major North American holdings to Britain. Spain, an ally of France toward the end of the war, gave Florida to the victors. France, meanwhile, ceded Louisiana west of the Mississippi to Spain, in partial compensation for its ally's losses elsewhere. The British thus gained control of the continent's fur trade. No longer would the English seacoast colonies have to worry about the threat to their existence posed by France's extensive North American territories (see Map 5.2).

Map 5.2 European Claims in North America

The dramatic results of the British victory in the Seven Years' (French and Indian) War are vividly demonstrated in these maps, which depict the abandonment of French claims to the mainland after the Treaty of Paris in 1763.

Source: Copyright © Cengage Learning

Link to Benjamin Franklin's "Join, or Die" cartoon.

The overwhelming British triumph stimulated some Americans to think expansively. Men like Benjamin Franklin, who had long touted the colonies' wealth and potential, predicted a glorious new future for British North America—a future that included not just geographical expansion but also economic development and population growth. Such men were to lead the resistance to British measures in the years after 1763. They uniformly opposed any laws that would retard America's growth and persistently supported steps to increase Americans' control over their own destiny. Many of them also speculated in western lands.

1763: A Turning Point

The great victory over France had an irreversible impact on North America, felt first by the indigenous peoples of the interior. With France excluded from the continent altogether and Spanish territory now confined to west of the Mississippi, the diplomatic strategy of playing Europeans off against one another, which the Indians had long adopted, became obsolete. The consequences were immediate and devastating.

Even before the Treaty of Paris, southern Indians had to adjust to new circumstances. After Britain gained the upper hand in the American war in 1758, Creeks and Cherokees lost their ability to force concessions by threatening to turn instead to France or Spain. In desperation, and in retaliation for British atrocities, Cherokees attacked the Carolina and Virginia frontiers in 1760. Though initially victorious, the Indians were defeated the following year by a force of British regulars and colonial militia. Late in 1761, the two sides concluded a treaty under which the Cherokees allowed the construction of British forts in their territories and opened a large tract to European settlement.

The fate of the Cherokees in the South portended events in the Ohio country. There, the Ottawas, Chippewas, and Potawatomis reacted angrily when Great Britain, no longer facing French competition, raised the price of trade goods and ended traditional gift-giving practices. Settlers rapidly moved into the Monongahela and Susquehanna valleys. A shaman named Neolin (also known as the Delaware Prophet) urged Indians to oppose the incursion on their lands and European influence on their culture. For the first time since King Philip in 1675, an influential native leader called for the unity of all tribes in the face of an Anglo-American threat. Contending that Indian peoples were destroying themselves by dependence on European goods (especially alcohol), Neolin

Neolin and Pontiac

advocated resistance, both peaceful and armed. If all Indians west of the mountains united to reject the invaders, Neolin declared, the Master of Life would replenish the depleted deer herds and once again look kindly upon his people. Ironically, Neolin's call for a return to native traditions itself revealed European origins; his reference to a single Master of Life showed the influence on his thinking of a syncretic Christianity.

Pontiac, war chief of an Ottawa village near Detroit, became the leader of a movement based on Neolin's precepts. In spring 1763, Pontiac forged an unprecedented alliance among Hurons, Chippewas, Potawatomis, Delawares, Shawnees, and Mingoes (Pennsylvania Iroquois). Pontiac besieged Fort Detroit while war parties attacked other British outposts in the Great Lakes. Detroit withstood the siege, but by late June all the other forts west of Niagara and north of Fort Pitt (formerly Fort Duquesne) had fallen to the alliance. Indians then raided the Virginia and Pennsylvania frontiers throughout the summer, slaying at least two thousand settlers. They carried off many enslaved African Americans, frightening planters, who feared an Indian-black alliance. Still, they could not take Niagara, Fort Pitt, or Detroit. In early August, colonial militiamen soundly defeated a combined Indian force at Bushy Run, Pennsylvania. Conflict ceased when Pontiac broke off the siege of Detroit in late October. A treaty ending the war was finally negotiated three years later.

The warfare on the Pennsylvania frontier in 1755–1757 and 1763 ended what had once been a uniquely peaceful relationship between European settlers and Indians in that province. For nearly eighty years, the residents of "Penn's Woods" had avoided major conflicts with each other. But first the Indian attacks and then the settlers' response—especially the massacre of several families of defenseless Conestoga Indians in December 1763 by fifty Scots-Irish men known as the Paxton Boys—revealed that violence in the region would subsequently become endemic.

Pontiac's war demonstrated that the huge territory Britain had acquired from France would be difficult to govern. London officials had no experience managing such vast area, particularly one inhabited by restive peoples: the remaining French settlers along the St. Lawrence and the many Indian communities. In October, the ministry issued the Proclamation of 1763, which designated the headwaters of rivers flowing into the Atlantic from the Appalachians as the temporary western boundary for colonial settlement (see Map 5.1). Its promulgators expected the proclamation to prevent clashes by forbidding colonists to move onto Indian lands until land cessions had been negotiated. But it infuriated two distinct groups of colonists: those who had already squatted west of the line (among them many Scots-Irish immigrants) and land speculation companies from Pennsylvania and Virginia.

Proclamation of 1763

Ohio Historical Society

▲ Benjamin West, the first well-known American artist, engraved this picture of a prisoner exchange at the end of Pontiac's Uprising, with Colonel Henry Bouquet supervising the return of settlers abducted during the war. In the foreground, a child resists leaving the Indian parents he had grown to love. Many colonists were fascinated by the phenomenon West depicted—the reluctance of captives to abandon their adoptive Indian families.

In the years after 1763, the latter groups (which included such men as George Washington, Thomas Jefferson, Patrick Henry, and Benjamin Franklin) lobbied vigorously to have their claims validated by colonial governments and London administrators. At a treaty conference in 1768 at Fort Stanwix, New York, they negotiated with Iroquois representatives to push the boundary line farther west and south, opening Kentucky to their speculations. The Iroquois, still claiming to speak for the Delawares and the Shawnees—who used Kentucky as their hunting grounds—agreed to the deal, which brought them valuable trade goods and did not affect their own territories. Yet even though the Virginia land companies eventually gained the support of the House of Burgesses for their claims, they never made any headway where it really mattered—in London—because administrators there realized that significant western expansion would require the expenditure of funds they did not have.

The hard-won victory in the Seven Years' War had cost Britain millions of pounds and created an immense war debt. The problem of paying it, and of finding the money to defend the newly acquired territories, bedeviled King George III, who in 1760 succeeded his grandfather, George II. The twenty-two-year-old monarch, an intelligent, passionate man with a mediocre education, was unfortunately an erratic judge of character. During the crucial years between 1763 and 1770, when the rift with the colonies grew ever wider and a series of political crises beset England, the king replaced ministries with bewildering rapidity. Although determined to assert the power of the monarchy, George III was immature and unsure of himself. He stubbornly regarded adherence to the status quo as the hallmark of patriotism.

George III

The man he selected as prime minister in 1763, George Grenville, believed the American colonies could be more tightly administered. Grenville confronted a financial crisis: England's burden of indebtedness had nearly doubled since 1754, from £73 million to £137 million. Annual expenditures before the war had amounted to no more than £8 million; now the yearly interest on the debt alone came to £5 million. Grenville's ministry had to find new sources of funds, and the British people themselves were already heavily taxed. Because the colonists had benefited greatly from wartime expenditures, Grenville concluded that Anglo-Americans should be asked to pay a larger share of the cost of running the empire.

Grenville did not question Great Britain's right to levy taxes on the colonies. Like all his countrymen, he believed that government's legitimacy derived ultimately from the consent of the people, but he defined consent differently than the colonists.

Theories of Representation

Americans had come to believe that they could be represented only by men who lived nearby and for whom they or their property-holding neighbors actually voted; otherwise, they could not count on legislators to represent their interests properly. Grenville and his English contemporaries, however, believed that Parliament—king, lords, and commons acting together—by definition represented all British subjects, wherever they resided (even overseas) and whether or not they could vote.

Parliament saw itself as collectively representing the entire nation; the particular constituency that chose a member of the House of Commons had no special claim on that member's vote, nor did the member have to live near his constituents. According to this theory, called *virtual representation*, all Britons—including colonists—were represented in Parliament. Thus, their consent to acts of Parliament could be presumed. In the colonies, by contrast, members of the lower houses of the assemblies were viewed as specifically representing the regions that had elected them. Before Grenville proposed to tax the colonists, the two notions coexisted because no conflict exposed the central contradiction. But events of the 1760s revealed the incompatibility of the two definitions of representation.

The same events threw into sharp relief Americans' attitudes toward political power. The colonists had

Real Whigs

become accustomed to a central government that wielded limited authority over them, affecting their daily lives very little. Consequently, they believed a good government was one that largely left them alone, a view in keeping with the theories of a group of British writers known as the Real Whigs. Drawing on a tradition of dissenting thought that reached back to John Locke and even to the English Civil War, the Real Whigs stressed the dangers inherent in a powerful government, particularly one headed by a monarch. Some of them even favored republicanism, which proposed to eliminate monarchs altogether and rest political power more directly on the people. Real Whigs warned the people to guard constantly against government's attempts to encroach on their liberty and seize their property. Political power was always to be feared, wrote John Trenchard and Thomas Gordon in their essay series *Cato's Letters* (originally published in London in 1720–1723 and reprinted many times thereafter in the colonies). The people had to exercise perpetual vigilance to prevent rulers' attempts to corrupt and oppress them.

Britain's efforts to tighten the reins of government and to raise revenues from the colonies in the 1760s and early 1770s convinced many Americans that the Real Whigs' reasoning applied to their circumstances, especially because of the link between liberty and property rights. Excessive and unjust taxation, they believed, could destroy their freedoms. They eventually interpreted British measures in light of the Real Whigs' warnings and saw oppressive designs behind the actions of Grenville and his successors. Historians disagree over the extent to which those perceptions were correct, but by 1775 a large number of colonists believed they were. In the mid-1760s, however, colonial leaders did not immediately accuse Grenville of conspiring to oppress them. Rather, they questioned the wisdom of the laws he proposed.

Parliament passed the first such measures, the Sugar and Currency Acts, in 1764. The Sugar Act (also known

Sugar and Currency Acts

as the Revenue Act) revised existing customs regulations and laid new duties on some foreign imports into the colonies. Its key provisions, strongly advocated in London by influential Caribbean sugar planters, aimed at discouraging American rum distillers from smuggling French West Indian molasses. It also established a vice-admiralty court at Halifax, Nova Scotia, to adjudicate violations of the law. Although the Sugar Act appeared to resemble the Navigation Acts, which the colonies had long accepted as legitimate, it broke with tradition in being explicitly designed to raise revenue, not to channel American trade through Britain. The Currency Act effectively outlawed most colonial paper money because British merchants had long complained that Americans were paying their debts in inflated local currencies. Americans could accumulate little sterling because they imported more than they exported; colonists complained that the act deprived them of a useful medium of exchange.

The Sugar and Currency Acts were imposed on an economy already in the midst of depression. A business boom accompanied the Seven Years' War, but the brief spell of prosperity ended abruptly in 1760 when the war shifted overseas. Urban merchants found few buyers for imported goods, and the loss of the military's demand for foodstuffs hurt American farmers. The bottom dropped out of the European tobacco market, threatening the livelihood of Chesapeake planters. Sailors were thrown out of work, and artisans had few customers. In such circumstances, the prospect of increased import duties and inadequate supplies of currency aroused merchants' hostility.

Individual American essayists and incensed colonial governments protested the new policies. But lacking any precedent for a united campaign against acts of Parliament, Americans in 1764 took only hesitant and uncoordinated steps. Eight colonial legislatures sent separate petitions to Parliament requesting the Sugar Act's repeal. They argued that its commercial restrictions would hurt Britain as well as the colonies and that they had not consented to its passage. The protests had no effect. The law remained in force, and Grenville proceeded with another revenue plan.

The Stamp Act Crisis

The Stamp Act (1765), Grenville's most important proposal, was modeled on a law that had been in effect in Britain for almost a century. It touched nearly every colonist by requiring tax

Link to the Virginia Stamp Act resolutions.

stamps on most printed materials, but it placed the heaviest burden on merchants and other members of the colonial elite, who used printed matter more frequently than did ordinary folk. Anyone who purchased a newspaper or pamphlet, made a will, transferred land, bought dice or playing cards, applied for a liquor license, accepted a government appointment, or borrowed money would have to pay the tax, which was doubled for foreign-language newspapers. Never before had a revenue measure of such scope been proposed for the colonies. The act also required that tax stamps be purchased with scarce sterling coin. Violators would be tried by vice-admiralty courts, in which judges alone rendered decisions, leading Americans to fear the loss of their right to trial by jury. Finally, such a law would break decisively with the colonial tradition of self-imposed taxation.

The most important colonial pamphlet protesting the Sugar Act and the proposed Stamp Act was *The Rights of the British Colonies Asserted and Proved*, by James Otis Jr., a brilliant young Massachusetts attorney. Otis starkly exposed the dilemma that confounded the colonists for the next decade. How could they justify their opposition to certain acts of Parliament without questioning Parliament's authority over them? On the one hand, Otis asserted, Americans were "entitled to all the natural, essential, inherent, and inseparable rights" of Britons, including the right not to be taxed without their consent. "No man or body of men . . . can take [those rights] away," he declared. On the other hand, Otis admitted that, under the British system established after the Glorious Revolution, "the power of parliament is uncontrollable but by themselves, and we must obey . . . Let the parliament lay what burthens they please on us, we must, it is our duty to submit and patiently bear them, till they will be pleased to relieve us."

James Otis's *Rights of the British Colonies*

Otis's first contention, drawing on colonial notions of representation, implied that Parliament could not constitutionally tax the colonies because Americans were not represented in its ranks. Yet his second point both

acknowledged political reality and accepted the prevailing theory of British government: that Parliament was the sole, supreme authority in the empire. Even unconstitutional laws enacted by Parliament had to be obeyed until Parliament decided to repeal them.

To resolve the dilemma, Otis proposed colonial representation in Parliament, but his idea was never taken seriously on either side of the Atlantic. The British believed colonists were already virtually represented in Parliament, and Anglo-Americans knew that a handful of colonial delegates to London would easily be outvoted. Otis published his pamphlet before the Stamp Act was passed. When Americans first learned of the act's adoption in the spring of 1765, they reacted indecisively. Few colonists—even appointed government officials—publicly favored the law. But colonial petitions had already failed to prevent its adoption, and further lobbying appeared futile. Perhaps Otis was correct: the only course open to Americans was to pay the stamp tax, reluctantly but loyally. Acting on that assumption, colonial agents in London sought the appointment of their American friends as stamp distributors so that the law would at least be enforced equitably.

Not all the colonists resigned themselves to paying the new tax. A twenty-nine-year-old lawyer serving his first term in the Virginia House of Burgesses was appalled by his fellow legislators' complacency. Patrick Henry later recalled that he was "young, inexperienced, unacquainted with the forms of the house and the members that composed it"—but he decided to act. "Alone, unadvised, and unassisted, on a blank leaf of an old law book," he wrote the Virginia Stamp Act Resolves.

Patrick Henry and the Virginia Stamp Act Resolves

Little in Henry's earlier life foreshadowed his success in the political arena that he entered so dramatically. The son of a prosperous Scots immigrant to western Virginia, Henry had little formal education. After marrying at eighteen, he failed at both farming and storekeeping before turning to the law as a means of supporting his wife and their six children. Henry lacked legal training, but his oratorical skills made him an effective advocate, first for his clients and later for his political beliefs. A prominent Virginia lawyer observed, "He is by far the most powerful speaker I ever heard. Every word he says not only engages, but commands the attention."

Patrick Henry introduced his seven proposals near the end of the legislative session, when many burgesses had already departed for home. Henry's fiery speech led the Speaker of the House to accuse him of treason, which Henry denied. The few burgesses remaining in Williamsburg adopted five of Henry's resolutions by a bare majority. Although they repealed the most radical of the five the next day, their action had far-reaching effects.

© Massachusetts Historical Society, Boston, MA, USA / The Bridgeman Art Library

▲ A selection of British tax stamps, ca. 1765, shows what the American colonists were protesting. Stamps for different purposes would have had different values, but even the least expensive would have significantly raised the cost of printed materials in North America.

Some colonial newspapers printed Henry's seven original resolutions as if they had been uniformly passed by the House, even though one was rescinded and two others were never debated or voted on at all.

The four propositions adopted by the burgesses repeated Otis's arguments, asserting that colonists had never forfeited the rights of British subjects, among which was consent to taxation. The other three resolutions went much further. The repealed resolution claimed for the burgesses "the only exclusive right" to tax Virginians, and the final two (those never considered) asserted that Virginians need not obey tax laws passed by other legislative bodies (namely, Parliament), terming any opponent of that opinion "an Enemy to this his Majesty's Colony."

The burgesses' decision to accept only the first four of Henry's resolutions anticipated the position most Americans would adopt throughout the following decade. Though willing to contend for their rights, the colonists did not seek independence.

Continuing Loyalty to Britain

The Maryland lawyer Daniel Dulany, whose *Considerations on the Propriety of Imposing Taxes on the British Colonies* was the most widely read pamphlet of 1765, expressed the consensus: "The colonies are dependent upon Great Britain, and the supreme authority vested in the king, lords, and commons, may justly be exercised to secure, or preserve their dependence." But, warned Dulany, a superior did not have the right "to seize the property of his inferior when he pleases"; there was a crucial distinction between a condition of "dependence and inferiority" and one of "absolute vassalage and slavery."

Over the next ten years, America's political leaders searched for a formula that would enable them to control their internal affairs, especially taxation, but remain under British rule. The chief difficulty lay in British officials' inability to compromise on the issue of parliamentary power. The notion that Parliament could exercise absolute authority over all colonial possessions inhered in the British theory of government. Even the harshest British critics of the ministries of the 1760s and 1770s questioned only the wisdom of specific policies, not the principles on which they rested. In effect, the Americans wanted British leaders to revise their fundamental understanding of the workings of their government. That was simply too much to expect.

◀ In 1795 the artist Lawrence Sully painted the only known life portrait of Patrick Henry. The old man's fierce gaze reflects the same intensity that marked his actions thirty years earlier, when he introduced the Virginia Stamp Act Resolves in the House of Burgesses.

Mead Art Museum, Amherst College, Amherst, Massachusetts, Bequest of Herbert L. Pratt (Class of 1895) AC 1945.115

The ultimate effectiveness of Americans' opposition to the Stamp Act rested on more than ideological arguments over parliamentary power. The decisive and inventive actions of some colonists during the late summer and fall of 1765 gave the resistance its primary force.

In August, the Loyal Nine, a Boston artisans' social club, organized a demonstration against the Stamp Act. Hoping to show that people of all ranks opposed the act, they approached the leaders of the city's rival laborers' associations, based in Boston's North End and South End neighborhoods. The two groups, composed of unskilled workers and poor tradesmen, often battled each other, but the Loyal Nine convinced them to lay aside their differences to participate in the demonstration. All colonists, not just affluent ones, would have to pay the stamp taxes.

Anti–Stamp Act Demonstrations

Early on August 14, the demonstrators hung an effigy of Andrew Oliver, the province's stamp distributor, from a tree on Boston Common. That night a large crowd led by a group of about fifty well-dressed tradesmen paraded the effigy around the city. The crowd built a bonfire near Oliver's house and added the effigy to the flames. Demonstrators broke most of Oliver's windows and threw stones at officials who tried to disperse them. In the midst of the melee, the North End and South End leaders drank a toast to their successful union. The Loyal Nine achieved success when Oliver publicly promised not to fulfill the duties of his office. One Bostonian jubilantly wrote to a relative, "I believe people never was more Universally pleased not so much one could I hear say he was sorry, but a smile sat on almost every ones countinance."

But another crowd action twelve days later, aimed this time at Oliver's brother-in-law, Lieutenant Governor Thomas Hutchinson, drew no praise from Boston's respectable citizens. On the night of August 26, a mob reportedly led by the South End leader Ebenezer MacIntosh attacked

Link to Hutchinson's account of the destruction of his house.

the homes of several customs officers. The crowd then destroyed Hutchinson's elaborately furnished townhouse in one of Boston's most fashionable districts. The lieutenant governor reported that by the next morning "one of the best finished houses in the Province had nothing remaining but the bare walls and floors." His trees and garden were ruined, his valuable library lost, and the mob "emptied the house of every thing whatsoever except a part of the kitchen furniture." But Hutchinson took some comfort in the fact that "the encouragers of the first mob never intended matters should go this length and the people in general express the utmost detestation of this unparalleled outrage."

The differences between the two Boston mobs of August 1765 exposed divisions that would continue to

Americans' Divergent Interests

characterize subsequent colonial protests. Few colonists sided with Britain during the 1760s, but various colonial groups had divergent goals. The skilled craftsmen who composed the Loyal Nine and merchants, lawyers, and other members of the educated elite preferred orderly demonstrations confined to political issues. For the city's laborers, by contrast, economic grievances may have been paramount. Certainly, their "hellish Fury" as they wrecked Hutchinson's house suggests resentment against his ostentatious display of wealth.

Colonists, like Britons, had a long tradition of crowd action in which disfranchised people took to the streets to redress deeply felt local grievances. But the Stamp Act controversy for the first time drew ordinary urban folk into transatlantic politics, including recent non-English-speaking immigrants targeted by the double taxation of foreign-language newspapers. Matters that previously had been of concern only to the gentry or to members of colonial legislatures were now discussed on every street corner and in every tavern. Benjamin Franklin's daughter observed as much when she informed her father, then serving as a colonial agent in London, that "nothing else is talked of, the Dutch [Germans] talk of the stompt act the Negroes of the tamp, in short every body has something to say."

The entry of unskilled workers, slaves, and women into the realm of imperial politics both threatened and aided the elite men who wanted to mount effective opposition to British measures. On the one hand, crowd action could have a stunning impact. Anti–Stamp Act demonstrations occurred in cities and towns stretching from Halifax in the north to the Caribbean island of Antigua in the south (see Map 5.3). They were so successful that, by November 1, when the law was scheduled to take effect, not one stamp distributor was

willing to carry out his duties. Thus, the act could not be enforced. On the other hand, wealthy men recognized that mobs composed of the formerly powerless—whose goals were not always identical to theirs (as the Boston experience showed)—could endanger their own dominance of the society. What would happen, they wondered, if the "hellish Fury" of the crowd turned against them?

They therefore attempted to channel resistance into acceptable forms by creating an intercolonial association,

Sons of Liberty

the Sons of Liberty. New Yorkers organized the first such group in early November, and branches spread rapidly through the coastal cities. Composed of merchants, lawyers, and prosperous tradesmen, the Sons of Liberty by early 1766 linked protest leaders from Charleston, South Carolina, to Portsmouth, New Hampshire. Not surprisingly, in light of the central role of taverns as settings for the exchange of news and opinions, a considerable number of members were tavern owners.

The Sons of Liberty could influence events but not control them. In Charleston (formerly Charles Town) in October 1765, a crowd shouting, "Liberty Liberty and stamp'd paper" forced the resignation of the South Carolina stamp distributor. The victory celebration a few days later—the largest demonstration the city had ever known—featured a British flag with the word "Liberty" emblazoned on it. But the new Charleston chapter of the Sons of Liberty was horrified when in January 1766 local slaves paraded through the streets similarly crying, "Liberty!" Freedom from slavery was not the sort of liberty elite slaveowners had in mind. In Virginia, plantation owners likewise expressed concern about the possibility that their slaves might make common cause with the Indian nations that had recently raided their frontiers.

In Philadelphia, too, resistance leaders were dismayed when an angry mob threatened to attack Benjamin Franklin's house. The city's laborers believed Franklin to be partly responsible for the Stamp Act because he had obtained the post of stamp distributor for a close friend. But Philadelphia's artisans—the backbone of the opposition movement there and elsewhere—were fiercely loyal to Franklin, one of their own who had made good. They gathered to protect his home and family from the crowd. The house was saved, but the resulting split between Philadelphia's better-off tradesmen and common laborers prevented the establishment of an alliance as successful as Boston's.

During the fall and winter of 1765–1766, opponents of the Stamp Act pursued several different strategies.

Opposition and Repeal

Colonial legislatures petitioned Parliament to repeal the hated law, and courts closed because they could not

Map 5.3 Sites of Major Demonstrations Against the Stamp Act

Every place named on these maps was the site of a demonstration against the Stamp Act of 1765; British colonies outside the eventual United States joined in the nearly universal opposition to the hated measure.

Source: Copyright © Cengage Learning

obtain the stamps now required for all legal documents. In October, nine colonies sent delegates to a general congress, the first since 1754. The Stamp Act Congress met in New York to draft a protest that stressed the law's adverse economic effects. At the same time, the Sons of Liberty held mass meetings, attempting to rally public support for the resistance movement. Finally, American merchants organized nonimportation associations to pressure British exporters. By the 1760s, one-quarter of all British exports went to the colonies, and American merchants reasoned that London merchants whose sales suffered severely would lobby for repeal. Because times were bad and American merchants were finding few customers for imported goods anyway, a general moratorium on future purchases would also help to reduce their bloated inventories.

In March 1766, Parliament repealed the Stamp Act. The nonimportation agreements had had the anticipated effect, creating allies for the colonies among wealthy London merchants. But boycotts, formal protests, and crowd actions were less important in winning repeal than was the appointment of a new prime minister, chosen by George III for reasons unrelated to colonial politics. Lord Rockingham, who replaced Grenville in the summer of 1765, had opposed the Stamp Act, not because he believed Parliament lacked power to tax the colonies, but because he thought the law unwise and divisive. Thus, although Rockingham proposed repeal, he linked it to passage of a Declaratory Act, which asserted Parliament's authority to tax and legislate for Britain's American possessions "in all cases whatsoever."

▲ In August 1766, after William Pitt became prime minister, a British artist depicted "The Triumph of America" as an impending disaster. America (an Indian) rides in a carriage driven by Pitt, heading directly for a chasm into which Britannia has already fallen. The six horses represent the members of Pitt's new ministry.

News of the repeal arrived in Newport, Rhode Island, in May, and the Sons of Liberty quickly dispatched messengers to carry the welcome tidings throughout the colonies. They organized celebrations commemorating the glorious event and Americans' loyalty to Britain. Their goal achieved, the Sons of Liberty dissolved. Few colonists saw the ominous implications of the Declaratory Act.

Resistance to the Townshend Acts

The colonists had accomplished their immediate aim, but the long-term prospects were unclear. In the summer of 1766, another change in the ministry in London revealed how fragile their victory had been. The new prime minister, William Pitt, had fostered cooperation between the colonies and Britain during the Seven Years' War. But Pitt fell ill, and another man, Charles Townshend, became the dominant force in the ministry. An ally of Grenville and a supporter of colonial taxation, Townshend decided to renew the attempt to obtain additional funds from Britain's American possessions (see Table 5.2).

The duties Townshend proposed in 1767 were to be levied on trade goods like paper, glass, and tea; thus they seemed to extend the existing Navigation Acts. But the Townshend duties differed from previous customs levies in two ways. First, they applied to items imported into the colonies from Britain, not to those from foreign countries. Accordingly, they violated mercantilist theory. Second, the revenues would be used to pay some colonial officials. Assemblies would no longer be able to threaten to withhold salaries in order to win those officials' cooperation. Additionally, Townshend's scheme established an American Board of Customs Commissioners and vice-admiralty courts at Boston, Philadelphia, and Charleston. Both moves angered merchants, whose profits would be threatened by more vigorous enforcement of the Navigation Acts.

In 1765, months passed before the colonists protested the Stamp Act. The passage of the Townshend Acts, however, drew a quick response. One series of essays in particular, *Letters from a Farmer in Pennsylvania*, by the prominent lawyer John Dickinson, expressed a broad consensus. Eventually, all but four colonial newspapers printed Dickinson's essays;

John Dickinson's Farmer's Letters

Table 5.2 British Ministries and Their American Policies

Head of Ministry	Major Acts
George Grenville	Sugar Act (1764)
	Currency Act (1764)
	Stamp Act (1765)
Lord Rockingham	Stamp Act repealed (1766)
	Declaratory Act (1766)
William Pitt/ Charles Townshend	Townshend Acts (1767)
Lord North	Townshend duties (except for the tea tax) repealed (1770)
	Tea Act (1773)
	Coercive Acts (1774)
	Quebec Act (1774)

in pamphlet form, they went through seven American editions. Dickinson contended that Parliament could regulate colonial trade but could not exercise that power to raise revenue. By distinguishing between trade regulation and unacceptable commercial taxation, Dickinson avoided the sticky issues of consent and the colonies' relationship to Parliament. But his argument created a different, and equally knotty, problem. In effect, it obligated the colonies to assess Parliament's motives in passing any law pertaining to trade before deciding whether to obey it. That was unworkable in the long run.

The Massachusetts assembly responded to the Townshend Acts by drafting a letter to the other colonial legislatures, suggesting a joint protest petition. Not the letter itself but the ministry's reaction to it united the colonies. When Lord Hillsborough, recently named to the new post of secretary of state for America, learned of the Massachusetts circular letter, he ordered the colony's Governor Francis Bernard to insist that the assembly recall it. He also directed other governors to prevent their assemblies from discussing the letter. Hillsborough's order gave colonial assemblies an incentive to join forces to oppose this new threat to their prerogatives. In late 1768, the Massachusetts legislature met, debated, and resoundingly rejected recall by a vote of 92 to 17. Bernard immediately dissolved the assembly, and other governors followed suit when their legislatures debated the circular letter.

The number of votes cast against recalling the circular letter—92—assumed ritual significance for the supporters of resistance. The number 45 already had symbolic meaning because John Wilkes, a radical Londoner sympathetic

Rituals of Resistance

to the American cause, had been jailed for publishing an essay entitled *The North Briton*, No. 45. In Boston, the silversmith Paul Revere made a punchbowl weighing 45 ounces that held 45 gills (half-cups) and was engraved with the names of opposition legislators; James Otis, John Adams, and others publicly drank 45 toasts from it. In Charleston, the city's tradesmen decorated a tree with 45 lights and set off 45 rockets. Carrying 45 candles, they adjourned to a tavern where 45 tables were set with 45 bowls of wine, 45 bowls of punch, and 92 glasses.

Such public rituals served important unifying and educational functions. Just as the pamphlets by Otis, Dulany, Dickinson, and others acquainted literate colonists with the issues raised by British actions, so public rituals taught illiterate Americans about the reasons for resistance and familiarized them with the terms of the argument. When Boston's revived Sons of Liberty invited hundreds of city residents to dine with them each August 14 to commemorate the first Stamp Act demonstration, and the Charleston Sons of Liberty held their meetings in public, crowds gathered to watch and listen. Likewise, the public singing of songs supporting the American cause helped to spread the word. The participants in such events openly expressed their commitment to the cause of resistance and encouraged others to join them.

The Sons of Liberty and other American leaders made a deliberate effort to involve ordinary folk in the campaign against the Townshend duties. Most important, they urged colonists of all ranks and both sexes to sign agreements not to purchase or consume British products. The new consumerism that previously had linked colonists economically now linked them politically as well, supplying them with a ready method of displaying their allegiance. As "A Tradesman" wrote in a Philadelphia paper in 1770, it was essential "for the Good of the Whole, to strengthen the Hands of the Patriotic Majority, by agreeing not to purchase British Goods."

As the primary purchasers of textiles and household goods, women played a central role in the nonconsumption movement. More than

Daughters of Liberty

three hundred Boston matrons publicly promised not to buy or drink tea, "Sickness excepted." As Janet Schaw later noted, the women of Wilmington, North Carolina, burned their tea after walking through town in a solemn procession. Women throughout the colonies exchanged recipes for tea substitutes or drank coffee instead. The best known of the protests, the so-called Edenton Ladies Tea Party, had little to do with tea. It was a meeting of prominent North Carolina women who pledged formally to work for the public good and to support resistance to British measures. (See the satirical cartoon on page 114.)

Visualizing THE PAST

The Revolutionary Symbolism of Female Spinners

By the 1760s, middling and well-to-do urban colonists purchased fabric and ordered clothing from tailors and dressmakers. Only the poorer residents of rural America continued to spin wool or flax into yarn, then wove that yarn into cloth and made their own wearing apparel. Urban dwellers, accustomed for decades to following the latest English fashions, had long looked down on rustics who wore homespun—and yet the ability to spin was still seen as a quintessentially feminine occupation, with many young girls being taught that skill. One wealthy Philadelphia poet wrote that working at her wheel reminded her of "a train of Female Hands / Chearful uniting in Industrious Bands." And so when colonists joined to boycott British goods, one of the key ways in which women could publicize their support for American resistance was to bring their wheels to a public location. What message does the poem convey about the spinners' aims and impact? What was the importance of women undertaking in public a task usually performed in their own homes, if at all?

A Boston poet in 1769 produced this broadside verse to praise spinners who had gathered in the North End of the city.

An eighteenth-century American flax wheel of the sort that would have been used in a public spinning demonstration. Wheels for spinning wool were too large to move easily.

Massachusetts Historical Society/Bridgeman Art Library Ltd.

National Museum of American History, Smithsonian Institution, Behring Center

Women also encouraged home manufacturing. In many towns, young women calling themselves Daughters of Liberty met to spin in public squares to try to persuade other women to make homespun and to encourage colonists to wear homespun clothing, thereby ending the colonies' dependence on British cloth. These symbolic displays of patriotism—publicized by newspapers and broadsides—served the same purpose as the male rituals involving the numbers 45 and 92. When young ladies from well-to-do families sat outdoors at spinning wheels all day, eating only American food, drinking local herbal tea, and listening to patriotic sermons, they served as political instructors. Many women took great satisfaction in their newfound role. When a satirist hinted that women discussed only "such triffling subjects as Dress, Scandal and Detraction" during their spinning bees, three Boston women replied angrily, "Inferior in abusive sarcasm, in personal invective, in low wit, we glory to be, but inferior in veracity, sincerity, love of virtue, of liberty and of our country, we would not willingly be to any."

But the colonists were by no means united in support of nonimportation and nonconsumption. If the Stamp Act protests had occasionally (as in Boston and Philadelphia) revealed a division between artisans and merchants on the one side and common laborers on the other, resistance to the Townshend Acts exposed new splits in American ranks. The most significant—which arose from a change in economic circumstances—divided urban artisans and merchants, allies in 1765.

Divided Opinion over Boycotts

The Stamp Act boycotts had helped to revive a depressed economy by creating a demand for local products and reducing merchants' inventories. But in 1768 and 1769, merchants were enjoying boom times and had no financial incentive to support a boycott. Consequently, merchants signed the agreements reluctantly and sometimes secretly violated them. In contrast, artisans supported nonimportation enthusiastically, recognizing that the absence of British goods would create a ready market for their own manufactures. Thus, tradesmen formed the core of the crowds that coerced both importers and their customers by picketing stores, publicizing offenders' names, and sometimes destroying property.

Such tactics were effective: colonial imports from England dropped dramatically in 1769, especially in New York, New England, and Pennsylvania. But the tactics also aroused heated opposition, dividing opinion in another way. Some Americans who supported resistance to British measures began to question the use of violence to force others to join the boycott. In addition, the threat to private property inherent in the campaign frightened wealthier and more conservative men and women. Political activism by ordinary colonists challenged the ruling elite's domination, just as its members had feared in 1765.

Disclosures that leading merchants had violated the nonimportation agreement caused dissension in the ranks of the boycotters, so Americans were relieved when news arrived in April 1770 that the Townshend duties had been repealed, with the exception of the tea tax. A new prime minister, Lord North, persuaded Parliament that duties on trade within the empire were ill-advised. Although some colonial leaders argued that nonimportation should continue until the tea tax was repealed, merchants quickly resumed importing. The other Townshend Acts remained in force, but repealing the duties made the provisions for paying officials' salaries and tightening customs enforcement appear less objectionable.

Confrontations in Boston

Initially, the new ministry did nothing to antagonize the colonists. Yet on the very day Lord North proposed repeal of the Townshend duties, a confrontation between civilians and soldiers in Boston led to five Americans' deaths. The origins of the event that patriots called the Boston Massacre lay in repeated clashes between customs officers and the people of Massachusetts. The decision to base the American Board of Customs Commissioners in Boston ultimately caused the confrontation.

Mobs targeted the customs commissioners from the day they arrived in November 1767. In June 1768, their seizure of the patriot leader John Hancock's sloop *Liberty* on suspicion of smuggling caused a riot in which customs officers' property was destroyed. The riot in turn helped to convince the ministry that troops were needed to maintain order in the unruly port. The assignment of two regiments of regulars to their city confirmed Bostonians' worst fears; the redcoats constantly reminded city dwellers of the oppressive potential of British power. Guards on Boston Neck, the entrance to the city, checked all travelers and their goods. Redcoat patrols roamed the city day and night, questioning and sometimes harassing passersby. Military parades on Boston Common were accompanied by martial music and often the public whipping of deserters and other violators of army rules. Parents began to fear for the safety of their daughters, who were subjected to soldiers' coarse sexual insults. But the greatest potential for violence lay in the uneasy relationship between the soldiers and Boston laborers. Many redcoats sought employment in their off-duty hours, competing for unskilled jobs with the city's workingmen. Members of the two groups brawled repeatedly in taverns and on the streets.

Early on the evening of March 5, 1770, a crowd of laborers began throwing hard-packed snowballs at soldiers guarding the Customs House. Goaded beyond endurance, the sentries acted against express orders and

Boston Massacre

fired on the crowd, killing four and wounding eight, one of whom died a few days later. Reportedly, the first to die was Crispus Attucks, a sailor of mixed Nipmuck and African origins. Resistance leaders idealized Attucks and the other dead rioters as martyrs for the cause of liberty, holding a solemn funeral and later commemorating March 5 annually with patriotic orations. Paul Revere's engraving of the massacre was part of the propaganda campaign.

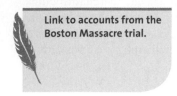

Link to accounts from the Boston Massacre trial.

Leading patriots wanted to ensure that the soldiers did not become martyrs as well. Despite the political benefits the patriots derived from the massacre, they probably did not approve of the crowd action that provoked it. Ever since the destruction of Hutchinson's house in August 1765, men allied with the Sons of Liberty had supported orderly demonstrations and expressed distaste at such uncontrolled riots as the one that provoked the Boston Massacre. Thus, when the soldiers were tried for the killings in November, John Adams and Josiah Quincy Jr., both unwavering patriots, acted as their defense attorneys. Almost all the accused were acquitted, and the two men convicted were released after being branded on the thumb. Undoubtedly, the favorable outcome of the trials persuaded London officials not to retaliate against the city.

For more than two years after the Boston Massacre and the repeal of the Townshend duties, a superficial calm descended on the colonies. In June 1772, Rhode Islanders, angry with overzealous customs enforcement by the British naval schooner *Gaspée*, attacked and burned it as it lay aground at low tide in Narragansett Bay near Providence, but because a subsequent investigation failed to identify the perpetrators, no adverse consequences followed for the colonists. The most outspoken newspapers, such as the

A British Plot?

▲ Shortly after the Boston Massacre, Paul Revere printed this illustration of the confrontation near the customs house on March 5, 1770. Offering visual support for the patriots' version of events, it showed the British soldiers firing on an unresisting crowd (instead of the aggressive mob described at the soldiers' trial) and—even worse—a gun firing from the building itself, which has been labeled "Butchers Hall."

Courtesy of the John Carter Brown Library at Brown University

Boston Gazette, the *Pennsylvania Journal*, and the *South Carolina Gazette*, published essays drawing on Real Whig ideology and accusing Great Britain of deliberately scheming to oppress the colonies. After the Stamp Act's repeal, the protest leaders had praised Parliament; following repeal of the Townshend duties, they warned of impending tyranny. What had seemed to be an isolated mistake, a single ill-chosen stamp tax, now appeared to be part of a plot against American liberties. Essayists pointed to Parliament's persecution of the British radical John Wilkes, the stationing of troops in Boston, and the growing number of vice-admiralty courts as evidence of plans to enslave the colonists. Indeed, patriot writers played repeatedly on the word *enslavement*. Most free colonists had direct knowledge of slavery (either as slaveholders themselves or as neighbors of slaveowners), and the threat of enslavement by Britain must have hit them with peculiar force.

Still, no one yet advocated independence from the mother country. Although some colonists were becoming increasingly convinced that they should seek freedom from parliamentary authority, they continued to acknowledge their British identity and allegiance to George III. They began, therefore, to envision a system that would enable them to be ruled by their own elected legislatures while remaining subordinate to the king. But any such scheme violated Britons' conception of the nature of their government, which posited that Parliament wielded sole, undivided sovereignty over the empire. Furthermore, in the British mind, Parliament encompassed the king as well as lords and commons, so separating the monarch from the legislature was impossible.

Then, in the fall of 1772, the North ministry began to implement the Townshend Act that provided for governors and judges to be paid from customs revenues. In early November, voters at a Boston town meeting established a Committee of Correspondence to publicize the decision by exchanging letters with other Massachusetts towns. Heading the committee was Samuel Adams, who had proposed its formation.

Fifty-one in 1772, Samuel Adams was about a decade older than the other leaders of American resistance, including his distant cousin John. He had been a Boston tax collector, a member and clerk of the Massachusetts assembly, an ally of the Loyal Nine, and one of the Sons of Liberty. Unswerving in his devotion to the American cause, Adams drew a sharp contrast between a corrupt, vice-ridden Britain and the colonies, peopled by simple, liberty-loving folk. An experienced political organizer, Adams continually stressed the necessity of prudent collective action in speeches in the Boston town meeting. His Committee of Correspondence thus undertook the task of creating an informed consensus among the residents of Massachusetts.

Samuel Adams and Committees of Correspondence

Such committees, which were eventually established throughout the colonies, represented the next logical step in the organization of American resistance. Until 1772, the protest movement was confined largely to the seacoast and primarily to major cities and towns (see Map 5.3). Adams realized the time had come to widen the movement's geographic scope, to attempt to involve more colonists in the struggle. Accordingly, the Boston town meeting directed the Committee of Correspondence "to state the Rights of the Colonists and of this Province in particular"; to list "the Infringements and Violations thereof that have been, or from time to time may be made"; and to send copies to the other towns in the province. In return, Boston requested "a free communication of their Sentiments on this Subject."

The statement of colonial rights prepared by the Bostonians declared that Americans had absolute rights to life, liberty, and property. The idea that "a British house of commons, should have a right, at pleasure, to give and grant the property of the colonists" was "irreconcileable" with "the first principles of natural law and Justice . . . and of the British Constitution in particular." The list of grievances complained of taxation without representation, the presence of unnecessary troops and customs officers on American soil, the use of imperial revenues to pay colonial officials, the expanded jurisdiction of vice-admiralty courts, and even the nature of the instructions given to American governors by their superiors in London.

The entire document, which was printed as a pamphlet for distribution to the towns, exhibited none of the hesitation that had characterized colonial claims against Parliament in the 1760s. No longer were resistance leaders—at least in Boston—preoccupied with defining the precise limits of parliamentary authority. No longer did they mention the necessity of obedience to Parliament. They were committed to a course that placed American rights first, loyalty to Great Britain a distant second.

The response of the Massachusetts towns to the committee's pamphlet must have caused Samuel Adams to rejoice. Some towns disagreed with Boston's assessment of the state of affairs, but most aligned themselves with the city. From Braintree came the assertion that "all civil officers are or ought to be Servants to the people and dependent upon them for their official Support, and every instance to the Contrary from the Governor downwards tends to crush and destroy civil liberty." The town of Holden declared that "the People of New England have never given the People of Britain any Right of Jurisdiction over us." The citizens of Petersham commented that resistance to tyranny was "the first and highest social Duty of this people." And Pownallborough warned, "Allegiance is a relative Term and like Kingdoms and commonwealths is local and has its bounds." Beliefs like these made the next crisis in Anglo-American affairs the last.

Tea and Turmoil

The tea tax was the only Townshend duty still in effect by 1773. In the years after 1770, some Americans continued to boycott English tea, while others resumed drinking it either openly or in secret. Tea figured prominently in both the colonists' diet and their social lives, so observing the boycott required them not only to forgo a favorite beverage but also to alter habitual forms of socializing. Tea thus retained an explosively symbolic character even though the boycott began to disintegrate after 1770.

In May 1773, Parliament passed an act designed to save the East India Company from bankruptcy. The company, which held a monopoly on British trade with the East Indies, was critically important to the British economy and to the financial well-being of many prominent British politicians who had invested in its stock. According to the Tea Act, legal tea would henceforth be sold in America only by the East India Company's designated agents, which would enable the company to avoid intermediaries in both Britain and the colonies, and to price its tea competitively with that offered by smugglers. The net result would be cheaper tea for American consumers. Resistance leaders, however, interpreted the new measure as a pernicious device to make them admit Parliament's right to tax them, for the

Reactions to the Tea Act

less expensive tea would still be taxed under the Townshend law. Others saw the Tea Act as the first step in the establishment of an East India Company monopoly on all colonial trade. Residents of the four cities designated to receive the first shipments of tea accordingly prepared to respond to what they perceived as a new threat to their freedom.

In New York City, tea ships never arrived. In Philadelphia, Pennsylvania's governor persuaded the captain to sail back to Britain. In Charleston, the tea was unloaded and stored; some was destroyed, the rest sold in 1776 by the new state government. The only confrontation occurred in Boston, where both sides—the town meeting, including participants from nearby towns, and Governor Thomas Hutchinson, two of whose sons were tea agents—rejected compromise.

The first of three tea ships, the *Dartmouth*, entered Boston harbor on November 28. The customs laws required cargo to be landed and the appropriate duty paid by its owners within twenty days of a ship's arrival; otherwise, the cargo would be seized by customs officers and sold at auction. After a series of mass meetings, Bostonians voted to post guards on the wharf to prevent the tea from being unloaded. Hutchinson refused to permit the vessels to leave the harbor.

On December 16, one day before the cargo would have been confiscated, more than five thousand people (nearly a third of the city's population) crowded into Old South Church. The meeting, chaired by Samuel

Courtesy, American Antiquarian Society

▲ The planners of the Boston Tea Party met here, at the Green Dragon Tavern, sketched later by one of their number, the portrait painter John Johnson.

Adams, made a final attempt to convince Hutchinson to send the tea back to England. But the governor remained adamant. In the early evening Adams reportedly announced "that he could think of nothing further to be done—that they had now done all they could for the Salvation of their Country." Cries then rang out from the back of the crowd: "Boston harbor a tea-pot tonight! The Mohawks are come!" Small groups pushed their way out of the meeting. Within a few minutes, about sixty men crudely disguised as Indians assembled at the wharf, boarded the three ships, and dumped the cargo into the harbor. By 9 P.M., their work was done: 342 chests of tea worth approximately £10,000 floated in splinters on the water.

Among the "Indians" were many representatives of Boston's artisans, including the silversmith Paul Revere. Five masons, eleven carpenters and builders, three leatherworkers, a blacksmith, two barbers, a coachmaker, a shoemaker, and twelve apprentices have been identified as participants. That their ranks also included four farmers from outside Boston, ten merchants, two doctors, a teacher, and a bookseller illustrated the widespread support for the resistance movement. The next day John Adams exulted in his diary that the protest was "so bold, so daring, so firm, intrepid and inflexible" that "I can't but consider it as an Epocha in history."

The North administration reacted with considerably less enthusiasm when it learned of the events in Boston. In

Coercive and Quebec Acts

March 1774, Parliament adopted the first of four laws that became known as the Coercive, or Intolerable, Acts. It ordered the port of Boston closed until the tea was paid for, prohibiting all but coastal trade in food and firewood. Later in the spring, Parliament passed three other punitive measures. The Massachusetts Government Act altered the province's charter, substituting an appointed council for the elected one, increasing the governor's powers, and forbidding most town meetings. The Justice Act provided that a person accused of committing murder in the course of suppressing a riot or enforcing the laws could be tried outside the colony where the incident had occurred. Finally, the Quartering Act allowed military officers to commandeer privately owned buildings

Legacy FOR A PEOPLE AND A NATION

Women's Political Activism

In the twenty-first century, female citizens of the United States participate at every level of American public life. In 1984, Geraldine Ferraro was the Democratic candidate for vice president; Nancy Pelosi was elected Speaker of the House, third in line for the presidency, in January 2007; Hillary Rodham Clinton ran for president in 2008; and Sonia Sotomayor joined the Supreme Court as its second current female member in 2009. Nearly one hundred women sit in the House and Senate; many serve as governors and in other state offices. But before the 1760s, American women as a group were seen as having no appropriate public role. A male essayist expressed the consensus in the mid-1730s: "Poli[ti]cks is what does not become them; the Governing Kingdoms and Ruling Provinces are Things too difficult and knotty for the fair Sex, it will render them grave and serious, and take off those agreeable Smiles that should always accompany them."

But that changed when colonists began to resist the imposition of new British taxes and laws in the mid- to late 1760s. Supporters of American resistance, men and women alike, realized that traditional forms of protest (for example, assemblies' petitions to Parliament) were too limited.

Because women made purchasing decisions for American households, and because in the case of spinning and cloth manufacture their labor could replace imported clothing, it was vital for them to participate in the cause. For the first time in American history, women began to take formal political stands. Women of all ranks had to decide whether they would join or oppose the movement to boycott British goods. The groups they established to promote home manufactures—dubbed "Daughters of Liberty"—constituted the first American women's political organizations, tentative and informal though they were.

Since then, American women have taken part in many political movements, among them antislavery societies, pro- and anti-woman suffrage organizations, the Women's Christian Temperance Union, and the civil rights movement. The legacy of revolutionary-era women for the nation continues today in such groups as the National Women's Political Caucus and Concerned Women for America. Indeed, contemporary Americans would undoubtedly find it impossible to imagine their country without female activists of all political and partisan affiliations.

to house their troops. Thus, the Coercive Acts punished not only Boston but also Massachusetts as a whole, alerting other colonies to the possibility that their residents, too, could be subject to retaliation if they opposed British authority.

After passing the last of the Coercive Acts, Parliament turned its attention to much-needed reforms in the government of Quebec. The Quebec Act thereby became linked with the Coercive Acts in the minds of the patriots. Intended to ease strains that had arisen since the British conquest of the formerly French colony, the Quebec Act granted greater religious freedom to Catholics—alarming Protestant colonists, who equated Roman Catholicism with religious and political despotism. It also reinstated French civil law, which had been replaced by British procedures in 1763, and it established an appointed council (rather than an elected legislature) as the governing body of the colony. Finally, in an attempt to provide northern Indians with some protection against Anglo-American settlement, the act annexed to Quebec the area west of the Appalachians, east of the Mississippi River, and north of the Ohio River. That region, still with few European inhabitants, was thus removed from the jurisdiction of the seacoast colonies. The wealthy colonists who hoped to develop the Ohio country to attract additional settlers now faced the prospect of dealing with officials in Quebec.

Members of Parliament who voted for the punitive legislation believed at long last they had solved the problem posed by the troublesome Americans. But resistance leaders showed little inclination to bow to Parliament's authority. In their eyes, the Coercive Acts and the Quebec Act proved what they had feared since 1768: that Britain had embarked on a deliberate plan to oppress them. If the port of Boston could be closed, why not the ports of Philadelphia or New York? If the royal charter of Massachusetts could be changed, why not the charter of South Carolina? If certain people could be transferred to distant locations for trial, why not any violator of any law? If troops could be forcibly quartered in private houses, did that not portend the occupation of all America? If the Catholic Church could receive favored status in Quebec, why not everywhere? It seemed as though the full dimensions of the plot against American rights and liberties had at last been revealed.

The Boston Committee of Correspondence urged all colonies to join an immediate boycott of British goods. But other provinces hesitated to take such a drastic step. Rhode Island, Virginia, and Pennsylvania each suggested another intercolonial congress be convened to consider an appropriate response, and in mid-June 1774 Massachusetts acquiesced. Few people wanted to take hasty action; even the most ardent patriots remained loyal Britons and hoped for reconciliation. Despite their objections to British policy, they continued to see themselves as part of the empire. Americans were approaching the brink of confrontation, but they had not committed themselves to an irrevocable break. So the colonies agreed to send delegates to Philadelphia in September to attend a Continental Congress.

SUMMARY

Just twenty years earlier, at the outbreak of the Seven Years' War in the wilderness of western Pennsylvania, no one could have predicted the future would bring such swift and dramatic change to Britain's mainland colonies. Yet that conflict simultaneously removed France from North America and created a huge debt that Britain had to find means to pay, developments with major implications for the imperial relationship.

In the years after the war ended in 1763, momentous changes occurred in the ways colonists thought about themselves and their allegiances. The number of colonists who defined themselves as political actors increased substantially. Once linked unquestioningly to Great Britain, they began to develop a sense of their own identity as Americans, including a recognition of the cultural and social gulf that separated them from Britons. They started to realize that their concept of the political process differed from that held by people in the mother country. Most important, they held a different definition of what constituted representation and appropriate consent to government actions. They also came to understand that their economic interests did not necessarily coincide with those of Great Britain. Colonial political leaders reached such conclusions only after a long train of events, some of them violent, had altered their understanding of their relationship with the mother country. Parliamentary acts such as the Stamp Act and the Townshend Acts elicited colonial responses—both ideological and practical—that produced further responses from Britain. Tensions escalated until they climaxed when Bostonians destroyed the East India Company's tea.

In the late summer of 1774, Americans were committed to resistance but not to independence. Even so, they had started to sever the bonds of empire. During the next decade, they would forge the bonds of a new American nationality to replace those rejected Anglo-American ties.

SUGGESTIONS FOR FURTHER READING

Fred Anderson, *The War That Made America: A Short History of the French and Indian War* (2005)

Bernard Bailyn, *The Ideological Origins of the American Revolution* (1967)

T. H. Breen, *The Marketplace of Revolution: How Consumer Politics Shaped American Independence* (2004)

Benjamin L. Carp, *Rebels Rising: Cities and the American Revolution* (2007)

Gregory Dowd, *War Under Heaven: Pontiac, the Indian Nations, and the British Empire* (2002)

Marc Egnal, *A Mighty Empire: The Origins of the American Revolution* (1988)

Merrill Jensen, *The Founding of a Nation: A History of the American Revolution, 1763–1776* (1968)

Pauline R. Maier, *From Resistance to Revolution: Colonial Radicals and the Development of American Opposition to Britain, 1765–1776* (1972)

Gary B. Nash, *The Unknown American Revolution: The Unruly Birth of Democracy and the Struggle to Create America* (2005)

Peter Silver, *Our Savage Neighbors: How Indian War Transformed Early America* (2008)

CourseMate

Go to the CourseMate website for primary source links, study tools, and review materials for this chapter. www.cengagebrain.com

A Revolution, Indeed 1774–1783

Fall of statue of George III, Lafayette College Art Collection, Easton, PA (Detail)

The Shawnee chief Blackfish named his new captive Sheltowee, or Big Turtle, and adopted him as his son. Blackfish's warriors had easily caught the lone hunter, who was returning with a slaughtered buffalo to an encampment of men making salt at the briny spring known as Blue Licks. The captive then persuaded his fellow frontiersmen to surrender to the Shawnees (allies of the British) without a fight. It was February 1778. The hunter, Daniel Boone, had moved his family from North Carolina to Kentucky about three years before, just as the Revolutionary War began. Both his contemporaries and some historians have wondered about Boone's allegiances during the American Revolution. His encounter with the Shawnees in 1778, which can be interpreted in several ways, highlights many ambiguities of revolutionary-era loyalties.

The Shawnees were seeking captives to cover the death of their chief, Cornstalk, who had been killed several months earlier while a prisoner of American militiamen in the Ohio country. Of the twenty-six men taken at the spring, about half were adopted into Shawnee families; the others—less willing to conform to Indian ways—were dispatched as prisoners to the British fort at Detroit. Boone, who assured Blackfish that in the spring he would negotiate the surrender of the women and children remaining at his home settlement of Boonesborough, watched and waited, outwardly content with his new life. In June 1778, he escaped, hurrying home to warn the Kentuckians of an impending attack.

When Blackfish's Shawnees and their British allies appeared outside the Boonesborough stockade in mid-September, Boone proved amenable to negotiations. Although the settlers adamantly refused to move back across the mountains, fragmentary evidence suggests that they agreed to swear allegiance to the British in order to avert a bloody battle. But the discussions dissolved into a melee, with the Indians futilely besieging the fort for a week before withdrawing. With the threat gone, Boone was charged with treason and court-martialed by the Kentucky militia. Although he was cleared, questions about the incident at Blue Licks and its aftermath haunted him for the rest of his life.

◄ A statue of George III standing in the Bowling Green in New York City was one of the first casualties of the American Revolution, as colonists marked the adoption of the Declaration of Independence by pulling it down. Much of the metal was melted to make bullets, but in the twentieth century the head—largely intact—was unearthed in Connecticut.

Chronology

1774
- First Continental Congress meets in Philadelphia, adopts Declaration of Rights and Grievances
- Continental Association implements economic boycott of Britain; committees of observation established to oversee boycott

1774–75
- Provincial conventions replace collapsing colonial governments

1775
- Battles of Lexington and Concord; first shots of war fired
- Second Continental Congress begins
- Washington named commander-in-chief
- Dunmore's proclamation offers freedom to patriots' slaves who join British forces

1776
- Paine publishes *Common Sense,* advocating independence
- British evacuate Boston
- Declaration of Independence adopted
- New York City falls to British

1777
- British take Philadelphia
- Burgoyne surrenders at Saratoga

1778
- French alliance brings vital assistance to America
- British evacuate Philadelphia

1779
- Sullivan expedition destroys Iroquois villages

1780
- British take Charleston

1781
- Cornwallis surrenders at Yorktown

1782
- Peace negotiations begin

1783
- Treaty of Paris signed, granting independence to the United States

Where did Daniel Boone's loyalties lie? With the British? the Americans? other Kentuckians? His actions could be viewed in all three lights. Had he betrayed the settlers to Shawnees and sought to establish British authority in Kentucky? Had he—as he later claimed—twice deceived the Shawnees? Or had he rather made the survival of the fragile settlements his highest priority? Kentucky was a

borderland—a region where British, Indians, and various groups of American settlers all vied for control. Boone and other residents of the Appalachian backcountry did not always face clear-cut choices as they struggled to establish themselves securely under such precarious circumstances.

Daniel Boone was not the only American of uncertain or shifting allegiances in the 1770s. As a civil war that affected much of North America east of the Mississippi River, the American Revolution uprooted thousands of families, disrupted the economy, reshaped society by forcing many colonists into permanent exile, led Americans to develop new conceptions of politics, and created a nation from thirteen separate colonies. Much more than a series of clashes between the British and patriot armies, it marked a significant turning point in Americans' collective history.

The struggle for independence required revolutionary leaders to accomplish three separate but closely related tasks. The first was political and ideological: transforming a consensus favoring loyal resistance into a coalition supporting independence. Pursuing a variety of measures (ranging from persuasion to coercion) to enlist all European-Americans in the patriot cause, the colonies' elected leaders also tried to ensure the neutrality of Indians and slaves in the impending conflict.

The second task involved foreign relations. To win independence, patriot leaders knew they needed international recognition and aid, particularly from France. Thus they dispatched to Paris the most experienced American diplomat, Benjamin Franklin, who had served for years as a colonial agent in London. Franklin skillfully negotiated the Franco-American alliance of 1778, which was to prove crucial to winning independence.

Only the third task directly involved the British. George Washington, commander-in-chief of the American army, soon recognized that his primary goal should be not to win battles, but to avoid losing them decisively. The outcome of any one battle was less important than ensuring that his army survived to fight another day. Consequently, the story of the Revolutionary War reveals British action and American reaction, British attacks and American defenses and withdrawals. The American war effort was aided by British military planners' failure to analyze the problem confronting them accurately. Until it was too late, they treated the war against the colonists as they treated wars against other Europeans: they concentrated on winning battles and did not consider the difficulties of achieving their main goal, retaining the colonies' allegiance. In the end, the Americans' triumph owed more to their endurance and to Britain's mistakes than to their military prowess.

- What choices of allegiance confronted residents of North America after 1774? Why did people of various descriptions make the choices they did?

- What military strategies did the British and American forces adopt?

- How did the new nation win independence?

Government by Congress and Committee

When the fifty-five delegates to the First Continental Congress convened in Philadelphia in September 1774, they knew any measures they adopted were likely to enjoy widespread support. That summer, well-publicized open meetings held throughout the colonies had endorsed the idea of another nonimportation pact. Participants in many such meetings promised (like some North Carolina men) to "strictly adhere to, and abide by, such Regulations and Restrictions as the Members of the said General Congress shall agree to." Most of the congressional delegates were selected by extralegal provincial conventions whose members were chosen at local gatherings because governors had forbidden regular assemblies to conduct formal elections. Thus the very act of designating delegates to attend the Congress involved Americans in open defiance of British authority.

The colonies' leading political figures—most of them lawyers, merchants, and planters representing every colony but Georgia—attended the Philadelphia Congress.

First Continental Congress

The Massachusetts delegation included Samuel Adams, the experienced organizer of Boston resistance, and his younger cousin John, an ambitious lawyer. Among others, New York sent John Jay, a talented young attorney. From Pennsylvania came the conservative Joseph Galloway and his long-time rival, John Dickinson. Virginia elected Richard Henry Lee and Patrick Henry, both noted for their patriotic zeal, as well as George Washington. Most of these men had never met, but in the weeks, months, and years that followed they became the chief architects of the new nation.

The congressmen faced three tasks when they convened at Carpenters' Hall on September 5. The first two were explicit: defining American grievances and developing a plan for resistance. The third—articulating their constitutional relationship with Great Britain—was less clear-cut and proved troublesome. The most radical congressmen, like Lee of Virginia, argued that colonists owed allegiance only to George III and that Parliament had no legitimate authority over the colonies.

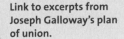

Link to excerpts from Joseph Galloway's plan of union.

The conservatives—Joseph Galloway and his allies—proposed a formal plan of union that would have required Parliament and a new American legislature to consent jointly to all laws pertaining to the colonies. After heated debate, delegates narrowly rejected Galloway's proposal, but they were not prepared to embrace the radicals' position either.

Finally, they accepted wording proposed by John Adams. The crucial clauses in the Congress's Declaration of Rights and Grievances declared that Americans would obey Parliament, but only voluntarily, and that they would resist all taxes in disguise, like the Townshend duties. Remarkably, such a position—which only a few years before would have been regarded as radical—represented a compromise in the fall of 1774. The Americans had come a long way since their first hesitant protests against the Sugar Act ten years earlier.

With the constitutional issue resolved, the delegates readily agreed on the laws they wanted repealed (notably the Coercive Acts) and decided to implement an economic boycott while petitioning the king for relief. They adopted the Continental Association, which called for nonimportation of British goods (effective December 1, 1774), nonconsumption of British products (effective March 1, 1775), and nonexportation of American goods to Britain and the British West Indies (effective September 10, 1775).

Continental Association

The provisions of the Association—far more comprehensive than any previous economic measure adopted by the colonies—were carefully designed to appeal to different groups and regions. For example, the inclusive language of the nonimportation agreement banned commerce in slaves as well as manufactures, which accorded with a long-standing desire of the Virginia gentry to halt, or at least to slow, the arrival of enslaved Africans on their shores. (Leading Virginians believed that continuing slave importations had discouraged the immigration to their colony of free Europeans with useful skills.) Delaying nonconsumption until three months after implementing nonimportation allowed northern urban merchants time to sell items they had acquired legally before December 1. And both the novel tactic of nonexportation and its postponement for nearly a year served other interests. In 1773, many Virginians had vowed to stop exporting tobacco, to raise prices in a then-glutted market. So they enthusiastically welcomed an Association that banned exportation while also permitting them to profit from higher prices for their 1774 crop, which needed to be dried and cured before shipment. Postponing the nonexportation agreement also benefited the northern exporters of wood and foodstuffs to the Caribbean, giving them a final season of sales before the embargo began.

To enforce the Continental Association, Congress recommended the election of committees of observation

Committees of Observation

and inspection in every American locality. By specifying that committee members be chosen by all men qualified to vote for members of the lower houses of assembly, Congress guaranteed the committees a broad popular base. The seven to eight thousand committeemen—some experienced officeholders, some new to politics—became the local leaders of American resistance.

Such committees were officially charged only with overseeing implementation of the boycott, but during the next six months they became de facto governments. They examined merchants' records, publicizing those who continued to import British goods. They promoted home manufactures, encouraging Americans to adopt simple modes of dress and behavior to symbolize their commitment to liberty and virtuous conduct. Because expensive leisure-time activities were believed to reflect vice and corruption, Congress (as Janet Schaw learned) urged Americans to forgo dancing, gambling, horseracing, cardplaying, cockfighting, and other forms of "extravagance and dissipation." Some committees extracted apologies from people caught gambling, drinking to excess, or racing. Thus, private activities acquired public significance.

The committees gradually extended their authority over many aspects of American life. They attempted to identify opponents of American resistance, developing elaborate spy networks, circulating copies of the Continental Association for signatures, and investigating reports of questionable remarks and activities. Suspected dissenters were urged to support the colonial cause publicly; if they refused, the committees had them watched, restricted their movements, or tried to force them into exile. People engaging in casual political exchanges with friends one day could find themselves charged with "treasonable conversation" the next. One Massachusetts man, for example, was called before his local committee for maligning the Congress as "a Pack or Parcell of Fools" that was "as tyrannical as Lord North and ought to be opposed & resisted." When he refused to recant, the committee put him under surveillance.

While the committees of observation were expanding their power during the winter and early spring of 1775,

Provincial Conventions

the regular colonial governments were collapsing. Only a few legislatures continued to meet without encountering

▲ In 1775, a British cartoonist demonstrated his contempt for the pronouncements of the Continental Congress by setting his satire in a privy, or "necessary house," and showing a politician who has used a torn congressional resolution as toilet paper. The person at right is poring over a political pamphlet while portraits of John Wilkes and a man who has been tarred and feathered decorate the walls.

challenges to their authority. In most colonies, popularly elected provincial conventions took over the task of running the government, sometimes entirely replacing the legislatures and at other times holding concurrent sessions. In late 1774 and early 1775, these conventions approved the Continental Association, elected delegates to the Second Continental Congress (scheduled for May), organized militia units, and gathered arms and ammunition. Unable to stem the tide of resistance, the British-appointed governors and councils watched helplessly as their authority crumbled.

Royal officials suffered humiliation after humiliation. Courts were prevented from meeting, taxes were paid to the conventions' agents rather than to provincial tax collectors, sheriffs' powers were challenged, and militiamen would muster only when committees ordered. In short, during the six months preceding the battles at Lexington and Concord, independence was being won at the local level, but without formal acknowledgment and for the most part without bloodshed. Not many Americans fully realized what was happening. The vast majority still proclaimed their loyalty to Great Britain, denying that they sought to leave the empire.

Contest in the Backcountry

While the committees of observation were consolidating their authority in the East, some colonists were heading west. Ignoring the Proclamation of 1763, pronouncements by colonial governors, and the threat of

Indian attacks, land-hungry folk—many of them recent immigrants from Ireland and soldiers who demobilized in North America after the Seven Years War—swarmed onto lands along the Ohio River and its tributaries after the mid-1760s. Sometimes, they purchased property from opportunists with grants of dubious origin; often, they simply surveyed and claimed land, squatting on it in hopes that their titles would eventually be honored. Britain's 1771 decision to abandon (and raze) Fort Pitt removed the final restraints on settlement in the region for the withdrawal rendered the Proclamation of 1763 unenforceable. By late 1775, thousands of new homesteads dotted the landscape of the backcountry from western Pennsylvania south through Virginia and eastern Kentucky into western North Carolina.

Few of the backcountry folk viewed the region's native peoples positively. (Rare exceptions were the

Distrust and Warfare

Moravian missionaries who settled with their Indian converts in three, small frontier communities in the upper Ohio valley.) The frontier dwellers had little interest in the small-scale trade that had once helped to sustain an uneasy peace in the region; they wanted only land on which to grow crops and pasture their livestock.

In 1774 Virginia, headed by a new governor, Lord Dunmore, moved vigorously to assert its title to the rapidly developing backcountry. During the spring and early summer, tensions mounted as Virginians surveyed land in Kentucky on the south side of the Ohio River—territory claimed by the Shawnees, who rejected the Fort Stanwix treaty of 1768. "Lord Dunmore's war" consisted of one large-scale confrontation between Virginia militia and some Shawnee warriors. Neither side won a clear-cut victory, but in the immediate aftermath thousands of settlers—including Daniel Boone and his associates—flooded across the mountains.

When war began just as large numbers of people were migrating into Kentucky, the loyalties of Indians and settlers in the backcountry remained, like Boone's, fluid and uncertain. They were hostile to each other, but which side should either take in the imperial struggle? The answer might well depend on which could better serve their interests. Understanding that, the Continental Congress moved to reoccupy the site of Fort Pitt and to establish other garrisons in the Ohio country. Relying on such protection, as many as twenty thousand settlers poured into Kentucky and western Pennsylvania by 1780. Yet frontier affiliations were not clear: the growing town of Pittsburgh, for example, harbored many active loyalists.

The native peoples' grievances against the European American newcomers predisposed many toward an alliance with Great Britain. Yet some chiefs urged caution: after all, the British abandonment of Fort Pitt (and

them) suggested that Britain lacked the will and ability to protect them in the future. Furthermore, Britain hesitated to make full, immediate use of its potential native allies. Officials on the scene understood that neither the Indians' style of fighting nor their war aims necessarily coincided with British goals and methods. Accordingly, they at first sought from Indians only a promise of neutrality.

Recognizing their poor standing with native peoples, patriots also sought Indians' neutrality. In 1775, the Second Continental Congress sent a general message to Indian communities, describing the war as "a family quarrel between us and Old England" and requesting that they "not join on either side" because "you Indians are not concerned in it." The Iroquois responded with a pledge of neutrality. But a group of Cherokees led by Chief Dragging Canoe decided to take advantage of the "family quarrel" to regain some land. In summer 1776, they attacked settlements in western Virginia and the Carolinas. After a militia campaign destroyed many Cherokee towns, along with crops and supplies, Dragging Canoe and his die-hard followers fled to the West, establishing new villages. Other Cherokees agreed to a treaty that ceded still more of their land.

Bands of Shawnees and Cherokees continued to attack settlements in the backcountry throughout the

Frontier Hostilities

war, but dissent in their own ranks crippled their efforts. The British victory over France in 1763 had destroyed the Indian nations' most effective means of maintaining their independence: playing European powers off against one another. Successful strategies were difficult to envision under these new circumstances, and Indian leaders no longer concurred on a unified course of action. Communities split asunder as older and younger men, or civil and war leaders, disagreed vehemently over what policy to adopt. Only a few communities (among them the Stockbridge Indians of New England and the Oneidas in New York) unwaveringly supported the American revolt; most other native villages either tried to remain neutral or sporadically aligned themselves with the British. And the settlers fought back: in 1778 and early 1779, a frontier militia force under George Rogers Clark captured British posts in modern Illinois (Kaskaskia) and Indiana (Vincennes). Still, the revolutionaries could never mount an effective attack against the redcoats' major stronghold at Detroit.

Warfare between settlers and Indians persisted in the backcountry long after fighting between patriot and redcoat armies had ceased. Indeed, the Revolutionary War itself constituted a brief chapter in the ongoing struggle for control of the region west of the Appalachians, which began in 1763 and continued into the next century.

Visualizing THE PAST

Frontier Refugees

As a result of its victory in the Seven Years' War, Great Britain in 1763 took command of Fort Detroit, located on the river that connected Lakes Huron and Erie, shown here in an eighteenth-century watercolor. The strategic site controlled water access to the three westernmost Great Lakes; such water travel was crucial in an era with few and poor frontier roads. The American revolutionaries tried twice to capture Detroit, from which Indian raiding parties attacked frontier settlements, but both times the colonial forces were

defeated by Britain's Native allies. Thus throughout the war Detroit served as a magnet for loyalist refugees, among them Marie-Therese Berthelet Lasselle, who fled with her family to the fort in 1780 from their trading post at what is now Fort Wayne, Indiana. Depicted here is her self-portrait in watercolor on silk, with additional silk embroidery. What can we learn about frontier female refugees from such sources? What does this tell us about her priorities, as well as her skills?

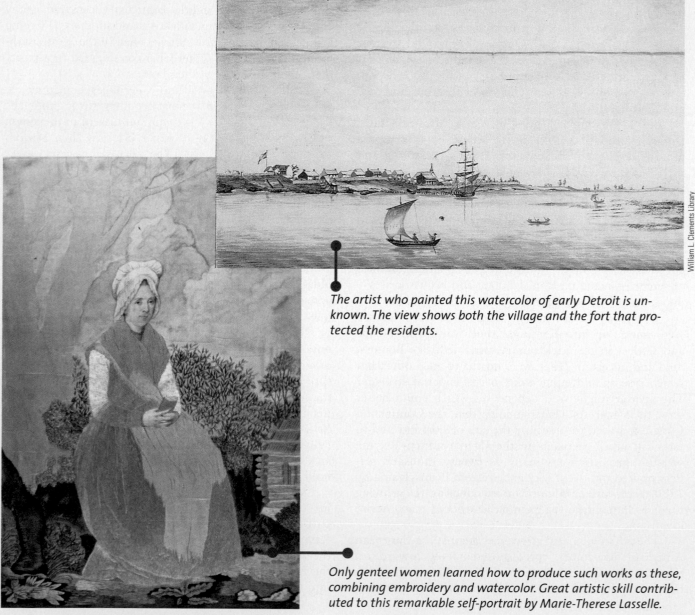

William L. Clements Library

The artist who painted this watercolor of early Detroit is unknown. The view shows both the village and the fort that protected the residents.

Monroe County Historical Commissions, Monroe, Michigan

Only genteel women learned how to produce such works as these, combining embroidery and watercolor. Great artistic skill contributed to this remarkable self-portrait by Marie-Therese Lasselle.

Choosing Sides

In 1765, protests against the Stamp Act had won the support of most colonists in the Caribbean and Nova Scotia as well as in the future United States. Demonstrations occurred in Halifax, Nova Scotia, St. Christopher, and Nevis as well as in Boston, New York, Charleston, and other mainland towns (see Map 5.3). When the Stamp Act went into effect, though, Caribbean islanders loyally paid the stamp duties until repeal. In Nova Scotia and the Caribbean, many colonists came to question both the aims and the tactics of the resistance movement, in large part because of their heavy military and economic dependence on Great Britain.

Despite the overwhelming British victory in the Seven Years War, the northern mainland and the southern island colonies believed themselves vulnerable to French counterattack and eagerly sought regular troops and naval vessels stationed within their borders. Additionally, sugar planters—on some islands outnumbered by their bondspeople twenty-five to one—feared the potential for slave revolts in the absence of British troops. Neither region had a large population of European descent, nor were local political structures very strong. Fewer people lived in Halifax in 1775 than in the late 1750s, and the sugar islands had only a few resident planters to provide leadership because successful men headed to England to buy great manors, leaving supervision of their property to hired managers.

Nova Scotia and the Caribbean

Both Nova Scotians and West Indians had major economic reasons for ultimately choosing to support the mother country. In the mid-1770s, the northerners finally broke into the Caribbean market with their cargoes of dried, salted fish. They reduced New England's domination of the northern coastal trade, and once the shooting started they benefited greatly from Britain's retaliatory measures against the rebels' commerce. British sugar producers relied for their profits primarily on their monopoly of trade within the empire, for more efficient French planters were able to sell their sugar for one-third less. Further, the British planters' effective lobbyists in London won the islands' exclusion from some provisions of the Townshend Acts. Accordingly, sugar producers logically concluded that their interests could be adequately protected within the empire. In short, neither islanders nor Nova Scotians had reason to believe they would be better off independent.

Many residents of the thirteen colonies—especially members of the groups that dominated colonial society numerically or politically—reached different conclusions, choosing to support resistance, then independence.

Patriots

Active revolutionaries accounted for about two-fifths of the European American population. Among them were small and middling farmers, members of dominant Protestant sects (both Old and New Lights), Chesapeake gentry, merchants handling American commodities, city artisans, elected officeholders, and people of English descent. Wives usually, but not always, agreed with their husbands about politics. Although such patriots supported the Revolution, they pursued divergent goals within the broader coalition, as they had in the 1760s. Some sought limited political reform; others, extensive political change; and still others, social and economic reforms. (The ways their concerns interacted are discussed in Chapter 7.)

Some colonists, though, could not endorse independence. Like their more radical counterparts, most objected to parliamentary policies, but they preferred the remedy of imperial constitutional reform. The events of the crucial year between the passage of the Coercive Acts and the outbreak of fighting in Massachusetts crystallized their thinking. Their objections to violent protest, their desire to uphold legally constituted government, and their fears of anarchy combined to make them sensitive to the dangers of resistance.

About one-fifth of the European American population remained loyal to Great Britain, firmly rejecting independence. Most loyalists had long opposed the men who became patriot leaders, though for varying reasons.

Loyalists

British-appointed government officials; Anglican clergy everywhere and lay Anglicans in the North, where their denomination was in the minority; tenant farmers, particularly those whose landlords sided with the patriots; members of persecuted religious sects; many of the backcountry southerners who had rebelled against eastern rule in the late 1760s and early 1770s; and non-English ethnic minorities, especially Scots—all these groups feared the power wielded by those who controlled the colonial assemblies and who had shown little concern for their welfare in the past. Joined by merchants whose trade depended on imperial connections and by former officers and enlisted men from the British army who had settled in America after 1763, they formed a loyalist core that remained true to a self-conception that revolutionaries proved willing to abandon.

During the war, loyalists congregated in cities held by the British army. When those posts were evacuated at war's end, loyalists scattered to different parts of the British Empire—Britain, the Bahamas, and especially Canada. In the provinces of Nova Scotia, New Brunswick, and Ontario they re-created their lives as colonists, laying the foundations of British Canada. All told, perhaps as many as seventy thousand Americans preferred exile to life in a nation independent of British rule.

Between the patriots and the loyalists, there remained in the middle perhaps two-fifths of the European American population. Some who tried to avoid taking sides were sincere pacifists, such as Quakers.

Neutrals

▲ Governor John Wentworth of New Hampshire, as painted by John Singleton Copley in 1769. Wentworth, a New Hampshire native, sympathized with early colonial protests against British policies, but ultimately remained loyal to the crown. He was one of the leaders of the loyalist exiles who gathered in London during the war, and in 1792 was named governor of Nova Scotia, serving until 1808.

Hood Museum of Art, Dartmouth College, Hanover, New Hampshire; gift of Mrs. Esther Lowell Abbott in memory of her husband, Gordon Abbott

voters (or, in some cases, all free adult men) to take oaths of allegiance; the penalty for refusal was usually banishment to England or extra taxes. After 1777, many states confiscated the property of banished persons, using the proceeds for the war effort.

The patriots' policies helped to ensure that their scattered and persecuted opponents could not band together to threaten the revolutionary cause. But loyalists and neutrals were not the patriots' only worry, for revolutionaries could not assume that enslaved people would support them.

In New England, with few resident bondspeople, revolutionary fervor was widespread, and free African Americans enlisted in local patriot militias. The middle colonies, where bondspeople constituted a small but substantial proportion of the population, were more divided but still largely revolutionary. In Virginia and Maryland, where free people constituted a slender majority, the potential for slave revolts raised occasional but not disabling fears. By contrast, South Carolina and Georgia, where slaves composed more than half of the population, were noticeably less enthusiastic about resistance to Britain. Georgia sent no delegates to the First Continental Congress and reminded its representatives at the second one to consider its circumstances, "with our blacks and tories [loyalists] within us," when voting on the question of independence. On the mainland as well as in the Caribbean islands, therefore, colonists feared the potential enemy in their midst.

African Americans

Bondspeople themselves faced a dilemma during the Revolution. Above all, their goal was *personal* independence. But how best could they escape from slavery? Should they fight with or against their masters? African Americans made different decisions, but to most slaves, supporting the British appeared more promising. In late 1774 and early 1775, groups of bondsmen began to offer to assist the British army in return for freedom. The most serious incident occurred in 1775 in Charleston, where Thomas Jeremiah, a free black harbor pilot, was brutally executed after convicted of attempting to foment a slave revolt.

The slaveowners' worst fears were realized in November 1775, when Virginia's royal governor, Lord Dunmore, offered to free any slaves and indentured servants who would leave their patriot masters to join the British forces. Dunmore hoped to use African Americans in his fight against the revolutionaries and to disrupt the economy by depriving planters of their labor force. About one thousand African Americans initially rallied to the British standard; although many of them perished in a smallpox epidemic, three hundred survived to reach occupied New York City under British protection. Because other commanders later renewed Dunmore's proclamation, tens of thousands of runaways eventually joined the British, and at the end of the war at least nine thousand left with the redcoats.

Others opportunistically shifted their allegiance to whatever side currently happened to be winning. Still others simply wanted to be left alone; they cared little about politics and usually obeyed whoever was in power. Such colonists also resisted British and Americans alike when the demands on them seemed too heavy—when taxes became too high or when calls for militia service came too often. Their attitude might best be summed up as "a plague on both your houses." Such people made up an especially large proportion of the population in the backcountry (including Boone's Kentucky), where Scots-Irish settlers had little love for either the patriot gentry or the English authorities.

To patriots, apathy or neutrality was as heinous as loyalism: those who were not for them were surely against them. By the winter of 1775–1776, the Second Continental Congress was recommending that all "disaffected" persons be disarmed and arrested. State legislatures passed laws prescribing severe penalties for suspected loyalists or neutrals. Many began to require all

New Nations

The American Revolution not only created the United States but led directly to the formation of three other nations: English-dominated Canada, Sierra Leone, and Australia.

In modern Canada before the Revolution, only Nova Scotia had a sizable number of English-speaking settlers. Those people, largely New Englanders, had been recruited after 1758 to repopulate the region forcibly taken from the exiled Acadians. During and after the Revolution, many loyalist families, especially those from the northern and middle colonies, moved to the region that is now

▲ An early view of the settlement of black loyalists in West Africa, the foundation of the modern nation of Sierra Leone.

Canada, which remained under British rule. The provinces of New Brunswick and Upper Canada (later Ontario) were established to accommodate them, and some exiles settled in Quebec as well. In just a few years, the loyalist refugees transformed the sparsely populated former French colony, laying the foundation of the modern bilingual (but majority English-speaking) Canadian nation.

Sierra Leone, too, was founded by colonial exiles—African Americans who had fled to the British army during the war, many of whom ended up in London. Seeing the refugees' poverty, a group of charitable merchants—calling themselves the Committee for Relief of the Black Poor—developed a plan to resettle the African Americans elsewhere. After the refugees refused to be sent to the Bahamas, fearing that in the Caribbean they would be reenslaved, they concurred in a scheme to return them to the land of their ancestors. In early 1787, vessels carrying about four hundred settlers reached Sierra Leone in West Africa, where representatives of the Black Poor Committee acquired land from local rulers. The first years of the new colony were difficult, and many of the newcomers died of disease and deprivation. But in 1792 they were joined by several thousand other loyalist African Americans who had originally moved to Nova Scotia. The influx ensured the colony's survival; it remained a part of the British Empire until achieving its independence in 1961.

While the Sierra Leone migrants were preparing to sail from London in late 1786, the first prison ships were simultaneously being readied for Australia. At the Paris peace negotiations in 1782, American diplomats adamantly rejected British suggestions that the United States continue to serve as a dumping ground for convicts, as had been true throughout the eighteenth century. Britain thus needed another destination for the convicts sentenced in its courts to transportation for crimes such as theft, assault, and manslaughter. It decided to send them halfway around the

world, to the continent Captain James Cook had explored and claimed in 1770. Britain continued to dispatch convicts to some parts of Australia until 1868, but long before then voluntary migrants had also begun to arrive. The modern nation was created from a federation of separate colonial governments on January 1, 1901.

Thus, the founding event in the history of the United States links the nation to the formation of its northern neighbor and to new nations in West Africa and the Asian Pacific.

▲ Thomas Rowlandson, an English artist, sketched the boatloads of male and female convicts as they were being ferried to the ships that would take them to their new lives in the prison colony of Australia. Note the gibbet on the shore with two hanging bodies—symbolizing the fate these people were escaping.

Although bondspeople did not pose a serious threat to the revolutionary cause in its early years, patriots turned rumors of slave uprisings to their own advantage. In South Carolina, resistance leaders argued that unity under the Continental Association would protect masters from their slaves at a time when royal government was unable to muster adequate defense forces. Undoubtedly, many wavering Carolinians were drawn into the revolutionary camp by fear that an overt division among the colony's free people would encourage rebellion by the bondspeople.

Patriots could never completely ignore the threats posed by loyalists, neutrals, slaves, and Indians as well, but only rarely did fear of these groups seriously hamper the revolutionary movement. Occasionally, backcountry militiamen refused to turn out for duty on the seacoast because they feared Indians would attack at home in their absence. Sometimes southern troops refused to serve in the North because they (and their political leaders) were unwilling to leave their regions unprotected against a slave insurrection. But the practical impossibility of a large-scale slave revolt, coupled with dissension in Indian communities and the patriots' successful campaign to disarm and neutralize loyalists, ensured that the revolutionaries would by and large remain firmly in control of the countryside as they fought for independence.

War and Independence

On January 27, 1775, Lord Dartmouth, secretary of state for America, addressed a fateful letter to General Thomas Gage in Boston, urging him to take a decisive step. Opposition could not be "very formidable," Dartmouth wrote, and even if it were, "it will surely be better that the Conflict should be brought on, upon such ground, than in a riper state of Rebellion."

After Gage received Dartmouth's letter on April 14, he sent an expedition to confiscate colonial military supplies stockpiled at Concord. Bostonians dispatched two messengers, William Dawes and Paul Revere (later joined by Dr. Samuel Prescott), to rouse the countryside. So, when the British vanguard of several hundred men approached Lexington at dawn on April 19, they found a ragtag group of seventy militiamen—about half of the adult male population of the town—mustered on the common. Realizing they could not halt the redcoats' advance, the Americans' commander ordered his men to withdraw. But as they began to disperse, a shot rang out; the British soldiers then fired several volleys. When they stopped, eight

Battles of Lexington and Concord

▲ In 1775, an unknown artist painted the redcoats entering Concord. The fighting at North Bridge, which occurred just a few hours after this triumphal entry, signaled the start of open warfare between Britain and the colonies.

Concord Museum, Concord, MA. www.concordmuseum.org.

Americans lay dead, and another ten had been wounded. The British moved on to Concord, 5 miles away.

There the contingents of militia were larger, Concord residents having been joined by groups of men from nearby towns. An exchange of gunfire at the North Bridge spilled the first British blood of the Revolution: three men were killed and nine wounded. Thousands of militiamen then fired from houses and from behind trees and bushes at the British forces as they retreated to Boston. By the end of the day, the redcoats had suffered 272 casualties, including seventy deaths. Only the arrival of reinforcements and the American militia's lack of coordination prevented much heavier British losses. The patriots suffered just ninety-three casualties.

By the evening of April 20, thousands of American militiamen had gathered around Boston, summoned by local committees that spread

First Year of War

the alarm across the countryside. Many did not stay long (they went home for spring planting), but those who remained, along with newer recruits, were organized into formal units. Officers under the command of General Artemas Ward of the Massachusetts militia ordered that latrines be dug, the water supply protected, supplies purchased, military discipline enforced, regular drills held, and defensive fortifications constructed.

For nearly a year, the two armies sat and stared at each other across those siege lines. The redcoats attacked their besiegers only once, on June 17, when they drove the Americans from trenches atop Breed's Hill in Charlestown. In that misnamed Battle of Bunker Hill, the British incurred their greatest losses of the entire war: more than eight hundred wounded and 228 killed. The Americans, though forced to abandon their position, lost less than half that number.

During the same eleven-month period, patriots captured Fort Ticonderoga, a British fort on Lake Champlain, acquiring much-needed cannon. Trying to bring Canada into the war on the American side, they also mounted a northern campaign that ended in disaster at Quebec in early 1776 after their troops were ravaged by smallpox. But the chief significance of the war's first year lay in the long lull in fighting between the main armies at Boston. The delay gave both sides a chance to regroup, organize, and plan their strategies.

Lord North and his new American secretary, Lord George Germain, made three central assumptions about the war they faced. First, they

British Strategy

concluded that patriot forces could not withstand the assaults of trained British regulars. They and their generals were convinced that the 1776 campaign would decide the war. Accordingly, they dispatched to America the largest force Great Britain had ever assembled anywhere: 370 transport ships carrying 32,000 troops and tons of supplies, accompanied by seventy-three naval vessels and thirteen thousand sailors. Such an extraordinary effort, they thought, would ensure a quick victory. Among the troops were thousands of professional German soldiers (many from the state of Hesse); the rulers of their principalities had hired them out to Britain.

Second, British officials and army officers treated this war as comparable to conflicts in Europe. They adopted a conventional strategy of capturing major American cities and defeating the rebel army decisively without suffering serious casualties themselves. Third, they assumed a clear-cut military victory would achieve their goal of retaining the colonies' allegiance.

All three assumptions proved false. North and Germain vastly underestimated Americans' commitment to armed resistance. Battlefield defeats did not lead patriots to abandon their political aims and sue for peace. London officials also failed to recognize the significance of the American population's dispersal over an area 1,500 miles long and more than 100 miles wide. Although Britain would control each of the largest American ports at some time during the war, less than 5 percent of the population lived in those cities. Furthermore, the coast offered so many excellent harbors that essential commerce was easily rerouted. In other words, the loss of cities did little to damage the American cause, while British generals repeatedly squandered their resources to capture such ports.

Most of all, London officials did not initially understand that military triumph would not necessarily bring political victory. Securing the colonies permanently would require hundreds of thousands of Americans to return to their original allegiance. After 1778, the ministry adopted a strategy designed to achieve that goal through the expanded use of loyalist forces and the restoration of civilian authority in occupied areas. But the new policy came too late. Britain's leaders never fully realized they were fighting, not a conventional European war, but an entirely new kind of conflict: the first modern war of national liberation.

At least Britain had a bureaucracy ready to supervise the war effort. The Americans had only the Second

Second Continental Congress

Continental Congress, originally intended to consider the ministry's response to the Continental Association. Instead, the delegates who convened in Philadelphia on May 10, 1775, had to assume the mantle of intercolonial government. "Such a vast Multitude of objects, civil, political, commercial and military, press and crowd upon us so fast, that we know not what to do first," John Adams wrote a close friend early in the session. Yet as the summer passed, Congress slowly organized the colonies for war. It authorized the printing of money with which to purchase necessary goods, established a committee to supervise relations with foreign countries, took steps to strengthen the militia, and ordered that thirteen frigates be built for a new Continental Navy (eventually, it comprised forty-seven vessels). Most important, it created the Continental Army and appointed its generals.

Until Congress met, the Massachusetts provincial congress supervised Ward and the militiamen encamped at Boston. But that army, composed of men from all over New England, constituted a heavy drain on limited local resources. Consequently, Massachusetts asked the Continental Congress to assume the task of directing the army. Initially, Congress had to choose a commander-in-chief, and many delegates recognized the importance of naming someone who was not a New Englander. John Adams later recalled that in mid-June he proposed the appointment of a Virginian "whose Skill and Experience as an Officer, whose independent fortune, great Talents and excellent universal Character, would command the Approbation of all America": George Washington. The Congress unanimously concurred.

Neither fiery radical nor reflective political thinker, Washington had not participated prominently in the pre-revolutionary agitation. Devoted to the American cause, he was dignified, conservative, and respectable—a man of unimpeachable integrity. The younger son of a Virginia planter, Washington did not expect to inherit substantial property and planned to work as a surveyor. But the early death of his older brother and his marriage to the wealthy widow Martha Custis made George Washington one of the largest slaveholders in Virginia. Though an aristocrat, he was unswervingly committed to representative government. After his mistakes at the beginning of the Seven Years War, he had repaired his reputation by rallying the troops and maintaining a calm demeanor under fire during Braddock's defeat in 1755.

George Washington

Washington also had remarkable stamina. In over eight years of war, he never had a serious illness and took only one brief leave of absence. Moreover, he both looked and acted like a leader. More than six feet tall in an era when most men were five inches shorter, he displayed a stately and commanding presence. Other patriots praised his judgment, steadiness, and discretion, and even a loyalist admitted that Washington could "atone for many demerits by the extraordinary coolness and caution which distinguish his character."

Washington needed all the coolness and caution he could muster when he took command of the army surrounding Boston in July 1775. The new general continued Ward's efforts to organize and sustain those troops. By March 1776, when the arrival of cannon from Ticonderoga finally enabled him to put direct pressure on the redcoats in the city, the army was prepared to act. Yet an assault on

British Evacuate Boston

Boston proved unnecessary. Sir William Howe, the new commander, had been considering an evacuation; he wanted to transfer his men to New York City. The patriots' cannon decided the matter. On March 17, the British and more than a thousand of their loyalist allies abandoned Boston forever.

That spring of 1776, as the British fleet left Boston for the temporary haven of Halifax, the colonies were moving inexorably toward independence. Although they had been at war for months, American leaders denied seeking a break with Great Britain until a pamphlet published in January 1776 advocated such a step.

Thomas Paine's *Common Sense* exploded on the American scene, quickly selling tens of thousands of copies. The author, a radical English printer who had lived in America only since 1774, called stridently for independence. Paine also challenged many common American assumptions about government and the colonies' relationship to Britain. Rejecting the notion that only a balance of monarchy, aristocracy, and democracy could preserve freedom, he advocated the establishment of a republic, a government by the people with no king or nobility. Instead of acknowledging the benefits of links to the mother country, Paine insisted that Britain had exploited the colonies unmercifully. And for the frequently heard assertion that an independent America would be weak and divided, he substituted an unlimited confidence in America's strength once freed from European control.

Common Sense

He expressed these striking sentiments in equally striking prose. Scorning the rational style of most other pamphleteers, Paine adopted an enraged tone, describing the king as a "royal brute," a "wretch" unconcerned for the colonists' welfare. His pamphlet reflected the oral culture of ordinary folk. Couched in everyday language, its primary source of authority was the Bible, the only book familiar to most Americans. No wonder the pamphlet had a wider distribution than any other political publication of its day.

It is unclear how many people were converted to the cause of independence by reading *Common Sense*. But by late spring, independence had become inevitable. On May 10, the Second Continental Congress formally recommended that individual colonies form new governments, replacing their colonial charters with state constitutions. Perceiving the trend, the few loyalists still connected with Congress severed their ties to that body.

Then on June 7 came confirmation of the movement toward independence. Richard Henry Lee of Virginia, seconded by John Adams, introduced the crucial resolution: "that these United Colonies are, and of right ought to be, free and independent States, that they are absolved of all allegiance to the British Crown, and that all political connection between them and the State of Great Britain is, and ought to be, totally dissolved." Congress debated but did not immediately adopt Lee's resolution.

▲ That America's patriot leaders read Thomas Paine's inflammatory *Common Sense* soon after it was published in early 1776 is indicated by this first edition, owned by George Washington himself.

his appointment to the committee. Jefferson, an intensely private man, loved his home and family deeply. This early stage of his political career was marked by his beloved wife Martha's repeated difficulties in childbearing. While he wrote and debated in Philadelphia, she suffered a miscarriage at their home, Monticello. Not until after her death in 1782, from complications following the birth of their sixth (but only third surviving) child in ten years of marriage, did Jefferson fully commit himself to public service.

The draft of the declaration was laid before Congress on June 28, 1776. The delegates officially voted for independence four days later, then debated the wording of the declaration for two more days, adopting it with some changes on July 4. Since Americans had long ago ceased to see themselves as legitimate subjects of Parliament, the Declaration of Independence (see appendix) concentrated on George III, who provided an identifiable villain. The document accused the king of attempting to destroy representative government in the colonies and of oppressing Americans through the unjustified use of excessive force.

The declaration's chief long-term importance, however, did not lie in its lengthy catalogue of grievances against George III (including, in a section deleted by Congress, Jefferson's charge that the British monarchy had forced slavery on America). It lay instead in the ringing statements of principle that have served ever since as the ideal to which Americans aspire: "We hold these truths to be self-evident: That all men are created equal; that they are endowed by their Creator with certain unalienable rights; that among these are life, liberty and the pursuit of happiness; that, to secure these rights, governments are instituted among men, deriving their just powers from the consent of the governed; that whenever any form of government becomes destructive of these ends, it is the right of the people to alter or to abolish it, and to institute new government." These phrases have echoed down through American history like no others.

The delegates in Philadelphia who voted to accept the Declaration of Independence could not predict the consequences of their audacious act. When they adopted the declaration, they were committing treason. Therefore, when they concluded with the assertion that they "mutually pledge[d] to each other our lives, our fortunes, and our sacred honor," they spoke no less than the truth. The real struggle still lay before them, and few had Thomas Paine's boundless confidence in success.

The Struggle in the North

In late June 1776, the first ships carrying Sir William Howe's troops from Halifax appeared off the coast of New York (see Map 6.1). On July 2, the day Congress voted for independence, redcoats landed on Staten Island, but Howe waited until more troops arrived from England before attacking. Washington therefore had time

Instead, it postponed a vote until early July, to allow time for consultation and public reaction. In the meantime, a five-man committee—including Thomas Jefferson, John Adams, and Benjamin Franklin—was directed to draft a declaration of independence.

The committee assigned primary responsibility for writing the declaration to Jefferson, who was well known for his eloquent style. Years later, Adams recalled that Jefferson had modestly protested his selection, suggesting that Adams prepare the initial draft. The Massachusetts revolutionary recorded his frank response: "You can write ten times better than I can."

Thirty-four-year-old Thomas Jefferson, a Virginia lawyer, had been educated at the College of William and Mary and in the law offices of a prominent attorney. A member of the House of Burgesses, he had read widely in history and political theory. That broad knowledge was evident not only in the declaration but also in his draft of the Virginia state constitution, completed just a few days before

Jefferson and the Declaration of Independence

to march his army of seventeen thousand south from Boston to defend Manhattan.

But Washington and his men, still inexperienced in fighting and maneuvering, made major mistakes, losing 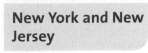**New York and New Jersey** battles at Brooklyn Heights and on Manhattan Island. The city fell to the British, who captured nearly three thousand American soldiers. (Those men spent most of the rest of the war on British prison ships anchored in New York harbor, where many died of smallpox and other diseases.) Washington slowly retreated across New Jersey into Pennsylvania, and British forces took control of most of New Jersey. Occupying troops met little opposition; the revolutionary cause appeared to be in disarray. "These are the times that try men's souls," wrote Thomas Paine in his pamphlet *The Crisis*. "The summer soldier and the sunshine patriot will, in this crisis, shrink from the service of his country; . . . yet we have this consolation with us, that the harder the conflict, the more glorious the triumph."

Map 6.1 The War in the North, 1775–1778

The early phase of the Revolutionary War was dominated by British troop movements in the Boston area, the redcoats' evacuation to Nova Scotia in the spring of 1776, and the subsequent British invasion of New York and New Jersey.

Source: Copyright © Cengage Learning

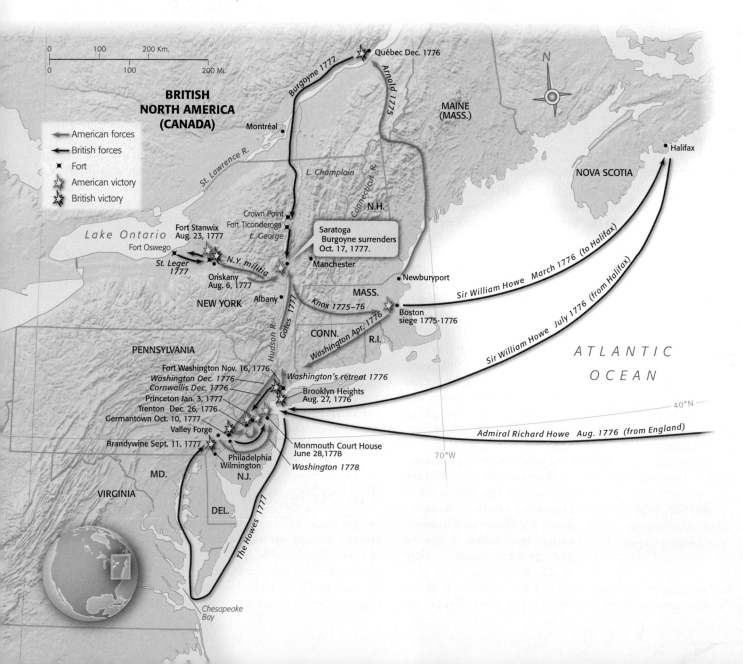

The British then forfeited their advantage as redcoats stationed in New Jersey went on a rampage of rape and plunder. Washington determined to strike back. Moving quickly, he crossed the Delaware River at night to attack a Hessian encampment at Trenton early on the morning of December 26, while the Germans were still recuperating from celebrating Christmas. The patriots captured more than nine hundred Hessians and killed another thirty; only three Americans were wounded. A few days later, Washington attacked again at Princeton. Having gained command of the field and buoyed American spirits with the two swift victories, Washington set up winter quarters at Morristown, New Jersey.

British strategy for 1777, sketched in London over the winter, aimed to cut New England off from the other

Campaign of 1777

colonies. General John Burgoyne, a subordinate of Howe and one of the planners, would lead an invading force of redcoats and Indians down the Hudson River from Canada to rendezvous near Albany with a similar force that would move east along the Mohawk River valley. The combined forces would then presumably link up with Howe's troops in New York City. But in New York, Howe simultaneously prepared his own plan to capture Philadelphia. Consequently, in 1777 the British armies in America would operate independently; the result would be disaster.

Howe took Philadelphia, but he did so in inexplicable fashion, delaying for months before beginning the campaign, then taking six weeks to transport his troops by sea instead of marching them overland. Incredibly, at the end of the lengthy voyage, he ended up only 40 miles closer to Philadelphia than when he started. By the time Howe advanced on Philadelphia, Washington had had time to prepare its defenses. Twice, at Brandywine Creek and again at Germantown, the two armies clashed near the patriot capital. Although the British won both engagements, the Americans handled themselves well. The redcoats captured Philadelphia in late September, but to little effect. The campaign season was nearly over; the revolutionary army had gained confidence in itself and its leaders; and far to the north, Burgoyne was going down to defeat.

Burgoyne and his men had set out from Montreal in mid-June, traveling first by boat on Lake Champlain, then later marching overland toward the Hudson, hampered by having to clear giant trees felled across their path by patriot militiamen. An easy triumph at Fort Ticonderoga in July was followed in August by two setbacks—the redcoats and Indians marching east along the Mohawk River turned back after a battle at Oriskany, New York; and in a clash near Bennington, Vermont, American militiamen nearly wiped out eight hundred

▲ Joseph Brant, the Iroquois leader who helped to persuade the Mohawks, Senecas, and Cayugas to support the British in the latter stages of the Revolution, as painted by Charles Willson Peale in 1797.

Independence National Historic Park Collection

of Burgoyne's German mercenaries. Burgoyne's sluggish progress had given American troops time to prepare for his arrival. After several skirmishes with an American army commanded by General Horatio Gates, Burgoyne was surrounded near Saratoga, New York. On October 17, 1777, he surrendered his entire force of more than six thousand men.

The August 1777 battle at Oriskany divided the Iroquois Confederacy. Although the Six Nations had for-

Iroquois Confederacy Splinters

mally pledged to remain neutral in the war, two influential Mohawk leaders, the siblings Mary and Joseph Brant, believed the Iroquois should ally themselves with the British to protect their territory from land-hungry colonists. The Brants won over the Senecas, Cayugas, and Mohawks, all of whom contributed warriors to the 1777 expedition. But the Oneidas—who had been converted to Christianity by Protestant missionaries—preferred the American side and brought the Tuscaroras with them. The Onondagas split into three factions, one on each side and one supporting neutrality. At Oriskany, some Oneidas and Tuscaroras joined patriot militiamen in fighting their Iroquois brethren, shattering a three-hundred-year-old league of friendship.

The collapse of Iroquois unity and the confederacy's abandonment of neutrality had significant consequences. In 1778, British-allied warriors raided frontier villages in Pennsylvania and New York. To retaliate, the following summer the Americans dispatched an expedition under General John Sullivan to burn Iroquois crops, orchards, and settlements. The resulting devastation led many bands to seek food and shelter north of the Great Lakes during the winter of 1779–1780. A large number of Iroquois people never returned to New York but settled permanently in Canada.

Burgoyne's surrender at Saratoga brought joy to patriots, discouragement to loyalists and Britons. In exile in London, Thomas Hutchinson wrote of "universal dejection" among loyalists there. "Everybody in a gloom," he commented, "most of us expect to lay our bones here." The disaster prompted Lord North to authorize a peace commission to offer the Americans what they had requested in 1774—in effect, a return to the imperial system of 1763. That proposal came far too late: the patriots rejected the overture, and the peace commission sailed back to England empty-handed in mid-1778.

Most important, the American victory at Saratoga drew France formally into the conflict. Since 1763, the French had sought to avenge their defeat in the Seven Years' War, and the American Revolution gave them that opportunity. Even before Benjamin Franklin arrived in Paris in late 1776, France covertly supplied the revolutionaries with military necessities. Indeed, 90 percent of the gunpowder used by the Americans during the war's first two years came from France, transported via the French Caribbean island of Martinique.

Benjamin Franklin worked tirelessly to strengthen ties between the two nations. He adopted a plain style of dress that made him conspicuous amid the luxury of the court of King Louis XVI. Presenting himself as a representative of American simplicity, Franklin played on the French image of Americans as virtuous farmers. His efforts culminated in 1778 when the countries signed two treaties. In the Treaty of Amity and Commerce, France recognized American independence, establishing trade ties with the new nation. In the Treaty of Alliance, France and the United States promised—assuming that France would declare war on Britain, which it soon did—that neither would negotiate peace with the enemy without consulting the other. France also formally abandoned any claim to Canada and to North American territory east of the Mississippi River. In the years that followed, the most visible symbol of Franco-American cooperation was the Marquis de Lafayette, a young nobleman who volunteered for service with George Washington in 1777 and fought with American forces until the conflict ended.

Franco-American Alliance of 1778

The French alliance had two major benefits for the patriot cause. First, France began to aid the Americans openly, sending troops and naval vessels in addition to arms, ammunition, clothing, and blankets. Second, Britain could no longer focus solely on the American mainland, for it had to fight France in the Caribbean and elsewhere. Spain's entry into the war in 1779 as an ally of France (but not of the United States) magnified Britain's problems, for the Revolution then became a global war. French, British, and American ships clashed in the West Indies, along the Atlantic coast of North America, and even in Britain's home waters. The French aided the Americans throughout the conflict, but in its last years that assistance proved vital.

Life in the Army and on the Home Front

Only in the first months of the war was the revolutionaries' army manned primarily by the semi-mythical "citizen-soldier," the militiaman who exchanged his plow for a gun to defend his homeland. After a few months or at most a year, the early arrivals went home. They reenlisted only briefly and only if the contending armies neared their farms and towns. In such militia units, elected officers and the soldiers who chose them reflected existing social hierarchies in their regions of origin, yet also retained a freedom and flexibility absent from the Continental Army, composed of men in formally organized statewide units led by appointed officers.

Continental soldiers, unlike militiamen, were primarily young, single, or propertyless men who enlisted for long periods or for the war's duration, in part to earn monetary bonuses or allotments of land after the war. They responded to calls for "manly resistance" to Britain, seeing in military service an opportunity to protect homes and families, assert their masculine identity, and claim postwar citizenship and property-owning rights. As the fighting dragged on, the bonuses grew larger and more enticing. To meet their quotas, towns and states eagerly recruited everyone they could. Regiments from the middle states contained an especially large proportion of recent immigrants; about 45 percent of Pennsylvania soldiers were of Irish origin, and about 13 percent were German, some serving in German-speaking regiments.

Continental Army

Dunmore's proclamation led Congress in January 1776 to modify an earlier policy that had prohibited the enlistment of African Americans in the regular American army, and recruiters in northern states turned increasingly to bondsmen, who were often promised freedom after the war. Enslaved substitutes for their masters constituted about 10 percent of eastern Connecticut enlistees, for example, along with another 5 percent identified as free blacks, who earned enlistment bounties. Southern states initially resisted the trend, but later all except

Georgia and South Carolina also enlisted black soldiers. Approximately five thousand African Americans eventually served in the Continental Army. They commonly served in racially integrated units but were assigned tasks that others shunned, such as burying the dead, foraging for food, and driving wagons. Overall, at any given time they composed about 10 percent of the regular army, but they seldom served in militia units.

Also attached to the American forces were a number of women, the wives and widows of poor soldiers, who came to the army with their menfolk because they were too impoverished to survive alone. Such camp followers—estimated to be about 3 percent of the total number of troops—worked as cooks, nurses, and launderers in return for rations and low wages. The women, along with civilian commissaries and militiamen who floated in and out of camp at irregular intervals, made up an unwieldy assemblage that officers found difficult to manage, especially because none of them could be subjected to the same military discipline as regular soldiers. Yet the army's shapelessness also reflected its greatest strength: an almost unlimited reservoir of manpower and womanpower.

The officers of the Continental Army developed an intense sense of pride and commitment to the revolutionary cause. The hardships they endured, the battles they fought, the difficulties they overcame all

Officer Corps

helped to forge an esprit de corps that outlasted the war. The realities of warfare were often dirty, messy, and corrupt, but the officers drew strength from a developing image of themselves as professionals who sacrificed personal gain for the good of the entire nation. When Benedict Arnold, an officer who fought heroically for the patriot cause early in the war, defected to the British, they made his name a metaphor for villainy. "How black, how despised, loved by none, and hated by all," wrote one officer.

The officers' wives, too, prided themselves on their and their husbands' service to the nation. Unlike poor women, they did not travel with the army but instead came for extended visits while the troops were in camp (usually during the winters). Martha Washington and other officers' wives, for example, lived at Valley Forge in the winter of 1777–1778. They brought with them food, clothing, and household furnishings to make their stay more comfortable, and they entertained each other and their menfolk at teas, dinners, and dances. Socializing and discussing current events created friendships later renewed in civilian life when some of their husbands became the new nation's leaders.

Life in the American army was difficult for everyone, although ordinary soldiers endured more hardships than their officers. Wages were low, and often the army could not meet the payroll. Rations (a daily standard

Hardship and Disease

Courtesy of Mae Theresa Bonitto

▲ Barzillai Lew, a free African American born in Groton, Massachusetts, in 1743, served in the Seven Years' War before enlisting with patriot troops in the American Revolution. An accomplished fifer, Lew fought at the Battle of Bunker Hill. Like other freemen in the north, he cast his lot with the revolutionaries, in contrast to southern bondspeople, who tended to favor the British.

allotment of bread, meat, vegetables, milk, and beer) did not always appear, and men had to forage for their own food. Clothing and shoes the army supplied were often of poor quality; soldiers had to make do or find their own. While in camp, soldiers occasionally hired themselves out as laborers to nearby farmers to augment their meager rations or earnings. When conditions deteriorated, troops threatened mutiny (though only a few carried out that threat) or, more often, simply deserted. Punishments for desertion or other offenses such as theft and assault were harsh; convicted soldiers were sentenced to hundreds of lashes, whereas officers were publicly humiliated, deprived of their commission, and discharged in disgrace.

Endemic disease in the camps—especially dysentery, various fevers, and, early in the war, smallpox—made matters worse, sometimes discouraging recruiting. Most native-born colonists had neither been exposed to smallpox nor inoculated against the disease, so soldiers and civilians were vulnerable when smallpox spread through the northern countryside after the early months of 1774. The disease

Link to excerpts from the journal of J.P. Martin, a revolutionary soldier.

ravaged residents of Boston during the British occupation, the troops attacking Quebec in 1775–1776, and the African Americans who fled to join Lord Dunmore (1775) or Lord Cornwallis (1781). Because most British soldiers had already survived smallpox (which was endemic in Europe), it did not pose a significant threat to redcoat troops.

Washington recognized that smallpox could potentially decimate the revolutionaries' ranks, especially after it helped cause the failure of the 1775 Quebec expedition. Thus, in Morristown in early 1777, he ordered that entire regular army and all new recruits be inoculated, although some would die from the risky procedure and survivors would be incapacitated for weeks. Those dramatic measures, coupled with the increasing numbers of foreign-born (and mostly immune) men who enlisted, helped to protect Continental soldiers later in the war, contributing significantly to the eventual American victory.

American soldiers and sailors unfortunate enough to be captured by the British endured great suffering, especially those held in makeshift prisons or on prison ships (known as hulks) in or near Manhattan. Because Britain refused to recognize the legitimacy of the American government, redcoat officers regarded the patriots as rebellious traitors rather than as prisoners of war with a right to decent treatment. The meager rations and crowded, unsanitary conditions of their confinement meant that half to two-thirds of the prisoners eventually fell victim to disease, especially dysentery. Particularly notorious was the hulk *Jersey*; survivors reported fighting over scraps of disgusting food, being covered with "bloody and loathesome filth," and each day having to remove the bodies of five to ten of their dead comrades.

Men who enlisted in the army, served in Congress, or were captured by the enemy were absent for long periods of time. Their womenfolk, who previously had handled only the "indoor affairs" of the household, thus shouldered the responsibility for "outdoor affairs" as well. As the wife of a Connecticut soldier later recalled, her husband "was out more or less during the remainder of the war [after 1777], so much so as to be unable to do anything on our farm. What was done, was done by myself." Similarly, John and Abigail Adams took great pride in Abigail's developing skills as a "farmeress." She stopped calling the farm "yours" in letters to her husband and began referring to it as "ours"— a revealing change of pronoun. Most women, like Abigail, did not work in the fields themselves, but they supervised field workers and managed their families' finances. Ever resourceful, Abigail sold small items (like handkerchiefs) that John sent her from Europe at her request, and she used the resulting profits to speculate successfully in state bonds, although John urged her to buy more land instead.

Home Front

Wartime disruptions affected the lives of all Americans. Even far from the battlefields, people suffered from shortages of necessities like salt, soap, and flour. Small luxuries like new clothing or even ribbons or gloves were essentially unavailable. Severe inflation added to the country's woes, eroding the value of any income. For those who lived near the armies' camps or lines of march, difficulties were compounded. Soldiers of both sides plundered farms and houses, looking for food or salable items; they burned fence rails in their fires and took horses and oxen to transport their wagons. Moreover, they carried smallpox and other diseases with them wherever they went. In such circumstances and in their husbands' absence, women had to make the momentous decision whether to deliberately risk their children's lives by inoculating them with smallpox or to take the chance of the youngsters' contracting the disease "in the natural way," with its even greater risk of death. Many, including Abigail Adams, chose the former course of action and were relieved when their children survived.

Victory in the South

In early 1778, in the wake of the Saratoga disaster, Lord George Germain and British military leaders reassessed their strategy. The loyalist exiles in London persuaded them to shift the field of battle southward, contending that loyal southerners would welcome the redcoat army as liberators. Southern colonies that had been pacified and returned to friendly civilian control could serve as bases for again attacking the middle and northern states.

Sir Henry Clinton, who replaced Sir William Howe, oversaw the regrouping of British forces in America. He ordered the evacuation of Philadelphia in June 1778 and sent a convoy that successfully captured the French

South Carolina and the Caribbean

Picture Research Consultants & Archives

▲ The *Jersey* prison hulk, shown here in an eighteenth-century print, was anchored in New York harbor. The stripped British vessel housed hundreds of American prisoners of war in appallingly bad conditions. The *Jersey*, just one of many such prisons, came to symbolize for Americans the mistreatment of their captured soldiers.

Caribbean island of St. Lucia, which thereafter served as a key base for Britain. He also dispatched a small expedition to Georgia at the end of the year. When Savannah and then Augusta fell easily into British hands, Clinton became convinced that a southern strategy would succeed. In late 1779, he sailed down the coast from New York to besiege Charleston, the most important city in the South (see Map 6.2). Although afflicted by smallpox, the Americans trapped in the city held out for months. Still, on May 12, 1780, General Benjamin Lincoln was forced to surrender the entire southern army—5,500 men—to the invaders. In the following weeks, the redcoats spread

Map 6.2 The War in the South

The southern war—after the British invasion of Georgia in late 1778—was characterized by a series of British thrusts into the interior, leading to battles with American defenders in both North and South Carolina. Finally, after promising beginnings, Cornwallis's foray into Virginia ended with disaster at Yorktown in October 1781.

Source: Copyright © Cengage Learning

through South Carolina, establishing garrisons at key points in the interior. Hundreds of South Carolinians renounced allegiance to the United States, proclaiming their renewed loyalty to the Crown. Clinton organized loyalist regiments, and the process of pacification began.

Yet the triumph was less complete than it appeared. The success of the southern campaign depended on control of the seas, for the British armies were so widely dispersed and travel by land was so difficult that only through British naval vessels could the armies coordinate their efforts. For the moment, the Royal Navy safely dominated the American coastline, but French naval power posed a threat to the entire southern enterprise. American privateers infested Caribbean waters, seizing valuable cargoes bound to and from the British islands. Furthermore, after late 1778, France picked off those islands one by one, including Grenada—second only to Jamaica in sugar production—and, in 1781, St. Christopher as well. Even though in early 1781 the British captured and plundered St. Eustatius (the Dutch island that, after French entry into the war, served as the main conduit for the movement of military supplies from Europe to America), the victory did them little good. Indeed, it might well have cost them the war, for Admiral Sir George Rodney, determined to secure the victory (and his personal profits from the plunder), failed to pursue the French fleet under Admiral François de Grasse when it subsequently sailed from the Caribbean to Virginia, where it played a major role in the battle at Yorktown.

Then, too, the redcoats never managed to establish full control of the areas they seized in South Carolina or Georgia. Patriot bands operated freely, and loyalists could not be adequately protected. The fall of Charleston failed to dishearten the patriots; instead, it spurred them to greater exertions. As one Marylander declared confidently, "The Fate of America is not to be decided by the Loss of a Town or Two." Patriot women in four states formed the Ladies Association, which collected money to purchase shirts for needy soldiers. Recruiting efforts were stepped up.

Nevertheless, the war in South Carolina went badly for the patriots throughout most of 1780. At Camden in August, forces under Lord Cornwallis, the new British commander in the South, crushingly defeated a reorganized southern army led by Horatio Gates. Thousands of enslaved African Americans joined the redcoats, seeking the freedom promised by Lord Dunmore and later by Sir Henry Clinton. Running away from their patriot masters individually and as families, they seriously disrupted planting and harvesting in the Carolinas and Georgia in 1780 and 1781. Tens of thousands of slaves were lost to their owners as a result of the war. Not all of them joined the British or won their freedom if they did, but their flight had exactly the effect the British sought. Many served the redcoats as scouts and guides, or as laborers in camps or occupied cities like New York.

After the Camden defeat, Washington (who had to remain in the North to contain the British army occupying New York) appointed General Nathanael Greene to command the southern campaign. Appalled by conditions in South Carolina, Greene told a friend that "the word difficulty when applied to the state of things here … is almost without meaning, it falls so far short" of reality. His troops needed clothing, blankets, and food, but "a great part of this country is already laid waste and in the utmost danger of becoming a desert." Incessant guerrilla warfare had, he commented, "so corrupted the principles

Greene and the Southern Campaign

▲ "A View from the Two-Gun Battery," St. Lucia, 1780, by Charles Forrest. Forrest, a British officer stationed in the West Indies during the Revolution, sketched this scene showing some of the island's defenses against a possible attack by the American or French Navy.

William L. Clements Library

of the people that they think of nothing but plundering one another."

In such dire circumstances, Greene had to move cautiously. He adopted a conciliatory policy toward the many Americans who had switched sides, an advantageous move in a region in which people could well have altered their allegiance up to seven times in less than two years. He also ordered his troops to treat captives fairly and not to loot loyalist property. Recognizing that the patriots needed to convince a war-weary populace that they could bring stability to the region, he helped the shattered provincial congresses of Georgia and South Carolina to reestablish civilian authority in the interior—a goal the British were never able to accomplish. Because he had so few regulars (only sixteen hundred when he took command), Greene had to rely on western volunteers and could not afford to have frontier militia companies occupied in defending their homes from Indian attack. He accordingly pursued diplomacy aimed at keeping the Indians out of the war. Although royal officials cooperating with the redcoat invaders initially won some Indian allies, Greene's careful maneuvers eventually proved successful. By war's end, only the Creeks remained allied with Great Britain.

Even before Greene took command of the southern army in December 1780, the tide had begun to turn. In October, at King's Mountain, a force from the backcountry defeated a large party of redcoats and loyalists. Then in January 1781, Greene's trusted aide Daniel Morgan brilliantly routed the British regiment Tarleton's Legion at Cowpens. Greene himself confronted the main body of British troops under Lord Cornwallis at Guilford Court House, North Carolina, in March. Although Cornwallis controlled the field at the end of the day, most of his army had been destroyed. He had to retreat to Wilmington, on the coast, to receive supplies and fresh troops from New York by sea. Meanwhile, Greene returned to South Carolina, where, in a series of swift strikes, he forced the redcoats to abandon their interior posts and retire to Charleston.

Cornwallis headed north into Virginia, where he joined forces with a detachment of redcoats commanded

Surrender at Yorktown

by the American traitor Benedict Arnold. Instead of acting decisively with his new army of 7,200 men, Cornwallis withdrew to the peninsula between the York and James Rivers, where he fortified Yorktown and awaited supplies and reinforcements. Seizing the opportunity, Washington quickly moved more than seven thousand French and American troops south from New York City. When De Grasse's fleet arrived from the Caribbean just in time to defeat the Royal Navy vessels sent to relieve Cornwallis, the British general was trapped. On October 19, 1781, Cornwallis surrendered.

When news of the defeat reached London, Lord North's ministry fell. Parliament voted to cease offensive operations in America, authorizing peace negotiations. Washington returned with the main army to the environs of New York, where his underpaid—and, they thought, underappreciated—officers grew restive. In March 1783, they threatened to mutiny unless Congress guaranteed them adequate compensation for their services. Washington, warned in advance of the so-called Newburgh Conspiracy, met the challenge brilliantly. Summoning his officers, he defused the crisis with a well-reasoned but emotional speech drawing on their patriotism. How could they, he asked, "open the flood Gates of Civil discord, and deluge our rising Empire in Blood"? When at one point he fumbled for glasses, remarking in passing that "I have grown gray in your service and now find myself growing blind," eyewitnesses reported that many of the rebellious officers began to cry. At the end of the year, he stood before Congress and formally resigned his commission as commander-in-chief. Through such actions at the end of the conflict, Washington established an enduring precedent: civilian control of the American military.

The war had been won, but at terrible cost. More than 35,000 American men died in the war, only about one-quarter of them from wounds suffered in battle and fully one-half while prisoners of the British. In the South, years of guerrilla warfare and the loss of thousands of runaway slaves shattered the economy. Indebtedness soared, and local governments were crippled for lack of funds, as few people could afford to pay their taxes. In the 1780s in Charles County, Maryland, for example, men commonly refused to serve in elective or appointive office because their personal estates would become liable for any taxes or fines they were unable to collect. Many of the county's formerly wealthy planters descended into insolvency, and in the 1790s a traveler observed that the countryside "wears a most dreary aspect," remarking on the "old dilapidated mansions" that had once housed well-to-do slaveowners.

Yet Charles County residents and Americans in general rejoiced when they learned of the signing of the pre-

Treaty of Paris

liminary peace treaty at Paris in November 1782. The American diplomats— Benjamin Franklin, John Jay, and John Adams—ignored their instructions from Congress to be guided by France and instead negotiated directly with Great Britain. Their instincts were sound: the French government was more an enemy to Britain than a friend to the United States. In fact, French ministers worked secretly behind the scenes to try to prevent the establishment of a strong, unified government in America. Spain's desire to lay claim to the region between the Appalachian Mountains and the Mississippi River further complicated the negotiations. But the American delegates proved adept

Legacy FOR A PEOPLE AND A NATION

Revolutionary Origins

The United States was created in an event universally termed the American Revolution. Yet many historians today would contend that it was not truly "revolutionary," if *revolution* means overturning an earlier power structure. The nation won its independence and established a republic, both radical events in the context of the eighteenth century, but essentially the same men who had led the colonies also led the new country (with the exception of British officials and appointees). In sharp contrast, the nearly contemporary French Revolution witnessed the execution of the monarch and many aristocrats, and consequently a significant redistribution of authority. So the legacy of the American Revolution appears ambiguous, at once radical and conservative.

Throughout the more than two hundred years since the "Revolution," groups of widely varying political views have claimed to represent its true meaning. From far left to far right, Americans frequently declare that they are acting in the spirit of the Revolution. People protesting discriminatory policies against women and minorities (usually "liberals") invoke the "created equal" language of the Declaration of Independence. Left-wing organizations rail against concentrations of wealth and power in the hands of

a few, again citing the Revolution's egalitarian thrust. Those protesting higher taxes (usually "conservatives" wanting a reduced role for government) often adopt the symbolism of the Boston Tea Party, as in the "tea-party" movement opposing Obama administration policies. Right-wing militias arm themselves, preparing to defend their homes and families against a malevolent government, just as they believe the minutemen did in 1775. Indeed, so-called minutemen have formed vigilante groups to guard the United States–Mexico border against illegal aliens. The message of the Revolution can be invoked to support extralegal demonstrations of any description, from invasions of military bases by antiwar protesters to demonstrations outside abortion clinics, all of which may be analogized to the demonstrations against British policies in the 1760s. But the Revolution can also be invoked to oppose such street protests because—some would argue—in a republic, change should come peacefully, via the ballot box and not in the streets.

Just as Americans in the eighteenth century disagreed over the meaning of their struggle against the mother country, so the legacy of revolution remains contested early in the twenty-first century, both for the nation thus created and for today's American people.

at power politics, achieving their main goal: independence as a united nation. Weary of war, the new British ministry, headed by Lord Shelburne (formerly an outspoken critic of Lord North's American policies), made numerous concessions—so many, in fact, that Parliament ousted the ministry shortly after peace terms were approved.

The treaty, signed formally on September 3, 1783, granted unconditional independence to a nation named "the United States of America." Generous boundaries delineated that new nation: to the north, approximately the present-day boundary with Canada; to the south, the 31st parallel (about the modern northern border of Florida); to the west, the Mississippi River. Florida, which Britain had acquired in 1763, reverted to Spain (see Map 7.2). The Americans also gained unlimited fishing rights off Newfoundland. In ceding so much land to the United States, Britain ignored the territorial rights of its Indian allies, sacrificing their interests to the demands of European politics. British diplomats also poorly served

loyalists and British merchants. The treaty's ambiguously worded clauses pertaining to the payment of prewar debts and the postwar treatment of loyalists caused trouble for years to come, proving impossible to enforce.

SUMMARY

The long war finally over, the victorious Americans could look back on their achievement with satisfaction and awe. Having unified the disparate mainland colonies, they had claimed

Link to the petition of Connecticut slaves for freedom.

their place in the family of nations and forged a successful alliance with France. With an inexperienced army composed of militia and regulars, they had defeated the professional soldiers of the greatest military power in the world. They accomplished their goal more through persistence and commitment than through brilliance on the battlefield, a persistence that involved wives and families on the home front as well as soldiers. They had won only a few actual victories—most notably, at Trenton, Saratoga, and Yorktown—but their army always survived defeats to fight again, even after the devastating losses at Manhattan and Charleston. Ultimately, the Americans wore their enemy down.

In winning the war, the Americans reshaped the physical and mental landscapes in which they lived. They abandoned the British identity once so important to them, excluding from their new nation their loyalist neighbors who were unwilling to make a break with the mother country. They established republican governments at state and national levels. In the families of Continental Army soldiers in particular they began the process of creating new national loyalties. They also laid claim to most of the territory east of the Mississippi River and south of the Great Lakes, thereby greatly expanding the land potentially open to their settlements and threatening the traditional Indian dominance of the continent's interior.

In achieving independence, Americans surmounted formidable challenges. But in the future they faced perhaps an even greater one: ensuring the survival of their republic in a world dominated by the bitter rivalries among Britain, France, and Spain.

SUGGESTIONS FOR FURTHER READING

Edwin G. Burrows, *Forgotten Patriots: The Untold Story of American Prisoners during the Revolutionary War* (2008)

Robert McCluer Calhoon, *The Loyalists in Revolutionary America, 1760–1781* (1973)

Colin Calloway, *The American Revolution in Indian Country* (1995)

Stephen Conway, *The War of American Independence, 1775–1783* (1995)

Sylvia Frey, *Water from the Rock: Black Resistance in a Revolutionary Age* (1991)

Pauline Maier, *American Scripture: Making the Declaration of Independence* (1997)

Charles Niemeyer, *America Goes to War: A Social History of the Continental Army* (1997)

Mary Beth Norton, *Liberty's Daughters: The Revolutionary Experience of American Women, 1750–1800* (2nd ed., 1996)

Cassandra Pybus, *Epic Journeys of Freedom: Runaway Slaves of the American Revolution and Their Global Quest for Liberty* (2006)

Charles Royster, *A Revolutionary People at War: The Continental Army and American Character, 1775–1783* (1980)

Chapter 7

Forging a National Republic 1776–1789

The Ramsay-Polk Family at Carpenter's Point, Cecil County, Maryland *by James Peale, ca. 1793. Oil on Canvas 49 1/8 x 39 3/8 inches. Anonymous. (Detail)/Crystal Bridges Museum of American Art*

On December 26, 1787, a group of Federalists—supporters of the proposed Constitution—gathered in Carlisle, a Pennsylvania frontier town. The men planned to fire a cannon to celebrate their state convention's ratification vote two weeks earlier, but a large crowd of Antifederalists prevented them from doing so. First, the Antis stood in front of the cannon, refusing to budge. Then, moving from passive to active resistance, they attacked the Federalists, who fled the scene as the angry Antis publicly burned a copy of the Constitution.

The next day, the Federalists returned to fire their cannon and to read the convention's ratification proclamation. Choosing to avoid another violent confrontation, Antifederalists instead paraded and then burned effigies of two Federalists. When Federalist officials later arrested several demonstrators on riot charges, the Antifederalist-dominated militia broke the men out of jail. Only a flaw in the warrant—which freed the arrestees legally—prevented another bloody brawl.

For several weeks thereafter, participants in these events argued in the Carlisle newspaper about the meaning of the demonstrations. Federalist authors proclaimed that the respectable initial celebrants acted with "good order and coolness," in contrast to their Antifederalist opponents who were "obscure" men, "a few worthless ragamuffins." Replying, "one of the People" pronounced the Federalists "an unhallowed riotous mob." Although the Constitution's supporters had declared themselves "friends of government," they were not: through their advocacy of government that aimed to suppress the people's liberties, they had revealed their true identity as secret aristocrats.

The Carlisle riots presaged violent disputes over the new Constitution in Albany (New York), Providence (Rhode Island), and other cities. In an ongoing struggle that began in 1775 and persisted until the end of the century, Americans argued

◄ Detail of *The Ramsay-Polk Family at Carpenter's Point, Cecil County, Maryland,* painted by James Peale about 1793. The sumptuous dresses and elaborate hats and hairdos mark these republican women as ladies of leisure. On the river wharf in the background, ready for shipping, are the hogsheads of tobacco (produced by slave labor) that made their leisure possible.

Chronology

1776	▪ Second Continental Congress directs states to draft constitutions
	▪ Abigail Adams advises her husband to "Remember the Ladies"
1777	▪ Articles of Confederation sent to states for ratification
	▪ Vermont becomes first jurisdiction to abolish slavery
1781	▪ Articles of Confederation ratified
1783	▪ Treaty of Paris signed, formalizing American independence
1784	▪ Diplomats sign treaty with Iroquois at Fort Stanwix, but Iroquois repudiate it two years later
1785	▪ Land Ordinance of 1785 provides for surveying and sale of national lands in Northwest Territory
1785–86	▪ United States negotiates treaties at Hopewell, South Carolina, with Choctaws, Chickasaws, and Cherokees
1786	▪ Annapolis Convention meets, discusses reforming government
1786–87	▪ Shays's Rebellion in western Massachusetts raises questions about future of the republic
1787	▪ Royall Tyler's *The Contrast*, first successful American play, performed
	▪ Northwest Ordinance organizes territory north of Ohio River and east of Mississippi River
	▪ Constitutional Convention drafts new form of government
1788	▪ Hamilton, Jay, and Madison write *The Federalist* to urge ratification of the Constitution by New York
	▪ Constitution ratified
1789	▪ William Hill Brown publishes *The Power of Sympathy*, first American novel
	▪ Massachusetts orders towns to support public schools
1800	▪ Weems publishes his *Life of Washington*

continually—in print and in person—over how to implement republican principles and who best represented the people. Easterners debated with westerners; in both regions, elites contended with ordinary folk. Public celebrations like those in the small Pennsylvania town played an important part in the struggle. After all, in a world in which only relatively few property-holding men had the right to vote, other people (even voters themselves) expressed their political opinions in the streets.

*R*epublicanism—the idea that governments should be based wholly on the consent of the people—originated with political theorists in ancient Greece and Rome. Republics, theorists declared, were desirable yet fragile forms of government. Unless their citizens were especially virtuous—that is, sober, moral, and industrious—and largely in agreement on key issues, republics were doomed to failure. When Americans left the British Empire, they abandoned the idea that the best system of government balanced monarchy, aristocracy, and democracy—or, put another way, that a stable polity required participation by a king, the nobility, and the people. They substituted a belief in the superiority of republicanism, in which the people, not Parliament, were sovereign. During and after the war, Americans had to deal with the potentially unwelcome consequences of that decision, such as those evident in the Carlisle demonstrations. How could they ensure political stability? How could they foster consensus among the populace? How could they create and sustain a virtuous republic?

America's political and intellectual leaders attempted to inculcate virtue in their fellow countrymen and countrywomen. After 1776, American literature, theater, art, architecture, and education all pursued explicitly moral goals. Women's education was considered particularly important, for the mothers of the republic's children were primarily responsible for ensuring the nation's future.

On such matters Americans could agree, but they disagreed on many other critical issues. Almost all white men assumed that women, African Americans, and Indians should have no formal role in politics; men saw the first two groups as household dependents, the last as outside the polity. Still, they found it difficult to reach a consensus on how many of their own number should be included in the political process, how often elections should be held, or how their new governments should be structured.

Republican citizens had to make many other decisions as well. Should a republic's diplomacy differ from that of other nations? (For example, should the United States work to advance the cause of republicanism elsewhere?) And then there were Thomas Jefferson's words in the Declaration of Independence: "all men are created equal." Given that bold statement of principle, how could white republicans justify holding African Americans in perpetual bondage? Some answered that question by freeing their slaves or by voting for state laws that abolished slavery. Others responded by denying that blacks were "men" in the same sense as whites.

The most important task facing Americans in these years was constructing a unified national government. Before 1765, the British mainland colonies had rarely cooperated on common endeavors. Many circumstances separated them: diverse economies, varying religious traditions and ethnic compositions, competing western land claims, and different polities. But fighting the Revolutionary War brought them together, creating a new nationalistic spirit, especially among those who served in the Continental Army or the diplomatic corps. Wartime experiences dissolved at least some of the boundaries that previously had divided Americans, replacing loyalties to state and region with loyalties to the nation.

Still, forging a national republic (as opposed to a set of loosely connected states) was neither easy nor simple. America's first such government, under the Articles of Confederation, proved too weak and decentralized. But political leaders tried another approach when they drafted the Constitution in 1787. Some historians have argued that the Articles of Confederation and the Constitution reflect opposing political philosophies, the Constitution representing an "aristocratic" counterrevolution against the "democratic" Articles. The two documents are more accurately viewed as successive attempts to solve the same problems—for instance, the relationship of states and nation, and the extent to which authority should be centralized. Both applied theories of republicanism to practical problems of governance; neither was entirely successful in resolving those difficulties.

- **What were the elements of the new national identity? How did women, Indians, and African Americans fit into that identity?**

- **What problems confronted the new nation's leaders as they attempted to establish the first modern republic?**

- **How and why were those problems resolved differently at different times?**

Creating a Virtuous Republic

When the colonies declared independence, John Dickinson recalled many years later, "there was no question concerning forms of Government, no enquiry whether a Republic or a limited Monarchy was best. . . . We knew that the people of this country must unite themselves under some form of Government and that this could be no other than the republican form"—in short, self-government by the people. But how should that goal be implemented?

Three different definitions of republicanism emerged in the new United States. Ancient history and political theory informed the first, held chiefly by members of the educated elite (such as the Adamses of Massachusetts). The histories of popular governments in Greece and Rome suggested that republics could succeed only if they were small in size and homogeneous in population. Unless a republic's citizens were willing to sacrifice their own private interests for the good of the whole, the government would collapse. A truly virtuous man, classical republican theory insisted, had to forgo personal profit and work solely for the best interests of the nation. In return for sacrifices, though, a republic offered its citizens equality of opportunity. Under such a government, rank would be based on merit rather than on inherited wealth and status. Society would be governed by members of a "natural aristocracy," men whose talent had elevated them from what might have been humble beginnings to positions of power and privilege. Rank would not be abolished but instead would be founded on merit.

A second definition, advanced by other members of the elite but also by some skilled craftsmen, drew more on economic theory than on political thought. Instead of perceiving the nation as an organic whole composed

Varieties of Republicanism

of people nobly sacrificing for the common good, this version of republicanism followed the Scottish theorist Adam Smith in emphasizing individuals' pursuit of rational self-interest. The huge profits some men reaped from patriotism by selling supplies to the army underscored such an approach. The nation could only benefit from aggressive economic expansion, argued men such as Alexander Hamilton. When republican men sought to improve their own economic and social circumstances, the entire nation would benefit. Republican virtue would be achieved through the pursuit of private interests, rather than through subordination to communal ideals. Such thinking decisively abandoned the old notion of the Puritan covenant, which the first definition perpetuated in its emphasis on consensus, though not in its stress on an aristocracy of talent rather than birth.

The third notion of republicanism was less influential but more egalitarian than the other two, both of which contained considerable potential for inequality. Many of its illiterate or barely literate proponents could write little to promote their beliefs. Men who advanced the third version of republicanism, most prominently Thomas Paine, called for widening men's participation in the political process. They also wanted government to respond directly to the needs of ordinary folk, rejecting any notion that the "lesser sort" should automatically defer to their "betters." They were, indeed, democrats in more or less the modern sense. For them, the untutored wisdom of the people embodied republican virtue.

Despite the differences, the three strands of republicanism shared many of the same assumptions. All three contrasted the industrious virtue of America with the corruption of Britain and Europe. In the first version, that virtue manifested itself in frugality and self-sacrifice; in the second, it would prevent self-interest from becoming vice; in the third, it was the justification for including propertyless free men in the ranks of voters. "Virtue, Virtue alone . . . is the basis of a republic," asserted Dr. Benjamin Rush of Philadelphia, an ardent patriot, in 1778. His fellow Americans concurred, even if they defined virtue differently. Most agreed that a virtuous country would be composed of hard-working citizens who would dress simply and live plainly, elect wise leaders to public office, and forgo the conspicuous consumption of luxury goods.

As citizens of the United States set out to construct their republic, they believed they were embarking on an unprecedented enterprise.

Virtue and the Arts

With great pride in their new nation, they expected to replace the vices of monarchical Europe—immorality, selfishness, and lack of public spirit—with the sober virtues of republican America. They sought to embody republican principles not only in their governments but also in their society and culture, expecting painting, literature, drama, and architecture to convey messages of nationalism and virtue to the public.

Americans faced a crucial contradiction at the outset of their efforts. To some republicans, fine arts were manifestations of vice. Their presence in a virtuous society, many contended, signaled the existence of luxury and corruption. Why did a frugal farmer need a painting or a novel? Why should anyone spend hard-earned wages to see a play in a lavishly decorated theater? The first American artists, playwrights, and authors confronted an impossible dilemma. They wanted to produce works embodying virtue, but many viewed those very works as corrupting, regardless of their content.

Still, authors and artists tried. William Hill Brown's *The Power of Sympathy* (1789), the first novel written in the United States, related a lurid tale of seduction as a warn-

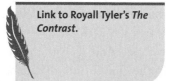

Link to Royall Tyler's *The Contrast.*

ing to young women. In Royall Tyler's *The Contrast* (1787), the first successful American play, the virtuous conduct of Colonel Manly was contrasted (hence the title) with the reprehensible behavior of the fop Billy Dimple. The most popular book of the era, Mason Locke Weems's *Life of Washington*, published in 1800 shortly after George Washington's death, was intended by its author to "hold up his great Virtues . . . to the imitation of Our Youth." Weems could hardly be accused of subtlety. The famous tale he invented—six-year-old George bravely admitting cutting down his father's favorite cherry tree—ended with George's father exclaiming, "Run to my arms, you dearest boy. . . . Such an act of heroism in my son, is worth more than a thousand trees, though blossomed with silver, and their fruit of purest gold."

Painting and architecture, too, were expected to exemplify high moral standards. Two of the most prominent artists of the period, Gilbert Stuart and Charles Willson Peale, painted innumerable portraits of upstanding republican citizens. John Trumbull's vast canvases depicted such milestones of American history as the Battle of Bunker Hill and Cornwallis's surrender at Yorktown. Such portraits and historical scenes were intended to instill patriotic sentiments in their viewers. Architects likewise hoped to convey in their buildings a sense of the young republic's ideals. When the Virginia government asked Thomas Jefferson, then minister to France, for advice on the design of the state capitol in Richmond, Jefferson unhesitatingly recommended copying a Roman building, the Maison Carrée at Nîmes. "It is very simple," he explained, "but it is noble beyond expression." Jefferson set forth ideals that would guide American architecture for a generation to come: simplicity of line, harmonious proportions, a feeling of grandeur.

Despite the artists' efforts (or, some would have said, because of them), some Americans began to detect signs of luxury and corruption by the mid-1780s. The resumption of European trade after the war brought a return to

Visualizing THE PAST

Depicting Virtue

In the 1780s, American printers began publishing magazines that became important vehicles for promoting their notions of virtue. For monthly or bi-monthly magazines filled with locally written poems and essays publishers needed illustrations—something not required by weekly newspapers. One of the most important and longest lasting of these publications was the *Columbian Magazine*, published in Philadelphia from 1786 to 1792. Seen here are two of the many illustrations its printer commissioned from local artists. *Venerate the Plow* celebrated American agriculture, with the female figure symbolizing America (note the thirteen stars in a circle over her head) holding a sheaf of grain. In the other, Columbia presents a girl and a boy (the "rising race") to Minerva (goddess of wisdom), who leans on a pedestal lauding independence as "the reward of wisdom, fortitude, and perseverance." In the background, a farmer plows his field and ships ply the ocean. What future did Americans see for themselves, as represented in these pictures?

Columbian Magazine, 1787

Columbian Magazine, 1786

up-to-date imported fashions for both men and women. Elite families again attended balls and concerts. Parties no longer seemed complete without gambling and card-playing. Social clubs for young people multiplied; Samuel Adams worried in print about the opportunities for corruption lurking behind plans for tea drinking and genteel conversation among Boston youths. Especially alarming to fervent republicans was the establishment in 1783 of the Society of the Cincinnati, a hereditary association for Revolutionary War officers and their firstborn male descendants. Although the organizers hoped to advance the notion of the citizen-soldier, opponents feared the group would become the nucleus of a native-born aristocracy. All these developments directly challenged the United States' self-image as a virtuous republic.

Americans' deep-seated concern for the future of the infant republic focused their attention on children, the "rising generation." Education had previously been seen as a private means to personal advancement, the concern of individual families. Now schooling would serve a public purpose. If young people were to resist the temptations of vice and become useful citizens prepared for self-government, they would need a good education. In fact, the very survival of the nation depended on it. The 1780s and 1790s thus witnessed two major changes in educational practice.

Educational Reform

First, some northern states began to use tax money to support public elementary schools. In 1789, Massachusetts became one of the first states to require towns to offer their citizens free public elementary education. Second, schooling for girls was improved. Recognizing the importance of the rising generation led Americans to conclude that mothers would have to be properly educated if they were to instruct their children adequately. Therefore, Massachusetts insisted that town elementary schools teach girls as well as boys. Throughout the United States, private academies were founded to give teenage girls from well-to-do families an opportunity for advanced schooling. No one yet proposed opening colleges to women, but a few fortunate girls could study history, geography, rhetoric, and mathematics. The academies also trained female students in fancy needlework—the only artistic endeavor considered appropriate for genteel women.

Judith Sargent Murray of Gloucester, Massachusetts, became the chief theorist of women's education in the early republic. Murray argued in several essays that women and men had equal intellectual capacities, although women's inadequate education might make them seem less intelligent. "We can only reason from what we know," she declared, "and if an opportunity of acquiring knowledge hath been denied us, the inferiority of our sex cannot fairly be deduced from

Judith Sargent Murray

Terra Foundation for American Art, Chicago/Art Resource, NY

▲ Judith Sargent Stevens (later Murray), by John Singleton Copley, ca. 1770–1772. The eventual author of tracts advocating improvements in women's education sat for this portrait two decades earlier, during her first marriage. Her clear-eyed gaze suggests both her intelligence and her seriousness of purpose.

thence." Therefore, concluded Murray, boys and girls should be offered equivalent schooling. She further contended that girls should be taught to support themselves by their own efforts: "Independence should be placed within their grasp."

Murray's direct challenge to the traditional colonial belief that, as one man put it, girls "knew quite enough if they could make a shirt and a pudding" was part of a general rethinking of women's position that occurred as a result of the Revolution. Both men and women realized that female patriots had made vitally important contributions to the American independence movement. Consequently, Americans began to develop new ideas about the roles women should play in a republican society.

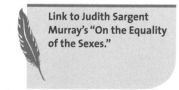

Link to Judith Sargent Murray's "On the Equality of the Sexes."

The best-known expression of those new ideas appeared in a letter Abigail Adams addressed to her husband in March 1776. "In the new Code of Laws which I suppose it will be necessary for you to make I desire you

Women and the Republic

would Remember the Ladies," she wrote. "Remember all Men would be tyrants if they could. . . . If perticuliar care and attention is not paid to the Laidies [sic] we are determined to foment a Rebelion, and will not hold ourselves bound by any Laws in which we have no voice, or Representation." With these words, Abigail Adams took a step that would be duplicated by other disfranchised Americans. She deliberately applied the ideology developed to combat parliamentary supremacy to purposes revolutionary leaders had never intended. They assumed that wives had no interests different from those of their husbands. Yet Abigail Adams argued that, because men were "Naturally Tyrannical," the United States should reform colonial marriage laws, which subordinated wives to their husbands, giving men control of family property and denying wives the right to independent legal action.

Abigail Adams did not ask for woman suffrage, but others claimed that right, and some male and female authors began to discuss and define the "rights of women" in general terms. The drafters of the New Jersey state constitution in 1776 defined voters carelessly as "all free inhabitants" who met certain property qualifications. They thereby unintentionally gave the vote to property-holding white spinsters and widows as well as to free black landowners. Qualified women and African Americans, politicized by their experiences during the Revolution, regularly voted in New Jersey's local and congressional elections until 1807, when they were disfranchised by the state legislature, which falsely charged them with widespread vote fraud. That women chose to vote was evidence of their altered perception of their place in the political life of the country.

Such dramatic episodes were unusual. After the war, most European-Americans still viewed women in traditional terms, affirming that women's primary function was to be good wives, mothers, and mistresses of households. They perceived significant differences between male and female character, which eventually enabled a resolution of the conflict between the two most influential strands of republican thought and led to new roles for some women. Because wives could not own property or participate directly in economic life, women came to be seen as the embodiment of self-sacrificing, disinterested republicanism. Through new female-run charitable associations founded after the war, better-off women assumed public responsibilities, in particular through caring for poor widows and orphaned children. Thus, men were freed from the naggings of conscience as they pursued their economic self-interest (that other republican virtue), secure in the knowledge that their wives and daughters were fulfilling the family's obligation to the common good. The ideal republican man, therefore, was an individualist, seeking advancement for himself and his family. The ideal republican woman, by contrast, always put the well-being of others ahead of her own.

Together, European American men and women established the context for the creation of a virtuous republic. But nearly 20 percent of the American population was of African descent. How did approximately 700,000 African Americans fit into the developing national plan?

The First Emancipation and the Growth of Racism

Revolutionary ideology exposed one of the primary contradictions in American society. Both European-Americans and African Americans saw the irony in slaveholders' claims that they sought to prevent Britain from "enslaving" them. Many revolutionary leaders voiced the theme. In 1773, Dr. Benjamin Rush called slavery "a vice which degrades human nature," warning ominously that "the plant of liberty is of so tender a nature that it cannot thrive long in the neighborhood of slavery." Common folk also pointed out the contradiction. When Josiah Atkins, a Connecticut soldier, saw Washington's plantation, he observed in his journal: "Alas! That persons who pretend to stand for the rights of mankind for the liberties of society, can delight in oppression, & that even of the worst kind!"

African Americans did not need revolutionary ideology to tell them that slavery was wrong, but they quickly took advantage of that ideology. In 1779, a group of slaves from Portsmouth, New Hampshire, asked the state legislature "from what authority [our masters] assume to dispose of our lives, freedom and property," pleading "that the name of slave may not more be heard in a land gloriously contending for the sweets of freedom." The same year, several bondsmen in Fairfield, Connecticut, petitioned the legislature for their freedom, characterizing slavery as a "dreadful Evil" and "flagrant Injustice." How could men who were "nobly contending in the Cause of Liberty," they asked, continue "this detestable Practice"?

Both legislatures responded negatively, but the postwar years witnessed the gradual abolition of slavery in the

Emancipation and Manumission

North, a process that has become known as "the first emancipation." Vermont, still an independent jurisdiction, banned slavery in its 1777 constitution. Responding to lawsuits filed by enslaved men and women, Massachusetts courts decided in 1783 that the state constitution prohibited slavery. Other states adopted gradual emancipation laws between 1780 (Pennsylvania) and 1804 (New Jersey). New Hampshire did not formally abolish slavery, but only eight slaves were reported on the 1800 census and none in 1810. Although

Writing and Stationery Supplies

In the seventeenth century, colonists stressed the importance of teaching children to read the Bible; writing was not seen as nearly so necessary, and many people who could read never learned to write. Yet as the eighteenth century progressed, and especially during and after the American Revolution, writing skills acquired new significance as family members parted by the war needed to communicate with each other and new opportunities arose for merchants who could deal with distant correspondents. After the war, such experiences led Americans to place greater emphasis on teaching youngsters to write as well as to read.

Most books were either imported from England or printed in the new United States, but writing drew on a wide range of items from around the world. Sheets of paper were either imported from Britain or manufactured at an increasing number of American paper mills; more than thirty were built between 1750 and 1780. The quill pens (goose feathers) that Americans used as writing implements often originated in Germany or Holland. Either on the continent or in Britain, the feathers would be heated to remove any fat or membrane and to harden the points before they were dispatched by the thousands across the Atlantic. Penknives, needed to sharpen blunt quills, and inkpots (made of brass, glass, or pewter, among other materials), also largely came from Britain. But the Americans could not write readily without additional items obtained from international trade.

For example, to absorb ink properly, paper needed to be treated with pounce, a powder made from a combination of gum sandarac (a tree resin from North Africa) and pumice, a powdered volcanic glass. Lacking envelopes, eighteenth-century writers folded their sheets of paper, addressed them on the outside, and sealed them with wax made in Holland or Britain from a combination of lac (a resinous secretion of insects, still used today for shellac) from India and cinnabar, a red quartz-like crystal, from Spain. Most notably, ink itself was manufactured from a set of diverse ingredients: oak galls from Aleppo (in Syria), gum arabic (sap from acacia trees) from Sudan, and alum and copperas (derived from different stones) from Britain. Most likely, the ink was shipped from Britain in powdered form; in America, another key ingredient, urine, would have to be added to cause the alum to blend properly with the other substances to create the liquid ink. Merchants who sold such supplies in the United States sometimes touted the virtues of the "Best Dutch Sealing Wax" or "Aleppo ink" they offered in their shops, but for the most part they simply advertised the wares without identifying their geographic origins.

Therefore, although a boy or girl learning how to write in one of the new academies—or their parents—might have been unaware of it, the implements they employed involved Americans in a long commercial chain that linked the seemingly mundane task of writing a letter or recording accounts to Great Britain, the European continent, North Africa, and the Middle East.

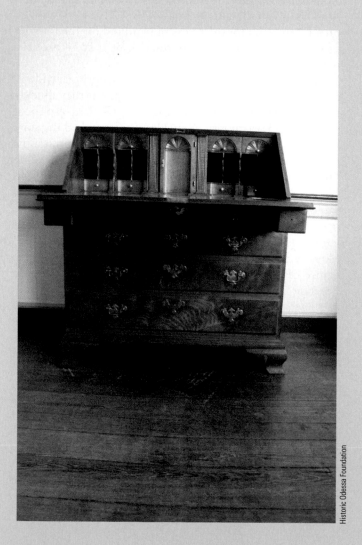

Historic Odessa Foundation

◀ This writing desk, made in Pennsylvania in the mid-to-late eighteenth century, would have been owned by a well-to-do family from the mid-Atlantic states. The pigeon holes would hold incoming and outgoing letters; the many drawers could store paper, ink, seals and sealing wax, and other supplies. The new importance of writing thus produced a perceived need for novel types of furniture.

no southern state adopted general emancipation laws, the legislatures of Virginia (1782), Delaware (1787), and Maryland (1790 and 1796) altered laws that earlier had restricted slaveowners' ability to free their bondspeople. Yet South Carolina and Georgia never considered adopting such acts, and North Carolina insisted that all manumissions (emancipations of individual slaves) be approved by county courts.

Revolutionary ideology thus had limited impact on the well-entrenched economic interests of large slaveholders. Only in the northern states—societies with slaves, not slave societies—could state legislatures vote to abolish slavery. Even there, legislators' concern for the *property* rights of owners of human chattel—the Revolution, after all, was fought for property as well as for life and liberty—led them to favor gradual emancipation over immediate abolition. For example, New York's law freed children born into slavery after July 4, 1799, but only after they had reached their mid-twenties (by then having through their labor more than paid back the cost of their upbringing). The laws failed to emancipate the existing slave population, thereby leaving the owners' current human property largely intact. For decades, then, African Americans in the North lived in an intermediate stage between slavery and freedom. Although

the emancipation laws forbade the sale of slaves to jurisdictions in which the institution remained legal, slaveowners regularly circumvented such provisions. The 1840 census recorded the presence of slaves in several northern states; not until later that decade did Rhode Island and Connecticut, for instance, abolish all vestiges of slavery.

Despite the slow progress of abolition, the number of free people of African descent in the United States grew dramatically in the first years after the Revolution. Before the war, they had been few in number; in 1755, for example, only 4 percent of African Americans in Maryland were free. Most slaves emancipated before the war were mulattos, born of unions between bondswomen and their masters, who then manumitted the children. But wartime disruptions radically augmented the freed population. Wartime escapees from plantations, slaves who had served in the American army, and still others who had been emancipated by their owners or by state laws were now free. By 1790, nearly sixty thousand free people of color lived in the United States; ten years later, they numbered more than 108,000, nearly 11 percent of the total African American population.

Growth of Free Black Population

In the Chesapeake, manumissions were speeded by economic changes, such as declining soil fertility and the shift from tobacco to grain production, as well as by the rising influence of antislavery Baptists and Methodists. One prominent Baptist convert, the immensely wealthy planter Robert Carter, manumitted all of his bondspeople after he became convinced that slaveowning was sinful. Because grain cultivation was less labor-intensive than tobacco growing, planters began to complain about "excess" slaves. They occasionally solved that problem by freeing some of their less productive or more favored bondspeople. The enslaved also seized the opportunity to negotiate agreements with their owners allowing them to live and work independently until they could purchase themselves with their accumulated earnings. The free black population of Virginia more than doubled between 1790 and 1810; by the latter year, nearly one-quarter of Maryland's African American population was no longer in legal bondage.

In the 1780s and thereafter, freedpeople from rural areas often made their way to northern port cities, such as Boston and Philadelphia.

Freedpeople's Lives

Women outnumbered men among the migrants by a margin of three to two, for they had better employment opportunities in the cities, especially in domestic service. Some freedmen also worked in domestic service, but larger numbers were employed as unskilled laborers and sailors. A few of the women and a sizable proportion of men (nearly one-third

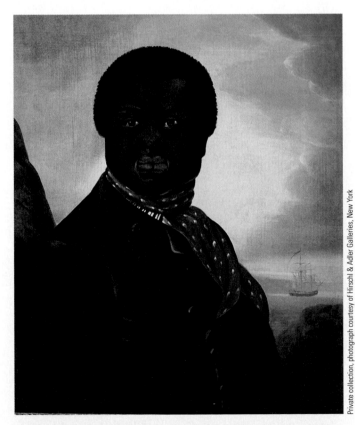

▲ A sailor of African descent posed proudly for this portrait around 1790. Unfortunately, neither the name of the sailor nor the name of the artist is known today.

Private collection, photograph courtesy of Hirschl & Adler Galleries, New York of those in Philadelphia in 1795) were skilled workers or retailers. These people chose new names for themselves, exchanging the surnames of former masters for names like Newman or Brown, and as soon as possible they established independent two-parent families instead of continuing to live in their employers' households. They also began to occupy distinct neighborhoods, probably as a result of discrimination.

Emancipation did not bring equality. Even whites who recognized African Americans' right to freedom were unwilling to accept them as equals. Laws discriminated against freedpeople as they had against slaves. Several states—among them Delaware, Maryland, and South Carolina—quickly adopted laws denying property-owning black men the vote. South Carolina forbade free blacks from testifying against whites in court. New Englanders used indenture contracts to control freed youths, who were also often denied education in public schools. Freedmen found it difficult to purchase property and find good jobs. And though in many areas African Americans were accepted as members—even ministers—of evangelical churches, they were rarely allowed an equal voice in church affairs.

Gradually, freedpeople developed their own institutions, often based in their own neighborhoods. In Charleston, mulattos formed the Brown Fellowship Society, which provided insurance coverage for its members, financed a school, and helped to support orphans. In 1794, former slaves in Philadelphia and Baltimore, led by the Reverend Richard Allen, founded societies that eventually formed the African Methodist Episcopal (AME) denomination. AME churches later sponsored schools and—along with African Baptist, African Episcopal, and African Presbyterian churches—became cultural centers of the free black community. Freedpeople quickly learned that, to survive and prosper, they had to rely on collective effort rather than on the goodwill of their white compatriots.

Their endeavors were all the more important because the postrevolutionary years witnessed the development of

Development of Racist Theory

formal racist theory in the United States. European-Americans had long regarded their slaves as inferior, but the most influential writers attributed that inferiority to environmental factors. They argued that African slaves' seemingly debased character derived from their enslavement, rather than enslavement's being the consequence of inherited inferiority. In the Revolution's aftermath, though, slaveowners needed to defend holding other human beings in bondage against the proposition that "all men are created equal." Consequently, they began to argue that people of African descent were less than fully human and that the principles of republican equality applied only to European-Americans. In other words, to avoid having to confront

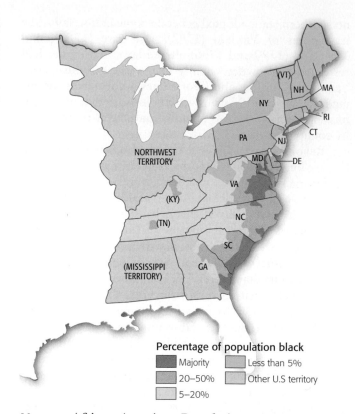

Map 7.1 African American Population, 1790: Proportion of Total Population

The first census clearly indicated that the African American population was heavily concentrated in just a few areas of the United States, most notably in coastal regions of South Carolina, Georgia, and Virginia. Although there were growing numbers of blacks in the backcountry—presumably taken there by migrating slaveowners—most parts of the North and East, with the exception of the immediate vicinity of New York City, had few African American residents.

Source: From Lester J. Cappon et al., eds., *Atlas of Early American History: The Revolutionary Era, 1760–1790.* Copyright © 1976 by Princeton University Press.

the contradiction between their practice and the egalitarian implications of revolutionary theory, they redefined the theory so that it would not apply to African Americans.

Simultaneously, the very notion of "race" appeared in coherent form applied to groups defined by skin color as "whites," "reds," and "blacks." The rise of egalitarian thinking among European-Americans both downplayed status distinctions within their own group and differentiated all "whites" from people of color—Indians and African Americans. (That differentiation soon manifested itself in new miscegenation laws adopted in both northern and southern states to forbid intermarriage between whites and blacks or Indians.) Indians from disparate nations, especially in the southeastern United States, had decades earlier begun to refer to themselves as "red."

Meanwhile, experience as slaves on American soil forged the identity "African" or "black" from the various ethnic and national affiliations of people who had survived the transatlantic crossing. Strikingly, among the first to term themselves "Africans" were oceanic sailors—men whose wide-ranging contacts with Europeans caused them to construct a unified (and separate) identity for themselves. Thus in the revolutionary era "whiteness," "redness," and "blackness"—along with the superiority of the first, the inferiority of the latter two—developed in tandem as contrasting terms.

Such racism had several intertwined elements. First came the assertion that, as Thomas Jefferson insisted in 1781, blacks were "inferior to the whites in the endowments both of body and mind." (He was less certain about the inferiority of Indians.) There followed the belief that blacks were congenitally lazy and disorderly. Even though owners had often argued, conversely, that slaves were "natural" workers, no one seemed to notice the inherent contradiction. Third was the notion that all blacks were sexually promiscuous and that African American men lusted after European American women. The specter of interracial sexual intercourse involving black men and white women haunted early American racist thought. Significantly, the more common reverse circumstance—the sexual exploitation of enslaved women by their masters—aroused little comment or concern.

African Americans did not allow these developing racist notions to go unchallenged. Benjamin Banneker, a free black mathematical genius, directly disputed Thomas Jefferson's belief in Africans' intellectual inferiority. In 1791, Banneker sent Jefferson a copy of his latest almanac (which included his astronomical calculations) as an example of blacks' mental powers. Jefferson's response admitted Banneker's intelligence but indicated that he regarded Banneker as exceptional; Jefferson insisted that he needed more evidence before he would change his mind about people of African descent generally.

At its birth, then, its leaders defined the republic as a white male enterprise. Even though men of African descent served with honor in the Continental Army, laws from the 1770s on linked "whiteness" and male citizenship rights. Indeed, some historians have argued that the subjugation of blacks, Indians, and women was a necessary precondition for theoretical equality among white men. They have pointed out that identifying common racial antagonists helped to create white solidarity and to lessen the threat to gentry power posed by the enfranchisement of poorer men. Moreover, excluding women from the political realm reserved all power for men, specifically those of the "better sort." That was perhaps one reason why after the

A White Men's Republic

Revolution the division of American society between slave and free was transformed into a division between blacks—some of whom were free—and whites. The white male wielders of power ensured their continued dominance in part by substituting race for enslavement as the primary determinant of African Americans' status.

Designing Republican Governments

In May 1776, even before adoption of the Declaration of Independence, the Second Continental Congress directed states to devise new republican governments to replace the popularly elected provincial conventions and committees that had met since colonial governments collapsed in 1774 and 1775. Thus, American men initially concentrated on drafting state constitutions and devoted little attention to their national government—an oversight they later had to remedy.

At the state level, political leaders immediately faced the problem of defining a "constitution." Americans wanted to create tangible documents specifying the fundamental structures of government, but at first legislators could not decide how to accomplish that goal. States eventually concluded that regular legislative bodies should not draft their constitutions. Following the lead established by Vermont in 1777 and Massachusetts in 1780, they began to elect conventions for the sole purpose of drafting constitutions. Thus, states sought direct authorization from the people—the theoretical sovereigns in a republic—before establishing new governments. After preparing new constitutions, delegates submitted them to voters for ratification.

State Constitutions

The framers of state constitutions concerned themselves primarily with outlining the distribution of and limitations on government power—both crucial to the survival of republics. If authority was not confined within reasonable limits, the states might become tyrannical, as Britain had. Americans' experience with British rule permeated every provision of their new constitutions. States experimented with different solutions to the problems the framers perceived, and the early constitutions varied considerably in specifics while remaining broadly comparable in outline.

Under their colonial charters, Americans had learned to fear the power of the governor—usually the appointed agent of the king or proprietor—and to see the legislature as their defender. Accordingly, the first state constitutions typically provided for the governor to be elected annually (commonly by the legislature), limited the number of terms he could serve, and gave him little independent authority. Simultaneously, the constitutions expanded the legislature's powers. Every state except Pennsylvania and Vermont retained a two-house structure, with members of the upper house having longer terms and required to meet higher property-holding standards than members of the lower house. But they also redrew electoral districts to more accurately reflect population patterns, and they increased the number of members in both houses. Finally, most states lowered property qualifications for voting. As a result, the legislatures came to include some members who before the war would not have been eligible to vote. Thus, the revolutionary era witnessed the first deliberate attempt to broaden the base of American government, a process that has continued to the present day.

But the state constitutions' authors knew that governments designed to be responsive to the people would not

Limiting State Governments

necessarily provide sufficient protection if tyrants were elected to office. They consequently included explicit limitations on government authority in the documents they composed, attempting to protect what they regarded as the inalienable rights of individual citizens. Seven constitutions contained formal bills of rights, and others had similar clauses. Most guaranteed citizens freedom of the press, rights to fair trials and to consent to taxation, and protection against general search warrants. An independent judiciary was charged with upholding such rights. Most states also guaranteed freedom of religion, but with restrictions. For example, seven states required that all officeholders be Christians, and some continued to support churches with tax money. (Not until 1833 did Massachusetts become the last state to remove all vestiges of a religious establishment.)

In general, the constitution makers put greater emphasis on preventing state governments from becoming tyrannical than on making them effective wielders of political authority. Their approach to shaping governments was understandable, given the American experience with Great Britain. But establishing such weak political units, especially in wartime, practically ensured that the constitutions would need revision. Soon, some states began to rewrite constitutions they had drafted in 1776 and 1777.

Invariably, the revised versions increased the powers of the governor and reduced the scope of the legislature's

Revising State Constitutions

authority. By the mid-1780s, some American political leaders had concluded that the best way to limit government power was to balance legislative, executive, and judicial powers, a design called checks and balances. The national Constitution they drafted in 1787 also embodied that principle.

Yet the constitutional theories that Americans applied at the state level did not immediately influence their conception of national government. Because American officials initially focused on organizing the military struggle against Britain, the powers and structure of the Continental Congress evolved by default. Not until late 1777 did Congress send the Articles of Confederation—the document outlining a national government—to the states for ratification, and those Articles simply wrote into law the unplanned arrangements of the Continental Congress.

The chief organ of national government was a unicameral (one-house) legislature in which each state had

Articles of Confederation

one vote. Its powers included conducting foreign relations, mediating interstate disputes, controlling maritime affairs, regulating Indian trade, and valuing state and national coinage. The Articles did not give the national government the ability to raise revenue effectively or to enforce a uniform commercial policy. The United States of America was described as "a firm league of friendship" in which each state "retains its sovereignty, freedom and independence, and every Power, Jurisdiction and right, which is not by this confederation expressly delegated to the United States, in Congress assembled."

The Articles required unanimous consent of state legislatures for ratification or amendment, and a clause concerning western lands proved troublesome. The draft accepted by Congress allowed states to retain all land claims derived from their original charters. But states with definite western boundaries in their charters (such as Maryland and New Jersey) wanted other states to cede to the national government their landholdings west of the Appalachian Mountains. Otherwise, they feared, states with large claims could expand and overpower their smaller neighbors. Maryland refused to accept the Articles until 1781, when Virginia finally promised to surrender its western holdings to national jurisdiction (see Map 7.2). Other states followed suit, establishing the principle that unorganized lands would be held by the nation as a whole.

The capacity of a single state to delay ratification for three years portended the fate of American government under the Articles of Confederation. The unicameral legislature, whether it was called the Second Continental Congress (until 1781) or the Confederation Congress (thereafter), was too inefficient and unwieldy to govern effectively. The Articles' authors had not given adequate thought to the distribution of power within the national government or to the relationship between the Confederation and the states. The Congress they created was simultaneously a legislative body and a collective executive (there was no judiciary), but it had no independent income and no authority to compel the states to accept its rulings. Under the Articles, national government lurched from crisis to crisis. (See the appendix or the text of the Articles of Confederation.)

Map 7.2 Western Land Claims and Cessions, 1782–1802

After the United States achieved independence, states competed with one another for control of valuable lands to which they had possible claims under their original charters. That competition led to a series of compromises among the states or between individual states and the new nation, indicated on this map.

Source: Copyright © Cengage Learning

Trials of the Confederation

Finance posed the most persistent problem faced by both state and national governments. Because legislators at all levels levied taxes only reluctantly, both Congress and the states at first tried to finance the war simply by printing currency. Even though the money was backed only by good faith, it circulated freely and without excessive depreciation during 1775 and most of 1776. Demand for military supplies and civilian goods was high, stimulating trade (especially with France) and local production. Indeed, the amount of money issued in those years was probably no more than what a healthy economy required as a medium of exchange.

But in late 1776, as the American army suffered reverses in New York and New Jersey, prices began to rise, and inflation set in. The currency's value rested on Americans' faith in their government, a faith that was sorely tested in the years that followed, especially during the dark days of British triumphs in the South (1779 and 1780). State governments fought inflation by controlling wages and prices and requiring acceptance of paper currency on an equal footing with specie (coins). States also borrowed funds, established lotteries, and levied taxes. Their efforts were futile. So, too, was Congress's attempt to stop printing currency altogether

Financial Affairs

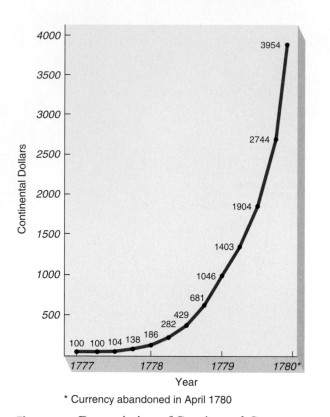

Figure 7.1 Depreciation of Continental Currency, 1777–1780

The depreciation of Continental currency accelerated in 1778, as is shown in this graph measuring its value against one hundred silver dollars. Thereafter, its value dropped almost daily.

Source: Data from John J. McCusker, "How Much Is That in Real Money? A Historical Price Index for Use as a Deflator of Money Values in the Economy of the United States," *Proceedings of the American Antiquarian Society,* Vol. 101, Pt. 2 [1991], Table C-1.

and to rely solely on money contributed by the states. By early 1780, it took forty paper dollars to purchase one silver dollar. Soon, Continental currency was worthless (see Figure 7.1).

In 1781, faced with total collapse of the monetary system, Congress undertook ambitious reforms. After establishing a department of finance under the wealthy Philadelphia merchant Robert Morris, it asked the states to amend the Articles of Confederation to allow a national duty of 5 percent on imported goods. Morris put national finances on a solid footing, but the customs duty was never adopted. First Rhode Island and then New York refused to agree to the tax. The states' resistance reflected fear of a too-powerful central government. As one worried citizen wrote in 1783, "If permanent Funds are given to Congress, the aristocratical Influence, which predominates in more than a major part of the United States, will fully establish an arbitrary Government."

Because the Articles denied Congress the power to establish a national commercial policy, the realm of foreign trade also exposed the new government's weaknesses. Immediately after the war, Britain, France, and Spain restricted American trade with their colonies. Americans, who had hoped independence would bring about trade with all nations, were outraged but could do little to change matters. Members of Congress watched helplessly as British manufactured goods flooded the United States while American produce could no longer be sold in the British West Indies, once its prime market. Although Americans reopened commerce with other European countries and started a profitable trade with China in 1784, neither substituted for access to closer and larger markets.

Foreign Affairs

Congress furthermore had difficulty dealing with the Spanish presence on the nation's southern and western borders. Determined to prevent the republic's expansion, Spain in 1784 closed the Mississippi River to American navigation, thereby depriving the growing settlements west of the Appalachians of access to the Gulf of Mexico. Congress, through its Department of Foreign Affairs, opened negotiations with Spain in 1785, but even John Jay, one of the nation's most experienced diplomats, could not win the necessary concessions. The talks collapsed the following year after Congress divided sharply: southerners and westerners insisted on navigation rights on the Mississippi, whereas northerners were willing to abandon that claim in order to win commercial concessions in the West Indies. The impasse made some congressmen question the possibility of a national consensus on foreign affairs.

Provisions of the 1783 Treaty of Paris, too, caused serious problems. Article Four, which promised payment of prewar debts (most of them owed by Americans to British merchants), and Article Five, which recommended that states allow loyalists to recover their confiscated property, aroused considerable opposition. States passed laws denying British subjects the right to sue for recovery of debts or property in American courts, and town meetings decried the loyalists' return. As residents of Norwalk, Connecticut, put it, few Americans wanted to permit the "Tory Villains" to return "while filial Tears are fresh upon our Cheeks and our Murdered Brethren scarcely cold in their Graves." State governments also had reason to oppose enforcement of the treaty. Sales of loyalists' land, houses, and other possessions had helped finance the war. Because many purchasers were prominent patriots, states hesitated to raise questions about the legitimacy of their property titles.

Peace Treaty Provisions

THE COMMISSIONERS·

▲ A British cartoon ironically reflected Americans' hopes for postwar trade, hopes that were dashed after 1783. The Indian woman symbolizing America sits on a pile of tobacco bales, with rice and indigo casks bound for Europe nearby. The artist was satirizing the failed 1778 British peace commission and Britons' willingness to make concessions to the rebellious colonies, but his image captured Americans' belief in the importance of their produce.

The refusal of state and local governments to comply with Articles Four and Five gave Britain an excuse to maintain military posts on the Great Lakes long after its troops were supposed to have withdrawn. Furthermore, Congress's inability to convince states to implement the treaty disclosed its lack of power, even in an area—foreign affairs—in which it had authority under the Articles. Concerned nationalists argued publicly that failure to enforce the treaty, however unpopular, challenged the republic's credibility. "Will foreign nations be willing to undertake anything with us or for us," asked Alexander Hamilton, "when they find that the nature of our governments will allow no dependence to be placed on our engagements?"

Order and Disorder in the West

Congressmen also confronted knotty problems when they considered the status of land beyond the Appalachians. Although British and American diplomats did not discuss tribal claims, the United States assumed the Treaty of Paris cleared its title to all land east of the Mississippi except the area still held by Spain. Still, recognizing that

land cessions should be obtained from the most powerful tribes, Congress initiated negotiations with both northern and southern Indians (see Map 7.3).

At Fort Stanwix, New York, in 1784, American diplomats negotiated a treaty with chiefs who claimed to represent the Iroquois; and at Hopewell, South Carolina, in late 1785 and early 1786, they did the same with emissaries from the Choctaw, Chickasaw, and Cherokee nations. In 1786, the Iroquois formally repudiated the Fort Stanwix treaty, denying that the men who attended the negotiations had been authorized to speak for the Six Nations. The confederacy threatened new attacks on frontier settlements, but everyone knew the threat was empty; the flawed treaty stood by default. At intervals until the end of the decade, New York purchased large tracts of land from individual Iroquois nations. By 1790, the once-dominant confederacy was confined to a few scattered reservations. In the South, too, the United States took the treaties as confirmation of its sovereignty, authorizing settlers to move onto the territories in question. European-Americans poured over the southern Appalachians, provoking the Creeks—who had not

Indian Relations

Map 7.3 Cession of Tribal Lands to the United States, 1775–1790

The land claims of the United States meant little as long as Indian nations still controlled vast territories within the new country's formal boundaries. A series of treaties in the 1780s and 1790s opened some lands to white settlement.

Source: From Lester J. Cappon et al., eds., *Atlas of Early American History: The Revolutionary Era, 1760–1790.* Copyright © 1976 by Princeton University Press.

agreed to the Hopewell treaties—to defend their territory by declaring war. Only in 1790 did they come to terms with the United States.

Western nations, such as the Shawnees, Chippewas, Ottawas, and Potawatomis, had already started to reject Iroquois hegemony as early as the 1750s. After the collapse of Iroquois power, they formed their own confederacy and demanded direct negotiations with the United States. They intended to present a united front to avoid the piecemeal surrender of land by individual bands and villages. But they faced a difficult task. In the postwar world, Indian nations could no longer pursue the diplomatic strategy that had worked so well for so long—playing off European and American powers against one another. France was gone; Spanish territory lay far to the west and south; and British power was confined to Canada, north of the Great Lakes. Only the United States remained.

At first, the national government ignored the western confederacy. Shortly after state land cessions were completed, Congress began to organize the Northwest Territory, bounded by the Mississippi River, the Great Lakes, and the Ohio River (see Map 7.2). Ordinances passed in 1784, 1785, and 1787 outlined the process through which the land could be sold to settlers and formal governments organized.

Ordinance of 1785

To ensure orderly development, Congress in 1785 directed that the land be surveyed into townships 6 miles square, each divided into thirty-six sections of 640 acres (1 square mile). Revenue from the sale of the sixteenth section of each township was to be reserved for the support of public schools—the first instance of federal aid to education in American history. One dollar was the minimum price per acre; the minimum sale was one section.

Thus Congress showed little concern for the small farmer: the resulting minimum outlay, $640, lay beyond the reach of ordinary Americans, except those veterans who received part of their army pay in land warrants. Proceeds from western land sales constituted the first independent revenues available to the national government.

The most important of the three land policies—the Northwest Ordinance of 1787—contained a bill of rights guaranteeing settlers freedom of religion and the right to a jury trial, forbidding cruel and unusual punishments, and nominally prohibiting slavery. Eventually, that prohibition became an important symbol for antislavery northerners, but at the time it had little effect. Some residents of the territory already held slaves, and Congress did not intend to deprive them of their property. Moreover, the ordinance also contained a

Northwest Ordinance

provision allowing slaveowners to "lawfully reclaim" runaway bondspeople who took refuge in the territory—the first national fugitive slave law. The ordinance prevented slavery from taking deep root by discouraging slaveholders from moving into the territory with their human chattel, but not until 1848 was enslavement abolished throughout the region, known as the Old Northwest. And by omission Congress implied that slavery was legal in the territories south of the Ohio River.

The ordinance of 1787 also specified the process by which territorial residents could organize state governments and seek admission to the Union "on an equal footing with the original States." Early in the nation's history, therefore, Congress laid down a policy of admitting new states on the same basis as the old and assuring residents of the territories the same rights held by citizens of the original states. Having suffered under the rule of a colonial power, congressmen understood the

Clements Library, University of Michigan

▲ In 1784, Thomas Jefferson proposed a scheme for organizing the new nation's western lands. His plan would have divided the region on a grid pattern, yielding fourteen new states (with names such as "Metropotamia" and "Pelisipia") composed of 10-mile-square "hundreds." After a year of debate, Jefferson's plan was replaced by the one adopted in the Land Ordinance of 1785, which is described in the text.

importance of preparing the new nation's first "colony" for eventual self-government. Nineteenth- and twentieth-century Americans were to be less generous in their attitudes toward residents of later territories, many of whom were non-European or non-Protestant. But the nation never fully lost sight of the egalitarian principles of the Northwest Ordinance.

In a sense, though, in 1787 the ordinance was purely theoretical. Miamis, Shawnees, and Delawares in the region refused to acknowledge American sovereignty. They opposed settlement violently, attacking unwary pioneers who ventured too far north of the Ohio River. In 1788, the Ohio Company, to which Congress had sold a large tract of land at reduced rates, established the town of Marietta at the juncture of the Ohio and Muskingum Rivers. But Indians prevented the company from extending settlement very far into the interior.

The problems the United States encountered in ensuring safe settlement of the Northwest Territory revealed the basic weakness of the Confederation government. Not until after the Articles of Confederation were replaced with a new constitution could the United States muster sufficient force to implement the Northwest Ordinance. Thus, although the ordinance is often viewed as one of the few lasting accomplishments of the Confederation Congress, it must be seen within a context of political impotence.

From Crisis to the Constitution

Americans involved in finance, overseas trade, and foreign affairs became acutely aware of the inadequacies of the Articles of Confederation. Congress could not levy taxes, nor could it impose its will on the states to establish a uniform commercial policy or ensure the enforcement of treaties. Partly as a result, the American economy slid into a depression less than a year after war's end. Exporters of staple crops (especially tobacco and rice) and importers of manufactured goods suffered from the postwar restrictions that European powers imposed on American commerce. Although recovery began by 1786, the war's effects proved impossible to erase, particularly in the Lower South. Some estimates suggest that between 1775 and 1790 America's per capita gross national product declined by nearly 50 percent.

The war wrought permanent change in the American economy. The near-total cessation of foreign commerce in nonmilitary items during the war stimulated domestic manufacturing. Consequently, despite the influx of European goods after 1783, the postwar period witnessed the stirrings of American industrial development. For example, the first American textile

Taxation and the Economy

mill began production in Pawtucket, Rhode Island, in 1793. Because of continuing population growth, the domestic market assumed greater relative importance in the overall economy. Moreover, foreign trade patterns shifted from Europe and toward the West Indies, continuing a trend that had begun before the war. Foodstuffs shipped to the French and Dutch Caribbean islands became America's largest single export, replacing tobacco (and thus accelerating the Chesapeake's conversion from tobacco to grain production). South Carolina resumed importing slaves on a large scale, as planters sought to replace workers lost to wartime disruptions. Yet without British subsidies, American indigo could not compete with that produced in the Caribbean, and even rice planters struggled to find new markets.

Recognizing the Confederation Congress's inability to deal with commercial matters, representatives of Virginia and Maryland met at Mt. Vernon (George Washington's plantation) in March 1785 to negotiate an agreement about trade on the Potomac River, which divided the two states for much of its length. The successful meeting led to an invitation to other states to discuss trade policy generally at a convention in Annapolis, Maryland. Although nine states named representatives to the meeting in September 1786, only five delegations attended. Those present realized that so few people could not have any significant impact on the political system. They issued a call for another convention, to be held in Philadelphia nine months later, "to devise such further provisions as shall . . . appear necessary to render the constitution of the federal government adequate to the exigencies of the Union."

At first, few other states responded. But the nation's economic problems also caused taxation woes. The states had run up huge debts to finance the war, issuing securities to soldiers in lieu of pay and to others in return for supplies and loans. During the hard times of the early 1780s, many veterans and other creditors sold those securities to speculators, who then stood to gain when states enacted taxes on the citizenry to pay them off. In 1785, Congress requisitioned still more taxes from the states to pay foreign and domestic holders of national war bonds. Most states tried to comply with the request, but succeeded primarily in arousing popular protests that led the legislatures to adopt laws relieving taxpayers of at least some of the obligations previously enacted. The most dramatic response came in Massachusetts, where the state legislature levied heavy taxes to pay the securities (plus interest) at full price in specie before the end of the decade. Farmers with little prospect of obtaining specie without selling their land responded furiously when the state moved to collect the new taxes. The actions of men from the state's western counties, many of them veterans from leading families, convinced doubters that reform was needed.

Daniel Shays, a former officer in the Continental Army, assumed nominal leadership of the disgruntled

Shays's Rebellion

westerners. On January 25, 1787, he led about fifteen hundred troops in an assault on the federal armory at Springfield, attempting to capture the military stores housed there. The militiamen mustered to defend the armory fired on their former comrades-in-arms, who withdrew after suffering twenty-four casualties. Some (including Shays) fled the state, never to return; two were hanged; and most escaped punishment by paying small fines and taking oaths of allegiance to Massachusetts. The state legislature, for its part, soon dramatically reduced the burden on landowners by enacting new import duties and by easing tax collections.

Even so, the words of the Shaysites reverberated around the new nation. Terming Massachusetts "tyrannical" and styling themselves "Regulators" (like backcountry Carolinians in the 1760s), they had insisted that "whenever any encroachments are made either upon the liberties or properties of the people, if redress cannot be had without, it is virtue in them to disturb government." Thus they linked their rebellion to the earlier independence struggle.

Such explosive assertions convinced many political leaders that the nation's problems extended far beyond

Constitutional Convention

trade and tax policies. To some, the rebellion confirmed the need for a much stronger federal government. After most of the states had already appointed delegates, the Confederation Congress belatedly endorsed the proposed convention, "for the sole and express purpose of revising the Articles of Confederation." In mid-May 1787, fifty-five men, representing all the states but Rhode Island, assembled in Philadelphia to begin deliberations.

The vast majority of delegates to the Constitutional Convention were substantial men of property. They all favored reform; otherwise, they would not have come to Philadelphia. Most wanted to give the national government new authority over taxation and foreign commerce. Yet simultaneously they sought to advance their states' interests. Many had been state legislators, and some had helped to draft state constitutions. Their understanding of the success or failure of those constitutions influenced their Philadelphia deliberations. Their ranks included merchants, planters, physicians, generals, governors, and especially lawyers—twenty-three had studied the law. Most had been born in America; many came from families that had arrived a century earlier. Most were Congregationalists, Presbyterians, or Anglicans. In an era when only a tiny handful of men had advanced education, more than half had attended college. A few

had been educated in Britain, but most had graduated from American institutions: Princeton, with ten, counted the most alumni participants. The youngest delegate was twenty-six, the oldest—Benjamin Franklin—eighty-one. Like George Washington, whom they elected their presiding officer, most were in their vigorous middle years. A dozen men did the bulk of the convention's work. Of those, James Madison of Virginia most fully deserves the title "Father of the Constitution."

The frail, shy James Madison was thirty-six years old in 1787. A Princeton graduate raised in western Virginia,

Madison and the Constitution

he served on the local Committee of Safety and was elected successively to the provincial convention, the state's lower and upper houses, and the Continental Congress (1780–1783). Although Madison returned to Virginia to serve in the state legislature in 1784, he remained in touch with national politics, partly through continuing correspondence with his close friend Thomas Jefferson. A promoter of the Annapolis Convention, he strongly supported its call for further reform.

Madison stood out among the delegates for his systematic preparation for the Philadelphia meeting. Through Jefferson, in Paris he bought more than two

▲ James Madison (1751–1836), the youthful scholar and skilled politician who earned the title "Father of the Consitution."

hundred books on history and government, carefully analyzing their accounts of past confederacies and republics. A month before the Constitutional Convention began, he summed up the results of his research in a lengthy paper entitled "Vices of the Political System of the United States." After listing the flaws he perceived in the current structure of the government (among them "encroachments by the states on the federal authority" and lack of unity "in matters where common interest requires it"), Madison revealed the conclusion that would guide his actions over the next few months. What the government most needed, he declared, was "such a modification of the sovereignty as will render it sufficiently neutral between the different interests and factions, to controul one part of the society from invading the rights of another, and at the same time sufficiently controuled itself, from setting up an interest adverse to that of the whole Society."

Madison thus believed government had to be constructed in such a way that it could not become tyrannical or fall wholly under the influence of a particular faction. He regarded the large size of a potential national republic as an advantage in that respect. Rejecting the common assertion that republics had to be small to survive, Madison asserted that a large, diverse republic should be preferred. Because the nation would include many different factions, no one of them would be able to control the government. Political stability would result from compromises among the contending parties.

The so-called Virginia Plan, introduced on May 29 by Edmund Randolph, embodied Madison's conception

Virginia and New Jersey Plans

of national government. The plan provided for a two-house legislature, the lower house elected directly by the people and the upper house selected by the lower; representation in both houses proportional to property or population; an executive elected by Congress; a national judiciary; and congressional veto over state laws. The Virginia Plan gave Congress the broad power to legislate "in all cases to which the separate states are incompetent." Had it been adopted intact, it would have created a government in which national authority reigned unchallenged and state power was greatly diminished. Proportional representation in both houses (however reckoned) would also have given large states a dominant voice in the national government.

The convention included many delegates who recognized the need for change but believed the Virginia Plan went too far in the direction of national consolidation. After two weeks of debate on Randolph's proposal, disaffected delegates—particularly those from small states—united under the leadership of William Paterson of New Jersey. On June 15, Paterson presented an alternative scheme, the New Jersey Plan, calling for strengthening the Articles rather than completely overhauling the govern-

ment. Paterson proposed retaining a unicameral Congress in which each state had an equal vote, but giving Congress new powers of taxation and trade regulation. Earlier, Paterson had made his position clear in debate. Asserting that the Articles were "the proper basis of all the proceedings of the convention," he contended that the delegates' proper task was "to mark the orbits of the states with due precision and provide for the use of coercion" by the national government. Although the convention initially rejected Paterson's position, he and his allies won a number of victories in the months that followed.

The delegates began their work by discussing the structure and functions of Congress. They readily agreed

Debates over Congress

that the new national government should have a two-house (bicameral) legislature. Further, in accordance with Americans' long-standing opposition to virtual representation, they concurred that "the people" (however that term was defined) should be directly represented in at least one house of Congress. But they discovered that they differed widely in their answers to three key questions: Should representation in both houses of Congress be proportional to population? How was representation in either or both houses to be apportioned among the states? And, finally, how were the members of the two houses to be elected?

The last issue proved the easiest to resolve. To quote John Dickinson, the delegates thought it "essential" that members of the lower branch of Congress be elected directly by the people and "expedient" that members of the upper house be chosen by state legislatures. Because legislatures had selected delegates to the Confederation Congress, they would expect a similar privilege in the new government. If the convention had not agreed to allow state legislatures to elect senators, the Constitution would have run into significant opposition among state political leaders. The plan also had the virtue of placing the election of one house of Congress one step removed from the "lesser sort," whose judgment the wealthy convention delegates did not wholly trust.

The possibility of representation proportional to population in the Senate caused considerably greater disagreement. The delegates accepted without much debate the principle of proportional representation in the House of Representatives. But small states, through their spokesman Luther Martin of Maryland, argued for equal representation in the Senate. Such a scheme, they rightly supposed, would give them relatively more power at the national level. Large states, on the other hand, supported a proportional plan, for they would then be allotted more votes in the upper house. For weeks, the convention deadlocked, neither side able to obtain a majority. A committee appointed to work out a compromise recommended equal representation in the Senate, coupled with a proviso that all appropriation bills originate in the lower house.

But only the absence of several opponents of the compromise at the time of the decisive vote averted a breakdown.

The remaining critical question divided the nation along sectional lines rather than by size of state: how was representation in the lower house to be apportioned among states? Delegates concurred that a census should be conducted every ten years to determine the nation's population, and they agreed that Indians who paid no taxes should be excluded for purposes of representation. Delegates from states with large numbers of slaves wanted African and European inhabitants to be counted equally; delegates from states with few slaves wanted only free people counted. Slavery thus became inextricably linked to the foundation of the new government. Delegates resolved the dispute by using a formula developed by the Confederation Congress in 1783 to allocate financial assessments among states: three-fifths of slaves would be included in population totals. (The formula reflected delegates' judgment that slaves were less efficient producers of wealth than free people, not that they were 60 percent human and 40 percent property.) The three-fifths compromise on representation won unanimous approval. Only two delegates, Gouverneur Morris of New York and George Mason of Virginia, later spoke out against the institution of slavery.

Slavery and the Constitution

Although the words *slave* and *slavery* do not appear in the Constitution (the framers used such euphemisms as "other persons"), the document contained both direct and indirect protections for slavery. The three-fifths clause, for example, assured white southern male voters not only congressional representation out of proportion to their numbers but also a disproportionate influence on the selection of the president because the number of each state's votes in the electoral college (see next section) was determined by the size of its congressional delegation. In return for southerners' agreement that commercial regulations could be adopted by a simple majority vote in Congress (rather than two-thirds), New Englanders agreed that Congress could not end the importation of slaves for at least twenty years. Further, the fugitive slave clause required all states to return runaways to their masters. By guaranteeing that the national government would aid any states threatened with "domestic violence," the Constitution promised aid in putting down future slave revolts, as well as incidents like Shays's Rebellion.

Once delegates agreed on the knotty, conjoined problems of slavery and representation, they achieved consensus on the other issues confronting them, aided by informal conversations at the taverns and boardinghouses where they lived that summer. All concurred that the national government needed the authority to tax and to regulate foreign and interstate

Congressional and Presidential Powers

commerce. But instead of giving Congress the nearly unlimited scope proposed in the Virginia Plan, delegates enumerated congressional powers and then provided for flexibility by granting it all authority "necessary and proper" to carry out those powers. Discarding the congressional veto contained in the Virginia Plan, the convention implied but did not explicitly authorize a national judicial veto of state laws. The Constitution plus national laws and treaties would constitute "the supreme law of the land; and the judges in every state shall be bound thereby," Article VI declared ambiguously. As another means of circumscribing state powers, delegates drafted a long list of actions forbidden to states, including impairing contractual obligations—in other words, preventing the relief of debtors. And—contrary to many state constitutions—they provided that religious tests could never be required of U.S. officeholders.

The convention placed primary responsibility for conducting foreign affairs in the hands of a new official, the president, who was also designated commander-in-chief of the armed forces. That decision raised the question, left unspecified in the Constitution's text, of whether the president or Congress acquired special powers in times of war. With the Senate's consent, the president could appoint judges and other federal officers. To select the president, delegates established an elaborate mechanism, the electoral college, whose members would be chosen in each state by legislatures or qualified voters. If a majority of electors failed to unite behind one candidate, the House of Representatives (voting as states, not as individuals) would choose the president. Delegates also agreed that the chief executive would serve for four years but be eligible for reelection, rejecting proposals that he serve one longer term.

The final document showed signs of its origins in the Virginia Plan, but compromises created a system of government less powerful at the national level than Madison and Randolph had envisioned. The key to the Constitution was the distribution of political authority—that is, separation of powers among executive, legislative, and judicial branches of the national government, and division of powers between states and nation (called *federalism*). Two-thirds of Congress and three-fourths of the states, for example, had to concur on amendments. The branches balanced one another, their powers deliberately entwined to prevent each from acting independently. The president could veto congressional legislation, but that veto could be overridden by two-thirds majorities in both houses, and his treaties and major appointments required the Senate's consent. Congress could impeach the president and federal judges, but courts appeared to have the final say on interpreting the Constitution. These checks and balances would make it difficult for the government to become tyrannical. At the same time, though, the elaborate system would sometimes prevent the government from acting quickly and decisively. Furthermore, the

Constitution drew such a vague line between state and national powers that the United States fought a civil war in the next century over that very issue.

The convention held its last session on September 17, 1787. Of the forty-two delegates present (others had returned home weeks earlier), only three refused to sign the Constitution, two of them in part because of the lack of a bill of rights. Benjamin Franklin had written a speech calling for unity; because his weak voice could not be heard, another delegate read it for him. "I confess that there are several parts of this constitution which I do not at present approve," Franklin admitted. Yet he urged its acceptance "because I expect no better, and because I am not sure,

that it is not the best." Only then was the Constitution made public. The convention's proceedings had been entirely secret—and remained so until the delegates' private notes were published in the nineteenth century. (See the appendix for the full text of the Constitution.)

Opposition and Ratification

Later the same month, the Confederation Congress submitted the Constitution to the states. The ratification clause provided for the new system to take effect once it was approved by special conventions in at least nine

▲ In August 1787, a first draft of the Constitution was secretly printed in Philadelphia for the use of convention members. Wide margins left room for additions and amendments, such as those made on this copy by South Carolina delegate Pierce Butler. Note that, in this early version, the preamble does not yet read "We the people of the United States," but instead begins by listing the individual states.

The Gilder Lehrman Collection, © Collection of the New York Historical Society states, with delegates elected by qualified voters. Thus, the national Constitution, unlike the Articles of Confederation, would rest directly on popular authority (and the presumably hostile state legislatures would be circumvented).

As states began to elect delegates to the special conventions, discussion of the proposed government grew more heated. Newspaper essays and pamphlets vigorously defended or attacked the Philadelphia convention's decisions. The extent of the debate was unprecedented. Every newspaper in the country printed the full text of the Constitution, and most supported its adoption. It quickly became apparent, though, that disputes within the Constitutional Convention had been mild compared to divisions of opinion within the populace as a whole. Although most citizens concurred that the national government should have more power over taxation and foreign and interstate commerce, some believed the proposed government held the potential for tyranny. As happened in Carlisle, Pennsylvania, the vigorous debate between the two sides frequently spilled out into the streets.

Those supporting the proposed Constitution called themselves Federalists. They built on the notions of classical republicanism, holding

Federalists and Antifederalists

forth a vision of a virtuous, collectivist, self-sacrificing republic vigorously led by a manly aristocracy of talent. Claiming the nation did not need to fear centralized authority when good men drawn from the elite were in charge, they argued that the carefully structured government would preclude the possibility of tyranny. A republic could be large, they declared, if the government's design prevented any one group from controlling it. The separation of powers among legislative, executive, and judicial branches, and the division of powers between states and nation, would accomplish that goal. Thus people did not need to be protected in a formal way from the powers of the new government. Instead, their liberties would be guarded by "distinguished worthies"—men of the "better sort" whose only goal (said George Washington) was "to merit the approbation of good and virtuous men."

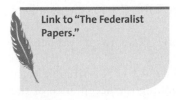

Link to "The Federalist Papers."

The Federalists termed those who opposed the Constitution Antifederalists, thus casting them in a negative light. Antifederalists, while recognizing the need for a national source of revenue, feared a too-powerful central government. They saw the states as the chief protectors of individual rights; consequently, weakening the states could bring the onset of arbitrary power. Antifederalist arguments against the Constitution often consisted of lists of potential abuses of government authority.

Heirs of the Real Whig ideology of the late 1760s and early 1770s, Antifederalists stressed the need for constant popular vigilance to avert oppression. Indeed, some of the Antifederalists had originally promulgated those ideas—Samuel Adams, Patrick Henry, and Richard Henry Lee led the opposition to the Constitution. Such older Americans, whose political opinions had been shaped prior to the centralizing, nationalistic Revolution, peopled the Antifederalist ranks. Joining them were small farmers preoccupied with guarding their property against excessive taxation, backcountry Baptists and Presbyterians, and ambitious, upwardly mobile men who would benefit from an economic and political system less tightly controlled than that the Constitution envisioned. Federalists denigrated such men as disorderly, licentious, and even "unmanly" and "boyish" because they would not follow the elites' lead in supporting the Constitution.

As public debate continued, Antifederalists focused on the Constitution's lack of a bill of rights. Even if the

Bill of Rights

new system weakened the states, critics believed, people could still be protected from tyranny by specific guarantees of rights. The Constitution did contain some prohibitions on congressional power. For example, the writ of habeas corpus, which prevented arbitrary imprisonment, could not be suspended except in "cases of rebellion or invasion." But Antifederalists found such constitutional provisions to be few and inadequate. Nor were they reassured by Federalist assertions that the new government could not violate people's rights because it had only limited powers. Opponents wanted the national governing document to incorporate a bill of rights, as had most state constitutions.

Letters of a Federal Farmer, perhaps the most widely read Antifederalist pamphlet, listed the rights that should be protected: freedom of the press and

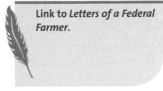

Link to *Letters of a Federal Farmer*.

religion, trial by jury, and guarantees against unreasonable searches. From Paris, Thomas Jefferson added his voice to the chorus. Replying to Madison's letter conveying a copy of the Constitution, Jefferson declared, "I like much the general idea" but not "the omission of a bill of rights. . . . A bill of rights is what the people are entitled to against every government on earth, general or particular, and what no just government should refuse, or rest on inference."

As state conventions considered ratification, delegates tended to put state and local interests first. Thus,

Ratification

many were persuaded when Federalists argued that the establishment of a national government with the power to tax foreign commerce would lessen the financial burdens that had prompted Shays's Rebellion and localized

FEDERAL HALL.

LET Trumpets found, and fwift wing'd Fame,
Thefe glorious tidings far proclaim ;
On Virtue's bafe, by Wifdom plann'd ;
And rear'd by Union's facred hand ;
The FEDERAL DOME, is rais'd fublime :
Its PILLARS folid, ftrong as time ;
Rife ! Commerce ! rife ! unfurl the fail,
Rich Golden harvefts blefs the vale :
Arts ! Science ! Genius ! fpring to light ;
And Freedom burft on realms of Night

American Antiquarian Society

▲ *The Federal Almanack* for 1789 trumpeted the virtues of the new Constitution. Not all Americans were so certain that the national government, here symbolized as an edifice supported by thirteen pillars, was as "solid, strong as time" as the printer proclaimed.

Table 7.1 Ratification of the Constitution by State Conventions

State	Date	Vote
Delaware	December 7, 1787	30–0
Pennsylvania	December 12, 1787	46–23
New Jersey	December 18, 1787	38–0
Georgia	January 2, 1788	26–0
Connecticut	January 9, 1788	128–40
Massachusetts	February 6, 1788	187–168
Maryland	April 28, 1788	63–11
South Carolina	May 23, 1788	149–73
New Hampshire	June 21, 1788	57–47
Virginia	June 25, 1788	89–79
New York	July 26, 1788	30–27
North Carolina	November 21, 1789	194–77
Rhode Island	May 29, 1790	34–32

and everyone realized the new Constitution could not succeed unless those key states accepted it.

Despite a valiant effort by Antifederalist Patrick Henry, pro-Constitution forces won by 10 votes in the Virginia convention, which likewise recommended the addition of specifications of rights. In New York, James Madison, John Jay, and Alexander Hamilton, writing collectively as "Publius," published *The Federalist*, a series of eighty-five political essays explaining the theory behind the Constitution and masterfully answering its critics. Their reasoned arguments, coupled with Federalists' promise to add a bill of rights to the Constitution, helped win the battle. On July 26, 1788, New York ratified the Constitution by the slim margin of 3 votes. Although the last states—North Carolina and Rhode Island—did not join the Union until November 1789 and May 1790, respectively, the new government was a reality. (See Table 7.1 for the details of ratifying convention votes.)

Americans in many cities celebrated ratification (somewhat prematurely) with a series of parades on

Celebrating Ratification

July 4, 1788, ritualistically linking the acceptance of the Constitution to the formal adoption of the Declaration of Independence. The carefully planned processions dramatized the history and symbolized the unity of the new nation, seeking to counteract memories of the dissent that had so recently engulfed such towns as Carlisle, Pennsylvania. Like pre-Revolution protest meetings, the parades served as political lessons for literate and illiterate Americans alike. The

protests in other states. Yet the lack of a bill of rights loomed ever larger as a flaw in the proposed government. Four of the first five states to ratify did so unanimously, but serious disagreements then surfaced. Massachusetts, in which Antifederalist forces had been bolstered by a backlash against the state government's heavy-handed treatment of the Shays rebels, ratified by a majority of only nineteen votes out of 355 cast and recommended amendments identifying rights. In June 1788, when New Hampshire ratified, the requirement of nine states was satisfied. But New York and Virginia had not yet voted,

▲ The Philadelphia State House (the building now known as Independence Hall, but without its familiar tower), on the left; and, to its right, Congress Hall, where Congress met when Philadelphia served as the U.S. capital. Portrayed in front of the state house in this 1792 watercolor is the 33-foot-long vessel *Union*, an elaborately constructed ship carried through the city streets in the grand ratification parade of July 4, 1788.

processions aimed to educate men and women about the significance of the new Constitution and to instruct them about political leaders' hopes for industry and frugality on the part of a virtuous American public.

Symbols expressing those goals filled the Philadelphia parade, planned by artist Charles Willson Peale. About five thousand people participated in the procession, which featured floats portraying such themes as "The Grand Federal Edifice" and stretched for a mile and a half. Marchers representing the first pioneers and Revolutionary War troops paraded with groups of farmers and artisans dramatizing their work. More than forty groups of tradesmen, including barbers, hatters, printers, cloth manufacturers, and clockmakers, sponsored floats. Lawyers, doctors, clergymen of all denominations, and congressmen followed the artisans. A final group of marchers symbolized the nation's future: students from the University of Pennsylvania and other city schools bore a flag labeled "The Rising Generation."

SUMMARY

During the 1770s and 1780s, the nation took shape as a political union. It began to develop an economy independent of the British Empire and attempted to chart its own course in the world in order to protect the national interest, defend the country's borders, and promote beneficial trade. Some Americans prescribed guidelines for the cultural and intellectual life they thought appropriate for a republic, outlining artistic and educational goals for a properly virtuous people. An integral part of the formation of the Union was the systematic formulation of American racist thought. Emphasizing race (rather than status as slave or free) as a determinant of African Americans' standing in the nation allowed men who now termed themselves "white" to define republicanism to exclude most men but themselves and to ensure that they would dominate the country for the foreseeable future. White women, viewed primarily as household dependents, had a limited role to play in the republic, as mothers of the next generation and as selfless contributors to the nation's welfare.

The experience of fighting a war and struggling for survival as an independent nation altered the political context of American life in the 1780s. In 1775, most Americans believed "that government which governs best governs least," but, by the late 1780s, many had changed their minds. They were the drafters and supporters of the Constitution, who concluded from the republic's vicissitudes under the Articles of Confederation that a more powerful central government was needed. During ratification debates, they contended that their proposals were

Legacy FOR A PEOPLE AND A NATION

The Township and Range System

Anyone flying over the American countryside west of the Appalachians today can see the impact of the township and range system inscribed on the landscape. Roads cross the land in straight lines, meeting at 90-degree angles, carving the terrain into a checkerboard pattern. That system of land surveys originated in the Land Ordinance of 1785, developed to organize land sales in the Northwest Territory.

Both English and native peoples traditionally bounded their lands by using such natural landmarks as hills, streams, large trees, and prominent rock outcroppings. That system, known as *metes and bounds*, produced such property descriptions as this one from 1667 in Maine: a "certen Parcell of upland . . . lying on the South West side of the . . . island, next [to] the Mussell Ridge & soe to the Sea Wall, & soe Joyneing to the Marsh." Even in the colonies' earliest days, though, some settlers employed surveyors who created lots of varying sizes divided by lines laid out abstractly on the soil. Sometimes those lines related to natural features such as the long, narrow lots in French Canada that fronted on the St. Lawrence River; other times, they bore little relationship to the land. But because North

America was settled in piecemeal fashion at various times and using different methods of land distribution, no one system dominated—not, at least, until the Land Ordinance of 1785. From then on, the system the ordinance described became the template for all land distributions by the U.S. government.

After a surveyor established an east-west baseline and a north-south meridian on a particular tract, he laid out rectangular townships composed of 36 numbered square-mile sections. He paid no attention to natural features; potential buyers were supposed to learn for themselves which sections had rivers, hills, or desirable assets like salt licks. The initial policy of selling sections as units, all priced the same, gave way by 1832 to a system in which individuals could purchase as few as forty acres and, after 1854, to price variations. As the United States expanded its reach westward across the continent, the township and range system followed, democratizing access to land and methodically opening land for settlement.

The legacy of the Land Ordinance of 1785 for the American people and nation still marks the landscape everywhere west of the Ohio River.

---

just as "republican" in conception as (if not more so than) the Articles.

Both sides concurred in a general adherence to republican principles, but they emphasized different views of republicanism. Federalists advanced a position based on the principles of classical republicanism, stressing the community over the individual. Antifederalists, fearing that elected leaders would not subordinate personal gain to the good of the whole, wanted a weak central government, formal protection of individual rights, and a loosely regulated economy. The Federalists won their point when the Constitution was adopted, however narrowly. The process of consolidating the states into a national whole was thereby formalized. The 1790s, the first decade of government under the Constitution, would witness hesi-

tant steps toward the creation of a true nation, the United States of America.

SUGGESTIONS FOR FURTHER READING

Richard Beeman, *Plain, Honest Men: The Making of the American Constitution* (2009)

Ira Berlin and Ronald Hoffman, eds., *Slavery and Freedom in the Age of the American Revolution* (1983)

Cathy N. Davidson, *Revolution and the Word: The Rise of the Novel in America* (1987)

Edith Gelles, *Portia: The World of Abigail Adams* (1992)

Woody Holton, *Unruly Americans and the Origins of the Constitution* (2007)

Peter S. Onuf, *Statehood and Union: A History of the Northwest Ordinance* (1987)

Jack N. Rakove, *Original Meanings: Politics and Ideas in the Making of the Constitution* (1996)

Leonard L. Richards, *Shays's Rebellion: The American Revolution's Final Battle* (2002)

David Waldstreicher, *In the Midst of Perpetual Fetes: The Making of American Nationalism, 1776–1820* (1997)

Gordon S. Wood, *The Creation of the American Republic, 1776–1787* (1969)

Go to the CourseMate website for primary source links, study tools, and review materials for this chapter. www.cengagebrain.com

Chapter 8

The Early Republic: Conflicts at Home and Abroad 1789–1800

In the last months of 1798, wealthy Philadelphia matron Deborah Norris Logan became the target of widespread public criticism. Her husband, Jefferson supporter Dr. George Logan, had undertaken a personal peace mission to France, fearing the looming prospect of war between the United States and its former ally. In her husband's absence, Logan's wife loyally defended his actions, and she in turn had to endure a campaign unlike any an American woman had previously experienced. That such an episode could occur at all suggests simultaneously the political symbolism now embodied by women, the growing division between the factions known as Federalists and Republicans, and the significance of foreign affairs in the early republic.

First to attack was "Peter Porcupine," the Federalist newspaper editor William Cobbett, who observed with sly sexual innuendo in his *Porcupine's Gazette* in July that "it is said that JEFFERSON went to his friend Doctor Logan's farm and spent three days there, soon after the Doctor's departure for France. *Query:* What did he do there? Was it to arrange the Doctor's *valuable manuscripts?*" Later Cobbett suggested that George and Deborah Logan should be placed in a pillory and publicly shamed for their actions—him, presumably, for treason (for that was the crime of which Federalists accused him) and her, Cobbett implied, for adultery. Understanding the symbolic significance of women's virtuous conduct in the fragile young republic, Republican newspapers leaped to Deborah's defense. They attacked the vulgarity of the suggestions about her and Vice President Jefferson, and insisted that not even a corrupt Londoner could have written "a greater libel upon public virtue or national morals."

Deborah Logan remained resolute in the face of such publicity. Although initially she secluded herself at her country estate, on Jefferson's advice she returned to

◀ George and Deborah Logan, whose activities caused so much political controversy in 1798. Their elegant house, Stenton, where Jefferson visited her in her husband's absence, is still preserved as a historic site.

Chronology

1789
- Washington inaugurated as first president
- Judiciary Act organizes federal court system
- French Revolution begins

1790
- Hamilton's *Report on Public Credit* proposes assumption of state debts

1791
- First ten amendments (Bill of Rights) ratified
- First national bank chartered

1793
- France declares war on Britain, Spain, and the Netherlands
- Washington's neutrality proclamation keeps the United States out of war
- Democratic societies founded, the first grassroots political organizations

1794
- Wayne defeats Miami Confederacy at Fallen Timbers
- Whiskey Rebellion in western Pennsylvania protests taxation

1795
- Jay Treaty with England resolves issues remaining from the Revolution
- Pinckney's Treaty with Spain establishes southern boundary of the United States
- Treaty of Greenville with Miami Confederacy opens Ohio to settlement

1796
- First contested presidential election: Adams elected president, Jefferson vice president

1798
- XYZ affair arouses American opinion against France
- Sedition Act penalizes dissent
- Virginia and Kentucky Resolutions protest suppression of dissent

1798–99
- Quasi-War with France
- Fries's Rebellion in Pennsylvania protests taxation

1800
- Franco-American Convention ends Quasi-War
- Gabriel's Rebellion threatens Virginia slaveowners

1801
- Thomas Jefferson elected president by the House of Representatives after stalemate in electoral college

Philadelphia to prove to the world George's "innocence and honor" and to show that she was "not afraid nor ashamed to meet the public eye." As reports emerged that her husband had been cordially received by French leaders and that he had had some success in quelling hostilities, she reveled in the praise showered on him, later recalling that "almost every day, wishes for his safety and speedy return greeted my ears." George Logan was indeed enthusiastically welcomed home, at least by Jeffersonian partisans. Congress, controlled by Federalists, was less impressed. In January 1799, it adopted the so-called Logan Act, still in effect, which forbids private citizens from undertaking unauthorized diplomatic missions.

The controversy caused by the Logans' actions was but one of many such battles in the 1790s. The fight over ratifying the Constitution turned out to presage an even wider division over the major political, economic, and diplomatic questions confronting the republic: the extent to which authority (especially fiscal authority and taxation) should be centralized in the national government, the relationship between national power and states' rights, the formulation of foreign policy in an era of continual warfare in Europe, and the limits of dissent. Americans had not anticipated the acrimonious disagreements that rocked the 1790s. Believing the Constitution would resolve the problems that had arisen under the Confederation, they mistakenly expected the new government to rule largely by consensus. And no one predicted the difficulties that would develop as the United States attempted to deal with Indian nations now wholly encompassed within its borders.

Most important, perhaps, Americans could not understand or fully accept the division of the nation's citizens into two competing factions. In republics, they believed, the rise of such factions signified decay and corruption. Yet on numerous occasions, as happened with Deborah and George Logan, Federalist and Republican leaders sought to mobilize their respective supporters through publications and public gatherings, thereby reworking the nation's political practice if not its theory. As the decade closed, Americans still had not come to terms with the implications of partisan politics, as was vividly illustrated by the fierce debates accompanying the election of 1800.

- What major challenges confronted the new republic?

- What disputes divided the nation's citizens?

- How did Americans react to those disputes?

Building a Workable Government

At first, consensus appeared possible. Only a few Antifederalists ran for office in the congressional elections held late in 1788, and even fewer were elected. Thus, most members of the First Congress supported a strong national government. The drafters of the Constitution had deliberately left many key issues undecided, so the nationalists' domination of Congress meant that their views quickly prevailed.

Congress faced four immediate tasks when it convened in April 1789: raising revenue to support the government, responding to states' calls for a bill of rights, setting up executive departments, and organizing the federal judiciary. The last task was especially important. The Constitution established a Supreme Court but left it to Congress to decide whether to have other federal courts.

First Congress

James Madison, representing Virginia in the House of Representatives, soon became as influential in Congress as he had been at the Constitutional Convention. A few months into the first session, he persuaded Congress to adopt the Revenue Act of 1789, imposing a 5 percent tariff on certain imports. Therefore, the First Congress quickly achieved what the Confederation Congress never had: an effective national tax law. The new government would have problems in its first years, but lack of revenue would not be one of them.

Madison also took the lead with respect to constitutional amendments. During the convention, he had opposed additional restrictions on the national government, believing that its limited powers made a Bill of Rights unnecessary. But

Bill of Rights

Madison subsequently changed his mind, observing to a friend that "in every Gov[ernmen]t power may oppress." When introducing nineteen proposed amendments in June, he told his fellow congressmen they needed to respond to the people's will as expressed in the state conventions, noting in particular that North Carolina had vowed not to ratify the Constitution without a Bill of Rights. Many initially resisted his arguments, yet after lengthy, heated debates, Congress approved twelve amendments. The states formally ratified ten, which officially became part of the Constitution on December 15, 1791 (see the appendix for the Constitution and all amendments, including the Twenty-seventh, which was one of the twelve). As Madison had predicted, their adoption defused Antifederalist opposition and rallied support for the new government.

 Link to Madison's original proposals for the Bill of Rights.

The First Amendment prohibited Congress from passing any law restricting the right to freedom of religion, speech, press, peaceable assembly, or petition. The next two amendments arose directly from the former colonists' fear of standing armies. The Second Amendment guaranteed the right "to keep and bear arms" because of the need for a "well-regulated Militia." The Third Amendment limited the conditions under which troops could be quartered in private homes. The next five pertained to judicial procedures. The Fourth Amendment prohibited "unreasonable searches and seizures," the Fifth and Sixth established the rights of accused persons, the Seventh specified the conditions for jury trials in civil (as opposed to criminal) cases, and the Eighth forbade "cruel and unusual punishments." The Ninth and Tenth Amendments reserved to the people and the states other unspecified rights and powers. In short, the amendments' authors insisted that, in listing some rights, they did not mean to preclude the exercise of others.

While debating proposed amendments, Congress also considered the organization of the executive branch. It readily agreed to continue the three administrative departments established under the Articles of Confederation: War, Foreign Affairs (renamed State), and Treasury. Congress instituted two lesser posts: the attorney general—the nation's official lawyer—and the postmaster general. Controversy arose over whether the president alone could dismiss officials whom he had originally appointed with the Senate's consent. After some debate, the House and Senate agreed he had such authority, which established the important principle that the heads of executive departments are accountable solely to the president.

Executive and Judiciary

The First Congress's most far-reaching law, the Judiciary Act of 1789, defined the jurisdiction of the federal judiciary and established a six-member Supreme Court, thirteen district courts, and three appellate courts. Its most important provision, Section 25, allowed appeals from state to federal courts when cases raised certain constitutional questions. The act presumed that Article VI of the Constitution, which stated that federal statutes and treaties were considered "the supreme Law of the Land," implied the right of appeal from state to federal courts, yet the Constitution did not explicitly permit such actions. In the nineteenth century, judges and legislators committed to states' rights would challenge the constitutionality of Section 25.

During its first decade, the Supreme Court handled few cases of any importance, and several members resigned. (John Jay, the first chief justice, served only six years.) But in a significant 1796 decision, *Ware v. Hylton*, the Court for the first time declared a state law unconstitutional. That same year, it also reviewed the constitutionality of an act of Congress, upholding its validity in the case of *Hylton v. U.S.* The most important case of the decade, *Chisholm v. Georgia* (1793), established that states could be sued in federal courts by citizens of other states. Five years later, the Eleventh Amendment to the Constitution overturned that decision, which was unpopular with state governments.

Despite the constitutional provisions forbidding Congress from prohibiting the importation of slaves for twenty years, in early 1790 three groups of Quakers submitted petitions to Congress favoring abolition and calling for an end to slave importations. In the ensuing debates, the nation's first political leaders directly addressed the questions they had suppressed in euphemisms in the Constitution. Southerners vigorously asserted that Congress should not even discuss the petitions. Had southern states thought that the federal government would consider interfering with the institution of slavery, such congressmen argued, they would never have ratified the Constitution. The legislators developed a positive defense of slavery that forecast most of the arguments offered on the subject during the next seven decades. They insisted that slavery was integral to the Union and that abolition would cause more problems than it solved, primarily by confronting the nation with the question of how to deal with a sizable population of freed people.

Some northern congressmen, and, in his last published essay, Benjamin Franklin, contested the southerners' position, but a consensus soon emerged to quash such discussions in the future. Congress accepted a committee report denying it the power either to halt slave importa-

| **Debate over Slavery** |

tions before 1808 or to emancipate slaves at any time, that authority "remaining with the several States alone." The precedent that Congress could not abolish slavery held until the Civil War.

Domestic Policy Under Washington and Hamilton

George Washington did not seek the presidency. In 1783, he returned to Mount Vernon eager for the peaceful life of a Virginia planter. But his fellow countrymen never regarded Washington as just another private citizen. Unanimously elected to preside at the Constitutional Convention, he did not participate in debates but consistently voted for a strong national government. After the adoption of the new governmental structure, Americans concurred that only George Washington had sufficient stature to serve as the republic's first president, an office designed largely with him in mind. The unanimous vote of the electoral college merely formalized that consensus.

Reluctant to return to public life, George Washington nevertheless knew he could not ignore his country's call. Awaiting the summons to New York City, the nation's capital, he wrote to an old friend, "My movements to the chair of Government will be accompanied by feelings not unlike those of a culprit who is going to the place of his execution. . . . I am sensible, that I am embarking the voice of my Countrymen and a good name of my own, on this voyage, but what returns will be made for them, Heaven alone can foretell." Symbolically, he donned a suit of homespun for the inaugural ceremony.

Washington acted cautiously during his first months in office in 1789, knowing that whatever he did would set precedents for the future. When the title by which he should be addressed aroused controversy (Vice President John Adams favored "His Highness, the President of the United States of America, and Protector of their Liberties"), Washington said nothing. The accepted title soon became a plain "Mr. President." By using the heads of the executive departments collectively as his chief advisers, he created the cabinet. As the Constitution required, he sent Congress an annual State of the Union message. Washington also concluded that he should exercise his veto power over congressional legislation sparingly—only, indeed, if he became convinced a bill was unconstitutional.

| **Washington's First Steps** |

Early in his term, Washington undertook elaborately organized journeys to all the states. At each stop, he was ritually welcomed by uniformed militia units, young women strewing flowers in his path, local leaders, groups of Revolutionary War veterans, and respectable citizens

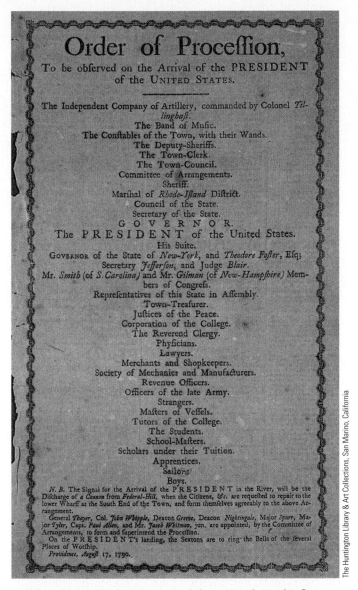

Order of Procession,

To be observed on the Arrival of the PRESIDENT of the UNITED STATES.

The Independent Company of Artillery, commanded by Colonel *Tillinghaft*.

The Band of Music.

The Constables of the Town, with their Wands.

The Deputy-Sheriffs.

The Town-Clerk.

The Town-Council.

Committee of Arrangements.

Sheriff.

Marshal of *Rhode-Island* District.

Council of the State.

Secretary of the State.

G O V E R N O R.

The P R E S I D E N T of the United States.

His Suite.

GOVERNOR of the State of *New-York*, and *Theodore Fofter*, Efq;

Secretary *Jefferfon*, and Judge *Blair*.

Mr. *Smith* (of *S. Carolina*) and Mr. *Gilman* (of *New-Hampfhire*) Members of Congrefs.

Representatives of this State in Affembly.

Town-Treasurer.

Justices of the Peace.

Corporation of the College.

The Reverend Clergy.

Physicians.

Lawyers.

Merchants and Shopkeepers.

Society of Mechanics and Manufacturers.

Revenue Officers.

Officers of the late Army.

Strangers.

Masters of Veffels.

Tutors of the College.

The Students.

School-Masters.

Scholars under their Tuition.

Apprentices.

Sailors.

Boys.

N. B. The Signal for the Arrival of the P R E S I D E N T in the River, will be the Difcharge of a Cannon from *Federal-Hill*, when the Citizens, &c. are requefted to repair to the lower Wharff at the South End of the Town, and form themfelves agreeably to the above Arrangement.

General *Thayer*, Col. *John Whipple*, Deacon *Greene*, Deacon *Nightingale*, Major *Spurr*, Major *Tyler*, Capt. *Paul Allen*, and Mr. *Jacob Whitman*, jun. are appointed, by the Committee of Arrangements, to form and fuperintend the Proceffion.

On the P R E S I D E N T's landing, the Sextons are to ring the Bells of the feveral Places of Worfhip.

Providence, Auguft 17, 1790.

▲ When George Washington toured the nation during his first term in office, he was greeted by local leaders in elaborately orchestrated rituals. The organizers of the ceremony at Providence, Rhode Island, on August 17, 1790, issued this broadside to inform participants of their plans for a formal procession. While some Americans gloried in such displays of pomp, others feared they presaged the return of monarchy.

who presented him with formal addresses reaffirming their loyalty to the United States. The president thus personally came to embody national unity, simultaneously drawing ordinary folk into the sphere of national politics.

Washington's first major task as president was to choose the heads of the executive departments. For the War Department, he selected an old comrade-in-arms, Henry Knox of Massachusetts, who had been his reliable artillery general during the war. His choice for the State Department was fellow Virginian Thomas Jefferson, who had just returned to the United States from his post as minister to France. And for the crucial position of secretary of the treasury, the president chose the brilliant, intensely ambitious Alexander Hamilton.

The illegitimate son of a Scottish aristocrat and a woman whose husband had divorced her for adultery and desertion, Hamilton was born in the British West Indies in 1757. His early years were spent in poverty; after his mother's death when he was eleven, he worked as a clerk for a mercantile firm. In 1773, with financial support from friends, Hamilton enrolled at King's College (later Columbia University). Only eighteen months later, the precocious seventeen-year-old contributed a pamphlet to the prerevolutionary publication wars. Devoted to the patriot cause, Hamilton volunteered for service in the American army, where he came to Washington's attention. In 1777, Washington appointed the young man as one of his aides, and the two developed great mutual affection.

Alexander Hamilton

The general's patronage helped the poor youth of dubious background to marry well. At twenty-three, he wed Elizabeth Schuyler, daughter of a wealthy New York family. After the war, Hamilton practiced law in New York City and served as a delegate to the Annapolis Convention and later the Constitutional Convention. Although he exerted little influence at either gathering, his contributions to *The Federalist* in 1788 revealed him as one of the chief political thinkers in the republic.

In his dual role as treasury secretary and presidential adviser, Hamilton exhibited two traits distinguishing him from most of his contemporaries. First, his primary loyalty lay with the nation. Caribbean-born, Hamilton had no natal ties to any state; he neither sympathized with nor fully understood demands for local autonomy. His fiscal policies always aimed at consolidating national power. Hamilton never feared the exercise of centralized executive authority, as did older compatriots who had clashed repeatedly with colonial governors, and he openly favored maintaining close political and economic ties with Britain.

Second, Hamilton regarded his fellow humans with unvarnished cynicism. Perhaps because of his difficult early life and his own overriding ambition, Hamilton believed people to be motivated primarily by economic self-interest. He placed no reliance on people's capacity for virtuous, self-sacrificing behavior. This outlook set him apart from those Americans who foresaw a rosy future in which public-spirited citizens would pursue the common good rather than their own private advantage. Although other Americans (for instance, James Madison) also stressed the role of private interests in a republic, Hamilton went further in his emphasis on self-interest as the major motivator of human behavior. Those beliefs significantly influenced the way he tackled the monumental task before him: straightening out the new nation's tangled finances.

Congress ordered the new secretary of the treasury to assess the public debt and to submit recommendations for supporting the government's credit. Hamilton found that the country's remaining war debts fell into three categories: those owed by the nation to foreign governments and investors, mostly to France (about $11 million); those owed by the national government to merchants, former soldiers, holders of revolutionary bonds, and the like (about $27 million); and, finally, similar debts owed by state governments (roughly $25 million). With respect to the national debt, few disagreed: Americans recognized that, if their new government was to succeed, it would have to repay at full face value those financial obligations the nation had incurred while winning independence.

National and State Debts

The state debts were another matter. Some states—notably, Virginia, Maryland, North Carolina, and Georgia—had already paid off most of their war debts by levying taxes and handing out land grants in lieu of monetary payments. They would oppose the national government's assumption of responsibility for other states' debts because their citizens would be taxed to pay such obligations. Massachusetts, Connecticut, and South Carolina, by contrast, still had sizable unpaid debts and would welcome a system of national assumption. The possible assumption of state debts also had political implications. Consolidating the debt in the hands of the national government would help to concentrate economic and political power at the national level. A contrary policy would reserve greater independence of action for the states.

Hamilton's first *Report on Public Credit*, sent to Congress in January 1790, stimulated lively debate. The treasury secretary proposed that Congress assume outstanding state debts, combine them with national obligations, and issue new securities covering both principal and accumulated unpaid interest. Hamilton thereby hoped to ensure that holders of the public debt—many of them wealthy merchants and speculators—had a significant financial stake in the new government's survival. The opposition coalesced around James Madison, who opposed the assumption of state debts for two reasons. First, his state of Virginia had already paid off most of its obligations, and second, he wanted to avoid rewarding wealthy speculators who had purchased state and national debt certificates at a small fraction of their face value from needy veterans and farmers.

Hamilton's Financial Plan

Prompted in part by Madison, the House initially rejected the assumption of state debts. The Senate, however, adopted Hamilton's plan largely intact. A series of compromises followed, in which the assumption bill became linked to the other major controversial issue of that congressional session: the location of the permanent national capital. Several related political deals were struck. A southern site on the Potomac River (favored by Washington and close to Mount Vernon) was selected for the capital, and the first part of Hamilton's financial program became law in August 1790.

Four months later, Hamilton submitted to Congress a second report on public credit, recommending the chartering of a national bank modeled on the Bank of England. This proposal, too, aroused much opposition, primarily after Congress had already voted to establish the bank.

First Bank of the United States

The Bank of the United States, to be chartered for twenty years, was to be capitalized at $10 million. Just $2 million would come from public funds, while private investors supplied the rest. The bank would act as collecting and disbursing agent for the Treasury, and its notes would circulate as the nation's currency. Most political leaders recognized that such an institution would be beneficial, especially because it would solve the problem of America's perpetual shortage of an acceptable medium of exchange. But another issue loomed large: did the Constitution give Congress the power to establish such a bank?

▲ Alexander Hamilton, by James Sharpless, about 1796. This profile of Hamilton, painted near the end of Washington's presidency, shows the secretary of the treasury as he looked during the years of his first heated partisan battles with Thomas Jefferson and James Madison.

National Portrait Gallery Smithsonian Institution

▲ The First Bank of the United States, constructed in the mid-1790s, as the building looked in Philadelphia in 1800. Its classical solidity visually concealed its contentious political origins.

James Madison answered that question with a resounding no. He pointed out that Constitutional Convention delegates had specifically rejected a clause authorizing Congress to issue corporate charters. Consequently, he argued, that power could not be inferred from other parts of the Constitution. Madison's contention disturbed President Washington, who decided to request other opinions before signing the bill into law. Edmund Randolph, the attorney general, and Thomas Jefferson, the secretary of state, agreed with Madison that the bank was unconstitutional. Jefferson referred to Article I, Section 8, of the Constitution, which gave Congress the power "to make all Laws which shall be necessary and proper for carrying into Execution the foregoing Powers." The key word, Jefferson argued, was *necessary*: Congress could do what was needed, but without specific constitutional authorization could not do what was merely desirable. Thus, Jefferson formulated the strict-constructionist interpretation of the Constitution.

Washington asked Hamilton to reply to the negative assessments of his proposal. Hamilton's *Defense of the Constitutionality of the Bank*, presented to the president in February 1791, brilliantly expounded a broad-constructionist view of the Constitution. Hamilton argued forcefully that Congress could choose any means not specifically prohibited by the Constitution to achieve a constitutional end. He reasoned thus: if the end was constitutional and the means was not *un*constitutional, then the means was constitutional.

Washington concurred, and the bill became law. The bank proved successful, as did the scheme for funding the national debt and assuming the states' debts. The new nation's securities became desirable investments for its own citizens and for wealthy foreigners, especially those in the Netherlands, who rushed to purchase American debt certificates. The influx of new capital, coupled with the high prices that American grain now commanded in European markets, eased farmers' debt burdens and contributed to a new prosperity. But two other aspects of Alexander Hamilton's wide-ranging financial scheme did not fare so well.

In December 1791, Hamilton presented to Congress his *Report on Manufactures*, the third and last of his prescriptions for the American economy. It outlined an ambitious plan for encouraging and protecting the United

Interpreting the Constitution

Report on Manufactures

States' infant industries, such as shoemaking and textile manufacturing. Hamilton argued that the nation could never be truly independent as long as it relied heavily on Europe for manufactured goods. He urged Congress to promote the immigration of technicians and laborers and to support industrial development through a limited use of protective tariffs. Many of Hamilton's ideas were implemented in later decades, but few congressmen in 1791 could see much merit in his proposals. They firmly believed America's future lay in agriculture and the carrying trade and that the mainstay of the republic was the yeoman farmer. Congress therefore rejected the report.

That same year, Congress accepted another feature of Hamilton's financial program, levying an excise tax on whiskey distilled within the United States. Although proceeds from the Revenue Act of 1789 covered the interest on the national debt, the decision to fund state debts meant that the national government required additional income. A tax on whiskey affected relatively few westerners—the farmers who grew corn and the small and large distillers who turned that corn into whiskey—and might also reduce the consumption of whiskey. (Eighteenth-century Americans, notorious for their heavy drinking, consumed about twice as much alcohol per capita as today's rate.) Moreover, Hamilton knew that those western farmers

and distillers were Jefferson's supporters, and he saw the benefits of taxing them rather than the merchants who favored his own policies.

News of the tax set off protests in the west, where residents were dissatisfied with the army's defense of their region from threats of Indian attack. To their minds, the same government that protected them inadequately was now proposing to tax them disproportionately. Unrest continued for two years on the frontiers of Pennsylvania, Maryland, and Virginia. Large groups of men drafted petitions protesting the tax, deliberately imitated crowd actions of the 1760s, and occasionally harassed tax collectors.

Whiskey Rebellion

President Washington responded with restraint until violence erupted in July 1794, when western Pennsylvania farmers resisted two excisemen trying to collect the tax. About seven thousand rebels convened on August 1 to plot the destruction of Pittsburgh but decided not to face the heavy guns of the fort guarding the town. Washington then took decisive action to prevent a crisis reminiscent of Shays's Rebellion. On August 7, he called on the insurgents to disperse and summoned nearly thirteen thousand militiamen. By the time federal forces marched westward in October and November (led

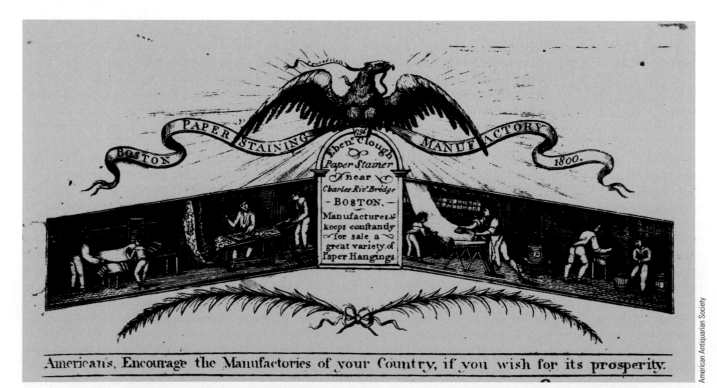

American Antiquarian Society

▲ Although Congress did not react positively to the arguments in Hamilton's *Report on Manufactures*, the owners of America's burgeoning industries recognized the importance of the policy Hamilton advocated. Ebenezer Clough, a Boston maker of wallpaper, incorporated into his letterhead the exhortation "Americans, Encourage the Manufactories of your Country, if you wish for its prosperity."

at times by Washington himself), the disturbances had ceased. The troops met no resistance and arrested only twenty suspects. Two men were convicted of treason, but—continuing his policy of restraint—Washington pardoned both. The leaderless and unorganized rebellion ended with little bloodshed.

The importance of the Whiskey Rebellion lay not in military victory over the rebels—for there was none—but in the forceful message it conveyed to the American people. The national government, Washington had demonstrated, would not allow violent resistance to its laws. In the republic, change would be effected peacefully, by legal means. People dissatisfied with the law should try to amend or repeal it, not take extralegal action as they had during the colonial era.

The French Revolution and the Development of Partisan Politics

By 1794, some Americans were already beginning to seek change systematically through electoral politics, even though traditional political theory regarded organized opposition—especially in a republic—as illegitimate. In a monarchy, formal opposition groups, commonly called factions, were to be expected. In a government of the people, by contrast, sustained factional disagreement was taken as a sign of corruption and subversion. Such negative judgments, though widely held, did not halt the growth of partisan sentiment.

Jefferson and Madison became convinced as early as 1792 that Hamilton's policies of favoring wealthy commercial interests at the expense of agriculture would eventually impose a corrupt government on the United States. Characterizing themselves as the true heirs of the Revolution, they charged Hamilton with plotting to subvert republican principles. To dramatize their point, Jefferson, Madison, and their followers in Congress began calling themselves Republicans. Hamilton in turn accused Jefferson and Madison of the same offense: attempting to destroy the republic. Hamilton and his supporters began calling themselves Federalists to legitimize their claims and link themselves with the Constitution. Each group accused the other of being an illicit faction working to sabotage the republican principles of the Revolution. Newspapers aligned with the two sides fanned the flames of partisanship, publishing virulent attacks on political opponents. Indeed, before parties fully coalesced, such newspapers not only provided a means of communication but also served as the very foundation of political identity.

At first, President Washington tried to remain aloof from the political dispute that divided Hamilton and

Republicans and Federalists

▲ A Federalist political cartoon from the 1790s shows "Mad Tom" Paine "in a rage," trying to destroy the federal government as carefully constructed (in classical style) by President Washington and Vice President Adams. That Paine is being aided by the Devil underscores the hostility to a partisanship common in the era.

Jefferson, his chief advisers. The growing controversy did help persuade him to promote political unity by seeking office again in 1792. But in 1793 and thereafter, developments in foreign affairs magnified the disagreements, for France (America's wartime ally) and Great Britain (America's most important trading partner) resumed the periodic hostilities that had originated a century earlier.

In 1789, many American men and women welcomed the news of the French Revolution. The French people's success in overthrowing an oppressive monarchy seemed to vindicate the United States' own revolution. Americans saw themselves as the vanguard of an inevitable historical trend that would reshape the world in a republican mold. Dinners, public ceremonies, and balls celebrated the French revolutionaries; women adorned their hats or clothing with revolutionary symbols; and some men

French Revolution

Erich Lessing/Art Resource, NY

▲ The violence of the French Revolution, especially the guillotining of King Louis XVI, shocked Americans, causing many to question whether the United States should remain that nation's ally.

began terming themselves "citizen" in the French manner, while women became "citizeness" or "citess." Yet one critical newspaper editor railed against "these fiery frenchified dames" whom he regarded as "monsters in human shape."

By 1793, the reports from France had become disquieting. Outbreaks of violence continued, and political leaders succeeded each other with bewildering rapidity. Executions mounted; the king himself was beheaded early that year. Although many Americans, including Jefferson and Madison, retained sympathy for the revolution, others—among them Alexander Hamilton—began to cite France as a prime example of the perversion of republicanism.

Debates within the United States intensified when the newly republican France became enmeshed in conflict with other European nations. Both because French leaders feared that neighboring monarchies would intervene to crush the revolution and because they sought to spread the republican gospel throughout the continent, they declared war first on Austria and then, in 1793, on Britain, Spain, and Holland. That confronted the Americans with a dilemma. The 1778 Treaty of Alliance with France bound them to that nation "forever," and

a mutual commitment to republicanism created ideological bonds. Yet the United States was connected to Great Britain as well. In addition to their shared history and language, America and Britain had again become important economic partners. Americans still purchased most of their manufactured goods from Great Britain. Indeed, because the revenues of the United States depended heavily on import tariffs, the nation's economic health in effect required uninterrupted trade with the former mother country.

The political and diplomatic climate grew even more complicated in April 1793, when Edmond Genêt, a representative of the French government, arrived in Charleston, South Carolina. Genêt's arrival raised troubling questions for President Washington. Should he receive Genêt, thus officially recognizing the French revolutionary government? Should he acknowledge an obligation to aid France under the terms of the 1778 Treaty of Alliance? Or should he proclaim American neutrality?

Edmond Genêt

Washington resolved his dilemma by receiving Genêt but also issuing a proclamation informing the world that the United States would adopt "a conduct friendly and impartial toward the belligerent powers." Federalist newspapers vociferously defended the proclamation, and partisan leaders organized rallies to praise the president's action. Republicans who favored assisting France reluctantly accepted the neutrality policy, which had overwhelming popular support.

Genêt's faction fell from power in Paris, and he subsequently sought political asylum in the United States. But his disappearance from the diplomatic scene did not diminish the impact of the French Revolution in America. The domestic divisions Genêt helped to widen were perpetuated by clubs called Democratic societies, formed by Americans sympathetic to the French Revolution and worried about the policies of the Washington administration. Such societies reflected a growing grassroots concern about the same developments that troubled Jefferson and Madison.

More than forty Democratic societies organized between 1793 and 1800. Their members saw themselves as seeking the same goal as the 1760s resistance movement: protecting people's liberties against encroachments by corrupt and self-serving rulers. To that end, they publicly protested government fiscal and foreign policy, repeatedly proclaiming their belief in "the equal rights of man," particularly the rights to free speech, free press, and assembly. Like the Sons of Liberty, the Democratic societies comprised chiefly artisans and craftsmen, although professionals, farmers, and merchants also joined. Although locally based, they communicated effectively through a network of newspapers and allied themselves nationally with congressional Republicans.

Democratic Societies

The rapid spread of such citizens' groups, outspokenly critical of the administration, disturbed Hamilton and Washington. Federalist writers charged that the organizations were dangerously subversive because elected officials, not "self-created societies," should formulate public policy. The groups' "real design," a newspaper asserted, was "to involve the country in war, to assume the reins of government and tyrannize over the people." The counterattack climaxed in the fall of 1794 when Washington accused the societies of fomenting the Whiskey Rebellion. Republican leaders and newspaper editors responded by defending the societies but condemning the insurgents.

In retrospect, Washington and Hamilton's reaction to the Democratic societies seems disproportionately hostile. But factional disputes were believed to endanger the survival of republics. As the first organized political dissenters in the United States, the Democratic societies alarmed administration officials, who had not yet accepted the idea that one component of a free government was an organized loyal opposition.

Partisan Politics and Relations with Great Britain

In 1794, George Washington dispatched Chief Justice John Jay to London to negotiate several unresolved questions in Anglo-American relations. The British had recently seized some American merchant ships trading in the French West Indies. The United States wanted to establish the countervailing principle of freedom of the seas and to assert its right, as a neutral nation, to trade freely with both combatants. Further, Great Britain still held posts in the American Northwest, thus violating the 1783 peace treaty. Settlers there believed that the British were responsible for renewed warfare with neighboring Indians, and they wanted that threat removed. The Americans also hoped for a commercial treaty and sought compensation for the slaves who left with the British army at the end of the war.

The negotiations in London proved difficult because Jay had little to offer in exchange for the concessions he sought. Britain did agree to evacuate the western forts and ease restrictions on American trade to England and the Caribbean. (Some limitations were retained, however, violating the Americans' desire for open commerce.) The treaty established two arbitration commissions—one to deal with prewar debts Americans owed to British creditors and the other to hear claims for captured American merchant ships—but Britain adamantly refused slaveowners compensation for their lost bondspeople. Under the circumstances, Jay had probably done the best he could. Nevertheless, most Americans, including the president, at first expressed dissatisfaction with at least some clauses of the treaty.

Jay Treaty Debate

The Senate debated the Jay Treaty in secret. Not until after ratification in late June 1795 (by 20 to 10, the exact two-thirds the Constitution required) did members of the public learn its provisions in the pages of the chief Republican newspaper, Benjamin Franklin Bache's *Aurora*. Bache organized the protests that followed, encouraging both publications and popular gatherings urging Washington to reject the treaty. Especially vehement opposition arose in the South, as planters criticized the lack of compensation for runaway slaves and objected to the commission on prewar debts, which might make them pay off obligations to British merchants dating back to the 1760s. But Federalists countered with meetings and essays of their own, contending that the Jay Treaty would prove preferable to the alternative—no treaty at all. The president, displeased by the Republicans' organized vocal opposition and convinced by pro-treaty arguments, signed the pact in mid-August. Just one opportunity remained to prevent it from going into effect: Congress had to appropriate funds to carry out the treaty, and, according to the Constitution, appropriation bills had to originate in the House of Representatives.

Washington delayed submitting the treaty to the House until March 1796, futilely hoping that by then the opposition would have dissipated. During the debate, Republicans argued against approving the appropriations, and they won a vote asking Washington to submit to the House all documents pertinent to the negotiations. In successfully resisting the request, Washington established a power still used today—executive privilege, in which the president may withhold information from Congress if he deems it necessary.

The treaty's opponents initially commanded a congressional majority, but pressure for appropriating the necessary funds built as time passed, fostered by an especially vigorous Federalist campaign of publications and petitions targeting middle-state congressmen whose districts would benefit from approval. Constituent petitions contended that failure to fund the treaty would lead to war with Britain, thus endangering Pennsylvania frontier settlements and New York and New Jersey commercial interests alike. Further, Federalists successfully linked the Jay Treaty with another, more popular pact. In 1795, Thomas Pinckney of South Carolina had negotiated a treaty with Spain giving the United States navigation privileges on the Mississippi River and the right to land and store goods at New Orleans tax free, thus boosting the nation's economy. The overwhelming support for Pinckney's Treaty (the Senate ratified it unanimously) helped to overcome opposition to the Jay Treaty. In late April, the House appropriated the money by the narrow margin of 51 to 48. The vote divided along partisan and regional lines: all but two southerners opposed the treaty, all but three congressional Federalists supported it, and a majority of middle-state representatives voted yes.

The Federalists' campaign to sway public opinion ironically violated their fundamental philosophy of government. They believed ordinary people should defer to the judgment of elected leaders, yet in order to persuade the House to follow the president's lead, they actively engaged in grassroots politicking. Even Federalist women became involved by presenting patriotic banners to militia companies or by taking formal roles in July fourth celebrations. The Federalists had won the battle, but in the long run they lost the war, for Republicans ultimately proved far more effective in appealing to the citizenry at large.

To describe the growing partisanship in Congress and the nation is easier than to explain such divisions in

Bases of Partisanship

the electorate. The terms used by Jefferson and Madison (the people versus aristocrats) or by Hamilton and Washington (true patriots versus subversive rabble) do not adequately explain the growing divisions. Simple economic differences

between agrarian and commercial interests do not provide the answer either, as more than 90 percent of Americans still lived in rural areas. Moreover, Jefferson's vision of a prosperous agrarian America rested on commercial farming, not rural self-sufficiency. Nor did the divisions in the 1790s simply repeat the Federalist-Antifederalist debate of 1787–1788. Even though most Antifederalists became Republicans, the party's leaders, Madison and Jefferson, had supported the Constitution.

Yet certain distinctions can be made. Republicans, especially prominent in the southern and middle states, tended to be self-assured, confident, and optimistic about both politics and the economy. Southern planters, in control of their region and dominating a class of enslaved laborers, foresaw a prosperous future based partly on continued westward expansion, a movement they expected to dominate. Republicans employed democratic rhetoric to win the allegiance of small farmers south of New England. Members of non-English ethnic groups—especially Irish, Scots, and Germans—found Republicans' words attractive. Artisans also joined the coalition; they saw themselves as the urban equivalent of small farmers, cherishing their independence from domineering bosses. Republicans of all descriptions emphasized developing America's own resources, worrying less than Federalists about the nation's place in the world. Republicans also remained sympathetic to France in international affairs.

By contrast, Federalists, concentrated among the commercial interests of New England, came mostly from English stock. Insecure, they stressed the need for order, hierarchy, and obedience to political authority. Wealthy New England merchants aligned themselves with the Federalists, but so, too, did the region's farmers who, prevented from expanding agricultural production because of New England's poor soil, gravitated toward the more conservative party. Federalists, like Republicans, assumed that southern and middle-state interests would dominate western lands, so they had little incentive to work actively to develop that potentially rich territory. In Federalist eyes, potential enemies—both internal and external—threatened the nation, necessitating a protective alliance with Great Britain. Given the dangers posed to the nation by European warfare, Federalists' vision of international affairs may have been accurate, but it was also unappealing. Because Federalists held out little hope of a better future to the voters of any region, it is not surprising that the Republicans prevailed in the end.

After the treaty debate, wearied by the criticism to which he had been subjected, George Washington decided to retire. (Presidents had not yet been limited to two

Washington's Farewell Address

terms, as they have been since the adoption of the Twenty-second Amendment in 1951.) In September,

Washington published his Farewell Address, most of which had been written by Hamilton. In it, Washington outlined two principles that guided American foreign policy at least until the late 1940s: to maintain commercial but not political ties to other nations and to enter no permanent alliances. He also drew sharp distinctions between the United States and Europe, stressing America's uniqueness—its exceptionalism—and the need for independent action in foreign affairs, today called unilateralism.

Washington lamented the existence of factional divisions among his countrymen. Some interpret his desire for an end to partisan strife as a call for politicians to consider only the good of the whole nation. But in the context of the impending presidential election, the Farewell Address appears rather as an attack on the legitimacy of the Republican opposition. Washington advocated unity behind the Federalist banner, which he viewed as the only proper political stance. The Federalists (like the Republicans) continued to see themselves as the sole guardians of the truth and the only true heirs of the Revolution. Both sides perceived their opponents as misguided, unpatriotic troublemakers who sought to undermine revolutionary ideals.

The two organized groups actively contending for office made the presidential election of 1796 the first serious contest for the position.

Election of 1796

To succeed Washington, the Federalists in Congress put forward Vice President John Adams, with the diplomat Thomas Pinckney as his running mate. Congressional Republicans chose Thomas Jefferson as their presidential candidate; the lawyer, Revolutionary War veteran, and active Republican politician Aaron Burr of New York agreed to run for vice president.

The election was contested, but not decided by popular vote. Most state legislatures appointed electors. Moreover, the method of voting in the electoral college did not take into account the possibility of party slates. The Constitution's drafters had not foreseen the development of competing national political organizations, so the Constitution provided no way to express support for one person for president and another for vice president. The electors simply voted for two people. The man with the highest total became president; the second highest, vice president.

That procedure proved to be the Federalists' undoing. Adams won the presidency with 71 votes, but a number of Federalist electors (especially those from New England) failed to cast ballots for Pinckney. Jefferson won 68 votes, 9 more than Pinckney, to become vice president. The incoming administration was thus politically divided. During the next four years, the new president and vice president, once allies and close friends, became bitter enemies.

John Adams and Political Dissent

John Adams took over the presidency peculiarly blind to the partisan developments of the previous four years. As president, he never abandoned an outdated notion discarded by George Washington as early as 1794: that the president should be above politics, an independent and dignified figure who did not seek factional advantage. Thus, Adams kept Washington's cabinet intact, despite its key members' allegiance to his chief Federalist rival, Alexander Hamilton. Adams often adopted a passive posture, letting others (usually Hamilton) take the lead when the president should have acted decisively. As a result, his administration gained a reputation for inconsistency. But Adams's detachment from Hamilton's maneuverings did enable him to weather the greatest international crisis the republic had yet faced: the Quasi-War with France.

The Jay Treaty improved America's relationship with Great Britain, but it provoked France to retaliate by

XYZ Affair

ordering its ships to seize American vessels carrying British goods. In response, Congress increased military spending, authorizing the building of ships and the stockpiling of weapons and ammunition. President Adams also sent three commissioners to Paris to negotiate a settlement. For months, the American commissioners sought talks with Talleyrand, the French foreign minister, but Talleyrand's agents demanded a bribe of $250,000 before negotiations could begin. The Americans retorted, "No, no; not a sixpence" and reported the incident in dispatches the president received in early March 1798. Adams informed Congress of the impasse and recommended further increases in defense appropriations.

Convinced that Adams had deliberately sabotaged the negotiations, congressional Republicans insisted that the dispatches be turned over to Congress. Adams complied, aware that releasing the reports would work to his advantage. He withheld only the names of the French agents, referring to them as X, Y, and Z. The revelation that the Americans had been treated with contempt stimulated a wave of anti-French sentiment in the United States. A journalist's version of the commissioners' reply, "Millions for defense, but not a cent for tribute," became the national slogan. Cries for war filled the air. Congress formally abrogated the Treaty of Alliance and authorized American ships to seize French vessels.

Thus began an undeclared war with France fought in Caribbean waters between warships of the U.S. Navy and

Quasi-War with France

French privateers. Although Americans initially suffered heavy losses of merchant shipping, by early 1799 the U.S. Navy had established its superiority. Its ships captured eight French privateers and naval vessels, easing the threat to America's vital Caribbean trade.

▲ This cartoon drawn during the XYZ affair depicts the United States as a maiden being victimized by the five leaders of the French government's directorate. In the background, John Bull (England) watches from on high, while other European nations discuss the situation.

The Republicans, who opposed war and continued to sympathize with France, could do little to stem the tide of anti-French feelings. Because Agent Y had boasted of the existence of a "French party in America," Federalists flatly accused Republicans (including the eccentric envoy George Logan) of traitorous designs. A New York newspaper declared that anyone who remained "lukewarm" after reading the XYZ dispatches was a "criminal—and the man who does not warmly reprobate the conduct of the French must have a soul black enough to be fit for treason Strategems and spoils." John Adams wavered between calling the Republicans traitors and acknowledging their right to oppose administration measures. His wife was less tolerant. "Those whom the French boast of as their Partizans," Abigail Adams declared, should be "adjudged traitors to their country." If Jefferson had been president, she added, "we should all have been sold to the French."

Federalists saw this climate of opinion as an opportunity to deal a death blow to their Republican opponents.

Alien and Sedition Acts

Now that the country seemed to see the truth of what they had been saying ever since the Whiskey Rebellion in 1794— that Republicans were subversive foreign agents—Federalists sought to codify that belief into law. In 1798, the Federalist-controlled Congress adopted a set of four laws known as the Alien and Sedition Acts, intended to suppress dissent and to prevent further growth of the Republican faction.

Three of the acts targeted recently arrived immigrants, whom Federalists accurately suspected of sympathizing with Republicans. The Naturalization Act lengthened the residency period required for citizenship and ordered all resident aliens to register with the federal government. The two Alien Acts, though not immediately implemented, provided for the detention of enemy aliens in time of war and gave the president authority to deport any alien he deemed dangerous to the nation's security.

The fourth statute, the Sedition Act, sought to control both citizens and aliens. It outlawed conspiracies to prevent the enforcement of federal laws, setting the maximum punishment for such offenses at five years in prison and a $5,000 fine. The act also tried to control speech. Writing, printing, or uttering "false, scandalous and malicious" statements against the government or the president "with intent to defame . . . or to bring them or either of them, into contempt or disrepute" became a crime punishable by as much as two years' imprisonment and a fine of $2,000. Today, a law punishing speech alone would be unconstitutional. But in the eighteenth century, when any organized political opposition was suspect, many Americans supported the Sedition Act's restrictions on free speech.

Visualizing THE PAST

Newspapers of the Early Republic

In the 1790s newspaper editors and publishers, unlike today, did not attempt to present news objectively, and indeed, none of their readers expected them to do so. Instead, newspapers were linked to the rapidly expanding political factions of the new nation—the partisan groupings (not yet political parties in the modern sense) terming themselves *Federalists* and *Republicans*. The "official" paper of the Federalists was *The Gazette of the United States* (colonial papers supported by individual governments too had been called *gazettes*—just as the *London Gazette* was tied to the English government). Among the Republicans'

many allied newspapers was *The New-York Journal, and Patriotic Register*. A reader comparing the front pages of two randomly selected issues could see at a glance the differences between the two. *The Gazette of the United States* filled its first page with sober news articles, whereas the face *The New-York Journal* presented to the world was consumed entirely with advertisements, some headed by intriguing design elements. Which would appeal more directly to America's artisans and forward-thinking agriculturalists: the dull newsprint of the Federalists, or the eye-catching ads of the Republicans?

Link to William Duane's A Letter to George Washington, President of the United States.

The Sedition Act led to fifteen indictments and ten guilty verdicts. Among those convicted were a congressman and former newspaper editor, Matthew Lyon of Vermont; and James Callender, a Scots immigrant and scandalmonger, whose exposés forced Alexander Hamilton to acknowledge an extramarital affair. After turning his attention to President Adams, Callender was convicted, fined, and jailed for nine months. Growing numbers of Republican newspaper editors nevertheless continued their relentless criticisms of Federalists, energized rather than quashed by the persecution. One of the most outspoken, William Duane—successor to Bache as the *Aurora's* editor—ignored a Sedition Act indictment, prosecutions in state and federal courts for other purported offenses, and even a vicious beating by Federalists thugs, to persist in partisan attacks. He and other Republicans created an informal network of newspapers that exchanged information and spread opposition ideas throughout the country.

Jefferson and Madison combated the acts in another way. Petitioning the Federalist-controlled Congress to repeal the laws would clearly fail, and Federalist judges refused to allow accused individuals to question the Sedition Act's constitutionality. Accordingly, the Republican leaders turned to the only other forum available for formal protest: state legislatures. Carefully concealing their own role—the vice president and congressman wanted to avoid being indicted for sedition—Jefferson and Madison drafted sets of resolutions that were introduced into the Kentucky and Virginia legislatures, respectively, in the fall of 1798. Because a compact among the states had created the Constitution, the resolutions contended, people speaking through their states had a legitimate right to judge the constitutionality of actions taken by the federal government. Both pronounced the Alien and Sedition Acts unconstitutional, and thus (declared Kentucky) "void and of no force," advancing the doctrine later known as nullification.

Although no other state endorsed them, the Virginia and Kentucky Resolutions nevertheless had considerable short- and long-term influence. First, they placed the opposition party squarely in the revolutionary tradition of resistance to tyrannical authority. Second, their theory of union inspired the Hartford Convention of 1814 and southern states' rights advocates in the 1830s and thereafter. Jefferson and Madison had identified a key constitutional issue: How far could states go in opposing the national government? How could a conflict between the two be resolved? These questions would not be definitively answered until the Civil War.

Virginia and Kentucky Resolutions

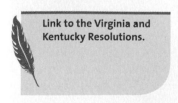

Link to the Virginia and Kentucky Resolutions.

Convention of 1800

Just as the Sedition Act was being implemented and northern legislatures were rejecting the Virginia and Kentucky Resolutions, Federalists split over the course of action the United States should take toward France. Hamilton and his supporters called for a declaration legitimizing the undeclared naval war. Adams, though, received a number of private signals—among them George Logan's report—that the French government regretted its treatment of the American commissioners.

Acting on such assurances, Adams dispatched William Vans Murray to Paris to negotiate with Napoleon Bonaparte, France's new leader, who was consolidating his hold on the country and eager to end messy foreign conflicts. The United States sought two goals: compensation for ships the French had seized since 1793 and abrogation of the treaty of 1778. The Convention of 1800, which ended the Quasi-War, provided for the latter but not the former. Still, it freed the United States from its only permanent alliance, thus allowing it to follow the independent diplomatic course George Washington had urged in his Farewell Address.

The West in the New Nation

By the end of the eighteenth century, the nation had added three states (Vermont, Kentucky, and Tennessee) to the original thirteen and more than 1 million people to the nearly 4 million counted by the 1790 census. It also nominally controlled all the land east of the Mississippi River and north of Spanish Florida, divided by the Ohio River. Control of the land north of the Ohio was achieved only after considerable bloodshed, for initially the land was dominated by a powerful western confederacy of eight Indian nations led by the Miamis.

General Arthur St. Clair, first governor of the Northwest Territory, futilely tried to open more land to settlement through failed treaty negotiations with the western confederacy in early 1789. Subsequently, Little Turtle, the confederacy's able war chief, defeated forces led by General Josiah Harmar (1790) and by St. Clair himself (1791) in major battles near the present border between Indiana and Ohio. More than six hundred of St. Clair's men died, and scores more were wounded, in the United States' worst defeat in the entire history of the American frontier.

In 1793, the Miami Confederacy declared that peace could be achieved only if the United States recognized

War in the Northwest Territory

Chicago History Museum

Independence National Historic Park

▲ The two chief antagonists at the Battle of Fallen Timbers and negotiators of the Treaty of Greenville (1795). On the left, Little Turtle, the leader of the Miami Confederacy; on the right, General Anthony Wayne. Little Turtle, in a copy of a portrait painted two years later, appears to be wearing a miniature of Wayne on a bear-claw necklace.

the Ohio River as its northwestern boundary. But the national government refused to relinquish its claims in the region. A reorganized and newly invigorated army under the command of General Anthony Wayne, a Revolutionary War hero, attacked and defeated the confederacy in August 1794 at the Battle of Fallen Timbers (near present-day Toledo, Ohio; see Map 7.3). Negotiating successfully with the confederacy was crucial for the new nation because without a treaty, warfare would continue indefinitely as American settlers—whom the government regarded as "white savages"—continued to push west. The United States lacked the will and the resources for a prolonged frontier conflict, so Wayne respectfully treated the confederacy's leaders, whom he saw as "red gentlemen." He reached agreement with them in August 1795.

The resulting Treaty of Greenville gave each side a portion of what it wanted. The United States gained the right to settle much of what was to become Ohio, the indigenous peoples retaining only the northwest corner of the region. Indians, though, received the acknowledgment they had long sought: American recognition of their rights to the soil. At Greenville, the United States formally accepted the principle of Indian sovereignty, by virtue of residence, over all lands the native peoples had not ceded. Never again would the U.S. government claim that it had

acquired Indian territory solely through negotiation with a European or North American country.

South of the Ohio, Pinckney's Treaty with Spain that same year established the 31st parallel as the boundary between the United States and Florida. Nevertheless, Spanish influence in the Old Southwest continued to raise questions about the loyalty of American settlers in the region, much of it still unceded and occupied by Creeks, Cherokees, and other Indian nations. A Southwest Ordinance (1790) attempted to organize the territory; by permitting slavery, it made the region attractive to slaveholders.

Increasingly, even Indian peoples who lived independent of federal authority came within the orbit of U.S. influence. The nation's stated goal was to "civilize" them. "Instead of exterminating a part of the human race," Henry Knox, Washington's secretary of war, contended in 1789, the government should "impart our knowledge of cultivation and the arts to the aboriginals of the country." The first step in such a project, Knox suggested, should be to introduce to Indian peoples "a love for exclusive property"; to that end, he proposed that the government give livestock to individual Indians. Four years later, the Indian Trade and Intercourse

"Civilizing" the Indians

▲ In 1805, an unidentified artist painted Benjamin Hawkins, a trader and U.S. agent to the Indians of the Southeast, at the Creek agency near Macon, Georgia. Hawkins introduced European-style agriculture to the Creeks, who are shown here with vegetables from their fields. Throughout the eastern United States, Indian nations had to make similar adaptations of their traditional lifestyles in order to maintain their group identity.

Greenville County Museum of Art

Act of 1793 codified Knox's plan, promising that the federal government would supply Indians with animals and agricultural implements, and also provide appropriate instructors.

The well-intentioned plan reflected federal officials' blindness to the realities of native peoples' lives. Not only did it incorrectly posit that the Indians' traditional commitment to communal notions of landowning could easily be overcome, it also ignored the centuries-long agricultural experience of eastern Indian peoples. The policymakers focused only on Indian men: because they hunted, male Indians were "savages" who had to be "civilized" by being taught to farm. That in these societies women traditionally did the farming was irrelevant because, in the eyes of the officials, Indian women—like those of European descent—should properly confine themselves to child rearing, household chores, and home manufacturing.

Indian nations at first responded cautiously to the "civilizing" plan. The Iroquois Confederacy had been devastated by the war; its people in the 1790s lived in what one historian has called "slums in the wilderness." Restricted to small reservations increasingly surrounded by

Iroquois and Cherokees

Anglo-American farmlands, men could no longer hunt and often spent their days in idle carousing. Quaker missionaries started a demonstration farm among the Senecas, intending to teach men to plow, but they quickly learned that women showed greater interest in their message. The same was true among the Cherokees of Georgia, where Indian agents found that women eagerly sought to learn both new farming methods and textile-manufacturing skills. As their southern hunting territories were reduced, Cherokee men did begin to raise cattle and hogs, but they startled the reformers by treating livestock like wild game, allowing the animals to run free in the woods and simply shooting them when needed, in the same way they had once killed deer. Men also started to plow the fields, although Cherokee women continued to bear primary responsibility for cultivation and harvest.

Iroquois men became more receptive to the Quakers' lessons after the spring of 1799, when a Seneca named Handsome Lake experienced a remarkable series of visions. Like other prophets stretching back to Neolin in the 1760s, Handsome Lake preached that Indian peoples should renounce alcohol, gambling, and other destructive European customs. Even though he directed his followers to reorient men's and women's work assignments as the Quakers advocated, Handsome Lake aimed above all to preserve Iroquois culture. He recognized that, because men could no longer obtain meat through hunting, only by adopting the European sexual division of labor could the Iroquois retain an autonomous existence.

"Revolutions" at the End of the Century

Three events in the last two years of the eighteenth century can be deemed real or potential revolutions: Fries's Rebellion, Gabriel's Rebellion, and the election of Thomas Jefferson. Although they differed significantly, these events mirrored the tensions and uncertainties of the young republic. The Fries rebels resisted national authority to tax. Gabriel and his followers directly challenged the slave system so crucial to the Chesapeake economy. And the venomous, hard-fought presidential election of 1800 exposed a structural flaw in the Constitution that would have to be corrected by amendment.

The tax resistance movement known by the name of one of its prominent leaders—militia captain and Revolutionary War veteran John Fries—arose among German American farmers in Pennsylvania's Lehigh Valley in 1798–1799. To

Fries's Rebellion

finance the Quasi-War, Congress enacted taxes on land, houses, and legal documents. German Americans, imbued with revolutionary ideals (at least two-fifths were veterans), saw in the taxes a threat to their liberties and livelihoods as well as an echo of the hated Stamp Act of 1765. Asserting a right of resistance to unconstitutional laws, they raised liberty poles, signed petitions to Congress, and nonviolently prevented assessors from evaluating their homes. They voiced repeated threats but harmed no one.

Even so, a federal judge ordered the arrest of twenty resisters. In response, in March 1799 Fries led a troop of 120 militiamen to Bethlehem where they surrounded a tavern temporarily housing the prisoners. Lengthy negotiations failed to win their release, but eventually, fearing a violent confrontation, a federal marshal let the men go. President Adams described the militiamen's actions as "treason, being overt acts of levying war against the United States." Fries and many of his neighbors were arrested and tried; he and two others were convicted of treason; thirty-two more, of violating the Sedition Act. Although Fries and the other "traitors" were sentenced to hang, Adams pardoned them (and all the others) just two days before their scheduled execution. Despite clemency from a Federalist president, the region's residents became, and remained, Republican partisans.

▲ Richmond, Virginia, at the time of Gabriel's Rebellion. This was the city as Gabriel knew it. The state capitol, the rebels' intended target, dominates the city's skyline as it dominated Gabriel's thinking.

Haitian Refugees

Although many European-Americans initially welcomed the news of the French Revolution in 1789, few expressed similar sentiments about the slave rebellion that broke out soon thereafter in the French colony of St. Domingue (later Haiti), which shared the island of Hispaniola with Spanish Santo Domingo. The large number of refugees who soon flowed into the new United States from that nearby revolt brought with them consequences deemed undesirable by most political leaders. Less than a decade after winning independence, the new nation confronted its first immigration crisis.

Among the approximately 600,000 residents of St. Domingue in the early 1790s were about 100,000 free people, almost all of them slaveowners; half were whites, the rest mulattos. When in the wake of the French Revolution those free mulattos split the slaveholding population by seeking greater social and political equality, the slaves seized the opportunity to revolt. By 1793, they had triumphed under the leadership of a former slave, Toussaint L'Ouverture, and in 1804 they finally ousted the French, thereafter establishing the republic of Haiti. Thousands of whites and mulattos, accompanied by as many slaves as they could readily transport, sought asylum in the United States during those turbulent years.

Although willing to offer shelter to refugees from the violence, American political leaders nonetheless feared the consequences of their arrival. Southern plantation owners shuddered at the thought that slaves so familiar with ideas of freedom and equality would mingle with their own bondspeople. Many were uncomfortable with the immigration of numerous free people of color, even though the immigrants were part of the slaveholding class. Most of the southern states adopted laws forbidding the entry of Haitian slaves and free mulattos, but the laws were difficult if not impossible to enforce, as was a later congressional act to the same effect. So, more than fifteen thousand refugees—white, black, and of mixed-race origins—flooded into the United States and Spanish Louisiana. Many ended up in Virginia (which did not pass an exclusion law) or the cities of Charleston, Savannah, and New Orleans.

There they had a considerable impact on the existing population. In both New Orleans and Charleston, the influx of mulattos gave rise to a heightened color consciousness that placed light-skinned people at the top of a hierarchy of people of color. Not coincidentally, the Charleston Brown Fellowship Society, composed exclusively of free mulattos, was founded in 1793. After the United States purchased Louisiana in 1803, the number of free people of color in the territory almost doubled in three years, largely because of a final surge of immigration from the new Haitian republic. And, in Virginia, stories of the successful revolt helped to inspire local slaves in 1800 when they planned the action that has become known as Gabriel's Rebellion.

The Haitian refugees thus linked both European-Americans and African Americans to current events in the West Indies, indelibly affecting both groups of people.

Louisiana State Museum

◀ A free woman of color in Louisiana early in the nineteenth century, possibly one of the refugees from Haiti. Esteban Rodriguez Mir, named governor of Spanish Louisiana in 1782, ordered all slave and free black women to wear head wraps rather than hats—which were reserved for whites—but this woman and many others subverted his order by nominally complying, but nevertheless creating elaborate headdresses.

Like their white compatriots in the Lehigh Valley and elsewhere, African Americans both slave and free became familiar with concepts of liberty and equality during the Revolution. They, too, witnessed the benefits of fighting collectively for freedom, rather than resisting individually or running away—a message reinforced by the dramatic news of the successful slave revolt in St. Domingue in 1793. Gabriel, an enslaved Virginia blacksmith who planned the second end-of-the-century revolution, drew on both Haitian and American experiences as well as his religious beliefs.

Gabriel's Rebellion

For months, often accompanied by his preacher brother, Martin, Gabriel visited Sunday services at black Baptist and Methodist congregations where bondspeople gathered free of the watchful eyes of their owners.

Gabriel first recruited to his cause other skilled African Americans who like himself lived in semi-freedom under minimal supervision. Next, he enlisted rural slaves. The rebels planned to attack Richmond on the night of August 30, 1800; set fire to the city; seize the state capitol; and capture the governor, James Monroe. At that point, Gabriel believed, other slaves and perhaps poor whites would join in.

The plan showed considerable political sophistication, but heavy rain forced a postponement. Several planters then learned of the plot from informers and spread the alarm. Gabriel avoided arrest for weeks, but militia troops quickly apprehended and interrogated most of the other leaders of the rebellion. Twenty-six rebels, including Gabriel himself, were hanged. Ironically, only those slaves who betrayed their fellows won freedom as a result of the rebellion.

Legacy FOR A PEOPLE AND A NATION

Dissent During Wartime

The Quasi-War with France in 1798 and 1799, the nation's first overseas conflict, brought the first attempt to suppress dissent. By criminalizing dissenting speech, the Sedition Act of 1798 tried to quiet the Republicans' criticism of the war and President John Adams. Fifteen men were indicted and ten fined and jailed (including a congressman) after being convicted under the statute's provisions.

Although Americans might assume that their right to free speech under the First Amendment, now more fully accepted than it was two centuries ago, protects dissenters during wartime, the history of the nation suggests otherwise. Every conflict has stimulated efforts by both government and individual citizens to suppress dissenters. During the Civil War, the Union jailed civilian Confederate sympathizers, holding them under martial law for long periods. During the First World War, a Sedition Act allowed the government to deport immigrant aliens who too vocally criticized the war effort, among them several outspoken Socialists and anarchists. Moreover, angry neighbors subjected citizens who objected to government policies to a variety of formal and informal sanctions. World War II brought the silencing of isolationists' voices, as those who had opposed American entry into the war were denied public outlets for their ideas.

The consequences of antiwar protests in the Vietnam era still affect the nation today, for the American people remain divided over whether the proper course of action in the 1960s and 1970s was dissent from, or acquiescence to, government policy. The USA PATRIOT Act, adopted after the attacks of September 11, 2001, removed long-standing restrictions on federal government surveillance of citizens, controversially granting access to library records. Criticism of the wars in Iraq and Afghanistan has raised questions that arouse heated debate: Do newspapers that publish classified information or pictures of abused prisoners overstep their proper bounds? Can political figures censure the conduct of the wars without being seen as unpatriotic?

Freedom of speech is never easy to maintain, and wartime conditions make it much more difficult. When the nation comes under attack, whether from a foreign country or from terrorists, many patriotic Americans argue that the time for dissent has ceased and that all citizens should support the government. Others contend that, if freedom in the nation is to mean anything, people must have the right to speak their mind freely at all times. Events in the United States since the 9/11 attacks suggest that this legacy remains extremely contentious for the American people.

At his trial, one of Gabriel's followers made explicit the links that so frightened Chesapeake slaveholders. He told his judges that, like George Washington, "I have adventured my life in endeavouring to obtain the liberty of my countrymen, and am a willing sacrifice in their cause." Southern state legislatures responded to such claims by increasing the severity of the laws regulating slavery. Before long, all talk of emancipation ceased in the South, and slavery became even more firmly entrenched as an economic institution and way of life.

The third end-of-the-century revolution was a Republican "takeover"—the election of Thomas Jefferson as president and a Congress dominated by Republicans—and the culmination of a decade of increasing partisanship. Prior to November 1800, Federalists and Republicans not only campaigned for congressional seats but also maneuvered furiously to control the outcome in the electoral college. Each side feared victory by the other, and both wanted to avoid reproducing the divided results of 1796. Republicans again nominated Thomas Jefferson and Aaron Burr; Federalists named John Adams, with Charles Cotesworth Pinckney of South Carolina as vice president. The network of Republican newspapers forged in the fires of Sedition Act prosecutions vigorously promoted the Jeffersonian cause. When the votes were counted, Jefferson and Burr had tied with seventy-three (no Republican elector wanted to chance omitting Burr's name from his ballot), while Adams had sixty-four and Pinckney sixty-three. Under the Constitution, the election had to be decided in the existing House of Representatives; the newly elected Jeffersonians would not take office until the president did.

Balloting continued for six days and thirty-five ballots, with Federalists uniformly supporting Burr, whereas Republicans held firm for Jefferson. Finally, James Bayard, a Federalist and the sole congressman from Delaware, concluded (perhaps correctly) that "we must risk the Constitution and a civil war or take Mr. Jefferson." He brokered a deal that gave the Virginian the presidency on the thirty-sixth ballot. A crucial consequence of the election was the adoption of the Twelfth Amendment, which provided that electors would henceforth cast separate ballots for president and vice president.

The defeated Federalists turned to strengthening their hold on the judiciary while they could. President Adams named his secretary of state, John Marshall, chief justice; Marshall would serve for thirty-four years, leaving a lasting imprint on constitutional interpretation. Adams spent his last hours in office on March 3, 1801, appointing so-called midnight justices to new positions created in the hastily adopted Judiciary Act of 1801, which also reduced the number of Supreme Court justices from six to five. The fiercely partisan Federalists thus hoped to prevent Jefferson from exerting immediate influence on the judicial branch, despite Republican control of the presidency and Congress.

Election of 1800

SUMMARY

As the nineteenth century began, inhabitants of the United States faced changed lives in the new republic. Indian peoples east of the Mississippi River found that they had to surrender some aspects of their traditional culture to preserve others. Some African Americans struggled unsuccessfully to free themselves from the inhuman bonds of slavery, then subsequently confronted more constraints than ever because of increasingly restrictive laws.

European-Americans, too, adjusted to changed circumstances. The first eleven years of government under the Constitution established many enduring precedents for congressional, presidential, and judicial action—among them establishment of the cabinet, interpretations of key clauses of the Constitution, and stirrings of judicial review of state and federal legislation. Building on successful negotiations with Spain (Pinckney's Treaty), Britain (the Jay Treaty), and France (the Convention of 1800), the United States developed its diplomatic independence, striving to avoid entanglement with European countries and their continental wars.

Yet especially after 1793 internal political consensus proved elusive. The 1790s spawned vigorous debates over foreign and domestic policy and saw the beginnings of a system of organized factionalism and grassroots politicking involving both men and women, if not yet formal parties. The Whiskey and Fries Rebellions showed that regional conflicts persisted even under the new government. The waging of an undeclared war against France proved extremely contentious, splitting one faction and energizing another. In 1801, after more than a decade of struggle, the Jeffersonian view of the future of agrarian, decentralized republicanism prevailed over Alexander Hamilton's vision of a powerful centralized economy and a strong national government.

SUGGESTIONS FOR FURTHER READING

Joyce Appleby, *Capitalism and a New Social Order: The Republican Vision of the 1790s* (1984)

Susan Branson, *These Fiery Frenchified Dames: Women and Political Culture in Early National Philadelphia* (2001)

Douglas Egerton, *Gabriel's Rebellion: The Virginia Slave Conspiracies of 1800 and 1802* (1993)

Stanley Elkins and Eric McKitrick, *The Age of Federalism, 1788–1800* (1993)

Joseph J. Ellis, *Founding Brothers: The Revolutionary Generation* (2000)

James Horn, Jan Ellen Lewis, and Peter S. Onuf, eds., *The Revolution of 1800: Democracy, Race, and the New Republic* (2002)

Richard Labunski, *James Madison and the Struggle for the Bill of Rights* (2006)

David Andrew Nichols, *Red Gentlemen & White Savages: Indians, Federalists, and the Search for Order on the American Frontier* (2008)

Jeffrey L. Pasley, *"The Tyranny of Printers": Newspaper Politics in the Early American Republic* (2001)

Thomas P. Slaughter, *The Whiskey Rebellion* (1986)

 CourseMate

Go to the CourseMate website for primary source links, study tools, and review materials for this chapter. www.cengagebrain.com

Chapter 9

Defining the Nation
1801–1823

Disinternment of the Mastodon by Charles Willson Peale, *1806. Courtesy of the Maryland Historical Society (Detail)*

*E*ager to set himself apart from the allegedly aristocratic ways of his Federalist predecessors, President Thomas Jefferson displayed impatience, even disdain, for ceremony. But on his first New Year's Day in office, the third president eagerly awaited the ceremonial presentation of a much-heralded tribute to his commitment, in the words of one of the gift's bearers, to "defend Republicanism and baffle all the arts of Aristocracy." Crafted in Massachusetts, the belated inaugural gift had been nearly a month en route, traveling amid much fanfare for more than 400 miles by sleigh, boat, and wagon. Weighing more than twelve hundred pounds and measuring four feet in diameter, it bore the inscription "THE GREATEST CHEESE IN AMERICA—FOR THE GREATEST MAN IN AMERICA."

The idea for the "mammoth cheese," as it became known, had been born the previous July in a small farming community in western Massachusetts. The "Ladies" of Cheshire—a town as resolutely Jeffersonian-Republican as it was Baptist—had made the cheese from the milk of nine hundred cows as "a mark of the exalted esteem" in which the town's residents held the Republican president. As members of a religious minority in New England, where Congregationalists still dominated the pulpits and statehouses, the Cheshire Baptists had much to celebrate in the election of a president whose vision for the nation featured not just agrarianism but also separation of church and state. Their fiery pastor, John Leland, presented the cheese to the president and, two days later, preached the Sunday sermon in the House of Representatives, where at least one genteel listener dismissed his brand of evangelicalism as "horrid."

Federalist editors delighted in poking fun at the mammoth cheese—especially at those who had made it. Its semirotten, maggot-infested condition upon delivery symbolized, they said, the nation under Republican rule. Its very existence, to say nothing of its size, resulted from the excesses of democracy, in which even women and backwoods preachers could play leading roles. The cheese, they scoffed, had been made of "*asses'* milk."

◄ Federalists derided the Cheshire cheese as the "mammoth" cheese, after the mastodon (similar to the "woolly mammoth") unearthed by naturalist Charles Willson Peale in 1801. Partially funded by the Jefferson administration, Peale's expedition was considered a boondoggle by Federalists.

Chronology

1801	■ Marshall becomes chief justice
	■ Jefferson inaugurated as president
1801–05	■ United States defeats Barbary pirates
1803	■ *Marbury v. Madison*
	■ Louisiana Purchase
1804	■ Jefferson reelected president, Clinton vice President
1804–06	■ Lewis and Clark expedition
1805	■ Tenskwatawa emerges as Shawnee leader
1807	■ *Chesapeake* affair
	■ Embargo Act
1808	■ Congress bans slave importation
	■ Madison elected president
1808–13	■ Tenskwatawa and Tecumseh organize Indian resistance
1811	■ National Road begun
1812	■ Madison reelected president
1812–15	■ War of 1812
1813	■ Tecumseh's death
	■ Boston Manufacturing Company starts textile mill in Waltham, Massachusetts
1814	■ Treaty of Ghent
1814–15	■ Hartford Convention
1815	■ Battle of New Orleans
1817	■ Regular steamboat travel begins on Mississippi
1817–25	■ Erie Canal constructed
1819	■ *McCulloch v. Maryland*
	■ Adams-Onis Treaty
1819– early 1820s	■ First major depression
1820–21	■ Missouri Compromise
1823	■ Monroe Doctrine

*Y*et the Federalists' derision of the mammoth cheese won them few new supporters and instead inspired additional showy expressions of democratic pride. In the following months, a Philadelphia baker sold "Mammoth Bread," while two butchers sent the president a "Mammoth veal." In Washington, a "Mammoth Eater" consumed forty-two eggs in ten minutes. Nor did the "mammoth" craze prove ephemeral: two years later, in 1804, a "mammoth loaf" was served—along with whiskey, hard cider, and wine—in the Capitol to a raucous crowd of Federalist-disparaging Republicans, including President Jefferson himself.

Seemingly frivolous in retrospect, political symbolism and rivalries were deadly serious in the early republic, as attested to by those, most famously Alexander Hamilton, who died in duels. People excluded from formal political participation often joined voting citizens in expressing ideal visions for the nation's future when they petitioned legislatures, marched in parades, engaged in heated tavern debates—and sent the president a mammoth cheese. Behind such symbolism lay serious political ideologies. Jeffersonians believed virtue derived from agricultural endeavors, and they thus celebrated the acquisition of the Louisiana Territory. Their efforts to expand their agriculturally based "empire of liberty" westward were resisted, however, by Native Americans and their European allies, and sometimes by Federalists, too. Not until the War of 1812 largely removed such resistance would the United States begin its nearly unbridled expansion across the continent. Although it resolved few of the issues that caused it, that war held profound consequences for American development. It secured the United States' sovereignty, opened much of the West to European-Americans and their African American slaves, and helped spur revolutions in transportation and industry.

Although contemporary observers noted that the postwar nationalism heralded an "Era of Good Feelings," it soon became apparent that good feelings had limits. When economic boom turned to bust, the postwar bubble of nationalistic optimism and ostensible unity may not have popped, but it never again proved quite so buoyant. No issue proved more divisive than slavery's future in the West, as Missouri's petition for statehood revealed.

- **What characterized the two main competing visions for national development?**

- **How did America's relationship with Europe influence political and economic developments?**

- In what ways did nonvoting Americans—most blacks, women, and Native Americans—take part in defining the new nation?

Political Visions

In his inaugural address, Jefferson appealed to his opponents. Standing in the Senate chamber, the Capitol's only completed part, he addressed the electorate not as party members but as citizens with common beliefs: "We are all republicans, we are all federalists." Nearly a thousand people strained to hear his vision of a restored republicanism: "A wise and frugal government, which shall restrain men from injuring one another, which shall leave them free to regulate their pursuits of industry and improvement, and shall not take from the mouth of labor the bread it had earned. This is the sum of good government."

But outgoing president John Adams did not hear Jefferson's call for unity, having left Washington before dawn. He and Jefferson, once close friends, now disliked each other intensely. Despite the spirit of Jefferson's inaugural address, the Democratic-Republicans—as the Republicans of the 1790s now called themselves, after the Democratic societies of the 1790s—and the Federalists remained bitter opponents. These parties held different visions of how society and government should be organized. The Federalists advocated a strong national government with centralized authority to promote economic development. The Democratic-Republicans sought to restrain the national government, believing that limited government would foster republican virtue, which derived from agricultural endeavors. Nearly two decades later, Jefferson would call his election "the revolution of 1800," which was "as real a revolution in the principles of our government as that of 1776 was in its form."

When the Cheshire farmers sent Jefferson a mammoth cheese, they did so largely to express gratitude for his commitment to the separation of church and state. On the very day he received the overripe cheese, Jefferson reciprocated by penning a letter to the Baptist association in Danbury, Connecticut, proclaiming that the Constitution's First Amendment supported a "wall of separation between church and state." Jefferson's letter articulated a core component of his vision of limited government. The president declared that "religion is a matter which lies solely between Man & his God." It lay beyond the government's purview. New England Baptists hailed Jefferson as a hero, but New England Federalists

Separation of Church and State

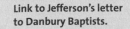

Link to Jefferson's letter to Danbury Baptists.

believed their worst fears were confirmed. During the election of 1800, Federalists had waged a venomous campaign against Jefferson, incorrectly labeling him an atheist. Their rhetoric proved so effective that, after Jefferson's election, some New England women hid their Bibles in their gardens and wells to foil Democratic-Republicans allegedly bent on confiscating them. Jefferson's letter to the Danbury Baptists seemingly vindicated such hysteria.

Jefferson became president during a period of religious revivalism, particularly among Methodists and Baptists, whose democratic preaching—all humans, they said, were equal in God's eyes—encouraged a growing democratic political culture. Emboldened by secular and religious ideologies about human equality, society's nonelites articulated their own political visions. Rather than simply taking stands in debates defined by social and political betters, they worked, to reshape the debates. When the Cheshire Baptists sent their cheese to President Jefferson, for example, they pointedly informed the Virginia planter that it had been made "without a single slave to assist."

Political Mobilization

The revolution of 1800, which gave the Democratic-Republicans majorities in both houses of Congress in addition to the presidency, resulted from an electorate limited largely, but not exclusively, to property-holding men. The Con-stitution left the regulation of voting to the individual states. In no state but New Jersey could women vote even when meeting property qualifications, and in New Jersey that right was granted inadvertently and later revoked in 1807. In 1800, free black men meeting property qualifications could vote in all states but Delaware, Georgia, South Carolina, and Virginia, but local custom often kept them from exercising that right. Nonetheless, partisan politics captured nearly all Americans' imaginations, and politicians actively courted nonvoters along with voters. Most political mobilization took place locally, where partisans rallied popular support for candidates and their ideologies on militia training grounds, in taverns and churches, at court gatherings, and during holiday celebrations. Voters and nonvoters alike expressed their views by marching in parades, signing petitions, singing songs, and debating politically charged sermons. Perhaps most important, they devoured a growing print culture of pamphlets, broadsides (posters), almanacs, and—especially—newspapers.

The Partisan Press

Newspapers provided a forum for sustained political conversation. Read aloud in taverns, artisans' workshops, and homes, newspapers gave national importance to local events. Without newspaper publicity, Cheshire's mammoth cheese would have been little more than a massive hunk of curdled milk. With it, a cheese became worthy of presidential

Courtesy, The Henry Francis du Pont Winterthur Museum

◄ Although most places limited the vote to property-owning white men, elections, such as this one in Philadelphia, drew multi-racial crowds of men, women, and children.

response. In 1800, the nation had 260 newspapers; by 1810, it had 396—virtually all of them unabashedly partisan.

The parties adopted official organs. Shortly after his election, Jefferson persuaded the *National Intelligencer* to move from Philadelphia to the new capital of Washington, where it became the Democratic-Republicans' voice. In 1801, Alexander Hamilton launched the *New York Evening Post* as the Federalist vehicle. It boosted Federalists while frequently calling Jefferson a liar and depicting him as the head of a slave harem. The party organs—published six or seven times a week, year in and year out—ensured that the growing American obsession with partisan politics extended beyond electoral campaigns.

Jefferson needed public servants as well as supporters. To bring into his administration men sharing his vision of individual liberty, an agrarian republic, and limited government, Jefferson refused to recognize appointments made by Adams in his presidency's last days and dismissed Federalist customs collectors. He awarded vacant treasury and judicial offices to Republicans. Federalists accused Jefferson of "hunting the Federalists like wild beasts" and abandoning his inaugural address' peaceful overtures. Jeffersonians worked to make the government leaner. If Alexander Hamilton had viewed the national debt as the engine of economic growth, Jefferson deemed it the source of government corruption. Secretary of the Treasury Albert Gallatin cut the army budget in half and reduced the 1802 navy budget by two-thirds. He moved to reduce the national debt from $83 million to $57 million, hoping to retire it altogether by 1817. Austerity motivated Jefferson to close two of the nation's five diplomatic missions abroad, at

Limited Government

The Hague and in Berlin. Jeffersonians attacked taxes as well as spending: the Democratic-Republican–controlled Congress oversaw the repeal of all internal taxes, including the despised whiskey tax of 1791.

Ideas of liberty also distinguished Democratic-Republicans from Federalists. The Alien and Sedition Acts of 1798 had helped unite the Republicans in opposition. Jefferson now declined to use the acts against his opponents, instead pardoning those already convicted of violating them.

Congress let the Sedition Act expire in 1801 and the Alien Act in 1802, and repealed the Naturalization Act of 1798, which had required fourteen years of residency for citizenship. The 1802 act that replaced it, while stipulating the registration of aliens, required of would-be citizens only five years of residency, loyalty to the Constitution, and the forsaking of foreign allegiances and titles. The new act remained the basis of naturalized American citizenship into the twentieth century.

To many Democratic-Republicans, the judiciary represented a centralizing and undemocratic force, especially because judges were appointed, not elected, and served for life. Partisan Democratic-Republicans thus targeted opposition judges. At Jefferson's prompting, the House impeached (indicted) and the Senate convicted Federal District Judge John Pickering of New Hampshire. Allegedly deranged and alcoholic, Pickering made an easy mark. On the same day in 1803 that Pickering was ousted from office, the House impeached Supreme Court Justice Samuel Chase for judicial misconduct. A staunch Federalist, Chase had pushed for prosecutions under the Sedition Act, had actively campaigned for Adams in 1800, and had repeatedly denounced Jefferson's administration from the

Judicial Politics

bench. But in the Senate, the Democratic-Republicans failed to muster the two-thirds majority necessary for conviction. The failure to remove Chase preserved the Court's independence and established the precedent that criminal actions, not political disagreements, justified removal from office.

Although Jefferson appointed three new Supreme Court justices during his two administrations, the Court remained a Federalist stronghold under the leadership of his distant cousin John Marshall. Marshall adopted some outward trappings of Republicanism—opting for a plain black gown over the more colorful academic robes of his fellow justices—but adhered steadfastly to Federalist ideology. Even after the Democratic-Republicans achieved a majority of Court seats in 1811, Marshall remained extremely influential as chief justice. Under the Marshall Court (1801–1835), the Supreme Court consistently upheld federal supremacy over the states while protecting the interests of commerce and capital.

The Marshall Court

Marshall made the Court an equal branch of the government in practice as well as theory. Previously regarded lightly, judicial service became a coveted honor for ambitious and talented men. Marshall, moreover, strengthened the Court by having it speak with a more unified voice; rather than issuing a host of individual concurring judgments, the justices now issued joint majority opinions. Marshall became the voice of the majority: from 1801 through 1805, he wrote twenty-four of the Court's twenty-six decisions; through 1810, he wrote 85 percent of the opinions, including every important one.

One of the most important involved Adams's midnight appointments. In his last hours in office, Adams had named Federalist William Marbury a justice of the peace in the District of Columbia. But Jefferson's secretary of state, James Madison, declined to certify the appointment, allowing the new president to appoint a Democratic-Republican instead. Marbury sued, requesting a writ of mandamus (a court order forcing the president to appoint him). *Marbury v. Madison* presented a political dilemma. If the Supreme Court ruled in Marbury's favor, the president probably would not comply with the writ, and the Court could not force him to do so. Yet by refusing to issue the writ, the Federalist-dominated bench would hand the Democratic-Republicans a victory.

Judicial Review

To avoid both pitfalls, Marshall brilliantly recast the issue. Writing for the Court, he ruled that Marbury had a right to his appointment but that the Supreme Court could not compel Madison to honor the appointment because the Constitution did not grant the Court power to issue a writ of mandamus. In the absence of any specific mention in the Constitution, Marshall wrote, the section of the Judiciary Act of 1789 authorizing the Court to issue writs was unconstitutional. Thus, the Supreme Court denied itself the power to issue writs of mandamus but established its far greater power to judge the constitutionality of laws passed by Congress. In doing so, Marshall fashioned the theory of judicial review. Because the Constitution was "the supreme law of the land," Marshall wrote, any federal or state act contrary to the Constitution must be null and void. The Supreme Court, whose duty it was to uphold the law, would decide whether a legislative act contradicted the Constitution. "It is emphatically the province and duty of the judicial department," Marshall ruled, "to say what the law is." This power of the Supreme Court to determine the constitutionality of legislation and presidential acts permanently enhanced the independence of the judiciary and breathed life into the Constitution. "Marshall found the Constitution paper and made it power," President James A. Garfield later observed.

In the first election after the Twelfth Amendment's ratification, Jefferson took no chances: he dropped Burr as his running mate and, in keeping with the already established convention of having a North-South balance on the ticket, chose George Clinton of New York. They swamped their opponents—South Carolinian Charles Cotesworth Pinckney and New Yorker Rufus King—in the electoral college by 162 votes to 14, carrying fifteen of the seventeen states. That 1804 election escalated the long-standing animosity between Burr and Hamilton, who supported Burr's rival in the New York gubernatorial election. When Hamilton called Burr a liar, Burr challenged Hamilton to a duel. Believing his honor was at stake, Hamilton accepted the challenge even though his son Philip had died in 1801 from dueling wounds. Because New York had outlawed dueling, the encounter took place across the Hudson River in New Jersey. Details of the duel itself remain hazy—did Hamilton withhold his fire, as he claimed he would?—but the outcome was clear: Hamilton died the following day, after being shot by Burr. In New York and New Jersey, prosecutors indicted Burr for murder.

Election of 1804

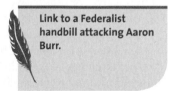

Link to a Federalist handbill attacking Aaron Burr.

Facing arrest if he returned to either state and with his political career in ruins, Burr fled to the West. While historians disagree about his motives, the "Burr Conspiracy" was understood at the time to involve a scheme with Brigadier General James Wilkinson to create a new empire by using military force to acquire what is now Texas and by persuading already existing western territories to leave the United States and join the new empire. Brought to trial for treason in 1807, Burr faced a prosecution aided by President Jefferson but overseen by Jefferson's political rival Chief Justice Marshall. (At the time, Supreme Court justices presided over circuit courts.) Prompted by Marshall to interpret treason narrowly, the jury acquitted Burr, who fled to Europe.

As statesmen bickered over how to realize the nation's potential, other Americans touted their own nationalist visions with paintbrushes and pens. Nearly three decades after the Constitution's ratification, painters continued to memorialize great birth scenes of American nationhood, such as the Declaration of Independence's signing, Revolutionary War battle scenes, and the Constitutional Convention. Four of John Trumbull's revolutionary scenes, commissioned in 1817, still hang on the rotunda of the Capitol building in Washington.

Nationalism and Culture

With architecture, Americans self-consciously constructed a new, independent nation. Designed by Major Pierre Charles L'Enfant, a French-born engineer who served under George Washington during the Revolution, the city of Washington was meant to embody a "reciprocity of sight": Each of the government's three branches—the legislative, judicial, and executive—should keep an eye on one another at all times. But nationalism could be easier to envision than to construct. Beset by pragmatic difficulties, L'Enfant's plan took nearly a century to implement. A French visitor in 1851 noted that Washington had "streets without houses," "houses without streets," and was "striking proof of this truth, that one cannot create a great city at will." In Washington and elsewhere, wealthier Americans commissioned homes in the "federal" style, which imitated classical architecture in its economy of decoration and which made use of indigenous, rather than imported, building materials.

The era's best-selling book was Noah Webster's spelling book, which proposed making English more "republican." By some estimates, the book sold nearly 100 million copies by the end of the nineteenth century. Webster believed Americans should speak and spell like one another—they should bind together by speaking a national language—but unlike "King's English," their language should not require elite training to master. Words should be spelled as they sound—for example, "honor" should replace "honour." A shared language would unite an increasingly farflung population.

National Expansion Westward

Little excited Jeffersonians' nationalistic imaginations more than the West and its seeming abundance of unoccupied land ripe for agrarian expansion. Federalists, though, often urged caution, fearing uncontrolled expansion would impede commercial development and federal oversight.

By 1800, hundreds of thousands of white Americans had settled in the rich Ohio River and Mississippi River valleys, intruding on Indian lands. In the Northwest they raised foodstuffs, primarily wheat, and in the Southwest they cultivated cotton. At the time of the American Revolution, cotton production was profitable only for the Sea Island planters in South Carolina and Georgia, who grew the long-staple variety. Short-staple cotton, which grew readily in the interior and in all kinds of soil, was unmarketable because its sticky seeds could be removed only by hand. After a young New England inventor named Eli Whitney designed a cotton gin (short for "engine") in 1793, allowing one person to remove the same number of seeds that previously required fifty people working by hand, the cultivation of short-staple cotton spread rapidly westward into the fertile lands of Louisiana, Mississippi, Alabama, Arkansas, and Tennessee. By exponentially increasing the efficiency with which cotton fiber could be extracted from raw cotton, the cotton gin greatly increased the demand for slaves who seeded, tended, and harvested cotton fields.

Whatever crops they marketed, American settlers depended on free access to the Mississippi River and its Gulf port, New Orleans. "The Mississippi," wrote Secretary of State James Madison, "is to them [western settlers] everything. It is the Hudson, the Delaware, the Potomac and all navigable rivers of the Atlantic States formed into one stream." Whoever controlled the port of New Orleans had a hand on the American economy's throat.

Spain, which had acquired France's territory west of the Mississippi in the settlement of the Seven Years' War (1763), secretly transferred it back to France in 1800 and 1801. American officials learned of the transfer only in 1802, when Napoleon seemed poised to rebuild a French empire in the New World. "Every eye in the United States is now focused on the affairs of Louisiana," Jefferson wrote to Robert R. Livingston, the American minister in Paris. American concerns intensified when Spanish officials, on the eve of ceding control to the French, violated Pinckney's treaty by denying Americans the privilege of storing their products (or exercising their "right of deposit") at New Orleans prior to transshipment to foreign markets. Western farmers and eastern merchants, who traded through New Orleans, thought a devious Napoleon had closed the port; they talked war.

New Orleans

To relieve the pressure for war and win western farmers' support, Jefferson urged Congress to authorize the call-up of eighty thousand militiamen but at the same time sent Virginia Governor James Monroe to join Robert Livingston in France with instructions to buy the port of New Orleans and as much of the Mississippi valley as possible. Arriving in Paris in April 1803, Monroe learned with astonishment that France had already offered to sell all 827,000 square miles of Louisiana to the United States

Map 9.1 Louisiana Purchase

The Louisiana Purchase (1803) doubled the area of the United States and opened the trans-Mississippi West for American settlement.

Source: Copyright © Cengage Learning

for a mere $15 million. With St. Domingue torn from French control by revolution and slave revolt, Napoleon gave up dreams of a New World empire and no longer needed Louisiana as its breadbasket. His more urgent need was for money to wage war against Britain. On April 30, Monroe and Livingston signed a treaty buying the vast territory whose exact borders and land remained uncharted (see Map 9.1).

The Louisiana Purchase appealed to Americans with divergent ideas about how best to achieve national greatness and personal prosperity.

Louisiana Purchase

The purchase ensured that the United States would control the Mississippi's mouth, giving peace of mind to western settlers who relied on the river to market their goods. It also inspired the commercial visions of those who imagined the United States as the nexus of international trade networks reaching between Europe and Asia. Louisiana promised to fulfill the dreams of easterners seeking cheap, fertile lands. Its vast expanse meant, too, that land could be set aside for Indians displaced by the incursion of white settlers and their black slaves, soothing the consciences of those white Americans who preferred to "civilize" rather than

to exterminate the continent's first settlers. The purchase had its critics, though: some doubted its constitutionality (even Jefferson agonized over it); others worried that it belied the Democratic-Republicans' commitment to debt reduction; some New England Federalists complained that it undermined their commercial interests and threatened the sustainability of the republic by spreading the population beyond where it could be properly controlled. Overall, though, the Louisiana Purchase was the most popular achievement of Jefferson's presidency.

Louisiana was not, however, the "vast wilderness" that some Federalists lamented and most Republicans coveted. When the United States acquired the territory, hundreds of thousands of people who had not been party to the agreement became American subjects. These included Native Americans from scores of nations who made their homes within the enormous territory, as well as people of European and African descent—or, often, a complex mixture of the two—who congregated primarily along the Gulf Coast. Around New Orleans, Louisiana's colonial heritage was reflected in its people: creoles of French and Spanish descent, slaves of African descent, free people of color, and Acadians, or Cajuns (descendants of French settlers in eastern Canada), as well as some Germans, Irish, and English. The 1810 census, the first taken after the purchase, reported that 97,000 non-Indians lived in the Louisiana Purchase area, of whom the great majority (77,000) lived in what is now the state of Louisiana. Not all these new Americans welcomed their new national identity. Although Jefferson imagined the West as an "empire of liberty," free people of color soon discovered their exclusion from the Louisiana Purchase treaty's provision that "the inhabitants of the ceded territory" would be accorded the rights of American citizenship. Denied the right to vote and serve on juries, New Orleans' people of color fought to retain their rights to form families and to bequeath as they pleased, and—with the help of sympathetic Anglos serving on juries, as justices, or as legislators—some of them succeeded.

Jefferson had a long-standing interest in the trans-Mississippi West, envisioning it as punctuated with volcanoes and mountains of pure salt, where llamas and mammoths roamed and Welshmen settled. He felt an urgent need to explore it, fearing that, if Americans did not claim it as their own, the British, who still controlled the northern reaches of the continent (in present-day Canada) and parts of the Pacific Northwest, surely would. He lost no time in launching a military-style mission that would chart the region's commercial possibilities—its water passages to the Pacific as well as its trading opportunities with Indians—while cataloguing its geography, peoples, flora, and fauna.

Lewis and Clark Expedition

The expedition, headed by Meriwether Lewis and William Clark, began in May 1804 and lasted for more than two years; it traveled up the Missouri River, across the Rockies, and then down the Columbia to the Pacific Ocean—and back. Along the way, the expedition's members "discovered" (as they saw it) dozens of previously unknown Indian tribes, many of whom had long before discovered Europeans. Lewis and Clark found the Mandans and Hidatsas already well supplied with European trade goods, such as knives, corduroy trousers, and rings. Although the Corps of Discovery, as the expedition came to be called, expected to find Indians and prepared for possible conflict, its goal was peaceable: to foster trade relations, win political allies, and take advantage of Indians' knowledge of the landscape. Accordingly, Lewis and Clark brought with them twenty-one bags of gifts for Native American leaders, both to establish goodwill and to stimulate interest in trading for American manufactured goods. Most of the corps' interactions with native peoples were cordial, but when Indians failed to be impressed by Lewis and Clark's gifts, tensions arose. After an encounter with the Lakota (or Sioux), Lewis denounced them as "the vilest miscreants of the savage race."

Although military in style, the Corps of Discovery proved unusually democratic in seating enlisted men on courts-martial and allowing Clark's black slave York as well as the expedition's female guide and translator Sacagawea to vote on where to locate winter quarters in 1805. But unlike the expedition's other members, neither York nor Sacagawea drew wages, and when York later demanded his freedom for his services, Clark repaid him instead with—in Clark's own words—"a severe trouncing."

Lewis and Clark failed to discover a Northwest Passage to the Pacific, and the route they mapped across the Rockies proved more perilous than practical, but their explorations contributed to nationalist visions of American expansion. Fossils and Native American artifacts collected during the expedition were displayed in Charles Willson Peale's museum at Independence Hall in Philadelphia, an institution emphasizing the uniqueness of America's geography and, especially, its republican experiment; in addition to housing natural and human "curiosities," Peale's museum displayed his own renowned portraits of Revolutionary heroes. Nationalists generally overlooked Indians' claims to American lands. Although Jefferson had more sympathy for Indians than did many of his contemporaries—he took interest in their cultures and believed Indians to be intellectually equal to whites—he nonetheless lobbied, unsuccessfully, for a constitutional amendment that would transport them west of the Mississippi into the newly acquired Louisiana Territory. He became personally involved in efforts to pressure the Chickasaws to sell their land, and in the event that legal methods for removing Indians should fail, he advocated trickery. Traders, he suggested, might run the "good and influential

▲ At the time of the Louisiana Purchase in 1803, New Orleans was already a bustling port, though boosters predicted an even brighter future under American "wings."

© Chicago History Museum, USA /The Bridgeman Art Library

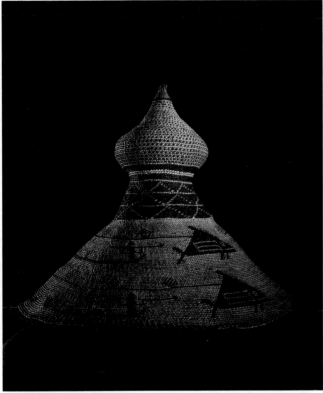

▲ Made by the Nootka Indians, this wicker hat was collected—either as a trade item or a gift—by Lewis and Clark during their expedition to the Columbia River.

American ones, becoming a shaman in 1804. But when European diseases ravaged his village, he despaired.

Lalawethika emerged from his own battle with illness in 1805 as a new man, renamed Tenskwatawa ("the Open Door") or—by whites—"the Prophet." Claiming to have died and been resurrected, he traveled widely in the Ohio River valley as a religious leader, attacking the decline of moral values among Native Americans, warning against whiskey, condemning intertribal battles, and stressing harmony and respect for elders. He urged Indians to return to the old ways and to abandon white ways: to hunt with bows and arrows, not guns; to stop wearing hats; and to give up bread for corn and beans. Tenskwatawa was building a religious movement that offered hope to the Shawnees, Potawatomis, and other displaced western Indians.

By 1808, Tenskwatawa and his older brother Tecumseh talked less about spiritual renewal and more about resisting American aggression. They invited Indians from all nations to settle in pan-Indian towns in Indiana,

Tenskwatawa and Tecumseh

individuals" into debt, which they would have to repay "by a cessation of lands."

Some Indian nations decided to deal with white intruders by adopting white customs as a means of survival and often agreeing to sell their lands and move west. These "accommodationists" (or "progressives") were opposed by "traditionalists," who urged adherence to native ways and refused to relinquish their lands. Distinctions between accommodationists and traditionalists were not always so clear-cut, however, as the Seneca Handsome Lake had demonstrated just a few years before.

Divisions Among Indian Peoples

In the early 1800s, two Shawnee brothers, Tenskwatawa (1775–1837) and Tecumseh (1768–1813), led a traditionalist revolt against American encroachment by fostering a pan-Indian federation that centered in the Old Northwest and reached into parts of the South. During the two brothers' lifetimes, the Shawnees had lost most of their Ohio land; by the 1800s, they occupied only scattered sites in Ohio and in the Michigan and Louisiana territories. Despondent, Lalawethika—as Tenskwatawa had been called as a youth—had turned to a combination of European remedies (particularly whiskey) and Native

▲ At his museum in Philadelphia, George Willson Peale displays some of the "natural curiosities" that many Americans believed contributed to the nation's uniqueness.

▲ This Charles M. Russell painting of the Lewis and Clark expedition depicts Sacagawea talking with Chinook Indians. A Shoshone, Sacagawea knew the land and the languages of the mountain Indians, and helped guide the Corps of Discovery.

first at Greenville (1806–1808) and then at Prophetstown (1808–1812), near modern-day Lafayette. The new towns challenged the treaty-making process by denying the claims of Indians who had been guaranteed the same land as part of the Treaty of Greenville of 1795 in exchange for enormous cessions. Younger Indians, in particular, flocked to Tecumseh, the more politically oriented of the two brothers.

Convinced that only an Indian federation could stop the advance of white settlement, Tecumseh sought to unify northern and southern Indians by preaching Indian resistance across a wide swath of territory, ranging from Canada to Georgia. Among southern Indians, only one faction of the Creek nation welcomed him, but his efforts to spread his message southward nonetheless alarmed white settlers and government officials. In November 1811, while Tecumseh was in the South, Indiana governor William Henry Harrison moved against Tenskwatawa and his followers. During the battle of Tippecanoe, the army burned their town; as they fled, the Indians exacted revenge on white settlers. "What other course is left for us to pursue," asked Harrison, "but to make a war of extirpation upon them." With the stakes raised, Tecumseh entered a formal alliance with the British, who maintained forts in southern Ontario. This alliance in the West, combined with issues over American neutral rights on the high seas, were propelling the United States toward war with Britain.

The Nation in the Orbit of Europe

A decade earlier, in 1801, when Jefferson had sought to set a new course for the nation, he tried to put tensions with France to rest. "Peace, commerce, and honest friendship with all nations, entangling alliances with none," he had proclaimed in his first inaugural address. Yet the economy of the early republic relied heavily on both fishing and the carrying trade, in which the American merchant marine transported commodities between nations. Merchants in Boston, Salem, and Philadelphia traded with China, sending cloth and metal to swap for furs with Chinook Indians on the Oregon coast, and then sailing to China to trade for porcelain, tea, and silk. The slave trade lured American ships to Africa. America's commercial interests were clearly focused on the seas, and not long after Jefferson's first inaugural address, the United States was at war with Tripoli—a state along the Barbary Coast of North Africa—over a principle that would long be a cornerstone of American foreign policy: freedom of the seas. In other words, outside national territorial waters, the high seas should be open for free transit of all vessels.

In 1801, the bashaw (pasha) of Tripoli declared war on the United States for its refusal to pay tribute for safe passage of its ships, sailors, and passengers through the Mediterranean. Jefferson deployed a naval squadron to protect American ships. After two years of stalemate, Jefferson declared a blockade of Tripoli, but when the American frigate *Philadelphia* ran aground in the harbor, its three hundred officers and sailors were imprisoned. Jefferson refused to ransom them, and a small American force accompanied by Arab, Greek, and African mercenaries marched from Egypt to the "shores of Tripoli" (memorialized to this day in the Marine Corps anthem) to seize the port of Derne. A treaty ended the war in 1805, but the United States continued to pay tribute to the three other Barbary states—Algiers, Morocco, and Tunis—until 1815. In the intervening years, the United States became embroiled in European conflicts.

First Barbary War

At first, Jefferson managed to distance the nation from the turmoil in Europe in the wake of the French Revolution. After the Senate ratified the Jay Treaty in 1795, the United States and Great Britain appeared to reconcile their differences. Britain withdrew from its western forts on American soil (while still retaining those in Canada and the Pacific Northwest) and interfered less in American trade with France. Then, in May 1803, two weeks after Napoleon sold Louisiana to the United States, France was at war against Britain and, later, Britain's continental allies, Prussia, Austria, and Russia. The Napoleonic wars again trapped the United States between belligerents on the high seas. But at first the United States—as the world's largest neutral shipping carrier—actually benefited from the conflict, and American merchants gained control of most of the West Indian trade. After 1805, however, when Britain defeated the French and Spanish fleets at Trafalgar, Britain's Royal Navy tightened its control of the oceans. Two months later, Napoleon crushed the Russian and Austrian armies

▲ During the War of 1812, British forces and their Indian allies seized Fort Shelby in Wisconsin, renaming it Fort McKay. After the Treaty of Ghent (1814) restored the installation to American hands, British Captain W. Andrew Bulger bid farewell to his Indian allies before withdrawing and burning the fort.

at Austerlitz. Stalemated, France and Britain launched a commercial war, blockading each other's trade. As a trading partner of both countries, the United States paid a high price.

One British tactic in particular threatened American sovereignty. To replenish their supply of sailors, British vessels stopped American ships and impressed (forcibly recruited) British deserters, British-born naturalized American seamen, and other sailors suspected of being British. Perhaps six to eight thousand Americans were impressed between 1803 and 1812. Moreover, alleged deserters—many of them American citizens—faced British courts-martial. Americans saw the principle of "once a British subject, always a British subject" as a mockery of U.S. citizenship and an assault on their national sovereignty. Americans also resented the British interfering with their West Indian trade as well as their searching and seizing American vessels within U.S. territorial waters.

Threats to American Sovereignty

In April 1806, Congress responded with the Non-Importation Act, barring British manufactured goods from entering American ports. Because the act exempted most cloth and metal articles, it had little impact on British trade; instead, it warned the British what to expect if they continued to violate American neutral rights. In November, Jefferson suspended the act temporarily while William Pinkney, a Baltimore lawyer, joined James Monroe in London to negotiate a settlement. But the treaty they carried home violated Jefferson's instructions—it did not so much as mention impressment—and the president never submitted it to the Senate for ratification.

Anglo-American relations steadily deteriorated, coming to a head in June 1807 when the USS *Chesapeake*, sailing out of Norfolk for the Mediterranean, was stopped by the British frigate *Leopard*, whose officers demanded to search the ship for British deserters. Refused, the *Leopard* opened fire, killing three Americans and wounding eighteen others, including the captain. The British then seized four deserters, three of whom held American citizenship; one of them was hanged. The *Chesapeake* affair outraged Americans while also exposing American military weakness.

Had the United States been better prepared militarily, public indignation might have resulted in a declaration of war. Instead, Jefferson opted for what he called "peaceable coercion." In July, the president closed American waters to British warships and soon thereafter increased military and naval expenditures. In December 1807, Jefferson again put economic pressure on Great Britain by invoking the Non-Importation Act, followed eight days later by a new restriction, the Embargo Act. Jefferson and his congressional supporters saw the embargo, which forbade all exports from the United States to any country, as a short-term measure to avoid war by pressuring Britain and France to respect American rights and by preventing confrontation between American merchant vessels and European warships.

The Embargo of 1807

The embargo's biggest economic impact, however, fell on the United States. Exports declined by 80 percent in 1808, squeezing New England shippers and their workers as economic depression set in. Manufacturers, by contrast, received a boost, as the domestic market became theirs exclusively, and merchants began to shift their

William L. Clements Library

▲ *Boarding and Taking of the American Ship* Chesapeake (1816) portrays crew from the British frigate *Leopard* fighting to search the USS *Chesapeake* for British navy deserters. The sailors of the *Chesapeake* resisted, but the British overpowered them and seized four deserters, three of them American citizens. Americans were humiliated and angered by the British violation of American rights.

capital from shipping to manufacturing. In 1807, there were twenty cotton and woolen mills in New England; by 1813, there were more than two hundred. Meanwhile, merchants who were willing to engage in smuggling profited enormously.

They had only to look at the vibrant slave trade to see how scarcity bred demand. With Jefferson's encourage-

International Slave Trade

ment, Congress had voted in 1807 to abolish the international slave trade as of January 1, 1808—the earliest date permissible under the Constitution. South Carolina alone still allowed the legal importation of slaves, but most of the state's influential planters favored a ban on the trade, nervous (having seen what happened in St. Domingue) about adding to the black population of a state in which whites were already outnumbered. Congressional debate focused not on whether it was a good idea to abolish the trade but on what should become of any Africans imported illegally after the ban took effect. The final bill provided that smuggled slaves would be sold in accordance with the laws of the state or territory in which they arrived. It underscored, in other words, that slaves (even illegal ones) were property. Had the bill not done so, threatened one Georgia congressman, the result might have been "resistance to the authority of the Government," even civil war. Although the debate over the slave trade did not fall along

strictly sectional (or regional) lines, sectional tensions never lay far beneath the surface in this era of heated partisan conflict.

In anticipation of the higher prices that their human property would fetch once the law took effect, traders temporarily withheld their slaves from the market in the months after the law's passage. During the last four months of 1807 alone, sixteen thousand African slaves arrived at Gadsden Wharf in Charleston, where they were detained by merchants eager to wait out the January 1 deadline. Although many of these slaves—hundreds, if not thousands—died in the cramped, disease-ridden holding pens before they could be sold, merchants calculated that the increased value of those who survived until the ban took effect would outweigh the losses. Not that January 1, 1808, brought an end to the international slave trade; a brisk—and profitable—illegal trade took over. As Justice Joseph Story noted in 1819, the slave trade "is still carried on with all the implacable ferocity and insatiable rapacity of former times. Avarice has grown more subtle in its evasions; and watches and seizes its prey with an appetite quickened rather than suppressed by its guilty vigils." In 1819,

> Link to Justice Joseph Story's indictment of the slave trade.

Congress passed a law authorizing the president to use force to intercept slave ships along the African coast, but the small American navy could not halt the illicit trade in human beings.

As discussion of the international slave trade subsided, debate over the embargo heated up, especially with the approach of the 1808 presidential election. Democratic Republicans suffered from factional dissent and dissatisfaction in seaboard states hobbled by the trade restrictions. Although nine state legislatures passed resolutions urging Jefferson to run again, the president followed George Washington's lead in declining a third term. He supported James Madison, his secretary of state, as the Democratic-Republican standard-bearer. For the first time, however, the Democratic-Republican nomination was contested. Madison won the endorsement of the party's congressional caucus, but Virginia Democratic-Republicans put forth James Monroe, who later withdrew, and some easterners supported Vice President George Clinton. Madison and Clinton headed the ticket. Charles Cotesworth Pinckney and Rufus King again ran on the Federalist ticket, but with new vigor.

Election of 1808

The younger Federalists made the most of the widespread disaffection with Democratic-Republican policy, especially the embargo. Pinckney received only 47 electoral votes to Madison's 122, but he carried all of New England except Vermont, won Delaware, and carried some electoral votes in two other states. Federalists also gained seats in Congress and captured the New York State legislature. Although the Federalist future looked promising, the transition from one Democratic-Republican administration to the next went smoothly.

This transition was eased, in part, by the wives of elected and appointed officials in the new capital, who encouraged political and diplomatic negotiation. Such negotiations often took place in social settings, even private homes, where people with divergent interests could bridge their ideological divides through personal relationships. Women played crucial roles, fostering conversation, providing an ear or a voice for unofficial messages, and—in the case of international affairs—standing as surrogates for their nation. Elite women hosted events that muted domestic partisan rivalries, events at which Federalists and Democratic-Republicans could find common ground in civility, if not always politics. Political wives' interactions among themselves served political purposes, too: when First Lady Dolley Madison visited congressmen's wives, she cultivated goodwill for her husband while collecting recipes that allowed her to serve regionally diverse cuisine at White House functions. Mrs. Madison hoped her menus would help keep simmering sectional tensions from reaching a boiling point.

Women and Politics

Private Collection/© Michael Graham-Stewart/The Bridgeman Art Library

▲ In an effort to win support for measures to end the international slave trade and slavery itself, abolitionists published drawings of the inhumanely cramped slave ships, where each person was allotted a space roughly the size of a coffin. Disease spread rapidly under such conditions, causing many slaves to die before reaching American shores.

But it was women's buying power that may have proved most influential in the era of the embargo. Recalling women's support of revolutionary-era boycotts, Jeffersonians appealed directly for women's support of their embargo. Sympathetic women responded by spurning imported fabric and making (or directing their slaves to make) homespun clothing for themselves and their families. Federalists, however, encouraged women to "keep commerce alive," and sympathetic women bought smuggled goods.

Under the pressure of domestic opposition, the embargo eventually collapsed. In its place, the Non-Intercourse Act of 1809 reopened trade with all nations except Britain and France, and authorized the president to resume trade with those two nations once they respected American neutral rights. In June 1809, President Madison reopened trade with Britain after its minister to the United States offered assurances that Britain would repeal restrictions on American trade. But his Majesty's government in London repudiated the minister's assurances, leading Madison to revert to nonintercourse.

Failed Policies

When the Non-Intercourse Act expired in 1810, Congress substituted Macon's Bill Number 2, reopening trade with both Great Britain and France but providing that, when either nation stopped violating American commercial rights, the president would suspend American commerce with the other. When Napoleon accepted the offer, Madison declared nonintercourse on Great Britain in 1811. Although the French continued to seize American ships, Britain became the main focus of American hostility because its Royal Navy dominated the seas.

In spring 1812, the British admiralty ordered its ships not to stop, search, or seize American warships, and in June Britain reopened the seas to American shipping. But before word of the change in British policy reached American shores, Congress declared war.

The vote was sharply divided. The House voted 79 to 49 for war; the Senate, 19 to 13. Democratic-Republicans

Mr. Madison's War

favored war by a vote of 98 to 23; Federalists opposed it 39 to 0. Those who favored war, including President Madison, pointed to assaults on American sovereignty and honor: impressment, violation of neutral trading rights, and British alliances with western Indians. Others saw an opportunity to conquer and annex British Canada. Most militant were land-hungry southerners and westerners—the "War Hawks"—led by John C. Calhoun of South Carolina and first-term congressman and House Speaker Henry Clay of Kentucky. John Randolph of

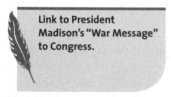
Link to President Madison's "War Message" to Congress.

Virginia, an opponent of war, charged angrily, "Agrarian cupidity, not maritime rights, urges war!" He heard "but one word" in Congress: "Canada! Canada! Canada!" Most representatives from the coastal states, and especially from the Northeast, feared disruption to commerce and opposed what they called "Mr. Madison's War."

Initially, the Federalists benefited from antiwar sentiment. They joined renegade Democratic-Republicans in supporting New York City mayor DeWitt Clinton for president in the election of 1812. Clinton lost to President Madison by 128 to 89 electoral votes—a respectable showing against a wartime president—and the Federalists gained some congressional seats and carried many local elections. But the South and the West—areas that favored the war—remained solidly Democratic-Republican.

The War of 1812

Lasting from 1812 to 1815, the war unfolded in a series of scuffles and skirmishes (see Map 9.2) for which the U.S. armed forces, kept lean by Jeffersonian fiscal policies, were ill prepared. With few experienced army officers— the U.S. Military Academy at West Point, founded in 1802, had produced only eighty-nine regular officers— campaigns were executed poorly. Although the U.S. Navy had a corps of experienced officers, it proved no match for the Royal Navy.

Nor did the United States succeed at enlisting sufficient forces. The government's efforts to lure recruits— with sign-up bonuses, and promises of three months' pay and rights to purchase 160 acres of western land upon discharge—met with mixed success. At first, recruitment went well among westerners, who were motivated by civic spirit, desire for land, strong anti-Indian sentiment, and fears of Tecumseh's pan-Indian organization. But after word spread of delays in pay, as well as inadequate supplies and rations, recruitment dwindled. In New England, raising an army was even more difficult. Federalists discouraged enlistments, and even some New England Democratic-Republicans declined to raise volunteer companies. Others promised their men that they would serve only in defensive roles, as in Maine, where they would guard the coastline. Militias in New England and New York often refused to fight outside their own states. Desperate for soldiers, New York offered freedom to slaves who enlisted, and compensation to their owners, and the U.S. Army made the same offer to slaves in the Old Northwest and in Canada. In Philadelphia, black leaders formed a "Black Brigade" to defend the city. But in the Deep South, fear of arming slaves kept them out of the military except in New Orleans, where a free black militia dated back to Spanish control of Louisiana. The British, on the other hand, recruited slaves by promising freedom in exchange for service. In the end, British forces—made up of British regulars, their Indian allies, fugitive slaves, and Canadians, many of whom were loyalists who had fled during the American Revolution—outnumbered the Americans overall.

Despite their recruitment problems, Americans expected to take Canada easily. Canada's population was

Invasion of Canada

sparse, its army small, and the Great Lakes inaccessible to the Royal Navy in the Atlantic. Americans hoped, too, that French Canadians might welcome U.S. forces.

American strategy aimed to split Canadian forces and isolate pro-British Indians, especially Tecumseh, whom the British had promised an Indian nation in the Great Lakes region. In July 1812, U.S. general William Hull, territorial governor of Michigan, marched his troops, who outnumbered those of the British and their allies, into Upper Canada (modern Ontario), hoping to conquer Montreal. But by abandoning Mackinac Island and Fort Dearborn, and by surrendering Fort Detroit, he left the entire Midwest exposed to the enemy. Captain Zachary Taylor provided the only bright spot, giving the Americans a land victory with his September 1812 defense of Fort Harrison in Indiana Territory. But by the winter of 1812–1813, the British controlled about half of the Old Northwest. The United States had no greater success on

Visualizing THE PAST

Selling War

The War of 1812 was not always a popular war, but in its aftermath many Americans trumpeted the war's successes. To the left, we see a recruitment poster from 1812, in which General William Henry Harrison seeks additional cavalrymen. Hampered in part by transportation difficulties, Harrison is unable to offer much—soldiers are even requested to supply their own bacon as well as their own horses—but he does promise that the expedition will be short, undoubtedly a concern to men eager to return to the fall harvest. To the right, we see a handkerchief made in 1815, after the Treaty of Ghent and the Battle of New Orleans; it features the United States' victories against the world's greatest naval power, Great Britain. Made with a decorative border, the kerchief may have been for display. What similar values do we see promoted in the two images, and what factors—such as their intended audiences, their purposes, and when they were created—might account for any differences between them?

Chicago History Museum

With a tiny regular army, the United States often had to rely on short-term recruits to wage war on the British.

Made in 1815 from cotton textiles—whose domestic production soared during the War of 1812, with trade cut off from Britain—this handkerchief helps promote American "liberty and independence."

Map 9.2 Major Campaigns of the War of 1812

The land war centered on the U.S.-Canadian border, the Chesapeake Bay, and the Louisiana and Mississippi Territories.

Source: Copyright © Cengage Learning

the Niagara Front, where New York borders Canada, in large part because New York militiamen refused to leave their state to join the invasion of Canada.

Despite victories on the Atlantic by the USS *Constitution* (nicknamed "Old Ironsides" after its rout of the HMS *Guerrière*), the USS *Wasp*, and the USS *United States*, the American navy—which began the war with just seventeen ships—could not match the powerful Royal Navy. The Royal Navy blockaded the Chesapeake and Delaware Bays in December 1812, and by 1814 the blockade covered nearly all American ports along the Atlantic and Gulf coasts. After 1811, American trade overseas declined by nearly 90 percent, and the decline in revenue from customs

Naval Battles

duties threatened to bankrupt the federal government and prostrate New England.

The contest for control of the Great Lakes, the key to the war in the Northwest, evolved as a shipbuilding race. Under Master Commandant Oliver Hazard Perry and shipbuilder Noah Brown, the United States outbuilt the British on Lake Erie and defeated them at the bloody Battle of Put-in-Bay on September 10, 1813, gaining control of Lake Erie.

General William Henry Harrison then began what would be among the United States' most successful land campaigns. A ragged group of Kentucky militia volunteers, armed only with swords and knives, marched 20 to 30 miles a day to join

Burning Capitals

The War of 1812 **233**

Harrison's forces in Ohio. Now 4,500 strong, Harrison's forces attacked and took Detroit before crossing into Canada, where at the Battle of the Thames they defeated British, Shawnee, and Chippewa forces in October 1813. Among the dead was Tecumseh. The Americans then razed the Canadian capital of York (now Toronto), looting and burning the Parliament building before withdrawing.

After defeating Napoleon in Europe in April 1814, the British launched a land counteroffensive against the United States, concentrating on the Chesapeake Bay region. In retaliation for the burning of York—and to divert American troops from Lake Champlain, where the British planned a new offensive—royal troops occupied Washington, D.C., in August and set it ablaze, leaving the presidential mansion and parts of the city burning all night. Chaos ruled. The president and cabinet fled. Dolley Madison stayed long enough to oversee the removal of cabinet documents and, famously, to save a Gilbert Stuart portrait of George Washington.

The British intended the attack on Washington only as a diversion. The major battle occurred in September 1814 at Baltimore, where the Americans held firm. Francis Scott Key, detained on a British ship, watched the bombardment of Fort McHenry from Baltimore harbor and the next morning wrote the verses of "The Star-Spangled Banner" (which became the national anthem in 1931). Although the British inflicted heavy damage, they achieved little militarily; their offensive on Lake Champlain proved equally unsuccessful. The war had reached a stalemate.

To the south, two wars were happening simultaneously. In what one historian calls "the other War of 1812"

War in the South

(or the Patriots War), a private army of Americans, with secret support from the Madison administration, tried to seize East Florida from Spain's control. What started as a settlers' rebellion along the Georgia-Florida border—in an effort to grab more land, strike at the Spaniards' Indian allies, and later to protest the Spaniards' arming of black soldiers (increasing white settlers' fears of slave rebellion)—turned into a war, with the Patriots receiving support from U.S. regular forces (land and naval) and Georgia militia units. Federalists condemned the invasion of a neutral territory, and the Senate refused twice (in 1812 and 1813) to support a military seizure of Florida. Politically embarrassed, Madison withdrew his support, and the movement collapsed in May 1814. Historians disagree about whether the Patriots War ultimately helped or hindered American efforts to win Florida from the Spanish.

In the war with Britain, the southern theater proved much more successful. The war's final campaign began with an American attack on the Red Stick Creeks along the Gulf of Mexico and the British around New Orleans,

and it ended with Americans gaining new territory for white settlement. The Red Sticks had responded to Tecumseh's call (his mother was a Creek) to resist U.S. expansion. Some had died in Indiana Territory, when General Harrison's troops routed Shawnee forces at Tippecanoe in 1811. In 1813, the Red Sticks attacked Fort Mims, about 40 miles from Mobile, killing hundreds of white men, women, and children seeking protection there. Looking for revenge, General Andrew Jackson of Tennessee rallied his militiamen as well as Indian opponents of the Red Sticks (including other Creeks favoring accommodation with whites) and crushed the Red Sticks at Horseshoe Bend (in present-day Alabama) in March 1814, leading to the Treaty of Fort Jackson, in which the Creeks ceded 23 million acres of their land, or about half of their holdings, and withdrew to the southern and western part of Mississippi Territory.

Jackson became a major general in the regular army and continued south toward the Gulf of Mexico, with his eye on New Orleans. After seizing Pensacola (in Spanish Florida) and then securing Mobile, Jackson's forces marched to New Orleans, where for three weeks they played a game of cat-and-mouse with the British soldiers. Finally, on January 8, 1815, the two forces met head-on. In fortified positions, Jackson's poorly trained army held its ground against two British frontal assaults. At day's end, more than two thousand British soldiers lay dead or wounded (a casualty rate of nearly one-third), while the Americans suffered only twenty-one casualties.

The Battle of New Orleans took place two weeks after the war's official conclusion: word had not yet reached America that British and United States diplomats had signed the Treaty of Ghent on December 24, 1814. Although militarily unnecessary, the Battle of New Orleans catapulted General Andrew Jackson to national political prominence, and the victory over a formidable foe inspired a sense of national pride.

The Treaty of Ghent essentially restored the prewar status quo. It provided for an end to hostilities with the

Treaty of Ghent

British and with Native Americans, release of prisoners, restoration of conquered territory, and arbitration of boundary disputes. But the United States received no satisfaction on impressment, blockades, or other maritime rights for neutrals, and the British demands for territorial cessions from Maine to Minnesota went unmet. The British dropped their promise to Tecumseh of an independent Indian nation.

Why did the negotiators settle for so little? Napoleon's defeat allowed the United States to discard its prewar demands because peace in Europe made impressment and interference with American commerce moot issues. Similarly, war-weary Britain—its treasury nearly depleted—stopped pressing for military victory.

Private Collection/Picture Research Consultants & Archives

▲ Americans rejoiced that the War of 1812 had reaffirmed their independence from the British monarchy. The sailor's foot here steps on the crown while broken chains of bondage lie nearby.

Yet the War of 1812 had significant consequences for America's status in the world. It affirmed the independence of the American republic and ensured Canada's independence from the United States. Trade and territorial disputes with Great Britain continued, but they never again led to war. Americans strengthened their resolve to steer clear of European politics.

American Sovereignty Reasserted

The return of peace allowed the United States to again focus on the Barbary Coast, where the dey (governor) of Algiers had taken advantage of the American preoccupation with British forces to declare his own war on the United States. In the Second Barbary War, U.S. forces captured and detained hundreds of Algerians while negotiating a treaty in the summer of 1815 that forever freed the United States from paying tributes for passage in the Mediterranean. The Second Barbary War reaffirmed America's sovereignty and its commitment to the principle of freedom of the seas.

The War of 1812 had profound domestic consequences. The Federalists' hopes of returning to national prominence all but evaporated with the Hartford Convention, when delegates from New England—frustrated by the stalemated war and the shattered New England economy—met in Hartford, Connecticut, for three weeks in the winter of

Domestic Consequences

1814–1815 to discuss revising the national compact or pulling out of the republic. Although moderates prevented a resolution of secession—a resolution to withdraw from the Union—the delegates condemned the war and the embargo while endorsing constitutional changes that would weaken the South's power vis-à-vis the North and make it harder to declare war. When news arrived in upcoming weeks of, first, Jackson's victory in New Orleans and, then, the Treaty of Ghent, the Hartford Convention made the Federalists look wrongheaded, even treasonous. Federalists survived in a handful of states until the 1820s, but the party faded from the national scene.

With Tecumseh's death, midwestern Indians lost their most powerful leader; with the withdrawal of the British, they lost their strongest ally. In the South, the Red Sticks had ceded vast tracts of fertile land. The war did not bring disaster to all Indians—some accommodationists, such as the Cherokees, temporarily flourished—but it effectively disarmed traditionalists bent on resisting American expansion. Although the Treaty of Ghent pledged the United States to end hostilities with Indians and to restore their prewar "possessions, rights, and privileges," Indians could not make the United States adhere to the agreement.

For American farmers, the war opened vast tracts of formerly Indian land for cultivating cotton in the Old Southwest and wheat in the Old Northwest. For young industries, the war also ultimately proved a stimulant, as Americans could no longer rely on overseas imports of manufactured goods, particularly textiles. The War of 1812 thus fueled demand for raw cotton, and the newly acquired lands in the Southwest beckoned southerners who migrated there with their slaves, or with expectations of someday owning slaves. The war's conclusion accelerated three trends that would dominate U.S. history for upcoming decades: westward expansion, industrial takeoff, and slavery's entrenchment.

The Nationalist Program

In his final year as president, James Madison and the Democratic-Republicans embraced a nationalist agenda, absorbing the Federalist idea that the federal government should encourage economic growth. In his December 1815 message to Congress, Madison recommended economic development and military expansion. His agenda, which Henry Clay later called the American System, included a national bank, improved transportation, and a protective tariff—a tax on imported goods that was designed to protect American manufacturers from foreign competition. Yet Madison did not stray entirely from his Jeffersonian roots; only a constitutional amendment, he argued, could authorize the federal government to build local roads and canals.

Clay and other congressional leaders, such as Calhoun of South Carolina, believed the American System would

American System

ease sectional divides in the expanding nation. The tariff would stimulate New England industry. New England manufactured goods would find markets in the South and West. At the same time, the South's and West's agricultural products—cotton and foodstuffs—would feed New England mills and their workers. Manufactured goods and agricultural products would move in all directions along roads and canals—what contemporaries called internal improvements—which tariff revenues would fund. A national bank would handle the transactions.

In the Madison administration's last year, the Democratic-Republican Congress enacted much of the nationalist program. In 1816, it chartered the Second Bank of the United States (the charter on the first bank had expired in 1811) to serve as a depository for federal funds and to issue currency, collect taxes, and pay the government's debts. The Second Bank of the United States would also oversee state and local banks, ensuring that their paper money had backing in specie (precious metals). Like its predecessor, the bank mixed public and private ownership; the government provided one-fifth of the bank's capital and appointed one-fifth of its directors.

Congress also passed a protective tariff to aid industries that flourished during the War of 1812 but that now were threatened by the resumption of overseas trade. The Tariff of 1816 levied taxes on imported woolens and cottons as well as on iron, leather, hats, paper, and sugar. Foreshadowing a growing trend, though, the tariff did more to divide than to unify the nation. New England as well as the western and Middle Atlantic states stood to benefit from it and thus applauded it, whereas many southerners objected that it raised the price of consumer goods while opening the possibility that Britain would retaliate with a tariff on cotton.

Some southerners did press for internal improvements. Calhoun vocally promoted roads and canals to "bind the republic together." However, on March 3, 1817, the day before leaving office, President Madison, citing constitutional scruples, stunned Congress by vetoing Calhoun's "Bonus Bill," which would have authorized federal funding for such public works.

Constitutional scruples aside, Federalists and Democratic-Republicans agreed that the nation's prosperity

Early Internal Improvements

depended on improved transportation. For Federalists, roads and canals were necessary for commercial development; for Jeffersonians, they would spur western expansion and agrarian growth. In 1806, Congress had passed (and Jefferson had signed) a bill

authorizing funding for the Cumberland Road (later, the National Road), running 130 miles between Cumberland, Maryland, and Wheeling, Virginia (now West Virginia). Construction began in 1811 and was completed in 1818. Two years later, Congress authorized a survey of the National Road to Columbus, Ohio, a project funded in 1825 and completed in 1833; the road would ultimately extend into Indiana.

After President Madison's veto of the Bonus Bill, though, most transportation initiatives received funding from states, private investors, or a combination of the two. Between 1817 and 1825, the State of New York constructed the Erie Canal, linking the Great Lakes to the Atlantic seaboard. Although southern states constructed modest canals, the South's trade depended on rivergoing steamboats after 1817, when steamboats began traveling regularly upriver on the Mississippi. With canals and steamboats, western agricultural products could travel to market much more quickly and inexpensively, fueling the nation's westward expansion. Unlike steamboats, though, canals expanded commercial networks into regions without natural waterways. Although the Mississippi provided the great commercial highway of the Early Republic, canals began to reorient midwestern commerce through the North.

James Monroe, Madison's successor, continued Madison's domestic program, supporting tariffs and veto-

The Era of Good Feelings

ing the Cumberland Road Bill (for repairs) in 1822. Monroe was the last president to have attended the Constitutional Convention and the third Virginian elected president since 1801. A former senator and twice governor of Virginia, he had served under Madison as secretary of state and of war and had used his close association with Jefferson and Madison to attain the presidency. In 1816, he and his running mate, Daniel Tompkins, trounced the last Federalist presidential nominee, Rufus King, garnering all the electoral votes except those of the Federalist strongholds of Massachusetts, Connecticut, and Delaware. A Boston newspaper dubbed this one-party period the "Era of Good Feelings."

Led by Federalist chief justice John Marshall, the Supreme Court became the bulwark of the nationalist agenda. In *McCulloch v. Maryland* (1819), the Court struck down a Maryland law taxing banks within the state that were not chartered by its legislature—a law aimed at hindering the Baltimore branch of the federally chartered Second Bank of the United States. The bank refused to pay the tax and sued. At issue was state versus federal jurisdiction. Writing for a unanimous Court, Marshall asserted the supremacy of the federal government over the states. "The Constitution and the laws thereof are supreme," he declared. "They control the constitution and laws of the respective states and cannot be

Courtesy of the Maryland Historical Society

▲ Travelers, mechants, and livestock clogged portions of the National Road, shown here alongside Milestone 3 in Baltimore in 1829.

controlled by them." The Court ruled, too, that Congress had the power to charter banks under the Constitution's clause endowing it with the authority to pass "all laws which shall be necessary and proper for carrying into execution" the enumerated powers of government. The Marshall Court thus supported the Federalist view that the federal government could promote interstate commerce.

Later Supreme Court cases validated government promotion of economic development and encouraged

Government Promotion of Market Expansion

business enterprise and risk taking. In *Gibbons v. Ogden* (1824), the Supreme Court overturned the New York law that had given Robert Fulton and Robert Livingston (and their successor, Aaron Ogden) a monopoly on the New York–New Jersey steamboat trade. Chief Justice Marshall ruled that the federal power to license new enterprises took precedence over New York's grant of monopoly rights and declared that Congress's power under the commerce clause of the Constitution extended to "every species of commercial intercourse," including transportation. The *Gibbons v. Ogden* ruling built on earlier Marshall Court decisions, such as those in *Dartmouth College v. Woodward* (1819), which protected the sanctity of contracts against state interference, and *Fletcher v. Peck* (1810), which voided a Georgia law that violated individuals' rights to make contracts. Within two years of *Gibbons v. Ogden*, the number of steamboats operating in New York increased from six to forty-three. A later ruling under Chief Justice Roger Taney, *Charles River Bridge v. Warren Bridge* (1837), encouraged new enterprises and technologies by favoring competition over monopoly, and the public interest over implied privileges in old contracts.

Federal and state courts, in conjunction with state legislatures, encouraged the proliferation of corporations—organizations entitled to hold property and transact business as if they were individuals. Corporation owners, called shareholders, were granted limited liability, or freedom from personal responsibility for the company's debts beyond their original investment. Limited liability encouraged investors to back new business ventures.

The federal government assisted the development of a commercial economy in other ways. The U.S. Post Office fostered the circulation of information, a critical element of the market economy. The number of post offices grew from three thousand in 1815 to fourteen thousand in 1845. To promote individual creativity and economic growth, the government protected inventions through patent laws and domestic industries through tariffs on foreign imports.

Monroe's secretary of state, John Quincy Adams, matched the Marshall Court in assertiveness and nationalism. Adams, the son of John

Boundary Settlements

and Abigail Adams, managed the nation's foreign policy from 1817 to 1825, pushing for expansion (through negotiations, not war), fishing rights for Americans in Atlantic waters, political distance from Europe, and peace. Under Adams's leadership, the United States settled points of conflict with both Britain and Spain. In 1817, the United States and Great Britain signed the Rush-Bagot Treaty limiting their naval forces to one ship each on Lake Champlain and Lake Ontario and to two ships each on the four other Great Lakes. This first disarmament treaty of modern times demilitarized the border between the United States and Canada. Adams then pushed for the Convention of 1818, which fixed the U.S.-Canadian border from Lake of the Woods in Minnesota westward to the Rockies along the 49th parallel. When they could not agree on the boundary west of the Rockies, Britain and the United States settled on joint occupation of Oregon for ten years (renewed indefinitely in 1827).

Adams's negotiations resulted in the Adams-Onís Treaty, in which the United States gained Florida, already occupied by General Andrew Jackson under pretext of suppressing Seminole raids against American settlements across the border during the First Seminole War of 1817–1818. Although the Louisiana Purchase had omitted reference to Spanish-ruled West Florida, the United States claimed the territory as far east as the Perdido River (the present-day Florida-Alabama border). During the War of 1812, the United States had seized Mobile and the remainder of West Florida, and after the war—with Spain preoccupied with its own domestic and colonial troubles—Adams had laid claim to East Florida. In 1819, Don Luís de Onís, the Spanish minister to the United States, agreed to cede Florida to the United States without payment if the United States renounced its dubious claims to northern Mexico (Texas) and assumed $5 million of claims by American citizens against Spain. The Adams-Onís (or Transcontinental) Treaty also defined the southwestern boundary of the Louisiana Purchase and set the line between Spanish Mexico and Oregon Country at the 42nd parallel.

John Quincy Adams's desire to insulate the United States and the Western Hemisphere from European conflict brought about his greatest achievement: the Monroe Doctrine. The immediate issue was recognition of new governments in Latin America. Between 1808 and 1822, the United Provinces of Río de la Plata (present-day northern Argentina, Paraguay, and Uruguay), Chile, Peru, Colombia, and Mexico all broke free from Spain (see Map 9.3). In 1822, shortly after the ratification of the Adams-Onís Treaty, the United States became the first nation outside Latin America to recognize the new states, including Mexico. But in Europe, reactionary regimes were ascending, and with France now occupying Spain to suppress a liberal rebellion, the United States feared that continental powers would attempt to return the new Latin American states to colonial rule. Having withdrawn from an alliance with continental nations, Britain proposed a joint declaration with the United States against European intervention in the Western Hemisphere. Adams rejected Britain's offer as just the kind of entanglement he sought to avoid, despite clear advantages to allying with the British and their powerful navy.

Monroe presented to Congress in December 1823 what became known as the Monroe Doctrine. His message announced that the American continents "are henceforth not to be considered subjects for future colonization by any European power." This principle addressed American anxiety not only about Latin America but also about Russian expansion beyond Alaska and its settlements in California. Monroe demanded nonintervention by Europe in the affairs of independent New World nations, and he pledged noninterference by the United States in European affairs, including those of Europe's existing New World colonies. Although Monroe's words carried no force—European nations stayed out of New World affairs because they feared the Royal Navy, not the United States' proclamations—they proved popular at home, tapping American nationalism as well as anti-British and anti-European feelings.

Sectionalism Exposed

The embargo, the War of 1812, and the postwar spurt of internal improvements encouraged the southern and northern economies to develop in different but interrelated ways. While the South became more dependent on cotton, the North underwent an accelerated industrial development, whose groundwork had been laid two decades earlier. With their commitment to frugal government and an agrarian nation, Jeffersonians did not promote industry, but a small number of entrepreneurs did.

Despite their efforts to define themselves as a separate nation, Americans relied on British technology to bring together the many steps of textile manufacturing—carding (or disentangling) fibers, spinning yarn, and weaving cloth—under one factory roof. The first American water-powered spinning mill was established in 1790 by Samuel Slater, a British immigrant who reconstructed from memory the complex machines he had used while working in a British cotton-spinning factory. But Slater's mill only carded and spun yarn; the yarn still needed to be hand-woven into cloth, work often done by farm women seeking to earn cash. In 1810, Bostonian Francis Cabot Lowell, determined to introduce water-powered mechanical weaving in the United States, visited the British textile center of Manchester, where he toured factories, later sketching from memory what he had seen. In 1813, he and his business associates, calling themselves the Boston Manufacturing Company, brought together all phases of textile manufacturing under one roof in Waltham, Massachusetts. A decade later, the Boston Manufacturing Company established what it saw as a model industrial village—named for its now-deceased founder—along the banks of the Merrimack River. At Lowell, Massachusetts, there would be boarding houses for workers, a healthy alternative to the tenements and slums of Manchester. American industrialists envisioned America industrializing without the poverty and degradation associated with European industrialization.

Monroe Doctrine

Early Industrial Development

Map 9.3 Latin American Independence, 1840

With Central and South American colonies triumphing in their wars of independence against European colonial powers, President Monroe sought to enhance the United States' security by warning European nations against meddling in the region.

Source: Copyright © Cengage Learning

Industrial Piracy

Although Americans pride themselves on inventiveness and hard work, their start in industrial development depended on importing technology, sometimes by stealth. Great Britain, which in the late eighteenth century had pioneered the invention of mechanical weaving and power looms, knew the value of its head start in the industrial revolution and prohibited the export of textile technology. But the British-born brothers Samuel and John Slater, their Scottish-born power-loom-builder William Gilmore, and Bostonians Francis Cabot Lowell and Nathan Appleton evaded British restrictions and patents to establish America's first textile factories.

As an apprentice and then a supervisor in a British cotton-spinning factory, Samuel Slater had mastered the machinery and the process. Britain forbade the export of textile technology, so Slater emigrated to the United States disguised as a farmer. In 1790 in Pawtucket, Rhode Island, he opened the first water-powered spinning mill in America on the Blackstone River, rebuilding the complex machines from memory. With his brother John and their Rhode Island partners, Moses and Obadiah Brown and William Almy, Slater later built and oversaw mills in Rhode Island and Massachusetts. In 1815, he hired a recent immigrant, William Gilmore, to build a water-powered loom like those used in Britain. The Slaters introduced British steam-powered looms in the 1820s. Spinning and weaving would now be done in New England factories organized along British models.

In 1810, Francis Cabot Lowell had the same idea as the Slaters: to build modern mills with mechanical, water-powered looms. Lowell took a family vacation to Britain, and in Edinburgh, Scotland, he met fellow Bostonian Nathan Appleton. Impressed by the textile mills they saw in Britain, they planned to introduce water-powered mechanical weaving into the United States. They knew they had to acquire the "improved manufactures" from Britain that had made Manchester famous as a textile center. Lowell went to Manchester, during the day visiting and observing the factories, and meeting the factory managers. At night, he returned to his hotel to sketch from memory the power looms and processes he had seen. Back in the United States, he and others formed the Boston Associates, which created the Waltham-Lowell mills based on Lowell's industrial piracy. Within a few years, textiles would be a major American industry, and the Boston Associates would dominate it.

Thus, the modern American industrial revolution began with international links, not homegrown American inventions. Ingenuity and industrial piracy put the United States on the road to industrial advancement.

Courtesy of Gore Place Society, Waltham, Massachusetts

◀ This contemporary painting shows the Boston Manufacturing Company's 1814 textile factory at Waltham, Massachusetts. All manufacturing processes were brought together under one roof, and the company built its first factories in rural New England to tap roaring rivers as a power source.

The American textile factory had been born in the midst of the War of 1812. When the British began flooding the American market with cheap textiles after the Treaty of Ghent, Lowell realized the market now needed to be protected. He lobbied hard for the inclusion of cotton textiles in the Tariff of 1816, playing a crucial role in persuading reluctant South Carolinians to support the provision.

Early industrialization, primarily in the northern states, was inextricably linked to slavery. Much of the capital came from merchants who made their fortunes at least in part through the trade in African slaves, and two of the most prominent industries—textiles and shoes—expanded in tandem with a growing southern cotton economy. Southern cotton fed northern textile mills, and northern shoe factories sold their "Negro brogans" (work shoes) to southern planters. Even in an older form of northern industrial labor which took place in private homes—outwork—the connections to the slave South were strong: New England farm girls wove palm-leaf hats for merchants who sold them to southern planters for their slaves.

Immediately after the war, the American economy boomed. The international demand for (and price of)

Panic of 1819

American commodities reached new heights. Poor weather in Europe led to crop failures, increasing demand for northern foodstuffs and Southern cotton, which, in turn, touched off western land speculation. Speculators raced to buy large tracts of land at modest, government-established prices and then to resell it at a hefty profit to would-be settlers. This expansion was built on easy credit. With easily obtained loans and paper money, farmers and speculators bought land, while manufacturers established new enterprises or enlarged existing ones.

Prosperity proved short-lived. Now recovered from war as well as weather, by the late 1810s Europeans could grow their own food, and Britain's new Corn Laws established a high tariff on imported foodstuffs, further lessening demand for American agricultural exports. Cotton prices fell in England. Wars in Latin America interfered with mining and reduced the supply of precious metals, leading European nations to hoard specie; in response, American banks furiously printed paper money and expanded credit even further. Fearful of inflation, the Second Bank of the United States, which had itself issued more loans than it could back in hard currency, demanded in 1819 that state banks repay loans in specie. State banks in turn called in the loans and mortgages they had made to individuals and companies. The falling prices of commodities meant that farmers could not pay their mortgages, and the decline of land values—from 50 to 75 percent in portions of the West—meant they could not meet their debts even by selling their farms. The

nation's banking system collapsed. The 1819 financial panic reminded Americans all too starkly that they still lived within the economic orbit of Europe.

Hard times came to countryside and city alike. Foreclosures soared. Unemployment skyrocketed, even in older manufacturing areas that had focused on industries like iron making and tobacco processing. In Philadelphia, unemployment reached 75 percent. The contraction devastated workers and their families. As a Baltimore physician noted in 1819, working people felt hard times "a thousand fold more than the merchants." They could not build up savings during boom times to get them through the hard times; often, they could not make it through the winter without drawing on charity for food, clothing, and firewood.

The depression sent tremors throughout American society. Americans from all regions contemplated the virtues and hazards of rapid market expansion, disagreeing most intensely on where to place the blame for its shortcomings. Westerners blamed easterners; farmers and workers blamed bankers. Even as the nation's economy began to rebound in the early 1820s amid a flurry of internal improvement projects, no one could predict with confidence where—in what region, in what sector—the nation's economic and political fortunes would lie.

Just as financial panic struck the nation in 1819, so, too, did political crisis. The issue was slavery's westward expansion. Although eco-

Missouri Compromise

nomic connections abounded between North and South, slavery had long been politically explosive. Since the drafting of the Constitution, Congress had tried to avoid the issue; the one exception had been debates over the international slave trade. In 1819, however, slavery once again burst onto the national political agenda when residents of the Missouri Territory—carved out of the Louisiana Territory—petitioned Congress for admission to the Union with a constitution permitting slavery. At stake was more than the future of slavery in an individual state. Missouri's admission to the Union would give the slaveholding states a two-vote majority in the Senate, and what happened in Missouri would set a precedent for all the new western states created from the vast Louisiana Purchase. "This momentous question," wrote former President Jefferson, fearful for the life of the Union, "like a fire bell in the night, awakened and filled me with terror."

Following the Louisiana Purchase and especially after the end of the War of 1812, the American population had surged westward, leading five new states to join the Union: Louisiana (1812), Indiana (1816), Mississippi (1817), Illinois (1818), and Alabama (1819). Of these, Louisiana, Mississippi, and Alabama permitted slavery.

Map 9.4 Missouri Compromise and the State of the Union, 1820

The compromise worked out by House Speaker Henry Clay established a formula that avoided debate over whether new states would allow or prohibit slavery. In the process, it divided the United States into northern and southern regions.

Source: Copyright © Cengage Learning

Because Missouri was on the same latitude as free Illinois, Indiana, and Ohio (a state since 1803), its admission as a slave state would thrust slavery not just westward but also northward, as well as tilt the uneasy balance in the Senate.

For two and a half years the issue dominated Congress, with the fiery debate transcending the immediate issue of slavery in Missouri. When Representative James Tallmadge Jr. of New York proposed gradual emancipation in Missouri, some southerners accused the North of threatening to destroy the Union. "If you persist, the Union will be dissolved," Thomas W. Cobb of Georgia shouted at Tallmadge. Only "seas of blood" could extinguish the fire Tallmadge had ignited, warned Cobb. "Let it come," retorted Tallmadge. The House, which had a northern majority, passed the Tallmadge Amendment, but the Senate rejected it.

House Speaker Henry Clay—himself a western slaveholder—put forward a compromise in 1820. Maine, carved out of Massachusetts, would enter as a free state, followed by Missouri as a slave state, maintaining the balance between slave and free states, at twelve to twelve. In the rest of the Louisiana Territory north of Missouri's southern border of 36°30′, slavery would be prohibited forever (see Map 9.4).

The compromise carried but almost unraveled when Missouri submitted a constitution barring free blacks from entering the state, a provision that opponents contended would violate the federal constitutional provision that citizens of each state were "entitled to all privileges and immunities of citizens in the several States." Proponents countered that many states, North and South, already barred free blacks from entering. In 1821, Clay proposed a second compromise: Missouri would guarantee that none of its laws would discriminate against citizens of other states. (The compromise carried, but once admitted to the Union, Missouri twice adopted laws barring free blacks.) For more than three decades, the Missouri Compromise would govern congressional policy toward admitting new slave states. But the compromise masked rather than suppressed the simmering political conflict over slavery's westward expansion.

Legacy FOR A PEOPLE AND A NATION

States' Rights and Nullification

When the Constitution replaced the Articles of Confederation, the United States had a much stronger central government, but the exact nature of the relationship between the states and the federal government was ambiguous because Constitutional Convention delegates could not agree on whether states or nation should prevail in the event of irreconcilable conflict. The Tenth Amendment to the Constitution offered only a slight clarification: powers not delegated to the central government, it said, were reserved to the states or to the people. The exact nature of the federal system's shared power, as well as who would determine which powers had been delegated to which authority, remained to be defined.

When New England Federalists met in Hartford at the end of 1814 to prepare a list of grievances against "Mr. Madison's War," they drew on the doctrine of nullification, first announced sixteen years earlier in the Kentucky and Virginia Resolutions, written by Thomas Jefferson and James Madison, respectively. Opposing the Alien and Sedition Acts, these founding fathers had asserted that, if the national government assumed powers not delegated to it by the Constitution, states could nullify federal actions—that is, declare them inoperative within state borders. At Hartford, Federalist representatives of New England states discussed taking nullification a step further by seceding. They backed away from this extreme step, but their formulation of states' rights to evaluate and nullify federal authority left a legacy for dissent that would be played out in crises up to the present day.

In the following decade, South Carolina nullified federal tariffs that it opposed, and in 1861 southern states threatened by Abraham Lincoln's election to the presidency claimed the right of secession. Although the Civil War supposedly settled the issue—states could neither nullify federal law nor secede—southern states opposing the Supreme Court's 1954 ruling in favor of school integration again claimed the right to nullify "unauthorized" federal policy within their borders. In the 1990s, some western states sought to nullify federal environmental laws. In the early twenty-first century, the issue of gay marriage once again exposed discord between the federal and state governments, though this time the states turned to neither secession nor nullification. Instead, as the U.S. Congress failed to muster a two-thirds majority to propose a constitutional amendment banning gay marriage, dozens of states asserted their rights by ratifying their own constitutional amendments banning gay marriage. Symbolically, the threat of secession remains potent more than two centuries after the Hartford Convention. Decrying the 2009 federal stimulus package, designed to jumpstart the ailing national economy, Texas Governor Rick Perry declared that his state might one day secede rather than face unwanted spending, taxation, and debt. The Hartford Convention's legacy for a people and a nation provides Americans who dissent from national policy with a model for using state governments, and threats of secession, as vehicles for their protests.

SUMMARY

The partisanship of the 1790s, though alarming to the nation's political leaders, captured Americans' imaginations, making the early republic a period of pervasive and vigorous political engagement. Troubled by vicious partisanship, President Jefferson sought both to unify the nation and to solidify Democratic-Republican control of the government. With a vision of an agrarian nation that protected individual liberty, Jeffersonians promoted a limited national government—one that stayed out of religious affairs and spent little on military forces, diplomatic missions, and economic initiatives. The rival Federalists, who exerted most of their influence through the judiciary, declared federal supremacy over the states even as the judiciary affirmed its own supremacy over other branches of the government. Federalists hoped a strengthened federal government would promote commerce and industry.

Despite his belief in limited government, Jefferson considered the acquisition of the Louisiana Territory and the commissioning of the Corps of Discovery among his most significant presidential accomplishments. The enormous expanse of fertile lands fueled the Jeffersonian dream of an agrarian republic: Americans soon streamed into the Louisiana Territory. Even more would have done so had it not been for the Indians (and their British allies) who stood in their way and for poorly developed transportation routes.

Jefferson's vision rested, too, on American disentanglement from foreign affairs. But with its economy so focused on international shipping, the United States soon faced its greatest threats from abroad, not from partisan or sectional divisions. In its wars with the Barbary states, the United States sought to guard its commerce and ships on the high seas. The second war with Britain—the War of 1812—was fought for similar reasons but against a much more formidable power. Although a military stalemate, the war inspired a new sense of nationalism and launched a new era of American development.

The Treaty of Ghent reaffirmed American independence; thereafter, the nation was able to settle disputes with Great Britain at the bargaining table. The war also dealt a serious blow to Indian resistance in the Midwest and Southwest. At the same time, embargoes and war accelerated the pace of American industrial growth. Because the Federalists' opposition to the war undermined their political credibility, their party all but disappeared from the national political scene by 1820. The absence of well-organized partisan conflict created what contemporaries called an Era of Good Feelings.

Although overt tension was muted in the heady postwar years, competing visions of America's route to prosperity and greatness endured. Under Chief Justice John Marshall, the Supreme Court supported the Federalist agenda, issuing rulings that stimulated commerce and industry through economic nationalism. The Democratic-Republicans looked, instead, toward the South and West, the vast and fertile Louisiana Territory. Whether they supported agrarian or industrial development, almost all Americans could agree on the need for improved transportation, though most internal improvements took place in the North.

During the first quarter of the nineteenth century, the United States vastly expanded its territorial reach, not just through the Louisiana Purchase but also with the acquisition of Florida. Fearful of European intentions to reassert influence in the Americas and emboldened by the nation's expanding boundaries, President Monroe proclaimed that the United States would not tolerate European intervention in American affairs. But even as its expanding boundaries strengthened the United States' international presence, that same territorial expansion would threaten the nation's newfound political unity at home.

That threat became most apparent in 1819, when the postwar economic boom came to a grinding halt and when congressmen predicted dire consequences could result from the dispute over whether to admit Missouri as a slave state. Henry Clay's compromise removed the issue of slavery's expansion from political center stage, but—by addressing only those territories already owned by the United States—it did not permanently settle the issue.

SUGGESTIONS FOR FURTHER READING

Stephen Aron, *American Confluence: The Missouri Frontier from Borderland to Border State* (2006)

David Edmunds, *Tecumseh and the Quest for Indian Leadership* (2006)

Joanne B. Freeman, *Affairs of Honor: National Politics in the New Republic* (2001)

Nancy Isenberg, *Fallen Founder: The Life of Aaron Burr* (2007)

John Lauritz Larson, *Internal Improvement: National Public Works and the Promise of Popular Government in the United States* (2001)

Jon Latimer, *1812: War with America* (2007)

Kent Newmyer, *John Marshall and the Heroic Age of the Supreme Court* (2001)

Jeffrey Ostler, *The Plains Sioux and U.S. Colonialism from Lewis and Clark to Wounded Knee* (2004)

Jeffrey Pasley, Andrew Robertson, and David Waldstreicher, eds., *Beyond the Founders: New Approaches to the Political History of the Early American Republic* (2004)

The Rise of the South
1815–1860

homas Jefferson died, as he had lived, in debt. Many Americans saw a providential hand at work when, on July 4, 1826, Jefferson and John Adams, rivals and founders of the American republic, died on the same day. But at Jefferson's home, Monticello, in Virginia, worldly anxiety abounded among the founder's white and black "families."

On January 15, 1827, a five-day estate sale took place at Monticello. Everything went up at auction, including paintings, furniture, and mementoes. Most expensive of all were "130 valuable negroes," described by Jefferson's grandson and executor, Thomas Jefferson Randolph, as "the most valuable for their number ever offered at one time in the state of Virginia." Large crowds gathered in frigid weather. Monticello's blacksmith, Joseph Fossett, watched his wife Edith and eight children sold at the auction to four different bidders.

By all accounts, Jefferson was a caring slaveholder, avoiding separation of families and whipping except in rare cases. But he was intensely involved in the domestic lives and labor efficiency of his slaves. After his wife, Martha (with whom he had two daughters), died in 1782, Jefferson also had at least six children, four of whom lived beyond infancy, with his slave woman, Sally Hemings. Sally was the half sister of Jefferson's wife, and part of a complex extended family of light-skinned Hemingses of Monticello.

Whole families of Jefferson's slaves were sold at the 1827 auction. Joe Fossett, as promised by Jefferson, became free exactly one year after his master's death. Jefferson had already earlier freed the four children he fathered with Sally Hemings: William Beverly Hemings, Harriet Hemings II, James Madison Hemings, and Thomas Eston Hemings. In 1822, Beverly and Harriet had left Monticello to pass as white people. Jefferson never freed Sally; Virginia law would have required him to attain, publicly, a dispensation from the state legislature in order to free her without removing her

◄ *Slave Market*, painting by unknown American artist, ca. 1850–1860. The scene condemns the cruelty and brutality of traders and planters at a slave auction, one of the most widely depicted images of slavery in antislavery culture. A young woman is separated from her lover and a child from the mother.

Chronology

1810–20	■ 137,000 slaves are forced to move from the Upper South to Alabama, Mississippi, and other western regions
1822	■ Vesey's insurrection plot is discovered in South Carolina
1830s	■ Vast majority of African American slaves are native-born in America
1830s–40s	■ Cotton trade grows into largest source of commercial wealth and America's leading export
1831	■ Turner leads a violent slave rebellion in Virginia
1832	■ Virginia holds the last debate in the South about the future of slavery; gradual abolition is voted down
	■ Publication of Dew's proslavery tract *Abolition of Negro Slavery*
1836	■ Arkansas gains admission to the Union as a slave state
1839	■ Mississippi's Married Women's Property Act gives married women some property rights
1845	■ Florida and Texas gain admission to the Union as slave states
	■ Publication of Douglass's *Narrative of the Life of Frederick Douglass, an American Slave, Written by Himself*
1850	■ Planters' share of agricultural wealth in the South is 90 to 95 percent
1850–60	■ Of some 300,000 slaves who migrate from the Upper to the Lower South, 60 to 70 percent go by outright sale
1857	■ Publication of Hinton R. Helper's *The Impending Crisis*, denouncing the slave system
	■ Publication of George Fitzhugh's *Southern Thought*, an aggressive defense of slavery
1860	■ 405,751 mulattos in the United States, 12.5 percent of the African American population
	■ Three-quarters of all southern white families own no slaves
	■ South produces largest cotton crop ever

from the state. The Sage of Monticello wanted no more salacious publicity about his long-time house servant and mistress than had already occurred for many years. Sally died a slave, living in Charlottesville, Virginia, in 1835 at the age of sixty-two; she left numerous heirlooms for her children from her life with Jefferson: a pair of his eyeglasses, a shoe buckle, and an inkwell.

"Thank heaven the whole of this dreadful business is over," wrote Jefferson's granddaughter, Mary, when the auction had ended. She consoled herself that the vast majority of slaves had been sold within the state. She likened the "sad scene," though, to a "captured village in ancient times when all were sold as slaves." Monticello itself was sold in 1831. But across the South in the 1820s the "business" of slavery expansion and cotton production was hardly over at all.

In 1815, the southern tier of states and territories, with fertile soil and a growing labor force of enslaved people to cultivate it, was poised for growth, prosperity, and power. New lands were settled, new states were peopled, and steadily the South emerged as the world's most extensive and vigorous commercial agricultural economy. The Old South's wealth came from export crops, land, and slaves, and its population was almost wholly rural. In the land where cotton became king, racial slavery affected not only economics but also values, customs, laws, class structure, and the region's relationship to the nation and the world. As slaves' bodies, labor, and lives came to be defined more and more as chattel, they struggled increasingly not only to survive but also to resist, sometimes overtly, but more often in daily life and cultural expression. By 1860, white Southerners not only asserted the moral and economic benefits of slavery with a vigorous defense of the system, but also sought to sustain and advance their political power over the national government.

- How and why was the Old South a "slave society," with slavery permeating every class and group within it, free or unfree?

- How and why did white southerners come to see cotton as "king" of a global economy, and how did the cotton trade's international reach shape southern society from 1815 to 1860?

- How did African American slaves build and sustain a meaningful life and a sense of community amid the potential chaos and destruction of their circumstances?

- How would you weigh the comparative significance of the following central themes in the history of the Old South: class, race, migration, power, liberty, wealth?

The "Distinctive" South

Not until the first half of the 1800s did the region of slaveholding states from the Chesapeake and Virginia to Missouri, and from Florida across to Texas, come to be designated as the South. Today, many still consider it America's most distinctive region. Historians have long examined how the Old South was like and unlike the rest of the nation. Because of its unique history, has the South, in the words of poet Allen Tate, always been "Uncle Sam's other province"? Or as southern writer W. J. Cash said in 1940, is the South "a tree with many age rings, with its limbs and trunk bent and twisted by all the winds of the years, but with its tap root in the Old South?" Analyzing just why the South seems more religious, more conservative, or more tragic than other regions of America has been an enduring practice in American culture and politics.

Certain American values, such as materialism, individualism, and faith in progress, have been associated with the North and values such as tradition, honor, and family loyalty, with the South. The South, so the stereotype has it, was static, even "backward," and the North was dynamic in the decades leading up to the Civil War. There are many measures of just how different South was from North in the antebellum era. At the same time, there were many Souths: low-country rice and cotton regions with dense slave populations; mountainous regions of small farmers and subsistence agriculture; semitropical wetlands in the Southeast; plantation culture in the Cotton Belt and especially the Mississippi valley; Texas grasslands; tobacco- and wheat-growing regions in Virginia and North Carolina; cities with bustling ports; wilderness areas with only the rare homestead of hillfolk.

The South was distinctive because of its commitment to slavery, but it also shared much in common with the rest of the nation. The geographic sizes of the South and the North were roughly the same. In 1815, white southerners shared with their fellow free citizens in the North a heritage of heroes and ideology from the era of the American Revolution and the War of 1812. With varying accents, southerners spoke the same language and worshiped the same Protestant God as northerners. Southerners lived under the same Constitution as northerners, and they shared a common mixture of nationalism and localism in their attitudes toward government. Down to the 1840s, northerners and southerners invoked with nearly equal frequency the doctrine of states' rights against federal authority. A sense of American mission and dreams inspired by the westward movement were as much a part of southern as of northern experience.

South-North Similarity

Indeed, some of the most eloquent visions of America as a land of yeomen—independent, self-sufficient farmers—expanding westward had come from a southerner, Thomas Jefferson. Jefferson believed that "virtue" rested in those who tilled the soil, that farmers made the best citizens. In 1804, Jefferson declared his "moral and physical preference of the agricultural over the manufacturing man." But as slavery and the plantation economy expanded (see Map 10.1), the South did not become a land of individual opportunity in the same manner as the North.

During the forty-five years before the Civil War, the South shared in the nation's economic booms and busts. Research has shown that, despite its enormous cruelties, slavery was a profitable labor system for planters. Southerners and northerners shared an expanding capitalist economy. As it grew, the slave-based economy of money-crop agriculture reflected the rational choices of planters. More land and more slaves generally converted into more wealth.

By the eve of the Civil War in 1860, the distribution of wealth and property in the two sections was almost identical: 50 percent of free adult males owned only 1 percent of real and personal property, and the richest 1 percent owned 27 percent of the wealth. One study comparing Texas and Wisconsin in 1850 shows that the richest 2 percent of families in each state owned 31 to 32 percent of the wealth. So both North

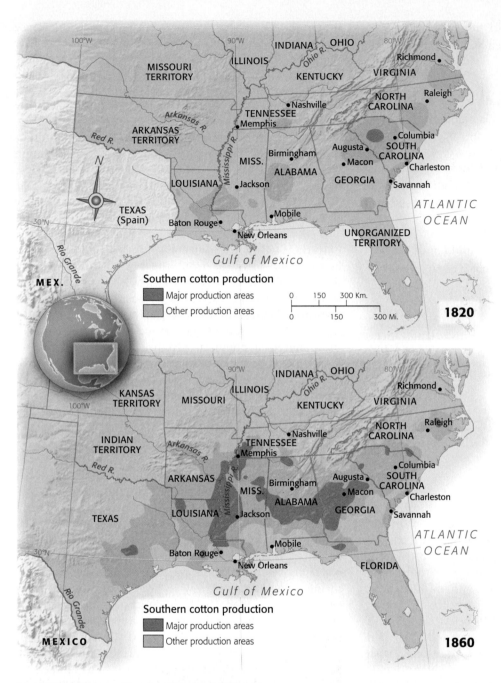

Map 10.1 Cotton Production in the South

These two maps reveal the rapid westward expansion of cotton production and its importance to the antebellum South.

Source: Copyright © Cengage Learning

and South had ruling classes, even if their wealth was invested in different kinds of property. Entrepreneurs in both sections, whether forging plantations out of Mississippi Delta land or shoe factories and textile mills in New England river towns, sought their fortunes in an expanding market economy. The southern "master class" was, in fact, more likely than propertied northerners to move west to make a profit.

There were important differences between the North and the South. The South's climate and longer growing season gave it an unmistakably rural and agricultural destiny. Many great rivers provided rich soil and transportation routes to market. The South's people, white and black, developed an

South-North Dissimilarity

intense attachment to place, to the ways people were related to the land and to one another. The South developed as a biracial society of brutal inequality, where the liberty of one race depended directly on the enslavement of another. White wealth was built on highly valued black labor.

Cotton growers spread out over as large an area as possible to maximize production and income. As a result, population density in the South was low; by 1860, there were only 2.3 people per square mile in vast and largely unsettled Texas, 15.6 in Louisiana, and 18.0 in Georgia. By contrast, population density in the nonslaveholding states east of the Mississippi River was almost three times higher. The Northeast had an average of 65.4 people per square mile. Massachusetts had 153.1 people per square mile, and New York City compressed 86,400 people into each square mile. When, in the 1850s, young Frederick Law Olmsted of Connecticut, later renowned as a landscape architect, toured the South as a journalist, he traveled mostly on horseback along primitive trails. Between Columbus, Georgia, and Montgomery, Alabama, Olmsted found "a hilly wilderness, with a few dreary villages, and many isolated cotton farms." For one who would design Central Park in New York City, this was just too much ruralness.

Where people were scarce, it was difficult to finance and operate schools, churches, libraries, and even inns and restaurants. Similarly, the rural character of the South and the significance of the plantation as a self-sufficient social unit meant that the section put few resources into improving disease control and public health. Southerners were strongly committed to their churches, and some believed in the importance of universities, but all such institutions were far less developed than those in the North. Factories were rare because planters invested most of their capital in slaves. A few southerners did invest in iron or textiles on a small scale. But the largest southern "industry" was lumbering, and the largest factories used slave labor to make cigars. More decisively, the South was slower than the North to develop a unified market economy and a regional transportation network. Despite concerted efforts, the South had only 35 percent of the nation's railroad mileage in 1860.

The Old South never developed its own banking and shipping capacity to any degree. If it had, its effort to be an international cartel might have succeeded longer. Most southern bank deposits were in the North, and southern cotton planters became ever more dependent on New York for shipping. As early as 1822, one-sixth of all southern cotton cleared for Liverpool or Le Havre from the port of New York and constituted two-fifths of all that city's exports. Many New York merchants and bankers developed deep interests in the fate of slavery and cotton prices. In a series of economic conventions held from 1837 to 1839, southern delegates debated the nature of foreign trade, dependence on northern importers and financiers, and other alleged threats to their commercial independence and security. But nothing, save rhetoric, came of these conventions; it was the last time southern planters would organize to break from their Yankee middlemen and shippers.

The South lagged far behind the North in nearly any measure of industrial growth. Its urban centers were mostly ports like New Orleans and Charleston, which became crossroads of commerce and small-scale manufacturing. In the interior were small market towns dependent on agricultural trade—"urbanization without cities," as one historian has said. Slavery slowed urban growth. As a system of racial control, slavery did not work well in cities. Likewise, because of a lack of manufacturing jobs, the South did not attract immigrants as readily as did the North. By 1860, only 13 percent of the nation's foreign-born population lived in the slave states.

Like most northerners, antebellum southerners were adherents to evangelical Christianity. Americans

▲ *America, 1841,* lithograph and watercolor by Edward Williams Clay. An idealized portrayal of loyal and contented slaves, likely distributed by northern apologists for slavery. All is well on the plantation as well-dressed slaves dance and express their gratitude to their master and his perfect family. The text includes the old slave saying: "God bless you master! You feed and clothe us. When we are sick you nurse us, and when too old to work, you provide for us!" The master replies piously: "These poor creatures are a sacred legacy from my ancestors and while a dollar is left me, nothing shall be spared to increase their comfort and happiness."

from all regions held in common a faith in a personal God and in conversion and piety as the means to salvation. But southern evangelicalism was distinct from its northern practice. In the South, Baptists and Methodists concentrated on personal rather than social improvement. By the 1830s in the North, evangelicalism was a major wellspring of reform movements (see Chapter 9); but in states where blacks were so numerous and unfree, and where the very social structure received increasingly aggressive attacks from abolitionists, religion, as one scholar has written, preached "a hands-off policy concerning slavery." Although slaves began to convert to Christianity in the early-nineteenth-century South, many southern whites feared a reform impulse that would foster what one historian has called an "interracial communion" in their churches. Moreover, those women who may have been reform minded were prevented from developing frequent associations with other reformers because of distance and sparse population. The only reform movements that did take hold in the emerging Bible Belt of the South, such as that for temperance, focused on personal behavior, not social reform.

The slave system made it inevitable that the interests and social structures of the North and the South would diverge after 1815. Because of its inherently conservative social structure, antebellum southern law restricted the authority of the courts, reinforcing a tradition of planter control. Penitentiaries tended to house only whites, as most blacks were under the authority of personal masters. Law-breaking in the South tended to involve crimes of violence rather than crimes against property.

Perhaps in no way was the South more distinctive than in its embrace of a particular world-view, a system of

A Southern World-View and the Proslavery Argument

thought and meaning held especially by the planter class, but also influencing the entire society. Like those of all people, southerners' justifications for slavery were not so different from those of any other civilization trying to defend the institutions it inherits. But at the heart of the proslavery argument was a deep and abiding racism. The persistence of modern racism in all sections of the United States is all the more reason to comprehend antebellum southerners' rationalizations for human slavery.

In the wake of the American Revolution, the Enlightenment ideas of natural rights and equality did stimulate antislavery sentiment in the Upper South, produced a brief flurry of manumissions, and led to considerable hope for gradual emancipation. In 1796, Virginian St. George Tucker argued that "slavery not only violates the laws of nature and of civil society, it also wounds the best forms of government." But confidence that the exercise of reason among gentlemen

might end such a profitable system as slavery waned in the new nation. As slavery spread, southerners soon vigorously defended it. In 1816, George Bourne, a Presbyterian minister exiled from Virginia for his antislavery sermons and for expulsion of slaveholders from his church, charged that, whenever southerners were challenged on slavery, "they were fast choked, for they had a Negro stuck fast in their throats." After walking home with South Carolina statesman and proslavery advocate John C. Calhoun from an 1820 cabinet meeting, John Quincy Adams confided to his diary that too many southerners "writhe in agonies of fear at the very mention of human rights as applicable to men of color."

By the 1820s, white southerners went on the offensive, actively justifying slavery as a "positive good" and not merely a "necessary evil." They used the antiquity of slavery, as well as the Bible's many references to slaveholding, to foster a historical argument for bondage. Slavery, they deemed, was the natural status of blacks. Whites were the more intellectual race, and blacks the race more inherently physical and therefore destined for labor. Whites were the creators of civilizations, blacks the appointed hewers of wood and drawers of water. Proslavery writers did not mince words. In a proslavery tract written in 1851, John Campbell confidently declared that "there is as much difference between the lowest tribe of negroes and the white Frenchman, Englishman, or American, as there is between the monkey and the negro."

Some southerners defended slavery in practical terms; they simply saw their bondsmen as economic necessities and symbols of their quest for prosperity. In 1845, James Henry Hammond of South Carolina argued that slaveholding was essentially a matter of property rights. Unwilling to "deal in abstractions" about the "right and wrong" of slavery, Hammond considered property sacred and protected by the Constitution, because slaves were legal property—end of argument. The deepest root of the proslavery argument was a hierarchical view of the social order as slavery's defenders believed God or nature had prescribed it. Southerners cherished tradition, duty, and honor, believing social change should come only in slow increments, if at all. As the Virginia legislature debated the gradual abolition of slavery in 1831–1832, in the wake of Nat Turner's rebellion, Thomas R. Dew, a slaveholder and professor of law and history at the College of William and Mary, contended that "that which is the growth of *ages* may require ages to remove." Dew's widely read work *Abolition of Negro Slavery* (1832) ushered in an outpouring of proslavery writing that would intensify over the next thirty years. Until Turner's bloody rebellion, Dew admitted, emancipation in the South had "never been seriously discussed." But as slavery expanded westward and fueled national prosperity, Dew cautioned southerners that any degree of gradual abolition threatened the whole region's "irremediable ruin." Dew declared black slavery part of the "order of nature," an indispensable part of the "deep and solid foundations of society" and the basis of the "well-ordered, well-established liberty" of white Americans. Dew's well-ordered society also included his conception of the proper division of men and women into separate spheres and functions.

Proslavery advocates held views very different from those of northern reformers on the concepts of freedom, progress, and equality. They turned natural-law doctrine to their favor, arguing that the natural state of humankind was inequality of ability and condition, not equality. A former U.S. senator in South Carolina, William Harper, charged in 1837 that Jefferson's famous dictum about equality in the Declaration of Independence was no more than a "sentimental phrase." "Is it not palpably nearer the truth to say that no man was ever born free," Harper argued, "and that no two men were ever born equal?" Proslavery writers believed that people were born to certain stations in life; they stressed dependence over autonomy and duty over rights as the human condition. As Virginia writer George Fitzhugh put it in 1854, "Men are not born entitled to equal rights. It would be far nearer the truth to say, that some were born with saddles on their backs, and others booted and spurred to ride them."

Many slaveholders believed their ownership of people bound them to a set of paternal obligations as guardians of a familial relationship between masters and slaves. Although contradicted by countless examples of slave resistance and escape, as well as by slave sales, planters needed to believe in and exerted great energy in constructing the idea of the contented slave. The slaveholders who promoted their own freedom and pursued personal profits through the bondage of blacks had to justify themselves endlessly.

Slavery and race affected everything in the Old South. Whites and blacks alike grew up, were socialized, married, reared children, worked, conceived of property, and honed their most basic habits of behavior under the influence of slavery. This was true of

A Slave Society

slaveholding and nonslaveholding whites as well as of blacks who were slave and free. Slavery shaped the social structure of the South, fueled almost anything meaningful in its economy, and came to dominate its politics. Rudolphe Lucien Desdunes, a Louisiana sugar planter, remembered growing up in a society where "slavery was the pivot around which everything revolved."

The South was interdependent with the North, the West, and even with Europe in a growing capitalist market system. To keep the cotton trade flowing,

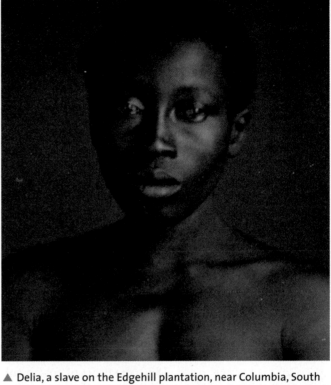

Peabody Museum of Archaeology and Ethnology, Harvard University

▲ Delia, a slave on the Edgehill plantation, near Columbia, South Carolina, photographed in 1850 by daguerrotypist, Joseph Zealy, for natural scientist, Louis Agassiz. Delia was among seven people Agassiz had photographed nude in an effort to investigate the alleged inferior physiogamy of Africans and African Americans. Delia's tearful gaze haunts the tragic process by which the "racial sciences" tried to categorize and rank human beings in the service of proslavery arguments.

southerners relied on northern banks, on northern steamship companies working the great western rivers, and on northern merchants. But there were elements of this system that southerners increasingly rejected during the antebellum era, especially urbanism, the wage labor system, a broadening right to vote, and any threat to their racial and class order.

In the antebellum era, as later, there were many Souths, but Americans have always been determined to define what one historian called the "Dixie difference." "The South is both American and something different," writes another historian, "at times a mirror or magnifier of national traits and at other times a counterculture." This was most acutely true in the decades before the Civil War.

Culturally, the South developed a proclivity to tell its own story. Its ruralness and its sense of tradition may have given southerners a special habit of telling tales. "Southerners . . . love a good tale," said Mississippi writer Eudora Welty. "They are born reciters, great memory retainers, diary keepers, letter exchangers, and letter savers, history tracers, and debaters, and—outstaying all the rest—great talkers." The South's story is both distinctive and national, and it begins in what we have come to call the Old South, a term only conceivable after the eviction of native peoples from the region.

Southern Expansion, Indian Resistance and Removal

Americans were a restless, moving people when the trans-Appalachian frontier opened in the wake of the War of 1812. Some 5 to 10 percent of the booming population moved each year, usually westward. In the first two decades of the century, they poured into the Ohio valley; by the 1820s, after the death of the Shawnee chief Tecumseh and the collapse of the pan-Indian federation, they were migrating into the Mississippi River valley and beyond. By 1850, two-thirds of Americans lived west of the Appalachians.

As much as in any other region, this surging westward movement was a southern phenomenon. After 1820, the heart of cotton cultivation and the slave-based plantation system shifted from the coastal states to Alabama and the newly settled Mississippi valley—Tennessee, Louisiana, Arkansas, and Mississippi. Southern slaveholders forced slaves to move with them to the newer areas of the South, and yeoman farmers followed, also hoping for new wealth through cheap land and the ownership of other people.

A Southern Westward Movement

A wave of migration was evident everywhere in the Southeast. As early as 1817, Georgian Samuel McDonald observed a "disease prevalent" in his region. "The patient," he said, first exhibited a "great love" of talking about "the new country" to the west. Then he tried to "make sale of his stock" and "lastly . . . to sell his plantation." Once attacked by this "Alabama fever," most never recovered and were carried "off to the westward." That same year, a Charleston, South Carolina, newspaper reported with alarm that migration out of that state had already reached "unprecedented proportions." Indeed, almost half of the white people born in South Carolina after 1800 left the state, most for the Southwest. And by 1833, Tyrone Power, an Irish actor riding a stagecoach from Georgia into Alabama, encountered many "camps of immigrants" and found the roads "covered" by such pilgrims.

The way to wealth for seaboard planters in the South was to go west to grow cotton for the booming world markets, by purchasing ever more land and slaves. The population of Mississippi soared from 73,000 in 1820 to 607,000 in 1850, with African American slaves in the majority. Across the Mississippi River, the population of Arkansas went from fourteen thousand in 1820 to 210,000 in 1850. By 1835, the American immigrant population in Texas reached 35,000, including three thousand slaves, and outnumbering Mexicans two to one. Aggressive American settlers declared Texas's independence from Mexico in 1836, spurring further American immigration into the region. By 1845, "Texas fever" had boosted the Anglo population to 125,000. Statehood that year opened the floodgates to more immigrants from the east and to a confrontation with Mexico that would lead to war.

As the cotton kingdom grew to what southern political leaders dreamed would be national and world dominion, this westward migration, fueled at first by an optimistic nationalism, ultimately made migrant planters more sectional and more southern. In 1817, Congressman John C. Calhoun embraced national expansion as the means to "bind the Republic together," as he provided the process its unquestioned assumption: "Let us conquer space." In time, political dominance in the South migrated westward into the Cotton Belt as well. By the 1840s and 1850s, these energetic capitalist planters, ever mindful of world markets and fearful that their slave-based economy was under attack, sought to protect and expand their system. Increasingly, they saw themselves, as one historian has written, less as "landowners who happened to own slaves" than as "slaveholders who happened to own land."

Before all this expansion could take place, other, older groups of Americans already occupied much of this land. Before 1830, large swaths of upper Georgia belonged to the Cherokees, and huge regions of Alabama and Mississippi were either Creek, Choctaw, or Chickasaw land. Indians were also on the move, but in forced migrations. The indigenous cultures of the eastern and southern woodlands had to be uprooted to make way for white expansion. For the vast majority of white Americans, the Indians were in the way of their growing empire. Taking Indian land, so the reasoning went, merely reflected the natural course of history: the "civilizers" had to displace the "children of the forest" in the name of progress. National leaders provided all the rhetoric and justification needed. "Nothing," said General Andrew Jackson as early as 1816, "can promote the welfare of the United States, and particularly the southwestern frontier so much as bringing into market . . . the whole of this fertile country." As president in 1830, Jackson spoke with certainty about why the Indians must go. "What good man would prefer a country," he asked, "covered with forests and ranged by a few thousand savages to our extensive Republic, studded with cities, towns, and prosperous farms?"

The Amistad Case

In April 1839, a Spanish slave ship, *Tecora*, sailed from Lomboko, the region of West Africa that became Sierre Leone. On board were Mende people, captured and sold by their African enemies. In June, they arrived in Havana, Cuba, a Spanish colony. Two Spaniards purchased fifty-three of the Mende and set sail aboard *La Amistad* for their plantations elsewhere in Cuba. After three days at sea, the Africans revolted. Led by a man the Spaniards called Joseph Cinque, they killed the captain and seized control of the vessel. They ordered the two Spaniard owners to take them back to Africa, but the slaveholders sailed east by day and north by night, trying to reach the shores of the American South. Far off course, *La Amistad* was seized by the USS *Washington* in Long Island Sound and brought ashore in Connecticut.

The "Amistad Africans" were soon a celebrated moral and legal cause for abolitionists and slaveholders, as well as in U.S.-Spanish relations. The Africans were imprisoned in New Haven, and a prolonged dispute ensued around many questions: Were they slaves and murderers, and the property of their Cuban owners, or were they free people exercising their natural rights? Were they Spanish property, seized on the high seas in violation of a 1795 treaty? If a northern state could "free" captive Africans, what did it mean for enslaved African Americans in the South? Connecticut abolitionists immediately went to court, where a U.S. circuit court judge dismissed the charges of mutiny and murder but refused to release the Africans because their Spanish owners claimed them as property.

Meanwhile, the Mende were desperate to tell their own story. A Yale professor of ancient languages, Josiah Gibbs, visited the captives and learned their words for numbers. In New York, he walked up and down the docks repeating the Mende words until an African seaman, James Covey, responded. Covey journeyed to New Haven, conversed with the jubilant Africans, and soon their harrowing tale garnered sympathy all over Yankee New England.

In a new trial, the judge ruled that the Africans were illegally enslaved and ordered them returned to their homeland. Although slavery might be legal in Cuba, the slave trade between Africa and the Americas had been outlawed in a treaty between Spain and Great Britain. Spain's lawyers demanded the return of their "merchandise." In need of southern votes to win reelection, President Martin Van Buren supported the Spanish claims and advocated the Africans' return to a likely death in Cuba.

The administration appealed the case to the Supreme Court in February 1841. Arguing the abolitionists' case, former president John Quincy Adams famously pointed to a copy of the Declaration of Independence on the wall of the court chambers, invoked the natural rights to life and liberty, and chastised the Van Buren administration for its "immense array of power . . . on the side of injustice." In a 7-to-1 decision, the Court ruled that the Africans were "free-born" with the right of self-defense, while remaining silent on slavery's legality in the United States.

Fund-raising and speaking tours featuring Cinque made the return voyage possible. On November 27, 1841, thirty-five survivors and five American missionaries disembarked for Africa. They arrived in Sierre Leone on January 15, 1842, whereupon Cinque wrote a letter to the Amistad Committee. "I thank all 'merican people," he said, "I shall never forget 'merican people." But the international meanings of the Amistad case would endure. Sarah Magru, one of the child captives on *La Amistad*, stayed in America to attend Oberlin College and later returned to work at the Mende mission in Sierre Leone.

The Amistad case showed how intertwined slavery was with freedom, and the United States with the world. It poisoned diplomatic relations between America and Spain for a generation, and stimulated Christian mission work in Africa.

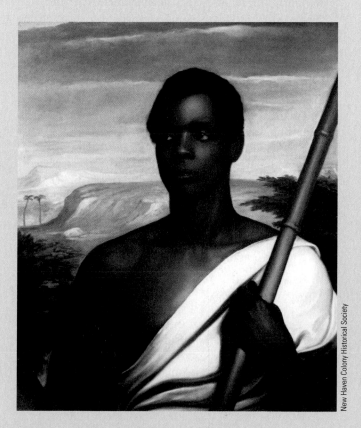

New Haven Colony Historical Society

◀ Joseph Cinque, by Nathaniel Jocelyn, 1840. Cinque led the rebellion aboard "The Amistad," a Spanish ship carrying captive Africans along the coast of Cuba in 1839. They commandeered the ship and sailed it north toward New England where they were rescued off the coast of Connecticut. Cinque, celebrated as a great leader, sat for the painting while he and his people awaited trial. They were freed by a decision of the U.S. Supreme Court in 1841 and returned to their homeland in Sierra Leone in West Africa.

In theory, under the U.S. Constitution, the federal government recognized Indian sovereignty and treated Indian peoples as foreign nations. Indeed, the United States received Indian delegations with pomp and ceremony, exchanging gifts as tokens of

Indian Treaty Making

friendship. Agreements between Indian nations and the United States were signed, sealed, and ratified like other international treaties. In practice, however, swindle and fraud dominated the government's approach to treaty making and Indian sovereignty. The United States imposed conditions on Indian representatives, and as the country expanded, new treaties replaced old ones, shrinking Indian landholdings.

Although Indian resistance persisted against such pressure after the War of 1812, it only slowed the process. In the 1820s, native peoples in the middle West, Ohio valley, Mississippi valley, and other parts of the cotton South ceded lands totaling 200 million acres for a pittance.

Increasingly, Indian nations east of the Mississippi sought to survive through accommodation. In the first three decades of the century, the Choctaw, Creek, and Chickasaw peoples in the lower Mississippi became

Indian Accommodation

suppliers and traders in the nation's expanding market economy. Under treaty provisions, Indian commerce took place through trading posts and stores that provided Indians with supplies, and purchased or bartered Indian-produced goods. The trading posts extended credit to chiefs, who increasingly fell into debt that they could pay off to the federal government only by selling their land.

By 1822, the Choctaw nation had sold 13 million acres but still carried a debt of $13,000. The Indians struggled to adjust, increasing agricultural production and hunting, working as farmhands and craftsmen, and selling produce at market stalls in Natchez and New Orleans. As the United States expanded westward, white Americans promoted their assimilation, through education and conversion to Christianity, with renewed urgency. "Put into the hand of [Indian] children the primer and the hoe," the House Committee on Indian Affairs recommended in 1818, "and they will naturally, in time, take hold of the plough; and, as their minds become enlightened and expand, the Bible will be their book, and they will grow up in habits of morality and industry." In 1819, in response to missionary lobbying, Congress appropriated $10,000 annually for "civilization of the tribes adjoining the frontier settlements." Protestant missionaries administered the "civilizing fund" and established mission schools.

Within five years, thirty-two boarding schools enrolled Indian students. They substituted English for American Indian languages and taught agriculture along-side the Christian gospel. But this emphasis on agriculture and the value of private property did not deter settlers eyeing Indian land. Wherever native peoples lived, illegal settlers disrupted their lives. The federal government only halfheartedly enforced the integrity of treaties, as legitimate Indian land rights gave way to the advance of white civilization.

Over time, however, the Indians could not prevent the spread of the cotton economy that arose all around them. With loss of land came dependency. The Choctaws came to rely on white Americans not only for manufactured goods but even for food. Dependency, coupled with disease, facilitated removal of American Indian peoples to western lands. While the population of other groups increased rapidly, the Indian population fell, some nations declining by 50 percent in only three decades. The French traveler and author Alexis de Tocqueville noticed the contrast. "Not only have these wild tribes receded, but they are destroyed," Tocqueville concluded, after personally observing the tragedy of forced removal in 1831, "and as they give way or perish, an immense and increasing people fill their place. There is no instance upon record of so prodigious a growth or so rapid a destruction." As many as 100,000 eastern and southern Indian peoples were removed between 1820 and 1850; about thirty thousand died in the process.

The wanderings of the Shawnees, the people of the Prophet and Tecumseh (see pages 229–230), illustrate the uprooting of Indian peoples. After giving up 17 million acres in Ohio in a 1795 treaty, the Shawnees scattered to Indiana and eastern Missouri. After the War of 1812, some Shawnees sought protection from either the British in Canada or from Mexico. Yet another group moved to the Kansas territory in 1825. By 1854, Kansas was open to white settlement, and the Shawnees had to cede seven-eighths of their land, or 1.4 million acres.

Removal had a profound impact on all Shawnees. The men lost their traditional role as providers; their skills hunting woodland animals were useless on the prairies of Kansas. As grain became the tribe's dietary staple, Shawnee women played a greater role as providers, supplemented by government aid under treaty provisions. Remarkably, the Shawnees preserved their language and culture in the face of these devastating dislocations.

Much of the land of the southeastern tribes—Cherokees, Creeks, Choctaws, Chickasaws, and Seminoles—had remained intact after the War of 1812,

Indian Removal as Federal Policy

and they had aggressively resisted white encroachment. In his last annual message to Congress in late 1824, President James Monroe proposed that all Indians be moved beyond the Mississippi River. Monroe described his proposal as an "honorable" one that would protect Indians from invasion and provide them with independence for "improvement and civilization." He believed force would be unnecessary.

But all four tribes unanimously rejected Monroe's proposition. Between 1789 and 1825, the four nations had negotiated thirty treaties with the United States, and they had reached their limit. Most wished to remain on what little was left of their ancestral land.

Pressure from Georgia had prompted Monroe's policy. In the 1820s, the state had accused the federal government of not fulfilling its 1802 promise to remove the Cherokees and Creeks from northwestern Georgia in return for the state's renunciation of its claim to western lands. In 1826, under federal pressure, the Creek nation ceded all but a small strip of its Georgia acreage, but Georgians remained unmoved. Only the complete removal of the Georgia Creeks to the West could resolve the conflict between the state and the federal government.

For the Creeks, the outcome was devastating. In an ultimately unsuccessful attempt to hold fast to the remainder of their traditional lands, which were in Alabama, they radically altered their political structure. In 1829, at the expense of traditional village autonomy, they centralized tribal authority and forbade any chief from ceding land.

In 1830, after extensive debate and a narrow vote in both houses, Congress passed the Indian Removal Act, authorizing the president to negotiate treaties of removal with all tribes living east of the Mississippi. The bill, which provided federal funds for such relocations, would likely not have passed the House without the additional representation afforded slave states due to the three-fifths clause in the Constitution.

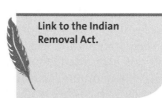

Link to the Indian Removal Act.

Adapting to American ways seemed no more successful than resistance in forestalling removal. No people met the challenge of assimilating to American standards more thoroughly than the Cherokees, whose traditional home centered on eastern Tennessee and northern Alabama and Georgia. Between 1819 and 1829, the tribe became economically self-sufficient and politically self-governing; during this Cherokee renaissance the nearly fifteen thousand adult Cherokees came to think of themselves as a nation, not a collection of villages. In 1821 and 1822, Sequoyah, a self-educated Cherokee, devised an eighty-six-character phonetic alphabet that made possible a Cherokee-language Bible and a bilingual tribal newspaper, *Cherokee Phoenix* (1828). Between 1820 and 1823, the Cherokees created a formal government with a bicameral legislature, a court system, and a salaried bureaucracy. In 1827, they adopted a written constitution modeled after that of the United States. They transformed their economy from hunting, gathering, and subsistence agriculture to commodity trade based on barter, cash, and credit.

Cherokees

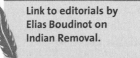

Link to editorials by Elias Boudinot on Indian Removal.

Cherokee land laws, however, differed from U.S. law. The nation collectively owned all Cherokee land and forbade land sales to outsiders. Nonetheless, economic change paralleled political adaptation. Many became individual farmers and slaveholders; by 1833, they held fifteen hundred black slaves, and over time Cherokee racial identity became very complex. Both before and after removal to the west, the designations of "mixed bloods" and "full bloods" were woven into

Joslyn Art Museum, Omaha, Nebraska. Gift of the Enron Art Foundation

◄ Southern Indians attempted to remain in their ancestral lands in the South. Karl Bodmer's watercolor portrayed a Choctaw camp on the Mississippi River near Natchez, before the Indians were forced out of Mississippi and Alabama in 1830.

the fabric of tribal society, and conflicts over membership as well as the legacy of Cherokee slaveholding still permeate the group today. But these Cherokee transformations failed to win respect or acceptance from white southerners. In the 1820s, Georgia pressed them to sell the 7,200 square miles of land they held in the state. Congress appropriated $30,000 in 1822 to buy the Cherokee land in Georgia, but the Cherokees resisted. Impatient with their refusals to negotiate cession, Georgia annulled the Cherokees' constitution, extended the state's sovereignty over them, prohibited the Cherokee National Council from meeting except to cede land, and ordered their lands seized. Then, the discovery of gold on Cherokee land in 1829 further whetted Georgia's appetite for Cherokee territory.

Backed by sympathetic whites but not by President Andrew Jackson, the Cherokees under Chief John Ross turned to the federal courts

Cherokee Nation v. Georgia

to defend their treaty with the United States. Their legal strategy reflected their growing political sophistication. In *Cherokee Nation v. Georgia* (1831), Chief Justice John Marshall ruled that under the federal Constitution an Indian tribe was neither a foreign nation nor a state and therefore had no standing in federal courts. Indians' relationship with the United States was "marked," said Marshall, "by cardinal and peculiar distinctions which exist nowhere else." They were deemed "domestic, dependent nations." Legally, they were in but not of the United States. Nonetheless, said Marshall, the Indians had an unquestionable right to their lands; they could lose title only by voluntarily giving it up.

A year later, in *Worcester v. Georgia*, Marshall defined the Cherokee position more clearly. The Indian nation was, he declared, a distinct political community in which "the laws of Georgia can have no force" and into which Georgians could not enter without permission or treaty privilege. The Cherokees celebrated. *Phoenix* editor Elias Boudinot called the decision "glorious news." Jackson, however, whose reputation had been built as an Indian fighter, did his best to usurp the Court's action. Newspapers widely reported that Jackson had said, "John Marshall has made his decision: now let him enforce it." Keen to open up new lands for settlement, Jackson favored expelling the Cherokees.

Georgians, too, refused to comply; they would not tolerate a sovereign Cherokee nation within their borders, and they refused to hear the pleas of Indian people to share their American dream. A Cherokee census indicated that they owned thirty-three grist mills, thirteen sawmills, one powder mill, sixty-nine blacksmith shops, two tanneries, 762 looms, 2,486 spinning wheels, 172 wagons, 2,923 plows, 7,683 horses, 22,531 cattle, 46,732 pigs, and 2,566 sheep. "You asked us to

throw off the hunter and warrior state," declared the Cherokee leader, John Ridge, in 1832. "We did so— you asked us to form a republican government: We did so—adopting your own as a model. You asked us to cultivate the earth, and learn the mechanic arts: We did so. You asked us to learn to read: We did so. You asked us to cast away our idols, and worship your God: We did so." But neither the plow nor the Bible earned the Cherokees respect in the face of the economic, imperial, and racial quests of their fellow southerners (see Map 10.2).

The Choctaws went first; they made the forced journey from Mississippi and Alabama to the West in

Trail of Tears

the winter of 1831 and 1832. Alexis de Tocqueville was visiting Memphis when they passed through: "The wounded, the sick, newborn babies, and the old men on the point of death. . . . I saw them embark to cross the great river," he wrote, "and the sight will never fade from my memory. Neither sob nor complaint rose from that silent assembly. Their afflictions were of long standing, and they felt them to be irremediable." Other tribes soon joined the forced march. The Creeks in Alabama resisted removal until 1836, when the army pushed them westward. A year later, the Chickasaws followed.

Having fought removal in the courts, the Cherokees were divided. Some believed that further resistance was hopeless and accepted removal as the only chance to preserve their civilization. The leaders of this minority agreed in 1835 to exchange their southern home for western land, in the Treaty of New Echota. Most, though, wanted to stand firm. John Ross, with petitions signed by fifteen thousand Cherokees, lobbied the Senate against ratification of the treaty. He lost. But when the time for evacuation came in 1838, most Cherokees refused to move. President Martin Van Buren sent federal troops to round them up. About twenty thousand Cherokees were evicted, held in detention camps, and marched under military escort to Indian Territory in present-day Oklahoma. Nearly one-quarter of them died of disease and exhaustion on what came to be known as the Trail of Tears.

When the forced march to the West ended, the Indians had traded about 100 million acres east of the Mississippi for 32 million acres west of the river plus $68 million. Only a few scattered remnants, among them the Seminoles in Florida and the Cherokees in the southern Appalachian Mountains, remained east of the Mississippi River.

Forced removal had a disastrous impact on the Cherokees and other displaced Indian nations. In the West, they encountered an alien environment. Unable to live off the land, many became dependent on government payments for survival. Removal also brought new internal conflicts. The Cherokees in particular struggled over their tribal government. In 1839, followers of John Ross assassinated the leaders of the protreaty faction. Violence continued sporadically until a new treaty in 1846 imposed a temporary truce. In time, the Cherokees managed to reestablish their political institutions and a governing body in Tahlequah, in northeastern Oklahoma.

In Florida, a small band of Seminoles continued to resist. Some Seminole leaders agreed in the 1832 Treaty of Payne's Landing to relocate to the West within three years, but others opposed the treaty, and some probably did not know it existed. A minority under Osceola, a charismatic leader, refused to vacate their homes and fought the protreaty group. When federal troops were sent to impose removal in 1835, Osceola waged a fierce guerrilla war against them.

Seminole Wars

The Florida Indians were a varied group that included many Creeks and mixed Indian–African Americans (ex-slaves or descendants of runaway slaves). The U.S. Army, however, considered them all Seminoles, subject to removal. General Thomas Jesup believed that the runaway slave population was the key to the war. "This, you may be assured, is a Negro, not an Indian war," he wrote a friend in 1836, "and if it be not speedily put down, the South will feel the effects of it on their slave population before the end of the next season."

Osceola was captured under a white flag of truce and died in an army prison in 1838, but the Seminoles fought on under Chief Coacoochee (Wild Cat) and other leaders. In 1842, the United States abandoned the removal effort. Most of Osceola's followers agreed to move west to Indian Territory after another war in 1858, but some Seminoles remained in the Florida Everglades.

Map 10.2 Removal of Native Americans from the South, 1820–1840

Over a twenty-year period, the federal government and southern states forced Native Americans to exchange their traditional homes for western land. Some tribal groups remained in the South, but most settled in the alien western environment.

Source: Copyright © Cengage Learning

▲ *The Trail of Tears*, by twentieth-century Pawnee artist Brummet Echohawk. About twenty thousand Cherokees were evicted in 1838–1839, and about one-quarter of them died on the forced march to present-day Oklahoma.

Social Pyramid in the Old South

As Indians increasingly were forced westward, their lands were now open to restless and mobile white settlers. A large majority of white southern families (three-quarters in 1860) owned no slaves. Most were yeoman farmers who owned their own land and grew their own food. The social distance between poorer whites and the planter class could be great, although the line between slaveholder and nonslaveholder was fluid. Still greater was the distance between whites and blacks with free status. White yeomen, landless whites, and free blacks occupied the broad base of the social pyramid in the Old South.

Many of the white farmers who pioneered the southern wilderness, moving into undeveloped regions or Indian land after removal, owned no slaves. After the War of 1812, they moved in successive waves down the southern Appalachians into the Gulf lands or through the Cumberland Gap into Kentucky and Tennessee. In large sections of the South, especially inland from the coast and away from large rivers, small, self-sufficient farms were the norm. Lured by stories of good land, many men repeatedly uprooted their wives and children. So many shared the excitement over new lands that one North Carolinian wrote in alarm, "The Alabama Fever rages here with great violence. . . . I am apprehensive if it continues to spread as it has done, it will almost depopulate the country."

Yeoman Farmers

These farmers were individualistic and hard working. Unlike their northern counterparts, their lives were not transformed by improvements in transportation. They could be independent thinkers as well, but their status as a numerical majority did not mean they set the political or economic direction of the larger society. Self-reliant and often isolated, absorbed in the work of their farms, they operated both apart from and within the slave-based staple-crop economy.

On the southern frontier, men cleared fields, built log cabins, and established farms while their wives labored in the household economy and patiently re-created the social ties—to relatives, neighbors, fellow churchgoers—that enriched everyone's experience. Women seldom shared the men's excitement about moving. They dreaded the isolation and loneliness of the frontier. "We have been [moving] all our lives," lamented one woman. "As soon as ever we get comfortably settled, it is time to be off to something new."

Some yeomen acquired large tracts of level land, purchased slaves, and became planters. They forged part of the new wealth of the cotton boom states of Mississippi and Louisiana, where mobility into the slaveowning class was possible. Others clung to familiar mountainous areas or sought self-sufficiency because, as one frontiersman put it, they disliked "seeing the nose of my neighbor sticking out between the trees." As one historian has written, though they owned no slaves, yeomen were jealous of their independence, and "the household grounded their own claims to masterhood." Whatever the size of their property, they wanted control over their economic and domestic lives.

Thomas Gilcrease Institute of American History and Art

▲ Eastman Johnson's *Fiddling His Way* (1866) depicts rural life by representing the visit of an itinerant black musician to a farm family. Expressions and gestures suggest a social mixing between the races at the yeoman level of southern society.

The Chrysler Museum of Art, Norfolk, Virginia. Bequest of Walter P. Chrysler, Jr.

Yeoman Folk Culture

The yeomen enjoyed a folk culture based on family, church, and local region. Their speech patterns and inflections recalled their Scots-Irish and Irish backgrounds. They flocked to religious revivals called camp meetings, and in between they got together for house-raisings, logrollings, quilting bees, corn-shuckings, and hunting for both food and sport. Such occasions combined work with fun and fellowship, offering food and liquor in abundance.

A demanding round of work and family responsibilities shaped women's lives in the home. They worked in the fields to an extent that astonished travelers like Frederick Law Olmsted and British writer Frances Trollope, who believed yeomen had rendered their wives "slaves of the soil." Throughout the year, the care and preparation of food consumed much of women's time. Household tasks continued during frequent pregnancies and childcare. Primary nursing and medical care also fell to mothers, who often relied on folk wisdom. Women, too, wanted to be masters of their household, the only space and power over which they could claim domain, although it came at the price of their health.

Yeomen's Livelihoods

Among the men, many aspired to wealth, eager to join the scramble for slaves and cotton profits. North Carolinian John F. Flintoff kept a diary of his struggle for success. At age eighteen in 1841, Flintoff went to Mississippi to seek his fortune. Like other aspiring yeomen, he worked as an overseer of slaves but often found it impossible to please his employers. At one point, he gave up and returned to North Carolina, where he married and lived for a while in his parents' house. But Flintoff was "impatient to get along in the world," so he tried Louisiana next and then Mississippi again.

Flintoff's health suffered in the Gulf region and, routinely, "first rate employment" alternated with "very low wages." Moreover, as a young man working on isolated plantations, Flintoff often felt lonely. Even at a revival meeting in 1844 he felt "little warm feeling." His employers found fault with his work, and in 1846 Flintoff concluded in despair that "managing negroes and large farms is soul destroying."

But a desire to succeed kept him going. At twenty-six, even before he owned any land, Flintoff bought his first slave, "a negro boy 7 years old." Soon he had purchased two more children, the cheapest slaves available.

◀ *North Carolina Emigrants: Poor White Folks,* oil on canvas, 1845, by James Henry Beard. This depicts a yeoman family, their belongings all on one hungry horse, as they migrate westward in search of new land and livelihood.

Cincinnati Museum of Art, Gift of the Proctor & Gamble Company. Accession #: 2003.52

Conscious of his status as a slaveowner, Flintoff resented the low wages he was paid. In 1853, with nine young slaves and a growing family, Flintoff faced "the most unhappy time of my life." Fired by his uncle, he returned to North Carolina, sold some of his slaves, and purchased 124 acres with help from his in-laws. As he began to pay off his debts, he looked forward to freeing his wife from labor and possibly sending his sons to college. Although Flintoff demonstrated that a farmer could move in and out of the slaveholding class, he never achieved the cotton planter status (owning roughly twenty or more slaves) that he desired.

Probably more typical of the southern yeoman was Ferdinand L. Steel, who as a young man moved from North Carolina to Tennessee to work as a river boatman but eventually took up farming in Mississippi. Steel rose every day at 5 A.M. and worked until sundown. He and his family raised corn and wheat, though cotton was his cash product: he sold five or six bales (about two thousand pounds) a year to obtain money for sugar, coffee, salt, calico, gunpowder, and a few other store-bought goods.

Thus, Steel entered the market economy as a small farmer, but with mixed results. He picked his own cotton and complained that it was brutal work and not profitable. He felt like a serf in cotton's kingdom. When cotton prices fell, a small grower like Steel could be driven into debt and lose his farm.

Steel's life in Mississippi in the 1840s retained much of the flavor of the frontier, and he survived on a household economy. He made all the family's shoes; his wife and sister sewed dresses, shirts, and "pantaloons." The Steel women also rendered their own soap and spun and wove cotton into cloth; the men hunted game. Steel doctored his illnesses with boneset tea and other herbs. As the nation fell deeper into crisis over the future of free or slave labor, this independent southern farmer never came close to owning a slave.

The focus of Steel's life was family and religion. Family members prayed together daily, and he studied Scripture for an hour after lunch. "My Faith increases, & I enjoy much of that peace which the world cannot give," he wrote in 1841. Seeking to prepare himself for Judgment Day, Steel borrowed histories, Latin and Greek grammars, and religious books from his church. Eventually, he became a traveling Methodist minister. "My life is one of toil," he reflected, "but blessed be God that it is as well with me as it is."

Toil with even less security was the lot of two other groups of free southerners: landless whites and free blacks. A sizable minority of

Landless Whites

white southern workers—from 25 to 40 percent, depending on the state—were hired hands who owned no land and worked for others in the countryside and towns. Their property consisted of a few household items and some animals—usually pigs—that could feed themselves on the open range. The landless included some immigrants, especially Irish, who did heavy and dangerous work, such as building railroads and digging ditches.

In the countryside, white farm laborers struggled to purchase land in the face of low wages or, if they rented, unpredictable market prices for their crops. By scrimping, saving, and finding odd jobs, some managed to climb into the ranks of yeomen. When James and Nancy Bennitt of North Carolina succeeded in their ten-year struggle to buy land, they decided to avoid the unstable market in cotton; thereafter they raised extra corn and wheat as sources of cash. People like the Bennitts were both participants in and victims of an economy dominated by cotton producers who relied on slave labor.

Herdsmen with pigs and other livestock had a desperate struggle to succeed. By 1860, as the South anticipated war to preserve its society, between 300,000 and 400,000 white people in the four states of Virginia, North and South Carolina, and Georgia—approximately one-fifth of the total white population—lived in genuine poverty. Their lives were harsh. An early antebellum traveler in central South Carolina described the white folk he encountered in the countryside: they "looked yellow, poor, and sickly. Some of them lived the most miserably I ever saw any poor people live." Land and slaves determined wealth in the Old South, and many whites possessed neither.

Class tensions emerged in the western, nonslaveholding parts of the seaboard states by the 1830s. There, yeoman farmers resented their

Yeomen's Demands and White Class Relations

underrepresentation in state legislatures and the corruption in local government. After vigorous debate, the reformers won many battles. Voters in the more recently settled states of the Old Southwest adopted white manhood suffrage and other electoral reforms, including popular election of governors, legislative apportionment based on white population only, and locally chosen county government. Slaveowners with new wealth, however, knew that a more open government structure could permit troubling class conflicts and were determined to hold the ultimate reins of power.

Given such tensions, it was perhaps remarkable that slaveholders and nonslaveholders did not experience more overt conflict. Historians have offered several explanations. One of the most important factors was race. The South's racial ideology stressed the superiority of all whites to blacks. Thus, slavery became the basis of equality among whites, and white privilege inflated the status of poor whites and gave them a common interest with the rich. At the same time, the dream of upward mobility blunted some class conflict.

Most important, before the Civil War many yeomen were able to pursue their independent lifestyle largely unhindered by slaveholding planters. They worked their farms, avoided debt, and marked progress for their families in rural habitats of their own making. Likewise, slaveholders pursued their goals quite independently of yeomen. Planters farmed for the market but also for themselves. Suppression of dissent also played an increasing role. After 1830, white southerners who criticized the slave system out of moral conviction or class resentment were intimidated, attacked, or rendered politically powerless in a society held together in part by white racial solidarity.

Still, there were signs of class conflict in the late antebellum period. As cotton lands filled up, nonslaveholders faced narrower economic prospects; meanwhile, wealthy planters enjoyed expanding profits. The risks of entering cotton production were becoming too great and the cost of slaves too high for many yeomen to rise in society. From 1830 to 1860, the percentage of white southern families holding slaves declined steadily from 36 to 25 percent. Although slaveowners were a distinct minority in the white population, planters' share of the South's agricultural wealth remained between 90 and 95 percent.

Anticipating possible secession, slaveowners stood secure. In the 1850s, they occupied from 50 to 85 percent of the seats in state legislatures and a similarly high percentage of the South's congressional seats. And planters' interests controlled all the other major social institutions, such as churches and colleges.

The nearly quarter-million free blacks in the South in 1860 also yearned for mobility. But their condition was

Free Blacks

generally worse than the yeoman's and often little better than the slave's. The free blacks of the Upper South were usually descendants of men and women manumitted by their owners in the 1780s and 1790s. A remarkable number of slaveholders in Virginia and the Chesapeake region had freed their slaves because of religious principles and revolutionary ideals in the wake of American independence (see Chapter 7). Many free blacks also became free as runaways, especially by the 1830s, disappearing into the southern population; a few made their way northward.

White southerners were increasingly desperate to restrict this growing free black presence in their midst. "It seems the number of free Negroes," complained a Virginia slaveholder, "always exceeds the number of Negroes freed." Some free blacks worked in towns or cities, but most lived in rural areas and struggled to survive. They usually did not own land and had to labor in someone else's fields, often beside slaves. By law, free blacks could not own a gun, buy liquor, violate curfew, assemble except in church, testify in court, or (throughout the South after 1835) vote. Despite these obstacles, a minority bought land, and others found jobs as skilled craftsmen, especially in cities.

A few free blacks prospered and bought slaves. In 1830, there were 3,775 free black slaveholders in the South; 80 percent lived in the four states of Louisiana, South Carolina, Virginia, and Maryland, and approximately half of the total lived in the two cities of New Orleans and Charleston. Most of them purchased their own wives and children, whom they nevertheless could not free because laws required newly emancipated blacks to leave their state. In order to free family members whom they had purchased, hundreds of black slaveholders petitioned for exemption from the antimanumission laws passed in most southern states. At the same time, a few mulattos in New Orleans were active slave traders in its booming market. The complex world of southern free blacks received new attention through Edward P. Jones's *The Known World*, a hugely successful novel published in 2003 about a Virginia family that rises from slavery to slaveownership. Although rare in the United States, the greed and the tragic quest for power that lay at the root of slavery could cross any racial or ethnic barrier.

In the Cotton Belt and Gulf regions, a large proportion of free blacks were mulattos, the privileged offspring of wealthy white planters.

Free Black Communities

Not all planters freed their mixed-race offspring, but those who did often recognized the moral obligation of giving their children a good education and financial backing. In a few cities like New Orleans, Charleston, and Mobile, extensive interracial sex, as well as migrations from the Caribbean, had produced a mulatto population that was recognized as a distinct class.

In many southern cities by the 1840s, free black communities formed, especially around an expanding number of churches. By the late 1850s, Baltimore had fifteen churches, Louisville nine, and Nashville and St. Louis four each—most of them African Methodist Episcopal. Class and race distinctions were important to southern free blacks, but outside a few cities, which developed fraternal orders of skilled craftsmen and fellowships of light-skinned people, most mulattos experienced hardship. In the United States, "one drop" of black "blood" (any observable racial mixture to white people's eyes) made them black, and potentially enslaveable.

The Planters' World

At the top of the southern social pyramid were slaveholding planters. As a group they lived well, but most lived in comfortable farmhouses, not on the opulent scale that legend suggests. The grand plantation mansions, with fabulous gardens and long rows of outlying slave quarters, are an enduring symbol of the Old South. But in 1850, 50 percent of southern slaveholders had fewer than five slaves; 72 percent had fewer than ten; 88 percent had

fewer than twenty. Thus, the average slaveholder was not a wealthy aristocrat but an aspiring farmer.

Louisiana cotton planter Bennet Barrow, a newly rich planter of the 1840s, was preoccupied with moneymak-

The Newly Rich

ing. He worried constantly over his cotton crop, filling his diary with weather reports and gloomy predictions of his yields. Yet Barrow also strove to appear above such worries. He hunted frequently and had a passion for racing horses and raising hounds. He could report the loss of a slave without feeling, but emotion broke through his laconic manner when illness afflicted his sporting animals. "Never was a person more unlucky than I am," he mourned. "My favorite pup never lives." His strongest feelings surfaced when his horse Jos Bell—equal to "the best Horse in the South"—"broke down running a mile . . . ruined for Ever." The same day, the distraught Barrow gave his human property a "general Whipping." In 1841 diary entries, he worried about a rumored slave insurrection. He gave a "severe whipping" to several of his slaves

Link to excerpts from Bennet Barrow's diary.

when they disobediently killed a hog. And when a slave named Ginney Jerry "sherked" his cotton-picking duties and was rumored "about to run off," Barrow whipped him one day and the next, recorded matter-of-factly: "took my gun found him in the Bayou behind the Quarter, shot him in his thigh—etc. raining all around."

The richest planters used their wealth to model genteel sophistication. Extended visits, parties, and balls to which women wore the latest fashions provided opportunities for friendship, courtship, and display. Such parties were held during the Christmas holidays, but also on such occasions as molasses stewing, a bachelors' ball, a horserace, or the crowning of the May queen. These entertainments were especially important as diversions for plantation women, and at the same time they sustained a rigidly gendered society. Young women relished social events to break the monotony of their domestic lives. In 1826, a Virginia girl was ecstatic about the "week . . . I was in Town. . . . There were five beaux and as many belles in the house constantly," she declared, and all she and her companions did was "eat, visit, romp, and sleep."

Most of the planters in the cotton-boom states of Alabama and Mississippi were newly rich by the 1840s. As one historian put it, "a number of men mounted from log cabin to plantation mansion on a stairway of cotton bales, accumulating slaves as they climbed." And many did not live like rich men. They put their new wealth into cotton acreage and slaves even as they sought refinement and high social status.

William Faulkner immortalized the new wealthy planter in a fictional character, Thomas Sutpen, in his novel *Absalom, Absalom!* (1936). After a huge win at riverboat gambling, Sutpen arrives in a Mississippi county in the 1830s, buys a huge plantation he calls Sutpen's Hundred, and with his troop of slaves converts it into a wealthy enterprise. Sutpen marries a local woman, and although he is always viewed as a mysterious outsider by earlier residents of the county, he becomes a pillar of the slaveholding class, eventually an officer in the Confederate Army. But Sutpen is a self-made man of indomitable will and slave-based wealth. Although his ambition is ultimately his undoing, one of the earliest lessons he learns about success in the South is that "you got to have land and niggers and a fine house."

The cotton boom in the Mississippi valley created one-generation aristocrats. A nonfictional case in point is Greenwood Leflore, a Chocktaw chieftain who owned a plantation in Mississippi with four hundred slaves. After selling his cotton on the world market, he spent $10,000 in France to furnish a single room of his mansion with handwoven carpets, furniture upholstered with gold leaf, tables and cabinets ornamented with tortoise-shell inlay, a variety of mirrors and paintings, and a clock and candelabra of brass and ebony.

Slave ownership was the main determinant of wealth in the South. Slaves were a commodity and an

Social Status and Planters' Values

investment, much like gold; people bought them on speculation, hoping for a steady rise in their market value. Many slaveholders took out mortgages on their slaves and used them as collateral. Especially in the growing states, people who could not pay cash for slaves would ask the sellers to purchase the mortgage, just as banks give mortgages on houses today. The slaveholder would pay back the loan in installments with interest. Slaveholders and the people who lent them money put their faith in this "human collateral," believing it would increase in value. Hundreds of thousands of slaves were thus mortgaged, many several times and with full awareness of their masters' financial methods. In St. Landry's Parish, Louisiana, between 1833 and 1837, an eight-year-old slave boy named Jacques was mortgaged three times, sold twice, and converted into what one historian has called a "human cash machine and an investment vehicle" before the age of twelve.

Slavery's influence spread throughout the social system, until even the values and mores of nonslaveholders bore its imprint. The availability of slave labor tended to devalue free labor: where strenuous work under supervision was reserved for an enslaved race, few free people relished it. When Alexis de Tocqueville crossed from Ohio into Kentucky in his travels of 1831, he observed "the effect that slavery produces on society. On the right bank of the Ohio [River] everything is activity, industry; labor is honoured; there are no slaves. Pass to the left bank and the scene changes so suddenly that you think yourself on the other side of the world; the enterprising spirit is gone. There, work is not only painful; it is shameful." Tocqueville's own class impulses found a home in the South, however. There he found a "veritable aristocracy which . . . combines many prejudices with high sentiments and instincts."

The values of the aristocrat—lineage, privilege, pride, honor, and refinement of person and manner—commanded respect throughout the South. Many of those qualities were in short supply, however, in the recently settled portions of the cotton kingdom, where frontier values of courage and self-reliance ruled during the 1820s and 1830s. By the 1850s, a settled aristocratic group of planters did rule, however, in much of the Mississippi valley. In this geographically mobile society, independence and codes of honor motivated both planter and frontier farmer alike.

Instead of gradually disappearing, as it did in the North, the Code Duello, which required men to defend their honor through violence, lasted much longer in the South. In North Carolina in 1851, wealthy planter Samuel Fleming sought to settle disputes with lawyer William Waightstill Avery by "cowhiding" him on a public street. According to the code, Avery had two choices: to redeem his honor violently or to brand himself a coward through inaction. Three weeks later, he shot Fleming dead at point-blank range during a session of the Burke County Superior Court. A jury took only ten minutes to find Avery not guilty, and the spectators gave him a standing ovation.

In their pride, aristocratic planters expected not only to wield power but also to receive deference from poorer whites. But the sternly independent yeoman class resented infringements of their rights, and many belonged to evangelical faiths that exalted values of simplicity and condemned the planters' love of wealth. Much of the planters' political power and their claims to leadership, after all, were built on their assumption of a monopoly on world cotton and on a foundation of black slave labor.

Planters always had their eyes on the international growth of the cotton markets. Cash crops such as cotton

King Cotton in a Global Economy

were for export; the planters' fate depended on world trade, especially with Europe. The American South so dominated the world's supply of cotton that southern planters gained enormous confidence that the cotton boom was permanent and that the industrializing nations of England and France in particular would always bow to King Cotton.

Made possible in part by the Eli Whitney's invention of the cotton gin in 1793, a device for cleaning the short staple variety of the crop that the British textile industry craved, American cotton production doubled in yield each decade after 1800 and provided three-fourths of the world's supply by the 1840s. Gins, which took on the scale of whole buildings with time, revolutionized cotton production and Southern wealth invested in land and slaves. In the first decade of the nineteenth century in South Carolina alone, wrote one planter, cotton "trebled the price of land suitable to its growth" and "doubled" the annual income of growers. Southern staple crops were fully three-fifths of all American exports by 1850, and one of every seven workers in England depended on American cotton for his job. Indeed, cotton production made slaves the single most valuable financial asset in the United States—greater in dollar value than all of America's banks, railroads, and manufacturing combined. In 1860 dollars, the slaves' total value as property came to an estimated $3.5 billion. In early-twenty-first-century dollars, that would be approximately $70 billion.

"Cotton is King," the *Southern Cultivator* declared in 1859, "and wields an astonishing influence over the world's commerce." Until 1840, the cotton trade furnished much of the export capital to finance northern economic growth. After that date, however, the northern economy expanded without dependence on cotton profits. Nevertheless, southern planters and politicians continued to boast of King Cotton's supremacy. "Our cotton is the most wonderful talisman in the world," announced a planter in 1853. "By its power we are transmuting whatever we choose into whatever we want." "No power on earth dares . . . to make war on cotton," James Hammond lectured the U.S. Senate in 1858; "Cotton is king." Although the South produced 4.5 million bales in 1861, its greatest cotton crop ever, such world dominance was about to collapse. Thereafter, cotton was more a shackle to the South than a king.

Slaveholding men often embraced a paternalistic ideology that justified their dominance over both black slaves and white women. Instead of stressing the profitable aspects of commercial agriculture, they stressed their obligations, viewing themselves as custodians of the welfare of society in general, and of the black families they owned in particular. The paternalistic planter saw himself not as an oppressor but as the benevolent guardian of an inferior race.

Paternalism

Paul Carrington Cameron, North Carolina's largest slaveholder, exemplifies this mentality. After a period of sickness among his one thousand North Carolina slaves (he had hundreds more in Alabama and Mississippi), Cameron wrote, "I fear the Negroes have suffered much from the want of proper attention and kindness under this late distemper no love of lucre shall ever induce me to be cruel." On another occasion, he described to his sister the sense of responsibility he felt: "Do you remember a cold & frosty morning, during [our mother's] illness, when she said to me Paul my son the people ought to be shod' this is ever in my ears, whenever I see any ones shoes in bad order; and in my ears it will be, so long as I am master."

It was comforting to rich planters to see themselves in this way, and slaves—accommodating to the realities of power—encouraged their masters to think that their benevolence was appreciated. Paternalism also served as a defense against abolitionist criticism. Still, paternalism was often a matter of self-delusion, a means of avoiding some harsh dimensions of slave treatment. In reality, paternalism grew as a give-and-take relationship between masters and slaves, each extracting from the other what they desired—owners took labor from the bondsmen, while slaves obligated masters to provide them a measure of autonomy and living space. As one historian has argued, paternalism "grew out of the necessity to discipline and morally justify a system of exploitation, . . . a fragile bridge across the intolerable contradictions inherent" in a slave society dependent on "the willing reproduction and productivity of its victims."

Even Paul Cameron's benevolence vanished with changed circumstances. After the Civil War, he bristled at African Americans' efforts to be free and made sweeping economic decisions without regard for their welfare. Writing on Christmas Day 1865, Cameron showed little Christian charity (but a healthy profit motive) when he declared, "I am convinced that the people who gets rid of the free negro first will be the first to advance in improved agriculture. Have made no effort to retain any of mine." With that, he turned off his land nearly a thousand black people, rented his fields to several white farmers, and invested in industry.

Relations between men and women in the planter class were similarly defined by paternalism. The upper-class southern woman was raised and educated to be a wife, mother, and subordinate companion to men. South Carolina's Mary Boykin Chesnut wrote of her husband, "He is master of the house. To hear is to obey. . . . All the comfort of my life depends upon his being in a good humor." In a social system based on the coercion of an entire race, women found it very difficult to challenge society's rules on sexual or racial relations.

Planters' daughters usually attended one of the South's rapidly multiplying boarding schools. There, they formed friendships with other girls and received an education. Typically, the young woman could entertain suitors whom her parents approved. But very soon she had to choose a husband and commit herself for life to a man whom she generally had known for only a brief time. Young women were often alienated and emotionally unfulfilled. They had to follow the wishes of their family, especially their father. "It was for me best that I yielded to the wishes of papa," wrote a young North Carolinian in 1823. "I wonder when my best will cease to be painful and when I shall begin to enjoy life instead of enduring it."

▲ A portrait of a planter-slaveholder, his two daughters, and their household slave who probably was "nurse" (caretaker) for the children. The picture vividly depicts the attempt at domestic tranquility as well as the prescribed roles of patriarch and slave.

birth rate for white southern women in their childbearing years was almost 30 percent higher than the national average. The average southern white woman could expect to bear eight children in 1800; by 1860, the figure had decreased to only six, with one or more miscarriages likely. Complications of childbirth were a major cause of death, occurring twice as often in the hot, humid South as in the Northeast.

Sexual relations between planters and slaves were another source of problems that white women had to endure but were not supposed to notice. "Violations of the moral law . . . made mulattos as common as blackberries," protested a woman in Georgia, but wives had to play "the ostrich game." "A magnate who runs a hideous black harem," wrote Mrs. Chesnut, " . . . poses as the model of all human virtues to these poor women whom God and the laws have given him." Such habits and dalliances, whatever the motives such as at Jefferson's Monticello, produced a very large mixed race population by the 1850s and a strained use of the term "family" across the South.

Southern men tolerated little discussion by women of the slavery issue. In the 1840s and 1850s, as abolitionist attacks on slavery increased, southern men published a barrage of articles stressing that women should restrict their concerns to the home. The *Southern Quarterly Review* declared, "The proper place for a woman is at home. One of her highest privileges, to be politically merged in the existence of her husband."

But some southern women were beginning to seek a larger role. A study of women in Petersburg, Virginia, a large tobacco-manufacturing town, revealed behavior that valued financial autonomy. Over several decades before 1860, the proportion of women who never married, or did not remarry after the death of a spouse, grew to exceed 33 percent. Likewise, the number of women who worked for wages, controlled their own property, and ran dressmaking businesses increased markedly.

Planters forged a society around their domestic lives and local mores. But they did so through the energies and lives of generations of enslaved African Americans who helped them extract great wealth from southern soil.

Upon marriage, a planter-class woman ceded to her husband most of her legal rights, becoming part of his family. Most of the year she was isolated on a large plantation, where she had to oversee the cooking and preserving of food, manage the house, supervise care of the children, and attend sick slaves. All these realities were more rigid and confining on the frontier, where isolation was even greater. Women sought refuge in their extended family and associations with other women. In 1821, a Georgia woman wrote to her brother of the distress of a cousin's wife: "They are living . . . in the frontiers of the state and [a] perfectly uncivilized place. Cousin W. gets a good practice [the husband] but she is almost crazy to get to Alabama where one of her sisters is living." Men on plantations could occasionally escape into the public realm—to town, business, or politics. Women could retreat from rural plantation culture only into kinship.

It is not surprising that a perceptive young white woman sometimes approached marriage with anxiety. Women could

Marriage and Family Among Planters

hardly help viewing their wedding day, as one put it in 1832, as "the day to fix my fate." Lucy Breckinridge, a wealthy Virginia girl of twenty, lamented the autonomy she surrendered at the altar. In her diary, she recorded this unvarnished observation on marriage: "If [husbands] care for their wives at all it is only as a sort of servant, a being made to attend to their comforts and to keep the children out of the way. A woman's life after she is married, unless there is an immense amount of love, is nothing but suffering and hard work."

Lucy loved young children but knew that childbearing often involved grief, poor health, and death. In 1840, the

Slave Life and Labor

For African Americans, slavery was a burden that destroyed some people and forced others to develop modes of survival. Slaves knew a life of poverty, coercion, toil, and resentment. They provided the physical strength, and much of the know-how, to build an agricultural empire. But their daily lives embodied the nation's most basic contradiction: in the world's model republic, they were on the wrong side of a brutally unequal power relationship.

Southern slaves enjoyed few material comforts beyond the bare necessities. Although they generally had

Slaves' Everyday Conditions

enough to eat, their diet was monotonous and nonnutritious. Clothing, too, was plain, coarse, and inexpensive. Few slaves received more than one or two changes of clothing for hot and cold seasons, and one blanket each winter. Children of both sexes ran naked in hot weather and wore long cotton shirts in winter. Many slaves had to go without shoes until December, even as far north as Virginia. The bare feet of slaves were often symbolic of their status and one reason why, after freedom, many black parents were so concerned with providing their children with shoes. These conditions were generally better in cities, where slaves frequently lived in the same dwelling as their owners and were hired out to employers on a regular basis, enabling them to accumulate their own money.

Some of the richer plantations provided substantial houses, but the average slave lived in a crude, one-room cabin. The gravest drawback of slave cabins was not lack of comfort but unhealthfulness. Each dwelling housed one or two entire families. Crowding and lack of sanitation fostered the spread of infection and such contagious diseases as typhoid fever, malaria, and dysentery. White plantation doctors were hired to care for sick slaves on a regular basis, but some "slave doctors" attained a degree of power in the quarters and with masters by practicing health care and healing through herbalism and spiritualism.

Hard work was the central fact of slaves' existence. The long hours and large work gangs that characterized

Slave Work Routines

Gulf Coast cotton districts operated almost like factories in the field. Overseers rang the morning bell before dawn, and black people of varying ages, tools in hand, walked toward the fields. Slaves who cultivated tobacco in the Upper South worked long hours picking the sticky, sometimes noxious, leaves under harsh discipline. And as one woman recalled when interviewed in the 1930s, "it was way after sundown fore they could stop that field work. Then they had to hustle to finish their night work [such as watering livestock or cleaning cotton] in time for supper, or go to bed without it."

Working "from sun to sun" became a norm in much of the South. As one planter put it, slaves were the best labor because "you could command them and make them do what was right." Profit took precedence over paternalism. Slave women did heavy fieldwork, often as much as the men and even during pregnancy. Old people were kept busy caring for young children, doing light chores, or carding, ginning, and spinning cotton. The black abolitionist orator Frances Ellen Watkins captured the grinding economic reality of slavery in an 1857 speech, charging that

slaveholders had "found out a fearful alchemy by which . . . blood can be transformed into gold. Instead of listening to the cry of agony, they listen to the ring of dollars and stoop down to pick up the coin."

By the 1830s, slaveowners found that labor could be similarly motivated by the clock. Incentives had to be part of the labor regime and the master-slave relationship as well. Planters in the South Carolina and Georgia low country used a task system whereby slaves were assigned measured amounts of work to be performed in a given amount of time. So much cotton on a daily basis was to be picked from a designated field, so many rows hoed or plowed in a particular slave's specified section. When their tasks were finished, slaves' time was their own for working garden plots, tending hogs, even hiring out their own extra labor. From this experience and personal space, many slaves developed their own sense of property ownership. When the task system worked best, slaves and masters alike embraced it, fostering a degree of reciprocal trust.

Slave children were the future of the system and widely valued as potential labor. Of the 1860 population of 4 million slaves, fully half were under the age of sixteen. "A child raised every two years," wrote Thomas Jefferson, "is of more profit than the crop of the best laboring man." And in 1858, a slaveowner writing in an agricultural magazine calculated that a slave girl he purchased in 1827 for $400 had borne three sons now worth $3,000 as his working field hands. Slave children gathered kindling, carried water to the fields, swept the yard, lifted cut sugar-cane stalks into carts, stacked wheat, chased birds away from sprouting rice plants, and labored at many levels of cotton and tobacco production. "Work," wrote one historian, "can be rightly called the thief who stole the childhood of youthful bond servants."

As slave children matured, they faced many psychological traumas. They faced a feeling of powerlessness as they became aware that their parents ultimately could not protect them. They had to muster strategies to fight internalizing what whites assumed was their inferiority. Thomas Jones, who grew up in North Carolina, remembered that his greatest struggle with the sense of "suffering and shame" as he "was made to feel . . . degraded." Many former slaves resented foremost their denial of education. "There is one sin that slavery committed against me which I will never forgive," recollected the minister James Pennington. "It robbed me of my education." And for girls reaching maturity, the potential trauma of sexual abuse loomed over their lives.

Slaves could not demand much autonomy, of course, because the owner enjoyed a monopoly on force and

Violence and Intimidation Against Slaves

violence. Whites throughout the South believed that slaves "can't be governed except with the whip." One South Carolinian frankly explained to a northern journalist that he whipped his slaves regularly, "say once a fortnight; . . . the fear of the lash kept them in good order." Evidence suggests that whippings were less frequent on small farms than on large plantations. But beatings symbolized authority to the master and tyranny to the slaves, who made them a benchmark for evaluating a master. In the words of former slaves, a good owner was one who did not "whip too much," whereas a bad owner "whipped till he's bloodied you and blistered you."

As these reports suggest, terrible abuses could and did occur. The master wielded virtually absolute authority on his plantation, and courts did not recognize the word of chattel. Slaveholders rarely had to answer to the law or to the state. Pregnant women were whipped, and there were burnings, mutilation, torture, and murder. Yet physical cruelty may have been less prevalent in the United States than in other slaveholding parts of the New World. Especially in some of the sugar islands of the Caribbean, treatment was so poor and death rates so high that the heavily male slave population shrank in size. In the United States, by contrast, the slave population experienced a steady natural increase, as births exceeded deaths and each generation grew larger.

The worst evil of American slavery was not its physical cruelty but the nature of slavery itself: coercion, belonging to another person, virtually no hope for mobility or change. Recalling their time in bondage, some former slaves emphasized the physical abuse, or the "bullwhip days," as one woman described her past. But memories of physical punishment focused on the tyranny of whipping as much as the pain. Delia Garlic made the essential point: "It's bad to belong to folks that own you soul an' body. I could tell you 'bout it all day, but even then you couldn't guess the awfulness of it." Thomas Lewis put it this way: "There was no such thing as being good to slaves. Many people were better than others, but a slave belonged to his master and there was no way to get out of it." To be a slave was to be the object of another person's will and material gain, to be owned, as the saying went, "from the cradle to the grave."

Most American slaves retained their mental independence and self-respect despite their bondage. Contrary to popular belief at the time, they were not loyal partners in their own oppression. They had to be subservient and speak honeyed words to their masters, but they talked and behaved quite differently among themselves. In *Narrative of the Life of Frederick Douglass, an American Slave, Written by Himself* (1845), Douglass wrote that most slaves, when asked about "their condition and the character of their masters, almost universally say they are contented, and that their masters are kind." Slaves did this, said Douglass, because they were governed by the maxim that "a still tongue makes a wise head," especially in the presence of unfamiliar people. Because they were "part of the human family," slaves often quarreled over who had the

best master. But at the end of the day, Douglass remarked, when one had a bad master, he sought a better master; and when he had a better one, he wanted to "be his own master."

Some former slaves remembered warm feelings between masters and slaves, and some "special" bondsmen,

Slave-Master Relationships

such as highly skilled jockeys for planters who were great horsemen, enjoyed autonomy, privilege, and even fame. But the prevailing attitudes were distrust and antagonism. Slaves saw through acts of kindness. One woman said her mistress was "a mighty good somebody to belong to" but only "'cause she was raisin' us to work for her." A man recalled that his owners took good care of their slaves, "and Grandma Maria say, 'Why shouldn't they—it was their money.'" Slaves also resented being used as beasts of burden. One man observed that his master "fed us reg'lar on good, 'stantial food, just like you'd tend to your horse, if you had a real good one."

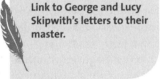

Link to George and Lucy Skipwith's letters to their master.

Slaves were alert to the thousand daily signs of their degraded status. One man recalled the general rule that slaves ate cornbread and owners ate biscuits. If blacks did get biscuits, "the flour that we made the biscuits out of was the third-grade sorts." A former slave recalled, "Us catch lots of 'possums," but "the white folks at [ate] 'em." If the owner took his slaves' garden produce to town and sold it for them, the slaves often suspected him of pocketing part of the profits.

Suspicion often grew into hatred. When a yellow fever epidemic struck in 1852, many slaves saw it as God's retribution. An elderly ex-slave named Minnie Fulkes cherished the conviction that God was going to punish white people for their cruelty to blacks. She described the whippings that her mother had to endure, and then she exclaimed, "Lord, Lord, I hate white people and the flood waters goin' to drown some more." On the plantation, of course, slaves had to keep such thoughts to themselves. Often they expressed one feeling to whites, another within their own household. In their daily lives, slaves created many ways to survive and to sustain their humanity in this world of repression.

Slave Culture and Resistance

A people is always "more than the sum of its brutalization," wrote African American novelist Ralph Ellison in 1967. What people create in the face of hard luck and oppression is what provides hope. The resource that enabled slaves to maintain such defiance was their culture: a body of beliefs, values, and practices born of their past and maintained in the present. As best they could, they built a community knitted together by stories, music, a religious world-view, leadership, the smells of their cooking, the sounds of their own voices, and the tapping of their feet. "The values expressed in folklore," wrote African American poet Sterling Brown, provided a "wellspring to which slaves . . . could return in times of doubt to be refreshed."

Slave culture changed significantly after 1808, when Congress banned further importation of slaves and the

African Cultural Survival

generations born in Africa died out. For a few years, South Carolina illegally reopened the international slave trade, but by the 1830s, the vast majority of slaves in the South were native-born Americans. Many blacks, in fact, can trace their American ancestry back further than most white Americans.

Yet African influences remained strong, despite lack of firsthand memory, especially in appearance and forms of expression. Some slave men plaited their hair into rows and fancy designs; slave women often wore their hair "in string"—tied in small bunches secured by a string or piece of cloth. A few men and many women wrapped their heads in kerchiefs of the styles and colors of West Africa. In burial practices, slaves used jars and other glass objects to decorate graves, following similar African traditions.

Music, religion, and folktales were parts of daily life for most slaves. Borrowing partly from their African background, as well as forging new American folkways, they developed what scholars have called a sacred world-view, which affected all aspects of work, leisure, and self-understanding. Slaves made musical instruments with carved motifs that resembled African stringed instruments. Their drumming and dancing followed African patterns that made whites marvel. One visitor to Georgia in the 1860s described a ritual dance of African origin: "A ring of singers is formed. . . . They then utter a kind of melodious chant, which gradually increases in strength, and in noise, until it fairly shakes the house, and it can be heard for a long distance." This observer of the "ring shout" also noted the agility of the dancers and the African call-and-response pattern in their chanting.

Many slaves continued to believe in spirit possession. Whites, too, believed in ghosts and charms, but the slaves' belief resembled the African concept of the living dead—the idea that deceased relatives visit the earth for many years until the process of dying is complete. Slaves also practiced conjuration and quasi-magical root medicine. By the 1850s, the most notable conjurers and root doctors were reputed to live in South Carolina, Georgia, Louisiana, and other isolated coastal areas with high slave populations.

These cultural survivals provided slaves with a sense of their separate past. Such practices and beliefs were not static "Africanisms" or mere "retentions." They were cultural adaptations, living traditions re-formed

in the Americas in response to new experience. African American slaves in the Old South were a people forged by two centuries of cultural mixture in the Atlantic world, and the South itself was a melding of many African and European cultural forces.

As they became African Americans, slaves also developed a sense of racial identity. In the colonial period, Africans had arrived in America from many different states and kingdoms, represented in distinctive languages, body markings, and traditions. Planters had used ethnic differences to create occupational hierarchies. By the early antebellum period, however, old ethnic identities gave way as American slaves increasingly saw themselves as a single group unified by race. Africans had arrived in the New World with virtually no concept of "race"; by the antebellum era, their descendants had learned through bitter experience that race was now the defining feature of their lives. They were a transplanted and transformed people.

As African culture gave way to a maturing African American culture, more and more slaves adopted

Slaves' Religion and Music

Christianity. But they fashioned Christianity into an instrument of support and resistance. Theirs was a religion of justice and deliverance, quite unlike their masters' religious propaganda directed at them as a means of control. "You ought to have heard that preachin'," said one man. "'Obey your master and mistress, don't steal chickens and eggs and meat,' but nary a word about havin' a soul to save." Slaves believed that Jesus cared about their souls and their plight. In their interpretations of biblical stories, as one historian has said, they were "literally willing themselves reborn."

For slaves, Christianity was a religion of personal and group salvation. Devout men and women worshiped every day, "in the field or by the side of the road" or in special "prayer grounds" that afforded privacy. Some slaves held fervent secret prayer meetings that lasted far into the night. Many slaves nurtured an unshakable belief that God would enter history and end their bondage. This faith—and the joy and emotional release that accompanied worship—sustained them.

Slaves also adapted Christianity to African practices. In West African belief, devotees are possessed by a god so thoroughly that the god's own personality replaces the human personality. In the late antebellum era, Christian slaves experienced possession by the Protestant "Holy Spirit." The combination of shouting, singing, and dancing that seemed to overtake black worshipers formed the heart of their religious faith. "The old meeting house caught fire," recalled an ex-slave preacher. "The spirit was there. . . . God saw our need and came to us. I used to wonder what made people shout but now I don't. There is a joy on the inside and it wells up so strong that we can't keep still. It is fire in the bones. Any time that fire touches a man, he will jump." Out in brush arbors

◀ Drawing by Lewis Miller of a *Lynchburg Negro Dance,* Lynchburg, Virginia, August 18, 1853. This work of art shows the slaves' use of elaborate costumes, string instruments, and "the bones"—folk percussion instruments of African origin, held between the fingers and used as clappers.

Abby Aldrich Rockefeller Folk Art Collection, Colonial Williamsburg Foundation

or in meetinghouses, slaves took in the presence of God, thrust their arms to heaven, made music with their feet, and sang away their woes. Some travelers observed "bands" of "Fist and Heel Worshippers." Many post-slavery black choirs could not perform properly without a good wooden floor to use as their "drum."

Rhythm and physical movement were crucial to slaves' religious experience. In black preachers' chanted sermons, which reached out to gather the sinner into a narrative of meanings and cadences along the way to conversion, an American tradition was born. The chanted sermon was both a message from Scripture and a patterned form that required audience response punctuated by "yes sirs!" and "amens!" But it was in song that the slaves left their most sublime gift to American culture.

Through the spirituals, slaves tried to impose order on the chaos of their lives. Many themes run through the lyrics of slave songs. Often referred to later as the "sorrow songs," they also anticipate imminent rebirth. Sadness could immediately give way to joy: "Did you ever stan' on a mountain, wash yo hands in a cloud?" Rebirth was at the heart as well of the famous hymn "Oh, Freedom": "Oh, Oh, Freedom / Oh, Oh, Freedom over me— / But before I'll be a slave, / I'll be buried in my grave, / And go home to my Lord, / And Be Free!"

This tension and sudden change between sorrow and joy animates many songs: "Sometimes I feel like a motherless chile . . . / Sometimes I feel like an eagle in the air, / . . . Spread my wings and fly, fly, fly!" Many songs also express a sense of intimacy and closeness with God. Some songs display an unmistakable rebelliousness, such as the enduring "He said, and if I had my way / If I had my way, if I had my way, / I'd tear this building down!" And some spirituals reached for a collective sense of hope in the black community as a whole.

> O, gracious Lord! When shall it be,
> That we poor souls shall all be free;
> Lord, break them slavery powers—
> Will you go along with me?
> Lord break them slavery powers,
> Go sound the jubilee!

In many ways, American slaves converted the Christian God to themselves. They sought an alternative world to live in—a home other than the one fate had given them on earth. In a thousand variations on the Br'er Rabbit folktales—in which the weak survive by wit and power is reversed—and in the countless refrains of their songs, they fashioned survival out of their own cultural imagination.

American slaves clung tenaciously to the personal relationships that gave meaning to life. Although American

The Black Family in Slavery

law did not recognize slave families, masters permitted them; in fact, slaveowners *expected* slaves to form families and have children. As a result, even along the rapidly expanding edge of the cotton kingdom, there was a normal ratio of men to women, young to old. On some of the largest cotton plantations of South Carolina, when masters allowed their slaves increased autonomy through work on the task system, the property accumulation in livestock, tools, and garden produce thus fostered led to more stable and healthier families.

▲ This photograph of five generations of a slave family, taken in Beaufort, South Carolina, in 1862, is silent but powerful testimony to the importance that enslaved African Americans placed on their ever-threatened family ties.

Following African kinship traditions, African Americans avoided marriage between cousins (commonplace among aristocratic slaveowners). By naming their children after relatives of past generations, African Americans emphasized their family histories. Kinship networks and broadly extended families are what held life together in many slave communities.

For slave women, sexual abuse and rape by white masters were ever-present threats to themselves and their family life. By 1860, there were 405,751 mulattos in the United States, comprising 12.5 percent of the African American population. White planters were sometimes open with their behavior toward slave women, but not in the way they talked about it. As Mary Chesnut remarked, sex between slaveholding men and their slave women was "the thing we can't name." Buying slaves for sex was all too common at the New Orleans slave market. In what was called the "fancy trade" (a "fancy" was a young, attractive slave girl or woman), females were often sold for prices as much as 300 percent higher than the average. At such auctions for young women, slaveholders exhibited some of the ugliest values at the heart of the slave system—patriarchal dominance demonstrated by paying

$3,000 to $5,000 for female "companions."

Slave women had to negotiate this confused world of desire, threat, and shame. Harriet Jacobs, who spent much of her youth and early adult years dodging her owner's relentless sexual pursuit, described this circumstance as "the war of my life." In recollecting her desperate effort to protect her children and help them find a way north to freedom, Jacobs asked a haunting question that many slave women carried with them to their graves: "Why does the slave ever love? Why allow the tendrils of the heart to twine around objects which may at any moment be wrenched away by the hand of violence?"

Separation by violence from those they loved, sexual appropriation, and sale were what slave families most feared and hated. Many struggled for years to keep their children together and, after emancipation, to reestablish contact with loved ones lost by forced migration and sale.

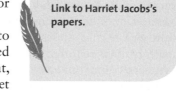

Link to Harriet Jacobs's papers.

The Domestic Slave Trade

Between 1820 and 1860, an estimated 2 million slaves were moved into the region extending from western Georgia to eastern Texas. When the Union Army registered thousands of black marriages in Mississippi and Louisiana in 1864 and 1865, fully 25 percent of the men over the age of forty reported that they had been forcibly separated from a previous wife. Thousands of black families were disrupted every year to serve the needs of the expanding cotton economy.

Many antebellum white southerners made their living from the slave trade. In South Carolina alone by the 1850s, there were more than one hundred slave-trading firms selling an annual average of approximately 6,500 slaves to southwestern states. Although southerners often denied it, vast numbers of slaves moved west by outright sale and not by migrating with their owners. A typical trader's advertisement read, "NEGROES WANTED. I am paying the highest cash prices for young and likely NEGROES, those having good front teeth and being otherwise sound." One estimate from 1858 indicated that slave sales in Richmond, Virginia, netted $4 million that year alone. A market guide to slave sales that same year in Richmond listed average prices for "likely ploughboys," ages twelve to fourteen, at $850 to $1,050; "extra number 1 fieldgirls" at $1,300 to $1,350; and "extra number 1 men" at $1,500.

Slave traders were practical, roving businessmen. They were sometimes considered degraded by white planters, but many slaveowners did business with them. Market forces drove this commerce in humanity. At slave "pens" in cities like New Orleans, traders promoted "a large and commodious showroom . . . prepared to accommodate over 200 Negroes for sale." Traders did their utmost to make their slaves appear young, healthy, and happy, cutting gray whiskers off men, using paddles as discipline so as not to scar their merchandise, and forcing people to dance and sing as buyers arrived for an auction. When transported to the southwestern markets, slaves were often chained together in "coffles," which made journeys of 500 miles or more on foot.

The complacent mixture of racism and business among traders is evident in their own language. "I refused a girl 20 year[s] old at 700 yesterday," one trader wrote to another in 1853. "If you think best to take her at 700 I can still get her. She is very badly whipped but good teeth." Some sales were transacted at owners' requests, often for tragically inhumane reasons. "Bought a cook yesterday that was to go out of state," wrote a trader; "she just made the people mad that was all." Some traders demonstrated how deeply slavery and racism were intertwined. "I have bought the boy Isaac for 1100," wrote a trader in 1854 to his partner. "I think him very prime. . . . He is a . . . house servant . . . first rate cook . . . and splendid carriage driver. He is also a fine painter and varnisher and . . . says he can make a fine panel door. . . . Also he performs well on the

Missouri Historical Society, St. Louis

▲ A bill of sale documents that this slave woman, Louisa, was owned by the young child whom she holds on her lap. In the future, Louisa's life would be subject to the child's wishes and decisions.

violin. . . . He is a genius and its strange to say I think he is smarter than I am."

Slaves brought to their efforts at resistance the same common sense and determination that characterized their struggle to secure their family lives. The scales weighed heavily against overt revolution, and they knew it. But they seized opportunities to alter their work conditions. They sometimes slacked off when they were not being watched. Thus, owners complained that slaves "never would lay out their strength freely."

Daily discontent and desperation were also manifest in sabotage of equipment; in wanton carelessness about work; in theft of food, livestock, or crops; or in getting drunk on stolen liquor. Some slaves who were hired out hoarded their earnings. Or they might just fall into recalcitrance. "I have a boy in my employ called Jim Archer," complained a Vicksburg,

Strategies of Resistance

▲ A slave coffle on the march toward newly settled states of the Southwest.

Mississippi, slaveholder in 1843. "Jim does not want to be under anyones control and says . . . he wants to go home this summer." A woman named Ellen, hired as a cook in Tennessee in 1856, quietly put mercury poison into a roasted apple for her unsuspecting mistress. And some slave women resisted as best they could by trying to control their own pregnancy, either by avoiding it or by seeking it as a way to improve their physical conditions.

Many male, and some female, slaves acted out their defiance by violently attacking overseers or even their owners. Southern court records and newspapers contain accounts of these resistant slaves who gave the lie to the image of the docile bondsman. The price they paid was high. Such lonely rebels were customarily secured and flogged, sold away, or hanged.

Many individual slaves attempted to run away to the North, and some received assistance from the loose network known as the Underground Railroad (see page 378). But it was more common for slaves to run off temporarily to hide in the woods. Approximately 80 percent of runaways were male; women simply could not flee as readily because of their responsibility for children. Fear, disgruntlement over treatment, or family separation might motivate slaves to risk all in flight. Only a minority of those who tried such escapes ever made it

to freedom in the North or Canada, but these fugitives made slavery a very insecure institution by the 1850s.

But American slavery also produced some fearless revolutionaries. Gabriel's Rebellion involved as many as a thousand slaves when it was discovered in 1800, just before it would have exploded in Richmond, Virginia (see pages 215–216). According to controversial court testimony, a similar conspiracy existed in Charleston in 1822, led by a free black named Denmark Vesey. Born a slave in the Caribbean, Vesey won a lottery of $1,500 in 1799, bought his own freedom, and became a religious leader in the black community. According to one long-argued interpretation, Vesey was a heroic revolutionary determined to free his people or die trying. But in a recent challenge, historian Michael Johnson points out that the court testimony is the only reliable source on the alleged insurrection. Might the testimony reveal less of reality than of white South Carolina's fears of slave rebellion? The court, says Johnson, built its case on rumors and intimidated witnesses, and "conjured into being" an insurrection that was not about to occur in reality. Whatever the facts, when the arrests and trials were over, thirty-seven "conspirators" were executed, and more than three dozen others were banished from the state.

The most famous rebel of all, Nat Turner, struck for freedom in Southampton County, Virginia, in 1831.

Nat Turner's Insurrection

The son of an African woman who passionately hated her enslavement, Nat Turner was a precocious child who learned to read when he was very young. Encouraged by his first owner to study the Bible, he enjoyed certain privileges but also endured hard work and changes of masters. His father successfully escaped to freedom.

Young Nat eventually became a preacher with a reputation for eloquence and mysticism. After nurturing his plan for several years, Turner led a band of rebels from farm to farm in the predawn darkness of August 22, 1831. The group severed limbs and crushed skulls with axes or killed their victims with guns. Before alarmed planters stopped them, Nat Turner and his followers had in forty-eight hours slaughtered sixty whites of both sexes and all ages. The rebellion was soon put down, and in retaliation whites killed slaves at random all over the region, including in adjoining states. Turner was eventually caught and then hanged. As many as two hundred African Americans, including innocent victims of marauding whites, lost their lives as a result of the rebellion.

Nat Turner remains one of the most haunting symbols in America's unresolved history with racial slavery and discrimination. While in jail awaiting execution, Turner was interviewed by a Virginia lawyer and slaveholder, Thomas R. Gray. Their intriguing creation, *The Confessions of Nat Turner*, became a bestseller within a

Visualizing THE PAST

Imaging Nat Turner's Rebellion

Below is the title page from *The Confessions of Nat Turner,* by Thomas R. Gray, 1832. This document of nearly twenty pages was published by the lawyer, Gray, who recorded and likely refashioned Turner's lengthy statement during an interview in his jail cell before his execution. *The Confessions* became a widely sold and sensational documentation of Turner's identity and especially his motivations and methods during the rebellion. It portrayed Turner as a religious mystic and fanatic and allowed the broad public to imagine the mind of a religiously motivated slave rebel.

Below and to the right is "Horrid Massacre in Virginia," 1831, woodcut. This composite of scenes depicts the slaughter of innocent women and children, as well as white men as both victims and resistants. The fear, confusion, and fierce retribution that dominated the aftermath of the Turner rebellion are on display here. Why was Nat Turner's insurrection such a shock to the nation as well as to the South? What kind of impact did Nat Turner's rebellion have on the South's evolving defense of slavery in the coming decades?

William L. Clements Library, University of Michigan

Library of Congress

Legacy FOR A PEOPLE AND A NATION

Reparations for Slavery

How should the United States come to terms with 250 years of racial slavery? Is this period best forgotten as a terrible passage that African Americans as well as the country transcended over time? Or does the nation owe a long-overdue debt to black people for their oppression? In the wake of emancipation in 1865, and rooted in vague federal promises, many former slaves believed they were entitled to "forty acres and a mule," but these never materialized.

In 1897, Callie House, a poor mother of four who had been born in 1865 in a contraband camp for ex-slaves, organized the National Ex-Slave Pension and Bounty Association, modeled after the pension system established for soldiers. House traveled all over the South, recruiting 250,000 members at 10-cent dues. Her lobbying of the federal government for slave pensions failed; she was accused of mail fraud and imprisoned for one year in 1916.

More recently, a widespread debate over "reparations" for slavery has emerged. In the rewriting of slavery's history since the 1960s, Americans have learned a great deal about how slave labor created American wealth: how insurance companies insured slaves, how complicit the U.S. government was in slavery's defense and expansion, and how slaves built the U.S. Capitol while their owners received $5 a month for their labor.

The debate is fueled by a wealth of analogies: the reparations paid to Japanese Americans interned during World War II; the reparations paid to several Native American tribes for their stolen land; the reparations paid to thousands of Holocaust survivors and victims of forced labor; and a suit settled in 1999 that will pay an estimated $2 billion to some twenty thousand black farmers for discrimination practiced by the Agriculture Department in the early twentieth century.

On the other side, some argue that, because there are no living former slaves or slaveholders, reparations for slavery can never take the form of money. But in 2002, a lawsuit was filed against three major corporations that allegedly profited from slavery, and the National Reparations Coordinating Committee promises a suit against the U.S. government itself. Some city councils have passed resolutions forcing companies that do business in their jurisdictions to investigate their possible past complicity with slave trading or ownership, which has prompted some banks and other firms to establish scholarship programs for African Americans.

Critics argue that resources would be better spent "making sure black kids have a credible education" and rebuilding inner cities. Advocates contend that, when "government participates in a crime against humanity," it is "obliged to make the victims whole." The movement for reparations has strong support in grassroots black communities, and the issue has become the subject of broad public debate. The legacy of slavery for a people and a nation promises to become America's most traumatic test of how to reconcile its history with justice.

---

month of Turner's hanging. Turner told of his early childhood, his religious visions, his zeal to be free; Gray called the rebel a "gloomy fanatic," but in a manner that made him fascinating and produced one of the most remarkable documents in the annals of American slavery. In the wake of Turner's insurrection, many states passed stiffened legal codes against black education and religious practice.

Most important, in 1832 the state of Virginia, shocked to its core, held a full-scale legislative and public debate over gradual emancipation as a means of ridding itself of slavery and of blacks. The plan debated would not have freed any slaves until 1858, and it provided that eventually all blacks would be colonized outside Virginia. But when the House of Delegates voted, gradual abolition lost, 73 to 58. In the end,

Virginia opted to do nothing except reinforce its own moral and economic defenses of slavery. It was the last time white southerners would debate any kind of emancipation until war forced their hand.

SUMMARY

During the four decades before the Civil War, the South grew in land, wealth, and power along with the rest of the country. Although the southern states were deeply enmeshed in the nation's heritage and political economy, they also developed as a distinctive region, ideologically and economically, because of slavery. Far more than the North, the antebellum South was a biracial society; whites grew up directly influenced by black folkways and culture; and blacks, the vast majority of whom were slaves, became predominantly native-born Americans and the cobuilders with whites of a rural, agricultural society. From the Old South until modern times, white and black southerners have always shared a tragic mutual history, and many are blood relatives.

With the cotton boom, as well as state and federal policies of Indian Removal, the South grew into a huge slave society. The coercive influence of slavery affected virtually every element of southern life and politics, and increasingly produced a leadership determined to preserve a conservative, hierarchical social and racial order. Despite the white supremacy that united them, the democratic values of yeomen often clashed with the profit motives of aristocratic planters. The benevolent self-image and paternalistic ideology of slaveholders ultimately had to stand the test of the slaves' own judgments. African American slaves responded by fashioning over time a rich, expressive folk culture and a religion of personal and group deliverance. Their experiences could be profoundly different from one region and kind of labor to another. Some blacks were crushed by bondage; many others transcended it in an epic of survival and resistance.

By 1850, through their own wits and on the backs of African labor, white southerners had aggressively built one of the last profitable, expanding slave societies on earth. North of them and deeply intertwined with them in the same nation, economy, constitutional system, and history, a different kind of society had grown even faster—driven by industrialism and free labor. The clash of these two deeply connected—yet mutually fearful and divided societies—would soon explode in political storms over the nation's future.

SUGGESTIONS FOR FURTHER READING

Ira Berlin, *Generations of Captivity: A History of African American Slaves* (2003)

David Brion Davis, *Inhuman Bondage: The Rise and Fall of Slavery in the New World* (2006)

Steven Deyle, *Carry Me Back: The Domestic Slave Trade in American Life* (2005)

Drew G. Faust, ed., *The Ideology of Slavery: Proslavery Thought in the Antebellum South, 1830–1860* (1981)

Annette Gordon-Reed, *The Hemingses of Monticello: An American Family* (2008)

Walter Johnson, *Soul by Soul: Life Inside the Antebellum Slave Market* (1999)

Charles Joyner, *Down by the Riverside: A South Carolina Slave Community* (1984)

James D. Miller, *South by Southwest: Planter Emigration and Identity in the Slave South* (2002)

James Oakes, *Slavery and Freedom: An Interpretation of the Old South* (1991)

Michael O'Brien, *Conjectures of Order: Intellectual Life and the American South, 1810–1860*, 2 vols. (2004)

Daniel H. Usner Jr., *American Indians in the Lower Mississippi Valley* (1998)

Go to the CourseMate website for primary source links, study tools, and review materials for this chapter. www.cengagebrain.com

Chapter 11

The Restless North
1815–1860

Nathaniel Currier, Preparing for Market, 1856, hand-colored lithograph. Gift of Lenore B. and Sidney A. Alpert, supplemented with Museum of Fine Arts Collections Funds, Springfield Museums Association. Detail used with permission.

he four children, all under the age of ten, struggled to find their land legs. It was April 17, 1807, and they had spent the last twenty-five days on a stormy voyage from Scotland to New York. Their parents, Mary Ann and James Archbald, had left their ancestral homeland reluctantly, but envisioned a future in which their children would be beholden to no one—neither landlord nor employer. They had set sail in search of the Jeffersonian dream of republican independence.

The Archbalds bought a farm in central New York, along a tributary of the Hudson River, where they raised a large flock of sheep, grew hay and vegetables, skinned rabbits for their meat and fur—and then sold whatever food or fur the family did not need to feed or clothe itself. From the wool shorn by her husband and sons, Mary Ann and her daughters spun thread and wove cloth for their own use and for sale. They used the cash to pay their mortgage. Twenty-one years after leaving Scotland, Mary Ann, in anticipation of making their last payment, declared herself wealthy: "being out of debt is, in my estimation, being rich." By then, though, her sons were young adults and had their own visions of wealth. Theirs centered on water, not land.

Ten years earlier, on April 17, 1817—a decade to the day after the Archbalds had stepped onto American shores—the New York State legislature authorized construction of a canal that would connect Lake Erie to the Hudson River, and surveyors mapped a route that ran through the Archbalds' farm. The sons (one in his early twenties, the other a teenager) helped dig the canal, while Mary Ann and her daughters cooked and cleaned for the twenty Irish laborers whom the sons hired. Bitten by canal fever, the Archbald sons soon tried their hands at commercial speculation, borrowing money to buy wheat and lumber in western New York with the idea of reselling it at substantial profits to merchants in Albany and New York City. This was not the future Mary Ann had envisioned for her sons, and their ventures distressed, but did not surprise, her. As early as 1808, she had reached an unpleasant conclusion

◀ Farm families transported their surplus produce and handicrafts to local marketplaces, where merchants purchased them for resale.

Chronology

1824	■ *Gibbons v. Ogden* prohibits steamboat monopolies
1825	■ Erie Canal completed
1827	■ Construction begins on Baltimore and Ohio (B&O) Railroad
1830	■ First locomotive runs on B&O Railroad
1830s	■ Penny press emerges
1830s–50s	■ Urban riots commonplace
1834	■ Women workers strike at Lowell
1835	■ Arkansas passes first women's property law
1836	■ Second Bank of the United States closes
1837	■ Panic of 1837 begins economic downturn
1839–43	■ Economic depression
1840s	■ Female mill workers' publications appear
1842	■ *Commonwealth v. Hunt* declares strikes lawful
1844	■ Federal government sponsors first telegraph line
	■ Lowell Female Reform Association formed
1845	■ Massive Irish immigration begins

about her new home: "We are a nation of traders in spite of all Mr. Jefferson can say or do."

The United States may have already been a "nation of traders" as early as 1808, but in the years after the War of 1812, the market economy took off in ways few could have anticipated when the Archbald family decided to seek its independence in America. In the North, steamboats, canals, and then railroads remapped the young republic's geography and economy, setting off booms in westward migration, industry, commerce, and urban growth, and fueling optimism among commercially minded Americans.

*a*lthough the transportation revolution would foster commercial exchange, technology alone could not make it happen. Even after the War of 1812, the United States' financial connections to Europe, particularly Britain, remained profound. When Europeans suffered hard times, so, too, did American merchants, manufacturers, farmers, workers—and their families. Particularly for those Americans who relied on wages for their livelihood, economic downturns often meant unemployment and destitution.

Economic downswings could shake even the most commercially minded northerners, as could other consequences of the economy's rapid expansion in the years after the War of 1812. Market expansion, some worried, threatened the nation's moral fiber if not properly controlled. It upset traditional patterns of

family organization, and it relied heavily on unskilled workers—many of whom were immigrants and free African Americans—who at best seemed unfit for republican citizenship and at worst seemed threatening. The burgeoning cities spawned by market expansion seemed to bear out Thomas Jefferson's opinion that they were "pestilential to the morals, the health and the liberties of man." Like Jefferson, who also acknowledged that cities nourished the arts, commercially minded Americans could see cities as both exemplars of civilization and breeding grounds of depravity and conflict. Only by maintaining a strong faith in improvement, progress, and upward mobility could these Americans remain hopeful that the nation's greatness lay with commercial expansion. They did so in part by articulating a free-labor ideology that at once rationalized the negative aspects of market expansion while promoting the northern labor system as superior to the South's.

- What factors contributed to the commercialization of northern society, and why did they have less of an influence on the South?

- How did the daily lives—work, family, leisure—of northerners change between 1815 and 1860?

- What factors contributed to rapid urbanization, and how did urban and rural life in the North compare with that in the South?

Or Is It the North That Was Distinctive?

Historian James McPherson has proposed a new twist to the old question of southern distinctiveness: perhaps it was the *North*—New England, the Middle Atlantic, and the Old Northwest—that diverged from the norm. At the republic's birth, the two regions had much in common, with some similarities persisting for decades: slavery, ethnic homogeneity, an overwhelming proportion of the population engaged in agricultural pursuits, a small urban population. As late as the War of 1812, the regions were more similar than dissimilar. But all that started to change with postwar economic development. Although often couched in nationalist terms, such development was undertaken mostly by state and local governments as well as private entrepreneurs, and it took place much more extensively and rapidly in the North. As the North embraced economic progress, it—rather than the South—diverged from the international norm. The North, writes McPherson, "hurtled forward toward a future that many Southerners found distasteful if not frightening." With its continual quest for improvement, the North—much more so than the South—embodied what Frenchman Alexis de Tocqueville, who toured the United States in 1831–1832, called the nation's "restless spirit."

While the South expanded as a slave society, the North changed rapidly and profoundly. It transformed, as one historian has put it, from a society with markets to a market society. In the colonial era, settlers lived in a society with markets, one in which they engaged in long-distance trade—selling their surpluses to merchants, who in turn sent raw materials to Europe, using the proceeds to purchase finished goods for resale—but in which most settlers remained self-sufficient. During and after the War of 1812, the North became more solidly a market society, one in which participation in long-distance commerce fundamentally altered individuals' aspirations and activities. With European trade largely halted during the war, entrepreneurs invested in domestic factories, setting off a series of changes in the organization of daily life. More men, women, and children began working for others in exchange for wages—rather than for themselves on a family farm—making the domestic demand for foodstuffs soar. The result was a transformation of agriculture itself. Farming became commercialized, with individual farmers abandoning self-sufficiency and specializing instead in crops that would yield cash on the market. With the cash that farmers earned when things went well, they now bought goods they had once made for themselves, such as cloth, candles, and soap as well as some luxuries. Unlike the typical southern yeoman, they were not self-reliant, and isolation was rare. In the North, market expansion altered, sometimes dramatically, virtually every aspect of life. Some historians see these rapid and pervasive changes as a market revolution.

At the beginning of the nineteenth century, few yeoman farmers, North or South, were entirely independent. Most practiced what is called mixed agriculture: they raised a variety of crops and livestock. Their goal was to procure what they called a "competence": everyday comforts and economic opportunities for their children. When they produced more than they needed, they traded the surplus with neighbors or sold it to local storekeepers. Such transactions often took place without money; farmers might trade eggs for shoes, or they might labor in their neighbor's fields in exchange for bales of hay. Even farmers like James and Mary Ann Archbald, whose main goals were to secure their own independence and seek opportunities for their children, engaged in long-distance market exchange. They did not simply trade their farm goods with neighbors but rather sold them for cash to merchants, who then sent the goods on their way to people whom the Archbalds would never meet, living perhaps hundreds of miles away. The Archbalds practiced mixed agriculture—they grew rye, corn, barley, peas, oats, and potatoes in addition to raising livestock—while also producing cloth to sell. But for Mary Ann Archbald, the main reason to earn cash was not to accumulate wealth but to pay off the family's land debt. Families like the Archbalds indulged in the occasional luxury—for Mary Ann Archbald, that meant buying books—but security mattered more than profit.

The main source of farm labor was family members, though some yeoman farmers, North and South, also relied on slaves or indentured servants. Work generally divided along gender lines. Men and boys worked in the fields, herded livestock, chopped firewood, fished, and hunted. Women and girls tended gardens, milked cows, spun and wove, processed and preserved food, prepared meals, washed clothes, and looked after infants and toddlers.

In their quest for independence, farmers cooperated with one another. They lent each other farm tools, harvested each other's fields, bartered goods, and raised their neighbors' barns and husked their corn. Little cash exchanged hands, in large part because money was in short supply. Still, New England farmers often kept elaborate account books in which they recorded what they owed and were owed (without assigning monetary value), whereas most farmers in the South rejected such formalities and simply made mental notes of debts. In both regions, years might pass without debts repaid, and when they were, they were not always repaid directly. A farmer who owed a neighbor two days' labor might bring the local storekeeper his eggs, to be credited to the neighbor's account.

Many farmers engaged simultaneously in this local economy and in long-distance trade. In the local economy—where they exchanged goods with people whom they knew—a system of "just price" prevailed, in which neighbors calculated value in terms of how much labor was involved in producing a good or providing a service. When the same farmers engaged in long-distance trade—when they sold their goods to merchants who resold it to other merchants before the goods eventually traveled as far away as coastal cities or even Europe—they set prices based on what the market would bear. In the long-distance market, credit and debt were reckoned in monetary value.

Farmers who lived near towns or villages often purchased crafted goods from local cobblers, saddlers,

Preindustrial Artisans

blacksmiths, gunsmiths, silversmiths, and tailors. Most artisans, though, lived in the nation's seaports, where master craftsmen (independent businessmen who owned their own shops and tools) oversaw workshops employing apprentices and journey-

men. Although the vast majority of craftsmen, North and South, were white, free blacks were well represented in some cities' urban trades, such as tailoring and carpentry in Charleston, South Carolina. Teenage apprentices lived with their masters, who taught them a craft, lodged and fed them, and offered parental oversight in exchange for labor. The master's wife, assisted by her daughters, cooked, cleaned, and sewed for her husband's workers. The relationship between a master craftsmen and his workers was often familial in nature, if not always harmonious. When the term of their apprenticeship expired, apprentices became journeymen who earned wages, usually with an eye toward saving money to open their own shops. The workplace had little division of labor or specialization. A tailor measured, designed, and sewed an entire suit; a cobbler did the same with shoes.

Men, women, and children worked long days on farms and in workshops, but the pace of work was generally uneven and unregimented. During busy periods, they worked dawn to dusk; the pace of work slowed after the harvest or after a large order had been completed. Market and court days were as much about exchanging gossip and offering toasts as exchanging

▲ Although separating flax fibers from their woody base could be arduous work, flax-scutching bees—much like corn-husking bees—brought together neighbors for frivolity as well as work.

goods and watching justice unfold. Husking bees and barn raisings brought people together not only to shuck corn and raise buildings, but also to eat, drink, dance, and flirt. Busy periods did not stop artisans from punctuating the day with grog breaks or from taking turns reading the newspaper aloud; they might even close their shops entirely to attend a political meeting. Nor did each workday adhere to a rigid schedule; journeymen craftsmen often staggered in late on Monday mornings, if they showed up at all, after a long night of carousing on their day off. Although the master craftsman was the boss, his workers exerted a good deal of influence over the workplace.

By the War of 1812, preindustrial habits had already changed, more noticeably in some places than in others.

Early Industrialization

Early industry in the United States reorganized daily work routines and market relationships. Women and children had long made the clothing, hats, soap, candles, and other goods on which their families relied. In the late eighteenth and early nineteenth centuries, a "putting-out" system—similar to one existing in parts of western Europe—developed in the Northeast, particularly in Massachusetts, New Jersey, and Pennsylvania. Women and children continued to produce goods as they always had but now did so in much greater quantities and for the consumption of people beyond their own families and communities. A merchant supplied them with raw materials, paid them a wage (usually a price for each piece they produced), and sold their wares in distant markets, pocketing the profit for himself. "Outwork," as it is sometimes called, appealed to women eager to earn cash, whether to secure some economic independence or to save money for additional land on which their children might establish their own farms. Particularly in New England— where population density, small farms, and tired soil conspired to constrict farming opportunities and thus to create a surplus labor pool—the putting-out system provided opportunities to earn money with which to buy cheaper, more fertile western lands without requiring that family members seek employment away from home.

Drawing on technology imported from Europe, the earliest factories grew up in tandem with the putting-out system. When Samuel Slater helped set up the first American water-powered spinning mill in Rhode Island in 1790—using children to card and spin raw cotton into thread—he sent the spun thread to nearby farm families who wove it into cloth before sending it back to Slater, from whom they received a wage. Early shoe factories relied on a similar system: factory workers cut cowhide into uppers and bottoms that were sent to rural homes. There, women sewed the uppers while men lasted (or shaped) and pegged the bottoms, a process that also sometimes took place in small workshops. The change was subtle but significant: although the work remained familiar, women now operated their looms for wages and produced cloth for the market, not primarily for their families, while male cobblers made shoes for feet that would never walk into their shops or homes.

The Transportation Revolution

In order to market goods at substantial distances from where they were produced, internal improvements were needed. Before the War of 1812, natural waterways provided the most readily available and cheapest transportation routes for people and goods, but their limitations were readily apparent. Boatmen poled bateaux (cargo boats) down shallow rivers or floated flatboats down deep ones. Cargo generally moved in one direction only—downstream—and most boats were broken up for lumber once they reached their destination. On portions of a few rivers, including the Mississippi and the Hudson, sailing ships could tack their way upstream under the right wind conditions, but upstream commerce was very limited.

Overland transport was limited, too. Although some roads had been built during the colonial and revolutionary eras, they often

Roads

became obstructed by fallen trees, soaked by mud, or clouded in dust. To reduce mud and dust, some turnpike companies built "corduroy" roads, whose tightly lined-up logs resembled the ribbed cotton fabric. But passengers complained of nausea from being continually jolted, and merchants remained wary of transporting fragile wares by wagon. Land transportation was slow and expensive, demanding a good deal of human and animal power. In 1800, according to a report commissioned by the federal government, it cost as much to ship a ton of goods 30 miles into the country's interior as to ship the same goods from New York to England. The lack of cheap, quick transportation impeded the westward expansion of the population as well as industrial growth. Fed up with the frigid winters in upstate New York, the Archbald family considered moving to Ohio in 1810 but decided against it because, as Mary Ann Archbald explained, "it is at a great distance from markets."

After the American Revolution, some northern states chartered private stock companies to build turnpikes (toll roads). These roads expanded commercial possibilities in southern New England and the Middle Atlantic, but during the War of 1812 the nation's lack of a road system in its more northerly and southerly reaches impeded the movement of troops and supplies, prompting renewed interest—in the name of defense—in building roads. Aside from the National Road, the financing fell on the states and private investors, and generally the enthusiasm for building turnpikes greatly outpaced the money and manpower expended. Turnpike companies sometimes adopted improvements, such as laying hard surfaces made of crushed stone and gravel, but many of the newly built roads suffered from old problems. With natural water routes unpredictable and roads predictably bad, an urgent need arose not just for more, but also for better transportation.

Steamboats

The first major innovation was the steamboat. In 1807, Robert Fulton's *Clermont* traveled between New York and Albany on the Hudson River in thirty-two hours, demonstrating the feasibility of using steam engines to power boats. After the Supreme Court's ruling against steamboat monopolies in *Gibbons v. Ogden* (1824), steamboat companies flourished on eastern rivers and, to a lesser extent, on the Great Lakes. These boats carried more passengers than freight, transporting settlers to the Midwest, where they would grow grain and raise pigs that fed northeastern factory workers. Along western rivers like the Mississippi and the Ohio, steamboats played a more direct commercial role, carrying midwestern timber and grain and southern cotton to New Orleans, where they were transferred to oceangoing vessels destined for northern and international ports. In the 1850s, steamboats began plying rivers as far west as California and Washington Territory. Privately owned and operated, steamboats became subject to federal regulations after frequent and deadly accidents in which boilers exploded, fires ignited, and boats collided.

To travel between Ohio and New Orleans by flatboat in 1815 took several months; in 1840, the same trip by steamboat took just ten days. But the steamboat did not supplant the flatboat. Rather, the number of flatboats traveling downstream to New Orleans more than doubled between 1816 and 1846. Now that flatboat crews could return upstream by steamboat rather than by foot, the greatest investment in flatboat travel—time—had been greatly reduced.

Canals

In the late eighteenth and early nineteenth centuries, private companies (sometimes with state subsidies) built small canals to transport goods and produce to and from interior locations previously accessible only by difficult-to-navigate rivers or by poorly maintained roads. These projects rarely reaped substantial profits, making it difficult to court investors for other projects. In 1815, only three canals in the United States measured more than 2 miles long; the longest was 27 miles. After Madison's veto of the Bonus Bill dashed commercially minded New Yorkers' hopes for a canal connecting Lake Erie to the port of New York, Governor DeWitt Clinton pushed hard and successfully for a state-sponsored initiative. What later became known as the Erie Canal was to run 363 miles between Buffalo and Albany, and was to be 4 feet deep. Skeptics derided it as "Clinton's Big Ditch."

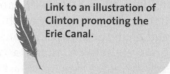

Link to an illustration of Clinton promoting the Erie Canal.

But the optimists prevailed. Construction began—amid much symbolism and fanfare—on July 4, 1817. The canal, its promoters emphasized, would help fulfill the nation's revolutionary promise by demonstrating how American ingenuity and hard work could overcome any obstacle, including imposing natural ones, such as the combined ascent and descent of 680 feet between Buffalo and Albany. By so doing, it would help unify the nation and secure its commercial independence from Europe.

Over the next eight years, nearly nine thousand laborers felled forests, shoveled and piled dirt, picked at tree roots, blasted rock, heaved and hauled boulders, rechanneled streams, and molded the canal bed. Stonemasons and carpenters built aqueducts and locks. The work was dangerous. Much of it took place in malaria- and rattlesnake-infested swamps. Where the landscape was rocksolid, gunpowder explosions blew up some workers along with the rock. Collapsing canal beds smothered yet others, while some fell to their death from aqueducts and locks.

The canal's promoters celebrated the waterway as the work of "republican free men," a tribute to the nation's republican heritage. But few of those involved in the canal's construction would have perceived their work as fulfilling Jefferson's notion of republican freedom. Although farmers and artisans provided important labor, unskilled laborers—including many immigrants and some convicts—outnumbered them. Once completed, the Erie Canal relied on the labor of children. Boys led the horses who pulled the canal boats between the canal's eighty-three locks, while girls cooked and cleaned on the boats. When the canal froze shut in winter, many canal workers found themselves with neither employment nor shelter. Some tried, successfully, to get themselves imprisoned as vagrants; many others experienced destitution.

The Erie Canal's completion in November 1825 brought immediate commercial success. Horse-drawn boats, stacked with bushels of wheat, barrels of oats, and piles of logs, streamed steadily eastward from western New York and Buffalo, where longshoreman transferred shipments from all around Lake Erie to canal boats. Tens of thousands of passengers—forty thousand in 1825 alone—traveled on the new waterway each year. The canal shortened the journey between Buffalo and

New York City from twenty to six days and reduced freight charges by nearly 95 percent—thus securing New York City's position as the nation's preeminent port. Goods that previously had not been readily available in the nation's interior now could be had easily and cheaply. Home production of cloth, for example, fell sharply after canal boats began carrying factory-made fabric from the eastern seaboard to central New York.

Other states rushed to construct their own canals. By 1840, canals crisscrossed the Northeast and Midwest, and total canal mileage reached 3,300. Because the South had easily navigable rivers, fewer canals were dug there. None of the new canals, North or South, enjoyed the Erie's financial success. As the high cost of construction combined with an economic contraction, investment in canals slumped in the 1830s. Several midwestern states could not repay their canal loans, leading them to bankruptcy or near-bankruptcy. By mid-century, more miles were abandoned than built. The canal era had ended, though the Erie Canal (by then twice enlarged and rerouted) continued to prosper, remaining in commercial operation until the late twentieth century.

The future belonged to railroads. Trains moved faster than canal boats and operated year-round. Railroads did

Railroads

not need to be built near natural sources of water and could therefore connect even the most remote locations to national and international markets. By 1860, the United States had 60,000 miles of track, most of it in the North, and railroads had dramatically reduced the cost and the time involved in shipping goods, exciting the popular imagination in the process.

The railroad era in the United States began in 1830 when Peter Cooper's locomotive, Tom Thumb, first steamed along 13 miles of Baltimore & Ohio Railroad track. In 1833, the nation's second railroad ran 136 miles from Charleston to Hamburg in South Carolina. Not until the 1850s, though, did railroads offer long-distance service at reasonable rates. Even then, the lack of a common standard for the width of track thwarted development of a national system. Pennsylvania and Ohio railroads, for example, had no fewer than seven different track widths. A journey from Philadelphia to Charleston involved eight different gauges, requiring passengers and freight to change trains seven times. Only at Bowling Green, Kentucky, did northern and southern railroads connect to one another. Although northerners and southerners alike raced to construct internal improvements, the nation's canals and railroads did little to unite the regions and promote nationalism, as the earliest proponents of government-sponsored internal improvements had hoped.

Northern state and local governments and private investors spent substantially more on internal improve-

Government Promotion of Internal Improvements

ments than did southerners. Pennsylvania and New York together accounted for half of all state monies invested. Southern states did invest in railroads, but—with smaller free populations—they collected fewer taxes, leaving them with less to spend.

For capitalists seeking dividends, southern railroads often seemed a poor bet. To be both profitable for investors and affordable for shippers, trains could not ship only

▲ Railroads, introduced in the 1830s, soon surpassed canals. Easier, quicker, and cheaper to build than canals, they moved goods and people faster. David Matthews, the engineer of the Mohawk & Hudson's John Bull, drew this picture of his early locomotive. The Mohawk & Hudson offered competition to the slower Erie Canal boats.

Map 11.1 Major Roads, Canals, and Railroads, 1850

A transportation network linked the seaboard to the interior. Settlers followed those routes westward, and they sent back grain, grain products, and cotton to the port cities.

Source: Copyright © Cengage Learning

one way; if they took agricultural products to market, their cars had to be filled with manufactured or finished goods for the return trip. But slaves and cash-strapped farmers did not provide much of a consumer base. Although planters bought northern ready-made clothes and shoes for their slaves, such purchases—made on an annual basis—did not constitute a regular source of incoming freight. Because the wealthiest men lived along rivers and could send their cotton to market on steamboats, they sometimes saw little need for railroads. Many reinvested in land and slaves, believing them a surer bet than risky railroad ventures.

The North and South laid roughly the same amount of railroad track per person before the Civil War, but when measured in terms of overall mileage, the more populous North had a web of tracks that stretched considerably farther, forming an integrated system of local lines branching off major trunk lines. In the South, railroads remained local in nature, leaving Southern travelers to patch together trips on railroads, stagecoaches, and boats.

Neither people nor goods moved easily across the South, unless they traveled via steamboat or flatboat along the Mississippi River system—and even then, flooded banks disrupted passage for weeks at a time.

Unlike southern investments in river improvements and steamboats, which disproportionately benefited planters whose lands bordered the region's riverbanks, the North's frenzy of canal and railroad building expanded transportation networks far into the hinterlands, proving not only more democratic but also more unifying. In 1815, nearly all the produce from the Old Northwest floated down the Mississippi to New Orleans, tying that region's fortunes to the South. By the 1850s, though, canals and railroads had strengthened the economic, cultural, and political links between the Old Northwest—particularly the more densely populated northern regions—and the Northeast. (See Map 11.1.)

Regional Connections

Internal improvements hastened the population's westward migration. They eased the journey itself while also making western settlement more appealing by providing easy access to eastern markets and familiar comforts. News, visitors, and luxuries now traveled regularly to previously remote areas of the Northeast and Midwest. Delighted that the Erie Canal brought fresh seafood to central New York, hundreds of miles from the sea, Mary Archbald explained that "distance . . . is reduced to nothing here."

Samuel F. B. Morse's invention of the telegraph in 1844 made the compression of distance and time even starker. News traveled almost instantaneously along telegraph wires. By 1852, more than 23,000 miles of lines had been strung nationwide. The telegraph enabled the birth of modern business practices involving the coordination of market conditions, production, and supply across great distances. Together, internal improvements and the telegraph allowed people in previously isolated areas to proclaim themselves—as did one western New Yorker—a "citizen of the world."

Many northerners hailed internal improvements as symbols of progress. Northerners proclaimed that, by building canals and railroads, they had completed God's design for the North American continent. On a more practical level, canals and railroads allowed them to seek opportunities in the West.

Ambivalence Toward Progress

But people who welcomed such opportunities could find much to lament. Mary Ann Archbald savored her fresh seafood dinners but regretted that her sons turned to speculation. Others decried the enormous numbers of Irish canal diggers and railroad track layers, whom they deemed depraved and racially inferior. Still others worried that, by promoting urban growth, transportation innovations fostered social ills.

The degradation of the natural world proved worrisome, too. When streams were rerouted, swamps drained, and forests felled, natural habitats were disturbed, even destroyed. Humans soon felt the consequences. Deprived of water power, mills no longer ran. Without forests to sustain them, wild animals—on which many rural people (Native American and European American) had relied for protein—sought homes elsewhere. Fishermen, too, found their sources of protein (and cash) dried up when natural waterways were dammed or rerouted to feed canals. If many northerners embraced progress, they also regretted its costs.

Henry David Thoreau, the prominent Transcendentalist (see Chapter 12), offered eloquent expressions of ambivalence toward progress. Even as he denounced the "devilish iron horse" (the railroad) for its shrieks and environmental degradation, he also recognized its awesome nature as a tribute to human inventiveness.

Factories and Industrialization

By dramatically lowering transportation costs, internal improvements made possible the Northeast's rapid manufacturing and commercial expansion. After canals and railroads opened the trans-Appalachian West for widescale settlement, western farmers supplied raw materials and foodstuffs for northeastern factories and their workers. They also created a larger domestic market for goods manufactured in the Northeast. With most of their time devoted to cultivating their lands, western settlers preferred to buy rather than make cloth, shoes, and other goods. They needed northeastern iron, too—for farm implements (plows, pitchforks, scythes), for nails (to build houses and other buildings, particularly in the Midwest's rapidly burgeoning cities), and for railroad tracks.

One of the oldest industries in North America, iron production was centered in the Middle Atlantic states, especially Pennsylvania, but stretched as far south as Richmond and as far north as Albany. Iron forges flourished wherever ore deposits lay and sources of fuel abounded. During the 1840s, ironworks, which previously heated their furnaces with charcoal, turned increasingly to coal and then steam. But production methods in iron making changed little, with smaller firms remaining more efficient than larger ones. Although the industry expanded, daily work stayed largely the same.

In many other industries, daily life changed dramatically. Much early industrialization involved processing raw materials—milling flour, turning hogs into packaged meat, sawing lumber—and the pork-packing industry illustrates strikingly how specialization turned skilled craftsmen into laborers. Traditionally, each butcher cut up an entire pig. Under the new industrial organization, each worker was assigned a particular task—such as cutting off the right front leg or scooping out the entrails—as the pig made its way down a "disassembly line."

Factory Work

The impersonal nature and formal rules of factory work contrasted sharply with the informal atmosphere of artisan shops and farm households. The bell, the steam whistle, or the clock governed the flow of work. In large factories, laborers never saw owners, working instead under paid supervisors, nor did they see the final product of their labor. Factory workers lost their sense of autonomy in the face of impersonal market forces. Competition from cheaper, less-skilled workers—particularly after European immigration soared in the 1840s—created job insecurity, while opportunities for advancement were virtually nonexistent.

Machinery made mass production possible in some industries. Although at first Americans imported machines or copied British designs, they soon built their own. The American System of manufacturing, as the British called

Internal Improvements

On July 4, 1827, ninety-one-year-old Charles Carroll, the only surviving signer of the Declaration of Independence, shoveled the first spadeful of earth on the Baltimore and Ohio Railroad, the nation's first westward railroad. "I consider this moment the most important act of my life," he declared, "second only to my signing the Declaration of Independence, if even it be second to that." Internal improvements, he and many others believed, would cement the United States' economic independence by supplying the nation's growing industrial centers with food and raw materials, while transporting manufactured goods back to its far-flung rural population.

Although boosters championed the era's canals and railroads as the triumph of American republicanism, such transportation projects often depended on technology, funding, and labor from abroad. American engineers scrutinized canals and, later, railroads in France, the Low Countries, and particularly England; one Erie Canal engineer spent nearly two years walking 2,000 miles alongside British canals. Railroad companies purchased locomotives from English manufacturers. Foreign investors, meanwhile, financed significant portions of projects heralded as symbols of American independence. In addition to borrowing know-how and money from abroad, Americans looked overseas for people to build their canals and railroads. Thousands of immigrants, mostly from Ireland, worked sunup to sundown blasting boulders, draining malaria-filled swamps, picking at roots and rocks, and heaving dirt. After the Civil War, Chinese immigrants performed similarly arduous and dangerous tasks on the transcontinental railroad.

When completed, internal improvements allowed people, raw materials, and goods to move inexpensively and quickly across the continent, spurring the young nation's growth—but also strengthening its ties to Europe. Eastward from the American heartland came cotton and grain, much of which was transferred to oceangoing vessels. The cotton fed European textile mills; the grain fed their workers. Thus, whenever economic conditions constricted in Europe, slowing textile production and leaving workers with smaller incomes with which to purchase food, reverberations could be felt on cotton and wheat farms across America.

Canals and railroads, hailed as great symbols of American independence, linked American farmers to an increasingly complex and volatile international economy.

◄ Workers repair a section of the Erie Canal, near Little Falls, in 1831. While hailed as a great achievement of human progress, the canal required frequent repairs, frustrating travelers, merchants, boat workers, and people living along its banks.

© Collection of the New York Historical Society, USA/The Bridgeman Art Library it, used precision machinery to produce interchangeable parts that did not require individual adjustment to fit. Eli Whitney, the cotton gin's inventor, promoted the idea of interchangeable parts in 1798, when he contracted with the federal government to make ten thousand rifles in twenty-eight months. In the 1820s, the United States Ordnance Department contracted with private firms to introduce machine-made interchangeable parts for firearms. The American System quickly produced the machine-tool industry—the manufacture of machines for the purpose of mass production. The new system permitted large-scale production at low costs: Waltham watches, Yale locks, and other goods became inexpensive but high-quality household items.

Mechanization was most dramatic in textiles, with production centered in New England, near sources of water

Textile Mills

to power spinning machines and looms. After 1815, New England's rudimentary cotton mills developed into modern factories in which machines mass-produced goods. Cotton cloth production rose from 4 million yards in 1817 to 323 million in 1840. Mechanization did not make workers obsolete; rather, more workers were needed to monitor the machines. In the mid-1840s, the cotton mills employed approximately eighty thousand "operatives," more than half of them women. Mill owners employed a resident manager to run the mills, thus separating ownership from management. Workers received wages, and the cloth they produced was sold throughout the United States.

Unable to find enough laborers in the vicinity of their mills, managers recruited New England farm daughters,

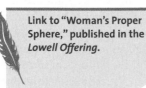
Link to "Woman's Proper Sphere," published in the *Lowell Offering*.

whom they paid wages and housed in dormitories and boarding houses in what became known as the Waltham or Lowell plan of industrialization. People who made their living off the land often harbored suspicions of those who did not—particularly in the young United States, where an agrarian lifestyle was often associated with virtue itself—causing some rural parents to hesitate from sending their daughters to textile mills. To ease such concerns, mill owners offered paternalistic oversight to the mill girls; they enforced curfews, prohibited alcohol, and required church attendance. Despite its restrictions, the system in Waltham offered farm girls opportunities to socialize with women of the same age and to gain a sense of independence that came from living away from home and earning wages. Workers wrote literary pieces for the owner-subsidized *Lowell Offering* and attended educational lectures in the evenings.

Most women imagined their factory stints as temporary, and the conditions of the work itself—the deafening roar of the power looms, the long hours, the regimentation—made few change their minds. Yet they

▲ This young mill girl at Waltham or Lowell, probably in the late 1840s, posed for an early daguerreotype. Her swollen and rough hands contrast with her youth, neat dress, and carefully tied, beribboned hair. Her hands suggest that she worked, as did most twelve- and thirteen-year-olds, as a warper, straightening the strands of cotton or wool as they entered the looms.

welcomed the social and cultural opportunities as well as the wages, which they used to help their families buy land or send a brother to college, to save for their own dowries or education, or to spend on personal items, such as fashionable clothing. The average girl arrived at sixteen and stayed five years, usually leaving to get married—often to men they met in town rather than to farm boys at home. When they left the mills, younger women took their places.

Although the Waltham plan drew international attention for its novelty, more common was the Rhode Island (or Fall River) plan employed by Samuel Slater, among others. Mills hired entire families, lodging them in company boarding houses. Men often worked farm plots near the factories while their wives and children worked in the mills, though as the system developed, men were more likely to work in the factories full-time, directly supervising the labor of their wives and children in small, family-based work units.

Mill life got harder over time, especially during the depression of 1837 to 1843, when demand for cloth

Labor Protests

declined, causing most mills to run part-time. To increase productivity, managers sped up machines and required each worker to operate more machines. Between 1836 and 1850, the number of spindles and looms in Lowell increased 150 and 140 percent, respectively, whereas the number of workers increased by only 50 percent. In the race for profits, owners lengthened hours, cut wages, tightened discipline, and packed the boarding houses.

Workers organized, accusing their bosses of treating them like wage slaves. In 1834, in reaction to a 25 percent wage cut, they unsuccessfully "turned out" (struck) against the Lowell mills. Two years later, when boarding house fees increased, they again turned out, unsuccessfully. With conditions worsening and strikes failing, workers resisted in new ways. In 1844, Massachusetts mill women formed the Lowell Female Reform Association and joined forces with other workers to press, unsuccessfully, for state legislation mandating a ten-hour day—as opposed to the fourteen-hour days that some workers endured.

Women aired their complaints in worker-run newspapers: in 1842, the *Factory Girl* appeared in New Hampshire, the *Wampanoag and Operatives' Journal* in Massachusetts. Two years later, mill workers founded the *Factory Girl's Garland* and the *Voice of Industry*, nicknamed "the factory girl's voice." Even the *Lowell Offering*, the owner-sponsored paper that was the pride of mill workers and managers alike, became embroiled in controversy when workers charged its editors with suppressing articles criticizing working conditions.

Worker turnover weakened organizational efforts. Few militant native-born mill workers stayed to fight the managers and owners, and gradually, fewer New England daughters entered the mills. In the 1850s, Irish immigrant women replaced them. Technological improvements made the work less skilled and more routine, enabling mills to hire unskilled laborers, who could be paid less. Male workers, too, protested changes wrought by the market economy and factories. But, unlike women, they could vote. Labor political parties first formed in Pennsylvania, New York, and Massachusetts in the 1820s, and then spread elsewhere; they advocated free public education and an end to imprisonment for debt, and opposed banks and monopolies. Some advocated for free homesteads, a reminder that most early industrial workers still aspired to land ownership.

The courts provided organized labor's greatest victory: protection from conspiracy laws. When journeyman shoemakers organized during the century's first decade, their employers accused them of criminal conspiracy. The cordwainers' (shoemakers') cases between 1806 and 1815 left labor organizations in an uncertain position. Although the courts acknowledged the journeymen's right to organize, judges viewed strikes as illegal until a Massachusetts case, *Commonwealth v. Hunt* (1842), ruled that Boston

Labor Unions

journeyman bootmakers could strike "in such manner as best to subserve their own interests."

The first unions arose among urban journeymen in printing, woodworking, shoemaking, and tailoring. Tending to be local, the strongest resembled medieval guilds, with members seeking protection against competition from inferior workmen by regulating apprenticeships and establishing minimum wages. Umbrella organizations composed of individual craft unions, like the National Trade Union (1834), arose in several cities in the 1820s and 1830s. But the movement disintegrated amid wage reductions and unemployment in the hard times of 1839–1843.

Permanent labor organizations were difficult to sustain. Skilled craftsmen disdained less skilled workers. Moreover, workers divided along ethnic, religious, racial, and gender lines.

Consumption and Commercialization

By producing inexpensive cloth, New England mills spawned the ready-made clothing industry. Before the 1820s, women sewed most clothing at home, and some people purchased used clothing. Tailors and seamstresses made wealthy men's and women's clothing to order. By the 1820s and 1830s, much clothing was mass-produced for sale in retail clothing stores. The process often involved little more than the reorganization of work; tailors no longer performed every task involved in making an article of clothing, from measuring to finishing work. Standard sizes replaced measuring, and a division of labor took hold: One worker cut patterns all day, another sewed hems, another affixed buttons, still another attached collars. The sewing machine's invention in 1846 sped the process along, especially with its wide availability in the 1850s. Many farm families still made their own clothing, yet bought clothes when they could afford to do so, creating more time for raising both crops and children.

Market expansion created a demand for mass-produced clothing. Rural girls who left farms for factories no longer had time to sew clothes. Young immigrant men—often separated by thousands of miles from mothers and sisters—bought the crudely made, loose-fitting clothing. But the biggest market for ready-made clothes, at least initially, was in the cotton South. With the textile industry's success driving up the demand and price for raw cotton, planters in the cotton kingdom bought ready-made shoes and clothes for slaves, in whose hands they would rather place a hoe than a needle and thread. Doing so made good economic sense.

The Garment Industry

Visualizing THE PAST

Images of Boom and Bust

The growth of the commercial economy, which saw the mass production of consumer items, also fostered economic boom and bust. To the right, we see an advertisement from the *Boston Directory* of 1848–1849 for readymade shirts, and below we see how *Harper's Weekly* portrayed New York City, the heart of the garment industry, in the heat of the financial panic of 1857, less than a decade later. To what values does F. B. Locke appeal in his choice of imagery for his advertisement? Why does *Harper's Weekly* refer to the discounted goods, and the scramble to purchase them, as an "epidemic"? What is the significance, on the image's left side, of the police officer escorting two children out of the store? What does it indicate about how *Harper's* saw the consequences of the "epidemic"? What else does the picture imply about the social consequences of financial collapse? Do the two images suggest that American values shifted in the intervening decade? Why or why not?

Although F. B. Locke continued to make shirts to order, he adapted to the new market for ready-made clothing by becoming a manufacturer, wholesaler, and retailer of men's shirts.

As the nation experienced a serious financial contraction in 1857, prices fell as business languished. But the availability of bargains did not compensate for widespread unemployment and falling wages.

Retailers often bought goods wholesale, though many manufactured shirts and trousers in their own factories. Lewis and Hanford of New York City boasted of cutting more than 100,000 garments in the winter of 1848–1849. The New York firm did business mostly in the South and owned its own retail outlet in New Orleans. Paul Tulane, a New Orleans competitor, owned a New York factory that made goods for his Louisiana store. In the Midwest, Cincinnati became the center of the men's clothing industry. But although southerners and westerners engaged in the clothing trade, its center remained in New York.

Commerce expanded with manufacturing. Commercial specialization transformed some traders in big cities, especially New York, into virtual merchant princes.

Specialization of Commerce

After the Erie Canal opened, New York City became a stop on every major trade route from Europe, southern ports, and the West. New York traders were the intermediaries for southern cotton and western grain. Merchants in other cities played a similar role. Traders in turn sometimes invested their profits in factories, further stimulating urban manufacturing. Some cities specialized: Rochester became a milling center ("The Flour City"), and Cincinnati ("Porkopolis") became the first meatpacking center.

Merchants who engaged in complex commercial transactions required large office staffs, mostly all male. At the bottom of the hierarchy were messenger boys, often preteens, who delivered documents. Above them were copyists, who hand-copied documents. Clerks processed documents and shipping papers, and did translations. Above them were the bookkeeper and the confidential chief clerk. Those seeking employment in such an office, called a counting house, often took a course from a writing master to acquire a "good hand." All hoped to rise some day to the status of partner, although their chances of success grew increasingly slim.

The specialization of commerce came more quickly to cities than to small towns, where merchants continued to exchange some goods with local farm women—trading flour or pots and pans for eggs and other produce. Local craftsmen continued to sell their own finished goods, such as shoes and clothing. In some rural areas, particularly newly settled ones, peddlers acted as general merchants. But as transportation improved and towns grew, small-town merchants increasingly specialized.

Even amid the manufacturing and commercial booms, agriculture remained the northern economy's backbone. But the transportation revolution and market expansion transformed formerly semisubsistence farms into commercial enterprises.

Commercial Farming

Many families stopped practicing mixed agriculture and began to specialize in cash crops. Although most northerners continued to farm, their daily lives and relationships often looked very different from those of their parents and grandparents.

By the 1820s, eastern farmers had cultivated nearly all the available land, and their small farms, often with uneven terrains, were not suited for the labor-saving farm implements introduced in the 1830s, such as mechanical sowers, reapers, and threshers. Many northern farmers thus either moved west or quit farming for jobs in merchants' houses and factories. Those farmers who remained, however, proved as adaptable on the farm as were their children working at water-powered looms or in countinghouses. State governments energetically promoted agricultural innovation. Massachusetts in 1817 and New York in 1819 began to subsidize agricultural prizes and county fairs. To spread innovation, New York published the winners' essays about how they grew their prize crops.

In 1820, about one-third of all northern produce was intended for the market, but by 1850 the amount surpassed 50 percent. As farmers shifted toward specialization and market-oriented production, they often invested in additional land (buying the farms of neighbors who moved west), new farming equipment (such as improved iron and steel plows), and new sources of labor (hired hands). Many New England and Middle Atlantic farm families faced steep competition from midwestern farmers after the opening of the Erie Canal, and began abandoning wheat and corn production. Instead, they raised livestock, especially cattle, and specialized in vegetable and fruit production. Much of what they produced ended up in the stomachs of the North's rapidly growing urban and manufacturing populations.

Farmers financed innovations through land sales and debts. Indeed, increasing land values, not the sale of agricultural products, promised the greatest profit. Farm families who owned their own land flourished, but it became harder to take up farming in the first place. By the 1840s, it took more than ten years for a rural laborer in the Northeast to save enough money to buy a farm. The number of tenant farmers and hired hands increased, providing labor to drive commercial expansion. Farmers who had previously employed unpaid family members and enslaved workers now leased portions of their farms or hired waged labor to raise their livestock and crops.

As the commercial economy expanded, rural women assumed additional responsibilities, increasing their already substantial farm and domestic work. Some did outwork. Many increased their production of eggs, dairy products, and garden produce for sale; others raised bees or silkworms.

Farm Women's Changing Labor

With the New England textile mills producing more and more finished cloth, farm women and children often abandoned time-consuming spinning and weaving, bought factory-produced cloth, and dedicated the saved time to producing additional products, such as butter and cheese, for the market. Women had always made butter and cheese; now they produced them in large quantities with intentions of profiting from their sale. Some mixed-agriculture farms converted entirely to dairy production, with men taking over formerly female tasks. Canals and railroads carried cheese to eastern ports, where wholesalers sold it around the world, shipping it to California, England, and China. In 1844, Britain imported more than 5 million pounds of cheese from the United States.

Although agricultural journals and societies exhorted farmers to manage their farms like time-efficient businesses, not all farmers abandoned the old practices of gathering at market, general stores, taverns, and church. They did not forgo barn raisings and husking bees, but by the 1830s there were fewer young people at such events to dance and flirt. Many young women had left for textile mills, and young men often worked as clerks or factory hands. Those who stayed behind were more likely to come dressed in store-bought clothing and to consume pies made with store-bought flour.

Rural Communities

Even as they continued to swap labor and socialize with neighbors, farmers became more likely to reckon debts in dollars. They kept tighter accounts and watched national and international markets more closely. When financial panics hit, cash shortages almost halted business activity, casting many farmers further into debt, sometimes to the point of bankruptcy. Faced with the possibility of losing their land, farmers did what many would have considered unthinkable before: they called in debts with their neighbors, sometimes causing fissures in long-established relationships.

Cycles of Boom and Bust

The market economy's expansion led to cycles of boom and bust. Prosperity stimulated demand for finished goods, such as clothing and furniture. Increased demand in turn led not only to higher prices and still higher production, but also, because of business optimism and expectations of higher prices, to land speculation. Investment money was plentiful as Americans saved and foreign, mostly British, investors bought U.S. bonds and securities. Then production surpassed demand, causing prices and wages to fall; in response, land and stock values collapsed, and investment money flowed out of the United States. This boom-and-bust cycle influenced every corner of the country, but particularly the Northeast, where even the smallest localities became enmeshed in regional and national markets.

Although the 1820s and 1830s were boom times, financial panic triggered a bust cycle in 1837, the year after the Second Bank of the United States closed. Economic contraction remained severe through 1843. Internal savings and foreign investments declined sharply. Many banks could not repay their depositors, and states, facing deficits because of the economy's decline, defaulted on their bonds. European, especially British, investors became suspicious of all U.S. loans and withdrew money from the United States.

Hard times had come. Philadelphia took on an eerie aura. "The streets seemed deserted," Sidney George Fisher observed in 1842. "The largest [merchant] houses are shut up and to rent, there is no business . . . no money, no confidence." New York countinghouses closed their doors. Former New York mayor Philip Hone later observed, "A deadly calm pervades this lately flourishing city. No goods are selling, no businesses stirring." The hungry formed lines in front of soup societies, and beggars crowded the sidewalks. Some workers looted. Crowds of laborers demanding their deposits gathered at closed banks. Sheriffs sold seized property at one-quarter of pre-hard-time prices. In smaller cities like Lynn, Massachusetts, shoemakers weathered the hard times by fishing and tending gardens, while laborers became scavengers, digging for clams and harvesting dandelions. Once-prosperous businessmen—some victims of the market, others of their own recklessness—lost nearly everything, prompting Congress to pass the Federal Bankruptcy Law of 1841; by the time the law was repealed two years later, 41,000 bankrupts had sought protection under its provisions.

Families in Flux

Anxieties about economic fluctuations reverberated beyond factories and countinghouses into northern homes. Sweeping changes in the household economy, rural as well as urban, led to new family ideals. In the preindustrial era, the family had been primarily an economic unit; now it became a moral and cultural institution, though in reality few families could live up to the new ideal.

In the North, the market economy increasingly separated the home from the workplace, leading to a new middle-class ideal in which men functioned in the public sphere, while women oversaw the private or domestic sphere. The home became, in theory, an emotional retreat from the competitive, selfish world of business, where men increasingly focused on their work, eager to prosper yet fearful of failure in the unpredictable market economy. At the home's center was a couple that married for love rather than for economic convenience or advantage.

The "Ideal" Family

Men provided and protected, while women nurtured and guarded the family's morality, making sure that capitalism's excesses did not invade the private sphere. Childhood focused more on education than on work, and the definition of childhood itself expanded: children were to remain at home until their late teens or early twenties. This ideal came to be known as separate-sphere ideology, or sometimes the cult of domesticity or the cult of true womanhood. Although it rigidly separated the male and female spheres, this ideology gave new standing to domestic responsibilities. In her widely read *Treatise on Domestic Economy* (1841), Catharine Beecher approached housekeeping as a science even as she trumpeted mothers' role as their family's moral guardian. Although Beecher advocated the employment of young, single women as teachers, she believed that, once married, women belonged at home. She maintained that women's natural superiority as moral, nurturing caregivers made them especially suited for teaching (when single) and parenting (once married). Although Beecher saw the public sphere as a male domain, she insisted that the private sphere be elevated to the same status as the public.

These new domestic ideals depended on smaller families in which parents, particularly mothers, could give

Shrinking Families

children more attention, better education, and more financial help. With the market economy, parents could afford to have fewer children because children no longer played a vital economic role. Urban families produced fewer household goods, and commercial farmers, unlike self-sufficient ones, did not need large numbers of workers year-round, turning instead to hired laborers during peak work periods. Although smaller families resulted in part from first marriages' taking place at a later age—shortening the period of potential childbearing—they also resulted from planning, made easier when cheap rubber condoms became available in the 1850s. Some women chose, too, to end accidental pregnancies with abortion.

In 1800, American women bore seven or eight children; by 1860, the figure had dropped to five or six. This decline occurred even though many immigrants with large-family traditions were settling in the United States; thus, the birth rate among native-born women declined even more sharply. Although rural families remained larger than urban ones, birth rates among both groups declined comparably.

Yet even as birth rates fell, few northern women could fulfill the middle-class ideal of separate spheres. Most wage-earning women provided essential income for their families and could not stay home. They often saw domestic ideals as oppressive, as middle-class reformers mistook poverty for immorality, condemning working mothers for letting their children work or scavenge rather

St. Louis Art Museum, Bequest of Edgar William and Bernice Chrysler Garbisch

▲ As they strove to live according to new domestic ideals, middle-class families often relied on African American or immigrant servants, who sacrificed time with their own children in order to care for their employers' children.

than attend school. Although most middle-class women could stay home, new standards of cleanliness and comfort weighed heavily on their time. These women's contributions to their families were generally assessed in moral terms, even though their economic contributions were significant. When they worked inside their homes, they provided, without remuneration, the labor for which wealthier women paid when they hired domestic servants to perform daily chores. Without servants, moreover, women could not devote themselves primarily to their children's upbringing, placing the ideals of the cult of domesticity beyond the reach of many middle-class families.

In working-class families, women left their parental home as early as age twelve, earning wages most of their

Women's Paid Labor

lives, with only short respites for bearing and rearing children. Unmarried girls and women worked primarily as domestic servants or in factories; married and widowed women worked as laundresses, seamstresses, and cooks. Some hawked food and wares on city streets; other did piecework at home, earning wages in the putting-out system; and some became prostitutes. Few of these occupations enabled women to support themselves or a family at a comfortable level.

Middle-class Americans sought to keep women closer to home. If young girls left the home to work—in New England's textile mills, in new urban stores as clerks—it was only for a brief interval before marriage. Otherwise, teaching was the only occupation consistent with genteel notions of femininity. In 1823, the Beecher sisters, Catharine and Mary, established the Hartford Female Seminary and offered history and science in addition to the traditional women's curriculum of domestic arts and religion. A decade later, Catharine Beecher successfully campaigned for teacher-training schools for women. She argued in part for women's moral superiority and in part for their economic value; because these women would be single, she contended, they need not earn as much as their male counterparts, whom she presumed to be married, though not all were. Unmarried women earned about half the salary of male teachers. By 1850, schoolteaching had become a woman's profession. Many women worked as teachers, usually for two to five years.

The proportion of single women in the population increased significantly in the nineteenth century. In the East, some single women would have preferred to marry but found market and geographic expansion working against them: more and more young men headed west in search of opportunity, leaving some eastern communities with a disproportionate number of young women. But other women chose to remain independent, seeking opportunities opened by the market economy and urban expansion. Because women's work generally paid poorly, those who forswore marriage faced serious challenges, leaving many single women to rely on charitable or family assistance.

The Growth of Cities

To many contemporary observers, cities came to symbolize what market expansion had wrought—for better or for worse—on northern society. No period in American history saw more rapid urbanization than the years between 1820 and 1860. The percentage of people living in urban areas (defined as a place with a population of 2,500 or more) grew from just over 7 percent in 1820 to nearly 20 percent in 1860. Most of this growth took place in the Northeast and the Midwest. Although most northerners continued to live on farms or in small villages, the population of individual cities boomed. Many of those residents were temporary—soon moving on to another city or the countryside—and many came from foreign shores.

Even as new cities sprang up, existing cities grew tremendously (see Map 11.2). In 1820, the United States had

Urban Boom

thirteen places with a population of ten thousand or more; in 1860, it had ninety-three. New York City, already the nation's largest city in 1820, saw its population grow from 123,709 people in that year to 813,669 in 1860—a growth factor of six and a half times. Philadelphia, the nation's second-largest city in both 1820 and 1860, saw the size of its population multiply ninefold during that same forty-year period. In 1815, Rochester, New York, had a population of just 300 persons. By 1830, the Erie Canal had turned the sleepy agricultural town into a bustling manufacturing center; it was now the nation's twenty-fifth-largest city, with a population of just over 9,000. Its population continued to multiply at fantastic rates, even doubling in a single decade. By 1860, it had more than 50,000 residents.

Cities experienced geographic expansion as well. New York City, for example, burst its boundaries around 1830. Until then, New Yorkers could walk from one end of the city to the other in an hour. In 1825, Fourteenth Street was the city's northern boundary. By 1860, 400,000 people lived above that divide, and Forty-second Street was the city's northern limit. Gone were the cow pastures, kitchen gardens, and orchards. Public transit made city expansion possible. Horse-drawn omnibuses appeared in New York in 1827, and the Harlem Railroad, completed in 1832, ran the length of Manhattan. By the 1850s, all big cities had horse-drawn streetcars, allowing wealthier residents who could afford the fare to settle on larger plots of land on the cities' outskirts.

Cities helped sustain the North's market revolution by serving as transportation hubs, commercial centers, and—

Market-Related Development

in some cases—manufacturing sites. Some cities grew up with manufacturing. The Boston Manufacturing Company selected the site for Lowell, Massachusetts, because of its proximity to the Merrimack River, whose rapidly flowing waters could power its textile mill. Incorporated in 1826, by the 1850s Lowell was the second-largest city in New England. Although most early manufacturing took place in rural areas, some commercial cities, such as New York, experienced what historians sometimes call metropolitan industrialization, a form relying not on mechanization but on reorganization of labor, similar to the earlier putting-out system. Much of the early production of ready-made clothing, for example, took place in tenements throughout New York City, where women performed an urban form of outwork, spending hour after hour sewing on buttons for a piece of ready-made clothing, while others sewed hem after hem. In 1860, 25,000 women worked in manufacturing jobs in New York City, where they constituted a

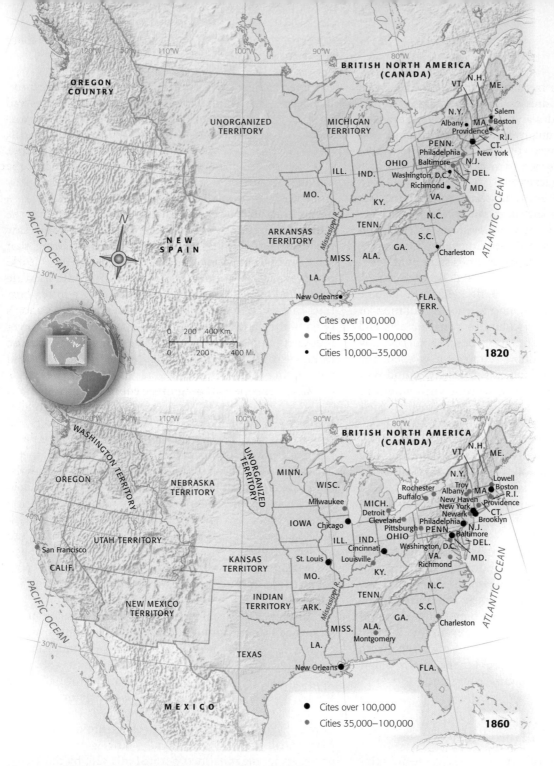

Map 11.2 Major American Cities in 1820 and 1860

The number of Americans who lived in cities increased rapidly between 1820 and 1860, and the number of large cities grew as well. In 1820, only New York City had a population exceeding 100,000; forty years later, eight more cities had surpassed that level.

Source: Copyright © Cengage Learning

quarter of the waged labor force. Two-thirds of them worked in the garment industry.

The North urbanized more quickly than the South, but what was most striking about northern urbanization was where it took place. With only a few exceptions, southern cities were seaports, whereas the period between 1820 and 1860 saw the creation of many inland cities in the North—usually places that sprang to life with

the creation of transportation lines or manufacturing establishments.

Northern cities developed elaborate systems of municipal services but lacked adequate taxing power to provide services for all. At best, they could tax property adjoining new sewers, paved streets, and water mains. New services and basic sanitation depended on residents' ability to pay. Another solution was to charter private companies to sell basic services, such as providing gas for lights. Baltimore first chartered a private gas company in 1816. By mid-century, every major city had done so. Private firms lacked the capital to build adequate water systems, though, and they laid pipe only in commercial and well-to-do residential areas, bypassing the poor. The task of supplying water ultimately fell on city governments.

Throughout the United States, wealth was concentrating in the hands of a relatively small number of people. By

Extremes of Wealth

1860, the top 5 percent of American families owned more than half of the nation's wealth, and the top 10 percent owned nearly three-quarters. In the South, the extremes of wealth were most apparent on rural plantations, but in the North, cities provided the starkest evidence of economic inequities.

Despite the optimistic forecasts of early textile manufacturers that American industrialization need not engender the poverty and degradation associated with European industrialization, America's industrial cities soon resembled European ones. A number of factors contributed to widespread poverty: poor wages, the inability of many workers to secure full-time employment, and the increasingly widespread employment of women and children, which further drove down wages for everyone. Women and children,

employers rationalized, did not need a living wage because they were—in the employers' way of thinking—dependent by nature, meaning that they relied on men to support them and did not need to earn a wage that allowed self-sufficiency. In reality, though, not all women or children had men to support them, nor were men's wages always adequate to support a family comfortably.

New York provides a striking example of the extremes of wealth accompanying industrialization. Where workers lived, conditions were crowded, unhealthy, and dangerous. Houses built for two families often held four; tenements built for six families held twelve. Some of those families took in lodgers to pay the rent, adding to the unbearably crowded conditions that encouraged poorer New Yorkers to spend as much time as possible outdoors. But streets in poor neighborhoods were filthy. Excess sewage from outhouses drained into ditches that carried urine and fecal matter into the streets. People piled garbage into gutters or left it to accumulate in backyards or alleys. Pigs, geese, dogs, and vultures scavenged the streets, while enormous rats roamed under cities' wooden sidewalks and through large buildings. Disease thrived. Typhoid, dysentery, malaria, and tuberculosis regularly visited the poorer sections of cities. Epidemics of cholera struck in 1831, 1849, and again in 1866, claiming thousands of victims.

Collection of the New York Historical Society

▲ Visible signs of urban poverty in the 1850s were the homeless and orphaned children, most of them immigrants, who wandered the streets of New York City. The Home for the Friendless Orphanage, at 29th Street and Madison Avenue, provided shelter for some of the orphan girls.

But within walking distance of poverty-stricken neighborhoods were lavish mansions, whose residents could escape to their country estates during the summer's brutal heat or during epidemics. Much of this wealth was inherited. For every John Jacob Astor, who became a millionaire in the western fur trade after beginning life in humble circumstances, ten others had inherited or married money. These rich New Yorkers were not idle, though; they worked at increasing their fortunes and power by investing in commerce and manufacturing.

Between the two extremes of wealth sat a distinct middle class, larger than the wealthy elite but substantially smaller than the working classes. They were businessmen, traders, and professionals, and the rapid turn toward industrialization and commercial specialization made them a much larger presence in northern cities than in southern ones. Middle-class families enjoyed new consumer items: wool carpeting, fine wallpaper, and rooms full of furniture replaced the bare floors, whitewashed walls, and relative sparseness of eighteenth-century homes. Houses were large, from four to six rooms. Middle-class children slept one to a bed, and by the 1840s and 1850s, middle-class families used indoor toilets that were mechanical, though not yet flushing. Middle-class families formed the backbone of urban clubs and societies, filled the family pews in church, and sent their sons to college. They were as distinct from the world of John Jacob Astor as they were from the milieu of the working class and the poor.

Many of the urban poor were immigrants. The 5 million immigrants who came to the United States between 1830 and 1860 outnumbered the country's entire population in 1790. The vast majority were Europeans, primarily from Ireland and the German states (see Figure 11.1). During the peak period of pre–Civil War immigration (1847–1857), 3.3 million immigrants entered the

Immigration

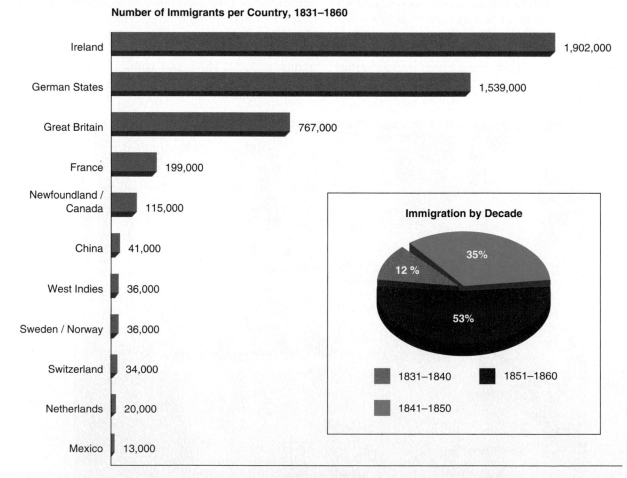

Figure 11-1 Major Sources of Immigration to the United States, 1831–1860

Most immigrants came from two areas: Great Britain, of which Ireland was a part, and the German states. These two areas sent more immigrants between 1830 and 1860 than the inhabitants of the United States enumerated at the first census in 1790. By 1860, 15 percent of the white population was of foreign birth.

Source: Data from Stephan Thernstrom, ed., *Harvard Encyclopedia of American Ethnic Groups* [Cambridge, Mass., and London: Harvard University Press, 1980], 1047.

United States, including 1.3 million Irish and 1.1 million Germans. By 1860, 15 percent of the white population was foreign-born, with 90 percent of immigrants living in northern states. Not all planned to stay permanently, and many, like the Irish, saw themselves as exiles from their homeland.

A combination of factors "pushed" Europeans from their homes and "pulled" them to the northern United States. In Ireland, the potato famine (1845–1850)—a period of widespread starvation caused by a diseased potato crop—drove millions from their homeland. Although economic conditions pushed most Germans as well, some were political refugees—liberals, free-thinkers, Socialists, communists, and anarchists—who fled after the abortive revolutions of 1848. Europeans' awareness of the United States grew as employers, states, and shipping companies promoted opportunities across the Atlantic. Often the message was stark: work and prosper in America, where everyone could aspire to be an independent farmer, or starve in Europe. Although boosters promised immigrants a land of milk and honey,

many soon became disillusioned; hundreds of thousands returned home.

Many early immigrants lived or worked in rural areas. Like the Archbalds, a few settled immediately on farms and eventually bought land. Others, unable to afford even a modest down payment on a farm, worked as hired farm hands, canal diggers, or railroad track layers—often hoping to buy land later. Pádraig Cúndún was among the lucky. The Irishman used his earnings as a canal laborer to buy land in western New York, pro-claiming proudly in 1834 that "I have a fine farm of land now, which I own outright. No one can demand rent from me. My family and I can eat our fill of bread and meat, butter and milk any day we like throughout the year, so I think being here is better than staying in Ireland, landless and powerless, without food or clothing." By the 1840s and 1850s—when the steady stream of immigration turned into a flood—the prospects of buying land became more remote.

By 1860, most immigrants settled in cities, often the port at which they arrived. The most destitute could not

North Carolina Museum of Art, Purchased with funds from the State of North Carolina (52.9.2)

◀ Immigrants often considered themselves superior to African Americans, fueling racial tensions. Here, a German immigrant demonstrates his sense of superiority even as he relies on an African American laborer for directions.

afford the canal or railroad fare to places farther inland. Others arrived with resources but fell victim to swindlers who preyed on newly arrived immigrants. Others liked the cities' ethnic flair. In 1855, 52 percent of New York's 623,000 inhabitants were immigrants, 28 percent from Ireland and 16 percent from the German states. Boston, another major entry port, took on a European tone; throughout the 1850s, the city was about 35 percent foreign-born, of whom more than two-thirds were Irish.

Most of the new immigrants from Ireland were young, poor, from rural districts, and Roman Catholic. Women found work as domestic servants or mill hands, while men worked in construction or transportation. Very few Germans settled in New England; most of them came with enough resources to head to the upper Mississippi and Ohio valleys, to states such as Ohio, Illinois, Wisconsin, and Missouri. Although some southern cities like Charleston and Savannah had significant numbers of Irish immigrants, the vast majority of European immigrants, many of whom arrived with aversions to slavery and to semitropical heat, settled in the Northeast or Midwest.

Tension—often resulting from anxieties over the era's economic changes—characterized the relationship between native-born Americans and immigrants, particularly Irish Catholics. Native-born workers blamed immigrants for scarce job opportunities and low wages. Middle-class whites blamed them for poverty and crime. As they saw it, immigrants' moral depravity—not poor wages—led to poverty.

Ethnic Tensions

Native-born Americans often associated the Irish with another group whom they deemed morally inferior: African Americans. White northerners often portrayed Irish immigrants as nonwhite, as African in appearance. But Irish and African Americans did not develop a sense of solidarity. Instead, some of the era's most virulent riots erupted between Irish immigrants and African Americans.

Closely related to racial stereotyping was anti-Catholicism, which became strident in the 1830s. In Boston, anti-Catholic riots occurred frequently. Nearby Charlestown, Massachusetts, saw a mob burn a convent in 1834. In Philadelphia, a crowd attacked priests

Link to the original report of the 1834 convent burning in Charlestown, MA.

and nuns, and vandalized churches in 1844, and in Lawrence, Massachusetts, a mob leveled the Irish neighborhood in 1854. Anti-Catholic violence spread beyond urban areas—riots between native-born and Irish workers erupted along the nation's canals and railroads—but urban riots usually attracted more newspaper attention, fueling fears that cities were violent, depraved places.

German immigrants, at least the majority who were Protestants, mostly fared better than the Irish. In part because Germans generally arrived with some resources and skills, Americans stereotyped them as hard working, self-reliant, and intelligent. But non-Protestant Germans—Catholics and Jews (whom white Americans considered a separate race) frequently encountered hostility fed by racial and religious prejudice.

Immigrants often lived in ethnic enclaves. Intolerance between Protestants and Catholics ran both ways, and Irish Catholics tended to live in their own neighborhoods,

Collection of The New York Historical Society, Museum Purchase, Abbott-Lenox Fund, 1959 (1959.46)

◄ Domestic servants await their fate at a hiring office. Because servants resided with their employers, concerns about honesty often topped an employer's list of priorities for a suitable servant.

The Fine Arts Museums of San Francisco, Mildred Anna Williams Collection

▲ Although African Americans could not make much money selling goods on the street, the job could provide them with a sense of independence and dignity.

where they established Catholic churches and schools. In larger cities, immigrants from the same German states clustered together. Immigrants set up social clubs and mutual-aid societies, such as the Hibernian Society and Sons of Erin (Irish), and B'nai B'rith (Jewish).

African Americans also forged their own communities and culture. As late as the 1830s, significant numbers of them remained enslaved in New York and New Jersey, but the numbers of free African Americans grew steadily, and by 1860 nearly 250,000 (many of them refugees from southern slavery) lived in the urban North. Despite differences in status, occupation, wealth, education, and religion, African Americans often felt a sense of racial solidarity. African Methodist Episcopal churches and preachers helped forge communities. Chapels and social halls functioned as town halls and school buildings.

People of Color

Ministers were political leaders, and their halls housed political forums, conventions, and protest meetings.

But white racism impinged on every aspect of northern African Americans' lives. Streetcars, hotels, restaurants, and theaters could turn away African Americans with no legal penalty. City laws barred African Americans from entering public buildings. Even where laws were more liberal, popular attitudes among whites constrained African Americans' opportunities. In Massachusetts, for example, African Americans enjoyed more legal rights than anywhere else in the country. Yet laws protecting civil and political rights could not make whites shop at black businesses. "Colored men in business in Massachusetts receive more respect, and less patronage than in any place I know of," proclaimed a prominent African American lawyer.

African Americans were excluded from factory and clerical jobs. Women worked as house servants, cooks, washerwomen, and child nurses. Most African American men worked as construction workers, porters, longshoremen, or day laborers—all jobs subject to frequent periods of unemployment. Others found employment in the lower-paying but more stable service industry, working as servants, waiters, cooks, barbers, and janitors. Many African American men became sailors and merchant seamen, as commercial sailing offered regular employment and opportunities for advancement, though not protection from racial taunts.

In the growing cities, African Americans turned service occupations into businesses, opening their own restaurants, taverns, hotels, barber shops, and employment agencies for domestic servants. Some became caterers. Others sold used clothing or were junk dealers or small-job contractors. A few became wealthy, invested in real estate, and loaned money. With professionals—ministers, teachers, physicians, dentists, lawyers, and newspaper editors—they formed a small but growing African American middle class.

In cities large and small, African Americans became targets of urban violence. White rioters clubbed and stoned African Americans, destroying their houses, churches, and businesses—and sent African Americans fleeing for their lives. Philadelphia experienced the most violence, with five major riots in the 1830s and 1840s, and major riots occurred in Providence and New York, where in July of 1834 more than sixty buildings were vandalized or destroyed during a three-day riot. By 1860, many hundreds of African Americans had died in urban riots.

Living in cramped, squalid conditions, working-class families—white and black, immigrant and native-born—spent little time indoors. In the 1840s, a working-class youth culture developed on the Bowery, one of New York's entertainment strips. The lamp-lit promenade, lined with theaters, dance halls, and cafés,

Urban Culture

became an urban midway. Older and more elite New Yorkers often feared the "Bowery boys and gals." The Bowery boys' greased hair, distinctive clothing, and swaggering gait frightened many middle-class New Yorkers, as did the Bowery girls' colorful costumes and ornate hats, which contrasted with genteel ladies' own modest veils and bonnets. Equally scandalous to an older generation were the middle-class clerks who succumbed to the city's temptations, most notably prostitution.

Gangs of garishly dressed young men and women—flaunting their sexuality, using foul language, sometimes speaking in foreign tongues, and drinking to excess—drove self-styled respectable citizenry to establish private clubs and associations. Some joined the Masonic order, which offered everything the bustling, chaotic city did not: an elaborate hierarchy, an older code of deference between ranks, harmony, and shared values. Although the Masons admitted men only, women organized their own associations, including literary clubs and benevolent societies.

Increasingly, urban recreation and sports became formal commodities to be purchased. One had to buy a ticket to go to the theater, the circus, P. T. Barnum's American Museum in New York City, the racetrack, or the ballpark. Horseracing, walking races, and, in the 1850s, baseball attracted large urban male crowds. Starting in 1831, enthusiasts could read the all-sports newspaper, *Spirit of the Times*. A group of Wall Street office workers formed the Knickerbocker Club in 1842 and in 1845 drew up rules for the game of baseball. By 1849, news of boxing was so much in demand that a round-by-round account of a Maryland boxing match was telegraphed throughout the East.

 Link to excerpts about promotion and marketing from P. T. Barnum's autobiography.

A theater was often the second public building constructed in a town, after a church. Large cities boasted two or more theaters catering to different classes. Some plays cut across class lines—Shakespeare was performed so often and appreciated so widely that even illiterate theatergoers knew his plays well—yet the same taste in plays did not soothe class tensions. In 1849, a dispute between an American and a British actor about how to properly stage Shakespeare's *Macbeth* escalated into a working-class riot at New York City's elitist Astor Place Opera House, which hosted the British actor. It was, as one observer explained, "the rich against the poor—the aristocracy against the people." As the disorder escalated, bringing thousands into the streets, militia fired into the working-class crowd, killing at least twenty-seven and injuring about 150.

In the 1840s, singing groups, theater troupes, and circuses traveled from city to city. Minstrel shows were particularly popular, featuring white men (often Irish) in burnt-cork makeup imitating African Americans in song, dance, and patter. In the early 1830s, Thomas D. Rice of New York became famous for his role as Jim Crow, an old southern slave. In ill-fitting patched clothing and torn shoes, the blackface Rice shuffled, danced, and sang. Minstrel performers told jokes mocking economic and political elites, and evoked nostalgia for preindustrial work habits and morality, as supposedly embodied by carefree black men. At the same time, the antics of blackface actors encouraged a racist stereotyping of African Americans as sensual and lazy.

Accounts of urban culture peppered the penny press, a new journalistic form that emerged in the 1830s, soon sweeping northern cities, particularly the ports of New York, Boston, Philadelphia, and Baltimore. Made possible by technological advances—the advent of the steam-powered press, improved methods for producing paper, and transportation innovations—the penny press (each newspaper cost one cent) contrasted in fundamental ways to the established six-cent newspapers. The older papers covered mostly commercial news and identified strongly with a political party; politicians themselves supplied much of the content, often reprinting their speeches. The penny press, by contrast, proclaimed political independence and dispersed paid reporters to cover local, national, and even international stories. Unlike six-cent newspapers, which relied primarily on mail subscriptions and contributions from political parties for their revenue, penny newspapers were sold by newsboys on the street, earned money by selling advertising, and circulated in much greater numbers to a more economically diverse readership. For the first time, working-class people could afford to buy newspapers regularly.

The Penny Press

Penny newspapers focused on daily life, what today would be called "human interest stories," giving individuals of one social class the opportunity to peer into the lives of different classes, ethnicities, and races. Working- and middle-class readers, for example, could read about high society—its balls, its horse-racing, its excesses of various sorts. Wealthy and middle-class readers encountered stories about life in poorer neighborhoods—its crime, poverty, and insalubrious conditions. The penny press often sensationalized or slanted the news, and, in the process, influenced urban dwellers' views of one another, and of cities themselves.

Many northerners saw cities—with their mixtures of people, rapid growth, municipal improvements, and violence—as symbolizing at once progress and decay. On the one hand, cities represented economic advancement; new ones grew at the crossroads of transportation and commerce. Cities nurtured churches, schools, civil governments, and museums—all signs of civilization and culture. As canals

Cities as Symbols of Progress

◄ Thomas D. Rice playing "Jim Crow" in blackface at the Bowery Theater in New York City, 1833. The rowdy audience climbed onto the stage, leaving Rice little room to perform. In representing African Americans on stage, Rice and other minstrels contributed to establishing both black and white as racial categories.

and railroads opened the West for mass settlement, many white northerners applauded the appearance of what they called "civilization"—church steeples, public buildings—in areas that had recently been what they called "savage wilderness"; that is, territory controlled by Native Americans. One Methodist newspaper remarked in 1846 that the nation's rapid expansion westward would outpace "our means of moral and intellectual improvement." But the remedies, the editor noted, were evident: bring churches, schools, and moral reform societies to the West. "Cities, civilization, religion, mark our progress," he declared. To many nineteenth-century white Americans, cities represented the moral triumph of civilization over savagery and heathenism.

Yet some of the same Americans deplored the everyday character of the nation's largest cities, which they saw as havens of disease, poverty, crime, and vice. To many middle-class observers, disease combined with crime to represent moral decline. They considered epidemics to be divine scourges, striking primarily those who were filthy, intemperate, and immoral. Many middle-class and wealthy people believed epidemics resulted from the urban poor's moral degradation. Theft and prostitution provided evidence of moral vice, and wealthy observers perceived these crimes not as by-products of poverty but as signs of individual failing. They responded by pressing for laws against vagrancy and disturbing the peace, and by pushing city officials to establish the nation's first police forces. Boston hired daytime policemen in 1838 to supplement its part-time night watchmen and constables, and New York formed its own police force, modeled on London's, in 1845.

How did northerners reconcile urban vice and depravity with their view of cities as symbols of progress? Middle-class reformers focused on purifying cities of disease and vice. If disease was a divine punishment—rather than an offshoot of cramped conditions engendered by economic change—then it was within Americans' power to fix things. Middle-class reformers took to the streets and back alleys, trying to convince the urban working classes that life would improve if they gave up alcohol, worked even harder, and prayed frequently. They talked about how the northern working poor—unlike southern slaves—could improve their condition through hard work and virtuous habits. This belief in upward mobility became central to many northerners' ideas about progress.

Belief in upward mobility related to the idea of free labor, the concept that, in a competitive marketplace, those who worked hard and lived virtuous lives could improve their status. Free-labor ideology appealed especially to manufacturers and merchants eager to believe that their own success emerged from hard work and moral virtue—and eager as well to encourage their factory hands and clerks to work hard and live virtuously, to remain optimistic despite current hardships. Many laborers initially rejected free-labor ideology, seeing it as a veiled attempt to tout industrial work habits, to rationalize poor wages, and to quell worker protest. But by the 1850s, when the question of slavery's westward expansion returned to the political foreground, more and more northerners would embrace free-labor ideology and come to see slavery as antithetical to the free-labor ideology of the North. It was this way of thinking, perhaps more than anything else, that made the North distinctive.

Legacy FOR A PEOPLE AND A NATION

P. T. Barnum's Publicity Stunts

Usually remembered for the Ringling Brothers and Barnum & Bailey Circus, P. T. Barnum (1810–1891) left another legacy: the publicity stunt. Using hoaxes and spectacles, Barnum's American Museum in New York City drew tens of millions of visitors between 1841 and 1868, making Barnum the era's second wealthiest American.

"I am indebted to the press . . . for almost every dollar that I possess," Barnum declared. Barnum first gained widespread publicity in 1835 with his traveling exhibition of Joice Heth, whom he claimed was the 161-year-old former slave of George Washington. When interest petered out, Barnum planted a rumor that she was a fake, a machine made of leather and bones. The penny press reveled in the ensuing controversy, swelling admissions and earning Barnum enough to purchase the American Museum, whose "500,000 natural and artificial curiosities" he promoted through similar stunts. The "Feejee [Fiji] Mermaid," for example, caused a national stir, as scientists debated its authenticity. (It was a monkey's head sewn to a fish's body.) Barnum hosted promotional events, too, including the nation's first beauty pageant in 1854. Offensive to middle-class sensibilities, it flopped, but Barnum persevered with pageants featuring dogs, babies, and chickens. The baby show alone attracted 61,000 visitors. As Barnum wrote, "Without promotion, something terrible happens . . . Nothing!" Selling more than a million copies, Barnum's autobiography inspired generations of entrepreneurs.

Many of today's cultural icons began as promotional gimmicks, including the Miss America Pageant (1921), the Macy's Thanksgiving Day parade (1924), and the Goodyear blimp (1925). Since 1916, Nathan's has hosted an annual Fourth of July hotdog eating contest, now attracting forty thousand live spectators and a national television audience; the event also includes acts from the circus that still bears Barnum's name. Nathan's rival, Oscar Meyer, launched its weinermobile in 1936; seven hot-dog-shaped cars now tour the country, with drivers selected from a nationally publicized competition. The *Guinness Book of World Records*, begun as an Irish beer company's promotional brochure, inspires pizza makers to attempt the world's largest pizza; ice-cream makers, the largest sundae; and billionaires to cross oceans in hot-air balloons sporting their conglomerate's logos. Even failed attempts generate publicity.

By staging stunts designed to garner free media exposure, today's entrepreneurs reveal the enduring legacy of P. T. Barnum, the self-proclaimed greatest showman on earth.

The Somers Historical Society

▲ P. T. Barnum's first great success came in 1835 when he charged admission to see Joice Heth, whom he claimed was the 161-year-old former slave of George Washington.

SUMMARY

During the first half of the nineteenth century, the North became rapidly enmeshed in a commercial culture. Northern states and capitalists invested heavily in internal improvements, helping to propel the North down a new development track. Most northerners now turned either toward commercial farming or, in smaller numbers, toward industrial wage labor. Farmers gave up mixed agriculture and specialized in cash crops, while their children often went to work in factories or countinghouses.

To many northerners, the market economy symbolized progress, in which they found much to celebrate: easier access to cheap western lands, employment for surplus farm laborers, and the ready commercial availability of goods that had once been time-consuming to produce. At the same time, though, the market economy led to increased specialization, a less personal workplace, complex market relationships, more regimentation, a sharper divide between work and leisure, and a degradation of natural resources. Northerners' involvement in the market economy also tied them more directly to fluctuating national and international markets, and during economic downturns, many northern families experienced destitution.

With parents relying less directly on children's labor, northerners began producing smaller families. Even as working-class children continued to work as canal drivers and factory hands (or to scavenge urban streets), middle-class families created a sheltered model of childhood in which they tried to shield children from the perceived dangers of the world outside the family. Their mothers, in theory, became moral guardians of the household, keeping the home safe from the encroachment of the new economy's competitiveness and selfishness. Few women, though, had the luxury to devote themselves entirely to nurturing their children and husbands.

Immigrants and free African Americans performed much of the lowest-paying work in the expanding economy, and many native-born whites blamed them for the problems that accompanied the era's rapid economic changes. Anti-immigrant (especially anti-Catholic) and antiblack riots became commonplace. At the same time, immigrants and African Americans worked to form their own communities.

Cities came to symbolize for many Americans both the possibilities and the limits of market expansion. Urban areas were marked by extremes of wealth, and they fostered vibrant working-class cultures even as they encouraged poverty, crime, and mob violence. To reconcile the seeming contradictions of progress—the coexistence, for example, of abundance and destitution—middle-class northerners articulated an ideology of free labor, touting the possibility for upward mobility in a competitive marketplace. This ideology would become increasingly central to northern regional identity.

SUGGESTIONS FOR FURTHER READING

Hal Barron, *Those Who Stayed Behind: Rural Society in Nineteenth-Century New England* (1984)

Jeanne Boydston, *Home and Work: Housework, Wages, and the Ideology of Labor in the Early Republic* (1990)

Nancy Cott, *The Bonds of Womanhood: "Women's Sphere" in New England, 1780–1835* (1977)

Daniel Walker Howe, *What Hath God Wrought: The Transformation of America, 1815–1848* (2007)

Bruce Laurie, *Artisans into Workers: Labor in Nineteenth-Century America* (1989)

Mary Ryan, *Cradle of the Middle Class: The Family in Oneida County, New York, 1790–1865* (1981)

Carol Sheriff, *The Artificial River: The Erie Canal and the Paradox of Progress, 1817–1862* (1996)

Christine Stansell, *City of Women: Sex and Class in New York, 1789–1860* (1986)

Melvyn Stokes and Stephen Conway, eds., *The Market Revolution in America: Social, Political, and Religious Expressions, 1800–1880* (1996)

George Rogers Taylor, *The Transportation Revolution, 1815–1860* (1951)

CourseMate

Go to the CourseMate website for primary source links, study tools, and review materials for this chapter. www.cengagebrain.com

Chapter 12

Reform and Politics
1824–1845

University of Delaware Library, Newark, Delaware (Detail)

The twenty-eight-year-old mill hand steadied himself atop a cliff in Paterson, New Jersey; peered down the seventy-foot precipice to the river below; and then leapt feet first, bending his knees to his chest before entering the water straight as an arrow, with legs extended and arms clasped to his sides. He resurfaced to cheers for his death-defying stunt—and what it symbolized. It was September 1827, and Sam Patch—a textile spinner who had worked in mills since he was seven or eight years old—wanted to make a point.

Jumping from waterfalls had long been a pastime among boys who labored in the nation's earliest textile mills; Sam Patch had made his own first leaps as a youth in Pawtucket, Rhode Island. But to Patch, jumping was more than a pastime: he considered it an "art" imbued with political meaning. He timed his Paterson leap to steal the show from Timothy B. Crane, an entrepreneur who had dreamed up Forest Garden, a pleasure park designed to provide "respectable" ladies and gentlemen a respite from the mill town. To get to the park, which had formerly been open to everyone, they would need to cross a toll bridge. The toll would raise revenue to sustain the park, but, more important, it would keep out those Paterson residents who could not afford it. To Crane, that meant keeping out the riffraff.

Patch and the mill hands understood that the riffraff meant *them*, and they saw in Forest Garden all that was wrong with the modernizing North. Forest Garden symbolized a world in which manual labor was devalued, in which artisans were turning into workers, in which industrialists and entrepreneurs increasingly held themselves to be morally superior to those who drew wages. In previous months, town residents had attacked (physically and verbally) the park, its workers, its buildings, and Timothy Crane himself. Then, when Crane planned elaborate celebrations to mark the completion of his toll bridge, Sam Patch decided to use the occasion to assert the pride of those workers who made the industrial revolution possible in the first place.

◄ Sam Patch and his daring exploits captured Americans' imaginations into the late nineteenth century.

Chronology

1790s–1840s	Second Great Awakening
1820s	Model penitentiaries established
1820s–40s	Utopian communities founded
1824	No electoral-college majority in presidential election
1825	House of Representatives elects Adams president
1826	American Society for the Promotion of Temperance founded
1828	Tariff of Abominations passed
	Jackson elected president
1830	Joseph Smith organizes Mormon Church
1830s–40s	Democratic-Whig competition gels in second party system
1831	Garrison first publishes *The Liberator*
	Antimasons hold first national political convention
1832	Jackson vetoes rechartering Second Bank of the United States
	Jackson reelected president
1832–33	Nullification Crisis
1836	Specie Circular
	Van Buren elected president
1837	*Caroline* affair
	Financial panic ends boom of the 1830s
1837–42	Croton Aqueduct constructed
1838–39	United States and Canada mobilize militias over border dispute
1839–43	Hard times spread unemployment and deflation
1840	Whigs win presidency under Harrison
1841	Tyler assumes presidency after Harrison's death
1846	Smithsonian Institution founded
1848	Seneca Falls Woman's Rights Convention
	American Association for the Advancement of Science established

In the two years following his Paterson leap—and before making his last, and fatal, jump at the 125-foot Genesee Falls in Rochester, New York—Sam Patch would become a professional waterfall jumper, taking on falls in some of the North's most rapidly industrializing areas. Even as some observers dismissed his leaps as mere drunken stunts, he costumed himself in the symbolic clothing of the textile spinner and associated socially and politically with a raucous crowd of skilled operatives. (As a boss spinner, Patch's job was highly skilled.) Along with his leaps, Patch's flaunting of respectable, middle-class values caught the attention of the political press. Members of the era's two main political parties—the Whigs and the Jacksonian Democrats—saw Patch through very different lenses. To Whigs, Patch exemplified what was, in one editor's words, "wrong with democracy," whereas Jacksonians hailed Patch as a heroic artisan. Patch captured the fancy of none other than President Andrew Jackson himself. When in 1833 the city of Philadelphia presented Jackson with a horse, the president named him Sam Patch. The horse became the president's favorite and would ultimately be buried with full military honors.

*M*any Americans joined Sam Patch in trying to reaffirm control over their lives in an era of rapid economic and social changes. The market economy, growing wealth and inequality, immigration, the westward thrust of settlement and slavery, and territorial expansion all contributed simultaneously to Americans' hopes and fears. Many Americans embraced progress even as they hoped to limit what they saw as its unpleasant side effects. These same Americans, though, often divided sharply among themselves over what defined progress, what constituted a social ill, and how those ills should be remedied.

Anxious about their personal status in a rapidly changing world, many Americans turned to evangelical religion, which in turn launched many of the era's myriad reform movements, most of them centered in the North. Believing in the notion of human perfectibility, reformers worked to free individuals and society from sin. In the Northeast and Midwest in particular, women and men organized to end the abuses of prostitution and alcohol, to improve conditions in prisons and asylums, and to establish public schools. Some embraced science as fervently as religion. Other reformers, instead of trying to fix society, established separate experimental communities that might model a new form of social relations. Opponents of slavery and proponents of women's rights, meanwhile, worked within the existing system but sought to radically alter Americans' premises about the practical implications of the revolutionary declaration that "all men are created equal."

Evangelical reformers generally aligned themselves with the Whig Party, but the Jacksonian Democrats, too, were concerned with what they saw as social problems, mostly class inequities. They grew suspicious of middle-class reformers who told working-class men and women how to live their lives, and they opposed special privileges bestowed by government policies and institutions, such as the Second Bank of the United States. Yet when it came to the era's most pressing issue—slavery—the national parties often remained silent, hoping to keep sectional conflict submerged.

The new system of political rivalry that emerged between the Democrats and Whigs did lay out distinct positions, however, on most other salient issues. Democrats emphasized that the best government is that which governs least, whereas the Whigs championed a strong federal government to promote economic development and maintain social order. Democrats saw the nation's agricultural expansion to the west as an urgent need, whereas Whigs actively promoted the nation's industrial and commercial growth in the East. They hoped to bring about that growth through their American System of high protective tariffs, centralized banking, and federal funding for internal improvements. Together, Democrats and Whigs constituted what is often called the second party system, characterized by strong organizations, intense loyalty, and religious and ethnic voting patterns.

- **What were the "evils" in society that reformers hoped to eliminate, and what motivated them to do so?**

- **What was the relationship between reform and politics?**

- **What were the main issues dividing Democrats and Whigs?**

From Revival to Reform

A series of religious revivals in the late eighteenth and early nineteenth centuries—sometimes called the Second Great Awakening for their resemblance to revivals of the Great Awakening of the eighteenth century—raised people's hopes for the Second Coming of the Christian messiah and the establishment of the Kingdom of God on earth. Revivalists resolved to speed the millennium, or the thousand years of peace on earth that would accompany Christ's Second Coming, by combating sin. Some believed the United States had a special mission in God's design and a special role in eliminating evil. If sin and evil could be eliminated, individuals and society could be perfected. Revivalists called on individuals to renounce personal sins, such as drinking, swearing, and licentiousness. They also called on individuals to combat social evils, including—most prominently—slavery, but also dueling and desecration of the Sabbath. Not until all Americans had been converted, and all social evils suppressed, would Christ make his Second Coming.

Because it was not enough for an individual to embrace God and godliness, revivalists strove for large-scale conversions. Rural women, men, and children traveled long distances to camp meetings, where they listened to fiery sermons preached day and night from hastily constructed platforms and tents in forests or open fields. In cities, women in particular attended daily church services and prayer meetings, sometimes for months on end. Converts renounced personal sin, vowed to live sanctified lives, and committed themselves to helping others see the light.

The most famous revival was at Cane Ridge, Kentucky, in August 1801. One report estimated 25,000 people attended, including men and women, free and enslaved, at a time when Kentucky's largest city, Lexington, had fewer than two thousand inhabitants. The call to personal repentance and conversion invigorated southern Protestantism, giving churches an evangelical base. Although laws often restricted or outlawed black churches and preachers, particularly after Nat Turner's bloody revolt in 1831, in practice black and mixed churches often flourished on the local level, with black and white evangelicals forging a united front against their profane neighbors. During the 1840s and 1850s, though, as the slavery issue increasingly entered public debate, southern Presbyterian, Baptist, and Methodist churches seceded from their denominations' national conferences. For the white leaders of these secessionist churches, slavery did not impede human perfectibility but rather ensured it; the paternal guidance of benevolent masters, they reasoned, would bring Africans to Christ.

Revivals

All revivalists shared a belief in individual self-improvement, but northern revivalists also emphasized communal improvement, becoming missionaries for

◄ Often attracting worshippers in the thousands, revivalist meetings became known as "camp meetings" because the faithful camped out for days at a time to hear charismatic preachers, who offered sermons day and night.

Old Sturbridge Village

both individual salvation and social reform. Northern evangelists generated new religious groups and voluntary reform societies. Preachers like Lyman Beecher, who made his base in New England before moving to Cincinnati, and Charles Finney, who traveled the canals and roads linking the Northeast to the Midwest, argued that evil was avoidable, that Christians were not doomed by original sin, and that anyone could achieve salvation. In everyday language, Finney—a former lawyer— preached that "God has made man a moral free agent." Finney's brand of revivalism transcended sects, class, and race. At first a Presbyterian, he eventually became a Methodist. Revivalism thrived among Methodists and Baptists, whose denominational structures maximized democratic participation and drew ministers from ordinary folk.

Finney achieved his greatest successes in the area of western New York that had experienced rapid changes in transportation and industrialization—in what he called the "Burned-Over District" because of the region's intense evangelical fires. Rapid change raised fears of social disorder—family dissolution, drinking, swearing, and prostitution. Many individuals worried, too, whether their status would improve or decline in an economy cycling through booms and busts.

When northern revivalist preachers emphasized the importance of good works—good deeds and piety—they helped ignite many of the era's social reform movements, which began in the Burned-Over District and spread eastward to New England and the Middle Atlantic and westward to the upper Midwest. Evangelically inspired reform associations together constituted what historians call the "benevolent empire." While advocating for distinct causes, these associations shared a commitment to human perfectibility, and they often turned to the same wealthy men for financial resources and advice.

Those resources enabled them to make good use of the era's new technologies—steam presses and railroads—to spread the evangelical word. By mass-producing pamphlets and newspapers for distribution far into the country's interior, reformers spread their message throughout the Northeast and Midwest, strengthening cultural connections between regions increasingly tied together economically. With canals and railroads making travel easier, reformers could attend annual conventions and contact like-minded people personally, and local reform societies could host speakers from distant places. Most reform organizations, like political parties, sponsored weekly newspapers, creating a virtual community of reformers.

Moral Reform

While industrialists and merchants provided financial resources for evangelical reform, their wives and daughters solicited new members and circulated petitions. The cult of domesticity, which arose in tandem with industrialization and the revivals, assigned women the role of moral guardianship of their families; reformers expanded that role beyond the domestic sphere into the public realm. Women undertook to do more than provide moral guidance to their own children; they would help run reformatories for wayward youth or establish asylums for orphans. Participation in reform movements thus allowed women to exercise moral authority outside the household, giving them a new sense of influence. They might both improve people's lives and hasten the millennium. Women also enjoyed the friendships and intellectual comraderie with other women that participation in benevolent societies fostered. Although some elite women in Upper South cities formed and joined reform societies, moral reform was primarily a northeastern and midwestern phenomenon.

Many female reformers had attended a female academy or seminary, where the curriculum included arts of "refinement"—music, dance, penmanship—but focused on science and literature. Based on the notion that women were men's intellectual equals, the curriculum was modeled on that of men's colleges, and by 1820, approximately the same number of men and women attended institutions of higher education. At the female academies and seminaries, and at the hundreds of reading circles and literary societies in which their alumnae participated, women honed their intellectual and persuasive skills, preparing themselves to influence public opinion even as many of them maintained substantial domestic responsibilities. A few of these women became prominent editors and writers, but most influenced society as educators and, especially, reformers.

For women and some men, reform represented their primary form of political influence at a time when the vote was restricted to property-owning men. The aftermath of an 1830 exposé of prostitution in New York City illustrates how reform led to political action. Even as female reformers organized a shelter for the city's prostitutes and tried to secure respectable employment for them, they publicized the names of brothel clients to shame the men contributing to the women's waywardness. The New York women organized themselves into the Female Moral Reform Society, expanding their geographic scope and activities. By 1840, it had 555 affiliated chapters across the nation. In the next few years, it entered the political sphere by lobbying successfully for criminal sanctions in New York State against men who seduced women into prostitution. If only prostitutes could be freed from the corrupting reach of the men who preyed on them, reformers believed, so-called fallen women might be morally uplifted.

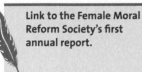

Link to the Female Moral Reform Society's first annual report.

A similar belief in perfectibility led reformers to establish penitentiaries for criminals and delinquents that aimed not simply to punish, as jails did, but to transform criminals into productive members of society through disciplined regimens. Under the "Auburn System," prisoners worked together in the daytime but were isolated at night, while under the "Philadelphia System," utter silence and isolation prevailed day and night. Isolation and silence were meant to enable reflection and redemption—to provide opportunities for penitence—within individual prisoners. When Frenchman Alexis de Tocqueville came to America in 1831 to study its prisons, he noted that the Philadelphia system made him feel as if he "had traversed catacombs; there were a thousand living beings, and yet it was desert solitude."

Penitentiaries and Asylums

Other reformers sought to improve treatment of the mentally ill, who were frequently imprisoned, often alongside criminals, and put in cages or dark dungeons, chained to walls, brutalized, or held in solitary confinement. Dorothea Dix, the movement's leader, exemplifies the early-nineteenth-century reformer who started with a religious belief in individual self-improvement and human perfectibility, and moved into social action by advocating collective responsibility. Investigating asylums, petitioning the Massachusetts legislature, and lobbying other states and Congress, Dix moved from reform to politics and helped create a new public role for women. In response to Dix's efforts, twenty-eight of thirty-three states built public institutions for the mentally ill by 1860.

Temperance advocates, who pushed for either partial or full abstinence from alcoholic beverages, likewise crossed from the personal into the political sphere. Drinking was widespread in the early nineteenth century, when men like Sam Patch gathered in public houses and rural inns to drink whiskey, rum, and hard cider while they gossiped, talked politics, and played cards. Contracts were sealed, celebrations commemorated, and harvests toasted with liquor. "Respectable" women did not drink in public, but many tippled alcohol-based patent medicines promoted as cure-alls.

Temperance

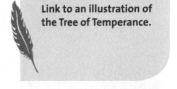

Link to an illustration of the Tree of Temperance.

Evangelicals considered drinking sinful, and in many denominations, forsaking alcohol was part of conversion. Preachers condemned alcohol for violating the Sabbath—the only day workers had off, which some spent at the public house. Factory owners condemned alcohol for making workers unreliable. Civic leaders connected alcohol with crime. Middle-class reformers, often women, condemned it for squandering wages, diverting men from their family responsibilities, and fostering abusive behavior at home. In the early 1840s, thousands of ordinary women formed Martha Washington societies to protect families by reforming alcoholics, raising children as teetotalers, and spreading the temperance message. Abstinence from alcohol, reformers believed, would foster both religious perfectibility and secular progress. They hoped to quash the raucous drinking culture of the likes of Sam Patch.

As the temperance movement gained momentum, its goal shifted from moderation to voluntary abstinence and finally to prohibition. By the mid-1830s, five thousand state and local temperance societies touted teetotalism, and more than a million people had taken the pledge of abstinence, including several hundred thousand children who enlisted in the Cold Water Army. Per capita consumption of alcohol fell from five gallons per year in 1800 to below two gallons in the 1840s. The American Society for the Promotion of Temperance, organized in 1826 to promote pledges of abstinence, became a pressure group for legislation to end alcohol manufacture and sale. In 1851, Maine became the first state to ban alcohol

Visualizing THE PAST

Engaging Children

Hundreds of thousands of children joined the temperance movement, often by enlisting in the so-called Cold Water Army. Like adult temperance societies, the Cold Water Army advocated for complete abstinence from alcoholic beverages. On holidays such as George Washington's birthday and the Fourth of July, they marched at public gatherings, singing temperance songs and carrying banners and fans such as the one pictured to the right. Reverend Thomas P. Hunt, a Presbyterian minister, founded the Cold Water Army because he believed that by recruiting children, he stood a much greater chance of eradicating alcohol consumption than if he aimed his temperance efforts directly at adults. What might have been his logic? Why might children have wanted to join a Cold Water Army? Do the images on the certificate and fan offer any clues? What were the benefits of participating in the movement? What were the implied consequences of failing to do so? Why might Hunt have chosen the term "army," and what about that choice might have proved appealing to his young recruits?

Collection of the New York Historical Society

Children who participated in a Cold Water Army often received a certificate that acknowledged their commitment to the cause while reiterating the pledge they had taken.

Museum of American Political Life

Children in Cold Water Army parades sometimes carried decorative fans, which they may have displayed in their homes as well, as reminders to themselves and their parents of temperance's virtues.

except for medicinal purposes; by 1855, similar laws had been enacted throughout New England and in New York, Pennsylvania, and the Midwest.

The temperance campaign had a nativist—or anti-immigrant and anti-Catholic—strain to it. The Irish and Germans, complained the *American Protestant Magazine* in 1849, "bring the grog shops like the frogs of Egypt upon us." Along the nation's canals, reformers lamented the hundreds of taverns catering to the largely Irish work force, and in the cities, they expressed outrage at the Sunday tradition of urban German families' gathering at beer gardens to eat and drink, to dance and sing, and sometimes to play cards. Some Catholics heeded the message, pledging abstinence and forming their own organizations, such as the St. Mary's Mutual Benevolence Total Abstinence Society in Boston.

But temperance spawned strong opposition, too. Many workers—Protestants as well as Catholics—rejected what they saw as reformers' efforts to impose middle-class values on people whose lives they did not understand, and they steadfastly defended their right to drink whatever they pleased. Workers agreed that poverty and crime were problems but believed that poor wages, not drinking habits, were responsible. Even some who abstained from alcohol opposed prohibition, believing that drinking should be a matter of self-control, not state coercion.

Protestants and Catholics often quarreled over education as well. Public education usually included religious education, but when teachers taught Protestant beliefs and used the King James version of the Bible, Catholics established their own schools, which taught Catholic doctrines. Some Protestants began to fear that Catholics would never assimilate into American culture, and some charged Catholics with being exclusionists, plotting to undermine the republic and impose papal control. Yet even as these conflicts brewed, public education touched the lives of more Americans than did any other reform movement.

Public Schools

The movement's leader was Horace Mann, a Massachusetts lawyer and reformer from humble beginnings. Mann advocated free, tax-supported education to replace church schools and the private schools set up by untrained, itinerant young men. Universal education, Mann proposed, would end misery and crime, and would help Americanize immigrants. "If we do not prepare children to become good citizens," he argued, "if we do not develop their capacities, imbue their hearts with the love of truth and duty, and a reverence for all things sacred and holy, then our republic must go down to destruction."

During Mann's tenure as secretary of the Massachusetts Board of Education from 1837 to 1848, Massachusetts led the "common school" movement, establishing schools for training teachers (the "normal school," modeled on the French *école normale*, and the forerunner of teacher-training colleges); lengthening the school year; and raising teachers' salaries to make the profession more attractive. In keeping with the era's notions that women had special claims to morality and that they could be paid less because they were by nature dependents, Mann envisioned a system in which women would prepare future clerks, farmers, and workers with a practical curriculum that deemphasized classics in favor of geography, arithmetic, and science. Like other reform movements, educational reform rested on the notions of progress and perfectibility; given the proper guidance, individuals could educate themselves out of their material and moral circumstances.

Thanks in part to expanding public education, by 1850 the vast majority of native-born white Americans were literate. Newspapers and magazines proliferated, and bookstores spread. Power printing presses and better transportation made possible wide distribution of books and periodicals. The religious press—of both traditional sects and revivalists—produced pamphlets, hymnals, Bibles, and religious newspapers. Secular newspapers and magazines—political organs, the penny press, and literary journals—also abounded from the 1830s on.

Public education's emphasis on science reflected a broader tendency to look not just to moral reform but also

Engineering and Science

to engineering and science to remedy the nation's problems. Not everyone blamed epidemics on immorality, for example; scientists and doctors saw unclean, stagnant water as the culprit. With its Fairmount Water Works, constructed between 1819 and 1822, Philadelphia took the lead in building municipal waterworks. After the devastating cholera epidemic of 1832, New York City planned its own massive waterworks: Between 1837 and 1842, it built the 41-mile Croton Aqueduct, an elaborate system of iron pipes encased in brick masonry that brought water from upstate New York to Manhattan.

Science became increasingly important nationally, too, with the founding of institutions that still exist today. After James Smithson, a wealthy British scientist, left his estate to the United States government, Congress established the Smithsonian Institution (1846), which acquired and disseminated scientific knowledge. The Smithsonian's director was Joseph Henry, one of the nation's most talented scientists; his experiments in electromagnetism helped make possible both the telegraph and, later in the century, the telephone. In 1848, Henry helped found the American Association for the Advancement of Science to promote scientific collaboration and, thus, advancement. That Henry was a devoutly religious man did not deter him from seeking scientific knowledge. For many nineteenth-century Americans, particularly those in nonrevivalist sects, religious devotion and scientific inquiry were compatible. They saw scientific discoveries as signs of progress, reassuring them that the millennium was approaching. God had created the natural world, they believed, and it was their Christian duty to perfect it in preparation for God's return.

◄ The Croton Aqueduct, shown here near Harlem, New York, was an engineering marvel of its time. It brought fresh water to New York City.

Miriam and Ira D. Wallach Division of Art, Prints and Photographs, The New York Public Library. Astor, Lenox and Tilden Foundations

Utopian Experiments

Some idealists dreamed of an entirely new social order. They established dozens of utopian communities—ideal communities designed as models for broader society—based on either religious principles, a desire to resist what they deemed the market economy's excessive individualism, or both. Some groups, like the Mormons, arose during the Second Great Awakening, while others, like the Shakers, had originated in eighteenth-century Europe. Utopian communities attempted to recapture what they perceived as the past's more communal nature, even as they offered sometimes-radical departures from established practices of marriage and child rearing.

No utopian experiment had a more lasting influence than the Church of Jesus Christ of Latter-day Saints, whose members were known as the Mormons. During the religious ferment of the 1820s in western New York, Joseph Smith, a young farmer, reported that an angel called Moroni had given him divinely engraved gold plates. Smith published his revelations as the *Book of Mormon* and organized a church in 1830. The next year, the community moved west to Ohio to build a "New Jerusalem" and await the Second Coming of Jesus.

Mormons

After angry mobs drove the Mormons from Ohio, they settled in Missouri. Anti-Mormons charged that Mormonism was a scam by Joseph Smith, and feared Mormon economic and political power. In 1838, Missouri's governor charged Smith with fomenting insurrection and worked to indict him and other leaders for treason.

Smith and his followers left for Nauvoo, Illinois. The state legislature gave them a city charter making them self-governing and authorized a local militia. But again the Mormons met antagonism, especially after Smith introduced the practice of polygamy in 1841, allowing men to have several wives at once. The next year, Smith became mayor, and this consolidation of religious and political power, as well as Nauvoo's petition to the federal government to be a self-governing territory, further antagonized opponents, now including some former Mormons. In 1844, after Smith and his brother were charged with treason and jailed, and then murdered, the Mormons left Illinois to seek security in the western wilderness. Under the leadership of Brigham Young, they established a cooperative community in the Great Salt Lake valley.

There, the Mormons distributed agricultural land according to family size. An extensive irrigation system, constructed by men who contributed their labor in proportion to the quantity of land they received and the amount of water they expected to use, transformed the arid valley into a rich oasis. As the colony developed, the church elders gained control of water, trade, industry, and eventually the territorial government of Utah.

The Shakers, the largest communal utopian experiment, reached their peak between 1820 and 1860, with six thousand members in twenty settlements in eight states. Shaker communities emphasized agriculture and handcrafts, selling their products beyond their own community; most became self-sufficient and profitable enterprises. The community's craft tradition contrasted with the new factory regime. But the Shakers were essentially a spiritual community. Founded in England in 1772 by Mother Ann Lee, their name derived from their worship service, which included shaking their entire bodies, singing, dancing, and shouting. Ann Lee's children had died in infancy, and she saw their deaths as retribution for her sin

Shakers

of intercourse; thus, she advocated celibacy. After imprisonment in England in 1773–1774, she settled in America.

In religious practice and social relations, Shakers offered an alternative to the era's rapid changes. Shakers lived communally, with men and women in separate quarters; individual families were abolished. Men and women shared leadership equally. Many Shaker settlements became temporary refuges for orphans, widows, runaways, abused wives, and laid-off workers. Their settlements depended on new recruits, not only because the practice of celibacy meant no reproduction, but also because some members left, unsuited to either communal living or the Shakers' spiritual message.

Other utopian communities joined in resisting the social changes accompanying industrialism. John

Oneidans, Owenites, and Fourierists

Humphrey Noyes, a lawyer converted by Finney's revivals, established two perfectionist communities: first in Putney, Vermont, in 1835, and then—after being indicted for adultery—in Oneida, New York, in 1848. Noyes decried individualism, advocating instead communal property ownership, communal child rearing, and "complex marriage," in which all the community's men were married to all its women, but in which a woman could accept or reject a sexual proposition. The Oneida Colony forbade exclusive sexual relationships and required men to practice "male continence," or intercourse without ejaculation, in order to promote relationships built on more than

sexual fulfillment. Pregnancies were to be planned; couples applied to Noyes for permission to have a child, or Noyes assigned two people to reproduce with each other. Robert Dale Owen's community in New Harmony, Indiana (1825–1828), also abolished private property and advocated communal child rearing. The Fourierists, named after French philosopher Charles Fourier, established more than two dozen communities in the Northeast and Midwest; these communities, too, resisted individualism and promoted equality between the sexes.

The most famous Fourier community was Brook Farm, in West Roxbury, Massachusetts, near Boston. Inspired by transcendentalism—the belief that the physical world is secondary to the spiritual realm, which human beings can reach not by custom and experience but only by intuition—Brook Farm's members rejected materialism. Their rural communalism combined spirituality, manual labor, intellectual life, and play. Originally founded in 1841 by the Unitarian minister George Ripley, Brook Farm attracted farmers, craftsmen, and writers, among them the novelist Nathaniel Hawthorne. Brook Farm residents contributed regularly to the *Dial*, the leading Transcendentalist journal. Although Unitarians were not evangelicals, their largely middle- and upper-class followers had a long-standing "devotion to progress," as one of their most influential ministers put it. In 1845, Brook Farm's one hundred members organized themselves into phalanxes (working-living units), following a model suggested by Fourier. As rigid regimentation replaced individualism, membership

▲ This bucolic image of New Harmony, painted several years after the experiment's collapse, belies the rancorous history of the short-lived community, which attracted many settlers who proved unwilling or unable to commit themselves fully to communitarian life. Pictured here on the far left is the "Hive," which housed the kitchen, office, and meeting rooms; along the hilltop are buildings that housed residents, a laundry, and printing presses.

Joslyn Art Museum, Omaha, Nebraska, Gift of Enron Art Foundation dropped. A year after a disastrous fire in 1846, the experiment collapsed.

After visiting Brook Farm in 1843, Transcendentalist Henry David Thoreau decided that organized utopian communities did not suit him: "As for these communities, I think I had rather keep bachelor's hall in hell than go to board in heaven." Two years later, Thoreau constructed his own one-man utopia in a small cabin along the shores of Walden Pond, in Massachusetts, where he mediated and wrote about nature, morality, spirituality, progress, society, and government.

Thoreau joined a literary outpouring known today as the American Renaissance. Ralph Waldo Emerson, a pillar of the transcendental movement, was its prime inspiration. After quitting his Boston Unitarian ministry in 1831, followed by a two-year sojourn in Europe, Emerson returned to lecture and write, preaching individualism and self-reliance. Widely admired, he influenced Hawthorne, *Dial* editor Margaret Fuller, Herman Melville, and Thoreau, among many others. In philosophical intensity and moral idealism, the American Renaissance was both distinctively American and an outgrowth of the European romantic movement. It addressed universal themes using American settings and characters. Hawthorne, for instance, used Puritan New England as a backdrop, and Melville wrote of great spiritual quests as seafaring adventures.

American Renaissance

Perhaps more than any other American Renaissance author, Thoreau emphasized individualism and its practical applications. In his 1849 essay on "Resistance to Civil Government" (known after his death as "Civil Disobedience"), Thoreau advocated individual resistance to a government engaged in immoral acts. Thoreau had already put into practice what he preached: In the midst of the War with Mexico (see Chapter 14), Thoreau refused to pay his taxes, believing they would aid an immoral war to expand slavery, and was briefly jailed. "I cannot for an instant recognize that political organization as my government which is the *slave's* government also," Thoreau wrote. Later, in defiance of federal law, Thoreau aided escaped slaves on their way to freedom.

Abolitionism

Thoreau joined evangelical abolitionists in trying to eradicate slavery, which they deemed both an individual and a communal sin suffusing American society. Their efforts built on an earlier generation of antislavery activism.

From the nation's earliest days—in places like Philadelphia, New York, Albany, Boston, and Nantucket—free blacks formed societies to petition legislatures, seek judicial redress, stage public marches, and, especially, publish tracts chronicling slavery's horrors. African American abolitionists wrote about slavery's devastating impact on both black and white families, advocated slavery's immediate termination, assisted escaped slaves, and promoted legal equality for free blacks. By 1830, the nation had fifty African American abolitionist societies. But more than anything else, David Walker's words captured white Americans' attention. In his *Appeal…to the Colored Citizens* (1829), Walker—a southern-born free African American—advocated slavery's violent overthrow, igniting fear throughout the white South and much of the North.

Early Abolitionism and Colonization

Violent overthrow did not figure in the goals of white abolitionists who, after the American Revolution, had come together in places like Boston and, especially, Philadelphia, with its large population of Quakers, whose religious beliefs emphasized human equality. These early antislavery advocates pressed for slavery's gradual abolition and an end to the international slave trade. Although they aided African Americans seeking freedom through judicial decisions, their assumptions about blacks' racial inferiority kept them from advocating for equal rights. Early white abolitionists tended to be wealthy, socially prominent men whose societies excluded women, African Americans, and less elite white men.

More often, elites supported the colonization movement, which crystallized in 1816 with the organization of the American Colonization Society. Its members planned to purchase and relocate American slaves, as well as free blacks, to Africa or the Caribbean. Among its supporters were Thomas Jefferson, James Madison, James Monroe, and Henry Clay, as well as many lesser-known men and women from the North and, especially, the Upper South. In 1824, the society founded Liberia, on Africa's west coast, and began a settlement for African Americans who were willing to go. The society had resettled nearly twelve thousand people in Liberia by 1860. Some colonizationists aimed to strengthen slavery by ridding the South of troublesome slaves or to purge the North of African Americans altogether. Others hoped colonization would improve African Americans' conditions. Although some African Americans supported the movement, black abolitionists generally denounced it.

In the early 1830s, a new group of more radical white abolitionists—most prominently, William Lloyd Garrison—rejected both the violent overthrow advocated by David Walker and the gradual approaches of white legal reformers and colonizationists. Instead, they demanded immediate, complete, and uncompensated emancipation. In the first issue of *The Liberator*, which he began publishing in 1831, Garrison declared, "I am in earnest—I will not equivocate—I will not excuse—I will not retreat a single inch—and *I will be heard.*" Two years later, he founded the American Antislavery Society, which became the era's largest abolitionist organization.

Immediatists, as they came to be called, believed slavery was an absolute sin needing urgent

Immediatism

eradication. They were influenced by African American abolitionist societies and by evangelicals' notion that humans, not God, determined their own spiritual fate by deciding whether to choose good or evil. In that sense, all were equal before God's eyes. When all humans had chosen good over evil, the millennium would come. Slavery, however, denied enslaved men and women the ability to make such choices, the ability to act as what Finney called "moral free agents." For every day that slavery continued, the millennium was postponed.

Because the millennium depended on *all* hearts being won over to Christ, because it depended on the perfectibility of everyone, including slaveowners, Garrison advocated "moral suasion." He and his followers hoped to bring about emancipation not through coercion, but by winning the hearts of slaveowners as well as others who supported or tolerated slavery. Evangelical abolitionism depended, then, on large numbers of ministers and laypeople spreading the evangelical message all across the nation.

In 1829, Congregationalists and Presbyterians founded the Lane Seminary in Cincinnati to train ministers who would carry the

The Lane Debates

evangelical message westward. With Lyman Beecher as president, it drew northern and southern students, and encouraged "people of color" to apply. Not long after Theodore Weld, one of Charles Finney's most faithful converts, arrived at the Lane Seminary in 1833, he organized what became known as the Lane Debates, eighteen days of discussion among the school's students and faculty about the relative merits of colonization and immediatism. Immediatism won.

Led by Weld, the Lane students and faculty next founded an antislavery society, and expanded their efforts to reach Cincinnati's growing African American population, which in 1829 had been brutally attacked by white people. Fearful of renewed disorder, white business leaders protested against the antislavery society. Lane's trustees, with Beecher's sanction, clamped down, barring further antislavery activities.

◀ After purchasing his own freedom in 1829, Gilbert Hunt left Virginia for Liberia under the auspices of the American Colonization Society. Although Hunt admired much of what he saw in Africa, he quickly became disillusioned with colonization and returned to Richmond, where he worked as a blacksmith and became a deacon in the First African Baptist Church.

Virginia Historical Society

The "Lane Rebels" publicly broke from the seminary and enrolled in a new seminary at Oberlin, a town in northern Ohio founded as a Christian perfectionist settlement. The new seminary, dedicated to immediatism, became the first college to admit women and one of the first to admit African Americans. Weld declined a faculty post at Oberlin, preferring instead to carry the abolitionist message directly into the western countryside as an agent for the American Antislavery Society.

By 1838, at its peak, the society had two thousand local affiliates and a membership of over 300,000. Unlike earlier white abolitionist soci-

The American Antislavery Society

eties, the immediatist organizations welcomed men and women of all racial and class backgrounds. Lydia Maria Child, Maria Chapman, and Lucretia Mott served on its executive committee; Child edited its official paper, the *National Anti-Slavery Standard*, from 1841 to 1843, and Chapman coedited it from 1844 until 1848. The society sponsored black and female speakers, and women undertook most of the day-to-day conversion efforts.

In rural and small-town northern and midwestern communities, women addressed mail, collected signatures, raised money, organized boycotts of textiles made from slave-grown cotton, and increased public awareness. With the "great postal campaign," launched in 1835, the society's membership flooded the mails with antislavery tracts. Women went door to door collecting signatures on antislavery petitions; by 1838, more than 400,000 petitions, each with numerous signatures, had been sent to Congress. Abolitionist-minded women met in "sewing circles," making clothes for escaped slaves while organizing future activities, such as antislavery fairs at which they sold goods—often items they had made themselves—whose proceeds they donated to antislavery causes. These fairs increased their cause's visibility and

The International Antislavery Movement

The heart of the international antislavery movement had been in Great Britain, but in the 1830s many of Britain's local antislavery societies thought they had accomplished their mission and disbanded. Over the previous three decades, the international slave trade had greatly diminished, and in 1833 Parliament ended slavery in the British Empire. At the same time, however, abolitionism in the United States was on the rise, and now American abolitionists extended their work across the Atlantic. They revived the international movement to end slavery where it still existed—in Spanish possessions like Cuba, in independent and colonial South America, in Africa and Asia, and in the United States.

American abolitionism in the 1830s was invigorated by the militancy of black abolitionists and by the conversion of William Lloyd Garrison to immediatism. Seeking to raise money and to put international pressure on the United States to abolish slavery, African American abolitionists in the 1840s toured Britain regularly. On the lecture circuit and in published narratives, they appealed for support. Especially effective were ex-slaves, who recounted their firsthand experiences of slavery and bared their scarred bodies.

Black abolitionists spoke in small towns and villages, and in Britain's industrial centers. After fugitive slave Moses Gandy toured England, he published his autobiography, the first of dozens of slave narratives published in London. The next year, 1845, Frederick Douglass began a nineteen-month tour, giving three hundred lectures in Britain.

In 1849, black abolitionists William Wells Brown, Alexander Crummell, and J. W. C. Pennington were among the twenty American delegates at the international Paris Peace Conference. There, Brown likened war to slavery, telling the eight hundred delegates from western Europe and the United States that "it is impossible to maintain slavery without maintaining war." His scheduled brief lecture tour in Britain turned into a five-year exile because, after passage of the 1850 Fugitive Slave Law, he feared being seized and sent back to slavery if he returned to the United States. In 1854, he became free when British abolitionists purchased his freedom from his former master.

Gandy, Douglass, Brown, and dozens of other former slaves helped revive abolitionism as an international issue. They energized the British and Foreign Anti-Slavery Society, founded in 1839, and hundreds of more militant local societies. By the early 1850s, national abolitionist movements succeeded in abolishing slavery in Colombia, Argentina, Venezuela, and Peru. Although the United States continued to resist internal and international pressure, its black abolitionists were instrumental not only in reviving the worldwide antislavery movement, but also, as advocates of women's rights, international peace, temperance, and other reforms, in linking Americans to reform movements around the world.

Used with Permission of Documenting the American South, The University of North Carolina at Chapel Hill Libraries

◀ William Wells Brown's autobiography stirred abolitionists in the United States and England. In 1849, Brown was among the American delegates to the Paris Peace Conference, then spent the next five years as an exile in Britain, fearing being sent back to slavery under the 1850 Fugitive Slave Act. He returned to the United States only after British abolitionists purchased his freedom from his former master.

drew more Americans into direct contact with abolitionists and their ideas.

Even as white abolitionist societies opened membership to African Americans and sponsored speaking tours by former slaves, African Americans continued into the 1840s and 1850s their independent efforts to end slavery and to improve the status of free African Americans. Former slaves—most famously, Frederick Douglass, Henry Bibb, Harriet Tubman, and Sojourner Truth—dedicated their lives to ending slavery through their speeches, publications, and participation in a secret network known as the Underground Railroad, which spirited enslaved men, women, and children to freedom. By the thousands, less famous African Americans continued the work of the postrevolutionary generation and established their churches, founded moral reform societies, published newspapers, created schools and orphanages for African American children, and held conventions to consider tactics for improving African Americans' status within the free states.

African American Abolitionists

Although genuine friendships emerged among white and black abolitionists, many white abolitionists treated blacks as inferiors, driving some African Americans to reject white antislavery organizations and to form their own. Others lacked the patience for the supposed immediatism of William Lloyd Garrison; they did not object to moral suasion, but they sought even more immediate solutions, such as legislation, to African Americans' problems in both the South and the North. African American

Collection of J. Paul Getty Museum, Los Angeles, California

▲ Women played an activist role in reform, especially in abolitionism. A rare daguerreotype from August 1850 shows women and men, including Frederick Douglass, on the podium at an abolitionist rally in Cazenovia, New York.

abolitionists nonetheless took heart in the immediatists' success at winning converts.

But that very success gave rise to a virulent, even violent, opposition. In the South, mobs blocked the distribution of antislavery tracts. In South Carolina, officials intercepted and burned abolitionist literature; in 1835, proslavery assailants killed four abolitionists in South Carolina and Louisiana as well as forty people allegedly plotting a slave rebellion in Mississippi and Louisiana.

Opposition to Abolitionism

White northerners had their own reasons for opposing abolition: they recognized cotton's vital economic role, and they feared emancipation would prompt an enormous influx of freed slaves into their own region. Like many southerners, they questioned the institution's morality but not its practicality: They believed blacks to be inherently inferior and incapable of acquiring the attributes—virtue and diligence—required of freedom and citizenship. Some northerners, too, objected to white women's involvement in abolitionism, believing that women's proper role lay within the home.

The North experienced its own anti-abolitionist violence. In Boston, David Walker died under mysterious circumstances in 1830. Among those northerners who most despised abolitionists were "gentlemen of property and standing"—a nineteenth-century term for commercial and political elites—who often had strong economic connections to the southern cotton economy and political connections to leading southerners. Northern gentlemen incited anti-abolitionist riots. In Utica, New York, in 1835 merchants and professionals broke up the state Anti-Slavery Convention, which had welcomed blacks and women. Mob violence peaked that year, with more than fifty riots aimed at abolitionists or African Americans. In 1837, in Alton, Illinois, a mob murdered white abolitionist editor Elijah P. Lovejoy, and rioters sacked his printing office. The following year, rioters in Philadelphia hurled stones and insults at three thousand black and white women attending the Anti-Slavery Convention of American Women in the brand-new Pennsylvania Hall, a building constructed to house abolitionist meetings and an abolitionist bookstore. The following day, a mob burned the building to the ground, three days after its dedication.

Such violence made some immediatists question whether moral suasion was a realistic tactic. Men like James G. Birney, the son of a Kentucky slaveowner, embraced immediatism but believed abolition could be effected only in the male sphere of politics. Involving women violated the natural order of things and detracted from the ultimate goal: freedom for slaves. Thus, with William Lloyd Garrison, an ardent supporter of wom

Moral Suasion Versus Political Action

rights, endorsed Abby Kelly's appointment to the American Antislavery Society's business committee, in 1840, he provoked an irreparable split in the abolitionist movement. Arthur Tappan and Theodore Weld led a dissident group that established the American and Foreign Anti-Slavery Society. That society in turn formed a new political party: the Liberty Party, which nominated Birney for president in 1840 and 1844.

Although committed to immediate abolitionism, the Liberty Party doubted the federal government's authority to abolish slavery where it already existed. States, not the federal government, had the jurisdiction to determine slavery's legality within their bounds. Where the federal government could act was in the western territories, and the party demanded that all new territories prohibit slavery. Some prominent black abolitionists, including Frederick Douglass, endorsed the party, whose leaders emphasized, too, the need to combat northern prejudice.

Women's Rights

Some female abolitionists, frustrated by their treatment, took the lead in advocating women's rights. At the first World Anti-Slavery Convention in London in 1840, abolitionists Lucretia Mott and Elizabeth Cady Stanton first met, united in their dismay that female abolitionists were denied seats in the convention's main hall; eight years later, the two would help organize the first American women's rights convention. Angelina and Sarah Grimké came from a slaveholding family but moved north and became active abolitionists. After critics attacked them for speaking to audiences that included men, they rejected claims that women should not lecture, but rather obey men, and they became vocal advocates for women's legal and social equality.

For many lesser-known women, too, their political consciousness developed from abolitionist activities, particularly petitioning campaigns. In the 1830s, women's petitions to Congress employed humbling language, with petitioners "praying" their political leaders to consider their grievances about slavery. After Congress voted to automatically table antislavery petitions in 1836, women defended their right to have their petitions considered. Women began employing more demanding language in their petitions, which now offered specific legislative advice. Female petitioners increasingly saw themselves as citizens and less as political subjects.

Religious revivalism and reform movements also led women to reexamine their positions in society. Revivals helped women to see themselves as inherently equal to men, and reform movements brought middle-class women outside the home and into the public sphere. Female reformers' lobbying helped to effect legal change, making some think the next step was obvious: full citizenship rights for women.

A great many legal obstacles had to be overcome. After independence, American states carried over traditional English marriage law, giving husbands absolute control over the family. Men owned their wives' personal property, were their children's legal guardians, and owned whatever family members produced or earned. A father could legally oppose his daughter's choice of husband, though by 1800 most American women chose their own marriage partner.

Legal Rights

Married women made modest gains in property and spousal rights from the 1830s on. Arkansas in 1835 passed the first married women's property law, and by 1860 sixteen more states had followed with laws allowing women—single, married, or divorced—to own and convey property. When a wife inherited property, it was hers, not her husband's, though money earned or acquired in some other way continued to belong to her husband. Women could also write wills. Such laws were particularly popular among wealthy Americans, South and North, hoping to protect their family fortunes during periods of economic boom and bust; property in a woman's name was safe from her husband's creditors. In the 1830s, states also liberalized divorce laws, adding cruelty and desertion as grounds for divorce, but divorce remained rare.

A few radical reformers still argued that marriage constituted a form of bondage. Among the most outspoken was Lucy Stone, who finally consented to marry fellow abolitionist Henry Blackwell, but only under the condition that she not take a vow of obedience and that she keep her own surname. The term "Lucy Stoner" entered common parlance as a reference to married women who did not adopt their husband's name.

By the time Lucy Stone and Harry Blackwell married in 1855, both were active in the organized movement to secure women's political rights. That movement had been launched in July 1848, when Elizabeth Cady Stanton,

Political Rights

Lucretia Mott, Mary Ann McClintock, Martha Wright, and Jane Hunt—all abolitionists and all, except Stanton, Quakers—organized the first Woman's Rights Convention at Seneca Falls, New York. Those at Seneca Falls were not the first women's rights activists: Radical reformers, such as Fanny Wright, had trumpeted the cause for decades, and two years earlier, in 1846, six rural New York women demanded—unsuccessfully but with little public outcry—their state's new constitution return to "true democratic principles" by guaranteeing women equal political and civil rights. But the Seneca Falls convention addressed national, not just state, citizenship, and it drew more attention—and rancor.

At Seneca Falls, three hundred women and men demanded women's social and economic equality, and

some advocated political equality, too. They protested women's legal disabilities and their social restrictions, such as exclusion from many occupations. Their Declaration of Sentiments, modeled on the Declaration of Independence, broadcast the injustices suffered by women and launched the women's rights movement. "All men and women are created equal," the declaration proclaimed. The similar premises of abolitionism and women's rights led many reformers, including former slaves like Sojourner Truth, to work simultaneously for both movements in the 1850s. Even among those supporting the movement's general aims, though, the question of female suffrage became divisive. William Lloyd Garrison and Frederick Douglass supported women's right to vote, but most men actively opposed it. At Seneca Falls, the resolution on woman suffrage passed only after Douglass passionately endorsed it, but some participants still refused to sign. In 1851, Elizabeth Cady Stanton joined with Susan B. Anthony, a temperance advocate, to become the most vocal and persistent activists for woman suffrage. They won relatively few converts and many critics.

Jacksonianism and Party Politics

No less than reformers, politicians sought to control the direction of change in the expanding nation. They reframed their political visions to appeal to an increasingly broad-based electorate. Hotly contested elections helped make politics the great nineteenth-century American pastime, drawing the interest and participation of voters and nonvoters alike. But intense interest also fueled bitter, even deadly, rivalries.

Property restrictions for voters, which states began abandoning during the 1810s, remained in only seven of

Expanding Political Participation

twenty-six states by 1840. Some states even allowed foreign nationals who had officially declared their intention of becoming American citizens to vote. The net effect was a sharply higher number of votes cast in presidential elections. Between 1824 and 1828, that number increased threefold, from 360,000 to over 1.1 million. In 1840, 2.4 million men cast votes. The proportion of eligible voters who cast ballots also grew, from about 27 percent in 1824 to more than 80 percent in 1840.

At the same time, the method of choosing presidential electors became more democratic. Previously, a caucus of party leaders had done so in most states, but by 1824 eighteen out of twenty-four states chose electors by popular vote, compared to just five of sixteen in 1800. As a result, politicians augmented their direct appeals to voters, and the election of 1824 saw the end of the congressional caucus, when House and Senate members

of the same political party came together to select their candidate.

As a result, five candidates, all of whom identified as Democratic-Republicans, came forward to run for presi-

Election of 1824

dent in 1824. The poorly attended Republican caucus chose William H. Crawford of Georgia, secretary of the treasury, as its presidential candidate. But other Democratic-Republicans boycotted the caucus as undemocratic, ending Congress's role in nominating presidential candidates. Instead, state legislatures nominated candidates, offering the expanded electorate a slate of sectional candidates. John Quincy Adams drew support from New England, while westerners backed House Speaker Henry Clay of Kentucky. Some southerners at first supported Secretary of War John C. Calhoun, who later dropped his bid for the presidency and ran for the vice presidency instead. The Tennessee legislature nominated Andrew Jackson, a military hero with unknown political views.

Among the four candidates remaining in the race until the election, Jackson led in both electoral and popular votes, but no candidate received an electoral college majority. Adams finished second; Crawford and Clay trailed far behind. Under the Constitution, the House of Representatives, voting by state delegation, one vote to a state, would select the next president from among the three leaders in electoral votes. Clay, with the fewest votes, was dropped, and the three others courted his support, hoping he would influence his electors to vote for them. Crawford, disabled from a stroke suffered before the election, never received serious consideration. Clay backed Adams, who won with thirteen of the twenty-four state delegations and thus became president (see Map 12.1). Adams named Clay to the cabinet position of secretary of state, the traditional steppingstone to the presidency.

Angry Jacksonians denounced the election's outcome as a "corrupt bargain," claiming Adams had stolen the election from their candidate by offering Clay a cabinet position in exchange for his votes. Jackson's bitterness fueled his later emphasis on the people's will. The Republican Party split. The Adams wing emerged as the National Republicans, and the Jacksonians became the Democrats; they immediately began planning for 1828.

As president, Adams proposed a strong nationalist policy incorporating Henry Clay's American System, a program of protective tariffs, a national bank, and internal improvements. Adams believed the federal government's active role should extend to education, science, and the arts, and he proposed a national university in Washington, D.C. Brilliant as a diplomat and secretary of state, Adams fared less well as chief executive. He underestimated the lingering effects of the Panic of 1819 and the resulting staunch opposition to a national bank and a protective tariff.

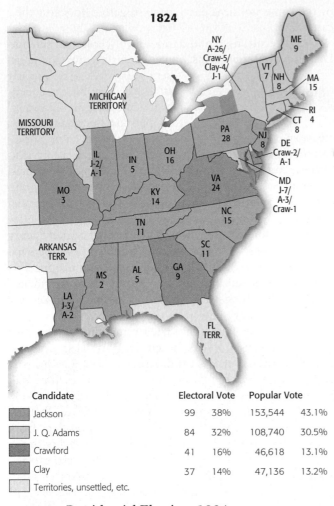

Map 12.1 Presidential Election, 1824

Andrew Jackson led in both electoral and popular votes but failed to win a majority of electoral college votes. The House elected John Quincy Adams president.

Source: Copyright © Cengage Learning

▲ Presidential candidate Andrew Jackson is portrayed on a trinket or sewing box in 1824. This is an example both of how campaigns entered popular culture and of the active role of women, excluded from voting, in politics.

Both voters and nonvoters displayed enthusiasm for Jackson with badges, medals, and other campaign paraphernalia, mass-produced for the first time. In an intensely personal contest, Jackson's supporters accused Adams of stealing the 1824 election and, when he was envoy to Russia, of having secured prostitutes for the czar. Anti-Jacksonians countered with reports that Jackson's wife, Rachel, had married Jackson before her divorce from her first husband was final, making her an adulterer and a bigamist. In 1806 Jackson, attempting to defend Rachel's integrity, had killed a man during a duel, and the cry of "murderer!" was revived in the election.

Although Adams kept the states he had won in 1824, his opposition now unified behind a single candidate, and Jackson swamped him, polling 56 percent of the popular vote and winning in the electoral college by 178 to 83 votes (Map 12.2). Jacksonians believed the people's will had finally prevailed. Through a lavishly financed coalition of state parties, political leaders, and newspaper editors, a popular movement had elected the president. The Democratic Party became the nation's first well-organized national party, and tight party organization became the hallmark of nineteenth-century American politics.

The Democrats represented a wide range of views but shared a fundamental commitment to the Jeffersonian

Election of 1828

The 1828 election pitted Adams against Jackson in a rowdy campaign. Nicknamed "Old Hickory" after the toughest of American hardwood, Andrew Jackson was a rough-and-tumble, ambitious man. Born in South Carolina in 1767, he rose from humble beginnings to become a wealthy Tennessee planter and slaveholder. After leading the Tennessee militia campaign to remove Creeks from the Alabama and Georgia frontier, Jackson burst onto the national scene in 1815 as the hero of the Battle of New Orleans; in 1818, he enhanced his glory in an expedition against Seminoles in Spanish Florida. Jackson served as a congressman and senator from Tennessee and as the first territorial governor of Florida (1821), before running for president in 1824.

Democrats

concept of an agrarian society. They viewed a strong central government as antithetical to individual liberty, and they condemned government intervention in the economy as favoring the rich at the expense of the artisan and the ordinary farmer. When it came to westward expansion, though, Jacksonians called for federal intervention, with Jackson

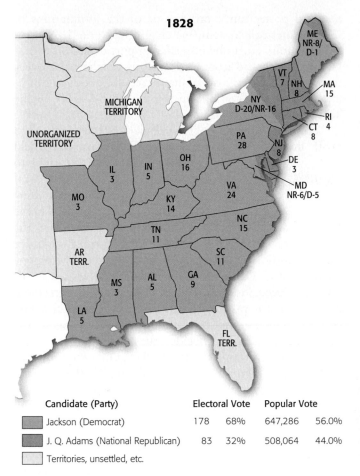

1828

Candidate (Party)		Electoral Vote		Popular Vote	
Jackson (Democrat)		178	68%	647,286	56.0%
J. Q. Adams (National Republican)		83	32%	508,064	44.0%
Territories, unsettled, etc.					

Map 12.2 Presidential Election, 1828

Andrew Jackson avenged his 1824 loss of the presidency, sweeping the election in 1828.

Source: Copyright © Cengage Learning

initiating Indian removal despite protests from northeastern reformers.

Like Jefferson, Jackson strengthened the government's executive branch even as he advocated limited government. In combining the roles of party leader and chief of state, he centralized power in the White House. He relied on political friends, his "Kitchen Cabinet," for advice, rarely consulting his official cabinet. Jackson commanded enormous loyalty and rewarded his followers handsomely. Rotating officeholders, Jackson claimed, made government more responsive to the public will, and he appointed loyal Democrats to office, a practice his critics called the spoils system, in which the victor gives the spoils of victory to his supporters. Although not the first president to do so—Jefferson had replaced many of Adams's appointees—Jackson's own outcry against corrupt bargains made him an easy target for inflammatory rhetoric. The spoils system, opponents charged, corrupted the government because it based appointments on loyalty, not competency.

Opponents mocked Jackson as "King Andrew I," charging him with abuse of power by ignoring the Supreme Court's ruling on Cherokee rights, by sidestepping his cabinet, and by replacing officeholders with his own political cronies. They rejected his claim of restoring republican virtue and accused him of recklessly destroying the economy.

King Andrew

Perhaps nothing rankled Jackson's critics more than his frequent use of the veto, which he employed to promote his vision of a limited government. In 1830, he vetoed the Maysville Road bill, which would have funded construction of a 60-mile turnpike from Maysville to Lexington, Kentucky. Constitutionally, he insisted, states not the federal government bore responsibility for funding internal improvements confined to a single state. The veto undermined Henry Clay's American System and personally embarrassed Clay because the project was in his home district.

▲ Whigs, who named themselves after the loyal opposition in Britain, delighted in portraying Andrew Jackson as a power-hungry leader eager to turn a republic into a monarchy.

The Hermitage: Home of President Andrew Jackson, Nashville, TN

▲ Even as his critics portrayed him as monarchical, Jackson presented himself as the president of the common man. Here he sits atop his prized horse, Sam Patch, named after the disgruntled factory worker and daring waterfall jumper.

From George Washington to John Quincy Adams, the first six presidents had vetoed nine bills; Jackson alone vetoed twelve. Previous presidents believed vetoes were justified only on constitutional grounds, but Jackson considered policy disagreements legitimate grounds as well. He made the veto an effective weapon for controlling Congress, which had to weigh the possibility of a presidential veto as it deliberated.

Federalism at Issue: The Nullification and Bank Controversies

Soon after the Maysville Road veto, Jackson directly faced the question of state versus federal power. The slave South feared federal power and no state more so than South Carolina, where the planter class was the strongest and slavery the most concentrated. Southerners also

resented protectionist tariffs, one of the foundations of Clay's American System, which in 1824 and 1828 protected manufactures by imposing import duties on manufactured cloth and iron. In protecting northern factories, the tariff raised the costs of manufactured goods to southerners, who quickly labeled the high tariff of 1828 the Tariff of Abominations.

South Carolina's political leaders rejected the 1828 tariff, invoking the doctrine of nullification, which held that a state had the right to overrule, or nullify, federal legislation. Nullification drew from the idea expressed in the Virginia and Kentucky Resolutions of 1798—that the states, representing the people, have a right to judge the constitutionality of federal actions. Jackson's vice president, John C. Calhoun of South Carolina, argued in his unsigned *Exposition and Protest* that, in any disagreement between the federal government and a state, a special state convention—like the conventions called to ratify the Constitution—should decide the conflict by either nullifying or affirming the federal law. Only the power of nullification, Calhoun asserted, could protect the minority against the majority's tyranny.

Nullification

As Jackson's running mate in 1828, Calhoun had avoided endorsing nullification and thus embarrassing the Democratic ticket; he also hoped to win Jackson's support as the Democratic presidential heir apparent. Thus, in early 1830, Calhoun presided silently over the Senate and its packed galleries when Senator Daniel Webster of Massachusetts and Senator Robert Y. Hayne of South Carolina debated states' rights. The debate started over a resolution to restrict western land sales, soon turned to the tariff, and from there focused on the nature of the Union, with nullification a subtext. Hayne charged the North with threatening to bring disunity. For two days, Webster eloquently defended New England and the republic, keeping supporters of nullification on the defensive. Although debating Hayne, he aimed his remarks at Calhoun. At the debate's climax, Webster invoked two powerful images. One was the outcome of nullification: "states dissevered, discordant, belligerent; on a land rent with civil feuds, or drenched…in fraternal blood!" The other was a patriotic vision of a great nation flourishing under the motto "Liberty and Union, now and forever, one and inseparable."

Though sympathetic to states' rights and distrustful of the federal government, Jackson rejected the idea of state sovereignty. He strongly believed sovereignty rested with the people. Believing deeply in the Union, he shared Webster's dread of nullification. Soon after the Webster-Hayne debate, the president made his position clear at a Jefferson Day dinner with the toast "Our Federal Union, it must and shall be preserved." Vice President Calhoun, when his turn came, toasted "The Federal Union—next to our liberty the most dear," revealing his adherence to states' rights. Calhoun and Jackson grew apart, and Jackson looked to Secretary of State Martin Van Buren, not Calhoun, as his successor.

Tension resumed when Congress passed a new tariff in 1832, reducing some duties but retaining high taxes on imported iron, cottons, and woolens. Although a majority of southern representatives supported the new tariff, South Carolinians did not, insisting that the constitutional right to control their own destiny had been sacrificed to northern industrialists' demands. They feared the act could set a precedent for congressional legislation on slavery. In November 1832, a South Carolina state convention nullified both the 1828 and the 1832 tariffs, declaring it unlawful for federal officials to collect duties in the state.

Privately, Jackson threatened to invade South Carolina and hang Vice President Calhoun; publicly, he took measured steps. In

The Force Act

December, Jackson issued a proclamation opposing nullification. He moved troops to federal forts in South Carolina and prepared U.S. marshals to collect the required duties. At Jackson's request, Congress passed the Force Act, authorizing the president to call up troops but also offering a way to avoid force by collecting duties before foreign ships reached Charleston's harbor. Jackson also extended an olive branch by recommending tariff reductions.

Link to Jackson's Proclamation against South Carolina's nullification.

Calhoun, disturbed by South Carolina's drift toward separatism, resigned as vice president and soon won election to the U.S. Senate, where he worked with Henry Clay to draw up the compromise Tariff of 1833. Quickly passed by Congress and signed by the president, the new tariff lengthened the list of duty-free items and reduced duties over nine years. Satisfied, South Carolina's convention repealed its nullification law. In a final salvo, it also nullified Jackson's Force Act. Jackson ignored the gesture.

Nullification offered a genuine debate on the nature and principles of the republic. Each side believed it was upholding the Constitution and opposing subversion of republican values. South Carolina's leaders opposed the tyranny of the federal government and manufacturing interests. Jackson fought the tyranny of South Carolina, whose refusal to bow to federal authority threatened to split the republic. Neither side won a clear victory, though both claimed to have done so. It took another crisis, over a central bank, to define the powers of the federal government more clearly.

At stake was survival of the Second Bank of the United States, whose twenty-year charter would expire in 1836.

Second Bank of the United States

The bank served as a depository for federal funds and provided credit for businesses. Its bank notes circulated as currency throughout the country; they could be readily exchanged for gold, and the federal government accepted them as payment in all transactions, including land sales. Through its twenty-five branch offices, the Second Bank acted as a clearing-house for state banks, refusing to accept bank notes of any state bank lacking sufficient gold reserves. Most state banks resented the central bank's police role, which they saw as potentially ruinous. Moreover, state banks were unable to compete equally with the Second Bank, which had more money in reserve.

Many state governments regarded the national bank as unresponsive to local needs, and many western settlers and urban workers remembered with bitterness the bank's conservative credit policies during the Panic of 1819. As a private, profit-making institution, its policies reflected the interest of its owners, especially its president, Nicholas Biddle, who controlled the bank completely. An eastern patrician, Biddle symbolized all that westerners found wrong with the bank, and all that eastern workers found wrong with the commercial elite.

Controversy over the Second Bank inflamed long-standing political animosities, bringing violence to the streets. Elections often

Political Violence

involved fraud, and with no secret ballot, political parties employed operatives to intimidate voters. New York City was home to the most powerful political machine, the Democrats' Tammany Hall, and thus while the bank controversy exacerbated tensions nationwide, New York's mayoral election of 1834 led to mayhem.

Three days of rioting began when Democratic operatives attacked Whig headquarters in the sixth ward. After beating some Whigs unconscious, the Democrats turned their fists and clubs against police, who tried to restore order; eight of them suffered severe wounds, and even the mayor was injured in the fray. Vowing revenge, more than five hundred Whigs stole weapons from the armory, but before they could use them, the state militia arrived to restore order.

A few months later, an election-day riot in Philadelphia left two dead and five substantial buildings burned to the ground. Although these two riots stood out for their proportions and intensity, voter intimidation and fraud—initiated by both Democrats and Whigs—characterized the second party system.

Violence was a catalyst for the formation of the Antimason Party, which had started in upstate New York in

Antimasonry

the mid-1820s as a grassroots movement against Freemasonry, a secret male fraternity that attracted middle- and upper-class men prominent in commerce and civic affairs. Opponents of Masonry claimed the fraternity to be unrepublican; Masons colluded to bestow business and political favors on each other, and—in the incident that sparked the organized Antimasonry movement—Masons had obstructed justice in the investigation of the 1826 disappearance and presumed murder of a disgruntled former member who had written an exposé of the society. Evangelicals denounced Masonry, claiming its members neglected their families for alcohol and ribald entertainment. Antimasonry soon developed into a vibrant political movement in the Northeast and parts of the Midwest. In the 1828 presidential election, the Antimasons opposed Jackson, himself a Mason. With their confidence bolstered by strong showings in gubernatorial elections in 1830, the Antimasons held the first national political convention in Baltimore in 1831, nominating William Wirt of Maryland for president and Amos Ellmaker of Pennsylvania for vice president.

Following the Antimasons' lead, the Democrats and National Republicans held their own conventions. The

Election of 1832

Democrats reaffirmed the choice of Jackson, who had already been nominated by state legislatures, for president and nominated Martin Van Buren of New York for vice president. The National Republican convention selected Clay and John Sergeant of Pennsylvania. The Independent Democrats ran John Floyd and Henry Lee of Virginia; as governor of Virginia, Floyd had supported nullification, winning him support from many South Carolinians.

The Bank of the United States became the election's main issue. Jacksonians denounced the bank as a vehicle for special privilege and economic power, while the Republicans supported it as a pillar of their plan for economic nationalism. The bank's charter was valid until 1836, but as part of his campaign strategy, Clay persuaded Biddle to ask Congress to approve an early rechartering. If Jackson signed the rechartering bill, then Clay could attack the president's inconsistency on the issue. If he vetoed it, then—Clay reasoned—the voters would give Clay the nod. The plan backfired. The president vetoed the bill and issued a pointed veto message appealing to voters who feared that the era's rapid economic development spread its advantages undemocratically. Jackson acknowledged that prosperity could never be evenly dispersed, but he took a strong stand against special interests that tried to use the government to their own unfair advantage. "It is to be regretted," he wrote, "that the rich and powerful too often bend the acts of government to their selfish purposes." The message proved powerful and successful. Jackson won 54 percent of the popular vote to Clay's 37 percent, and he captured 76 percent of the electoral college. Although the Antimasons won just one state, Vermont, they nonetheless helped galvanize the anti-Jackson opposition.

After a sweeping victory and second inauguration,

Jackson's Second Term

Jackson began in 1833 dismantling the Second Bank and depositing federal funds in state-chartered banks (termed "pet banks" by critics). Without federal money, the Second Bank shriveled. When its federal charter expired in 1836, it became just another Pennsylvania-chartered private bank. Five years later, it closed its doors.

As Congress allowed the Bank of the United States to die, it passed the Deposit Act of 1836, authorizing the secretary of the treasury to designate one bank in each state and territory to provide services formerly performed by the Bank of the United States. The act also provided that the federal surplus in excess of $5 million—income derived from the sale of public lands to speculators, who bought large quantities of land to re-parcel and sell, they hoped, at a profit—be distributed to the states as interest-free loans (or "deposits") beginning in 1837. (The loans were understood to be forgiven and, in fact, they were never repaid.) Eager to use the money for state-funded internal improvements, Democrats joined Whigs in supporting the measure overwhelmingly. Fearing that the act would fuel speculation, promote inflation, and thus undermine farmers' interests, Jackson opposed the bill. Because support was strong enough to override a veto, Jackson signed the bill but first insisted on a provision prohibiting state banks from issuing or accepting small-denomination paper money. Jackson hoped that by encouraging the use of coins, the provision would prevent unscrupulous businessmen from defrauding workers by paying them in devalued paper bills.

The president then ordered Treasury Secretary Levi Woodbury to issue the Specie Circular, which provided

Specie Circular

that, after August 1836, only settlers could use paper money to buy land; speculators would have to use specie (gold or silver). The policy proved disastrous, significantly reducing public-land sales, which in turn reduced the federal government's surplus and its loans to the states.

Meanwhile, a banking crisis emerged. One western banker remarked that people "appear to distrust all Banks, they think Govt. has no confidence in them." Fearful that their banknotes would lose value, people sought to redeem them for specie, creating a shortage that forced the banks to suspend payment, further reducing confidence.

Jackson's opponents were irate, largely because the Senate, fearing such consequences, had defeated a bill similar to the Specie Circular just three months earlier. Now "King Andrew" had used presidential powers to defy legislative will, and with disastrous consequences. In the waning days of Jackson's administration, Congress repealed the circular, but the president pocket-vetoed the bill by holding it unsigned until Congress adjourned. Finally, in May 1838, after Jackson had left office, a joint resolution of Congress overturned the circular.

The Whig Challenge and the Second Party System

In the 1830s, opponents of the Democrats, including remnants of the National Republican and Antimason parties, joined together to become the Whig Party. Resentful of Jackson's domination of Congress, the Whigs borrowed the name of the eighteenth-century British party that opposed the Hanoverian monarchs' tyranny. They, too, were the loyal opposition. From 1834 through the 1840s, the Whigs and the Democrats competed on nearly equal footing, and each drew supporters from all regions. The era's political competition—the second party system—was more intense and better organized than what scholars have labeled as the first party system of Democratic-Republicans versus Federalists.

Whigs favored economic expansion through an activist government. They supported corporate charters,

Whigs and Reformers

a national bank, and paper currency; Democrats opposed all three. Whigs generally professed a strong belief in progress and perfectibility, and they favored social reforms, including public schools, prison and asylum reform, and temperance. Jacksonians criticized reform associations for undermining the people's will by giving undue influence to political minorities; Whigs countered they served the common good. Nor did Whigs object to helping special interests if doing so promoted the general welfare. The chartering of corporations, they argued, expanded economic opportunity for everyone, laborers and farmers alike. Democrats, distrustful of concentrated economic power and of moral and economic coercion, held fast to the Jeffersonian principle of limited government.

Whigs stressed a "harmony of interests" among all classes and interests. Their philosophy was one of equal opportunity. Democrats tended to see society as divided into the "haves" and the "have nots," and they embraced a motto of "equal rights." They championed "heroic artisans" like Sam Patch, whereas Whigs remained wary of the "excesses of democracy" and preferred to see society ruled from the top down. Whigs believed in free-labor ideology and thought that society's wealthy and powerful had risen by their own merits. Democrats alleged that, instead, their political opponents had benefited from special favors.

But religion and ethnicity, as much as class, influenced party affiliation. The Whigs' support for energetic government and moral reform won the favor of evangelical Protestants. Methodists and Baptists were overwhelmingly Whigs, as were the small number of free black voters. In many locales, the membership rolls of reform societies overlapped those of the party. Indeed, Whigs practiced a kind of political revivalism. Their rallies resembled camp meetings; their speeches employed pulpit rhetoric; their programs embodied reformers' perfectionist beliefs.

By appealing to evangelicals, Whigs alienated members of other faiths. The evangelicals' ideal Christian state had no room for nonevangelical Protestants, Catholics, Mormons, or religious freethinkers. Those groups opposed Sabbath laws and temperance legislation in particular, and state interference in moral and religious questions in general. In fact, they preferred to keep religion and politics separate. As a result, more than 95 percent of Irish Catholics, 90 percent of Reformed Dutch, and 80 percent of German Catholics voted Democratic.

The parties' platforms thus attracted what might seem to be an odd coalition of voters. Favoring government-sponsored commercial development and fearful of social disorder, the Whigs wanted a slower, more controlled settlement of western lands; later, they opposed slavery's westward expansion. Groups as diverse as black New Englanders and well-settled slave owners, especially in the Upper South, found these ideas appealing; the former, to undercut slavery itself, and the latter to protect their own investments from cheap western competition. Democrats' promises to open additional lands for settlement attracted yeoman farmers, wage earners, frontier slaveowners, and immigrants. With such broad coalitions of voters, there was room within each party for a broad spectrum of beliefs, particularly when it came to slavery.

Politicians recognized, however, the potentially divisive nature of slavery, and some went to extremes to keep it out of national political debate. In response to the American Antislavery Society's petitioning campaign, the House of Representatives in 1836 adopted what abolitionists labeled the "gag rule," which automatically tabled abolitionist petitions, effectively preventing debate on them. Former president John Quincy Adams, now a representative from Massachusetts, dramatically defended the right to petition and took to the floor many times to speak against the gag rule, which was ultimately repealed in 1844.

Vice President Martin Van Buren, handpicked by Jackson, headed the Democratic ticket in the 1836

Election of 1836

presidential election. A career politician, Van Buren had built a political machine—the Albany Regency—in New York and then left to join Jackson's cabinet in 1829, first as secretary of state and then as American minister to Great Britain.

Because the Whigs in 1836 had not yet coalesced into a national party, they entered three sectional candidates: Daniel Webster (New England), Hugh White (the South), and William Henry Harrison (the West). By splintering the vote, they hoped to throw the election into the House of Representatives. Van Buren, however, comfortably captured the electoral college even though he had only a 25,000-vote edge out of a total of 1.5 million votes

Table 12.1 United States Presidents, 1824–1845

President	Party	Years in Office
James Monroe	Democratic-Republican	1817–1825
John Quincy Adams	Democratic-Republican	1825–1829
Andrew Jackson	Democratic	1829–1837
Martin Van Buren	Democratic	1837–1841
William Henry Harrison	Whig	1841
John Tyler	Elected as Whig, but broke with party	1841–1845

cast. No vice-presidential candidate received a majority of electoral votes, and for the only time in American history, the Senate decided a vice-presidential race, selecting Democratic candidate Richard M. Johnson of Kentucky.

Van Buren took office just weeks before the American credit system collapsed. With banks refusing to redeem paper currency with gold in response to the Specie Circular, a downward economic spiral began, curtailing bank loans and strangling business confidence. Credit contraction made things worse. After a brief recovery, hard times persisted from 1839 until 1843.

Van Buren and Hard Times

Van Buren followed Jackson's hard-money policies. He cut federal spending, causing prices to drop further, and opposed a national bank, which would have expanded credit. The president proposed a new regional treasury system for government deposits. The proposed treasury branches would accept and disperse only gold and silver coin; they would not accept paper currency or checks drawn on state banks. Van Buren's independent treasury bill became law in 1840. By increasing the demand for hard coin, it deprived banks of gold and accelerated price deflation. These issues dominated state elections. Whigs favored new banks, more paper currency, and readily available corporate and bank charters. As the party of hard money, Democrats favored eliminating paper currency altogether. Increasingly, the Democrats became distrustful even of state banks; by the mid-1840s, a majority favored eliminating all bank corporations.

Amid hard times came a renewal of Anglo-American tensions. One of the most troublesome disputes arose from the *Caroline* affair. After the privately owned steamer *Caroline* carried supplies to aid an unsuccessful Canadian uprising against Great Britain, a group of British loyalists burned the ship, killing an American citizen in the process. Britain refused to apologize, and American newspapers called for revenge. Fearing that popular support for the Canadian rebels would ignite war, President Van Buren posted troops under General Winfield Scott at the border to discourage

Anglo-American Tensions

Americans from seeking vigilante retaliation. Tensions subsided in late 1840 when New York authorities arrested a Canadian deemed responsible for the American's death aboard the *Caroline*. The alleged murderer was acquitted. Had the verdict gone otherwise, Lord Palmerston, the British foreign minister, might have sought war.

At almost the same time, an old border dispute between Maine and New Brunswick disrupted Anglo-American relations. Great Britain had accepted an 1831 arbitration decision fixing a new boundary, but the U.S. Senate rejected it. Thus, when Canadian lumbermen cut trees in the disputed region in the winter of 1838–1839, a posse of Maine citizens assembled to expel them. The lumbermen captured the posse, both sides mobilized their militias, and Congress authorized a call-up of fifty thousand men. General Scott was dispatched to Aroostook, Maine, where he arranged a truce. The Webster-Ashburton Treaty (1842) settled the boundaries between Maine and New Brunswick, and along the Great Lakes, but left unresolved the still-disputed northern boundary of Oregon, joint occupancy of which had been renewed in 1827.

With the nation gripped by hard times, the Whigs confidently approached the election of 1840. Their strategy was simple: maintain loyal supporters and court independents by blaming hard times on the Democrats. The Whigs rallied behind a military hero, General William Henry Harrison, conqueror of the Shawnees at Tippecanoe Creek in 1811. The Democrats renominated President Van Buren, and the newly formed Liberty Party ran James Birney.

William Henry Harrison and the Election of 1840

Harrison, or "Old Tippecanoe," and his running mate, John Tyler of Virginia, ran a "log cabin and hard cider" campaign—a people's crusade—against the aristocratic president in "the Palace." Although descended from a Virginia plantation family, Harrison presented himself as an ordinary farmer. While party hacks blamed Democrats for hard times, Harrison remained silent, earning the nickname "General Mum." Whigs wooed voters with huge rallies, parades, songs, posters, campaign mementos, and a party newspaper, *The Log Cabin*.

Link to Ellen Kay Bond's speech in support of William Henry Harrison.

They appealed to voters as well as nonvoters, including women, who attended their rallies and speeches, and women actively promoted the Whig cause; one Virginia woman, for example, published two pamphlets backing Harrison's candidacy. In a huge turnout, 80 percent of eligible voters cast ballots. Winning the popular vote by a narrow margin, Harrison swept the electoral college, 234 to 60.

Immediately after taking office in 1841, President Harrison convened Congress in special session to pass the Whig program: repeal of the independent treasury system, a new national bank, and a higher protective tariff. But the sixty-eight-year-old Harrison caught pneumonia and died within a month of his inauguration. His vice president, John Tyler, who had left the Democratic Party to protest Jackson's nullification proclamation, now became the first vice president whose president had died in office. The Constitution did not stipulate what should happen, but Tyler quickly took full possession of executive powers, setting a crucial precedent that would not be codified in the Constitution until 1967 with the Twenty-fifth Amendment's ratification.

In office, Tyler became more a Democrat than a Whig. He repeatedly vetoed Clay's protective tariffs, internal improvements, and bills to revive the Bank of the United States. Two days after

President Tyler

Legacy FOR A PEOPLE AND A NATION

Moral Reformers' Abstinence Campaigns

Reform organizations, seeking to perfect society and thus hasten Christ's return, commanded a large following in the 1830s and 1840s. From western New York in 1837, merchant Silas Marks remarked that women were engrossed in the "Great objects of the day ... such as supporting societies such as abolitionism, Moral Reform &c." By "moral reform," reformers meant establishing and enforcing a new sexual propriety: premarital celibacy for both men and women. One hears echoes of their calls in today's "purity" movements, which advocate sexual abstinence until marriage.

Moral reformers worried that devastating social byproducts accompanied economic expansion. As young people left home for jobs or schooling—leaving behind parental controls—society (in reformers' estimation) plunged into licentiousness and obscenity, threatening the nation's physical and spiritual health. Northern women formed nearly six hundred local reform associations to ward off such threats. They lobbied against prostitution, assisted "fallen" women, preached chastity, and publically shamed men seeking sexual gratification outside marriage by either frequenting brothels or "seducing" virtuous young women. Some men openly criticized reformers' tactics, but few publically questioned their goals. It was, wrote Silas Marks, "heresy not to wink at their proceedings."

Modern purity campaigns also emerged from both secular and religious concerns. They began in the early 1990s, amid escalating AIDS awareness alongside public outcries over teen pregnancies. Purity activists encourage youth to pledge abstinence in order to honor "God with your body,

which is the temple of the Holy Spirit," and they promise practical benefits from doing so. Pledging purity, notes one organization's web site, means avoiding pregnancy and sexually transmitted diseases while maintaining "every opportunity to fulfill your dreams." Nineteenth-century reformers, too, reminded youth that their dreams—business ownership, middle-class respectability—depended on sexual propriety. And just as moral reformers offered redemption for wayward youths who mended their ways, today's purity advocates talk about "second virginity."

Like nineteenth-century reformers, today's purity activists emphasize community and conversion. To foster a sense of fellowship among purity-minded youth, and to encourage new pledges, purity organizations sponsor concert-like events, modern adaptations of energetic, revival-inspired reform meetings. At highly publicized purity balls, daughters and fathers exchange vows: Fathers promise to "cover my daughter as her authority and protection in the area of purity;" daughters, to remain chaste until marriage. Young men and women wear purity rings to proclaim their pledges and to encourage friends to join them. Today, some youthful pop stars, such as the Jonas Brothers and Jordin Sparks, highlight their own purity pledges in their publicity campaigns. But now as then, purity advocates face criticism for their tactics, whose effectiveness has been questioned.

By advocating premarital celibacy as a weapon against society's religious, medical, and social ills, moral reformers left to a people and a nation an enduring, if controversial, legacy.

Franklin D. Roosevelt Library

▲ Even as the Whigs opposed the Democrats, they adopted many of the Democrats' campaign techniques, appealing to the common man with their "log cabin and cider" campaign of 1840. The band in this street scene is riding a wagon decorated with a log-cabin painting. The campaign's excitement appealed to nonvoters as well as voters, and eighty percent of eligible voters cast ballots.

Tyler's second veto of a bank bill, the entire cabinet except Secretary of State Daniel Webster resigned; Webster, once done negotiating the Webster-Ashburton treaty, followed. Tyler became a president without a party, and the Whigs lost the presidency without losing an election. Disgusted Whigs referred to Tyler as "His Accidency."

Like Jackson, Tyler expanded presidential powers and emphasized westward expansion. His expansionist vision contained Whig elements, though: he eyed commercial markets in Hawaii and China. During his presidency, the United States negotiated its first treaties with China, and Tyler expanded the Monroe Doctrine to include Hawaii (or the Sandwich Islands). But Tyler's vision for the nation's path to greatness fixed mostly on Texas and the westward expansion of slavery.

SUMMARY

Religion and reform shaped politics from 1824 through the 1840s. Driven by a belief in human perfectibility, many evangelicals, especially women, worked tirelessly to right the wrongs of American society. They hoped to trigger the millennium, the thousand years of earthly peace accompanying Christ's return. Reformers battled the evils of prostitution and alcohol, and they sought to reform criminals and delinquents, improve insane asylums, and establish public schools. Some rejected the possibility of reforming American society from within and instead joined experimental communities that modeled radical alternatives to the social and economic order. Abolitionists combined the reformers' and utopians' approaches; they worked to perfect American society from within but through radical means—the eradication of slavery. As women entered the public sphere as advocates of reform and, especially, abolitionism, some of them turned toward the equally radical proposition of full legal and political rights for women.

Reform remade politics, and politicians reshaped public discourse to appeal to the broadening electorate. As did reformers, President John Quincy Adams raised expectations about an expanded governmental role. The struggles between the National Republicans and the Democrats, then between the Democrats and the Whigs, stimulated even greater interest in campaigns and political issues. The Democrats and Whigs competed almost equally for voter loyalty by building strong organizations that faced off in national and local elections often characterized by fraud, and sometimes by violence. Both parties favored economic development but by different means: The Whigs advocated centralized government initiative to spur commercial growth, whereas Democrats advocated limited government and sought agricultural expansion. Jackson did not hesitate, however, to use presidential authority; his opponents dubbed him King Andrew. The controversies over the Second Bank of the United States and nullification exposed different interpretations of the nation's founding principles.

The late 1830s and early 1840s brought uncertainty: The economy once again cycled through a period of bust; tensions with the British resurfaced; and—for the first time—a president died in office. As John Tyler, derided by his critics as "His Accidency," took office, he tenaciously articulated a vision of American greatness that depended on its westward expansion.

SUGGESTIONS FOR FURTHER READING

Philip F. Gura, *American Transcendentalism: A History* (2007)

Daniel Walker Howe, *What Hath God Wrought: The Transformation of America, 1815–1848* (2007)

Paul E. Johnson, *Sam Patch, the Famous Jumper* (2003)

Mary Kelley, *Learning to Stand and Speak: Women, Education, and Public Life in America's Republic* (2006)

Steven Mintz, *Moralists and Modernizers: America's Pre-Civil War Reformers* (1995)

Richard S. Newman, *The Transformation of American Abolitionism: Fighting Slavery in the Early Republic* (2002)

Harry L. Watson, *Liberty and Power: The Politics of Jacksonian America* (2006)

Susan Zaeske, *Signatures of Citizenship: Petitioning, Antislavery, and Women's Political Identity* (2003)

Go to the CourseMate website for primary source links, study tools, and review materials for this chapter. www.cengagebrain.com

Chapter 13

The Contested West
1815–1860

The Steamboat Napoleon, *1833 by Karl Bodmer, Josslyn Art Museum, Omaha, NE (Detail)*

To eight-year-old Henry Clay Bruce, moving west was an adventure. In April 1844, the Virginia boy began a 1,500-mile, two-month trip to his new home in Missouri. Henry marveled at the newness of it all—beautiful natural terrain, impressive towns, different styles of dress. Nothing awed him more than the steamboat ride from Louisville to St. Louis; it felt like "a house floating on the water." Upon his arrival in Missouri, Henry was struck by how much the West differed from the East. The farms lay at much greater distances apart, and the countryside abounded with berries, wild fruits, game, and fish. But it was not paradise. Rattlesnakes, wolves, and vicious hogs roamed the countryside, keeping Henry and his playmates close to home.

Only one thing matched the wildlife's ferocity: Jack Perkinson, the owner of the plantation on which Henry now lived. For Henry was a slave boy who had been relocated, along with his mother and siblings, because his master decided to seek a new beginning in the West. Pettis Perkinson (Jack's brother and Henry's owner) and three other white Virginians had crammed their families, their slaves, and whatever belongings they could fit into three wagons—two for slaves, one for whites. Once in Missouri, Pettis resided with Jack Perkinson, who—according to Henry—readily yelled at and whipped his own slaves. Henry's first year in Missouri was as carefree as a slave child's life could be. The boy fished, hunted (with dogs, not guns), and gathered prairie chickens' eggs. But as his ninth birthday approached, Henry was hired out, first to a brickmaker, then to a tobacco factory. He worked sunup to sundown, and when he failed to satisfy his bosses, he was whipped.

Meanwhile, Pettis Perkinson, unenamored with Missouri, returned home to Virginia, only later summoning some of his slaves, including Henry, who returned "contrary to our will." A less rigorous work routine awaited the Perkinson slaves in Virginia, but that did not compensate for leaving loved ones behind in Missouri.

◄ Like Henry Clay Bruce, many emigrants in the 1840s traveled west by steamboat for part of their journey, making the rest of the trip on foot, horseback, wagon, canal boat, or—often—by some combination of means.

Chronology

1812	■ General Land Office established
1820	■ Price lowered on public lands
1821	■ Santa Fe Trail charted
	■ Mexico's independence
1823	■ Mexico allows Stephen Austin to settle U.S. citizens
1824	■ Congressional General Survey Act
	■ Jedediah Smith's South Pass publicized
	■ Indian Office established
1825–32	■ *Empresario* contracts signed
1826	■ Fredonia rebellion fails
1830	■ Indian Removal Act (see Chapter 10)
1832	■ Black Hawk War
1834	■ McCormick reaper patented
1836	■ Lone Star Republic founded
	■ U.S. Army Corps of Topographical Engineers established
1840–60	■ 250,000 to 500,000 migrants travel overland
1841	■ Log Cabin Bill
1844	■ Presidential campaign features Texas annexation
1845	■ "Manifest destiny" coined
	■ Texas annexed (March 1) and becomes twenty-eighth state (December 29)
1846–48	■ War with Mexico (see Chapter 14)
1847	■ Mormons settle Great Salt Lake valley
1848	■ California gold discovered
1849–50s	■ Migrants stream into Great Plains and Far West
1855	■ Ash Hollow Massacre
1857–58	■ Mormons and U.S. Army in armed conflict
1862	■ Homestead Act

*S*oon Pettis Perkinson again grew weary of the tired, rocky soil on his Virginia farm, and with renewed determination to seek opportunity in the West, he moved to Mississippi, where his sister lived. But life on a cotton plantation suited neither Henry nor his master, who now decided—to his slaves' joy—to give Missouri a second chance.

Henry's master remained restless: two years after returning to Missouri, he decided to head for Texas. Henry, now in his late teens, and his brothers refused to go. Although livid, Pettis Perkinson abandoned his plans, apparently not wishing to contend with recalcitrant slaves. After being hired out several more times, Henry became the foreman on Perkinson's Missouri farm, where he remained until escaping during the Civil War to the free state of Kansas. Finally, Henry Clay Bruce found the opportunity and freedom that so many sought when they first headed westward.

In 1820, about 20 percent of the nation's population lived west of the Appalachian Mountains. By 1860, nearly 50 percent did. Most white people and free blacks moved west because they—or their heads of household—believed better opportunities awaited them there. When easterners envisioned the West, they generally saw enormous tracts of fertile, uncultivated land. Or, beginning in the late 1840s, they imagined getting rich quick in the West's gold or silver mines. Some saw opportunities for lumbering or ranching or for selling goods or services to farmers, miners, lumbermen, and cattlemen.

Many of those heading west had no say in the matter. Men often made the decision without consulting their wives and children, and slaves' wishes received even less consideration. Nor did western settlers give much, if any, thought to how their migration would influence the Indian peoples already living in the West—on lands they had occupied in some cases for generations and, in other cases, since being relocated by the U.S. government.

The federal government's involvement in westward expansion extended far beyond removing Indians. The government-sponsored exploration made laws regulating settlement and the establishment of territorial governments, surveyed and fixed prices on public lands, sold those lands, invested in transportation routes, and established a military presence.

The Mexican government, too, played a role in Anglo-American settlement in the West—one it would later regret—by encouraging immigration to its northern borderlands in the 1820s. From the United States came settlers who vied with the region's other inhabitants—Indians, Hispanics, and people of mixed heritage—for land and other natural resources. A decade later, Texas, one of Mexico's northern provinces, declared its independence and sought annexation by the United States. Thus began an era of heightened tensions—not only between the United States and Mexico, but also within the United States as Texas's future became entangled with the thorny issue of slavery.

For some white Americans, mostly from the South, the ability to own slaves in the West signaled the epitome of their own freedom. For others, from both the North and the South, slavery's westward expansion frustrated dreams for a new beginning in a region free from what they saw as slavery's degrading influence on white labor. Northerners, in particular, often set their sights on the Oregon Territory. They believed the sacrifices brought about by an arduous transcontinental journey would be outweighed by the rewards: agricultural prosperity in a land free from blacks, enslaved and free.

Even as Democrats and Whigs skirted the slavery issue, they took distinct stands on westward expansion's role in national economic development. But once the spotlight focused on Texas, political leaders would find it increasingly difficult to disentangle the issues of westward expansion and slavery.

Human interactions in the West involved both cooperation and conflict, but with each passing decade conflict—between expectations and reality, between people with different aspirations and world-views—increasingly defined daily life. By the mid-1840s, events in the West would, in turn, aggravate long-simmering discord between southern and northern political interests.

- How did tensions in the East influence western migration and settlement?

- How did public, private, and individual initiatives converge to shape the West's development?

- What motivated cooperation in the West, and what spurred conflict?

The West in the American Imagination

For historian Frederick Jackson Turner, writing in the late nineteenth century, it was the West, not the South or the North, that was distinctive. With its abundance of free land, the western frontier—what he saw as the "meeting point between savagery and civilization"—bred American democracy, shaped the American character, and made the United States exceptional among nations. Modern historians generally eschew the notion of American exceptionalism, stressing instead the deep and complex connections between the United States and the rest of the world. Although today's scholars also reject the racialist assumptions of Turner's definition of *frontier*, some see continued value in using the term to signify a meeting place of different cultures. Others see the West as fundamentally a place, not a process, though they disagree over what delineates it.

For early-nineteenth-century Americans of European descent, the West included anything west of the Appalachian Mountains. But it was, first and foremost, a place representing the future—a place offering economic and social betterment for themselves and their children. For many, betterment entailed land ownership; the West's seeming abundance of land meant that anyone could hope to own a farm and achieve economic and political independence. Men who already owned land, like Pettis Perkinson, looked westward for cheaper, bigger, and more fertile landholdings. With the discovery of gold in California in 1848, the West became a place to strike it rich before returning home to live in increased comfort or even opulence.

Defining the West

Many people arrived in the West under the threat of force. These included enslaved men, women, and children whose owners moved them, often against their will, as well as Indians removed from their eastern homelands by the U.S. military under provisions of the Indian Removal Act of 1830.

To others, the very notion of the West would have been baffling. Emigrants from Mexico and Central or South America traveled north to get to what European-Americans called the West. Chinese nationals traveled eastward to California. Many Indians simply considered the West home. Other Indians and French Canadians journeyed southward to the West. All these people, much like European-Americans, arrived in the western portion of the North American continent because of a combination of factors pushing and pulling them.

For European-Americans, Daniel Boone became the archetypal frontiersman, a man whose daring individualism opened the Eden-like West for virtuous and hard-working freedom lovers. Through biographies published by John Filson during Boone's lifetime and by Timothy Flint after Boone's death (in 1784 and 1833, respectively), Boone became a familiar figure in American and European households. The mythical Boone lived in the wilderness, became "natural" himself, and shrank from society, feeling compelled to relocate upon seeing smoke billowing from a

Frontier Literature

neighboring cabin. He single-handedly overpowered bears and Indians. Even as he adopted wilderness ways, according to legend, Boone became the pathfinder for civilization. As a friend wrote, Boone "has been the instrument of opening the road to millions of the human family from the pressure of sterility and want, to a Land flowing with milk and honey." By borrowing biblical language—the land of milk and honey denoting the Promised Land, the idyllic place that God promised to the beleaguered Israelites— Boone's friend suggested that Boone was Moses-like, leading his people to a land of abundance.

Such stories mythologized not only Boone, but the West itself. The Indian-fighting Boone, according to Flint's bestselling biography, had wrested for civilized society "the great west—the garden of the earth." Little matter that the real Boone regretted having killed

Indians and often struggled to support his family. When Boone became the heroic model for James Fenimore Cooper's *Leatherstocking Tales* (1823–1841)—set on the frontier of western New York—he came to symbolize not only American adventure but also individualism and freedom.

With the invention of the steam press in the early 1830s, western adventure stories became cheap and widely read. Davy Crockett, another real-life figure turned into mythical hero, was featured in many of them. In real life, Crockett had first fought the Creeks under Andrew Jackson but later championed Indian rights, rebuking the removal bill. After losing his life defending the Alamo mission during Texas's fight for independence (1836), though, Crockett often appeared in stories portraying the West as violent, a place where one escaped civilized

Map 13.1 Westward Expansion, 1800–1860

Through exploration, purchase, war, and treaty, the United States became a continental nation, stretching from the Atlantic to the Pacific.

Source: Copyright © Cengage Learning

society and fought Indians and Mexicans. But even in this version of the western myth, the American West symbolized what white Americans saw as their nation's core value: freedom.

Inspired partly by such literature, many easterners yearned to see the West and its native peoples, and artists hastened to accommodate

Western Art

them. Yet the images they produced often revealed more about white Americans' ideals than about the West itself. In these portrayals, the West was sometimes an untamed wilderness inhabited by savages (noble or otherwise), and sometimes a cultivated garden, a land of milk and honey where the Jeffersonian agrarian dream was realized.

The first Anglo-American artists to travel west were Samuel Seymour and Titian Ramsay Peale, whom the federal government hired to accompany explorer Stephen H. Long on his 1820 expedition to the Rocky Mountains. They pioneered an influential art genre: facsimiles in government reports. Between 1840 and 1860, Congress published nearly sixty works on western exploration, featuring hundreds of lithographs and engravings of plants, animals, and people. Some reports became bestsellers. The most popular was the twelve-volume Pacific Railway Survey (1855–1860), chronicling expeditions to explore four possible railroad routes. The government distributed more than 53,000 copies, helping easterners visualize for themselves the continent's western reaches.

Although government reports often faithfully reproduced original paintings, they sometimes made telling alterations. When Richard Kern accompanied explorer James H. Simpson in 1849 to the Southwest, for example, he painted a Navajo man in a submissive pose. The painting's reproduction for general distribution transformed the man's pose into a rebellious one. In other cases, the government reports transformed artists' depictions of Indian-occupied landscapes into empty terrain seemingly free for the taking.

Yet the original artwork did not necessarily offer an accurate view of the West either. Artists' own cultural assumptions colored their portrayals, and commercial artists produced what they thought the public craved. When George Catlin traveled west in the early 1830s, he may have genuinely hoped to paint what he saw as the Indians' vanishing way of life. But he also aimed to attract a paying public of easterners to his exhibitions. Traveling and painting immediately following the Indian Removal Act of 1830, Catlin painted the West with a moral in mind. Indians came in two varieties—those who preserved their original, almost noble qualities, characterized by freedom and moderation, and those who, after coming in contact with whites, had become "dissolute." Indians, he implied, benefited from removal from white Americans' corrupting influence.

Smithsonian American Art Museum, Washington, DC

▲ In one of his most famous portraits, George Catlin painted Wi-Jun-Jon, an Assiniboine Indian, both before and after he had mingled with white men. In the "before" stance, the Indian is a dignified, peace-pipe-bearing warrior; in the "after" portrait, the "corrupted" Indian has abandoned dignity for vanity and his peace pipe for a cigar.

Western artwork became widely viewed as facsimiles appeared in magazines and books and even on banknotes. Such images nurtured easterners' curiosities and fantasies— and sometimes their itch to move westward.

But western realities often clashed with promoters' promises, and disappointed settlers sometimes tried to

Countering the Myths

clarify matters for future migrants. From Philadelphia in the 1850s came a song parodying the familiar call of "to the West":

At the west they told me there was wealth to be won,
The forest to clear, was the work to be done;
I tried it—couldn't do it—gave it up in despair,
And just see if you'll ever again catch me there.
The little snug farm I expected to buy,
I quickly discovered was just all in my eye,
I came back like a streak—you may go—but I'm bless'd
If you'll ever again, sirs, catch me at the west.

Rebecca Burlend, an English immigrant in Illinois, encountered hardships aplenty—intemperate weather, difficult working conditions, swindlers—and with her son wrote an autobiographical account, *A True Picture of Emigration* (1831), alerting her countrymen to what awaited them in the American West. The Burlends had been lured to Illinois by an Englishman's letters extolling "a land flowing with milk and honey." Burlend reckoned that he must have "gathered his honey rather from thorns than flowers." Her account sought not to discourage emigration, but to substitute a realistic for a rosy description.

Expansion and Resistance in the Trans-Appalachian West

Americans had always been highly mobile, but never to the extent following the War of 1812, which weakened Indian resistance and set off a flurry of transportation projects. In the 1820s and 1830s, settlers streamed west of the Appalachian Mountains into the Old Northwest and the Old Southwest. They traveled by foot, horseback, wagon, canal boat, steamboat, or—often—by some combination of means. Many people, like Pettis Perkinson and his slaves, moved several times, looking for better opportunities, and when opportunities failed to materialize, some returned home.

Both the Old Northwest and the Old Southwest saw population explosions during the early nineteenth century. But while the Old Southwest grew by an impressive 50 percent each decade, the Northwest's population grew exponentially. In 1790, the region's white population numbered just a few hundred people. By 1860, nearly 7 million people called the region home. Between 1810 and 1830, the population of Ohio more than quadrupled, while Indiana and Illinois grew fourteenfold and thirteenfold, respectively. Michigan's population multiplied by fifty times in the thirty years between 1820 and 1850. Migration rather than birth rates accounted for most of this growth, and once in the Old Northwest, people did not stay put. By the 1840s, more people left Ohio than moved into it. Geographic mobility, the search for more and better opportunities, and connections to the market economy defined the region that became known as the Midwest following the acquisition of U.S. territory farther west. This region came to symbolize, for many northerners, the heart of American values: freedom and upward mobility, both of which could be achieved (for white Americans and European immigrants) through hard work and virtuous behavior.

The decision to move west—and then to move again—could be difficult, even heart-wrenching. Moving

Deciding Where to Move

west meant leaving behind worn-out soil and settled areas with little land available for purchase, but it also meant leaving behind family, friends, and communities. One woman remembered how on the evening before her departure for the West, her entire family gathered together for the last time "looking as if we were all going to our graves the next morning." The journey promised to be arduous and expensive, as did the backbreaking labor of clearing new lands. The West was a land of opportunity but also of uncertainty. What if the soil proved less fertile than anticipated? What if neighbors—white as well as Indian—proved unfriendly, or worse? What if homesickness became unbearable?

Given all that western settlers risked, they tried to control as many variables as possible. Like Pettis Perkinson, people often relocated to communities where they had relatives or friends, and they often traveled with acquaintances from home. They moved to climates similar to those they left behind. Massachusetts farmers headed to western New York or Ohio, Virginians and North Carolinians went to Missouri, Georgians populated Mississippi and Texas, and Europeans—mostly Germans and Irish—headed to the Old Northwest in much larger numbers than to the Old Southwest. Migrants settled in ethnic communities or with people of similar religious values and affiliations. As a result, the Midwest was—in the words of two of its historians—"more like an ethnic and cultural checkerboard than the proverbial melting pot."

When westward-bound Americans fixed on particular destinations, their decisions often rested on slavery's status there. Some white southerners, tired of the planter elite's social and political power, sought homes in areas free from slavery—or at least where there were few plantations. Many others, though, went west to improve their chances of owning slaves, or of purchasing additional slaves. White northerners also resented elite slaveowners' economic and political power and hoped to distance themselves from slavery as well as from free blacks. In the 1850s, many midwestern states passed "black laws" prohibiting African Americans, free or enslaved, from living within their boundaries. (Oregon passed a similar law.) Ironically, many free blacks migrated west to free themselves from eastern prejudice.

Between 1815 and 1860, few western migrants settled on the Great Plains, a region reserved for Indians until the 1850s, and relatively few easterners risked the overland journey to California and Oregon before the transcontinental railroad's completion in 1869. Although at first the Southwest seemed to hold the edge in attracting new settlers, the Midwest—with its better-developed transportation routes, its more democratic access to economic markets, its smaller African American population, its smaller and cheaper average landholding, and its climatic similarity to New England and northern Europe—proved considerably more attractive in the decades after 1820. The Old Northwest's

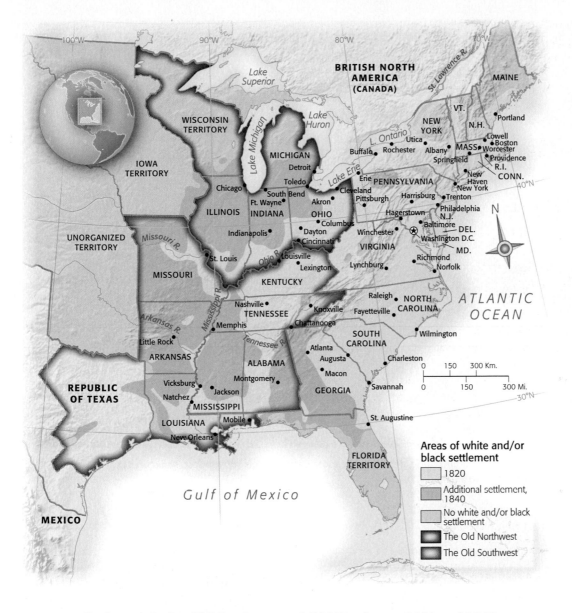

Map 13.2 Settlement in the Old Southwest and Old Northwest, 1820 and 1840

Removal of Indians and a growing transportation network opened up land to white and black settlers in the regions known as the Old Southwest and the Old Northwest, as the U.S. population grew from 9.6 million in 1820 to 17.1 million in 1840.

Source: Copyright © Cengage Learning

thriving transportation hubs also made good first stops for western migrants lacking cash to purchase land. They found work unloading canal boats, planting and harvesting wheat on nearby farms, grinding wheat into flour, or sawing trees into lumber—or, more often, cobbling together a combination of these seasonal jobs. The South offered fewer such opportunities. With the Old Northwest's population growing more quickly, white southerners worried increasingly about congressional representation and laws regarding slavery.

In both the Midwest and the Southwest, the expansion of white settlement depended on Indian removal.

Indian Removal and Resistance

Even as the U.S. Army escorted Indians from the Old Southwest (see Chapter 10), the federal government arranged treaties in which northeastern Indian nations relinquished their land titles in exchange for lands west of the Mississippi River. Between 1829 and 1851, the U.S. government and northern Indian

▲ In 1834, Karl Bodmer painted a farm on the Illinois prairie, depicting the more permanent, if still modest, structures that farmers built after the initial urgency to clear fields for cultivation had subsided.

tribes signed eighty-six such treaties. Some northern Indians evaded removal, including the Miamis in Indiana, the Ottawas and Chippewas in the upper Midwest, and the Winnebagos in southern Wisconsin. In 1840, for example, Miami chiefs had acceded to pressure to exchange 500,000 acres in Indiana for equivalent acreage in Indian Country. Under the treaty's terms, their people had five years to move. When they did not, federal troops arrived to escort them. But about half of the Miami nation dodged the soldiers—and many of those who did trek to Indian Country later returned unauthorized. In Wisconsin, some Winnebagos similarly eluded removal or returned to Wisconsin after being escorted west by soldiers.

The Sauks (or "Sacs") and Fox fared much less well. In a series of treaties between 1804 and 1830, their leaders exchanged lands in northwestern Illinois and southwestern Wisconsin for lands across the Mississippi River in Iowa Territory. Black Hawk, a Sauk warrior who had sided with the British during the War of 1812, disputed the treaties' validity and vowed his people would return to their ancestral lands. In 1832, he led a group of Sauk

Black Hawk War

and Fox families to Illinois, causing panic among white settlers. The state's governor activated the militia, who were later joined by militia from surrounding states and territories as well as by U.S. Army regular soldiers. Over the next several months, hundreds of Indians and dozens of whites died under often-gruesome circumstances in what is known as the Black Hawk War. As the Sauks and Fox tried to flee across the Mississippi River, American soldiers on steamboats and on land fired indiscriminately. Those men, women, and children who survived the river crossing met gunfire on the western shore from Lakota (Sioux), their longtime enemies now allied with the Americans.

Black Hawk survived to surrender, and U.S. officials undertook to impress on him and the uprising's other leaders the futility of resistance. After being imprisoned, then sent to Washington, D.C., along a route meant to underscore the United States' immense size and population, and then imprisoned again, the Indians were returned to their homes. The Black Hawk War marked the end of militant Indian uprisings in the Old Northwest, adding to the region's appeal to white settlers.

Land speculators, developers of "paper towns" (ones existing on paper only), steamboat companies, and manu-

Selling the West

facturers of farming implements all promoted the Midwest as a tranquil place of unbounded opportunity. Land proprietors emphasized the region's connections to eastern customs and markets. They knew that, when families uprooted themselves and headed west, they did not—the mythical Daniel Boone and Davy Crockett aside—seek to escape civilization. When Michael D. Row, the proprietor of Rowsburg in northern Ohio, sought to sell town lots in 1835, he emphasized that Rowsburg was in a "thickly settled" area, stood at the crossroads of public transportation leading in every direction, and had established mills and tanning yards.

Western settlement generally followed rather than preceded connections to national and international markets. Eastern farmers, looking to escape tired soil or tenancy, sought fertile lands for growing commercial crops. Labor-saving devices, such as Cyrus McCormick's reaper (1834) and John Deere's steel plow (1837), made the West more alluring. McCormick, a Virginia inventor, patented a horse-drawn reaper that allowed two men to harvest the same number of acres of wheat that previously required between four and sixteen men, depending on which hand-held tool they wielded. Because the reaper's efficiency achieved its greatest payoffs on the prairies, where tracts of land were larger and flatter than in the Shenandoah valley, McCormick relocated his factory to Chicago in 1847 and began a dogged campaign to sell his reaper—which at $100 was an expensive investment for the average farmer—and, along with it, the West itself. Without John Deere's steel plow, which unlike wooden and iron plows could break through tough grass and roots and did not require constant cleaning, "breaking the plains" might not have been possible at all.

Most white migrants intended to farm. After locating a suitable land claim, they immediately constructed a

Clearing the Land

rudimentary cabin if none already existed. Time did not permit more elaborate structures, for—contrary to McCormick reaper ads—few settlers found plowed fields awaiting them. First they had to clear the land.

For those settling in wooded areas, the quickest and easiest way to get crops in the ground was to girdle, or to cut deep notches with an ax around a tree's base, cutting off the flow of sap. A few weeks later, the trees would lose their leaves, which farmers burned for fertilizer. As soon as enough light came through, settlers planted corn—a durable and nutritious crop. Eventually the dead trees fell and were chopped for firewood and fences, leaving stumps whose removal was a backbreaking task. At the rate of five to ten acres a year, depending on a family's size, the average family needed ten years to fully clear a farm, assuming they did not relocate sooner. Prairie land took less time. Throughout the 1850s, though, many farmers dismissed lands free of timber as equivalent to deserts, unfit for cultivation.

MᶜCORMICKS MACHINES.

Wisconsin Historical Society

◄ In his advertisements, Cyrus McCormick portrayed his reapers as making the West into a place of prosperity and leisure.

Whereas farming attracted families, lumbering and mining appealed mostly to single young men. By the 1840s, the nation's timber industry centered around the Great Lakes. As eastern forests became depleted, northeastern lumber companies and their laborers migrated to Wisconsin, Michigan, and Minnesota. Recently arrived Scandinavians and French Canadians also worked in the booming lumber industry, which provided construction materials for growing cities and wooden ties for expanding railroads. As the Great Lakes forests thinned, lumbermen moved again—some to the Gulf States' pine forests, some to Canada, and some to the Far West, where Mexicans in California and British in Canada had already established flourishing lumber industries. With the rapid growth of California's cities following the Gold Rush of 1849, timber's demand soared, drawing midwestern lumbermen farther west.

The Midwest's own cities nurtured the surrounding countryside's settlement. Steamboats turned river settlements like Louisville and Cincinnati into vibrant commercial centers, while Chicago, Detroit, and Cleveland grew up on the Great Lakes' banks. By the mid-nineteenth century, Chicago, with its railroads, stockyards, and grain elevators, dominated the region's economy; western farmers transported livestock and grain by rail to that city, where pigs became packed meat and grain became flour before being shipped east. The promise of future flour and future pigs gave rise to commodities markets. Some of the world's most sophisticated and speculative economic practices took place in Chicago.

Courtesy of the Eiteljorg Museum of American Indians and Western Art, Indianapolis

▲ Artist Alfred Jacob Miller portrayed a marriage *à la façon du pays* (in the custom of the country) in which an Indian woman is given in marriage by her father to a *métis* man at a Rocky Mountain *rendezvous* in 1837.

The Federal Government and Westward Expansion

Few white Americans considered settling in the West before the region had been explored, surveyed, secured, and "civilized," by which they meant not only the removal of native populations but also the establishment of churches, businesses, and American legal structures. Although some individuals headed west in advance of European civilization, wide-scale settlement depended on the federal government's sponsorship.

No figure better represents the mythical westerner than the mountain man: the loner who wandered the mountains, trapping beaver, living off the land, casting off all semblance of civilization, and daring to go where no white person had ever trod. Fur trappers were, in fact, among the first white Americans in the trans-Appalachian West, but in reality, their lives bore faint resemblance to the myth. Although many had little contact with American society, they interacted regularly with the West's native peoples. Fur trappers lived among Indians, became multilingual, and often married Indian women. Indian women

The Fur Trade

transformed animal carcasses into finished pelts, and they also smoothed trade relations between their husbands and their own native communities. The offspring of such marriages—métis or mestizos (people of mixed Indian and European heritage)—often entered the fur trade and added to the West's cultural complexity.

The fur trade was an international business, with pelts from deep in the American interior finding their way to Europe and Asia. Until the 1820s, British companies dominated the trade, but American ventures prospered in the 1820s and 1830s. The American Fur Company made John Jacob Astor the nation's wealthiest man. While Astor lived lavishly in his New York City mansion, his business employed hundreds of trappers and traders who lived and worked among native peoples in the Great Lakes and Pacific Northwest regions. From its base in Astoria on the Columbia River, just a few miles from the Pacific Ocean in present-day Oregon, the American Fur Company made millions by sending furs to China.

Even for the great majority of trappers who never made it to Astoria, the fur trade had an international dimension. Beginning in the 1820s, they came together annually for a "rendezvous"—a multiday gathering where they traded fur

Map 13.3 Western Indians and Routes of Exploration

Although western explorers believed they were discovering new routes and places, Indians had long lived in most of the areas through which explorers traveled.

Source: Robert Utley, *The Indian Frontier of the American West*, 1846–1890, University of New Mexico Press, 1984, p. 5. Reprinted by permission of the University of New Mexico Press.

for guns, tobacco, and beads that they could later exchange with Indians. They also shared stories and alcohol, and gambled. Modeled on similar Indian gatherings that had occurred for generations, the rendezvous brought together Americans, Indians, Mexicans, and people of mixed heritage from all over the West—as far north as Canada and as far south as Mexico. Rendezvous took place in remote mountain locations but were cosmopolitan affairs.

By the 1840s, the American fur trade was declining. Beavers had been overhunted and fashions had shifted, with silk supplanting beaver fur as the preferred material for hats. The traders' legacy includes setting a pattern of resource extraction and depletion (and boom and bust), introducing native peoples to devastating diseases, and developing trails across the trans-Mississippi West.

A desire for quicker and safer routes for transporting goods to trading posts drove much early exploration.

Transcontinental Exploration

William Becknell, an enterprising merchant, helped in 1821 to chart the Santa Fe Trail running between Missouri and Santa Fe, New Mexico, where it connected to the Chihuahua Trail running southward into Mexico, allowing American and Mexican merchants to develop a vibrant exchange of American manufactured goods for furs and other items. Fur trader Jedediah Smith rediscovered in 1824 the South Pass; this 20-mile break in the Rocky Mountains in present-day Wyoming had previously been known only to Native Americans and a handful of fur trappers from the Pacific Fur Company who had passed through in 1812. The South Pass became the route followed by most overland travelers to California and Oregon. Less well-known traders, trappers, missionaries, and gold seekers, often assisted by Native American guides, also discovered traveling routes throughout the West, and some—most famously, mountain man Kit Carson—aided government expeditions.

Lewis and Clark's Corps of Discovery was only the first of many federally sponsored expeditions to chart the trans-Mississippi West. These expeditions often had diplomatic goals, aiming to establish cordial relations with Indian groups with whom Americans might trade or enter military alliances. Some had scientific missions, charged with recording information about the region's native inhabitants, flora, and fauna. But they were always also commercial in purpose. Just as Lewis and Clark had hoped to find what proved to be an elusive Northwest Passage to the Pacific, so, too, did later explorers hope to locate land, water, and rail routes that would allow American businessmen and farmers to trade nationally and internationally.

In 1805, the U.S. Army dispatched Zebulon Pike to find the Mississippi River's source and a navigable route west. He was instructed to collect information on natural resources and native peoples, and foster diplomatic relationships with Indian leaders. He was also to purchase land from Indians; before the Supreme Court ruled in *Johnson v. M'Intosh* (1823) that Indians did not own land but rather had only a "right of occupancy," government officials instructed Pike and other explorers to identify and purchase lands suitable for military garrisons.

Although Pike failed to identify the Mississippi's source and had limited success in cultivating relationships and purchasing land, he nonetheless gathered important information. Shortly after returning from present-day Minnesota, he left for what are now Missouri, Nebraska, Kansas, and Colorado. After Pike and his men wandered into Spanish territory to the south, military officials held Pike captive for several months in Mexico, inadvertently giving him a tour of areas that he might not have otherwise explored. After his release, Pike wrote an account of his experiences describing a potential market in southwestern cities as well as bountiful furs and precious metals. The province of Tejas (Texas), with its fertile soil and rich grasslands, enchanted him. At the same time, Pike dismissed the other northern provinces of Mexico, whose boundaries stretched to the northern borders of present-day Nevada and Utah, as unsuitable for human habitation. Although nomadic Indians might sustain

themselves there, he explained, the region was unfit for cultivation by civilized people.

Stephen Long, another army explorer, similarly declared in 1820 that the region comprising modern-day Oklahoma, Kansas, and Nebraska was "the Great American Desert," incapable of cultivation. Until the 1850s, when a transcontinental railroad was planned, this "desert" was reserved for Indian settlement, and most army-sponsored exploration focused elsewhere. In 1838, Congress established the U.S. Army Corps of Topographical Engineers to systematically explore the West in advance of widespread settlement. As a second lieutenant in that corps, John C. Frémont undertook three expeditions to the region between the upper Mississippi and Missouri rivers, the Rockies, the Great Basin, Oregon, and California. He helped survey the Oregon Trail. With the assistance of his wife, Jessie Benton Frémont, Frémont published best-selling accounts of his explorations, earning him the nickname "The Pathfinder" and paving the way for a political career. The Corps of Topographical Engineers' most significant contributions came in the 1850s with its surveying of possible routes for a transcontinental railroad.

The federal government spent millions publicizing the results of its explorations, much more than it allotted for exploration itself. Westward migrants often carried two books with them: the Bible and Frémont's account of his army explorations.

The army did more than explore. It also helped ready the West for settlement. With the General Survey Act of

A Military Presence

1824, Congress empowered the military to chart transportation improvements deemed vital to the nation's military protection or commercial growth. In addition to working on federally funded projects, army engineers helped design state- and privately sponsored roads, canals, and railroads, and its soldiers cleared forests and lay roadbeds. A related bill, also in 1824, authorized the army to improve the Ohio and Mississippi rivers; a later amendment did the same for the Missouri.

By the 1850s, 90 percent of the U.S. military was stationed west of the Mississippi River. When Indians refused to relinquish their lands, the army escorted them westward; when they inflicted harm on whites or their property, the army waged war. The army sometimes destroyed the crops and buildings of white squatters refusing to vacate lands settled without legal title. But, primarily, the army assisted overland migration. Army forts on the periphery of Indian Country intimidated Indians, defended settlers and migrants from Indian attacks, and supplied information and provisions. In theory, the army was also supposed to protect Indians by driving settlers off Indian lands and enforcing laws prohibiting the sale of alcohol to Indians. Yet even when officers were disposed

Gold in California

When James Marshall discovered gold in Sutter's Mill, California, in January 1848, word spread quickly—and quite literally around the world. Within a year, tens of thousands of adventurers from other countries rushed to California, making it the most cosmopolitan place in North America, and perhaps the entire world.

In an era before the telegraph crossed the oceans, the news traveled surprisingly fast. Mexicans heard first. Next, word spread to Chile, Peru, and throughout South America; then across the Pacific to Hawai'i, China, and Australia; and then to Europe—Ireland, France, and the German states. How did the news travel? Overland travelers brought the news south to Baja California and Sonora in Mexico. By spring 1849, some six thousand Mexicans were panning for gold around the newly established town of Sonora, California. Many of the Mexicans came north seasonally to seek gold, spreading news of California on every trip home.

Sailing ships brought news of California gold to Hawai'i. The newspaper *Honolulu Polynesian* announced it in the kingdom on June 24, 1848. "Honolulu has never before witnessed such an excitement as the gold fever has created," the *Polynesian* reported later that summer. Gold seekers and merchants sailed from Hawai'i to California, and their letters home recruited others. The constant traffic led to regular steamship service between Hawai'i and California as early as 1853.

A ship brought news of California gold discoveries to Valparaiso, Chile, in August 1848. More dramatically, a few weeks later, another sailing vessel landed with $2,500 in gold dust aboard. Although Chilean newspapers initially ignored the discovery, people in Chile's cities talked feverishly about gold. By November, newspapers reported rumors of California's overnight riches. Before year's end, two thousand Chileans had left for California, and many Chilean merchants opened branch stores in San Francisco.

Word of gold and California reached Australia in December 1848. Gold seekers quickly made travel arrangements, and by 1850 every ship in Sydney Harbour was destined for California. News had already reached China in mid-1848. A San Francisco merchant headed for the gold fields, Chum Ming, had written a cousin about his hopes for wealth. Four months later, the cousin arrived in San Francisco—with fellow villagers. Widespread poverty and gold's allure prompted many other Chinese to follow. By the mid-1850s, one in five gold miners was Chinese.

Californians, new and old, foreign and native-born, expressed amazement at the ethnic variety. One described it as "the most curious Babel of a place imaginable." In 1850, the new state of California had nearly 40 percent foreign-born inhabitants, the majority non-European. Through word of mouth, rumor, letters home, and newspaper reports, the discovery of gold in 1848 linked California to millions of ordinary people around the globe.

Collection of the New York Historical Society

◀ This 1855 Frank Marryat drawing of a San Francisco saloon dramatizes the international nature of the California gold rush. Like theater performers, the patrons of the saloon dress their parts as Yankees, Mexicans, Asians, and South Americans.

The Center for American History, The University of Texas at Austin

▲ Charles Koppel portrayed the Colorado Desert and Signal Mountain for the *Pacific Railway Reports* (1853). The desert appears vast and unlimited, and those who travel through it seem to be advancing into the unknown.

to enforce such policies, the army's small size relative to the territory it regulated made it virtually impossible to do so.

The Office of Indian Affairs handled the government's other Indian interactions, including treaty negotiations, school management, and trade oversight. Created in 1824 as part of the War Department, the Indian Office cooperated with the military in removing Indians from lands that stood in the way of American expansion and in protecting those citizens who staked their future in the West. In 1849 the Indian Office became part of the newly established Department of the Interior, and soon shifted its focus from removal to civilization, through a reservation system. Whereas some Indians accepted reservations as the best protection from white incursion, others rejected them, sometimes setting off deadly intratribal disagreements.

The federal government controlled vast tracts of land, procured either from the states' cessions of their western claims after the Revolution or through treaties with foreign powers, including Indian nations. The General Land Office, established in 1812 as part of the Treasury Department, handled those lands' distribu-

Public Lands

tion. Its earliest policies, designed to raise revenue, divided western lands into 640-acre tracts to be sold at public auction at a minimum price of $2 an acre. These policies favored speculators over individual, cash-poor farmers. Speculators bought up millions of acres of land. Unable to afford federal lands, many settlers became squatters, prompting Congress in 1820 to lower the price of land to $1.25 per acre and to make available tracts as small as 80 acres. Twelve years later, it began selling forty-acre tracts. Yet it demanded that the land be bought outright, and in a cash-poor society (particularly in the aftermath of the Panic of 1819), few would-be western settlers had enough cash to purchase government land. Because speculators sold land on credit, many small-time farmers bought from them instead, but at inflated prices.

Farmers pressed for a federal policy of preemption— that is, the right to settle on land without obtaining title, to improve it, and to buy it later at the minimum price ($1.25 an acre) established by law. Although some states offered lands through preemption, and although Congress authorized preemption of federal lands in particular instances in the 1820s and 1830s, the first general preemption law, the so-called Log Cabin Bill, came in 1841, and even then, it applied only to surveyed land. The right of preemption extended to unsurveyed lands with the Homestead Act of 1862, which provided that land would be provided free to any U.S. citizen (or foreigner who had declared the intention of becoming a citizen), provided he or she resided on it for five years and improved it. Alternatively, settlers could buy the land outright at $1.25 an acre after six months of residency, an arrangement that allowed them to use the land as collateral for loans to purchase additional land, farming supplies, or machinery. By the time of the Homestead Act, though, much of the remaining federal land was arid, and 160 acres was not always enough for an independent farm. Most of the best land, moreover, ended up in speculators' hands.

The Southwestern Borderlands

Along the Louisiana Territory's southwestern border lay vast provinces controlled mostly by the Comanches and other Indians but claimed first by Spain and then—after 1821—by the newly independent nation of Mexico. New Mexico, with its bustling commercial centers of Albuquerque and Santa Fe, remained under Mexican federal control until the United States conquered the territory during its War with Mexico. Texas, by contrast, had a much more attenuated relationship with the Mexican government; in 1824, it became an autonomous state, giving it substantially more political independence from federal authorities than New Mexico enjoyed. This situation fostered Texas's struggle for national independence and then annexation to the United States, which in turn returned the divisive issue of slavery to the forefront of American political debate.

By the time Anglo-Americans became interested in Mexico's northern reaches, slavery in the Southwest was centuries-old. Yet as practiced by indigenous peoples— Comanches, Apaches, Kiowas, Navajos, Utes, and Pueblos— and by Spaniards, slavery differed from the chattel slavery of Africans and African Americans in the American South. Southwestern slavery was no less violent, but it centered on capturing women and children, who were then assimilated into their captors' communities, where they provided labor and status while fostering economic and diplomatic exchanges with the communities from which they had been captured.

| Southwestern Slavery |

This system of "captives and cousins," as one scholar terms it, was built on racial mixing—a practice anathema to most white Americans. As white slaveholders from the Southeast pushed their way into Mexican territory during the 1820s and 1830s, they often justified their conquest in racial terms. Even the region's Hispanic settlers, they reasoned, had been rendered lazy and barbarous by racial intermixing and were thus destined to be supplanted, whether peaceably or otherwise.

When Mexico gained independence from Spain in 1821, the Hispanic population of New Mexico outnumbered the indigenous Pueblo peoples by three to one. There were 28,000 Hispanics, including people born in Spain and, especially, criollos, people born in New Spain to parents of Spanish descent. Whether Spanish, Indian, criollo, or mestizo, most New Mexicans engaged in irrigated agriculture. To the north of Santa Fe, they farmed small plots, but to the south, larger farms and ranches predominated. Rancheros' wealth came from selling their wool and corn in distant markets, and from relying on unpaid laborers: farm hands, often their own relatives, bound to the rancheros by debt. United by a threat from the province's raiding Indian tribes—Apaches, Utes, Navajos, and Comanches—Hispanics, Pueblos, and mestizos sometimes united in common defense. But relations among Hispanics and the sedentary Pueblos were not always peaceful. Their numerical superiority allowed Hispanics to seize many of the Pueblos' villages and lands in the rich northern river valleys of an otherwise arid region.

| The New Mexican Frontier |

The Santa Fe Trail caused a commercial explosion in New Mexico, doubling the value of imports in just two years. Whereas the Spanish had tried to keep foreigners out, the Mexican government offered enormous land grants to Anglo-American and French entrepreneurs, sometimes in partnership with the region's Hispanic residents, hoping they would develop the region's industry and agriculture, and strengthen commercial ties with the United States.

Although commercial ties did strengthen, very few Americans settled permanently in New Mexico during the 1820s and 1830s. Most of the best lands had already been taken by Indians and Hispanics. And Americans in search of cheap, fertile land did not need to travel that far west; they could find what they were looking for in Texas.

That they would do so, however, was not evident at the time of Mexican independence. Unlike in New Mexico, indigenous Indians remained the dominant group in Texas in 1821, though the population also included Hispanics, Anglos, mestizos, and immigrant Indians. Of the thirty thousand indigenous people, most were Comanches, but there were also Jumanos, Coahuiltecans, Tonkawas, Karankawas, Apaches, Caddos, and Wichitas. Texas was part of what one historian has called the Comanche Empire, an enormous territory spreading from northern Mexico to Louisiana that the Comanches dominated through a combination of kinship ties, trade, diplomacy, and violence. People of European heritage were a relatively small presence in Texas in 1821. Hispanic peoples had been there since the

| The Texas Frontier |

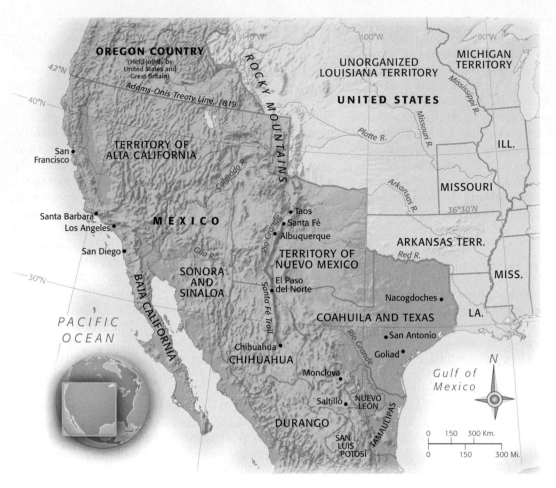

Map 13.4 Mexico's Far North

What is now considered the American Southwest was made up of the northern provinces of Mexico until the United States conquered the territory during the Mexican War (1846–1848).

Source: Copyright © Cengage Learning

1500s, establishing missions and presidios, but by 1820, they numbered only five thousand. Most raised livestock on ranches, while others made their living from trading with Indians. Living so distant from the Spanish colonial capital in Mexico City, they formed a distinctive identity, seeing themselves as Tejanos (or Texans) rather than as Spaniards. Many intermarried with Indians.

After the War of 1812, Anglo-Americans had begun entering Texas, where they sought furs, silver, or adventure. They traded manufactured goods—such as guns, ammunition, and kettles—for animal hides, horses, and mules; soon they largely supplanted the Tejanos as the Indians' trading partners. Although some Anglos settled in Texas, often living among Indians, most simply traveled the Santa Fe and Chihuahua trails without settling. They were deterred in part by the region's violence.

As Indians competed with one another for resources, the southwestern borderlands experienced intermittent but often brutal violence. Mounted on horses, the Comanches hunted bison, took captives, and stole horses, livestock, and crops from their enemies, among whom were the Pawnees, Arapahos, Cheyennes, and Osage. Other, smaller Indian groups, such as the Wichitas and Caddos, mostly farmed, growing enough corn, beans, squash, and pumpkin to feed themselves and to trade with the more mobile Comanches. When crops failed, farmers often turned to bison hunting as well, sometimes causing conflict with the Comanches.

Tensions increased around the time of Mexican independence, when another ten thousand Indians began

The Comanche Empire

Visualizing THE PAST

Paintings and Cultural Impressions

Although few people of Spanish descent settled in Texas, those who did developed a distinctive and proud cultural identity. Calling themselves Tejanos, they adapted their inherited culture—music, dances, and cuisine—to their new surroundings. In the painting below of an 1844 celebration in San Antonio, French-born painter Theodore Gentilz captures the mixture of cultural carryovers and frontier adaptations. Which elements of the scene seem reminiscent of life in Spain or in the colonial capital of Mexico City? Which elements seem to be adaptations to life along a cultural frontier and political borderland? Which elements of the painting seem to celebrate Tejanos culture, and which, if any, seem critical of it? If you were using this painting as a source of information about Tejano culture and its influence on contemporary music and dance, what else would you want to know about the artist and the scene he has captured?

Photo by Robert Corwin

Although the musician in Gentilz's painting is playing the fiddle, other artistic depictions record the widespread use of the guitar, which helped give rise to the corridor, a folk ballad whose legacy is still apparent in today's country and western music.

Daughters of the Republic of Texas Library

Theodore Gentilz arrived in Texas in the 1840s and soon began portraying the region's culture with his paintbrush. Here, Tejano settlers perform the fandango, a Spanish dance.

migrating into the region. From the Old Northwest came Shawnees and Kickapoos—former members of Tecumseh's confederacy—who after their defeat during the War of 1812 had headed north to Canada before heading back southward into Kansas, Indian Territory, and then Texas. From the Old Southwest came Cherokees, Creeks, Choctaws, Chickasaws, and Seminoles, some with African American slaves. Indian newcomers often clashed with indigenous Indians, with whom they vied for land and animals. The conflict was cultural, too: Some immigrant Indians, having adopted Anglo clothing and racial ideologies, dismissed as "savage" the indigenous Indians who hunted buffalo, wore skins, and did not value land as a commodity.

Because such violence threatened the viability of southeastern Indian removal and disrupted trade, the U.S. government brokered a treaty in 1835: The Comanches agreed to allow immigrants onto their lands in exchange for trade opportunities. Before long, trade boomed. Immigrant Indians swapped agricultural products and manufactured goods, such as rifles and ammunition, for the Comanches' meats, robes, and horses. The Comanches also traded human captives, seized in Texas or northern Mexico. That same year, the Comanches ended more than a century of war with the Osages. As peace returned, so too did American traders, who now built permanent trading posts. Meanwhile, the U.S. government's Indian removal continued apace, fueling Americans' commitment to cotton cultivation and expansionism. Mexican officials feared for the region's future.

More than a decade earlier, before Mexican independence, the Spanish had worried about the security of Texas, which they saw as a buffer between hostile Indians, particularly Comanches, and the United States. Their solution was to populate the region.

American Empresarios

Thus when Moses Austin, a miner and trader from Missouri, approached Spanish authorities in Mexico City in January 1821 about settling Americans in Texas, they were willing to make a deal as long as Austin brought with him Americans willing to assimilate into Texas society. In exchange for promising to bring three hundred Catholic families—and no slaves—Austin would receive an enormous land grant of approximately 200,000 acres along the Brazos River. Before Austin could act, though, he died, and Mexico won its independence from Spain in September 1821.

Austin's son, Stephen, pursued his father's scheme, pressing the new Mexican government to honor the grant, which it did in 1823, provided that the younger Austin renounce his American citizenship and become a Mexican national. By 1825, Stephen Austin had settled three hundred families (two thousand white people) and, despite the promise of no slaves, four hundred "contract laborers" of African descent. With contracts that ran for ninety-nine years, these African Americans were essentially slaves. Still, Austin's success at luring settlers to Texas encouraged the Mexican government to sign three more contracts granting Austin land in exchange for his bringing nine hundred additional families.

Generally satisfied with the Austin experiment, in 1824 Mexico passed a Colonization Law providing land and tax incentives to future foreign settlers and leaving the details of colonization to the individual Mexican states. Coahuila y Texas specified that the head of a family could obtain as much as 4,428 acres of grazing land or 177 acres of farming land. The land was cheap, and—unlike land in the United States—could be paid for in installments over six years, with no money due until the fourth year. To be eligible, foreigners had to be upstanding Christians with "good habits," and they had to establish permanent residency. As an incentive for these new settlers to assimilate into Mexican society, the Coahuila y Texas government provided additional land to those who married Mexican women.

Most U.S. citizens who settled in Mexico did so under the auspices of an *empresario,* or immigration agent, who took responsibility for selecting "moral" colonists, distributing lands, and enforcing regulations. In exchange, he received nearly 25,000 acres of grazing land and 1,000 acres of farming land for every hundred families that he settled. Between 1825 and 1832, approximately twenty-four *empresario* contracts (seventeen of which went to Anglo-Americans) had been signed, with the *empresarios* agreeing to bring eight thousand families total. The land grants were so vast that together they covered almost all of present-day Texas.

During the 1820s, Anglo-Americans emigrated, with their slaves, to Texas, motivated by a combination of push and pull factors. Some felt pushed by the hard times following the Panic of 1819; at the same time, they were drawn by cheap land and, especially, generous credit terms. Despite Mexican efforts to encourage assimilation, these Americans tended to settle in separate communities and to interact little with the Tejanos. Even more troubling to the Mexican government, the Anglo-Americans outnumbered the Tejanos two to one. Authorities worried that the transplanted Americans would try to make Texas part of the United States.

In 1826, their fears seemed to materialize when an *empresario* named Haden Edwards called for an independent Texas, the "Fredonia Republic." Other *empresarios,* reasoning that they had more to gain than to lose from peaceful relations with the Mexican government, resisted Edwards's secessionist movement. Austin even sent militia to help quash the rebellion. Although the Fredonia revolt failed, Mexican authorities dreaded what it might foreshadow.

Texas Politics

The answer to the secessionist threat, Mexican authorities thought, was to weaken the American presence in Texas. In 1830, they terminated legal immigration from the United States while simultaneously encouraging immigration from Europe and other parts of Mexico in order to dilute the American influence. They prohibited American slaves from entering Texas, a provision that brought Texas in line with the rest of Mexico—where slavery had been outlawed the previous year—and that was meant to repel American slaveholders. Yet these laws did little to discourage Americans and their slaves from coming; soon they controlled most of the Texas coastline and its border with the United States. Mexican authorities repealed the anti-immigration law in 1833, reasoning that it discouraged upstanding settlers but did nothing to stem the influx of undesirable settlers. By 1835, the non-Indian population of Texas was nearly thirty thousand, with Americans outnumbering Tejanos seven to one.

White Texans divided into two main factions. There were those, like Stephen Austin, who favored staying in Mexico but demanding more autonomy, the legalization of slavery, and free trade with the United States. Others pushed for Texas secession from Mexico and asked to be annexed to the United States. In 1835, the secessionists overtook a Mexican military installation charged with collecting taxes at Galveston Bay. Austin advocated a peaceful resolution to the crisis, but Mexican authorities nonetheless considered him suspicious and jailed him for eighteen months, an act that helped convert him to the independence cause. But it would be Sam Houston and Davy Crockett—newly arrived Americans—who would lead the movement.

With discontent over Texas increasing throughout Mexico, Mexican president General Santa Anna declared

The Lone Star Republic

himself dictator and marched his army toward Texas. Fearing Santa Anna would free their slaves, and citing similarities between their own cause and that of the American colonies in the 1770s, Texans staged an armed rebellion. After initial defeats at the Alamo mission in San Antonio and at Goliad in March 1836, the Texans easily triumphed by year's end. They declared themselves the Lone Star Republic and elected Sam Houston as president. Their constitution legalized slavery and banned free blacks from living within Texas.

Texas then faced the challenge of nation building, which to its leaders involved Indian removal. When the Indians refused to leave, Mirabeau Lamar, the nation's second president, mobilized the Texas Rangers—mounted nonuniformed militia—to drive them out through terror. Sanctioned by the Texas government, but sometimes acting on their own, the Rangers raided Indian villages, where they robbed, raped, and murdered. Although some Texas officials tried to negotiate with the Indians and Tejanos, it was what one historian has called "ethnic cleansing" that cleared the land of its native settlers to make room for white Americans and their African American slaves. Before long, the surviving Comanches would face starvation and depopulation—weakened by European disease, drought, and overhunting—but not before fighting back with devastating raids on northern Mexico, ravaging its inhabitants and countryside, and inadvertently paving the way for American conquest.

After annexing Texas in 1845, the United States, seeking to further expand its territorial reach, waged war

Wartime Losses and Profits

against Mexico from 1846 to 1848 (see Chapter 14). In the borderlands, as in Mexico itself, civilians—Indians,

▲ Like George Allen, many Texas settlers relied on slave labor to work their fields and maintain their households.

The Center for American History, The University of Texas at Austin tejanos, californios, and Mexicans—got caught in the fray. Some lost their lives, and many more, precariously caught between the two sides, suffered wartime depredations. If they aided the Mexicans, the U.S. Army destroyed their homes; if they refused aid to the Mexicans, then the Mexicans destroyed their homes. A U.S. army report in 1847 acknowledged that its "wild volunteers . . . committed . . . all sorts of atrocities on the persons and property of Mexicans." Many civilians fled. Even once the war ended in the borderlands, violence did not stop. From 1847 to 1848, Texas Rangers slaughtered Indians. "They think that the death of an Indian is a fair offsett [sic] to the loss of a horse," wrote one Anglo American.

Yet some civilians profited from the war. Farmers sold provisions and mules to the armies, peddlers sold alcohol and food to soldiers, and others set up gambling and prostitution businesses near army camps. Even still, tension generally characterized the relationship between civilians and soldiers, largely because of the American soldiers' racial attitudes.

Cultural Frontiers in the Far West

Even before the United States seized tremendous amounts of new territory during the War with Mexico, some Americans took the gamble of a lifetime and moved to the Far West, often to places—such as California and Utah—that Mexico controlled. Some sought religious freedom or to convert others to Christianity, but most wanted fertile farmland. Whatever their reasons for moving west, they often encountered people from different cultures. Such encounters sometimes led to cooperation, but more often to tension or open conflict.

Catholic missionaries maintained a strong presence in the Far West. In the Spanish missions, priests treated Indians as "spiritual children," introducing them to Catholic sacraments; holding them to a rigid system of prayer, sexual conduct, and work; and treating them as legal minors. When they failed to live up to priests' or soldiers' expectations, they were subject to corporeal punishment. When they ran away, they were forcibly returned. With no political voice and few other choices, Indians often responded to abusive practices with armed uprisings, in the process helping to weaken the mission system itself.

Western Missionaries

A Mexican law secularized the California missions in 1833, removing them from ecclesiastical control and using them primarily to organize Indian labor. Some Indians stayed at the missions, others left to farm their own land or to find employment elsewhere, but for almost all, secularization brought enhanced personal freedom despite persistent limitations to their legal rights.

Even after the missions' secularization, Catholic missionaries—Americans, Europeans, and converted Indians—continued ministering to immigrants, working to convert Indians, and encouraging specifically Roman Catholic colonies. Missionaries founded schools and colleges, introduced medical services, and even aided in railroad explorations.

In the Pacific Northwest, Catholics vied directly with Protestants for Indian souls. Although evangelicals focused on the Midwest, a few hoped to bring Christianity to the Indians of the Far West. Under the auspices of the American Board of Commissioners for Foreign Missions, two missionary couples—generally credited as being the first white migrants along the Oregon Trail—traveled to the Pacific Northwest in 1836. Narcissa and Marcus Whitman built a meetinghouse for Cayuse Indians in Waiilatpu, near present-day Walla Walla, Washington, while Eliza and Henry Spalding worked to convert the Nez Percé at Lapwai, in what is now Idaho. With their air of cultural superiority, the Whitmans did little to endear themselves to the Cayuses, none of whom converted. The Whitmans redirected their efforts toward the ever-increasing stream of white migrants flowing into Oregon beginning in the 1840s.

These migrants' arrival escalated tensions with the Cayuses, and when a devastating measles epidemic struck in 1847, the Cayuses saw it as a calculated assault. They retaliated by murdering the Whitmans and twelve other missionaries. After the Whitmans' violent deaths, the Spaldings abandoned their own, more successful mission; blamed Catholics for inciting the massacre; and became farmers in Oregon, not returning to Lapwai for another fifteen years.

The Mormons, who had been persecuted in Missouri and Illinois, sought religious sanctuary in the West. In 1847, Brigham Young led them to their "Promised Land" in the Great Salt Lake valley, still under Mexican control but soon to become part of the unorganized U.S. territory of Utah. As non-Mormons began to settle in Utah, Brigham Young tried to dilute their influence by attracting new Mormon settlers to what he called the state of Deseret. In 1849, Young and his associates established the Perpetual Emigration Fund, which sponsored "handcart companies" of poor migrants, particularly from Europe, who pushed all their belongings to Utah in small handcarts.

Mormons

The Mormon's arrival in the Great Basin complicated the region's already complex relations among Indians. The Utes, for example, had long traded in stolen goods and captured people, particularly Paiutes. After Mormons tried to curtail the slave trade, Ute slavers tortured their Paiute captives, particularly children, calculating that Mormons would buy them. The ploy often worked; when it did not, Ute slavers sometimes killed the children, in one case dangling them by their feet and thrashing them against stones. The purchased children often worked as servants in Mormon homes, which encouraged their distraught families, eager for proximity to their children, to settle near Mormon villages. Although the Mormons tried to bring the Paiutes into their religious fold, they—much like Catholic missionaries in California—treated adult Indians as children, causing friction, even violence, when the Paiutes sought to secure their autonomy. Sharing the Utes as a common enemy, the Mormons and Paiutes nonetheless formed an uneasy alliance in the early 1850s.

With their slave trade threatened and their economy in shambles, the Utes attacked Mormon and Paiute settlements to steal livestock and horses for resale, and then to vandalize their crops and property in an effort to drive away the Mormons. War erupted in 1853, and although an uneasy truce was reached in 1854, tensions continued between the Mormons and their Indian neighbors.

And between Mormons and their white neighbors. Although Mormons prospered from providing services, such as ferries, and supplies to tens of thousands of California-bound settlers and miners passing by their settlements, Young discouraged "gentiles" (his term for non-Mormons) from settling in Deseret and advocated boycotts of gentile businesses. When in 1852 the Mormons openly sanctioned polygamy, which some of its followers had practiced for more than a decade, anti-Mormon sentiment increased throughout the nation. After some young Mormons vandalized federal offices in Utah, President James Buchanan—hoping to divert Americans' attention from the increasingly divisive slavery issue—dispatched 2,500 federal troops in June 1857 to suppress an alleged Mormon rebellion.

Anxious over their own safety, a group of Mormons joined some Paiutes in attacking a passing wagon train of non-Mormon migrants. Approximately 120 men, women, and children died in the so-called Mountain Meadows Massacre in August 1857. In the next two years, the U.S. Army and the Mormons engaged in armed conflict, resulting in much property destruction but no fatalities. As the Mormons' relationships with their neighbors and passersby indicate, western violence often emerged from complex interactions and alliances which did not simply pit natives against newcomers.

Nor were all encounters between natives and newcomers violent. From 1840 until 1860, between 250,000 and 500,000 people, including many children, walked across much of the continent, a trek that took seven months on average. Although they traveled armed for conflict, most of their encounters with Indians were peaceful, if tense.

Oregon and California Trails

The overland journeys began at one of the so-called jumping-off points—towns such as Independence, St. Joseph, and Westport Landing—along the Missouri River, where migrants bought supplies for the 2,000-mile trip still ahead of them. After cramming supplies into wagons already overflowing with household possessions, they set out either in organized wagon trains or on their own. While miners frequently traveled alone or in groups of fortune-seeking young men, farmers—including many women migrating only at their husbands' insistence—often traveled with relatives, neighbors, church members, and other acquaintances.

They timed their departures to be late enough that they could find forage grass for their oxen and livestock, but not so late that they would encounter the treacherous snows that came early to the Rockies and the Sierra Nevada. Not all were successful. From 1846 to 1847, the Donner Party took a wrong turn, got caught in a blizzard, and resorted to cannibalism. More fortunate overland migrants trudged alongside their wagons, beginning their days well before dawn, pausing only for a short midday break, and walking until late afternoon. They covered on average 15 miles a day, in weather ranging from freezing cold to blistering heat. In wagon trains composed of families, men generally tended livestock during the day, while women—after an energy-draining day on the trail—set up camp, prepared meals, and tended small children. Many women gave birth on the trail, where an always-difficult experience could become excruciating. "Her sufferings were so great," one woman wrote about her sister. "It all seems like a jumble of jolting wagon, crying baby, dust, sagebrush and the never ceasing pain." Even under normal circumstances, trail life was exhausting, both physically and emotionally. Overlanders worried about Indian attack, getting lost, running out of provisions or water, and losing loved ones, who would have to be buried along the trail, in graves never again to be visited. But for most adults, trail life did not prove particularly dangerous, with Indian attacks rare and death rates approximating those of society at large. Children, though, had a greater risk than adults of being crushed by wagon wheels or drowning during river crossings.

Indians were usually peaceful, if cautious. Particularly during the trails' early days, Indians provided food and information or ferried migrants across rivers; in exchange, migrants offered wool blankets, knives, metal pots, tobacco, ornamental beads, and other items in short supply in

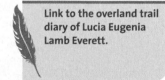

Link to the overland trail diary of Lucia Eugenia Lamb Everett.

Indian societies. When exchanges went bad—when one of the parties misunderstood the other's cultural practices or tried to swindle the other—relationships grew tense, not just between the particular persons involved, but between Indians and migrants more generally. Indians grew suspicious of all white people, just as migrants failed to distinguish different native bands or tribes.

A persistent aggravation among migrants was the theft of livestock, which they usually blamed on Indians even though white thieves stole livestock, too. Indians who took livestock often did so when whites failed to offer gifts in exchange for grazing rights. One such incident, the so-called Mormon Cow Incident (or the Grattan Massacre), resulted in human bloodshed, forever altering relationships along the Oregon Trail.

In August 1854, a Lakota in present-day Wyoming slaughtered a cow that had strayed from a nearby Mormon camp. When Lakota leaders offered compensation, U.S. Army Lieutenant John Grattan, intent on making a point, refused the offer. Tempers flared, Grattan ordered his men to shoot, and after a Lakota chief fell dead, the Indians returned the fire, killing Grattan and all twenty-nine of his men. In retaliation, the following year General William Harney led six hundred soldiers to a village near Ash Hollow, where migrants and Indians had traded peaceably for many years. When Indian leaders refused to surrender any of their people to Harney, the general ordered his men to fire. Thirty minutes later, eighty-seven Indians lay dead, and seventy women and children had been taken prisoner. The event disrupted peaceful exchange along the trail and laid the groundwork for nearly two decades of warfare between the Lakotas and the U.S. Army.

Even as the U.S. Army became embroiled in armed conflict, the Indian Office worked to negotiate treaties to keep Indians—and their intertribal conflicts—from interfering with western migration

Indian Treaties

and commerce. The Fort Laramie Treaty of 1851 (or the Horse Creek Council Treaty) was signed by the United States and eight northern Plains tribes—the Lakotas, Cheyennes, Arapahos, Crows, Assiniboines, Gros-Ventres, Mandans, and Arrickaras—who occupied the Platte River valley through which the three great overland routes westward—the Oregon, California, and Mormon Trails—all passed. Two years later, in 1853, the United States signed a treaty with three southwestern nations, the Comanches, Kiowas, and Apaches, who lived in the vicinity of the Sante Fe Trail. Under the terms of both treaties, the Indians agreed to maintain peace among themselves, to recognize government-delineated tribal boundaries, to allow the United States to construct roads and forts within those boundaries, to refrain from depredations against western migrants, and to issue restitution for any depredations nonetheless committed. In return, they would receive annual allotments from the U.S. government for ten years, to be paid with provisions, domestic animals, and agricultural implements. These allotments could be renewed for another five years at the discretion of the president of the United States.

But these treaties often meant different things to their Indian signatories and to the U.S. officials who brokered them. Contrary to U.S. expectations, Indian chiefs did not see such treaties as perpetually binding. Government

▲ This rare stereocard shows an emigrant train, including two women and possibly a child, dwarfed by the natural landscape in Strawberry Valley, Califonia, in the 1860s.

Library of Congress

The Walters Art Museum, Baltimore

▲ Established in 1834, Fort Laramie—pictured here three years later by Alfred Jacob Miller— served as a fur-trading site, where Indians and trappers of European or mixed heritage came together not only to exchange goods but also to socialize. In 1849, as interactions between Indians and overland migrants to Oregon grew increasingly tense, the U.S. Army took over the fort, now designed to protect overland emigrants. Located in eastern Wyoming, the fort stood at the beginning of the Oregon Trail.

officials, meanwhile, promised allotments but did little to ensure their timely arrival, often leaving Indians starving and freezing. The treaties did not end intratribal warfare, nor did they fully secure the overlanders' safety. But they did represent the U.S. government's efforts to promote expansion and to protect those citizens who caught the western fever.

Armed conflict took relatively few lives compared to cholera, smallpox, and other maladies. The trails' jumping-off points, where migrants camped in close quarters while preparing for their journeys, bred disease, which migrants inadvertently carried to the Indians with whom they traded. Fearful of infection, Indians and migrants increasingly shied away from trading.

Ecological Consequences of Cultural Contact

The disappearance of the buffalo (American bison) from the trails' environs further inflamed tensions. The buffalo not only provided protein to Plains Indians; they also held great spiritual significance. Many Native Americans blamed the migrants for the buffalo's disappearance, even though most overlanders never laid eyes on a buffalo. By the time the overland migration reached its peak in the late 1840s and 1850s, the herds had already been overhunted, in part by Native Americans eager to trade their hides. As traffic increased along the trail, the surviving buffalo scattered to where the grass was safe from the voracious appetites, and trampling feet, of the overlanders' livestock. But on those rare occasions when wagon trains did stumble upon bison herds, men rushed to fulfill their frontier fantasies—nurtured by the literature they had read—and shot the animals; such buffalo chases provided diversions from the trail's drudgery. Overlanders hunted other animals for sport, too, leaving behind rotting carcasses of antelopes, wolves, bears, and birds—animals that held spiritual significance for many Native Americans.

Overland migrants also sparked prairie fires. Indians had long used fire to clear farm land, to stimulate the growth of grasslands, and to create barren zones that would discourage bison from roaming into a rival nation's territory. But now emigrants—accustomed to stoves, not open fires— accidentally started fires that raged across the prairies, killing animals and the vegetation on which they survived. On rarer occasions, Indians started fires in the hope of capturing the migrants' fleeing livestock. Stories about intentionally lit fires exaggerated their extent, but they, too, contributed to increasing hostility between Indians and overlanders.

Nowhere did migrants intrude more deeply on Indian life than near the California gold strikes. In January 1848, John Wilson Marshall discovered gold on John Sutter's property along a shallow tributary to the American River near present-day Sacramento, California. During the next year, tens of thousands of "forty-niners" rushed to California, where they practiced what is called placer mining, panning and dredging for gold in the hope of instant riches.

Gold Rush

Some did indeed make fortunes. Peter Brown, a black man from Ste. Genevieve, Missouri, wrote his wife in 1851 that "California is the best country in the world to make money. It is also the best place for black folks on the globe." But not everyone reveled in the gold strikes. John Sutter complained that gold "destroyed" his milling and tanning businesses, as his Indians and Mormon workers left him for the mines and vandals stole his property. Most forty-niners never found enough gold to pay their expenses. "The stories you hear frequently in the States," one gold seeker wrote home, "are the most extravagant lies imaginable—the mines are a humbug." With their dreams dashed—and

> Link to John Sutter's account of discovering gold in California and its consequences.

too poor or embarrassed to return home—many forty-niners took wage-paying jobs with large mining companies that used dangerous machinery to cut deep into the earth's surface to reach mineral veins.

The discovery of gold changed the face of California. (See Map 13.5.) As a remote Mexican province, California had a chain of small settlements surrounded by military forts (presidios) and missions, and it was inhabited mostly by Indians, along with a small number of Mexican rancheros, who raised cattle and sheep on enormous landholdings worked by coerced Indian laborers. As word spread of gold strikes, new migrants—from South America, Asia, Australia, and Europe—rushed to California. Although a California Supreme Court ruling—*People v. Hall* (1854)—made it virtually impossible to prevent violence against Chinese immigrants, Chinese citizens continued to seek their fortunes in California; by 1859, approximately 35,000 of them worked in the goldfields.

With so many hungry gold miners to feed, California experienced an agricultural boom. Although the immediate vicinity of mines became barren, when hydraulic mining washed away surface soil to expose buried lodes, California agriculture thrived overall, with wheat becoming the preferred crop: it required minimal investment, was easily planted, and had a relatively short growing

> Link to the original text of "Ahine, Chinaman."

Library of Congress

▲ The vibrant trade in buffalo hides prompted both Indians and whites to over hunt the American bison, leading to near extinction for the animal by the latter part of the nineteenth century.

Map 13.5 The California Gold Rush

Gold was discovered at Sutter's Mill in 1848, sparking the California gold rush that took place mostly along the western foothills of the Sierra Nevada mountains.

Source: Copyright © Cengage Learning

season. In contrast to the Midwest's and Oregon's family farms, though, California's large-scale wheat farming depended on bonded Indian laborers.

Mining brought commercial and industrial boom, too, as enterprising merchants rushed to supply, feed, and clothe the new settlers. Among them was Levi Strauss, a German Jewish immigrant, whose tough mining pants found a ready market among the prospectors. Because men greatly outnumbered women, women's skills (and company) were in great demand. Even as men set up all-male households and performed tasks that bent prevailing notions of gender propriety, women received high fees for cooking, laundering, and sewing. Women also ran boarding houses, hotels, and brothels.

Mining Settlements

Cities sprang up. In 1848, San Francisco had been a small mission settlement of about 1,000 Mexicans, Anglos, soldiers, friars, and Indians. With the gold rush, it became an instant city, ballooning to 35,000 people in 1850. It was the West Coast gateway to the interior, and ships bringing people and supplies jammed the harbor. A French visitor in that year wrote, "At San Francisco, where fifteen months ago one found only a half-dozen large cabins, one finds today a stock exchange, a theater, churches of all Christian cults, and a large number of quite beautiful homes."

Yet as the Anglo-American, European, Hispanic, Asian, and African American populations swelled, the Indian population experienced devastation. Although California was admitted into the Union as a free state in 1850, its legislature soon passed "An Act for the Government and Protection of Indians" that essentially legalized Indians' enslavement. The practice of using enslaved Indians in the mines between 1849 and 1851 ended only when newly arrived miners brutally attacked the Indian workers, believing they degraded white labor and gave an unfair advantage to established miners. Those slaves who survived the violence were sent to work instead as field workers and house servants. Between 1821 and 1860, the Indian population of California fell from 200,000 to 30,000, as Indians died from disease, starvation, and violence. Because masters separated male and female workers, even Indians who survived failed to reproduce in large numbers.

The Politics of Territorial Expansion

With the population's westward movement shifting the locus of political power, Democratic and Whig politicians tried to keep the slavery issue out of the politics of territorial expansion. But they could not. Westward expansion was central to Democratic ideology, which saw the West's fertile and abundant lands as essential for creating a society in which white men could establish independent livelihoods and receive equal rights, freed from the undue influence of established slaveholders or urban elites. Whigs were more suspicious of rapid westward expansion, though they welcomed the commercial opportunities it might bring. Instead, they pushed harder for industrial and commercial development within the nation's current boundaries. Henry Clay, a leading Whig, explained that it "is much more important that we unite, harmonize, and improve what we have than attempt to acquire more."

The Texas issue, however, made it impossible to disentangle westward expansion and slavery. Soon after establishing the Lone Star Republic, Sam Houston approached American authorities to propose annexation as a state. But a new slave state would upset the balance of slave and free states in the Senate, a balance maintained since before the Missouri Compromise. Neither Whigs nor Democrats, wary of causing sectional divisions within their ranks, were inclined to confront the issue. In the 1830s, Democratic presidents Andrew Jackson and Martin Van Buren—one a strong proponent of slavery, the other a mild opponent—sidestepped the issue. But by the mid-1840s—with cotton cultivation expanding rapidly—some Democratic politicians began to equate the annexation of Texas with the nation's manifest destiny.

Manifest Destiny

The belief that American expansion westward and southward was inevitable, just, and divinely ordained dated to the nation's founding but was first labeled "manifest destiny" in 1845, by John L. O'Sullivan, editor of the *United States Magazine and Democratic Review*. O'Sullivan claimed that Texas annexation would be "the fulfillment of our manifest destiny to overspread the continent allotted by Providence for the free development of our yearly multiplying millions." The nation's destiny, he and others believed, was to encompass the continent. Manifest destiny implied that Americans had a God-given right, perhaps even an obligation, to expand their republican and Christian institutions to less fortunate and less civilized peoples. Manifest destiny motivated few Americans to pack their wagons and head westward. It did, however, provide a political rationale for territorial expansion.

Implicit in the idea of manifest destiny was the belief that American Indians and Hispanics, much like people of African descent, were inferior peoples best controlled or conquered. White racial theorists believed that, unlike white people, pure-blooded Indians and blacks were not capable of self-improvement. Nor, according to these racial theorists, were Hispanics because intermarriage with Indians had left them incapable of improvement. Lansford Hastings, an Ohio native who ventured west and authored *The Emigrants' Guide to Oregon and California* (1845) noted that a *Californio* (a Mexican living in California) was "scarcely a visible grade, in the scale of intelligence, above the barbarous tribes by whom he is surrounded." Hastings hoped that, if enough Anglo-Saxons migrated to California, they could conquer the Mexicans with sheer numbers. And if they did so, they could congratulate themselves for carrying out God's will. Others, however, felt that an expanding American empire defied God's will. During debates over Texas annexation, Transcendentalist William Ellery Channing argued that the United States should expand its empire by example not conquest: It should "assume the role of sublime moral empire, with a mission to diffuse freedom by manifesting its fruits, not to plunder, crush, and destroy."

In June 1846, impatient expansionists, including John C. Frémont, staged an armed rebellion against Mexican authorities and declared California an independent republic. Because the U.S. military soon conquered California in its War with Mexico, the "Bear Flag Rebellion"—so named for the symbol on the revolutionaries' flag—was short-lived but further inflamed racial tensions in California.

To the north, Britain and the United States had jointly occupied the disputed Oregon Territory since 1818.

Fifty-Four Forty or Fight

Beginning with John Quincy Adams's administration, the United States had tried to fix the boundary at the 49th parallel, but Britain was determined to maintain access to Puget Sound and the Columbia River. As migrants streamed into Oregon in the early 1840s, expansionists demanded the entire Oregon Country for the United States, up to its northernmost border at latitude 54° 40'. Soon "fifty-four forty or fight" became their rallying cry.

President Tyler wanted both Oregon and Texas, but was obsessed with Texas. He argued that there was little to fear from slavery's expansion, for it would spread the nation's black population more thinly, causing the institution's gradual demise. But when word leaked out that Secretary of State John Calhoun had written to the British minister in Washington to justify Texas annexation as a way of protecting slavery—"a political institution essential to the peace, safety, and prosperity of those States in which it exists"—the Senate rejected annexation in 1844 by a vote of 35 to 16.

Worried southern Democrats persuaded their party's 1844 convention to adopt a rule requiring that

Polk and the Election of 1844

the presidential nominee receive two-thirds of the convention votes, effectively giving the southern states a veto and allowing them to block the nomination of Martin Van Buren, an opponent of annexation. Instead, the party ran "Young Hickory," House Speaker James K. Polk, an avid expansionist and slaveholding cotton planter from Tennessee. The Democratic platform, designed to appeal to voters across regional lines, called for occupation of the entire Oregon Territory and annexation of Texas. The Whigs, who ran Henry Clay, argued that the Democrats' belligerent nationalism would lead to war with Great Britain or Mexico or both. Clay favored expansion through negotiation, whereas many northern Whigs opposed annexation altogether, fearful it would lead to additional slave states and strained relations with vital trading partners.

Polk and the Democrats won the election by 170 electoral votes to 105, though with a margin of just 38,000 out of 2.7 million votes cast. Polk won New York's 36 electoral votes by just 6,000 popular votes. Abolitionist James G. Birney, the Liberty Party candidate, had drawn almost 16,000 votes away from Clay by running on a

▲ This 1845 portrayal of Oregon City, the western terminus of the Oregon Trail, was provided by a British army officer sent to investigate the influence of large-scale American immigration into a territory jointly occupied by Great Britain and the United States. After the Oregon Treaty (1846) drew the boundary between British and American territory at the forty-ninth parallel, Oregon City became the capital of the Oregon Territory from 1848 to 1851.

Free-Soil platform. Without Birney, Clay might have won New York, giving him an edge of 141 to 134 in the electoral college. Abolitionist forces thus unwittingly helped elect a slaveholder as president.

Interpreting Polk's victory as a mandate for annexation, President Tyler proposed that Texas be admitted by joint resolution of Congress. The usual method of annexation, by treaty negotiation, required a two-thirds vote in the Senate—which expansionists did not have because there were sufficient opponents to slavery who stood against annexation. Joint resolution required only a simple majority in each house. On March 1, 1845, the resolution passed the House by 120 to 98 and the Senate by 27 to 25. Three days before leaving office, Tyler signed the measure. Mexico, which had never recognized Texas independence, immediately broke relations with the United States. In October, the citizens of Texas ratified annexation, and Texas joined the Union, with a constitution permitting slavery, in December 1845. The nation was on the brink of war with Mexico. That conflict—like none other before it—would lay bare the inextricable relationships among westward expansion, slavery, and sectional discord.

Annexation of Texas

SUMMARY

Encouraged by literary and artistic images of the frontier, easterners often viewed the West as a place of natural abundance, where hard-working individuals could seek security, freedom, and perhaps even fortune. By the millions they poured into the Old Southwest and Old Northwest in the early decades of the nineteenth century. Although the federal government promoted westward expansion—in the form of support for transportation improvements, surveying, cheap land, and protection from Indians—western migrants did not make the decision to head west lightly. Nor did they always find what they were looking for. Some returned home, some moved to new locations, and some—too poor or too embarrassed—stayed in the West, where they reluctantly abandoned their dreams of economic independence. Others found what they were looking for in the West, though often the road to success proved much slower and more circuitous than they had anticipated.

Not everyone who went west did so voluntarily, nor did everyone in the West think of it as an expanding region. African American slaves were moved westward by their owners in enormous numbers in the years between 1820 and 1860. Native Americans saw their lands and their livelihoods constrict, and their environments so altered that their economic and spiritual lives were threatened. Some Indians responded to the white incursion through accommodation and peaceful overtures; others resisted, sometimes forcefully. If their first strategy failed, then they tried another. But the sheer force of numbers favored whites. For Indians in Texas and California, white incursions brought devastation.

Legacy FOR A PEOPLE AND A NATION

Descendants of Early Latino Settlers

Today, the American news media are filled with stories about Latinos in the United States, for current census figures identify them as the nation's largest racial or ethnic minority. Newspapers, magazines, television, and radio focus on the growing number of documented and undocumented Latino immigrants, the increasing impact of Latinos in the communities where they live and work, and the occasionally difficult relationships of such immigrants and African Americans. Yet all the attention devoted to recent arrivals overlooks a considerable proportion of the Latino population: those who are descended not from immigrants but from people whose residency in North America predated the existence of the United States.

When the region stretching from eastern Texas to California was acquired by the United States in the 1840s, its population included not only the members of indigenous Indian nations, but also scattered settlements composed of thousands of people with at least partial European ancestry, primarily Spanish or Portuguese. Their descendants have included such U.S. congressmen as Manuel Luján (1969–1988) and such senators as Kenneth Salazar (who served from 2004 to 2009, when he resigned to become Secretary of the Interior). Today, when asked about their immigrant ancestors, they commonly reply that the country came to them rather than the reverse. Their families have resided in what is now U.S. territory for as long as twelve or fourteen generations.

Intriguingly, persuasive evidence suggests that many of the early Iberian settlers in New Mexico were *conversos*, or of New Christian descent—that is, people whose Jewish ancestors formally converted to Catholicism in the fifteenth century in order to avoid religious persecution. After Jews were expelled from Spain and Portugal in 1492, many fled to the Spanish empire's far corners. Some participated in Juan de Oñate's 1598 expedition to New Mexico, and others subsequently moved to the remote settlement. There, some secretly continued to follow such Jewish customs as Sabbath observances and food restrictions (not eating pork, for example). When the Inquisition took note of these practices in the 1660s, among those charged with such offenses were a former governor of the colony and his wife. Today, some Latino residents of New Mexico have acknowledged their *converso* roots and reclaimed a Jewish identity.

All the long-standing Latino citizens of the United States, not just those of *converso* descent, have given the nation and its people an important multicultural legacy.

Although their belief in Native Americans' inferiority allowed many white Americans to rationalize the Indians' fate, it was white attitudes toward black people and slavery that drove their decisions about where to locate in the West. Those who believed that slavery degraded white labor headed along a northern trajectory, whereas those who dreamed of slave ownership headed southward, where they clashed with yet another group of people whom they deemed racially inferior: Mexicans. When American settlers in Texas achieved their independence from Mexico, legalized slavery, and applied for annexation by the United States, they brought the divisive issue of slavery's westward expansion to the surface of American politics. Although Democratic politicians at first tried to maintain a geographic equilibrium by proposing an ambitious territorial agenda in Oregon as well, it would be Texas annexation that set the stage for military conflict, the addition of vast territories in the Southwest, and reinvigorated sectional conflict.

SUGGESTIONS FOR FURTHER READING

Gary Clayton Anderson, *The Conquest of Texas: Ethnic Cleansing in the Promised Land, 1820–1875* (2005)

Stuart Banner, *How the Indians Lost Their Land: Law and Power on the Frontier* (2005)

Ned Blackhawk, *Violence over the Land: Indians and Empires in the Early American West* (2006)

Andrew R. L. Cayton and Peter S. Onuf, *The Midwest and the Nation: Rethinking the History of an American Region* (1990)

Pekka Hämäläinen, *The Comanche Empire* (2008)

Robert V. Hine and John Mack Faragher, *The American West: A New Interpretive History* (2000)

Albert L. Hurtado, *Indian Survival on the California Frontier* (1998)

Susan L. Johnson, *Roaring Camp: The Social World of the California Gold Rush* (2000)

Andrés Reséndez, *Changing National Identities at the Frontier: Texas and New Mexico, 1800–1850* (2005)

Michael L. Tate, *Indians and Emigrants: Encounters on the Overland Trails* (2006)

CourseMate

Go to the CourseMate website for primary source links, study tools, and review materials for this chapter. www.cengagebrain.com

Chapter 14

Slavery and America's Future: The Road to War 1845–1861

On a stiflingly hot evening, June 16, 1858, former one-term congressman Abraham Lincoln stepped onto the raised platform of the legislative chamber in the state house at Springfield, Illinois, to accept the Republican Party's nomination to run for the U.S. Senate against the most famous Democrat in America—the incumbent, Stephen A. Douglas. At six feet, four inches, Lincoln towered over the packed hall, his head nearly level with the edge of the balcony. The nation was at a historic crossroads, and he had worked on this speech for weeks. He loved to recite poetry and delivered his poetic prose with unmatched intellectual power. His body angular, his hands large and awkward, his voice strong but high-pitched, Lincoln quickly gained his audience's attention. "Slavery agitation" had convulsed American politics and exploded in guerrilla war in Kansas. "In my opinion," ventured Lincoln, "it will not cease, until a crisis shall have been reached, and passed." Then, in imagery familiar to his Bible-reading listeners, he gave the crisis its unforgettable metaphor.

"A house divided against itself cannot stand." I believe this government cannot endure permanently half slave and half free. I do not expect the Union to be dissolved—I do not expect the house to *fall*—but I *do* expect it will cease to be divided. It will become *all* one thing, or *all* the other. Either the *opponents* of slavery will arrest the further spread of it, and place it where the public mind shall rest in the belief that it is in the course of ultimate extinction; or its *advocates* will push it forward, till it shall become alike lawful in *all* the States, *old* as well as *new*—North as well as South.

In much of the remainder of the thirty-minute speech, Lincoln contended that a conspiracy—a "design" led by the Democratic Party's "chief bosses"—sought to make slavery a *national* institution. With partisan fervor, he charged Douglas with not caring "whether slavery be voted down or voted up." For Lincoln, this was a choice history would no longer allow Americans to avoid.

◀ Abraham Lincoln (right) and Stephen A. Douglass (left), 1860. The formal studio photographs depict each man in a stance he might have assumed in the famous debates of 1858 as they squared off for the U. S. Senate election in Illinois.

Chronology

1846
- War with Mexico begins
- Oregon Treaty negotiated
- Wilmot Proviso inflames sectional divisions

1847
- Cass proposes idea of popular sovereignty

1848
- Treaty of Guadalupe Hidalgo gives United States new territory in the Southwest
- Free-Soil Party formed
- Taylor elected president
- Gold discovered in California, which later applies for admission to Union as free state

1850
- Compromise of 1850 passes, containing controversial Fugitive Slave Act

1852
- Stowe publishes *Uncle Tom's Cabin*
- Pierce elected president

1854
- Publication of "Appeal of the Independent Democrats"
- Kansas-Nebraska Act wins approval and ignites controversy
- Republican Party formed
- Return of fugitive Burns to slavery in Virginia

1856
- Bleeding Kansas troubles nation
- Brooks attacks Sumner in Senate chamber
- Buchanan elected president, but Republican Frémont wins most northern states

1857
- *Dred Scott v. Sanford* endorses southern views on black citizenship and slavery in territories
- Economic panic and widespread unemployment begin

1858
- Kansas voters reject Lecompton Constitution
- Lincoln-Douglas debates attract attention
- Douglas contends popular sovereignty prevails over Dred Scott decision in territories

1859
- Brown raids Harpers Ferry

1860
- Democratic Party splits in two; southern Democrats demand constitutional guarantee for the territories
- Lincoln elected president in divided, sectional election
- Crittenden Compromise fails
- South Carolina secedes from Union

1861
- Six more Deep South states secede
- Confederacy established at Montgomery, Alabama
- Attack on Fort Sumter begins Civil War
- Four states in the Upper South join the Confederacy

In the ensuing campaign, Lincoln and Douglas squared off over the great issues dividing the country: the westward expansion of slavery, the meaning of abolitionism, the character of federal authority over property in slaves, whether the Declaration of Independence had signaled some form of racial equality, and ultimately the moral integrity and future existence of the American republic. Both candidates crisscrossed Illinois, with Lincoln traveling 4,350 miles and delivering some 63 major speeches, and Douglas logging over 5,000 miles and speaking 130 times. Reluctantly, Douglas agreed to seven debates, one in each congressional district of Illinois, with the exception of Chicago and Springfield, where the candidates had already appeared.

*T*he format for the Lincoln-Douglas debates inspires envy in twenty-first-century Americans: they were three-hour marathons of direct confrontation, political analysis, and theater, with the candidates alternately speaking in long addresses and rebuttals. Tens of thousands of people attended these outdoor events, arriving by foot, by wagon, on trains, and accompanied by brass bands. Perhaps never before or since have Americans demonstrated such an appetite for democratic engagement. "The prairies are on fire," wrote an eastern journalist. "It is astonishing how deep an interest in politics this people takes."

Over and over, Douglas accused his opponent and all Republicans of radicalism, of being "abolitionists" and favoring racial equality. Lincoln was forced to admit that he opposed social equality between whites and blacks, but he embraced the natural-rights doctrine of the Declaration of Independence and morally condemned slavery as an "evil" that must be constrained. Lincoln insisted on stopping slavery's expansion, while maintaining that the federal government could not legally end it in the South. He accused Douglas of a dangerous neutrality, even indifference, about slavery's future.

Link to excerpts from the Lincoln-Douglas debates.

A foot shorter than Lincoln, better dressed, and resplendent in oratorical manner, Douglas appealed to racial prejudice and to a vague, if eloquent, unionism. Lincoln cast the election as a moral choice between free-labor–Free-Soil doctrine and a republic ultimately dominated by an oligarchy of slaveholders and their abettors, determined to snuff out the liberties of ordinary citizens. In 1858, Lincoln and Douglas debated the nature of American democracy. Both appealed to fear and to hope; the citizens of Illinois listened, learned, and voted for different futures.

Of the quarter-million votes cast, Lincoln received four thousand more than Douglas. But senators were elected by state legislatures in the nineteenth century; due to an outdated apportionment, Democrats maintained a 54-to-46 margin and returned Douglas to the U.S. Senate. Lincoln would be heard from again, however. "I am glad I made the late race," he said. "It gave me a hearing on the great and durable question of the age."

Well before 1858, a larger drama of conflict and violence had begun to envelop the nation. From 1846 to 1848, the United States aggressively went to war against Mexico, unleashing the problem of slavery's expansion as never before. In Kansas Territory, open warfare had exploded between proslavery and antislavery settlers. On the floor of the U.S. Senate, a southern representative had beaten a northern senator senseless. A new fugitive slave law had sent thousands of free and fugitive blacks fleeing into Canada in fear for their liberty and their lives. The tradition of compromise on political problems related to slavery teetered on the brink of collapse. The Supreme Court had just issued a dramatic decision about slavery's constitutionality in westward expansion, as well as the status of African American citizenship—to the delight of most southerners and the dread of many northerners. And abolitionist John Brown was planning a raid into Virginia to start a slave rebellion.

The political culture of the American republic was disintegrating. As the 1850s advanced, slavery pulled Americans, North and South, into a maelstrom of dispute that its best statesmen ultimately could not subdue. Divergent economic and political aims, which had long been held in check, now flew apart over the issue of slavery. The old nationwide political parties fractured, and a realignment that reinforced sectional interests took their place. What began as a dark cloud over the western territories became a storm engulfing the nation. Each time the nation expanded, it confronted a thorny issue: should new territories and states be slave or free?

A feeling grew in both North and South that America's future was at stake—the character of its economy, its labor system, its definition of constitutional liberty, and its racial self-definition. For blacks, the growing dispute brought both hope and despair. They could take heart that political strife over slavery might somehow lead to their liberation. But in a nation now trying to define its future, blacks had to wonder whether they had a future at all in America. In 1855, Frederick Douglass spoke for the enslaved when he wrote that "the thought of only being a creature of the present and the past, troubled me, and I longed to have a future—a future with hope in it." In those words, Douglass spoke as well to the nation's central dilemma.

- After 1845, how and why did westward expansion become so intertwined with the future of slavery and freedom?
- During the 1850s, why did Americans (white males, virtually all of whom could vote, and blacks, few of whom had the franchise) seem to care so deeply about electoral politics?
- What were the long-term and immediate causes of the Civil War?

The War with Mexico and Its Consequences

In the 1840s, territorial expansion surged forward under the leadership of President James K. Polk of North Carolina. The annexation of Texas just before his inauguration did not necessarily make war with Mexico inevitable, but through a series of calculated decisions, Polk brought the conflict on. Mexico broke off relations with the United States, and during the annexation process, Polk urged Texans to seize all land to the Rio Grande and claim the river as their southern and western border. Mexico held that the Nueces River was the border; hence, the stage was set for conflict. Nothing could weaken Polk's determination to fulfill the nation's manifest destiny to rule the continent. He wanted Mexico's territory all the way to the Pacific, and all of Oregon Country as well. He and his expansionist cabinet achieved their goals but were largely unaware of the price in domestic harmony that expansion would exact.

During the 1844 campaign, Polk's supporters had threatened war with Great Britain to gain all of Oregon.

Oregon

As president, however, Polk turned first to diplomacy. Not wanting to fight Mexico and Great Britain at the same time, he tried to avoid bloodshed in the Northwest, where America and Britain had since 1819 jointly occupied disputed territory. Dropping the demand for a boundary at latitude 54°40', he pressured the British to accept the 49th parallel. In 1846, Great Britain agreed. The Oregon Treaty gave the United States all of present-day Oregon, Washington, and Idaho, and parts of Wyoming and Montana (see Map 14.1). Thus, a new era of land acquisition and conquest had begun under the eleventh president of the United States, the sixth to be a slaveholder and one who, through an agent, secretly bought and sold slaves from the White House.

Toward Mexico, Polk was more aggressive. In early 1846, he ordered American troops under "Old Rough

"Mr. Polk's War"

and Ready," General Zachary Taylor, to march south and defend the contested border of the Rio Grande across from the town of Matamoros, Mexico (see Map 14.2). Polk especially desired California as the prize in his expansionist strategy, and he attempted to buy from Mexico a huge tract of land extending to the Pacific. When that effort failed, Polk waited for war. Negotiations between troops on the Rio Grande were awkwardly conducted in French because no American officer spoke Spanish and no Mexican spoke English. After a three-week standoff, the tense situation came to a head. On April 24, 1846, Mexican cavalry ambushed a U.S. cavalry unit on the north side of the river; eleven Americans were killed, and sixty-three were taken captive. On April 26, Taylor sent a dispatch overland to Washington, D.C., which took two weeks to arrive, announcing, "Hostilities may now be considered as commenced."

Polk now drafted a message to Congress: Mexico had "passed the boundary of the United States, had invaded our territory and shed American blood on American soil." In the bill accompanying the war message, Polk deceptively declared that "war exists by the act of Mexico itself" and summoned the nation to arms. Two days later, on May 13, the House recognized a state of war with Mexico by a vote of 174 to 14, and the Senate, by 40 to 2, with numerous abstentions. Some antislavery Whigs had tried to oppose the war in Congress but were barely allowed to speak. Because Polk withheld key facts, the full reality of what had happened on the distant Rio Grande

Map 14.1 American Expansion in Oregon

The slogan of Polk's supporters had been "fifty-four forty or fight," but negotiation of a boundary at the 49th parallel avoided the danger of war with Great Britain.

Source: Copyright © Cengage Learning

was not known. But the theory and practice of manifest destiny had launched the United States into its first major war on foreign territory.

The idea of war unleashed great public celebrations. Huge crowds gathered in southern cities, such as Richmond and Louisville, to voice

Foreign War and the Popular Imagination

support for the war effort. Twenty thousand Philadelphians and even more New Yorkers rallied in the same spirit. After news came of General Taylor's first two battlefield victories at Palo Alto and Resaca de la Palma, volunteers swarmed recruiting stations. From his home in Lansingburgh, New York, writer Herman Melville remarked that "the people here are all in a state of delirium. . . . A military ardor pervades all ranks. . . . Nothing is talked of but the Halls of the Montezumas." Publishers rushed books about Mexican geography into print; "Palo Alto" hats and root beer went on sale. And new daily newspapers, now printed on rotary presses, boosted their sales by giving the war a romantic appeal.

Here was an adventurous war of conquest in a far-off, exotic land. Here was the fulfillment of an Anglo-Saxon–Christian destiny to expand and possess the North American continent and to take civilization to the "semi-Indian" Mexicans. For many, racism fueled the expansionist spirit. In 1846, an Illinois newspaper justified the war on the basis that Mexicans were "reptiles in the path of progressive democracy." For those who read newspapers, the War with Mexico became the first national event experienced with immediacy. The battles south of the border were reported by war correspondents. From Vera Cruz on the Gulf Coast of Mexico, ships carried news dispatches to New Orleans, whose nine daily newspapers ran a faster steamer out to meet them. With stories set in type before they even reached shore, riders carried the news to the North. Near the end of the war, news traveled by telegraph in only three days from New Orleans to Washington, D.C.

The war spawned an outpouring of poetry, song, drama, travel literature, and lithographs that captured the popular imagination and glorified the conflict. New lyrics to the tune of "Yankee Doodle" proclaimed: "They attacked our men upon our land / and crossed our river too sir / now show them all with sword in hand / what yankee boys can do sir." Most of the war-inspired flowering of the popular arts was patriotic. But not everyone cheered. Abolitionist James Russell Lowell considered the war a "national crime committed in behoof of slavery, our common sin." Ralph Waldo Emerson confided to his journals in 1847, "The United States will conquer Mexico, but it will be as the man swallows arsenic, which brings

Map 14.2 The War with Mexico

This map shows the territory disputed between the United States and Mexico. After U.S. gains in northeastern Mexico, in New Mexico, and in California, General Winfield Scott captured Mexico City in the decisive campaign of the war.

Source: Copyright © Cengage Learning

Link to John C. Calhoun's 1850 speech on preserving the Union.

him down in turn. Mexico will poison us." Even pro-slavery spokesman John C. Calhoun saw the perils of expansionism. Mexico, he said, was "the forbidden fruit; the penalty of eating it would be to subject our institutions to political death."

The troops proved unruly and undisciplined, and their politically ambitious commanders often quarreled among themselves. Nevertheless, early in the war, U.S. forces made significant gains. In May 1846, Polk ordered Colonel Stephen Kearny and a small detachment to invade the remote and thinly populated provinces of New Mexico and California. Taking Santa Fe largely without opposition, Kearny pushed into California, where he joined forces with two U.S. naval units and rebellious American settlers led by Captain John C. Férmont. General Zachary Taylor's forces attacked and occupied Monterrey, which surrendered in September, securing northeastern Mexico (see Map 14.2).

Conquest

New Mexico did not prove easy for U.S. forces to subdue, however. In January 1847, in Taos, northwest of Santa Fe, Hispanics and Indians led by Pablo Montoya and Tomas Romero rebelled against the Americans and killed numerous government officials. In what came to be known as the Taos Revolt, some 500 Mexican and Indian insurgents laid siege to a mill in Arroyo Hondo, outside Taos. The U.S. command acted swiftly to suppress the revolt with 300 heavily armed troops. The growing band of insurgents eventually retreated to Taos Pueblo and held out in a thick-walled church. With cannon, the U.S. Army succeeded in killing some 150 and capturing 400 of the rebels. After many arrests, approximately 28 insurgent leaders were hanged in the Taos plaza, ending the bloody resistance to U.S. occupation of lands still claimed by Mexican and Indian peoples.

Before the end of 1846, American forces had also established dominion over California. Because losses on the periphery of their large country had not broken Mexican resistance, General Winfield Scott carried the war to the enemy's heartland. Landing at Veracruz, he led fourteen thousand men toward Mexico City. This daring invasion proved the decisive campaign of the war. Scott's men, outnumbered and threatened by yellow fever, encountered a series of formidable Mexican defenses, but engineers repeatedly discovered flanking routes around their foes. After a series of hard-fought battles, U.S. troops captured the Mexican capital.

Representatives of both countries signed the Treaty of Guadalupe Hidalgo in February 1848. The United States gained California and New Mexico (including present-day Nevada, Utah, and Arizona, and parts of Colorado

Treaty of Guadalupe Hidalgo

and Wyoming), and recognition of the Rio Grande as the southern boundary of Texas. In return, the American government agreed to settle the claims of its citizens (mostly Texans) against Mexico ($3.2 million) and to pay Mexico a mere $15 million. On the day Polk received the treaty from the Senate, a mob in Paris forced Louis Philippe to abdicate the throne of France, and a German writer, Karl Marx, published a pamphlet, *The Communist Manifesto*, in London. The enormous influence of Marx's work would be many years away, but as the 1848 nationalistic revolutions against monarchy spread to Italy, Austria, Hungary, and Germany, republican America seized a western empire.

The costs of the war included the deaths of thirteen thousand Americans (mostly from disease) and fifty thousand Mexicans. Moreover, enmity between Mexico and the United States endured into the twentieth century. The domestic cost to the United States was even higher. Public opinion was sharply divided. Southwesterners were enthusiastic about the war, as were most southern planters; New Englanders strenuously opposed it. Whigs in Congress charged that Polk, a Democrat, had "provoked" an unnecessary war and "usurped the power of Congress." The aged John Quincy Adams denounced the war, and an Illinois Whig named Abraham Lincoln called Polk's justifications the "half insane mumbling of a fever-dream." Abolitionists and a small minority of antislavery Whigs charged that the war was a plot to extend slavery. Congressman Joshua Giddings of Ohio charged that Polk's purpose was "to render slavery secure in Texas" and to extend slavery's dominion over the West.

These charges fed northern fear of the "Slave Power." Abolitionists had long warned of a slaveholding oligarchy that intended to dominate the nation through its hold on federal power. Slaveholders had gained control of the South by suppressing dissent. They had forced the gag rule on Congress in 1836 and threatened northern liberties. To many white northerners, even those who saw nothing wrong with slavery, it was the battle over free speech that first made the idea of a Slave Power credible. The War with Mexico deepened such fears. Had this questionable war, asked antislavery northerners, not been launched for vast, new slave territory?

"Slave Power Conspiracy"

Northern opinion on slavery's expansion began to shift, but the impact of the war on southern opinion was even more dramatic. At first, some southern Whigs attacked the Democratic president for causing the war, and few southern congressmen saw slavery as the paramount issue. Many whites in both North and South feared that large land seizures would bring thousands of nonwhite Mexicans into the United States and upset the racial order. An Indiana politician did not want "any mixed races in our Union, nor men of any color except white, unless they be slaves." And the *Charleston* (South

Visualizing THE PAST

The Mexican War in Popular Imagination

The War with Mexico was the first American foreign conflict to be covered by the press with actual correspondents and the first to stimulate the creation of widespread promotional popular art and commemorative objects. General Zachary Taylor, the American commander in Mexico, became the hero of the war, and in its wake, was elected president in 1848 in a campaign that featured countless forms of this art. Why was the War with Mexico the first American foreign war to be covered by journalists and so widely depicted in political and military art? Do you think the artistic depictions of the War with Mexico increased or decreased the popularity of the war?

Presentation pitcher: ca. 1848–1850 (porcelain), French School, (nineteenth century) Portrait of Zachary Taylor (1784–1850) on one side, twelfth president of the United States (1849–1850); landscape with battle on the other side, hero of the Mexican war (1846–1848), commemorates Taylor's triumph in the 1847 battle of Buena Vista.

Museum of Fine Arts, Houston, Texas, the Bayou Bend Collection, gift of Miss Ima Hogg. Bridgeman Art Library

Chicago History Museum, Bridgeman Art Library

Painting, General Zachary Taylor in command at the Battle of Buena Vista, in Mexico, 1847, oil on canvas, by William Henry Powell (1823–79).

Carolina) *Mercury* asked if the nation expected "to melt into our population eight millions of men, at war with us by race, by language, by religion, manners and laws." Yet, despite their racism and such numerical exaggerations, many statesmen soon saw other prospects in the outcomes of a war of conquest in the Southwest.

In August 1846, David Wilmot, a Pennsylvania Democrat, proposed an amendment, or proviso, to a military tary appropriations bill: that "neither slavery nor involuntary servitude shall ever exist" in any territory gained from Mexico. Although the proviso never passed both houses of Congress, its repeated introduction by northerners transformed the debate over the expansion of slavery. Southerners suddenly circled their wagons to protect the future of a slave society. Alexander H. Stephens, only recently "no defender of slavery," now declared that slavery was based on the Bible and above moral criticism, and John C. Calhoun took an aggressive stand. The territories, Calhoun insisted, belonged to all the states, and the federal government could do nothing to limit the spread of slavery there. Southern slaveholders had a constitutional right rooted in the Fifth Amendment, Calhoun claimed, to take their slaves (as property) anywhere in the territories.

Wilmot Proviso

This position, often called "state sovereignty," which quickly became a test of orthodoxy among southern politicians, was a radical reversal of history. In 1787, the Confederation Congress had discouraged if not fully excluded slavery from the Northwest Territory; Article IV of the U.S. Constitution had authorized Congress to make "all needful rules and regulations" for the territories; and the Missouri Compromise had barred slavery from most of the Louisiana Purchase. Now, however, southern leaders demanded future guarantees for slavery.

In the North, the Wilmot Proviso became a rallying cry for abolitionists. Eventually the legislatures of fourteen northern states endorsed it—and not because all of its supporters were abolitionists. David Wilmot, significantly, was neither an abolitionist nor an antislavery Whig. He denied having any "squeamish sensitiveness upon the subject of slavery" or "morbid sympathy for the slave." Instead, his goal was to defend "the rights of white freemen" and to obtain California "for free white labor." Wilmot's involvement in antislavery controversy is a measure of the remarkable ability of the territorial issue to alarm northerners of many viewpoints.

As Wilmot demonstrated, it was possible, however, to be both a racist and an opponent of slavery. The vast majority of white northerners were not active abolitionists, and their desire to keep the West free from slavery was often matched by their desire to keep blacks from settling there. Fear of the Slave Power was thus building a potent antislavery movement that united abolitionists and antiblack voters. At stake was an abiding version of the American Dream: the free individual's access to social mobility through acquisition of land in the West. This

sacred ideal of free labor, and its dread of concentrated power, fueled a new political persuasion in America. A man's ownership and sale of his own labor, wrote British economist Adam Smith, was "the most sacred and inviolable foundation of all property." Slave labor, thousands of northerners had come to believe, would degrade the honest toil of free men and render them unemployable. The West must therefore be kept free of slaves.

The divisive slavery question now infested national politics. After Polk renounced a second term as president, the Democrats nominated Senator Lewis Cass of Michigan for president and General William Butler of Kentucky for vice president. Cass, a party loyalist who had served in Jackson's cabinet, had devised in 1847 the idea of "popular sovereignty"—letting residents in the western territories decide the question of slavery for themselves. His party's platform declared that Congress lacked the power to interfere with slavery's expansion. The Whigs nominated General Zachary Taylor, a southern slaveholder and war hero; Congressman Millard Fillmore of New York was his running mate. The Whig convention similarly refused to assert that Congress had power over slavery in the territories.

The Election of 1848 and Popular Sovereignty

But the issue could not be avoided. Many southern Democrats distrusted Cass and eventually voted for Taylor because he was a slaveholder. Among northerners, concern over slavery led to the formation of a new party. New York Democrats committed to the Wilmot Proviso rebelled against Cass and nominated former president Martin Van Buren. Antislavery Whigs and former supporters of the Liberty Party then joined them to organize the Free-Soil Party, with Van Buren as its candidate (see Table 14.1). This party, which sought to restrict slavery expansion to any western territories and whose slogan was "Free Soil, Free Speech, Free Labor, and Free Men," won almost 300,000 northern votes. For a new third party to win 10 percent of the national vote was unprecedented. Taylor polled 1.4 million votes to Cass's 1.2 million and won the White House, but the results were more ominous than decisive.

American politics had split along sectional lines as never before. Religious denominations, too, severed into northern and southern wings. As the 1850s dawned, the legacies of the War with Mexico and the conflicts of 1848 dominated national life and threatened the nature of the Union itself.

1850: Compromise or Armistice?

The first sectional battle of the new decade involved California. More than eighty thousand Americans flooded into California during the gold rush of 1849. With Congress unable to agree on a formula to govern the territories,

Table 14.1 New Political Parties

Party	Period of Influence	Area of Influence	Outcome
Liberty Party	1839–1848	North	Merged with other antislavery groups to form Free-Soil Party
Free-Soil Party	1848–1854	North	Merged with Republican Party
Know-Nothings (American Party)	1853–1856	Nationwide	Disappeared, freeing most to join Republican Party
Republican Party	1854–present	North (later nationwide)	Became rival of Democratic Party and won presidency in 1860

President Taylor urged these settlers to apply directly for admission to the Union. They promptly did so, proposing a state constitution that did not allow for slavery. Because California's admission as a free state would upset the sectional balance of power in the Senate (the ratio of slave to free states was fifteen to fifteen), southern politicians wanted to postpone admission and make California a slave territory, or at least extend the Missouri Compromise line west to the Pacific.

Henry Clay, the venerable Whig leader, sensed that the Union was in peril. Twice before—in 1820 and 1833—Clay, the "Great Pacificator," had taken the lead in shaping sectional compromise; now he struggled one last time to preserve the nation. To hushed Senate galleries Clay presented a series of compromise measures in the winter of 1850. At one point, he held up what he claimed was a piece of George Washington's coffin as a means of inspiring unity. Over the weeks that followed, he and Senator Stephen A. Douglas of Illinois steered their compromise package through debate and amendment.

Debate over Slavery in the Territories

The problems to be solved were numerous and difficult. Would California, or part of it, become a free state? How should the territory acquired from Mexico be organized? Texas, which allowed slavery, claimed large portions of the new land as far west as Santa Fe. Southerners complained that fugitive slaves were not returned as the Constitution required, and northerners objected to slave auctions held in the nation's capital. Eight years earlier, in *Prigg v. Pennsylvania* (1842), the Supreme Court had ruled that enforcement of the fugitive slave clause in the Constitution was a federal, not a state, obligation, buttressing long-standing southern desires to bring this issue to a head. Most troublesome of all, however, was the status of slavery in the territories.

Clay and Douglas hoped to avoid a specific formula, and in the idea of popular sovereignty they discovered what one historian called a "charm of ambiguity." Ultimately Congress would have to approve statehood for a territory, but "in the meantime," said Lewis Cass, it should allow the people living there "to regulate their own concerns in their own way."

Those simple words proved all but unenforceable. When could settlers prohibit slavery? To avoid dissension within their party, northern and southern Democrats explained Cass's statement to their constituents in two incompatible ways. Southerners claimed that neither Congress nor a territorial legislature could bar slavery. Only late in the territorial process, when settlers were ready to draft a state constitution, could they take that step, thus allowing time for slavery to take root. Northerners, however, insisted that Americans living in a territory were entitled to local self-government and thus could outlaw slavery at any time.

The cause of compromise gained a powerful supporter when Senator Daniel Webster committed his prestige and eloquence to Clay's bill. "I wish to speak today," Webster declaimed on March 7 in a scene of high drama, "not as a Massachusetts man, nor as a Northern man, but as an American. I speak today for the preservation of the Union." Abandoning his earlier support for the Wilmot Proviso, Webster urged northerners not to "taunt or reproach" the

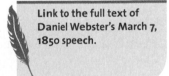

Link to the full text of Daniel Webster's March 7, 1850 speech.

South with antislavery measures. To southern firebrands, he issued a warning that disunion inevitably would cause violence and destruction. For his efforts at compromise, Webster was condemned by many former abolitionist friends in New England who accused him of going over to the "devil."

Only three days earlier, with equal drama, Calhoun had been carried from his sickbed to deliver a speech opposing the compromise. As Calhoun was unable to stand and speak, Senator James Mason of Virginia read his address for him. Grizzled and dying, the South's intellectual defender warned that the "cords which bind these states" were "already greatly weakened." Calhoun did not address the specific measures in the bill; he predicted disunion if southern demands were not met, thereby frightening some into support of compromise.

With Clay sick and absent from Washington, Douglas reintroduced the compromise measures one at a time. Although there was no majority for compromise, Douglas shrewdly realized that different majorities might be created for the separate measures. Because southerners favored some bills and northerners the rest, a small majority for compromise could be achieved on each distinct issue. The strategy worked, and Douglas's resourcefulness alleviated the crisis as the Compromise of 1850 became law.

The compromise had five essential measures:

1. California became a free state.
2. The Texas boundary was set at its present limits (see Map 14.3), and the United States paid Texas $10 million in compensation for the loss of New Mexico Territory.

Compromise of 1850

3. The territories of New Mexico and Utah were organized on a basis of popular sovereignty.
4. The fugitive slave law was strengthened.
5. The slave trade was abolished in the District of Columbia.

Jubilation greeted passage of the compromise; crowds in Washington and other cities celebrated the happy news. "On one glorious night," records a modern historian, "the word went abroad that it was the duty of every patriot to get drunk. Before the next morning many a citizen had proved his patriotism."

In reality, there was less cause for celebration than people hoped. At best, the Compromise of 1850 was an artful evasion. As one historian has argued, the legislation was more an "armistice," delaying greater conflict, than a compromise. Douglas had found a way to pass the five proposals without convincing northerners and southerners to agree on fundamentals. The compromise bought time for the nation, but it did not provide a real settlement of the territorial questions.

Furthermore, the compromise had two basic flaws. The first concerned the ambiguity of popular sovereignty. Southerners insisted there would be no prohibition of slavery during the territorial stage, and northerners declared that settlers could bar slavery whenever they wished. The compromise even allowed for the appeal of a territorial legislature's action to the Supreme Court. One witty politician remarked that the legislators had enacted a lawsuit instead of a law.

The second flaw lay in the Fugitive Slave Act, which gave new—and controversial—protection to slavery. The

Fugitive Slave Act

law empowered slaveowners to go into court in their own states to present evidence that a slave who owed them service had escaped. The resulting transcript and a description of the fugitive would then serve as legal proof of a person's slave status, even in free states and territories. Specially appointed court officials adjudicated the identity of the person described, not whether he or she was indeed a slave. Penalties made it a felony to harbor fugitives, and

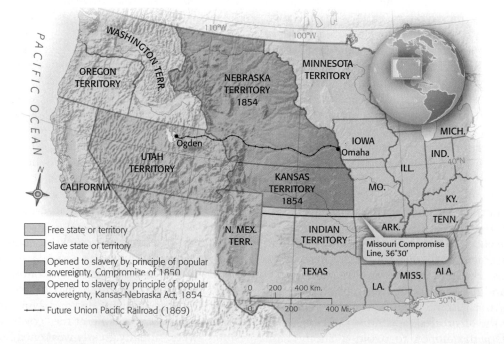

Map 14.3 The Kansas-Nebraska Act and Slavery Expansion, 1854

The vote on the Kansas-Nebraska Act in the House of Representatives (see also Table 14.2) demonstrates the sectionalization of American politics due to the slavery question.

Source: Copyright © Cengage Learning

Table 14.2 The Vote on the Kansas-Nebraska Act

The vote was 113 to 100 in favor.

	Aye	Nay
Northern Democrats	44	42
Southern Democrats	57	2
Northern Whigs	0	45
Southern Whigs	12	7
Northern Free-Soilers		4

the law stated that northern citizens could be summoned to hunt fugitives. The fees paid to U.S. marshals favored slaveholders: $10 if the alleged fugitive was returned to the slaveowner, $5 if not returned.

Abolitionist newspapers quickly attacked the Fugitive Slave Act as a violation of fundamental American rights. Why were alleged fugitives denied a trial by jury? Why were they given no chance to present evidence or cross-examine witnesses? Why did the law give authorities a financial incentive to send suspected fugitives into bondage, and why would northerners now be arrested if they harbored runaways? These arguments convinced some northerners that all free blacks were vulnerable to kidnapping and enslavement. The "free" states were no longer a safe haven for black folk, whatever their origins; an estimated twenty thousand fled to Canada in the wake of the Fugitive Slave Act.

Link to Frederick Douglass's "What to the Slave is the Fourth of July," speech at the Rochester Ladies' Anti-Slavery Society in 1852.

Between 1850 and 1854, protests and violent resistance to slave catchers occurred in dozens of northern towns. Sometimes a captured fugitive was broken out of jail or from the clutches of slave agents by abolitionists, as in the 1851 Boston case of Shadrach Minkins, who was spirited by a series of wagons and trains across Massachusetts, up through Vermont, to Montreal, Canada. Also in 1851, a fugitive named Jerry McHenry was freed by an abolitionist mob in Syracuse, New York, and hurried to Canadian freedom. That same year as well, the small black community in Lancaster County, Pennsylvania, rose up in arms to defend four escaped slaves from a federal posse charged with reenslaving them. At this "Christiana riot," the fugitives shot and killed Edward Gorsuch, the Maryland slaveowner who sought the return of his "property." Amid increasing border warfare over fugitive slaves, a headline reporting the Christiana affair screamed, "Civil War, The First Blow Struck!"

Many abolitionists became convinced by their experience of resisting the Fugitive Slave Act that violence was a legitimate means of opposing slavery. In an 1854 column entitled "Is It Right and Wise to Kill a Kidnapper?" Frederick

Douglass said that the only way to make the fugitive slave law "dead letter" was to make a "few dead slave catchers."

At this point, a novel portrayed the humanity and suffering of slaves in a way that touched millions of northerners. Harriet Beecher

Uncle Tom's Cabin

Stowe, whose New England family had produced many prominent ministers, wrote *Uncle Tom's Cabin* out of deep moral conviction. Her story, serialized in 1851 and published as a book in 1852, conveyed the agonies faced by slave families and described a mother's dash to freedom with her child across the frozen Ohio River. Stowe also portrayed slavery's evil effects on slaveholders, indicting the institution itself more harshly than she indicted the southerners caught in its web. Moreover, Stowe exposed northern racism and complicity with slavery by making the worst slaveholder a man of New England birth and a visiting relative on a plantation a squeamish Vermont woman who could hardly cope with the near presence of blacks.

In nine months, the book sold over 300,000 copies and by mid-1853 over 1 million. Countless people saw *Uncle Tom's Cabin* performed as a stage play, heard the story in dramatic readings, or read similar novels inspired by it. Stowe brought home the evil of slavery to many who had never given it much thought. Indeed, for generations, the characters in *Uncle Tom's Cabin*—Eliza, Little Eva, Simon Legree, and Uncle Tom himself—entered the American imagination as symbols of slavery and its demise.

The popularity of *Uncle Tom's Cabin* alarmed anxious southern whites. In politics and now in popular literature they saw threats to their way of life. Behind the South's aggressive claims about territorial rights lay the fear that, if nearby areas outlawed slavery, they would be used as bases from which to spread abolitionism into the slave states. To most white southerners, a moral condemnation of slaveholding anywhere meant the same thing everywhere.

To protect slavery in the arena of ideas, southerners needed to counter indictments of the institution as a moral wrong. Accordingly, some fifteen to twenty proslavery novels were published in the 1850s as responses to *Uncle Tom's Cabin*. Most of these paled in comparison to Mrs. Stowe's masterpiece, but southern writers continued to defend their system as more humane than wage labor, and they blamed the slave trade on the "outside interference" of Yankee speculators. In awkward stories, such as J. W. Page's *Uncle Robin in His Cabin and Tom Without One in Boston*, slaves were induced to run away by visiting abolitionists, and then all but starved in northern cities.

In reality, slaveholders were especially disturbed by the 1850s over what was widely called the Underground Railroad. This loose, illegal network of civil disobedience, spiriting runaways to freedom, had never been

The Underground Railroad

Courtesy Amherst College Archives and Special Collections

▲ Eliza crossing the Ohio River, leaping on icebergs, is perhaps the most famous and oft-repeated image from *Uncle Tom's Cabin*. The drawing is from a series by 20th century Mexican artist Miguel Covarrubias.

Louis Psihoyos/Science Faction

▲ In *Still Life of Harriet Tubman with Bible and Candle*, we see the youthful, calm, determined leader of the Underground Railroad. Appearing gentle, Tubman was in her own way a revolutionary who liberated nearly three hundred of her people.

very organized. Thousands of slaves did escape by these routes, but largely through their own wits and courage, and through the assistance of blacks in some northern cities. Lewis Hayden in Boston, David Ruggles in New York, William Still in Philadelphia, John Parker in Ripley, Ohio, and Jacob Gibbs in Washington, D.C., were only some of the many black abolitionists who managed fugitive slave escapes through their regions.

Moreover, Harriet Tubman, herself an escapee in 1848, returned to her native Maryland and to Virginia at least a dozen times, and through clandestine measures helped possibly as many as three hundred slaves, some of them her own family members, to freedom. Maryland planters were so outraged at her heroic success that they offered a $40,000 reward for her capture.

In Ohio, numerous white abolitionists, often Quakers, joined with blacks as agents of slave liberation at various points along the river border between slavery and freedom. The Underground Railroad also had numerous maritime routes, as coastal slaves escaped aboard ship out of Virginia or the Carolinas, or from New Orleans, and ended up in northern port cities, the Caribbean, or England. Many fugitive slaves from the Lower South and Texas escaped to Mexico, which had abolished slavery

in 1829. Some slaves escaped by joining the Seminole communities in Florida, where they fought with them against the U.S. Army in the Seminole Wars of 1835–1842 and 1855–1858.

This constant, dangerous flow of humanity was a testament to human courage and the will for freedom. It never reached the scale believed by some angry slaveholders or that of the countless safe houses and hideaways claimed by hundreds of northern towns and local historical societies today. But in reality and in legend, the Underground Railroad applied pressure to the institution of slavery and provided slaves with a focus for hope.

The 1852 election gave southern leaders hope that slavery would be secure under the administration of a new

Election of 1852 and the Collapse of Compromise

president. Franklin Pierce, a Democrat from New Hampshire, won an easy victory over the Whig presidential nominee, General Winfield Scott.

Southerners hoped that Pierce firmly supported the Compromise of 1850. Because Scott's views on the compromise had been unknown and the Free-Soil candidate, John P. Hale of New Hampshire, had openly rejected it, Pierce's victory suggested widespread support for the compromise.

The Whig party was weak, however, and by 1852 sectional discord had rendered it all but dead. President Pierce's embrace of the compromise appalled many northerners. His vigorous enforcement of the Fugitive Slave Act provoked outrage and fear of the Slave Power, especially in the case of the fugitive slave Anthony Burns, who had fled Virginia by stowing away on a ship in 1852. In Boston, thinking he was safe in a city known for abolitionism, Burns began a new life. But in 1854, federal marshals found and placed him under guard in Boston's courthouse. An interracial crowd of abolitionists attacked the courthouse, killing a jailer in an unsuccessful attempt to free Burns, whose case attracted nationwide attention.

Pierce moved decisively to enforce the Fugitive Slave Act. He telegraphed local officials to "incur any expense to insure the execution of the law" and sent marines, cavalry, and artillery to Boston. U.S. troops marched Burns to Boston harbor through streets that his supporters had draped in black and hung with American flags at half-mast. At a cost of $100,000, a single black man was returned to slavery through the power of federal law.

The national will to sustain the future of slavery was now tested at every turn. This demonstration of federal support for slavery radicalized opinion, even among many conservatives. Textile manufacturer Amos A. Lawrence observed that "we went to bed one night old fashioned, conservative, Compromise Union Whigs & waked up stark mad Abolitionists." Juries refused to convict the abolitionists who had stormed the Boston courthouse, and New England states began to pass personal liberty laws designed to impede or block federal enforcement. In such laws, local judges were absolved from enforcing the Fugitive Slave Act, in effect nullifying federal authority. What northerners now saw as evidence of a dominating Slave Power, outraged slaveholders saw as the legal defense of their rights.

Pierce confronted sectional conflict at every turn. His proposal for a transcontinental railroad derailed when congressmen fought over its location, North or South. His attempts to acquire foreign territory stirred more trouble. An annexation treaty with Hawai'i failed because southern senators would not vote for another free state, and efforts to acquire slaveholding Cuba through the Ostend Manifesto angered northerners. Written after a meeting among the U.S. foreign ministers to Britain, France, and Spain, the document advocated conquest of Cuba if it could not be "purchased." The ministers predicted that Cuba "would be Africanized and become a second St. Domingo, with all its attendant horrors to the white race." Antislavery advocates once again saw schemes of the Slave Power.

Events in the Pacific also caused division at home over just how far American expansion should extend. With two orchestrated landings in the Bay of Tokyo, in 1853 and 1854, Commodore Matthew Perry established U.S. intentions to trade with Japan. Offended and intrigued, the Japanese were impressed with Perry's steam-powered warships, the first such black smoke–belching, floating machines they had seen. Perry's Treaty of Kanagawa in March 1854 negotiated two ports as coaling stations for American ships. The much sought-after trading arrangements were slow in coming, although this did not stop merchants and bankers from lavishing on Perry a hero's honors when he returned to the United States. In his meetings with the Japanese, the pompous Perry had given his hosts, whom he considered an inferior people, a telegraph system, a quarter-scale railroad train, a bound history of the War with Mexico, and one hundred gallons of Kentucky whiskey.

Soon, back home, another territorial bill threw Congress and the nation into even greater turmoil, and the Compromise of 1850 fell into complete collapse.

Slavery Expansion and Collapse of the Party System

The new controversy began in a surprising way. Stephen A. Douglas, one of the architects of the Compromise of 1850, introduced a bill to establish the Kansas and Nebraska Territories. Talented and ambitious for the presidency, Douglas was known for compromise, not sectional quarreling. But he did not view slavery as a fundamental problem, and he was willing to risk some controversy to win economic benefits for Illinois, his home state. A transcontinental railroad would encourage settlement of the Great Plains and stimulate the economy of Illinois, but no company would build such a railroad before Congress organized the territories it would cross. Thus, interest in promoting the construction of such a railroad drove Douglas to introduce a bill that inflamed sectional passions.

The Kansas-Nebraska Act exposed the conflicting interpretations of popular sovereignty. Douglas's bill left "all

The Kansas-Nebraska Act

questions pertaining to slavery in the Territories . . . to the people residing therein." Northerners and southerners, however, still disagreed violently over what territorial settlers could constitutionally do. Moreover, the Kansas and Nebraska Territories lay within the Louisiana Purchase, and the Missouri Compromise prohibited slavery in all that land from latitude 36°30' north to the Canadian border. If popular sovereignty were to mean anything in Kansas and Nebraska, it had to mean that the Missouri Compromise was no longer in effect and that settlers could establish slavery there.

Southern congressmen, anxious to establish slaveholders' right to take slaves into any territory, pressed Douglas to concede this point. They demanded an explicit repeal of the 36°30' limitation as the price of their support. During a carriage ride with Senator Archibald Dixon of Kentucky, Douglas debated the point at length. Finally, he made an impulsive decision: "By God, Sir, you are right. I will incorporate it in my bill, though I know it will raise a hell of a storm."

Perhaps Douglas underestimated the storm because he believed that conditions of climate and soil would keep slavery out of Kansas and Nebraska. Nevertheless, his bill threw open to slavery land from which it had been prohibited for thirty-four years. Opposition from Free-Soilers and antislavery forces was immediate and enduring; many considered this turn of events a betrayal of a sacred trust. The titanic struggle in Congress lasted three and a half months. Douglas won the support of President Pierce and eventually prevailed: the bill became law in May 1854 by a vote that demonstrated the dangerous sectionalization of American politics (see Map 14.3 and Table 14.2).

But the storm was just beginning. Northern fears of slavery's influence deepened. Opposition to the Fugitive Slave Act grew dramatically; between 1855 and 1859, Connecticut, Rhode Island, Massachusetts, Michigan, Maine, Ohio, and Wisconsin passed personal-liberty laws. These laws enraged southern leaders by providing counsel for alleged fugitives and requiring trial by jury. More important was the devastating impact of the Kansas-Nebraska Act on political parties. The weakened Whig Party broke apart into northern and southern wings that could no longer cooperate nationally. The Democrats survived, but their support in the North fell drastically in the 1854 elections. Northern Democrats lost sixty-six of their ninety-one congressional seats and lost control of all but two free-state legislatures.

The beneficiary of northern voters' wrath was a new political party. During debate on the Kansas-Nebraska Act,

Birth of the Republican Party

six congressmen had published an "Appeal of the Independent Democrats." Joshua Giddings, Salmon Chase, and Charles Sumner—the principal authors of this protest—attacked Douglas's legislation as a "gross violation of a sacred pledge" (the Missouri Compromise) and a "criminal betrayal of precious rights" that would make free territory a "dreary region of despotism." Their appeal tapped a reservoir of deep concerns in the North, cogently expressed by Illinois's Abraham Lincoln.

Although Lincoln did not personally condemn southerners—"They are just what we would be in their situation"—he exposed the meaning of the Kansas-Nebraska Act. Lincoln argued that the founders, from love of liberty, had banned slavery from the Northwest Territory, kept the word *slavery* out of the Constitution, and treated it overall as a "cancer" on the republic. Rather than encouraging liberty, the Kansas-Nebraska Act put slavery "on the high road to extension and perpetuity," and that constituted a "moral wrong and injustice." America's future, Lincoln warned, was being mortgaged to slavery and all its influences.

Thousands of ordinary white northerners agreed. During the summer and fall of 1854, antislavery Whigs and Democrats, Free-Soilers, and other reformers throughout the Old Northwest met to form the new Republican Party, dedicated to keeping slavery out of the territories. The influence of the Republicans rapidly spread to the East, and they won a stunning victory in the 1854 elections. In their first appearance on the ballot, Republicans captured a majority of northern House seats. Antislavery sentiment had created a new party and caused roughly a quarter of northern Democrats to desert their party.

For the first time, too, a sectional party had gained significant power in the political system. Now the Whigs were gone, and only the Democrats struggled to maintain national membership. The Republicans absorbed the Free-Soil Party and grew rapidly in the North. Indeed, the emergence of the Republican coalition of antislavery interests is the most rapid transformation in party allegiance and voter behavior in American history.

Republicans also drew into their coalition a fast-growing nativist movement that called itself the American

Know-Nothings

Party, or Know-Nothings (because its first members kept their purposes secret, answering, "I know nothing" to all questions). This group exploited fear of foreigners and Catholics. Between 1848 and 1860, nearly 3.5 million immigrants entered the United States—proportionally the heaviest inflow of foreigners ever in American history. Democrats courted the votes of these new citizens, but many native-born Anglo-Saxon Protestants believed that Irish and German Catholics would owe primary allegiance to the pope in Rome and not to the American nation.

In 1854, anti-immigrant fears gave the Know-Nothings spectacular success in some northern states. They triumphed especially in Massachusetts, electing 11 congressmen, a governor, all state officers, all state senators, and all but 2 of 378 state representatives. The temperance movement also gained new strength early in the 1850s with its promises to stamp out the evils associated with liquor and immigrants (a particularly anti-Irish campaign). In this context, the Know-Nothings strove

PEOPLE'S MEETING!!

CITIZENS OF CHESTER COUNTY:—The time has arrived when it is necessary to make preparations for the next general election. In view of existing circumstances, it is proper that the citizens of this County

WITHOUT RESPECT TO PARTY,

Should meet for the purpose of Conferring together, and forming such an organization as will give effect to their views on important public questions. A fixed and resolute determination has recently been manifested on the part of the

SLAVE POWER,

To extend its dominion—to carry its blighting influence to territory now free—to control the government of the nation, and make it subservient to its wicked designs. Compacts entered into, under circumstances the most solemn, have been violated; an extended territory, dedicated by the MISSOURI COMPROMISE to Freedom, in violation of faith and honor, has been thrown open to the traffickers in human flesh, who in disregard of law and order, have seized upon its fertile plains with a view of adding

OTHER SLAVE STATES TO THE UNION

And giving to the Slave Power an ascendancy over freedom in the Nation. Experience has satisfied the people that while the emigration to this country of the peaceable industrious foreigner, should be regarded with favor, the facility with which persons reared abroad, under systems of government radically different from our own, approach the ballot box, and influence our elections, is an evil dangerous alike to the adopted and native citizen. We therefore demand an alteration of our

NATURALIZATION LAWS

Extending the probative period of the alien—the separation of Church and State in practice as well as in theory—the freedom of the government from all improper foreign influence—and the protection of the

AMERICAN LABORER

Are believed to be essential to the welfare of all classes of the people. All persons who are willing to co-operate upon the principles here indicated and which we believe to be those of a true democracy, are earnestly invited to meet at the

COURT HOUSE IN THE BOROUGH OF WEST CHESTER

On Saturday the 18th instant at ten o'clock A. M. August 1855

U. V. Pennypacker,   French James,   Joseph Painter,   Wm. Butler,   Samuel Way,   James Sweney,
Hickman James.   William Hoopes,   Wm. Sweney,   N. Mendenhall,   John B. Brinton,   Isaac Sweney,
Jonathan T. Marshall,   Jesse C. Green,   Mordecai T. Ruth,   Wm. Darlington,   E. D. Haines,   J. B. Wood,
Joshua Darlington,   J. B. Jeffris,   Benj. J. Passmore,   Samuel S. Heed,   Wm. S. Kirk,   Reuben White,
Geo. F. Worrall,   C. P. Sweney,   Whitldin M. Foster,   William Hoopes,   W. W. Sweney,   Wm. Windle,
Thos. W. Parker,   Wm. Whitehead,   C. M. Valentine,   Sam. J. Parker,   Z. C. Wollerton,   Thos. H. Hall,
Other names omitted for want of room.

Independent Herald Steam Press, Mar. et Street, West Chester Pa.

▲ Throughout the North, the Kansas-Nebraska Act kindled fires of alarm over the Slave Power's "determination to extend its dominion" and "control the government of the nation." Public meetings like the one announced here, held in West Chester, Pennsylvania, aided the new Republican Party.

to reinforce Protestant morality and to restrict voting and office holding to the native-born. As the Whig Party faded from the scene, the Know-Nothings temporarily filled the void. But like the Whigs, the Know-Nothings could not keep their northern and southern wings together in the face of the slavery expansion issue, and they dissolved after 1856. The growing Republican coalition wooed the nativists with temperance ordinances and laws postponing suffrage for naturalized citizens (see Table 14.1).

With nearly half of the old electorate up for grabs, the demise of the Whig Party ensured a major realignment of the political system. The remaining parties made appeals to various segments of the electorate. Immigration, temperance, homestead bills, the tariff, internal improvements—all played important roles in attracting voters during the 1850s. The Republicans appealed strongly to those interested in the economic development of the West. Commercial agriculture was booming in the

Party Realignment and the Republicans' Appeal

Ohio–Mississippi–Great Lakes area, but residents of that region desired more canals, roads, and river and harbor improvements. Because credit was scarce, a homestead program—the idea that western land should be free to individuals who would farm it and make a home on it—attracted many voters. The Republicans seized on these political desires.

Partisan ideological appeals became the currency of the realigned political system. As Republicans preached, "Free Soil, Free Labor, Free Men," they captured a self-image of many northerners. These phrases resonated with traditional ideals of equality, liberty, and opportunity under self-government—the heritage of republicanism. Invoking that heritage also undercut charges that the Republican Party was radical and abolitionist.

The northern economy was booming, and thousands of migrants had moved west to establish productive farms and growing communities. Midwesterners multiplied their yields by using new machines, such as mechanical reapers. Railroads were carrying their crops to urban markets. And industry was beginning to perform wonders of production, making available goods that only recently had been beyond the reach of the average person.

The key to progress appeared, to many people, to be free labor—the dignity of work and the incentive of opportunity. Any hard-working and virtuous man, it was thought, could improve his condition and achieve economic independence by seizing the main chance. Republicans argued that the South, with little industry and slave labor, was backward by comparison. Their arguments captured the spirit of the age in the North.

Republican Ideology

Traditional republicanism hailed the virtuous common man as the backbone of the country. In Abraham Lincoln, a man of humble origins who had become a successful lawyer and political leader, Republicans had a symbol of that tradition. They portrayed their party as the guardian of economic opportunity, giving individuals a chance to work, acquire land, and attain success. In the words of an Iowa Republican, the United States was thriving because its "door is thrown open to all, and even the poorest and humblest in the land, may, by industry and application, gain a position which will entitle him to the respect . . . of his fellow-men."

At stake in the crises of the 1850s were thus two competing definitions of "liberty": southern planters' claims to protection of their liberty in the possession and transport of their slaves anywhere in the land, and northern workers' and farmers' claims to protection of their liberty to seek a new start on free land, unimpeded by a system that defined labor as slave and black.

Opposition to the extension of slavery had brought the Republicans into being, but party members carefully

William Walker and Filibustering

Between 1848 and1861, the United States was officially at peace with foreign nations. But that did not stop private citizens, sometimes with the support of politicians and businessmen, from launching adventurous attempts to take over foreign lands, especially in Mexico, Central America, and the Caribbean. The 1850s was the heyday of "filibustering," defined in this era as private military expeditions designed to destabilize or conquer foreign lands in the name of Manifest Destiny, commerce, the spread of slavery and white supremacy, or masculine daring.

At least a dozen filibustering schemes emerged in this era of expansion and sectional crises, all of them illegal and often opposed by American presidents as blatant violations of a Neutrality Act of 1818 that outlawed the attempted overthrow of foreign "dominions." Such laws did not stop some senators, railroad and shipping entrepreneurs, and especially the self-styled soldier of fortune, William Walker, from flaunting law and seeking the "Southern dream" of a Latin American empire. The law also did not stop several American presidents from engaging in numerous more official attempts to annex Cuba in these years.

Born in Tennessee, Walker traveled and studied in Europe as the 1848 revolutions rocked that continent. After a short stint editing a newspaper in New Orleans, he moved to California, practiced law, and courted conflict by fighting at least three duels. After an ill-fated but determined attempt in 1853 to create by force an American "colony" in Sonora and the Baja peninsula in Mexico, Walker turned his sights to Nicaragua, already of great interest to thousands of Americans using its isthmus as the fastest route to the California gold fields.

With a small army of mercenaries, Walker invaded Nicaragua in 1856, exploited its ongoing civil war, seized its government, declared himself president, and reintroduced slavery into a society that had banned it. Defeated by a coalition of Nicaraguans and British in 1857, Walker returned to the United States and launched a fund-raising and speaking campaign on which he was often treated as a romantic hero. On his return to Nicaragua, he was arrested by a U.S. Navy squadron, brought once again to American soil, tried and acquitted.

In 1860, Walker published an account of his exploits, *War in Nicaragua*. His wide fame was due in part to his swashbuckling character; some saw him as a pirate serving the "Slave Power Conspiracy," and others as the "grey-eyed man of destiny" advancing the causes of slavery and American hegemony. Walker became more aggressively proslavery in Nicaragua when he desperately needed Southern political support to supply his plots. On Walker's third return to Central America in 1860 to pursue his insatiable dream of fame and power, he was arrested by a British captain who turned him over to Honduran authorities who promptly executed him by firing squad. These filibustering adventures fired the imagination of Manifest Destiny and were merely small precursors of a larger Latin American exploitation and conquest by the United States in the century to follow. Walker's legend lives on today in Central America, both heroic and notorious, as well as in two American movies, *Burn* (1969), starring Marlon Brando, and *Walker* (1987), starring Ed Harris. Filibusters were links to the world that gave the United States a difficult legacy to overcome with its neighbors from Cuba to Hawaii.

Library of Congress

◀ Portrait of William Walker, Tennessee-born filibusterer, a self-styled soldier of fortune who attempted to create his own empire in Nicaragua, where he reinstituted slavery. To some, especially Southerners, he was a romantic hero, but to others, especially Northerners and the U.S. government, he was a notorious villain and arch proponent of the worst aspects of Manifest Destiny.

broadened their appeal by adopting the causes of other groups. Their coalition ideology consisted of many elements: resentment of southern political power, devotion to unionism, antislavery based on free-labor arguments, moral revulsion to slavery, and racial prejudice. As *New York Tribune* editor Horace Greeley wrote in 1856, "It is beaten into my bones that the American people are not yet anti-slavery." Four years later, Greeley again observed that "an Anti-Slavery man per se cannot be elected." But, he added, "a Tariff, River-and-Harbor, Pacific Railroad, Free Homestead man, may succeed although he is Anti-Slavery." As these elements placed their hopes in the Republican Party, they also grew to fear slavery even more.

In the South, the disintegration of the Whig Party had left many southerners at loose ends politically; they

Southern Democrats

included a good number of wealthy planters, smaller slaveholders, and urban businessmen. In the increasingly tense atmosphere of sectional crisis, these people were highly susceptible to strong states' rights positions and the defense of slavery. The security of their own communities seemed at stake, and in the 1850s, most formerly Whig slaveholders converted to the Democratic Party.

Since Andrew Jackson's day, however, nonslaveholding yeomen had been the heart of the Democratic Party. Democratic politicians, though often slaveowners themselves, lauded the common man and argued that their policies advanced his interests. According to the southern version of republicanism, white citizens in a slave society enjoyed liberty and social equality because black people were enslaved. As Jefferson Davis put it in 1851, in other societies distinctions were drawn "by property, between the rich and the poor." But in the South, slavery elevated every white person's status and allowed the nonslaveholder to "stand upon the broad level of equality with the rich man." To retain the support of ordinary whites, southern Democrats appealed to racism, warning starkly of the main issue: "shall negroes govern white men, or white men govern negroes?"

Southern leaders also portrayed sectional controversies as matters of injustice and insult to the honor and prestige of the South. The rights of all southern whites were in jeopardy, they argued, because antislavery and Free-Soil forces threatened an institution protected in the Constitution. The stable, well-ordered South was the true defender of constitutional principles; the rapidly changing North, their destroyer.

Racial fears and traditional political loyalties helped keep the volatile political alliance between yeoman farmers and planters largely intact through the 1850s. Across class lines, white southerners joined together in the interest of community security against what they perceived as the Republican Party's capacity to cause slave unrest in their midst. In the South, no viable party emerged to replace the Whigs, and as in the North, political realignment sharpened sectional identities.

Political leaders of both sections used race in their arguments about opportunity, but northerners and southerners saw different futures. The *Montgomery* (Alabama) *Mail* warned southern whites in 1860 that the Republicans intended "to free the negroes and force amalgamation between them and the children of the poor men of the South. The rich will be able to keep out of the way of the contamination." Republicans warned northern workers that, if slavery entered the territories, the great reservoir of opportunity for ordinary citizens would be poisoned.

The Kansas-Nebraska Act spawned hatred and violence as land-hungry partisans in the sectional struggle

Bleeding Kansas

clashed repeatedly in Kansas Territory. Abolitionists and religious groups sent in armed Free-Soil settlers; southerners sent in their reinforcements to establish slavery and prevent "northern hordes" from stealing Kansas away. Conflicts led to vicious bloodshed, and soon the whole nation was talking about "Bleeding Kansas."

Politics in the territory resembled war more than democracy. During elections for a territorial legislature in 1855, thousands of proslavery Missourians—known as Border Ruffians—invaded the polls and ran up a large but fraudulent majority for proslavery candidates. They murdered and intimidated free state settlers. At one rally of such ruffians with other southerners, flags flapped in the breeze with the mottoes "Southern Rights," "Supremacy of the White Race," and "Alabama for Kansas." The resulting legislature legalized slavery, and in response Free-Soilers held an unauthorized convention at which they created their own government and constitution. Kansas was a tinderbox. By the spring of 1856, newspapers screamed for violence. "In a fight, let our motto be War to the knife, and knife to the hilt," demanded the proslavery *Squatter Sovereign*. Slavery's advocates taunted their adversaries as cowards and likened "abolitionists" to "infidels" worthy only of "total extermination."

In May, a proslavery posse sent to arrest the Free-Soil leaders sacked the Kansas town of Lawrence, killing several people and destroying a hotel with cannon shot. In revenge, John Brown, a radical abolitionist with a band of followers, murdered five proslavery settlers living along Pottawatomie Creek. The victims were taken in the dark of night from the clutches of their families, their heads and limbs hacked to pieces by heavy broadswords, their bodies heaved into dead brush. Brown himself did not wield the swords, but he did fire a single shot into the head of one senseless foe to assure his death. Soon, armed bands of guerrillas roamed the territory, battling over land claims as well as slavery.

These passions brought violence to the U.S. Senate in May 1856, when Charles Sumner of Massachusetts denounced "the Crime against Kansas." Radical in his anti-slavery views, Sumner bitterly assailed the president, the South, and Senator Andrew P. Butler of South Carolina. Soon thereafter, Butler's cousin, Representative Preston Brooks, approached Sumner at the latter's Senate desk, raised his cane, announced the defense of his kin's honor, and mercilessly beat Sumner on the head. The senator collapsed, bleeding, on the floor while unsympathetic colleagues watched.

Shocked northerners recoiled from what they saw as another case of wanton southern violence and an assault on free speech. William Cullen Bryant, editor of the *New York Evening Post,* asked, "Has it come to this, that we must speak with bated breath in the presence of our southern masters?" As if in reply, the *Richmond Enquirer* denounced "vulgar Abolitionists in the Senate" who "have been suffered to run too long without collars. They must be lashed into submission." Popular opinion in Massachusetts strongly supported Sumner; South Carolina voters reelected Brooks and sent him dozens of commemorative canes.

The election of 1856 showed how extreme such polarization had become. For Republicans, "Bleeding Sumner" and "Bleeding Kansas" had become rallying cries. When Democrats met to select a nominee, they shied away from prominent leaders whose views on the territorial question would invite controversy. Instead, they chose James Buchanan of Pennsylvania, whose chief virtue was that for the past four years he had been ambassador to Britain, uninvolved in territorial controversies. Superior party organization helped Buchanan win 1.8 million votes and the election, but he owed his victory to southern support. Hence, he was tagged with the label "a northern man with southern principles."

Election of 1856

Eleven of sixteen free states voted against Buchanan, and Democrats did not regain ascendancy in those states for decades. The Republican candidate, John C. Frémont, famous as a western explorer, won those eleven free states and 1.3 million votes; Republicans had become the dominant party in the North after only two years of existence. The Know-Nothing candidate, Millard Fillmore, won almost 1 million votes, but this election was that party's last hurrah. The coming battle would pit a sectional Republican Party against an increasingly divided Democratic Party. With huge voter turnouts, as high as 75 to 80 percent in many states, Americans were about to learn that elections really matter.

Slavery and the Nation's Future

For years, the issue of slavery in the territories had convulsed Congress, and Congress had tried to settle the issue with vague formulas. In 1857, the Supreme Court stepped into the fray, took up this emotionally charged subject, and attempted to silence controversy with a definitive verdict.

A Missouri slave named Dred Scott and his wife, Harriet Robinson Scott, had sued for their freedom. Scott based his claim on the fact that his former owner, an army surgeon, had taken him for several years into Illinois, a free state, and to Fort Snelling in the Minnesota Territory, from which slavery had been barred by the Missouri Compromise. Scott first won and then lost his case as it moved on appeal through the state courts into the federal system and, finally, after eleven years, to the Supreme Court.

Dred Scott Case

The impetus for the lawsuit likely came as much from Harriet as from Dred Scott. They were legally married at Fort Snelling (free territory) in 1836 when Dred was forty and Harriet seventeen. She had already lived as a slave on free soil for at least five years and had given birth to four children, also born on free soil: two sons who died in infancy and two daughters, Eliza and Lizzie, who lived. In all likelihood, the quest to achieve "freedom papers" through a lawsuit—begun in 1846 as two separate cases, one in his name and one in hers—came as much from Harriet's desire to sustain her family and protect her two teenage daughters from potential sale and sexual abuse as from the aging and sickly Dred. Indeed, her legal case for freedom may have been even stronger than Dred's, but their lawyers subsumed her case into his during the long appeal process.

Normally, Supreme Court justices were reluctant to inject themselves into major political issues. An 1851 decision had declared that state courts determined the status of blacks who lived within their jurisdictions. The Supreme Court had only to follow this precedent to avoid ruling on substantive, and very controversial, issues: Was a black person like Dred Scott a citizen of the United States and thus eligible to sue in federal court? Had residence in a free state or territory made him free? Did Congress have the power to prohibit or promote slavery in a territory?

After hesitation, the Supreme Court agreed to hear *Dred Scott v. Sanford* and decided to rule on the Missouri Compromise after all. Two northern justices indicated they would dissent from the assigned opinion and argue for Scott's freedom and the constitutionality of the Missouri Compromise. Their decision emboldened southerners on the Court, who were growing eager to declare the 1820 geographical restriction on slavery unconstitutional. Southern sympathizers in Washington were pressing for a proslavery verdict, and several justices felt they should simply try to resolve sectional strife once and for all.

In March 1857, Chief Justice Roger B. Taney of Maryland delivered the majority opinion of a divided Court (the vote was 7 to 2). Taney declared that Scott was not a citizen of either the United States or Missouri, that residence in free territory did not make Scott free, and that Congress had no power to bar slavery from any

FRANK LESLIE'S
ILLUSTRATED
NEWSPAPER

NEW YORK, SATURDAY, JUNE 27, 1857.

▲ Frank Leslie's *Illustrated Newspaper*, June 27, 1857. Dred Scott and his wife, Harriet, below, and their two children, Eliza and Lizzie, above. Such dignified pictures and informative articles provided Americans broadly with images of the otherwise mysterious Dred Scott and his family in the landmark Supreme Court case.

territory. The decision not only overturned a sectional compromise that had been honored for thirty-seven years, it also invalidated the basic ideas of the Wilmot Proviso and popular sovereignty.

The Slave Power seemed to have won a major constitutional victory. African Americans were especially dismayed, for Taney's decision asserted that the founders had never intended for black people to be citizens. At the nation's founding, the chief justice wrote, blacks had been regarded "as beings of an inferior order" with "no rights which the white man was bound to respect." Taney was mistaken, however. African Americans had been citizens in several of the original states and had in fact voted.

 Link to excerpts from Chief Justice Roger B. Taney's ruling in the Dred Scott case.

Nevertheless, the ruling seemed to shut the door permanently on black hopes for justice. After 1857, African Americans lived in the land of the *Dred Scott* decision. In northern black communities, rage and despair prevailed. Many who were still fugitive slaves sought refuge in Canada; others considered emigration to the Caribbean or even to Africa. Mary Ann Shadd Cary, who was free and the leader of an emigration movement to Canada, advised her fellow blacks, "Your national ship is rotten and sinking, why not leave it?" Another black abolitionist said that the *Dred Scott* decision had made slavery "the supreme law of the land and all descendants of the African race denationalized." In this state of social dislocation and fear, blacks contemplated whether they had any future in the United States.

Northern whites who rejected the decision's content were suspicious of the circumstances that had produced it. Five of the nine justices were southerners; three of the northern justices actively dissented or refused to concur in parts of the decision. The only northerner who supported Taney's opinion, Justice Robert Grier of Pennsylvania, was known to be close to President Buchanan. In fact, Buchanan had secretly brought to bear improper but effective influence.

A storm of angry reaction broke in the North. The decision seemed to confirm every charge against the aggressive Slave Power. "There is such a thing as the slave power," warned the *Cincinnati Daily Commercial*. "It has marched over and annihilated the boundaries of the states. We are now one great homogenous slaveholding community." The *Cincinnati Freeman* asked, "What security have the Germans and the Irish that their children will not, within a hundred years, be reduced to slavery in this land of their adoption?" Poet James Russell Lowell expressed the racial and economic anxieties of poor northern whites when he had his Yankee character Ezekiel Biglow say, in the language of the day,

> Wy, it's just ez clear ez figgers,
> Clear ez one an' one make two,
> Chaps thet make black slaves o' niggers,
> Want to make wite slaves o' you.

Republican politicians used these fears to strengthen their antislavery coalition. Abraham Lincoln stressed that

Abraham Lincoln and the Slave Power

the territorial question affected every citizen. "The whole nation," he had declared as early as 1854, "is interested that the best use shall be made of these Territories. We want them for homes of free white people. This they cannot be, to any considerable extent, if slavery shall be planted within them." The territories must be reserved, he insisted, "as an outlet for free white people everywhere" so that immigrants could come to America and "find new homes and better their condition in life."

More important, Lincoln warned of slavery's increasing control over the nation. The founders had created a government dedicated to freedom, Lincoln insisted. Admittedly they had recognized slavery's existence, but the public mind, he argued in the "House Divided" speech of 1858, had always rested in the belief that slavery would die either naturally or by legislation. The next step in the unfolding Slave Power conspiracy, Lincoln alleged, would be a Supreme Court decision "declaring that the Constitution does not permit a State to exclude slavery from its limits. . . . We shall lie down pleasantly, dreaming that the people of Missouri are on the verge of making their State free; and we shall awake to the reality instead, that the Supreme Court has made Illinois a slave State." This charge was not hyperbole, for lawsuits soon challenged state laws that freed slaves brought within their borders. Countless northerners heeded Lincoln's warnings, as events convinced them that slaveholders were intent on making slavery a national institution. Southerners, fatefully, never forgot Lincoln's use of the direct words "ultimate extinction."

Politically, Republicans were now locked in conflict with the *Dred Scott* decision. By endorsing the South's doctrine of state sovereignty, the Court had in effect declared that the central position of the Republican Party—no extension of slavery—was unconstitutional. Republicans could only repudiate the decision, appealing to a "higher law," or hope to change the personnel of the Court. They did both and gained politically as fear of the Slave Power grew. But fear also deepened among free blacks. Frederick Douglass continued to try to fashion hope among his people but concluded a speech in the wake of the *Dred Scott* decision bleakly: "I walk by faith, not by sight."

For northern Democrats like Stephen Douglas, the Court's decision posed an awful dilemma. Northern voters were alarmed by the prospect that the territories would be opened to slavery. To retain their support, Douglas had to find some way to reassure these voters. Yet given his presidential ambitions, Douglas could not afford to alienate southern Democrats.

The Lecompton Constitution and Disharmony Among Democrats

Douglas chose to stand by his principle of popular sovereignty, even if the result angered southerners. In 1857, Kansans voted on a proslavery constitution that had been drafted at Lecompton. It was defeated by more than ten thousand votes in a referendum boycotted by most proslavery voters. The evidence was overwhelming that Kansans did not want slavery, yet President Buchanan tried to force the Lecompton Constitution through Congress in an effort to hastily organize the territory.

Never had the Slave Power's influence over the government seemed more blatant; the Buchanan administration and southerners demanded a proslavery outcome, contrary to the majority will in Kansas. Breaking with the administration, Douglas threw his weight against the Lecompton Constitution. But his action infuriated southern Democrats. After the *Dred Scott* decision, southerners like Senator Albert G. Brown of Mississippi believed

slavery was protected in the territories: "The Constitution as expounded by the Supreme Court awards it. We demand it; we mean to have it." Increasingly, though, many southerners believed their sectional rights and slavery would be safe only in a separate nation. And northern Democrats, led by Douglas, found it harder to support the territorial protection for slavery that southern Democrats insisted was theirs as a constitutional right. Thus, in North and South, the issue of slavery in the territories continued to destroy moderation and promote militancy.

Disunion

It is worth remembering that, in the late 1850s, most Americans were not always caught up daily in the slavery crisis. They were preoccupied with personal affairs, especially coping with the effects of the economic panic that had begun in the spring of 1857. They were worried about widespread unemployment, the plummeting price of wheat, the declining wages at a textile mill, or sons who needed land. In the Midwest, clerks, mechanics, domestics, railroad hands, and lumber camp workers lost jobs by the thousands. Bankers were at a loss for what to do about a weak credit system caused by frenzied western land speculation that began early in the decade. In parts of the South, such as Georgia, the panic intensified class divisions between upcountry yeomen and coastal slaveholding planters. Farmers blamed the tight money policies of Georgia's budding commercial banking system on wealthy planters who controlled the state's Democratic Party.

The panic had been caused by several shortcomings of the unregulated American banking system, by frenzies of speculation in western lands and railroads, and by a weak and overburdened credit system. By 1858, Philadelphia had 40,000 unemployed workers and New York City, nearly 100,000. Fear of bread riots and class warfare gripped many cities in the North. True to form, blame for such economic woe became sectionalized, as southerners saw their system justified by the temporary collapse of industrial prosperity and northerners feared even more the incursions of the Slave Power on an insecure future.

Soon, however, the entire nation's focus would be drawn to a new dimension of the slavery question—armed rebellion, led by the abolitionist who had killed proslavery settlers along Pottawatomie Creek in "Bleeding Kansas." Born in Connecticut in 1800, John Brown had been raised by staunchly religious antislavery parents. Between 1820 and 1855, he engaged in some twenty business ventures, including farming, nearly all of them failures. But Brown had a distinctive vision of abolitionism. He relied on an Old Testament conception of justice—"an eye for an eye"—and he had a puritanical obsession with the wickedness of others, especially southern

John Brown's Raid on Harpers Ferry

slaveowners. Brown believed that slavery was an "unjustifiable" state of war conducted by one group of people against another. He also believed violence in a righteous cause was a holy act, even a rite of purification for those who engaged in it. To Brown, the destruction of slavery in America required revolutionary ideology and revolutionary acts.

On October 16, 1859, Brown led a small band of eighteen whites and blacks in an attack on the federal arsenal at Harpers Ferry, Virginia. Hoping to trigger a slave rebellion, Brown failed miserably and was quickly captured. In a celebrated trial in November and a widely publicized execution in December, in Charles Town, Virginia, Brown became one of the most enduring martyrs, as well as villains, of American history. His attempted insurrection struck fear into the South.

Then it became known that Brown had received financial backing from several prominent abolitionists. When such northern intellectuals as Ralph Waldo Emerson and Henry David Thoreau praised Brown as a holy warrior who "would make the gallows as glorious as the cross," white southerners' outrage intensified. The South almost universally interpreted Brown's attack at Harpers Ferry as an act of midnight terrorism, as the fulfillment of their long-stated dread of "abolition emissaries" who would infiltrate the region to incite slave rebellion.

Perhaps most telling of all was the fact that the pivotal election of 1860 was less than a year away when Brown went so eagerly to the gallows, handing a note to

▲ The earliest known photograph of John Brown, probably taken in 1846 in Massachusetts, shows him pledging his devotion to an unidentified flag, possibly an abolitionist banner. Already Brown was aiding runaway slaves and pondering ways to strike at slavery.

his jailer with the famous prediction "I John Brown am now quite certain that the crimes of this guilty land will never be purged away, but with blood." Most troubling to southerners, perhaps, was their awareness that, though Republican politicians condemned Brown's crimes, they did so in a way that deflected attention onto the still-greater crime of slavery.

Many Americans believed the election of 1860 would decide the fate of the Union. The Democratic Party was the only party that was truly national in scope. "One after another," wrote a Mississippi editor, "the links which have bound the North and South together, have been severed . . . [but] the Democratic party looms gradually up . . . and waves the olive branch over the troubled waters of politics." But, fatefully, at its 1860 convention in Charleston, South Carolina, the Democratic Party split.

Election of 1860

Stephen Douglas wanted his party's presidential nomination, but he could not afford to alienate northern voters by accepting the southern position on the territories. Southern Democrats, however, insisted on recognition of their rights—as the *Dred Scott* decision had defined them—and they moved to block Douglas's nomination. When Douglas obtained a majority for his version of the platform, delegates from the Deep South walked out of the convention. After efforts at compromise failed, the Democrats presented two nominees: Douglas for the northern wing, and Vice President John C. Breckinridge of Kentucky for the southern.

The Republicans nominated Abraham Lincoln at a rousing convention in Chicago. The choice of Lincoln reflected the growing power of the Midwest, and he was perceived as more moderate on slavery than the early front runner, Senator William H. Seward of New York. A Constitutional Union Party, formed to preserve the nation but strong only in the Upper South, nominated John Bell of Tennessee.

Bell's only issue in the ensuing campaign was the urgency of preserving the Union; Constitutional Unionists hoped to appeal to history, sentiment, and moderation to hold the country together. Douglas desperately sought to unite his northern and southern supporters, while Breckinridge quickly backed away from the appearance of extremism, and his supporters in several states stressed his unionism. Although Lincoln and the Republicans denied any intent to interfere with slavery in the states where it existed, they stood firm against the extension of slavery into the territories.

The election of 1860 was sectional in character, and the only one in American history in which the losers refused to accept the result. Lincoln won, but Douglas, Breckinridge, and Bell together received a majority of the votes. Douglas had broad-based support but won few states. Breckinridge carried nine southern states, all in the Deep South. Bell won pluralities in Virginia, Kentucky, and

Table 14.3 Presidential Vote in 1860 (by State)

Lincoln (Republican)*	Carried all northern states and all electoral votes except 3 in New Jersey
Breckinridge (Southern Democrat)	Carried all slave states except Virginia, Kentucky, Tennessee, Missouri
Bell (Constitutional Union)	Carried Virginia, Kentucky, Tennessee
Douglas (Northern Democrat)	Carried only Missouri

*Lincoln received only 26,000 votes in the entire South and was not even on the ballot in ten slave states. Breckinridge was not on the ballot in three northern states.

Tennessee. Lincoln prevailed in the North, but in the four slave states that ultimately remained loyal to the Union (Missouri, Kentucky, Maryland, and Delaware—the border states) he gained only a plurality, not a majority (see Table 14.3). Lincoln's victory was won in the electoral college. He polled only 40 percent of the total vote and was not even on the ballot in ten slave states.

Opposition to slavery's extension was the core issue for Lincoln and the Republican Party. Moreover, abolitionists and Free-Soil supporters in the North worked to keep the Republicans from compromising on their territorial stand. Meanwhile, in the South, proslavery advocates and secessionists whipped up public opinion and demanded that state conventions assemble to consider secession.

Lincoln made the crucial decision not to soften his party's position on the territories. He wrote of the necessity of maintaining the bond of faith between voter and candidate and of declining to set "the minority over the majority." Although many conservative Republicans—eastern businessmen and former Whigs who did not feel strongly about slavery—hoped for a compromise, the original and most committed Republicans—old Free-Soilers and antislavery Whigs—held the line on slavery expansion.

In the winter of 1860–1861, Senator John J. Crittenden of Kentucky tried to craft a late-hour compromise. Hoping to don the mantle of Henry Clay and avert disunion, Crittenden proposed that the two sections divide the territories between them at the Missouri Compromise line, 36°30'. But this well-worn and controversial idea did not work. When Lincoln ruled out concessions on the territorial issue, Crittenden's peacemaking effort, based on discredited measures, collapsed.

Meanwhile, on December 20, 1860, South Carolina passed an ordinance of secession amid jubilation and cheer-

Secession and the Confederate States of America

ing. Secession strategists concentrated their efforts on the most extreme proslavery state, hoping that South Carolina's bold act would create momentum and induce other states to follow.

By reclaiming its independence, South Carolina raised the stakes in the sectional confrontation. No longer was secession an unthinkable step; the Union was broken. Secessionists now argued that other states should follow South Carolina and that those who favored compromise could make a better deal outside the Union than in it. Moderates from regions with fewer slaves and more diversified economies than the cotton belt, fearing economic chaos and arguing for "resistance short of secession," still felt deep affection for the Union and had family ties in the North; secession was by no means inevitable or widely popular in upper South states like Virginia or Tennessee.

Southern extremists soon got their way in the Deep South. Overwhelming their opposition, they called separate state conventions and passed secession ordinances in Mississippi, Florida, Alabama, Georgia, Louisiana, and Texas. By February 1861, these states had joined South Carolina to form a new government in Montgomery, Alabama: the Confederate States of America. The delegates at Montgomery chose Jefferson Davis of Mississippi as their president, and the Confederacy began to function independently of the United States.

This apparent unanimity of action was deceiving. Confused and dissatisfied with the alternatives, many southerners—perhaps as much as 40 percent even in the deep South—opposed immediate secession. In some state conventions, the secession vote was close and decided by overrepresentation of plantation districts. In Georgia, where more than three in five voters were nonslaveholders, the secession convention voted 166–130 to secede after a bitterly divided debate. Four states in the Upper South where wheat production and commerical ties to the North had grown steadily in the 1850s—Virginia, North Carolina, Tennessee, and Arkansas—flatly rejected secession and did not join the Confederacy until after fighting had begun. In Augusta County, Virginia, in the Shenandoah Valley, where one-fifth of households held slaves, the majority steadfastly sought alternatives to secession until after Fort Sumter. In the border states, popular sentiment was deeply divided; minorities in

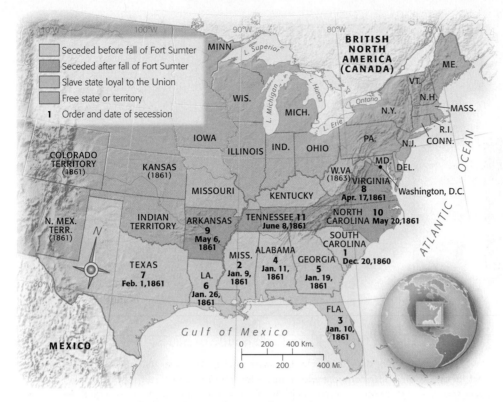

Map 14.4 The Divided Nation—Slave and Free Areas, 1861

After fighting began, the Upper South joined the Deep South in the Confederacy. How does the nation's pattern of division correspond to the distribution of slavery and the percentage of blacks in the population?

Source: Copyright © Cengage Learning

Kentucky and Missouri tried to secede, but these slave states ultimately came under Union control, along with Maryland and Delaware (see Map 14.4).

Such misgivings were not surprising. Secession posed new and troubling issues for southerners. Analysis of election returns from 1860 and 1861 indicates that slaveholders and nonslaveholders were beginning to part company politically. Heavily slaveholding counties strongly supported secession. But nonslaveholding areas that had favored Breckinridge in the presidential election proved far less willing to support secession: economic interests and fear of war on their own soil provided a potent, negative reaction to abstractions such as "state rights" (see Figure 14.1). With war on the horizon, yeomen were beginning to consider their class interests and to ask themselves how far they would go to support slavery and slaveowners.

As for why the Deep South bolted, we need look no further than the speeches and writings of the secession commissioners sent out by the seven seceded states to try to convince the other slave states to join them. Repeatedly, they stressed independence as the only way to preserve white racial security and the slave system against the hostile Republicans. Upon "slavery,"

said the Alabama commissioner, Stephen Hale, to the Kentucky legislature, rested "not only the wealth and prosperity of the southern people, but their very existence as a political community." Only secession, Hale contended, could sustain the "heaven-ordained superiority of the white over the black race." This combination of economic interests and beliefs fueled the tragedy about to happen.

The dilemma facing President Lincoln on inauguration day in March 1861 was how to maintain the authority of the federal government without provoking war. Proceeding cautiously, he sought only to hold onto forts in the states that had left the Union, reasoning that in this way he could assert federal sovereignty while waiting for a restoration. But Jefferson Davis, who could not claim to lead a sovereign nation if the Confederate ports were under foreign (that is, U.S.) control, was unwilling to be so patient. A collision soon came.

It arrived in the early morning hours of April 12, 1861, at Fort Sumter in Charleston harbor. A federal garrison there ran low on food, and Lincoln notified

Fort Sumter and Outbreak of War

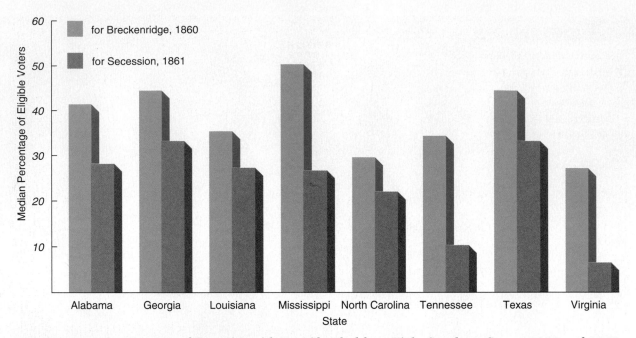

Figure 14-1 Voting Returns of Counties with Few Slaveholders, Eight Southern States, 1860 and 1861

This graph depicts voting in counties whose percentage of slaveholders ranked them among the lower half of the counties in their state. How does voters' support for secession in 1861 compare with support for John Breckinridge, the southern Democratic candidate in 1860? Why was their support for secession so weak? At this time counties with many slaveholders were giving increased support to secession.

the South Carolinians that he was sending a ship to resupply the fort. For the Montgomery government, the alternatives were to attack the fort or to acquiesce to Lincoln's authority. After the Confederate cabinet met, the secretary of war ordered local commanders to obtain a surrender or attack the fort. After two days of heavy bombardment, the federal garrison finally surrendered. No one died in battle, though an accident during post-battle ceremonies killed two Union soldiers. Confederates permitted the U.S. troops to sail away on unarmed vessels while Charlestonians celebrated wildly. The Civil War—the bloodiest war in America's history—had begun.

Historians have long debated the immediate and long-term roots of the Civil War. Some have interpreted it as an "irrepressible conflict," the clash of two civilizations on divergent trajectories of history. Another group saw the war as "needless," the result of a "blundering generation" of irrational politicians and activists who trumped up an avoidable conflict. But the issues dividing Americans in 1861 were fundamental to the future of the republic. The logic of Republican ideology tended in the direction of abolishing slavery, even though Republicans denied any such intention. The logic of southern arguments led to establishing slavery everywhere, though southern leaders, too, denied such a motive. Republicans were devoted to promoting the North's free labor economy, burgeoning

Causation

in the Great Lakes region through homesteading, internal improvements, and protective tariffs. The lords of the cotton kingdom, owners of $3 billion in slave property and the largest single asset in the American economy, were determined to protect and expand their "way of life." Small investors in land and large investors in slaves were on a collision course.

Lincoln put these facts succinctly. In a postelection letter to his old congressional colleague, Alexander Stephens of Georgia, soon to be vice president of the Confederacy, Lincoln offered assurance that Republicans would not attack slavery in the states where it existed. But Lincoln continued, "You think slavery is right and ought to be expanded; while we think it is wrong and ought to be restricted. That I suppose is the rub." Frederick Douglass demonstrated that he understood this in a postwar speech in which he declared that the "fight" had not been between "rapacious birds and ferocious beasts, a mere display of brute courage... but it was a war between men of thought, as well as of action, and in dead earnest for something beyond the battlefield."

Directly or indirectly, as a matter of *interests* and *morality*, Douglass's "something" had to do with slavery. Without slavery, there would have been no war. Many Americans still hold to a belief that the war was about states' rights, the theory and practice of the proper relationship of state to federal authority. But the significance of states' rights, then as now, is always in

▲ R. H. Howell, after Henry Cleenewerck, *The First Flag of Independence Raised in the South*. Lithograph, Savannah, Georgia, 1860. On the night of November 8, 1860, a huge crowd gathered in Johnson Square, Savannah, to protest Lincoln's election victory. The special banner on the obelisk reads "Our Motto Southern Rights, Equality of the States, Don't Tread on Me," drawing on traditions from the Revolutionary War.

the cause in which it is employed. If secession was an exercise in states' rights—to what end? To borrow from Douglass, it is the meaning within the fight that we must understand.

SUMMARY

Events often seem inevitable after they have occurred. We should never fall into the trap of seeing big events in history only through a lens of inevitability. The events and ideas that Americans clashed over were links in a chain leading to conflict; humans made choices all along the way and to go to war.

The War with Mexico fostered massive land acquisition, which in turn forced an open debate about slavery in the West. The Compromise of 1850 attempted to settle the dispute but only added fuel to the fires of sectional contention, leading to the fateful Kansas-Nebraska Act of 1854, which tore asunder the political party system and gave birth to a genuine antislavery coalition. With Bleeding Kansas and the *Dred Scott* decision by 1857, Americans North and South faced clear and dangerous choices about the future of labor and the meaning of liberty in an ambitious and expanding society. And finally,

by 1859, when radical abolitionist John Brown attacked Harpers Ferry to foment a slave insurrection, southerners and northerners came to see each other in conspiratorial terms. Meanwhile, African Americans, slave and free, fled from slave catchers in unprecedented numbers and grew to expect violent if uncertain resolutions to their dreams of freedom in America. No one knew the future, but all knew the issues and conflicts were real.

Throughout the 1840s and 1850s, many able leaders had worked to avert the outcome of disunion. As late as 1858, even Jefferson Davis had declared, "This great country will continue united." Secession dismayed northern editors and voters, and it also plunged some planters into depression. Paul Cameron, the largest slaveowner in North Carolina, confessed that he was "very unhappy. I love the Union." Many blacks, however, shared Frederick Douglass's outlook. "The contest must now be decided," he wrote in March 1861, "and decided forever, which of the two, Freedom or Slavery, shall give law to this Republic. Let the conflict come."

Why had war broken out? Why had all efforts to prevent it failed? The emotions bound up in attacking and defending slavery's future were too powerful, and the interests it affected too vital for a final compromise.

Legacy FOR A PEOPLE AND A NATION

Terrorist or Freedom Fighter?

The greatest significance of John Brown's raid on Harpers Ferry in 1859 rests in its long aftermath in American memory. "Men consented to his death," wrote Frederick Douglass of Brown, "and then went home and taught their children to honor his memory." Brown is as important as a symbol as he is for his deeds. He has been at once one of the most beloved and most loathed figures in American history. In the song that bears his name, "John Brown's Body," a popular marching tune during the Civil War, his "soul goes marching on." As poet Stephen Vincent Benet wrote: "You can weigh John Brown's body well enough, / But how and in what balance weigh John Brown?"

In the wake of his execution, in painting, song, and poetry people constructed a John Brown mythology. Was he a Christ-like figure who died for the nation's sins, who had to commit crimes in order to expose the nation's larger crime? Or was he a terrorist, who murdered in the name of his own vision of God's will? Brown can be inspiring and disturbing, majestic and foolish, a warrior saint and a monster. He represents the highest ideals and the most ruthless deeds. He killed for justice and was hanged as a traitor. Perhaps Brown was one of the avengers of history who does the work the rest of us will not, could not, or should not.

Over the years, many organizations have adopted John Brown as their justifying symbol, from left-wing students opposing American foreign policy to current anti-abortion groups who target clinics and doctors. In today's world, terrorism and revolutionary violence are more often in the news. Suicide bombers attack buses and restaurants in Israel; a federal building explodes in Oklahoma City; Al Qaeda operatives blow up trains in Madrid; American embassies are attacked in Africa and Europe; on September 11, 2001, four hijacked passenger airplanes become weapons of death that bring terrorism to American soil as never before; and in Iraq, a lethal insurgency resists the American occupation, as a country falls into sectarian civil war between Shi'ites and Sunnis. The story of John Brown's raid in 1859 continues to force us to ask when and how revolutionary violence—violence in the name of a political or spiritual end—is justified. That is his legacy for a people and a nation.

Advocates of compromise anticipated that the tradition of conciliation and sectional adjustment would yet again save the Union in 1860, but their hopes were dashed.

During the 1850s, every southern victory in territorial expansion increased fear of the Slave Power, and each new expression of Free-Soil sentiment prompted slaveholders to harden their demands. In the profoundest sense, slavery was the root of the war. But as the fighting began, the fate of the war's central issue was shrouded in confusion. As a people and a nation, Americans had reached the most fateful turning point in their history. Answers would now come from the battlefield and from the mobilization of two societies to wage war on a scale they had not imagined.

SUGGESTIONS FOR FURTHER READING

Edward L. Ayers, *What Caused the Civil War: Reflections on the South and Southern History* (2005)

Richard J. Carwardine, *Lincoln* (2003)

Charles Dew, *Apostles of Disunion: Southern Secession Commissioners and the Causes of the Civil War* (2001)

Marc Egnal, *Clash of Extremes: The Economic Origins of the Civil War* (2009)

Nicole Etcheson, *Bleeding Kansas: Contested Liberty in the Civil War Era* (2004)

Don E. Fehrenbacher, *The Slaveholding Republic: An Account of the United States Government's Relations to Slavery* (2001)

Eric Foner, *Free Soil, Free Labor, Free Men: The Ideology of the Republican Party* (1970)

Robert W. Johannsen, *To the Halls of the Montezumas: The Mexican War and the American Imagination* (1985)

David S. Reynolds, *John Brown, Abolitionist: The Man Who Killed Slavery, Sparked the Civil War, and Seeded Civil Rights* (2005)

Elizabeth R. Varon, *Disunion! The Coming of the American Civil War, 1789–1859* (2008)

Go to the CourseMate website for primary source links, study tools, and review materials for this chapter. www.cengagebrain.com

Transforming Fire: The Civil War 1861–1865

*S*lave pens were the dark and ugly crossroads of American history. To see, hear, and smell one was to understand why the Civil War happened. Wallace Turnage, a seventeen-year-old slave from a cotton plantation in Pickens County, Alabama, entered wartime Mobile in December 1862 through the slave traders' yard; he would leave Mobile from that same yard a year and eight months later.

Turnage was born in 1846 on a remote tobacco farm near Snow Hill, North Carolina. In mid-1860, as the nation teetered on the brink of disunion, he was sold to a Richmond, Virginia, slave trader named Hector Davis. Turnage worked in Davis's three-story slave jail, organizing daily auctions until he was sold for $1,000 in early 1861 to a cotton planter from Pickens County, Alabama. Frequently whipped and longing for escape, the desperate teenager tried four times over the next two years to run away to Mississippi, seeking the lines of the Union armies. Although he remained at large for months, he was captured each time and returned to his owner in southeastern Alabama.

In frustration, his owner took Turnage to the Mobile slave traders' yard, where the youth was sold for $2,000 to a wealthy merchant in the port city. During 1864, as Union Admiral David Farragut prepared his fleet for an assault on Mobile Bay and the city came under siege, its slaves were enlisted to build elaborate trenchworks. Meanwhile, Turnage labored at all manner of urban tasks for his new owner's family, including driving their carriage on errands.

One day in early August, Turnage crashed the old carriage on a Mobile street. In anger, his owner took him to the slave pen and hired the jailer to administer thirty lashes in the pen's special "whipping house." Stripped naked, his hands tied in ropes, Turnage was hoisted up on a hook on the wall. At the end of the gruesome ritual, his owner instructed Wallace to walk home. Instead, Turnage "took courage," as he wrote in his postwar narrative, "prayed faithfully," and walked steadfastly southwest, right through the Confederate encampment and trenchworks. The soldiers took the bloodied and

◀ Lithograph of a runaway slave, which was one of the most common depictions of slavery generally in northern popular culture. Part of Wallace Turnage's final escape occurred in a setting much like this image.

Chronology

1861
- Battle of Bull Run
- McClellan organizes Union Army
- Union blockade begins
- U.S. Congress passes first confiscation act
- *Trent* affair

1862
- Union captures Fort Henry and Fort Donelson
- U.S. Navy captures New Orleans
- Battle of Shiloh shows the war's destructiveness
- Confederacy enacts conscription
- McClellan's peninsula campaign fails to take Richmond
- U.S. Congress passes second confiscation act, initiating emancipation
- Confederacy mounts offensive in Maryland and Kentucky
- Battle of Antietam ends Lee's drive into Maryland in September
- British intervention in the war on Confederate side is averted

1863
- Emancipation Proclamation takes effect
- U.S. Congress passes National Banking Act
- Union enacts conscription
- African American soldiers join Union Army
- Food riots occur in southern cities
- Battle of Chancellorsville ends in Confederate victory but Jackson's death
- Union wins key victories at Vicksburg and Gettysburg
- Draft riots take place in New York City

1864
- Battles of the Wilderness and Spotsylvania produce heavy casualties on both sides
- Battle of Cold Harbor continues carnage in Virginia
- Sherman captures Atlanta
- Confederacy begins to collapse on home front
- Lincoln wins reelection, eliminating any Confederate hopes for negotiated end to war
- Jefferson Davis proposes arming slaves
- Sherman marches through Georgia to the sea

1865
- Sherman marches through Carolinas
- U.S. Congress approves Thirteenth Amendment
- Lee abandons Richmond and Petersburg
- Lee surrenders at Appomattox Court House
- Lincoln assassinated
- Death toll in war reaches 620,000

tattered black teenager for simply one among the hundreds of slaves who did camp labor.

For the next three weeks, Turnage crawled and waded for 25 miles through the snake-infested swamps of the Foul River estuary, down the west edge of Mobile Bay. Nearly starved and narrowly escaping Confederate patrols, Turnage made it all the way to Cedar Point, where he could look out at the forbidding mouth of Mobile Bay to Dauphin Island, now occupied by Union forces. Alligators swam in their wallows nearby, delta grass swayed waist-high in the hot breezes, and the laughing gulls squawked around him as Turnage hid from Confederate lookouts in a swampy den. He remembered his choices starkly: "It was death to go back and it was death to stay there and freedom was before me; it could only be death to go forward if I was caught and freedom if I escaped."

*T*urnage barely survived a desperate attempt to ride a log out into the ocean and narrowly made it back to shore. Then, one day at the water's edge, he noticed an old rowboat that had rolled in with the tide. The veteran runaway now took a "piece of board" and began to row out into the bay. As a squall with "water like a hill coming" at him nearly swamped him, he suddenly "heard the crash of oars and behold there was eight Yankees in a boat." Following the rhythm of the oars, Turnage jumped into the Union gunboat. For a stunning few moments, he remembered, the oarsmen in blue "were struck with silence" as they contemplated the frail young black man crouched in front of them. Turnage turned his head and looked back at Confederate soldiers on the shore and measured the distance of his bravery at sea. Then he took his first breaths of freedom.

The Civil War brought astonishing changes to individuals everywhere in North and South. It obliterated the normal patterns of life. Millions of men were swept away into training camps and regiments. Armies numbering in the hundreds of thousands marched over the South, devastating the countryside. Families struggled to survive without their men; businesses tried to cope with the loss of workers. Women in both North and South took on extra responsibilities in the home and moved into new jobs in the work force. Many women joined the ranks of nurses and hospital workers. No sphere of life went untouched.

But southern soldiers and their families also experienced what few other groups of Americans have—utter defeat. For most of them, wealth changed to poverty and hope to despair as countless southern farms were ruined. Late in the war, many southerners yearned only for an end to inflation, to shortages, to the escape of their slaves, and to the death that visited nearly every family. Even the South's slaves, who eventually placed great hope in the war, did not always encounter sympathetic liberators such as those who took Turnage from his drowning boat, fed and clothed him in a tent, and took him before a Union general, where the freedman was given two choices: join a black regiment or become a camp servant for a white officer. For the remainder of the war, Turnage cooked for a Maryland captain.

In the North, farm boys and mechanics from all regions would be asked for heretofore unimagined sacrifices. The conflict ensured vast government expenditures and lucrative federal contracts. *Harper's Monthly* reported that an eminent financier expected a long war, fostering huge purchases, active speculation, and rising prices. "The battle of Bull Run," predicted the financier, "makes the fortune of every man in Wall Street who is not a natural idiot."

Change was most drastic in the South, where secessionists had launched a conservative revolution for their section's national independence. Born of states' rights doctrine, the Confederacy now had to be transformed into a centralized nation to fight a vast war. Southern whites had feared that a peacetime government of Republicans would interfere with slavery and ruin plantation life. Instead, their own actions led to a war that turned southern society upside down and imperiled the very existence of slavery.

The war created social strains in both North and South. To the alarm of many, the powers of the federal government and of the president increased during the war. Disaffection was strongest, though, in the Confederacy, where poverty and class resentment threatened the South from within as federal armies assailed it from without. In the North, dissent also flourished, and antiwar sentiment occasionally erupted into violence.

Ultimately, the Civil War forced on the nation a social and political revolution regarding race. Its greatest effect was to compel leaders and citizens to finally face the great question of slavery. And blacks themselves embraced what was for them the most fundamental turning point in their experience as Americans.

- How and why did the Civil War bring social transformations to both South and North?

- How did the war to preserve the Union or for southern independence become the war to free the slaves?

- By 1865, when Americans on all sides searched for the *meaning* of the war they had just fought, what might some of their answers have been?

America Goes to War, 1861–1862

Few Americans understood what they were getting into when the war began. The onset of hostilities sparked patriotic sentiments, optimistic speeches, and joyous ceremonies in both North and South. Northern communities raised companies of volunteers eager to save the Union and sent them off with fanfare. In the South, confident recruits boasted of whipping the Yankees and returning home before Christmas. Southern women sewed dashing uniforms for men who would soon be lucky to wear drab gray or butternut homespun. Americans went to war in 1861 with decidedly romantic notions of what they would experience.

Through the spring of 1861, both sides scrambled to organize and train their undisciplined armies. On July 21, 1861, the first battle took place outside Manassas Junction, Virginia, near a stream called Bull Run. General Irvin McDowell and thirty thousand Union troops attacked General P. G. T. Beauregard's twenty-two thousand southerners (see Map 15.1). As raw recruits struggled amid the confusion of their first battle, federal forces began to gain ground. Then they ran into a line of Virginia troops under General Thomas Jackson. "There is Jackson standing like a stone wall," shouted one Confederate. "Stonewall" Jackson's line held, and the arrival of nine thousand Confederate reinforcements by train won the day for the South. Union troops fled back to Washington, observed by shocked northern congressmen and spectators who had watched the battle; a few sightseers were actually captured for their folly.

The unexpected rout at Bull Run gave northerners their first hint of the nature of the war to come. Although the United States enjoyed an enormous advantage in resources, victory would not be easy. Pro-Union feeling was growing in western Virginia, and loyalties were divided in the four border slave states—Missouri,

First Battle of Bull Run

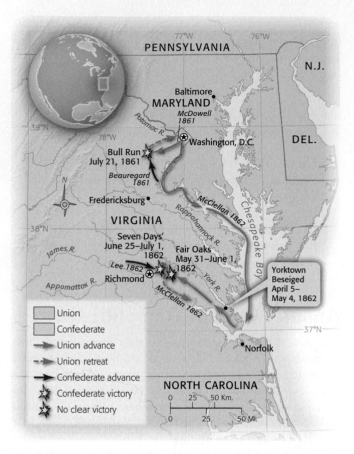

Map 15.1 McClellan's Campaign

The water route chosen by McClellan to threaten Richmond during the peninsular campaign.

Source: Copyright © Cengage Learning

Kentucky, Maryland, and Delaware. But the rest of the Upper South—the states of North Carolina, Virginia, Tennessee, and Arkansas—had joined the Confederacy in the wake of the attack on Fort Sumter. Moved by an outpouring of regional loyalty, half a million southerners volunteered to fight—so many that the Confederate government could hardly arm them all. The United States therefore undertook a massive mobilization of troops around Washington, D.C.

Lincoln gave command of the army to General George B. McClellan, an officer who proved better at organization and training than at fighting. McClellan put his growing army into camp and devoted the fall and winter of 1861 to readying a formidable force of a quarter-million men whose mission would be to take Richmond, established as the Confederate capital by July 1861. "The vast preparation of the enemy," wrote one southern soldier, produced a "feeling of despondency" in the South for the first time. But southern morale remained high early in the war. Most Americans still possessed a rather romantic conception of the war looming on their horizon.

While McClellan prepared, the Union began to implement other parts of its overall strategy, which called

Grand Strategy

for a blockade of southern ports and eventual capture of the Mississippi River. Like a constricting snake, this "Anaconda plan" would strangle the Confederacy (see Map 15.2). At first, the Union Navy had too few ships to patrol 3,550 miles of coastline and block the Confederacy's avenues of supply. Gradually, however, the navy increased the blockade's effectiveness, though it never stopped southern commerce completely.

The Confederate strategy was essentially defensive. A defensive posture was not only consistent with the South's claim of independence, but also reasonable in light of the North's advantage in resources (see Figure 15.1). But Jefferson Davis called the southern strategy an "offensive defensive," taking advantage of opportunities to attack and using its interior lines of transportation to concentrate troops at crucial points. In its war aims, the Confederacy did not need to conquer the North; the Union effort, however, as time would tell, required conquest of the South.

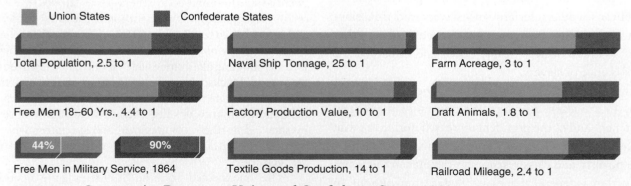

Figure 15-1 Comparative Resources, Union and Confederate States, 1861

The North had vastly superior resources. Although the North's advantages in manpower and industrial capacity proved very important, the South still had to be conquered, its society and its will crushed.

Source: The Times Atlas of World History. Used with permission.

Map 15.2 The War in the West

Here is an overview of the Union's successful campaigns in the West and its seizure of the key points on the Mississippi River, as well as along the Atlantic coast in 1862 and 1863. These actions were decisive in paving the way for ultimate northern victory.

Source: Copyright © Cengage Learning

Strategic thinking on both sides slighted the importance of the West, that vast expanse of territory between Virginia and the Mississippi River and beyond. Guerrilla warfare broke out in 1861 in the politically divided state of Missouri, and key locations along the Mississippi and other major western rivers would prove crucial prizes in the North's eventual victory. Beyond the Mississippi River, the Confederacy hoped to gain an advantage by negotiating treaties with the Creeks, Choctaws, Chickasaws, Cherokees, Seminoles, and smaller groups of Plains Indians. Meanwhile, the Republican U.S. Congress carved the West into territories in anticipation of state making. For most Indians west of the Mississippi, what began during the Civil War was nearly three decades of offensive warfare against them, an enveloping strategy of conquest, relocation, and slaughter.

The last half of 1861 brought no major land battles, but the North made gains by sea. Late in the summer,

Union Naval Campaign

Union naval forces captured Cape Hatteras and then Hilton Head, one of the Sea Islands off Port Royal, South Carolina. A few months later, similar operations secured vital coastal points in North Carolina as well as Fort Pulaski, which defended Savannah. Federal naval operations established significant beachheads along the Confederate coastline (see Map 15.2).

The coastal victories off South Carolina foreshadowed a revolution in slave society. At the federal gunboats' approach, planters abandoned their land and fled. For a while, Confederate cavalry tried to round up slaves and move them to the interior as well. But thousands of slaves greeted what they hoped to be freedom with rejoicing and broke the hated cotton gins. Some entered their masters' homes and took clothing and furniture, which they conspicuously displayed. A growing stream of runaways poured into Union lines. Unwilling at first to wage a war against slavery, the federal government did not acknowledge the slaves' freedom—though it began to use their labor in the Union cause. This swelling tide of emancipated slaves, defined by many Union officers as "contraband" of war (confiscated enemy property), forced first a bitter and confused debate within the Union Army and government over how to treat the freedmen, and then a forthright attempt to harness their labor and military power.

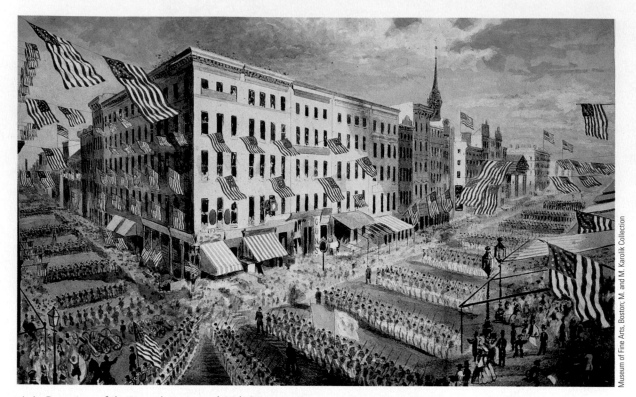

▲ In *Departure of the Seventh Regiment* (1861), flags and the spectacle of thousands of young men from New York marching off to battle give a deceptively gay appearance to the beginning of the Civil War.

Museum of Fine Arts, Boston; M. and M. Karolik Collection

The coastal incursions worried southerners, but the spring of 1862 brought even stronger evidence of the war's gravity. In March, two ironclad ships—the *Monitor* (a Union warship) and the *Merrimack* (a Union ship seized by the Confederacy)—fought each other for the first time off the coast of Virginia. Their battle, though indecisive, ushered in a new era in naval design. In April, Union ships commanded by Admiral David Farragut smashed through log booms blocking the Mississippi River and fought their way upstream to capture New Orleans. The city at the mouth of the Mississippi, the South's greatest seaport and slave-trading center, was now in federal hands.

Farther west, three full Confederate regiments were organized, mostly of Cherokees, from Indian Territory, but a Union victory at Elkhorn Tavern, Arkansas, shattered southern control of the region. Thereafter, dissension within Native American groups and a Union victory the following year at Honey Springs, Arkansas, reduced Confederate operations in Indian Territory to guerrilla raids.

War in the Far West

In the westernmost campaign of the war, from February to May 1862, some three thousand Confederate and four thousand Union forces fought for control of New Mexico Territory. The military significance of the New Mexico campaign was limited, but the Confederate invasion had grander aims: access to the trade riches of the Santa Fe Trail and possession of gold mines in Colorado and California. If the campaign had endured long enough, the Confederacy would have been much stronger with a western empire. But Colorado and New Mexico Unionists fought for their region, and in a series of battles at Glorieta Pass, 20 miles east of Santa Fe, on March 26 through 28, they blocked the Confederate invasion. By May 1, Confederate forces straggled down the Rio Grande River back into Texas, ending their effort to take New Mexico.

Meanwhile, in February 1862, land and river forces in northern Tennessee won significant victories for the Union.

Grant's Tennessee Campaign and the Battle of Shiloh

A Union commander named Ulysses S. Grant saw the strategic importance of Fort Henry and Fort Donelson, the Confederate outposts guarding the Tennessee and Cumberland Rivers. If federal troops could capture these forts, Grant realized, they would open two prime routes into the heartland of the Confederacy. In just ten days, he seized the forts—completely cutting off the Confederates and demanding "unconditional surrender" of Fort Donelson. A path into Tennessee, Alabama, and Mississippi now lay open before the Union Army. Grant's achievement of such a surrender from his former West Point roommate, Confederate commander Simon Bolivar Buckner, inspired northern public opinion.

Grant moved on into southern Tennessee and the first of the war's shockingly bloody encounters, the Battle of

◄ Steamboats at Pittsburgh Landing, Tennessee, during the Shiloh campaign, April 1862. These riverboats and their cargoes arrived along with reinforcements of troops to help save Ulysses S. Grant's army at the crucial battle of Shiloh.

Massachuessetts Commandery Military Order of the Loyal Legion and the U.S. Army Military History Institute

Shiloh (see Map 15.2). On April 6, Confederate general Albert Sidney Johnston caught federal troops with their backs to the water awaiting reinforcements along the Tennessee River. The Confederates attacked early in the morning and inflicted heavy damage all day. Close to victory, General Johnston was shot from his horse and killed. Southern forces almost achieved a breakthrough, but Union reinforcements arrived that night. The next day, the tide of battle turned and, after ten hours of terrible combat, Grant's men forced the Confederates to withdraw.

Neither side won a decisive victory at Shiloh, yet the losses were staggering, and the Confederates were forced to retreat into northern Mississippi. Northern troops lost thirteen thousand men (killed, wounded, or captured) out of sixty-three thousand; southerners sacrificed eleven thousand out of forty thousand. Total casualties in this single battle exceeded those in all three of America's previous wars combined. Now both sides were beginning to sense the true nature of the war. "I saw an open field," Grant recalled, "over which Confederates had made repeated charges . . . so covered with dead that it would have been possible to walk across the clearing, in any direction, stepping on dead bodies, without a foot touching the ground." Shiloh utterly changed Grant's thinking about the war. He had hoped that southerners would soon be "heartily tired" of the conflict. After Shiloh, "I gave up all idea of saving the Union except by complete conquest." Memories of the Shiloh battlefield, and many others to come, would haunt the soldiers who survived for the rest of their lives. Herman Melville's "Shiloh, A Requiem" captures the pathos of that spring day when armies learned the truth about war:

Skimming lightly, wheeling still,
The swallows fly low
Over the field in clouded days,
The forest-field of Shiloh—

Over the field where April rain
Solaced the parched ones stretched in pain
Through the pause of night
That followed the Sunday fight
Around the church of Shiloh—
The church so lone, the log-built one,
That echoed to many a parting groan
And natural prayer
Of dying foemen mingled there—
Foemen at morn, but friends at eve—
Fame or country least their care:
(What like a bullet can undeceive!)
But now they lie low,
While over them the swallows skim,
And all is hushed at Shiloh.

On the Virginia front, President Lincoln had a different problem. General McClellan was slow to move. Only thirty-six, McClellan had already achieved notable success as an army officer and railroad president. Habitually overestimating the size of enemy forces, he called repeatedly for reinforcements and ignored Lincoln's directions to advance. McClellan advocated war of limited aims that would lead to a quick reunion. He intended neither disruption of slavery nor war on noncombatants. McClellan's conservative vision of the war was practically outdated before he even moved his army into Virginia. Finally, he chose to move by a water route, sailing his troops down the Chesapeake, landing them on the peninsula between the York and James Rivers, and advancing on Richmond from the east (see Map 15.1).

McClellan and the Peninsula Campaign

After a bloody but indecisive battle at Fair Oaks on May 31 through June 1, the federal armies moved to within 7 miles of the Confederate capital. They could see the spires on Richmond churches. The Confederate commanding general, Joseph E. Johnston, was badly wounded at Fair Oaks, and President Jefferson Davis placed his chief military adviser, Robert E. Lee, in command. The fifty-five-year-old Lee was an aristocratic Virginian, a lifelong military officer, and a veteran of distinction from the War with Mexico. Although he initially opposed secession, Lee loyally gave his allegiance to his state and became a staunch Confederate nationalist. He soon foiled McClellan's legions.

First, Lee sent Stonewall Jackson's corps of seventeen thousand northwest into the Shenandoah valley behind Union forces, where they threatened Washington, D.C., and with rapid-strike mobility drew some federal troops away from Richmond to protect their own capital. Further, in mid-June, in an extraordinary four-day ride around the entire Union Army, Confederate cavalry under J. E. B. Stuart, a self-styled Virginia cavalier with red cape and plumed hat, confirmed the exposed position of a major portion of McClellan's army north of the rain-swollen Chickahominy River. Then, in a series of engagements known as the Seven Days Battles, from June 26 through July 1, Lee struck at McClellan's army. Lee never managed to close his pincers around the retreating Union forces, but the daring move of taking the majority of his army northeast and attacking the Union right flank, while leaving only a small force to defend Richmond, forced McClellan (always believing he was outnumbered) to retreat toward the James River.

During the sustained fighting of the Seven Days, the Union forces suffered 20,614 casualties and the Confederates, 15,849. After repeated rebel assaults against entrenched positions on high ground at Malvern Hill, an officer concluded, "It was not war, it was murder." By August 3, McClellan withdrew his army back to the Potomac and the environs of Washington. Richmond remained safe for almost two more years.

Buoyed by these results, Jefferson Davis conceived an ambitious plan to turn the tide of the war and gain recognition of the Confederacy by European nations. He ordered a general offensive, sending Lee north into Maryland and Generals Kirby Smith and Braxton Bragg into Kentucky. Calling on residents of Maryland and Kentucky, still slave states, to make a separate peace with his government, Davis also invited northwestern states like Indiana, which sent much of their trade down the Mississippi to New Orleans, to leave the Union. This was a coordinated effort to take the war to the North and to try to force both a military and a political turning point.

Confederate Offensive in Maryland and Kentucky

The plan was promising, but in the end the offensive failed. Lee's forces achieved a striking success at the battle of Second Bull Run, August 29 through 30, just southwest of Washington, D.C. On the same killing fields along Bull Run Creek where federal troops had been defeated the previous summer, an entire Union army was sent in retreat back into the federal capital.

◀ In October 1862 in New York City, photographer Mathew Brady opened an exhibition of photographs from the Battle of Antietam. Although few knew it, Brady's vision was very poor, and this photograph of Confederate dead was actually made by his assistants, Alexander Gardner and James F. Gibson.

Library of Congress

Thousands of wounded occupied schools and churches, and two thousand suffered on cots in the rotunda of the U.S. Capitol.

But in the bloodiest day of the entire war, September 17, 1862, McClellan turned Lee back from Sharpsburg, Maryland. In this Battle of Antietam, five thousand men died, and another eighteen thousand were wounded. Lee was lucky to escape destruction, for McClellan had intercepted a lost battle order, wrapped around cigars for each Confederate corps commander and inadvertently dropped by a courier. But McClellan moved slowly, failed to use his larger forces in simultaneous attacks, and allowed Lee's stricken army to retreat to safety across the Potomac. In the wake of Antietam, Lincoln removed McClellan from command.

In Kentucky, Generals Smith and Bragg secured Lexington and Frankfort, but their effort to force the Yankees back to the Ohio River was stopped at the Battle of Perryville on October 8. Bragg's army retreated back into Tennessee, where—from December 31, 1862, to January 2, 1863—they fought an indecisive but much bloodier battle at Murfreesboro. Casualties exceeded even those of Shiloh, and many lives were sacrificed on a bitter winter landscape.

Confederate leaders marshaled all their strength for a breakthrough but failed. Outnumbered and disadvantaged in resources, the South could not continue the offensive. Profoundly disappointed, Davis admitted to a committee of Confederate representatives that southerners were entering "the darkest and most dangerous period we have yet had."

But 1862 also brought painful lessons to the North. Confederate general J. E. B. Stuart executed a daring cavalry raid into Pennsylvania in October. Then, on December 13, Union general Ambrose Burnside, now in command of the Army of the Potomac, unwisely ordered his soldiers to attack Lee's army, which held fortified positions on high ground at Fredericksburg, Virginia. Lee's men performed so efficiently in killing northerners that Lee was moved to say, "It is well that war is so terrible. We should grow too fond of it." Burnside's repeated assaults up Marye's Heights shocked even the opponents. "The Federals had fallen like the steady dripping of rain from the eaves of a house," remarked Confederate general James Longstreet. And a Union officer observed of the carnage of thirteen hundred dead and ninety-six hundred wounded Union soldiers, "The whole plain was covered with men, prostrate and dropping. . . . I had never before seen fighting like that . . . the next brigade coming up in succession would do its duty, and melt like snow coming down on warm ground." The scale of carnage now challenged people on both sides to search deeply for the meaning of such a war. At the front some soldiers lost their sense of humanity in the face of the challenge. In the wake of Antietam's death toll, one Union burial

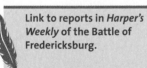
Link to reports in *Harper's Weekly* of the Battle of Fredericksburg.

crew, exhausted and perhaps inebriated, threw fifty-eight Confederate bodies down the well of a local farmer.

War Transforms the South

The war caused tremendous disruptions in civilian life and altered southern society beyond all expectations. One of the first traditions to fall was the southern preference for local and limited government. States' rights had been a formative ideology for the Confederacy, but state governments were weak operations. To withstand the massive power of the North, the South needed to centralize; like the colonial revolutionaries, southerners faced a choice of joining together or dying separately.

Jefferson Davis moved promptly to bring all arms, supplies, and troops under centralized control. But by early 1862, the scope and duration of the conflict required something more. Tens of thousands of Confederate soldiers had volunteered for just one year's service, planning to return home in the spring to plant their crops. More recruits were needed constantly to keep southern armies in the field. However, as one official admitted, "the spirit of volunteering had died out." Finally, faced with a critical shortage of troops, in April 1862 the Confederate government enacted the first national conscription (draft) law in American history. Thus, the war forced unprecedented change on states that had seceded out of fear of change.

The Confederacy and Centralization

Davis adopted a firm leadership role toward the Confederate Congress, which raised taxes and later passed a tax-in-kind—paid in farm products. Nearly forty-five hundred agents dispersed to collect the tax. Where opposition arose, the government suspended the writ of habeas corpus (which prevented individuals from being held without trial) and imposed martial law. Despite Davis's unyielding stance, this tax system proved inadequate for the South's war effort.

To replace the food that men in uniform would have grown, Davis exhorted state governments to require farmers to switch from cash crops to food crops. But the army remained short of food and labor. The War Department resorted to impressing slaves to work on fortifications, and after 1861 the government relied heavily on confiscation of food to feed the troops. Officers swooped down on farms in the line of march and carted away grain, meat, wagons, and draft animals. Such raids caused increased hardship and resentment for women managing farms in the absence of husbands and sons.

Soon, the Confederate administration in Richmond gained virtually complete control over the southern economy. The Confederate Congress also gave the central government almost complete control of the railroads. A large bureaucracy sprang up to administer these operations: over seventy thousand civilians staffed the Confederate administration. By war's end, the southern bureaucracy was larger in proportion to population than its northern counterpart.

Historians have long argued over whether the Confederacy itself was a "rebellion," a "revolution," or the creation of a genuine "nation."

Confederate Nationalism

Whatever label we apply, Confederates created a culture and an ideology of nationalism. Southerners immediately tried to forge their own national symbols and identity. In flags, songs, language, seals, school readers, and other national characteristics, Confederates created their own story.

In its conservative crusade to preserve states' rights, the social order, and racial slavery, southerners believed the Confederacy was the true legacy of the American Revolution—a bulwark against centralized power in keeping with the war for independence. In this view, southern "liberty" was no less a holy cause than that of the patriots of 1776. To southerners, theirs was a continuing revolution against the excesses of Yankee democracy, and George Washington (a Virginian) on horseback formed the center of the official seal of the Confederacy.

Also central to Confederate nationalism was a refurbished defense of slavery as a benign, protective institution. In wartime schoolbooks, children were instructed in the divinely inspired, paternalistic character of slavery. And the idea of the "faithful slave" was key to southerners' nationalist cause. A poem popular among whites captured an old slave's rejection of the Emancipation Proclamation:

> Now, Massa, dis is berry fine, dese words
> You've spoke to me,
> No doubt you mean it kindly, but ole Dinah
> Won't be free . . .

Ole Massa's berry good to me—and though I am
His slave,
He treats me like I'se kin to him—and I would
Rather have
A home in Massa's cabin, and eat his black
Bread too,
Dan leave ole Massa's children and go and
Lib wid you.

In the face of defeat and devastation, this and other forms of Confederate nationalism collapsed in the final year of the war. But much of the spirit and substance of Confederate nationalism would revive in the postwar period in a new ideology of the Lost Cause.

Clerks and subordinate officials crowded the towns and cities where Confederate departments set up their offices.

Southern Cities and Industry

Clerks had always been males, but now "government girls" staffed the Confederate bureaucracy. The sudden urban migration that resulted overwhelmed the housing supply and stimulated new construction. The pressure was especially great in Richmond, whose population increased 250 percent. Mobile's population jumped from twenty-nine thousand to forty-one thousand; Atlanta, too, began to grow; and ten thousand people poured into war-related industries in little Selma, Alabama.

As the Union blockade disrupted imports of manufactured products, the traditionally agricultural South forged new industries. Many planters shared Davis's hope that industrialization would bring "deliverance, full and unrestricted, from all commercial dependence" on the North or the world. Indeed, beginning almost from

The Panhandle-Plains Historical Society, Canyon, Texas

◀ Five Texans in the Confederate cavalry sitting for a formal photograph. Four have the "lone star" on their hats. Like thousands of others, these men posed to send their image to the folks back home, but also perhaps as an act of comradeship at the war front.

scratch, the Confederacy achieved tremendous feats of industrial development. Chief of Ordnance Josiah Gorgas increased the capacity of Richmond's Tredegar Iron Works and other factories to the point that by 1865, his Ordnance Bureau was supplying all Confederate small arms and ammunition. Meanwhile, the government constructed new railroad lines and ironworks, and much of the labor consisted of slaves relocated from farms and plantations.

White women, restricted to narrow roles in antebellum society, gained substantial new responsibilities in war-

Changing Roles of Women

time. The wives and mothers of soldiers now headed households and performed men's work, including raising crops and tending animals. Women in nonslaveowning families cultivated fields themselves, while wealthier women suddenly had to perform as overseers and manage field work. In the cities, white women— who had been largely excluded from the labor force—found a limited number of respectable paying jobs, often in the Confederate bureaucracy, where some found clerks' jobs as "government girls." And female schoolteachers appeared in the South for the first time.

Women experienced both confidence and agony from their new responsibilities. Among them was Janie Smith, a young North Carolinian. Raised in a rural area by prosperous parents, she now faced grim realities as the war reached her farm and troops turned her home into a hospital. "It makes me shudder when I think of the awful sights I witnessed that morning," she wrote to a friend. "Ambulance after ambulance drove up with our wounded. . . . Under every shed and tree, the tables were carried for amputating the limbs. . . . The blood lay in puddles in the grove; the groans of the dying . . . were horrible." But Janie Smith learned to cope with crisis. She ended her account with the proud words "I can dress amputated limbs now and do most anything in the way of nursing wounded soldiers."

Patriotic sacrifice appealed to some women, but others resented their new burdens. A Texas woman who had struggled to discipline slaves pronounced herself "sick of trying to do a man's business." Others grew angry over shortages and resented cooking and unfamiliar contact with lower-class women. Some women grew scornful of the war and demanded that their men return to help provide for their families.

For millions of ordinary southerners, the war brought privation and suffering. Mass poverty descended for the

Human Suffering, Hoarding, and Inflation

first time on a large minority of the white population. Many yeoman families had lost their breadwinners to the army. As a South Carolina newspaper put it, "The duties of war have called away from home the sole supports of many, many families. . . . Help must be given, or the poor will suffer." Women on their own sought help from relatives, neighbors, friends, anyone. Sometimes they pleaded their case to the Confederate government. "In the name of humanity," begged one woman, "discharge my husband he is not able to do your government much good and he might do his children some good . . . my poor children have no home nor no Father." To the extent that the South eventually lost the will to fight in the face of defeat, women played a role in demanding an end to the war.

The South was in many places so sparsely populated that the conscription of one skilled craftsman could wreak hardship on the people of an entire county. Often, they begged in unison for the exemption or discharge of the local miller, or the neighborhood tanner or wheelwright. Physicians were also in short supply. Most serious, however, was the loss of a blacksmith. As a petition from Alabama explained, "Our Section of County [is] left entirely Destitute of any man that is able to keep in order any kind of Farming Tules."

The blockade of Confederate shipping created shortages of important supplies—salt, sugar, coffee, nails—and speculation and hoarding made the shortages worse. Greedy businessmen cornered the supply of some commodities; prosperous citizens stocked up on food. The *Richmond Enquirer* criticized a planter who purchased so many wagonloads of supplies that his "lawn and paths looked like a wharf covered with a ship's loads." North Carolina's Governor Zebulon Vance worried about "the cry of distress . . . from the poor wives and children of our soldiers. . . . What will become of them?"

Inflation raged out of control, fueled by the Confederate government's heavy borrowing and inadequate taxes, until prices had increased almost 7,000 percent. Inflation particularly imperiled urban dwellers without their own sources of food. As early as 1861 and 1862, newspapers reported that "want and starvation are staring thousands in the face," and troubled officials predicted that "women and children are bound to come to suffering if not starvation." Hoarding continued to cause local conflict, and a rudimentary relief program organized by the Confederacy failed to meet the need.

As their fortunes declined, people of once-modest means looked around and found abundant evidence that

Inequities of the Confederate Draft

all classes were not sacrificing equally. The Confederate government enacted policies that decidedly favored the upper class. Until the last year of the war, for example, prosperous southerners could avoid military service by hiring substitutes. Prices for substitutes skyrocketed until it cost a man $5,000 or $6,000 to send someone to the front in his place. Well over fifty thousand upper-class southerners purchased such substitutes. Mary Boykin Chesnut knew of one young aristocrat who "spent a fortune in substitutes. . . . He is at the end of his row now, for all able-bodied men are ordered to the front. I hear he is going as some general's courier."

Anger at such discrimination exploded in October 1862, when the Confederate Congress exempted from military duty anyone who was supervising at least twenty slaves. "Never did a law meet with more universal odium," observed one representative. "Its influence upon the poor is most calamitous." Protests poured in from every corner of the Confederacy, and North Carolina's legislators formally condemned the law. Its defenders argued, however, that the exemption preserved order and aided food production, and the statute remained on the books.

This "twenty Negro" law is indicative of the racial fears many Confederates felt as the war threatened to overturn southern society. But it also fueled desertion and stimulated new levels of overt Unionism in nonslaveholding regions of the South. In Jones County, Mississippi, an area of piney woods and few slaves or plantations, Newt Knight, a Confederate soldier, led a band of renegades who took over the county, declared their allegiance to the Union, and called their district the "Free State of Jones." They held out for the remainder of the war as an enclave of independent Union sympathizers.

The bitterness of letters to Confederate officials suggests the depth of the dissension and class anger. "If I and my little children suffer [and] die while there Father is in service," threatened one woman, "I invoke God Almighty that our blood rest upon the South." Another woman swore to the secretary of war that, unless help was provided to poverty-stricken wives and mothers, "an allwise god . . . will send down his fury . . . [on] those that are in power." War magnified existing social tensions in the Confederacy, and created a few new ones.

Wartime Northern Economy and Society

With the onset of war, a tidal wave of change rolled over the North as well. Factories and citizens' associations geared up to support the war, and the federal government and its executive branch gained new powers. The energies of an industrializing society were harnessed to serve the cause of the Union. Idealism and greed flourished together, and the northern economy proved its awesome productivity.

At first, the war was a shock to business. Northern firms lost their southern markets, and many companies had to change their products and find new customers. Southern debts became uncollectible, jeopardizing not only northern merchants but also

Northern Business, Industry, and Agriculture

many western banks. Farm families struggled with a shortage of labor caused by army enlistments. A few enterprises never pulled out of the tailspin caused by the war. Cotton mills lacked cotton; construction declined; and shoe manufacturers sold few of the cheap shoes that planters had bought for their slaves.

But certain entrepreneurs, such as wool producers, benefited from shortages of competing products, and soaring demand for war-related goods swept some businesses to new success. To feed the hungry war machine, the federal government pumped unprecedented sums into the economy. The Treasury issued $3.2 billion in bonds and paper money called "greenbacks," and the War Department spent over $360 million in revenues from new taxes, including the nation's first income tax.

War-related spending revived business in many northern states. In 1863, a merchants' magazine examined the effects of the war in Massachusetts: "Seldom, if ever, has the business of Massachusetts been more active or profitable than during the past year. . . . In every department of labor the government has been, directly or indirectly, the chief employer and paymaster." Government contracts saved Massachusetts shoe manufacturers, as well as many firms in other states, from ruin.

The northern economy also grew because of a complementary relationship between agriculture and industry. Mechanization of agriculture had begun before the war. Wartime recruitment and conscription, however, gave western farmers an added incentive to purchase labor-saving machinery. The shift from human labor to machines created new markets for industry and expanded the food supply for the urban industrial work force. The boom in the sale of agricultural tools was tremendous. Cyrus and William McCormick built an industrial empire in Chicago from the sale of their reapers. Between 1862 and 1864, the manufacture of mowers and reapers doubled to 70,000 yearly; by war's end, 375,000 reapers were in use, triple the number in 1861. Thus northern farm families whose breadwinners went to war did not suffer as much as did their counterparts in the South. "We have seen," one magazine observed, "a stout matron whose sons are in the army, cutting hay with her team . . . and she cut seven acres with ease in a day, riding leisurely upon her cutter." Northern farms, generally not ravaged by foraging armies and devastation, thrived during wartime.

This government-business marriage emerged from a greatly empowered Quartermaster Department, which as a bureaucracy grew to be the single largest employer in the United States, issuing thousands of manufacturing contracts to hundreds of firms. The 100,000 civilian employees of the Quartermaster Department labored throughout a network of procurement centers,

The Quartermaster and Military-Government Mobilization

especially in the cities of Washington, D.C., Phildelphia, New York, Cincinnati, and St. Louis. Many of the senior military officers in the department had considerable prewar experience, especially in the West.

A portion of Secretary of War Edwin M. Stanton's list of the weapons supplies alone needed by the Ordnance Department indicates the scope of the demand for government and business cooperation: "7,892 cannon, 11,787 artillery carriages, 4,022,130 small-arms, . . . 1,022,176,474 cartridges for small-arms, 1,220,555,435 percussion caps, . . . 26,440,054 pounds of gunpowder, . . . and 90,416,295 pounds of lead." In an unprecedented military mobilization, the government also purchased huge quantities of uniforms, boots, food, camp equipment, saddles, horses, ships, and other necessities. By 1865, the government had purchased some 640,000 horses and 300,000 mules at a cost well over $100 million.

Two-thirds of all U.S. war spending went to supply the forces in the field and, to command that process, President Lincoln appointed the talented West Point–trained engineer, Montgomery Meigs. Meigs, whose experience included overseeing the building of the Capitol dome, insisted on issuing government contracts only with competitive bidding. He spent $1.8 billion of the public's money to wage the war, a figure larger than all previous U.S. government expenditures combined since

independence. His efforts, argued one historian, made the Union army "the best fed, most lavishly supplied army that had ever existed." Many historians consider Meigs the "unsung hero of Northern victory," a claim hard to deny, although he benefitted from his corps of Quartermaster officers who won the war one contract at a time. The success of such military mobilization left an indelible mark on American political-economic history and provided perhaps the oldest root of the modern American military-industrial state.

Nothing illustrated the wartime partnership between business and government better than the work of Jay Cooke, a wealthy New York financier. Cooke threw himself into the marketing of government bonds to finance the war effort. With imagination and energy, he convinced both large investors and ordinary citizens to invest enormous sums, in the process earning hefty commissions for himself. But the financier's profit served the Union cause, as the interests of capitalism and government merged in American history's first era of "big government."

Northern industrial and urban workers did not fare as well as many of the companies for which they labored.

Northern Workers' Militancy

After the initial slump, jobs became plentiful, but inflation ate up much of a worker's paycheck. The price of

Collection of The New York Historical Society

▲ Despite initial problems, the task of supplying a vast war machine kept the northern economy humming. This photograph shows businesses on the west side of Hudson Street in New York City in 1865.

coffee had tripled; rice and sugar had doubled; and clothing, fuel, and rent had all climbed. Between 1860 and 1864, consumer prices rose at least 76 percent, while daily wages rose only 42 percent. Workers' families consequently suffered a substantial decline in their standard of living.

As their real wages shrank, industrial workers lost job security. To increase production, some employers replaced workers with labor-saving machines. Other employers urged the government to promote immigration to secure cheap labor. Workers responded by forming unions and sometimes by striking. Skilled craftsmen organized to combat the loss of their jobs and status to machines; women and unskilled workers, who were excluded by the craftsmen, formed their own unions. Indeed, thirteen occupational groups—including tailors, coal miners, and railway engineers—formed national unions during the Civil War, and the number of strikes climbed steadily.

Employers reacted with hostility to this new labor independence. Manufacturers viewed labor activism as a threat to their freedom of action and accordingly formed statewide or craft-based associations to cooperate and pool information. These employers shared blacklists of union members and required new workers to sign "yellow dog" contracts (promises not to join a union). To put down strikes, they hired strikebreakers from among blacks, immigrants, and women, and sometimes used federal troops to break the unions' will.

Labor militancy, however, prevented employers neither from making profits nor from profiteering on government contracts. Unscrupulous businessmen took advantage of the suddenly immense demand for army supplies by selling clothing and blankets made of "shoddy"—wool fibers reclaimed from rags or worn cloth. Shoddy goods often came apart in the rain; most of the shoes purchased in the early months of the war were worthless. Contractors sold inferior guns for double the usual price and passed off tainted meat as good. Corruption was so widespread that it led to a year-long investigation by the House of Representatives. These realities of everyday economic life eroded the early romance for war among many Americans.

Legitimate enterprises also made healthy profits. The output of woolen mills increased so dramatically that

Economic Nationalism and Government-Business Partnership

dividends in the industry nearly tripled. Some cotton mills made record profits on what they sold, even though they reduced their output. Brokerage houses worked until midnight and earned unheard-of commissions. Railroads carried immense quantities of freight and passengers, increasing their business to the point that railroad stocks skyrocketed in value.

Railroads were also a leading beneficiary of government largesse. With southern representatives absent from Congress, the northern route of the transcontinental railroad quickly prevailed. In 1862 and 1864, Congress chartered two corporations—the Union Pacific Railroad and the Central Pacific Railroad—and assisted them financially in connecting Omaha, Nebraska, with Sacramento, California. For each mile of track laid, the railroads received a loan of from $16,000 to $48,000 in government bonds plus 20 square miles of land along a free 400-foot-wide right of way. Overall, the two corporations gained approximately 20 million acres of land and nearly $60 million in loans.

Other businessmen benefited handsomely from the Morrill Land Grant Act (1862). To promote public education in agriculture, engineering, and military science, Congress granted each state thirty thousand acres of federal land for each of its congressional districts. The law eventually fostered sixty-nine colleges and universities as it also enriched a few prominent speculators. At the same time, the Homestead Act of 1862 offered cheap, and sometimes free, land to people who would settle the West and improve their property.

Before the war, adequate national banking, taxation, and currency did not exist. Banks operating under state charters issued no fewer than seven thousand different kinds of notes. During the war, Congress and the Treasury Department established a national banking system empowered to issue national bank notes and, by 1865, most state banks were forced by a prohibitive tax to join the national system. This process created sounder currency but also inflexibility in the money supply and an eastern-oriented financial structure that, later in the century, pushed farmers in need of credit and cash to revolt.

Republican economic policies expanded the scope of government and bonded people to the nation as never before. Yet ostentation coexisted with idealism. In the excitement of wartime moneymaking, an eagerness to display one's wealth flourished in the largest cities. *Harper's Monthly* reported that "the suddenly enriched contractors, speculators, and stock-jobbers . . . are spending money with a profusion never before witnessed in our country. . . . The men button their waistcoats with diamonds . . . and the women powder their hair with gold and silver dust." The *New York Herald* summarized that city's atmosphere: "This war has entirely changed the American character. . . . The individual who makes the most money—no matter how—and spends the most—no matter for what—is considered the greatest man."

In thousands of self-governing towns and communities, northern citizens felt a personal connection to representa-

The Union Cause

tive government. Secession threatened to destroy their system, and northerners rallied to its defense. In the first two years of the war, northern morale remained remarkably high for a cause that today may seem abstract—the Union—but at the time meant the preservation of a social and political order that people cherished.

▲ Union women's volunteer defense unit, ca. 1864. The soldiers' cap and muskets make this a rare image of women's lives on the home front during the Civil War.

National Archives

Secular and church leaders supported the cause, and even ministers who preferred to separate politics and pulpit denounced "the iniquity of causeless rebellion. Abolitionists campaigned to turn the war into a crusade against slavery." Free black communities and churches, both black and white, responded to the needs of slaves who flocked to the Union lines, sending clothing, ministers, and teachers to aid the freedpeople. Indeed, northern blacks gave wholehearted support to the war, volunteering by the thousands at first and in spite of the initial rejection they received from the Lincoln administration.

Thus, northern society embraced strangely contradictory tendencies. Materialism and greed flourished alongside idealism, religious conviction, and self-sacrifice. In decades to come, Americans would commemorate and build monuments to soldiers' sacrifice and idealism, not to opportunism and sometimes not even to the causes for which they fought, which was a way of forgetting the deeper nature of the conflict.

Northern women, like their southern counterparts, took on new roles. Those who stayed home organized over ten thousand soldiers' aid societies, rolled bandages, and raised $3 million to aid injured troops. Women were instrumental in pressing for the first trained ambulance corps in the Union Army, and they formed the backbone of the U.S. Sanitary Commission, a civilian agency officially recognized by the War Department in 1861. The Sanitary Commission provided crucial nutritional and medical aid to soldiers. Although most of its officers were

Northern Women on Home Front and Battlefront

men, the bulk of the volunteers who ran its seven thousand auxiliaries were women. Women organized elaborate "Sanitary Fairs" to raise money and awareness for soldiers' health and hygiene.

Approximately thirty-two hundred women also served as nurses in frontline hospitals. Yet women had to fight for a chance to serve at all; the professionalization of medicine since the Revolution had created a medical system dominated by men, and many male physicians did not want women's aid. Even Clara Barton, famous for her persistence in working in the worst hospitals at the front, was ousted from her post in 1863. But along with Barton, women such as the stern Dorothea Dix, well known for her efforts to reform asylums for the insane, and an Illinois widow, Mary Ann Bickerdyke, who served tirelessly in Sherman's army in the West, established a heroic tradition for Civil War nurses. They also advanced the professionalization of nursing, as several schools of nursing were established in northern cities during or after the war.

Women also wrote popular fiction about the war. In sentimental war poetry, short stories, and novels, and in printed war songs that reached thousands of readers, women produced a commercial literature in illustrated weeklies, monthly periodicals, and special "story papers." In many stories, female characters seek recognition for their loyalty and service to the Union, while others probe the suffering and death of loved ones at the front. One woman writer was Louisa May Alcott, arrived at her job as a nurse in Washington, D.C., just after the horrific Union defeat at Fredericksburg, in December 1862, and later immortalized her experience in *Hospital Sketches* (1863), a popular book in which she described

◄ Nurse Anne Bell tending to wounded soldiers in a federal hospital, Nashville, Tennessee, ca. 1863. The distant gaze of the man on the left and the grateful gaze of the one on the right realistically represent agonies of military hospitals.

U.S. Army Center of Military History

shattered men, "riddled with shot and shell," who had "borne suffering for which we have no name." Alcott provided northern readers a clear-eyed view of the hospitals in which so many of their loved ones agonized and perished.

At its heart, in what one historian has called a "feminized war literature," woman writers explored the relationship between individual and national needs, between home and "the cause." And by 1863, many women found the liberation of slaves an inspiring subject, as Julia Ward Howe did in her immortal "Battle Hymn of the Republic":

As He died to make men holy
Let us die to make men free.

The poet Walt Whitman also left a record of his experiences as a volunteer nurse in Washington, D.C. As he

Walt Whitman's War

dressed wounds and tried to comfort suffering and lonely men, Whitman found "the marrow of the tragedy concentrated in those Army Hospitals." But despite "indescribably horrid wounds," he also found inspiration in such suffering and a deepening faith in American democracy. Whitman celebrated the "incredible dauntlessness" and sacrifice of the common soldier who fought for the Union. As he had written in the preface to his great work *Leaves of Grass* (1855), "The genius of the United States is not best or most in its executives or legislatures, but always most in the common people." Whitman worked this idealization of the common man into his poetry, which also explored homoerotic themes and rejected the lofty meter and rhyme of European verse to strive for a "genuineness" that would appeal to the masses.

In "The Wound Dresser," Whitman meditated unforgettably on the deaths he had witnessed on both sides:

On, on I go, (open doors of time! open hospital doors!)
The crush'd head I dress, (poor crazed hand tear not the bandage away,)
The neck of the cavalry-man with the bullet through and through I examine,
Hard the breathing rattles, quite glazed already the eye, yet life struggles hard, (Come sweet death! be persuaded O beautiful death!
In mercy come quickly.)

Whitman mused for millions in the war who suffered the death of a husband, brother, father, or friend. Indeed, the scale of death in this war shocked many Americans into believing that the conflict had to be for purposes larger than themselves.

The Advent of Emancipation

Despite the sense of loyalty to cause that animated soldiers and civilians on both sides, the governments of the United States and the Confederacy lacked clarity about the purpose of the war. Throughout the first several months of the struggle, both Davis and Lincoln studiously avoided references to slavery. Davis realized that emphasis on the issue could increase class conflict in the South. To avoid identifying the Confederacy only with the interests of slaveholders, he articulated a broader, traditional ideology. Davis told southerners they were fighting for constitutional liberty: northerners had betrayed the founders' legacy, and southerners had seceded to preserve it. As long as Lincoln also avoided making slavery an issue, Davis's strategy seemed to work.

Lincoln had his own reasons for avoiding slavery. It was crucial at first not to antagonize the Union's border slave states, whose loyalty was tenuous. Also, for many months Lincoln hoped that a pro-Union majority would assert itself in the South. It might be possible, he thought, to coax the South back into the Union and stop the fighting, short of what he later called "the result so fundamental and astounding"—emancipation. Raising the slavery issue would severely undermine both goals. Powerful political considerations also dictated Lincoln's reticence. The Republican Party was a young and unwieldy coalition. Some Republicans burned with moral outrage over slavery; others were frankly racist, dedicated to protecting free whites from the Slave Power and the competition of cheap slave labor. No Republican, or even northern, consensus on what to do about slavery existed early in the war.

The president's hesitancy ran counter to some of his personal feelings. Lincoln's compassion, humility, and moral anguish during the war were evident in his speeches and writings. But as a politician, Lincoln distinguished

Lincoln and Emancipation

between his own moral convictions and his official acts. His political positions were studied and complex, calculated for maximum advantage.

Many blacks attacked Lincoln furiously during the first year of the war for his refusal to convert the struggle into an "abolition war." When Lincoln countermanded General John C. Frémont's order of liberation for slaves owned by disloyal masters in Missouri in September 1861, the *Anglo-African* declared that the president, by his actions, "hurls back into the hell of slavery thousands . . . rightfully set free." As late as July 1862, Frederick Douglass condemned Lincoln as a "miserable tool of traitors and rebels," and characterized administration policy as reconstruction of "the old union on the old and corrupting basis of compromise, by which slavery shall retain all the power that it ever had." Douglass wanted the old Union destroyed and a new one created in the crucible of a war that would destroy slavery and rewrite the Constitution in the name of human equality. To the black leader's own amazement, within a year, just such a profound result began to take place.

Lincoln first broached the subject of slavery in a substantive way in March 1862, when he proposed that the states consider emancipation on their own. He asked Congress to promise aid to any state that decided to emancipate, appealing especially to border state representatives. What Lincoln proposed was gradual emancipation, with compensation for slaveholders and colonization of

▲ A group of "contrabands" (liberated slaves), photographed at Cumberland Landing, Virginia, May 14, 1862, at a sensitive point in the war when their legal status was still not fully determined. The faces and generations of the women, men, and children represent the human drama of emancipation.

Library of Congress

the freed slaves outside the United States. To a delegation of free blacks in August 1862, he explained that "it is better for us both . . . to be separated."

Until well into 1864, Lincoln's administration promoted an impractical scheme to colonize blacks in Central America or the Caribbean. Lincoln saw colonization as one option among others in dealing with the impending freedom of America's 4.2 million slaves. He was as yet unconvinced that America had any prospect as a biracial society, and he desperately feared that white northerners might not support a war for black freedom. Led by Frederick Douglass, black abolitionists vehemently opposed these machinations by the Lincoln administration.

Other politicians had much greater plans for a struggle against slavery. A group of Republicans in Congress, known as the Radicals and led by men such as George Julian, Charles Sumner, and Thaddeus Stevens, dedicated themselves to a war for emancipation. They were instrumental in creating a special House-Senate committee on the conduct of the war, which investigated Union reverses, sought to make the war effort more efficient, and prodded the president to take stronger measures against slavery.

In August 1861, at the Radicals' instigation, Congress passed its first confiscation act. Designed to punish the Confederates, the law confis-

Confiscation Acts

cated all property used for "insurrectionary purposes." Thus, if the South used slaves in a hostile action, those slaves were seized and liberated as "contraband" of war. A second confiscation act (July 1862) went much further: it confiscated the property of anyone who supported the rebellion, even those who merely resided in the South and paid Confederate taxes. Their slaves were declared "forever free of their servitude." These acts stemmed from the logic that, in order to crush the southern rebellion, the government had to use extraordinary powers.

Lincoln refused to adopt that view in the summer of 1862. He stood by his proposal of voluntary gradual emancipation by the states and made no effort at first to enforce the second confiscation act. His stance provoked a public protest from Horace Greeley, editor of the powerful *New York Tribune*. In an open letter to the president entitled "The Prayer of Twenty Millions," Greeley pleaded with Lincoln to "execute the laws" and declared, "On the face of this wide earth, Mr. President, there is not one . . . intelligent champion of the Union cause who does not feel that all attempts to put down the Rebellion and at the same time uphold its inciting cause are preposterous and futile." Lincoln's reply was an explicit statement of his calculated approach to the question. He disagreed, he said, with all those who would make slavery the paramount issue of the war. "I would save the Union," announced Lincoln. "If I could save the Union without freeing any

slave I would do it, and if I could save it by freeing all the slaves I would do it; and if I could save it by freeing some and leaving others alone I would also do that. What I do about slavery, and the colored race, I do because I believe it helps to save the Union." Lincoln closed with a personal disclaimer: "I have here stated my purpose according to my view of official duty; and I intend no modification of my oft-expressed personal wish that all men everywhere could be free."

When he wrote those words, Lincoln had already decided to boldly issue a presidential Emancipation Proclamation. He was waiting, however, for a Union victory so that it would not appear to be an act of desperation. Yet the letter to Greeley represents Lincoln's concern with conditioning public opinion as best he could for the coming social revolution, and he needed to delicately consider international opinion as well.

On September 22, 1862, shortly after Union success at the Battle of Antietam, Lincoln issued the first part of

Emancipation Proclamations

his two-part proclamation. Invoking his powers as commander-in-chief of the armed forces, he announced that on January 1, 1863, he would emancipate the slaves in the states "in rebellion." Lincoln made plain that he would judge a state to be in rebellion in January if it lacked legitimate representatives in the U.S. Congress. Thus, his September 1862 proclamation was less a declaration of the right of slaves to be free than a threat to southerners: unless they put down their arms and returned to Congress, they would lose their slaves. "Knowing the value that was set on the slaves by the rebels," said Garrison Frazier, a black Georgia minister, "the President thought that his proclamation would stimulate them to lay down their arms . . . and their not doing so has now made the freedom of the slaves a part of the war." Lincoln had little expectation that southerners would give up their effort, but he was determined to make them reply.

In the fateful January 1, 1863, proclamation, Lincoln declared that "all persons held as slaves" in areas in rebellion "shall be then, thenceforward, and forever free." But he excepted (as areas in rebellion) every Confederate county or city that had fallen under Union control. Those areas, he declared, "are, for the present, left precisely as if this proclamation were not issued." Nor did Lincoln liberate slaves in the border slave states that remained in the Union. "The President has purposely made the proclamation inoperative in all places where . . . the slaves [are] accessible," charged the anti-administration *New York World*. "He has proclaimed emancipation only where he has notoriously no power to execute it." Partisanship aside, even Secretary of State Seward said sarcastically, "We show our sympathy with slavery by emancipating slaves where we cannot reach them and holding them in bondage where we can set them free."

But Lincoln was worried about the constitutionality of his acts, and he anticipated that after the war southerners might sue in court for restoration of their "property." Making the liberation of the slaves "a fit and necessary war measure" raised a variety of legal questions: How long did a war measure remain in force? Did it expire with the suppression of a rebellion? The proclamation did little to clarify the status or citizenship of the freed slaves, although it did open the possibility of military service for blacks. How, indeed, would this change the character and purpose of the war?

Thus the Emancipation Proclamation was legally an ambiguous document. But as a moral and political document it had great meaning. Because the proclamation defined the war as a war against slavery, congressional Radicals could applaud it. Yet at the same time, it protected Lincoln's position with conservatives, leaving him room to retreat if he chose and forcing no immediate changes on the border slave states. It was a delicate balancing act, but one from which there was no real turning back.

Most important, though, thousands of slaves had already reached Union lines in various sections of the South. They had "voted with their feet" for emancipation, as many said, well before the proclamation. And now, every advance of federal forces into slave society was a liberating step.

Across the North and in Union-occupied sections of the South, blacks and their white allies celebrated the Emancipation Proclamation with unprecedented fervor. Full of praise songs, these celebrations demonstrated that, whatever the fine print of the proclamation, black folks knew they had lived to see a new day. At a large "contraband camp" in Washington, D.C., some six hundred black men, women, and children gathered at the superintendent's headquarters on New Year's Eve and sang through the night. In chorus after chorus of "Go Down, Moses" they announced the magnitude of their painful but beautiful exodus. One newly supplied verse concluded with "Go down, Abraham, away down in Dixie's land, tell Jeff Davis to let my people go!"

The need for men soon convinced the administration to recruit northern and southern blacks for the Union Army.

African American Recruits

By the spring of 1863, African American troops were answering the call of a dozen or more black recruiters barnstorming the cities and towns of the North. Lincoln came to see black soldiers as "the great available and yet unavailed of force for restoring the Union."

African American leaders hoped that military service would secure equal rights for their people. Once the black soldier had fought for the Union, wrote Frederick Douglass, "there is no power on earth which can deny that he has earned the right of citizenship in the United States." If black soldiers turned the tide, asked another man, "would the nation refuse us our rights?"

In June 1864, with thousands of black former slaves in blue uniforms, Lincoln gave his support to a constitutional ban on slavery. On the eve of the Republican national convention, Lincoln called on the party to "put into the platform as the keystone, the amendment of the Constitution abolishing and prohibiting slavery forever." The party promptly called for the Thirteenth Amendment. Republican delegates probably would have adopted such a plank without his urging, but Lincoln demonstrated his commitment by lobbying Congress for quick approval of the measure. The proposed amendment passed in early 1865 and was sent to the states for ratification. The war to save the Union had also become the war to free the slaves.

It has long been debated whether Abraham Lincoln deserved the label (one he never claimed for himself) of

Who Freed the Slaves?

"Great Emancipator." Was Lincoln ultimately a reluctant emancipator, following rather than leading Congress and public opinion? Or did Lincoln give essential presidential leadership to the most transformative and sensitive aspect of the war by going slow on emancipation but, once moving, never backpedaling on black freedom? Once he had realized the total character of the war and decided to prosecute it to the unconditional surrender of the Confederates, Lincoln made the destruction of slavery central to the war's purpose.

Others have argued, however, that the slaves themselves are the central story in the achievement of their own freedom. When they were in proximity to the war zones or had opportunities as traveling laborers, slaves fled for their freedom by the thousands. Some worked as camp laborers for the Union armies, and eventually more than 180,000 black men served in the Union Army and Navy. Sometimes freedom came as a combination of confusion, fear, and joy in the rural hinterlands of the South. Some found freedom as individuals in 1861, and some not until 1865, as members of trains of refugees trekking great distances to reach contraband camps.

However freedom came to individuals, emancipation was a historical confluence of two essential forces: one, a policy directed by and dependent on the military authority of the president in his effort to win the war; and the other, the will and courage necessary for acts of self-emancipation. Wallace Turnage's escape in Mobile Bay in 1864 demonstrates that emancipation could result from both a slave's own extraordinary heroism and the liberating actions of the Union forces. Most blacks comprehended their freedom as both given and taken, but also as their human right. "I now dreaded the gun and handcuffs . . . no more," remembered Turnage of his liberation. "Nor the blowing of horns and running of hounds, nor the threats of death from rebels' authority." He was free in body and mind. "I could now speak my opinion" Turnage concluded, "to men of all grades and colors."

Before the war was over, the Confederacy, too, addressed the issue of emancipation. Late in the war, Jefferson Davis himself was willing to sacrifice slavery to achieve independence. He proposed that the Confederate government purchase forty thousand slaves to work for the army as laborers, with a promise of freedom at the end of their service. Soon Davis upgraded the idea, calling for the recruitment and arming of slaves as soldiers, who likewise would gain their freedom at war's end. The wives and children of these soldiers, he made plain, must also receive freedom from the states. Davis and his advisers envisioned an "intermediate" status for ex-slaves of "serfage or peonage." Thus, at the bitter end, a few southerners were willing to sacrifice some of the racial, if not class, destiny for which they had launched their revolution.

A Confederate Plan of Emancipation

Bitter debate over Davis's plan resounded through the Confederacy. When the Confederate Congress finally approved slave enlistments in March 1865, owners had to comply only on a "voluntary" basis. In sheer desperation for manpower, General Lee also supported the idea of slave soldiers. Against the reality all around them of slaves fleeing to Union lines, some southern leaders mistakenly hoped that they could still count on the "loyalty" of their bondsmen. Most Confederate slaveholders and editors vehemently opposed the enlistment plan; those who did support it acknowledged that the war had already freed some portion of the slave population. Their aim was to fight to a stalemate, achieve independence, and control the postwar racial order through their limited wartime emancipation schemes. It was too late. As a Mississippi planter wrote to his state's governor, the plan seemed "like a drowning man catching at straws."

By contrast, Lincoln's Emancipation Proclamation stimulated a vital infusion of forces into the Union armies. Before the war was over, 134,000 former slaves (and 52,000 free blacks) had fought for freedom and the Union. Their participation was pivotal for northern victory. As both policy and process, emancipation had profound practical and moral implications for the new nation to be born out of the war.

The Soldiers' War

The intricacies of policymaking and social revolutions were often far from the minds of most ordinary soldiers. Military service completely altered their lives. Enlistment took young men from their homes and submerged them in large organizations whose military discipline ignored their individuality. Army life meant tedium, physical hardship, and separation from loved ones. Yet the military experience had powerful attractions as well.

Most common soldiers, according to recent studies, were also committed to the ideological purposes of the war on both sides and not merely pawns caught up in a struggle they did not comprehend. The thousands of soldiers' letters, as well as regimental newspapers, indicate a deep awareness, if varying degrees of resolve, about slavery as the principle reason for the war.

Ordinary Soldiers and Ideology

The old idea that Civil War soldiers fought largely because of unit cohesion and the devotion of the men next to them is no longer an adequate explanation of why so many endured so much hardship for so long. Comradeship, duty, and honor were all powerful motivators for the men of the line. So were "union," "home," "the government," "freedom," "flag," "liberty," and "states' rights." But multitudes of literate soldiers left testimony of how much they saw slavery at the heart of the matter. In typical phrasing, members of the Thirteenth Wisconsin Infantry declared the conflict "a war of, by and for Slavery . . . as plain as the noon day sun." And their foes in Morgan's Confederate Brigade from Virginia agreed with different intentions: "any man who pretends to believe that this is not a war for the emancipation of the blacks . . . is either a fool or a liar."

The soldiers' lot was often misery. They benefited from certain new products, such as canned condensed milk, but blankets, clothing, and arms were often of poor quality. Hospitals were badly managed at first. Rules of hygiene in large camps were scarcely enforced; latrines were poorly made or carelessly used. One investigation turned up "an area of over three acres, encircling the camp as a broad belt, on which is deposited an almost perfect layer of human excrement." Water supplies were unsafe and typhoid epidemics common. About 57,000 men died from dysentery and diarrhea; in fact, 224,000 Union troops died from disease or accidents, far more than the 110,100 who died as a result of battle. Confederate troops were less well supplied, especially in the latter part of the war, and they had no sanitary commission. Still, an extensive network of hospitals, aided by many white female volunteers and black woman slaves, sprang up to aid the sick and wounded.

Hospitals and Camp Life

On both sides, troops quickly learned that soldiering was far from glorious. "The dirt of a camp life knocks all its poetry into a cocked hat," wrote a North Carolina volunteer in 1862. One year later, he marveled at his earlier innocence. Fighting had taught him "the realities of a soldier's life. We had no tents after the 6th of August, but slept on the ground, in the woods or open fields. . . . I learned to eat fat bacon raw, and to like it. . . . Without time to wash our clothes or our persons . . . the whole army became lousy more or less with body lice." Union troops "skirmished" against lice by boiling their clothes, but, reported one soldier, "I find some on me in spite of all I can do."

Few had seen violent death before, but war soon exposed them to the blasted bodies of their friends and comrades. "Any one who goes over a battlefield after a battle," wrote one Confederate, "never cares to go over another. . . . It is a sad sight to see the dead and if possible more sad to see the wounded—shot in every possible way you can imagine." Many men died gallantly; there were innumerable striking displays of courage. But often soldiers gave up their lives in mass sacrifice, in tactics that made little sense.

Still, Civil War soldiers developed deep commitments to each other and to their task. As campaigns dragged on, most soldiers who did not desert grew determined to see the struggle through. "We now, like true Soldiers go determined not to yield one inch," wrote a New York corporal. When at last the war was over, "it seemed like breaking up a family to separate," one man observed. Another admitted, "We shook hands all around, and laughed and seemed to make merry, while our hearts were heavy and our eyes ready to shed tears."

Advances in technology made the Civil War particularly deadly. By far the most important were the rifle and the "minie ball." Bullets fired from smoothbore musket tumbled and wobbled as they flew through the air, and thus were not accurate at distances over eighty yards. Cutting spiraled grooves inside the barrel gave the projectile a spin and much greater accuracy, but rifles remained difficult to load and use until Frenchman Claude Minie and American James Burton developed a new kind of bullet. Civil War bullets were lead slugs with a cavity at the bottom that expanded on firing so that the bullet "took" the rifling and flew accurately. With these bullets, rifles were deadly at four hundred yards.

The Rifled Musket

This meant, of course, that soldiers assaulting a position defended by riflemen were in greater peril than ever before; the defense thus gained a significant advantage. While artillery now fired from a safe distance, there was no substitute for the infantry assault or the popular turning movements aimed at an enemy's flank. Thus, advancing soldiers had to expose themselves repeatedly to accurate rifle fire. Because medical knowledge was rudimentary, even minor wounds often led to amputation and death through infection. Never before in Europe or America had such massive forces pummeled each other with weapons of such destructive power. As losses mounted, many citizens wondered at what Union soldier (and future Supreme Court justice) Oliver Wendell Holmes Jr. called "the butcher's bill."

The Black Soldier's Fight for Manhood

At the outset of the war, racism in the Union Army was strong. Most white soldiers wanted nothing to do with black people and regarded them as inferior. "I never came out here for to free the black devils," wrote one soldier, and another objected to fighting beside African Americans because "[w]e are a too superior race for that." For many, acceptance of black

troops grew only because they could do heavy labor and "stop Bullets as well as white people." A popular song celebrated "Sambo's Right to Be Kilt" as the only justification for black enlistments.

But among some, a change occurred. While recruiting black troops in Virginia in late 1864, Massachusetts soldier Charles Brewster sometimes denigrated the very men he sought to enlist. But he was delighted at the sight of a black cavalry unit because it made the local "secesh" furious, and he praised black soldiers who "fought nobly" and filled hospitals with "their wounded and mangled bodies." White officers who volunteered to lead segregated black units only to gain promotion found that experience altered their opinions. After just one month with black troops, a white captain informed his wife, "I have a more elevated opinion of their abilities than I ever had before. I know that many of them are vastly the superiors of those . . . who would condemn them all to a life of brutal degradation." One general reported that his "colored regiments" possessed "remarkable aptitude for military training."

Black troops created this change through their own dedication. They had a mission to destroy slavery and demonstrate their equality. "When Rebellion is crushed," wrote a black volunteer from Connecticut, "who will be more proud than I to say, I was one of the first of the despised race to leave the free North with a rifle on my shoulder, and give the lie to the old story that the black man will not fight." Corporal James Henry Gooding of Massachusetts's black Fifty-fourth Regiment explained that his unit intended "to live down all prejudice against its color, by a determination to do well in any position it is put." After an engagement, he was proud that "a regiment of white men gave us three cheers as we were passing them" because "it shows that we did our duty as men should."

Link to Hannah Johnson's letter to President Lincoln, asking the government to protect black soldiers.

Through such experience under fire, the blacks and whites of the Fifty-fourth Massachusetts forged deep bonds. Just before the regiment launched its costly assault on Fort Wagner in Charleston harbor, in July 1863, a black soldier called out to abolitionist Colonel Robert Gould Shaw, who would perish that day, "Colonel, I will stay by you till I die." "And he kept his word," noted a survivor of the attack. "He has never been seen since." Indeed, the heroic assault on Fort Wagner was celebrated for demonstrating the valor of black men. This bloody chapter in the history of American racism proved many things, not least of which that black men had to die in battle to be acknowledged as men.

Such valor emerged despite persistent discrimination. The Union government paid white privates $13 per month plus a clothing allowance of $3.50, whereas black privates earned only $10 per month less $3 for clothing. Outraged by this injustice, several regiments refused to accept any

Visualizing THE PAST

Black Soldiers in the Civil War

The image below is of the storming of Fort Wagner, July 1863, by the Fifty-fourth Massachusetts regiment, in Charleston, South Carolina, by Chicago printmakers, Kurtz and Allison. Kurtz and Allison issued vivid and colorful chromolithographs in the 1880s, celebrating the military valor of African Americans. This scene depicts the most famous combat action of black troops in the Civil War; the Fifty-fourth was the first northern-recruited black unit, and their bravery and sacrifice served as a measure of African American devotion to the Union cause. At right is a medal for valor won by a member of the 54th Massachusetts Regiment. Why was the 54th Massachusetts regiment such a symbolic test case for the military ability and political meaning of black soldiers in the Civil War? Why did black men have to die on battlefields for many Americans in the Civil War era to consider them fully men and citizens?

Private Collection/Picture Research Consultants & Archives

THE GALLANT CHARGE OF THE FIFTY FOURTH MASSACHUSETTS (COLORED) REGIMENT.
On the Rebel works at Fort Wagner, Morris Island, near Charleston, July 18th, 1863, and death of Colonel Robt. G. Shaw.

The Granger Collection, New York

pay whatsoever, and Congress eventually remedied the inequity. In this instance at least, the majority of legislators agreed with a white private that black troops had "proved their title to manhood on many a bloody field fighting freedom's battles."

1863: The Tide of Battle Turns

The fighting in the spring and summer of 1863 did not settle the war, but it began to suggest the outcome. The campaigns began in a deceptively positive way for Confederates, as Lee's army performed brilliantly in battles in central Virginia.

For once, a large Civil War army was not slow and cumbersome, but executed tactics with speed and precision. On

Battle of Chancellorsville

May 2 and 3, west of Fredericksburg, Virginia, some 130,000 members of the Union Army of the Potomac bore down on fewer than 60,000 Confederates. Boldly, Lee and Stonewall Jackson divided their forces, ordering 30,000 men under Jackson on a day-long march westward to prepare a flank attack.

This classic turning movement was carried out in the face of great numerical disadvantage. Arriving at their position late in the afternoon, Jackson's seasoned "foot cavalry" found unprepared Union troops laughing, smoking, and playing cards. The Union soldiers had no idea they were under attack until frightened deer and rabbits bounded out of the forest, followed by gray-clad troops. The Confederate attack drove the entire right side of the Union Army back in confusion. Eager to press his advantage, Jackson rode forward with a few officers to study the ground. As they returned at twilight, southern troops mistook them for federals and fired, fatally wounding their commander. The next day, Union forces left in defeat. Chancellorsville was a remarkable southern victory, but costly because of the loss of Stonewall Jackson, who would forever remain a legend in Confederate memory.

July brought crushing defeats for the Confederacy in two critical battles—Vicksburg and Gettysburg—that sev-

Siege of Vicksburg

erely damaged Confederate hopes for independence. Vicksburg was a vital western citadel, the last major fortification on the Mississippi River in southern hands (see Map 15.2). After months of searching through swamps and bayous, General Ulysses S. Grant found an advantageous approach to the city. He laid siege to Vicksburg in May, bottling up the defending army of General John Pemberton. If Vicksburg fell, Union forces would control the river, cutting the Confederacy in two and gaining an open path into its interior. To stave off such a result, Jefferson Davis gave command of all other forces in the area to General Joseph E. Johnston and beseeched him to go to Pemberton's aid. Meanwhile, at a council of war in Richmond, General Robert E. Lee proposed a Confederate invasion of the

North. Although such an offensive would not relieve Vicksburg directly, it could stun and dismay the North and, if successful, possibly even lead to peace. By invading the North a second time, Lee hoped to take the war out of war-weary Virginia, garner civilian support in Maryland, win a major victory on northern soil, threaten major cities, and thereby force a Union capitulation on his terms.

As Lee's emboldened army advanced through western Maryland and into Pennsylvania, Confederate prospects to the south along the Mississippi darkened. Davis repeatedly wired General Johnston, urging him to concentrate his forces and attack Grant's army. Johnston, however, did little, telegraphing back: "I consider saving Vicksburg hopeless." Grant's men, meanwhile, were supplying themselves from the abundant crops of the Mississippi River valley and could continue their siege indefinitely. Their rich meat-and-vegetable diet became so tiresome, in fact, that one day, as Grant rode by, a private looked up and muttered, "Hardtack," referring to the dry biscuits that were the usual staple of soldiers' diets. Soon a line of soldiers was shouting, "Hardtack! Hardtack!" demanding respite from turkey and sweet potatoes.

In such circumstances, the fall of Vicksburg was inevitable, and on July 4, 1863, its commander surrendered.

Battle of Gettysburg

The same day, a battle that had been raging for three days concluded at Gettysburg, Pennsylvania (see Map 15.3). On July 1, Confederate forces hunting for a supply of shoes had collided with part of the Union Army. Heavy fighting on the second day over two steep hills left federal forces in possession of high ground along Cemetery Ridge, running more than a mile south of the town. There, they enjoyed the protection of a stone wall and a clear view of their foe across almost a mile of open field.

Undaunted, Lee believed his reinforced troops could break the Union line and, on July 3, he ordered a direct assault. Full of foreboding, General James Longstreet warned Lee that "no 15,000 men ever arrayed for battle can take that position." But Lee stuck to his plan. Virginians under General George E. Pickett and North Carolinians under General James Pettigrew methodically marched up the slope in a doomed assault known as Pickett's Charge. For a moment, a few hundred Confederates breached the enemy's line, but most fell in heavy slaughter. On July 4, Lee had to withdraw, having suffered almost four thousand dead and about twenty-four thousand missing and wounded. The Confederate general reported to President Davis that "I am alone to blame" and offered to resign. Davis replied that to find a more capable commander was "an impossibility." The Confederacy had reached what many consider its "high water mark" on that ridge at Gettysburg.

Southern troops displayed unforgettable courage and dedication at Gettysburg, and under General George G. Meade, the Union Army, which suffered twenty-three thousand casualties (nearly one-quarter of the force),

Map 15.3 Battle of Gettysburg

In the war's greatest battle, fought around a small market town in southern Pennsylvania, Lee's invasion of the North was repulsed. Union forces had the advantage of the high ground, shorter lines, and superior numbers. The casualties for the two armies—dead, wounded, and missing—exceeded 50,000 men.

Source: Copyright © Cengage Learning

exhibited the same bravery in stopping the Confederate invasion. But the results there and at Vicksburg were disastrous for the South. The Confederacy was split in two; west of the Mississippi, General E. Kirby Smith had to operate on his own, virtually independent of Richmond. Moreover, the heartland of Louisiana, Tennessee, and Mississippi lay exposed to invasion. Far to the north, Lee's defeat spelled the end of major southern offensive actions. Too weak to prevail in attack, the Confederacy henceforth would have to conserve its limited resources and rely on a prolonged defense. By refusing to be beaten and by wearing down northern morale, the South might yet win, but its prospects were darker than before.

Disunity: South, North, and West

Both northern and southern governments waged the final two years of the war in the face of increasing opposition at home. Dissatisfactions that had surfaced earlier grew more intense and sometimes violent. The gigantic costs of a civil war that neither side seemed able to win fed the unrest. But protest also arose from fundamental stresses in the social structures of North and South.

Wherever Union forces invaded, they imposed a military occupation consisting roughly of three zones: garrisoned towns, with large numbers of troops in control of civilian and economic life; the Confederate frontier, areas still under southern control but also with some federal military penetration; and "no man's land," the land between the two armies, beyond Confederate authority and under frequent Union patrols.

Union Occupation Zones

As many as one hundred southern towns were garrisoned during the war, causing severe disruption to the social landscape. Large regions of Tennessee, Virginia, Louisiana, Mississippi, and Georgia fell under this pattern of occupation and suffered food shortages, crop and property destruction, disease, roadway banditry, guerrilla warfare, summary executions, and the random flow of escaped slaves. After two years of occupation, a southern white woman wrote to a kinsman about their native Clarksville, Tennessee. "You would scarcely know the place," she lamented, "it is nothing but a dirty hole filled . . . with niggers and Yankees."

Vastly disadvantaged in industrial capacity, natural resources, and labor, southerners felt the cost of the war more directly and more painfully than northerners. But even more fundamental were the Confederacy's internal problems; the southern class system threatened the Confederate cause.

Disintegration of Confederate Unity

One ominous development was the planters' increasing opposition to their own government. Along with new taxation, Confederate military authorities also impressed slaves to build fortifications. And when Union forces advanced on plantation areas, Confederate commanders burned stores of cotton that lay in the enemy's path. Many planters bitterly complained about such interference with their agricultural production and financial interests.

Nor were the centralizing policies of the Davis administration popular. In fact, the Confederate constitution had granted substantial powers to the central government, especially in time of war. But many planters took the position articulated by R. B. Rhett, editor of the *Charleston Mercury*, that the Confederate constitution "leaves the States untouched in their Sovereignty, and commits to the Confederate Government only a few simple objects, and a few simple powers to enforce them." Governor Joseph E. Brown of Georgia took a similar states' rights position, occasionally prohibiting supplies and that state's soldiers from leaving its borders.

Years of opposition to the federal government within the Union had frozen southerners in a defensive posture. Now they erected the barrier of states' rights as a defense against change, hiding behind it while their capacity for creative statesmanship atrophied. Planters sought, above all, a guarantee that their plantations and their lives would remain untouched. As secession revolutionized their world and hard war took so many lives, some could never fully commit to the cause.

Confused and embittered planters struck out at Jefferson Davis. Conscription, thundered Governor Brown, was "subversive of [Georgia's] sovereignty, and at war with all the principles for the support of which Georgia entered into this revolution." Searching for ways to frustrate the law, Brown ordered local enrollment officials not to cooperate with the Confederacy. The *Charleston Mercury* told readers that "conscription . . . is . . . the very embodiment of Lincolnism, which our gallant armies are today fighting." In a gesture of stubborn selfishness, Robert Toombs of Georgia, a former U.S. senator, refused to switch from cotton to food crops, defying the wishes of the government, the newspapers, and his neighbors' petitions.

The southern courts ultimately upheld Davis's power to conscript. Davis was deeply devoted to southern independence, but some of his actions earned him the hatred of influential and elite citizens.

Meanwhile, for ordinary southerners, the dire predictions of hunger and suffering were becoming a reality. Food riots occurred in the spring of 1863 in Atlanta, Macon, Columbus, and Augusta, Georgia, and in

Food Riots in Southern Cities

Salisbury and High Point, North Carolina. On April 2, a crowd assembled in Richmond to demand relief. A passerby, noticing the excitement, asked a young girl, "Is there some celebration?" "We celebrate our right to live," replied the girl. "We are starving. As soon as enough of us get together we are going to the bakeries and each of us will take a loaf of bread." Soon they did just that, sparking a riot that Davis ordered quelled at gunpoint.

Throughout the rural South, ordinary people resisted more quietly—by refusing to cooperate with conscription, tax collection, and impressments of food. "In all the States impressments are evaded by every means which ingenuity can suggest, and in some openly resisted," wrote a commissary officer. Farmers who did provide food for the army refused to accept payment in certificates of credit or government bonds, as required by law. Conscription officers increasingly found no one to draft. "The disposition to avoid military service is general," observed one of Georgia's senators in 1864. In some areas, tax agents were killed in the line of duty.

Jefferson Davis was ill-equipped to deal with such discontent. Austere and private by nature, he failed to communicate with the masses. His class perspective also distanced him from the sufferings of the common people. While his social circle in Richmond dined on duck and oysters, ordinary southerners recovered salt from the drippings on their smokehouse floors and went hungry.

Such discontent was certain to affect the Confederate armies. "What man is there that would stay in the army

Desertions from the Confederate Army

and no that his family is suffering at home?" an angry citizen wrote anonymously to the secretary of war. Worried about their loved ones and

◀ Refugees driven from their homes in the South as armies, seen in the distant camp in the background, move through the countryside. Hundreds of thousands of southerners, white and black, were displaced people by 1864–1865.

National Archives

resentful of what they saw as a rich man's war, large numbers of men did indeed leave the armies. Their friends and neighbors gave them support. Mary Chesnut observed a man being dragged back to the army as his wife looked on. "Desert agin, Jake!" she cried openly. "You desert agin, quick as you kin. Come back to your wife and children."

Desertion did not become a serious problem for the Confederacy until mid-1862, and stiffer policing solved the problem that year. But from 1863 on, the number of men on duty fell rapidly. By mid-1863, John A. Campbell, the South's assistant secretary of war, wondered whether "so general a habit" as desertion could be considered a crime. Campbell estimated that 40,000 to 50,000 troops were absent without leave and that 100,000 were evading duty in some way. Furloughs, amnesty proclamations, and appeals to return had little effect; by November 1863, Secretary of War James Seddon admitted that one-third of the army could not be accounted for.

The defeats at Gettysburg and Vicksburg dealt a heavy blow to Confederate morale. When the news reached Josiah Gorgas, the genius of Confederate ordnance operations, he confided to his diary, "Today absolute ruin seems our portion. The Confederacy totters to its destruction." In desperation, President Davis and several state governors resorted to threats and racial scare tactics to drive southern whites to further sacrifice. Defeat, Davis warned, would mean "extermination of yourselves, your wives, and children." Governor Charles Clark of Mississippi predicted "elevation of the black race to a position of equality—aye, of superiority, that will make them your masters and rulers."

From this point on, the internal disintegration of the Confederacy quickened. A few newspapers began to call openly for peace. "We are for peace," admitted the *Raleigh* (North Carolina) *Daily Progress*, "because there has been enough of blood and carnage, enough of widows and orphans." Confederate leaders began to realize they were losing the support of the common people. It is, indeed, remarkable how long and how effectively the Confederacy sustained a military effort in the face of such internal division.

In North Carolina, a peace movement grew under the leadership of William W. Holden, a popular Democratic politician and editor. He and his followers convened over one hundred public meetings in support of peace negotiations, which took place during the summer of 1863. In Georgia early in 1864, Governor Brown and Alexander H. Stephens, vice president of the Confederacy, led a similar effort. Ultimately, however, these movements came to naught. The lack of a two-party system threw into question the legitimacy of any criticism of the gov-

Antiwar Sentiment, South and North

Link to Alexander H. Stephens's "Slavery is the Cornerstone of the Confederacy" speech.

ernment; even Holden and Brown could not entirely escape the taint of dishonor and disloyalty.

The results of the 1863 congressional elections strengthened dissent in the Confederacy. Everywhere, secessionists and supporters of the administration lost seats to men not identified with the government. In the last years of the war, Davis's support in the Confederate Congress dwindled. Some newspaper editors and a core of courageous, determined soldiers, especially in Lee's Army of Northern Virginia, kept the Confederacy alive in spite of disintegrating popular support.

By 1864, much of the opposition to the war had moved entirely outside the political sphere. Southerners were simply giving up the struggle. Deserters dominated some whole towns and counties. Active dissent was particularly common in upland and mountain regions, where support for the Union had always been genuine. "The condition of things in the mountain districts of North Carolina, South Carolina, Georgia, and Alabama," admitted Assistant Secretary of War Campbell, "menaces the existence of the Confederacy as fatally as either of the armies of the United States."

Opposition to the war, though less severe, existed in the North as well. Alarm intensified over the growing centralization of government and, by 1863, war-weariness was widespread. Resentment of the draft sparked protest, especially among poor citizens, and the Union Army, too, struggled with a troubling desertion rate. But the Union was so much richer than the South in human resources that none of these problems ever threatened the effectiveness of the government.

Moreover, Lincoln possessed a talent that Davis lacked: he knew how to stay in touch with the ordinary citizen. Through public letters to newspapers and private ones to soldiers' families, he reached the common people. The battlefield carnage, the tortuous political problems, and the ceaseless criticism weighed heavily on him, but his administration never lost control of the federal war effort.

Much of the wartime protest in the North was political in origin. The Democratic Party fought to regain power by blaming Lincoln for the war's death toll, the expansion of federal powers, inflation and the high tariff, and the emancipation of blacks. Appealing to tradition, its leaders called for an end to the war and reunion on the basis of "the Constitution as it is and the Union as it was." The Democrats denounced conscription and martial law, and defended states' rights. They charged repeatedly that Republican policies were designed to flood the North with blacks, threatening white men's privileges. In the 1862 congressional elections, the Democrats made a strong comeback, with peace Democrats wielding influence in New York State and majorities in the legislatures of Illinois and Indiana.

Peace Democrats

Led by outspoken men like Representative Clement L. Vallandigham of Ohio, the peace Democrats became

Library of Congress

▲ In the Union government's conscription system, a draftee could hire a "substitute" to replace him in the army, lending credence to the claim by some that the conflict became a "rich man's war but a poor man's fight." Less than 7 percent of all Union soldiers were draftees, but this practice caused problems in northern morale.

highly visible. Vallandigham criticized Lincoln as a "dictator" who had suspended the writ of habeas corpus without congressional authority, arrested thousands of innocent citizens, and shut down opposition newspapers (which was true). He condemned both conscription and emancipation, and urged voters to use their power at the polls to depose "King Abraham." Vallandigham stayed carefully within legal bounds, but his attacks seemed so damaging to the war effort that military authorities arrested him for treason. Lincoln wisely decided against punishment—and martyr's status—for the Ohioan and exiled him to the Confederacy. Vallandigham eventually returned to the North through Canada.

Some antiwar Democrats did encourage draft resistance, discourage enlistment, sabotage communications, and generally plot to aid the Confederacy. Likening such groups to a poisonous snake, Republicans sometimes branded them—and by extension the peace Democrats—as "Copperheads." Although some Confederate agents were active in the North and Canada, they never genuinely

threatened the Union war effort and their suppression remains a vexing legal legacy.

More violent opposition to the government arose from ordinary citizens facing the draft, which became law in 1863. Although many soldiers risked their lives willingly out of a desire to preserve the Union or extend freedom, others openly sought to avoid service. Under the law, a draftee could stay at home by providing a substitute or paying a $300 commutation fee. Many wealthy men chose these options and—in response to popular demand—clubs, cities, and states provided the money for others to escape conscription. In all, 118,000 substitutes were provided and 87,000 commutations paid before Congress ended the commutation system in 1864.

New York City Draft Riots

The urban poor and immigrants in strongly Democratic areas were especially hostile to conscription. Federal enrolling officers made up the lists of eligibles, a procedure open to personal favoritism and prejudice. The North's poor viewed the system as discriminatory, and many immigrants suspected (wrongly, on the whole) that they were called in disproportionate numbers. (Approximately 200,000 men born in Germany and 150,000 born in Ireland served in the Union Army.)

As a result, there were scores of disturbances. Enrolling officers received rough treatment in many parts of the North, and riots occurred in New Jersey, Ohio, Indiana, Pennsylvania, Illinois, and Wisconsin. By far, the most serious outbreak of violence occurred in New York City in July 1863. The war was unpopular in that Democratic stronghold, and racial, ethnic, and class tensions ran high. Shippers had recently broken a longshoremen's strike by hiring black strikebreakers to work under police protection. Working-class New Yorkers feared an inflow of black labor from the South and regarded blacks as the cause of the war. Poor Irish workers resented being forced to serve in the place of others who could afford to avoid the draft.

Military police officers came under attack first, and then mobs crying, "Down with the rich" looted wealthy homes and stores. But blacks became the special target. The mob rampaged through African American neighborhoods, beating and murdering people in the streets, and burning an orphan asylum. At least seventy-four people died in the violence, which raged out of control for three days. Only the dispatch of army units directly from Gettysburg ended this tragic episode of racism and class resentment.

East and West, over race, land, and culture, America was a deeply divided country. A civil war of another kind raged on the Great Plains and in the Southwest. By 1864, U.S. troops under the command of Colonel John Chivington waged full-scale

War Against Indians in the Far West

war against the Sioux, Arapahos, and Cheyennes in order to eradicate Indian title to all of eastern Colorado. Indian chiefs sought peace, but American commanders had orders to "burn villages and kill Cheyennes whenever and wherever found." A Cheyenne chief, Lean Bear, was shot from his horse as he rode toward U.S. troops, holding in his hand papers given him by President Lincoln during a visit to Washington, D.C. Another chief, Black Kettle, was told by the U.S. command that, by moving his people to Sand Creek, Colorado, they would find a safe haven. But on November 29, 1864, 700 cavalrymen, many drunk, attacked the Cheyenne village. With most of the men absent hunting, the slaughter included 105 Cheyenne women and children and 28 men. American soldiers scalped and mutilated their victims, carrying women's body parts on their saddles or hats back to Denver. The Sand Creek Massacre, and the retaliation against white ranches and stagecoaches by Indians in 1865, would live in western historical memory forever.

In New Mexico and Arizona Territories, an authoritarian and brutal commander, General James Carleton, waged war on the Apaches and the Navajos. Both tribes had engaged for generations in raiding the Pueblo and Hispanic peoples of the region to maintain their security and economy. During the Civil War years, Anglo-American farms also became Indian targets. In 1863, the New Mexico Volunteers, commanded in the field by former mountain man Kit Carson, defeated the Mescalero Apaches and forced them onto a reservation at Bosque Redondo in the Pecos River valley.

But the Navajos, who lived in a vast region of canyons and high deserts, resisted. In a "scorched earth" campaign, Carson destroyed the Navajos' livestock, orchards, and crops. On the run, starving and demoralized, the Navajos began to surrender for food in January 1864. Three-quarters of the twelve thousand Navajos were rounded up and forced to march 400 miles (the "Long Walk") to the Bosque Redondo Reservation, suffering malnutrition and death along the way. When General William T. Sherman visited the reservation in 1868, he found the Navajos "sunk into a condition of absolute poverty and despair." Permitted to return to a fraction of their homelands later that year, the Navajos carried with them searing memories of the federal government's ruthless policies of both removal and eradication of Indian peoples.

Back east, war-weariness reached a peak in the summer of 1864, when the Democratic Party nominated the popular general George B. McClellan for president and inserted a peace plank into its platform. The plank, written by Vallandigham, called for an armistice and spoke vaguely about preserving the Union. The Democrats made racist appeals to white insecurity, calling Lincoln "Abe the nigger-lover" and "Abe the widow-maker." Lincoln con-

Election of 1864

cluded that it was "exceedingly probable that this Administration will not be reelected." No incumbent president had been reelected since 1832, and no nation had ever held a general election in the midst of all-out civil war. Some Republicans worked to dump Lincoln from their ticket in favor of either Salmon P. Chase or John C. Frémont, although little came of either effort. Even a relatively unified Republican Party, declaring itself for "unconditional surrender" of the Confederacy and a constitutional amendment abolishing slavery, had to contend with the horrible casualty lists and the battlefield stalemate of the summer of 1864.

The fortunes of war soon changed the electoral situation. With the fall of Atlanta and Union victories in the Shenandoah Valley by early September, Lincoln's prospects rose. Decisive in the election was that eighteen states allowed troops to vote at the front; Lincoln won an extraordinary 78 percent of the soldier vote. In taking 55 percent of the total popular vote, Lincoln's reelection—a referendum on the war and emancipation—had a devastating impact on southern morale. Without such a political outcome in 1864, a Union military victory and a redefined nation might never have been possible.

1864–1865: The Final Test of Wills

During the final year of the war, the Confederates could still have won their version of victory if military stalemate and northern antiwar sentiment had forced a negotiated settlement. But events and northern determination prevailed, as Americans endured the bloodiest nightmare in their history.

The North's long-term diplomatic strategy succeeded in 1864. From the outset, the North had pursued one paramount goal: to prevent recognition of the Confederacy by European nations. Foreign recognition would belie Lincoln's claim that the United States was fighting an illegal rebellion and would open the way to the financial and military aid that could ensure Confederate independence. Both England and France stood to benefit from a divided and weakened America. Thus, to achieve their goal, Lincoln and Secretary of State Seward needed to avoid both serious military defeats and controversies with the European powers.

Northern Diplomatic Strategy

Aware that the textile industry employed one-fifth of the British population directly or indirectly, southerners banked on British recognition of the Confederacy. But at the beginning of the war, British mills had a 50 percent surplus of cotton on hand, and they later found new sources of supply in India, Egypt, and Brazil. And throughout the war, some southern cotton continued to reach Europe, despite the Confederacy's embargo on cotton production, an ill-fated policy aimed at securing British support. The British government flirted with recognition of the Confederacy but awaited battlefield demonstrations of southern success. France, though sympathetic to the South, was unwilling to act independently of Britain. Confederate agents managed to purchase valuable arms and supplies in Europe and obtained loans from European financiers, but they never achieved a diplomatic breakthrough.

More than once, the Union strategy nearly broke down. An acute crisis occurred in 1861 when the overzealous commander of an American frigate stopped the British steamer *Trent* and removed two Confederate ambassadors, James Mason and John Slidell, sailing to Britain. When they were imprisoned in Boston, northerners cheered, but the British interpreted the capture as a violation of freedom of the seas and demanded the prisoners' release. Lincoln and Seward waited until northern public opinion cooled and then released the two southerners. The incident strained U.S.-British relations.

Then the sale to the Confederacy of warships constructed in England sparked vigorous protest from U.S. ambassador Charles Francis Adams. A few English-built ships, notably the *Alabama*, reached open water to serve the South. Over a period of twenty-two months, without entering a southern port (because of the Union blockade), the *Alabama* destroyed or captured more than sixty U.S. ships, leaving a bitter legal legacy to be settled in the postwar period.

On the battlefield, northern victory was far from won in 1864. General Nathaniel Banks's Red River campaign, designed to capture more of Louisiana and Texas, fell apart, and the capture of Mobile Bay in August did not cause the fall of Mobile. Union general William Tecumseh Sherman commented that the North had to "keep the war South until they are not only ruined, exhausted, but humbled in pride and spirit." Sherman soon brought total war to the southern heartland. On the eastern front during the winter of 1863–1864, the two armies in Virginia settled into a stalemate awaiting yet another spring offensive by the North.

Battlefield Stalemate and a Union Strategy for Victory

Military authorities throughout history have agreed that deep invasion is very risky: the farther an army penetrates enemy territory, the more vulnerable are its own communications and supply lines. Moreover, observed the Prussian expert Karl von Clausewitz, if the invader encounters a "truly national" resistance, his troops will be "everywhere exposed to attacks by an insurgent population." The South's vast size and a determined resistance could yet make a northern victory elusive.

National Archives

National Archives

▲ ▶ Both General Grant (left) and General Lee (right) were West Point graduates and had served in the U.S. Army during the War with Mexico. Their bloody battles against each other in 1864 stirred northern revulsion to the war even as they brought its end in sight.

The Civil War in Britain

So engaged was the British public with America's disunion and war that an unemployed weaver, John Ward, frequently trekked many miles from Britain's Low Moor to Clitheroe just to read newspaper accounts of the strife.

Because of the direct reliance of the British textile industry on southern cotton (cut off by the war) as well as the many ideological and familial ties between the two nations, the American war was significant in Britain's economy and domestic politics. The British aristocracy and most cotton mill owners were solidly pro-Confederate and proslavery, whereas a combination of clergymen, shopkeepers, artisans, and radical politicians worked for the causes of Union and emancipation. Most British workers saw their future at stake in a war for slave emancipation. "Freedom" to the huge British working class (who could not vote) meant basic political and civil rights as well as the bread and butter of secure jobs in an industrializing economy,
now damaged by a "cotton famine" that threw millhands out of work.

English aristocrats saw Americans as untutored, wayward cousins and took satisfaction in America's troubles. Conservatives believed in the superiority of the British system of government and looked askance at America's leveling tendencies. And some aristocratic British Liberals also saw Americans through their class bias and sympathized with the Confederacy's demand for "order" and independence. English racism also intensified in these years, exemplified by the popularity of minstrelsy and the employment of science in the service of racial theory.

The intensity of the British propaganda war over the American conflict is evident in the methods of their debate: public meetings organized by both sides were huge affairs, with cheering and jeering, competing banners, carts and floats, orators and resolutions. In a press war, the British argued over when rebellion is justified, whether secession was right or legal, whether slavery was at the heart of the conflict, and especially over the democratic image of America itself. This bitter debate about America's trial became a test of reform in Britain: those eager for a broadened franchise and increased democracy were pro-Union, and those who preferred to preserve Britain's class-ridden political system favored the Confederacy.

The nature of the internal British debate was no better symbolized than by the dozens of African Americans who served as pro-Union agents in England. The most popular was William Andrew Jackson, Confederate president Jefferson Davis's former coachman, who had escaped from Richmond in September 1862. Jackson's articulate presence at British public meetings countered pro-Confederate arguments that the war was not about slavery.

In the end, the British government did not recognize the Confederacy and, by 1864, English cotton lords had found new sources of the crop in Egypt and India. But in this link between America and its English roots at its time of greatest travail, we can see that the Civil War was a transformation of international significance.

Granger Collection

▲ Some southern leaders pronounced that cotton was king and would bring Britain to their cause. This British cartoon shows King Cotton brought down in chains by the American eagle, anticipating the cotton famine to follow and the intense debate in Great Britain over the nature and meaning of the American Civil War.

General Grant, by now in command of all the federal armies, decided to test southern will with a strategic innovation of his own: raids on a massive scale. Less tied to tradition and textbook maneuver than most other Union commanders, Grant proposed to use armies to destroy Confederate railroads, thus ruining the enemy's transportation and economy. Abandoning their lines of support, Union troops would live off the land while laying waste all resources useful to the military and to the civilian population of the Confederacy. After General George H. Thomas's troops won the Battle of Chattanooga in November 1863, the heartland of Georgia lay open. Grant entrusted General Sherman with 100,000 men for an invasion deep into the South, toward the rail center of Atlanta.

Jefferson Davis countered by positioning the army of General Joseph E. Johnston in Sherman's path. Davis's entire political strategy for 1864 was based on demonstrating Confederate military strength and successfully defending Atlanta. Davis hoped that southern resolve would lead to the political defeat of Lincoln and the elec-

Fall of Atlanta

tion of a president who would sue for peace. When General Johnston slowly but steadily fell back toward Atlanta, Davis grew anxious and sought assurances that Atlanta would be held. From a purely military point of view, Johnston maneuvered skillfully. But when Johnston fell silent and continued to retreat, Davis replaced him with the one-legged General John Hood, who knew his job was to fight. "Our all depends on that army at Atlanta," wrote Mary Chesnut. "If that fails us, the game is up."

For southern morale, the game *was* up. Hood attacked but was beaten, and Sherman's army occupied Atlanta on September 2, 1864. The victory buoyed northern spirits and ensured Lincoln's reelection. A government clerk in Richmond wrote, "Our fondly-cherished visions of peace have vanished like a mirage of the desert." Davis exhorted southerners to fight on and win new victories before the federal elections, but he had to admit that "two-thirds of our men are absent . . . without leave." In a desperate diversion, Hood's army marched north to cut Sherman's supply lines and force him to withdraw, but Sherman began to march sixty thousand of his marauding men straight to the sea, destroying Confederate resources as he went (see Map 15.4).

Map 15.4 Sherman's March to the Sea

The Deep South proved a decisive theater at the end of the war. From Chattanooga, Union forces drove into Georgia, capturing Atlanta. Following the fall of Atlanta, General Sherman embarked on his march of destruction through Georgia to the coast and then northward through the Carolinas.

Source: Copyright © Cengage Learning

Sherman's army was an unusually formidable force, composed almost entirely of battle-tested veterans and

Sherman's March to the Sea

officers who had risen through the ranks from the midwestern states. Before the march began, army doctors weeded out any men who were weak or sick. Weathered, bearded, and tough, the remaining veterans were determined, as one put it, "to Conquer this Rebelien or Die." They believed "the South are to blame for this war" and were ready to make the South pay. Although many harbored racist attitudes, most had come to support emancipation because, as one said, "Slavery stands in the way of putting down the rebellion." Confederate General Johnston later commented, "There has been no such army since the days of Julius Caesar."

As Sherman's men moved across Georgia, they cut a path 50 to 60 miles wide and more than 200 miles long. The totality of the destruction they caused was awesome; indeed, it was Sherman's campaign that later prompted many historians to deem this the first modern "total war." A Georgia woman described the "Burnt Country" this way: "The fields were trampled down and the road was lined with carcasses of horses, hogs, and cattle that the invaders, unable either to consume or to carry with them, had wantonly shot down to starve our people. . . . The stench in some places was unbearable." Such devastation diminished the South's material resources and sapped its will to resist.

After reaching Savannah in December, Sherman marched his armies north into the Carolinas. To his soldiers, South Carolina was "the root of secession." They burned and destroyed as they marched, encountering little resistance. The opposing army of General Johnston was small, but Sherman's men should have been prime targets for guerrilla raids and harassing attacks by local defense units. The absence of both led South Carolina's James Chesnut Jr. (a politician and the husband of Mary Chesnut) to write that his state "was shamefully and unnecessarily lost. . . . We had time, opportunity and means to destroy him. But there was wholly wanting the energy and ability required." Southerners had lost the will to continue the struggle.

Sherman's march drew additional human resources to the Union cause. In Georgia alone, as many as nineteen thousand slaves gladly embraced emancipation and followed the marauding Union troops. Others remained on the plantations to await the end of the war because of either an ingrained wariness of whites or negative experiences with federal soldiers. The destruction of food harmed slaves as well as white rebels, and many blacks lost livestock, clothing, crops, and other valuables to their liberators. In fact, the brutality of Sherman's troops shocked some liberated slaves. "I've seen them cut the hams off of a live pig or ox and go off leavin' the animal groanin'," recalled one man. "The master had 'em kilt then, but it was awful."

It was awful, too, in Virginia, where the path to victory proved protracted and ghastly. Throughout the spring

Virginia's Bloody Soil

and summer of 1864, intent on capturing Richmond, Grant hurled his troops at Lee's army and suffered appalling losses: almost eighteen thousand casualties in the Battle of the Wilderness, where skeletons poked out of the shallow graves dug one year before; more than eight thousand at Spotsylvania; and twelve thousand in the space of a few hours at Cold Harbor (see Map 15.5).

Before the assault at Cold Harbor (which Grant later admitted was a grave mistake), Union troops pinned scraps of paper bearing their names and addresses to their backs, certain they would be mowed down as they rushed Lee's trenches. In four weeks in May and June, Grant lost as many men as were enrolled in Lee's entire army. From early May until July, when Union forces had marched and fought all the way from forests west of Fredericksburg to Petersburg, south of Richmond, which they besieged, the two armies engaged each other nearly every day. The war had reached a horribly modern scale. Wagon trains carrying thousands of Union wounded crawled back toward Washington. "It was as if war," wrote historian Bruce Catton, "the great clumsy machine for maiming people, had at last been perfected. Instead of turning out its grist spasmodically, with long waits between each delivery, it was at last able to produce every day, without any gaps at all."

Undaunted, Grant kept up the pressure, saying, "I propose to fight it out along this line if it takes all summer." Although costly, and testing northern morale to its limits, these battles prepared the way for eventual victory: Lee's army shrank until offensive action was no longer possible, while Grant's army kept replenishing its forces with new recruits. The siege of Petersburg, with the armies facing each other in miles of trenches, lasted throughout the winter of 1864–1865.

The end finally came in the spring of 1865. Grant kept battering Lee, who tried but failed to break through

Surrender at Appomattox

the Union line. With the numerical superiority of Grant's army now greater than two to one, Confederate defeat was inevitable. On April 2, Lee abandoned Richmond and Petersburg. On April 9, hemmed in by Union troops, short of rations, and with fewer than thirty thousand men left, he surrendered at Appomattox Court House. Grant treated his rival with respect and paroled the defeated troops, allowing cavalrymen to keep their horses and take them home. The war was over at last. Within weeks, Confederate forces under Johnston surrendered to Sherman in North

Map 15.5 The War in Virginia

At great cost, Grant hammered away at Lee's army until the weakened southern forces finally surrendered at Appomattox Court House.

Source: Copyright © Cengage Learning

Carolina, and Davis, who had fled Richmond but wanted the war to continue, was captured in Georgia. The North rejoiced, and most southerners fell into despair, expecting waves of punishment. In the profound relief and stillness of the surrender field at Appomattox, no one could know the harrowing tasks of healing and justice that lay ahead.

With Lee's surrender, Lincoln knew the Union had been preserved, yet he lived to see but a few days of war's aftermath. On the evening of Good Friday, April 14, he accompanied his wife to Ford's Theatre in Washington to enjoy a popular comedy. There John Wilkes Booth, an embittered southern sympathizer, shot the president in the head at point-blank range. Lincoln died the next day. Twelve days later, troops tracked down and killed Booth. The Union had lost its wartime leader, and millions publicly mourned the martyred chief executive along the route of the funeral train that took his body home to Illinois. Relief at the war's end mingled hauntingly with a renewed sense of loss and anxiety about the future. Millions never for-

got where they were and how they felt at the news of Lincoln's assassination.

Property damage and financial costs were enormous, though difficult to tally. U.S. loans and taxes during the

Financial Tally

conflict totaled almost $3 billion, and interest on the war debt was $2.8 billion. The Confederacy borrowed over $2 billion but lost far more in the destruction of homes, crops, livestock, and other property. In southern war zones, the landscape was desolated. Over wide regions, fences and crops were destroyed; houses, barns, and bridges burned; and fields abandoned and left to erode. Union troops had looted factories and put two-thirds of the South's railroad system out of service.

Estimates of the total cost of the war exceed $20 billion—five times the total expenditures of the federal government from its creation until 1861. By 1865, the federal government's spending had soared to twenty times the prewar level and accounted for over 26 percent of the gross national product. Many of these changes

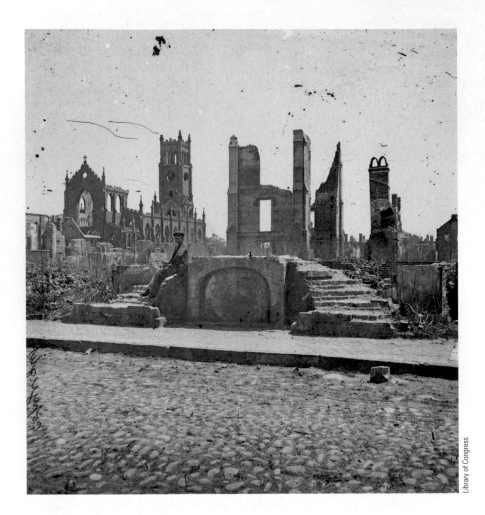

◄ The ruins of Charleston, South Carolina, late spring 1865. The city fell and was evacuated on February 18, 1865. Union gunboats and siege cannons had bombarded Charleston during the final year of the war, leaving much of the beautiful neoclassical architecture of that city, where secession had begun four years earlier, in devastation. An African American regiment accepted the formal surrender of the city.

Library of Congress

were more or less permanent, as wartime measures left the government more deeply involved in manufacturing, banking, and transportation.

The human costs of the Civil War were especially staggering. The total number of military casualties on both sides exceeded 1 million—a frightful toll for a nation of 31 million people. Approximately 360,000 Union soldiers died, the majority from disease. Another 275,175 Union soldiers were wounded but survived. On the Confederate side, an estimated 260,000 lost their lives, and almost as many suffered wounds. More men died in the Civil War than in all other American wars combined until Vietnam. Not all died on the battlefield: 30,218 northerners died in southern prisons, and 25,976 Confederates died in Union prisons.

The scale and the anonymous nature of death overwhelmed American culture and led to the establishment of national cemeteries, where the large majority of the fallen were buried without identification. This prompted

Death Toll and Its Impact

desperate efforts by families to find their loved ones, usually in vain. In a Christian culture believing in the "good death," where the deceased is surrounded by family and a clear narrative of the final hours could be remembered, mass death and dismembered bodies strewn on war-ravaged landscapes violated the values of a romantic age. On the mass private level, countless Americans, soldiers, and family members alike never psychologically recovered or found true consolation from the war's personal loss. The age's earlier belief that suffering was always purposeful underwent fundamental shock. The desperate urge to memorialize individual soldiers in this war, writes historian Drew Faust, stemmed from "the anguish of wives, parents, siblings, and children who found undocumented, unconfirmed, and unrecognizable loss intolerable." For some, the magnitude of death meant living could never be the same.

These unprecedented losses (approximately 620,000 total dead) flowed from fundamental strife over the nature of the Union and the liberty of black people. Both sides saw vital interests in the struggle but lost control of its

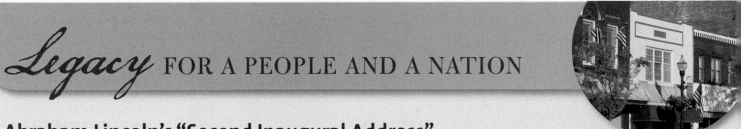

Legacy FOR A PEOPLE AND A NATION

Abraham Lincoln's "Second Inaugural Address"

Historian Don Fehrenbacher wrote that "some of Lincoln's words have acquired transcendent meaning as contributions to the permanent literary treasure of the nation." How is this so with the short oration Lincoln delivered from the north portico of the Capitol on March 4, 1865? Why have so many book titles been drawn from its text?

In a 701-word prose poem at the occasion of his second inauguration, Lincoln chose not to celebrate the Union armies' impending victory, nor his own at the polls. Instead, he probed the tragedy at the heart of the Civil War and interpreted its ultimate meanings. The prosaic first paragraph acknowledges wide understanding of the "progress of our arms" over four years of war. In the second paragraph, Lincoln entwines North and South in a mutual fate, but suggests responsibility for which side "would make war," and which side "would accept war," and leaves it to posterity: "And the war came."

Then, the speech transforms and Lincoln boldly offers a theological-historical explanation of the war that still resonates today in how Americans interpret this crucial turning point in their history. Evenhandedly, but forcefully, Lincoln declares that "all knew . . . somehow" slavery was the "cause" of the conflict. Both sides appealed to the "same God" to favor their cause. But quoting Mathew 18:17, he warned that the "Almighty has his own purposes," and though "offences" will always come from human frailty, "woe to that man by whom the offence cometh!" Wary of judging, but unrestrained, Lincoln called it "strange that any men should dare to ask a just God's assistance in ringing their bread from the sweat of other men's faces." Lincoln did not claim to utterly know God's will, but he imagined slavery as an "offence" that came "in the providence of God," and brought "this mighty scourge of war" as its awful price.

Suddenly, in rhetoric so unusual for presidential inaugurals, Lincoln assumed the prophet's mantle: "Yet if God wills that it [the war] continue, until all the wealth piled by the bond-man's two hundred and fifty years of unrequited toil shall be sunk, and until every drop of blood drawn by the lash, shall be paid by another drawn with the sword, as was said three thousand years ago, so still it must be said the judgments of the Lord are true and righteous altogether."

Famously, Lincoln ended with a single-sentence paragraph where he declared "malice toward none . . . charity for all" the healing balm for the "nation's wounds." But in that third paragraph—less popular or savored in modern memory—Lincoln transcended time and place and delivered what Frederick Douglass would call a "sacred effort" to explain what the Civil War was really about. Whether Lincoln was the nation's healer or its war-maker who would demand any sacrifice to restore the Union and destroy slavery has always animated the endless study of his personal story. The legacy of the Civil War, and Lincoln's place in it, are forever enmeshed in how we interpret this oratorical masterpiece.

---

scope. As Julia Ward Howe wrote in her famous "Battle Hymn of the Republic," they had heard "the trumpet that shall never call retreat." And so the war took its horrifying course.

SUMMARY

The Civil War altered American society forever. The first great legacy of the war in the lives of its survivors was, therefore, death itself. Although precise figures on enlistments are unavailable, it appears that 700,000 to 800,000 men served in the Confederate armies. Far more, possibly 2.3 million, served in the Union armies. All of these men were taken from home, family, and personal goals; their lives, if they survived, were disrupted in

> Link to the text of Abraham Lincoln's Second Inaugural Address.

◀ Abraham Lincoln delivering his Second Inaugural Address from the steps of the U.S. Capitol, March 4, 1865. Among the audience that day were Frederick Douglass, the great black orator, and John Wilkes Booth, the president's would-be assassin. In the address, Lincoln declared that "all knew" that slavery had been "somehow, the cause of the war...."

Library of Congress

ways that were never repaired. During the war, in both North and South, women, too, took on new roles as they struggled to manage the hardships of the home front, to grieve, and to support the war effort.

Industrialization and economic enterprises grew exponentially in tandem with the war. Ordinary citizens found that their futures were increasingly tied to huge organizations. The character and extent of government power, too, changed markedly. Under Republican leadership, the federal government expanded its power not only to preserve the Union but also to extend freedom. A social revolution and government authority emancipated the slaves. A republic desperately divided against itself had survived, but in new constitutional forms yet to take shape during Reconstruction.

It was unclear at the end of the war how or whether the nation would use its power to protect the rights of the former slaves. Secession was dead, but whether Americans would continue to embrace a centralized nationalism remained to be seen. The war ended decisively after tremendous sacrifice, but it left many unanswered questions: How would white southerners, embittered and impoverished, respond to efforts to reconstruct the nation? How would the country care for the maimed, the orphans, the farming women without men to work their land, and all the dead who had to be found and properly buried? What would be the place of black men and women in American life?

In the West, two civil wars had raged: one between Union and Confederate forces and the other resulting in

a conquest of southwestern Indians by U.S. troops and land-hungry settlers. On the diplomatic front, the Union government had delicately managed to keep Great Britain and other foreign powers out of the war. Dissent flourished in both North and South, playing a crucial role in the ultimate collapse of the Confederacy.

In the Civil War, Americans had undergone an epic of destruction and survival—a transformation like nothing else in their history. White southerners had experienced defeat that few other Americans had ever faced. Blacks were moving proudly but anxiously from slavery to freedom. White northerners were, by and large, self-conscious victors in a massive war for the nation's existence and for new definitions of freedom. The war, with all of its drama, sacrifice, and social and political change, would leave a compelling memory in American hearts and minds for generations.

SUGGESTIONS FOR FURTHER READING

Stephen V. Ash, *When the Yankees Came: Conflict and Chaos in the Occupied South* (1995)

Edward L. Ayers, *In the Presence of Mine Enemies: War in the Heart of America, 1859–1863* (2002)

Ira Berlin et al., eds., *Freedom: A Documentary History of Emancipation, 1861–1867*, 3 vols. (1979–1982)

David W. Blight, *Frederick Douglass' Civil War: Keeping Faith in Jubilee* (1989)

Alice Fahs, *The Imagined Civil War: Popular Literature of the North and South* (2001)

Drew G. Faust, *This Republic of Suffering: Death and the American Civil War* (2008)

Gary W. Gallagher, *The Confederate War* (1997)

Bruce Levine, *Confederate Emancipation: Southern Plans to Free and Arm Slaves During the Civil War* (2006)

Chandra Manning, *What This Cruel War Was Over: Soldiers, Slavery, and the Civil War* (2007)

James M. McPherson, *Battle Cry of Freedom: The Civil War Era* (1987)

Philip S. Paludan, *"A People's Contest": The Union and the Civil War* (1989)

Mark R. Wilson, *The Business of Civil War: Military Mobilization and the State, 1861–1865* (2006)

CourseMate

Go to the CourseMate website for primary source links, study tools, and review materials for this chapter. www.cengagebrain.com

Reconstruction: An Unfinished Revolution 1865–1877

Museum of Fine Arts, Boston. Gift of Maxim Karolik for the M. & M. Karolik Collection of American Watercolors and Drawings. Photograph @ 2008 Museum of Fine Arts, Boston (Detail)

The lower half of the city of Charleston, South Carolina, the seedbed of secession, lay in ruin when most of the white population evacuated on February 18, 1865. A prolonged bombardment by Union batteries and gunboats around Charleston harbor had already destroyed many of the lovely town homes of the low-country planters. Then, as the city was abandoned, fires broke out everywhere, ignited in bales of cotton left in huge stockpiles in public squares. To many observers, the flames were the funeral pyres of a dying civilization.

Among the first Union troops to enter Charleston was the Twenty-first U.S. Colored Regiment, which received the surrender of the city from its mayor. For black Charlestonians, most of whom were former slaves, this was a time of celebration. In symbolic ceremonies, they proclaimed their freedom and announced their rebirth. Whatever the postwar order would bring, the freedpeople of Charleston converted Confederate ruin into a vision of Reconstruction based on Union victory and black liberation.

Still, in Charleston as elsewhere, death demanded attention. During the final year of the war, the Confederates had converted the planters' Race Course, a horseracing track, and its famed Jockey Club, into a prison. Union soldiers were kept in terrible conditions in the interior of the track, without shelter. The 257 who died there of exposure and disease were buried in a mass grave behind the judges' stand. After the fall of the city, Charleston's blacks organized to create a proper burial ground for the Union dead. During April, more than twenty black workmen reinterred the dead in marked graves and built a high fence around the cemetery. On the archway over the cemetery's entrance they painted the inscription "Martyrs of the Race Course."

And then they planned an extraordinary ceremony. On the morning of May 1, 1865, a procession of ten thousand people marched around the planters' Race Course, led by three thousand children carrying armloads of roses and singing "John Brown's

◄ "Entrance of the 55th Massachusetts (Colored) Regiment into Charleston, S. C., February 21, 1865." Thomas Nast, pencil, oil, and wash on board, 1865. Black troops celebrated as they marched into the Confederate stronghold, hoisting their caps on their bayonets, and singing "John Brown's Body" as they marched up Meeting Street, Charleston's main thoroughfare.

Chronology

1865
- Johnson begins rapid and lenient Reconstruction
- White southern governments pass restrictive black codes
- Congress refuses to seat southern representatives
- Thirteenth Amendment ratified, abolishing slavery

1866
- Congress passes Civil Rights Act and renewal of Freedmen's Bureau over Johnson's veto
- Congress approves Fourteenth Amendment
- In *Ex parte Milligan*, the Supreme Court reasserts its influence

1867
- Congress passes First Reconstruction Act and Tenure of Office Act
- Constitutional conventions called in southern states

1868
- House impeaches and Senate acquits Johnson
- Most southern states readmitted to Union under Radical plan
- Fourteenth Amendment ratified
- Grant elected president

1869
- Congress approves Fifteenth Amendment (ratified in 1870)

1871
- Congress passes second Enforcement Act and Ku Klux Klan Act
- Treaty with England settles Alabama claims

1872
- Amnesty Act frees almost all remaining Confederates from restrictions on holding office
- Grant reelected

1873
- *Slaughter-House* cases limit power of Fourteenth Amendment
- Panic of 1873 leads to widespread unemployment and labor strife

1874
- Democrats win majority in House of Representatives

1875
- Several Grant appointees indicted for corruption
- Congress passes weak Civil Rights Act
- Democratic Party increases control of southern states with white supremacy campaigns

1876
- *U.S. v. Cruikshank* further weakens Fourteenth Amendment
- Presidential election disputed

1877
- Congress elects Hayes president

Body." The children were followed by black women with baskets of flowers and wreaths, and then by black men. The parade concluded with members of black and white Union regiments, along with white missionaries and teachers led by James Redpath, the supervisor of freedmen's schools in the region. All who could fit assembled at the gravesite; five black ministers read from Scripture, and a black children's choir sang "America," "We'll Rally 'Round the Flag," "The Star-Spangled Banner," and Negro spirituals. When the ceremony ended, the huge crowd retired to the Race Course for speeches, picnics, and military festivities.

The war was over in Charleston, and "Decoration Day"—now Memorial Day, the day to remember the war dead and decorate their graves with flowers—had been founded by African Americans. Black people—by their labor, their words, their songs, and their marching feet on the old planters' Race Course—had created an American tradition. In their vision, they were creating the Independence Day of a Second American Revolution.

Reconstruction would bring revolutionary circumstances, but revolutions can also go backward. The Civil War and its aftermath wrought unprecedented changes in American society, law, and politics, but the underlying realities of economic power, racism, and judicial conservatism limited Reconstruction's revolutionary potential. As never before, the nation had to determine the nature of federal-state relations, whether confiscated land could be redistributed, and how to bring justice to both freedpeople and aggrieved white southerners whose property and lives had been devastated. Americans faced the harrowing challenge of psychological healing from a bloody and fratricidal war. How they would negotiate the tangled relationship between healing and justice would determine the extent of change during Reconstruction.

Nowhere was the turmoil of Reconstruction more evident than in national politics. Lincoln's successor, Andrew

Johnson, fought bitterly with Congress over the shaping of Reconstruction policies. Although a southerner, Johnson had always been a foe of the South's wealthy planters, and his first acts as president suggested that he would be tough on "traitors." Before the end of 1865, however, Johnson's policies changed direction, and he became the protector of southern interests.

Johnson imagined a lenient and rapid "restoration" of the South to the Union rather than the fundamental "reconstruction" that Republican congressmen favored. Between 1866 and 1868, the president and the Republican leadership in Congress engaged in a bitter power struggle over how to put the United States back together again. Before the struggle ceased, Congress had impeached the president, enfranchised freedmen, and given them a role in reconstructing the South. The nation also adopted the Fourteenth and Fifteenth Amendments, ushering equal protection of the law, a definition of citizenship, and universal manhood suffrage into the Constitution. But little was done to open the doors of economic opportunity to black southerners, and the cause of equal rights for African Americans fell almost as fast as it had risen.

By 1869, the Ku Klux Klan employed extensive violence and terror to thwart Reconstruction and undermine black freedom. As white Democrats in the South took control of state governments, they encountered little opposition from the North. Moreover, the wartime industrial boom had created new opportunities and priorities. The West, with its seemingly limitless potential and its wars against Indians, drew American resources and consciousness like never before. Political corruption became a nationwide scandal, and bribery a way of doing business.

Thus, Reconstruction became a revolution eclipsed. The white South's desire to reclaim control of its states and of race relations overwhelmed the national interest in stopping it. But Reconstruction left enduring legacies with which the nation has benefitted and struggled ever since.

- Should the Reconstruction era be considered the Second American Revolution? By what criteria should we make such a judgment?

- What were the origins and meanings of the Fourteenth Amendment in the 1860s? What is its significance today?

- Reconstruction is judged to have "ended" in 1877. Over the course of the 1870s, what caused its end?

Wartime Reconstruction

Civil wars leave immense challenges of healing, justice, and physical rebuilding. Anticipating that process, reconstruction of the Union was an issue as early as 1863, well before the war ended. Many key questions loomed on the horizon when and if the North succeeded on the battlefield: How would the nation be restored? How would southern states and leaders be treated—as errant brothers or as traitors? What was the constitutional basis for readmission of states to the Union, and where, if anywhere, could American statesmen look for precedence or guidance? More specifically, four vexing problems compelled early thinking and would haunt the Reconstruction era throughout. One, who would rule in the South once it was defeated? Two, who would rule in the federal government—Congress or the president? Three, what were the dimensions of black freedom, and what rights under law would the freedmen enjoy? And four, would Reconstruction be a preservation of the old republic or a second Revolution, a reinvention of a new republic?

Abraham Lincoln had never been antisouthern, though he had become the leader of an antislavery war.

Lincoln's 10 Percent Plan

He lost three brothers-in-law, killed in the war on the Confederate side. His worst fear was that the war would collapse at the end into guerrilla warfare across the South, with surviving bands of Confederates carrying on resistance. Lincoln insisted that his generals give lenient terms to southern soldiers once they surrendered. In his Second Inaugural Address, delivered only a month before his assassination, Lincoln promised "malice toward none; with charity for all," as Americans strove to "bind up the nation's wounds."

Lincoln planned early for a swift and moderate Reconstruction process. In his "Proclamation of Amnesty and Reconstruction," issued in December 1863, he proposed to replace majority rule with "loyal rule" as a means of reconstructing southern state governments. He proposed pardons to all ex-Confederates except the highest-ranking military and civilian officers. Then, as soon as 10 percent of the voting population in the 1860 general election in a given state had taken an oath to the United States and established a government, the new state would be recognized. Lincoln did not consult Congress in these plans, and "loyal" assemblies (known as "Lincoln governments") were created in Louisiana, Tennessee, and Arkansas in 1864, states largely occupied by Union troops. These governments were weak and dependent on northern armies for survival.

Congress and the Wade-Davis Bill

Congress responded with great hostility to Lincoln's moves to readmit southern states in what seemed such a premature manner. Many Radical Republicans, strong proponents of emancipation and of aggressive prosecution of the war against the South, considered the 10 percent plan a "mere mockery" of democracy. Led by Thaddeus Stevens of Pennsylvania in the House and Charles Sumner of Massachusetts in the Senate, congressional Republicans locked horns with Lincoln and proposed a longer and harsher approach to Reconstruction. Stevens advocated a "conquered provinces" theory, arguing that southerners had organized as a foreign nation to make war on the United States and, by secession, had destroyed their status as states. They therefore must be treated as "conquered foreign lands" and returned to the status of "unorganized territories" before any process of readmission could be entertained by Congress.

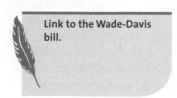

Link to the Wade-Davis bill.

In July 1864, the Wade-Davis bill, named for its sponsors, Senator Benjamin Wade of Ohio and Congressman Henry W. Davis of Maryland, emerged from Congress with three specific conditions for southern readmission.

1. It demanded a "majority" of white male citizens participating in the creation of a new government.

2. To vote or be a delegate to constitutional conventions, men had to take an "iron-clad" oath (declaring that they had never aided the Confederate war effort).

3. All officers above the rank of lieutenant and all civil officials in the Confederacy would be disfranchised and deemed "not a citizen of the United States."

The Confederate states were to be defined as "conquered enemies," said Davis, and the process of readmission was to be harsh and slow. Lincoln, ever the adroit politician, pocket-vetoed the bill and issued a conciliatory proclamation of his own, announcing that he would not be inflexibly committed to any "one plan" of Reconstruction.

This exchange came during Grant's bloody campaign against Lee in Virginia, when the outcome of the war and Lincoln's reelection were still in doubt. On August 5, Radical Republicans issued the "Wade-Davis Manifesto" to newspapers. An unprecedented attack on a sitting president by members of his own party, it accused Lincoln of usurpation of presidential powers and disgraceful leniency toward an eventually conquered South. What emerged in 1864–1865 was a clear debate and a potential constitutional crisis. Lincoln saw Reconstruction as a means of weakening the Confederacy and winning the war; the Radicals saw it as a longer-term transformation of the political and racial order of the country.

In early 1865, Congress and Lincoln joined in two important measures that recognized slavery's centrality to the war. On January 31, with strong administration backing, Congress passed the Thirteenth Amendment, which had two provisions: first, it abolished involuntary servitude everywhere in the United States; second, it declared that Congress shall have the power to enforce this outcome by "appropriate legislation." When the measure passed by 119 to 56, a mere 2 votes more than the necessary two-thirds, rejoicing broke out in Congress. A Republican recorded in his diary, "Members joined in the shouting and kept it up for some minutes. Some embraced one another, others wept like children. I have felt ever since the vote, as if I were in a new country."

Thirteenth Amendment

But the Thirteenth Amendment had emerged from a long congressional debate and considerable petitioning and public advocacy. One of the first and most remarkable petitions for a constitutional amendment abolishing slavery was submitted early in 1864 by Elizabeth Cady Stanton, Susan B. Anthony, and the Women's Loyal National League. Women throughout the Union accumulated thousands of signatures, even venturing into staunchly pro-Confederate regions of Kentucky and Missouri to secure supporters. It was a long road from the Emancipation Proclamation to the Thirteenth Amendment—through treacherous constitutional theory about individual "property rights," a bedrock of belief that the sacred document ought never to be altered, and partisan politics. But the logic of winning the war by crushing slavery, and of securing a new beginning under law for the nation that so many had died to save, won the day.

Potentially as significant, on March 3, 1865, Congress created the Bureau of Refugees, Freedmen, and Abandoned Lands—the Freedmen's Bureau, an unprecedented agency of social uplift necessitated by the ravages of the war. Americans had never engaged in federal aid to citizens on such a scale. With thousands of refugees, white and black, displaced in the South, the government continued what private freedmen's aid societies had started as early as 1862. In the mere four years of its existence, the Freedmen's Bureau supplied food and medical services, built several thousand schools and some colleges, negotiated several hundred thousand employment contracts between freedmen and their former masters, and tried to manage confiscated land.

Freedmen's Bureau

The Bureau would be a controversial aspect of Reconstruction—within the South, where whites generally hated it, and within the federal government, where politicians divided over its constitutionality. Some bureau agents were devoted to freedmen's rights, whereas others were opportunists who exploited the chaos of the postwar

South. The war had forced into the open an eternal question of republics: what are the social welfare obligations of the state toward its people, and what do people owe their governments in return? Apart from their conquest and displacement of the eastern Indians, Americans were relatively inexperienced at the Freedmen's Bureau's task—social reform through military occupation.

In 1865, due to the devastation of the war, America was now a land with ruins. Like the countries of Europe, it now seemed an older, more

Ruins and Enmity

historic landscape. It had torn itself asunder—physically, politically, spiritually. Some of its cities lay in rubble, large stretches of the southern countryside were depopulated and defoliated, and thousands of people, white and black, were refugees. Some of this would in time seem romantic to northern travelers in the postwar South.

Thousands of yeoman farmer-soldiers, some paroled by surrenders and others who had abandoned Confederate ranks earlier, walked home too late in the season to plant a crop in a collapsed economy. Many white refugees faced genuine starvation. Of the approximately 18,300,000 rations distributed across the South in the first three years of the Freedmen's Bureau, 5,230,000 went to whites. In early 1866, in a proud agricultural society, the legislature of South Carolina issued $300,000 in state bonds to purchase corn for the destitute.

In October 1865, just after a five-month imprisonment in Boston, former Confederate Vice President Alexander H. Stephens rode a slow train southward. In Virginia he found "the desolation of the country . . . was horrible to behold." When Stephens reached northern Georgia, his native state, his shock ran over: "War has left a terrible impression. . . . Fences gone, fields all a-waste, houses burnt." A northern journalist visiting Richmond that same fall observed a city "mourning for her sins . . . in dust and ashes." The "burnt district" was a "bed of cinders . . . broken and blackened walls, impassable streets deluged with debris." Above all, every northern traveler encountered a wall of hatred among white southerners for their conquerors. An innkeeper in North Carolina told a journalist that Yankees had killed his sons in the war, burned his house, and stolen his slaves. "They left me one inestimable privilege," he said, "to hate 'em. I git up at half-past four in the morning, and sit up 'til twelve at night, to hate 'em."

The Meanings of Freedom

Black southerners entered into life after slavery with hope and circumspection. A Texas man recalled his father's telling him, even before the war was over, "Our forever was going to be spent living among the Southerners, after they got licked." Freed men and women tried to gain as much as they could from their new circumstances. Often the changes they valued the most were personal—alterations in location, employer, or living arrangements.

For America's former slaves, Reconstruction had one paramount meaning: a chance to explore freedom. A

The Feel of Freedom

southern white woman admitted in her diary that the black people "showed a natural and exultant joy at being free." Former slaves remembered singing far into the night after federal troops, who confirmed rumors of their emancipation, reached their plantations. The slaves on a Texas plantation shouted for joy, their leader proclaiming, "We is free—no more whippings and beatings." A few people gave in to the natural desire to do what had been impossible before. One angry grandmother dropped her hoe and ran to confront her mistress. "I'm free!" she yelled. "Yes, I'm free! Ain't got to work for you no more! You can't put me in your pocket now!" Another man recalled that he and others "started on the move," either to search for family members or just to exercise the human right of mobility.

Many freed men and women reacted more cautiously and shrewdly, taking care to test the boundaries of their new condition. "After the war was over," explained one man, "we was afraid to move. Just like terrapins or turtles after emancipation. Just stick our heads out to see how the land lay." As slaves, they had learned to expect hostility from white people, and they did not presume it would instantly disappear. Life in freedom might still be a matter of what was possible, not what was right. Many freedpeople evaluated potential employers with shrewd caution. "Most all the Negroes that had good owners stayed with 'em, but the others left. Some of 'em come back and some didn't," explained one man. After considerable wandering in search of better circumstances, a majority of blacks eventually settled as agricultural workers back on their former farms or plantations. But they relocated their houses and did their utmost to control the conditions of their labor.

Throughout the South, former slaves devoted themselves to reuniting their families, separated during slavery

Reunion of African American Families

by sale or hardship, and during the war by dislocation and the emancipation process. With only shreds of information to guide them, thousands of freedpeople embarked on odysseys in search of a husband, wife, child, or parent. By relying on the black community for help and information, and by placing ads that continued to appear in black newspapers well into the 1880s, some succeeded in their quest, while others searched in vain.

Husbands and wives who had belonged to different masters established homes together for the first time, and, as they had tried under slavery, parents asserted the

▲ *The Armed Slave*, William Sprang, oil on canvas, ca. 1865. This remarkable painting depicts an African American veteran soldier, musket with fixed bayonet leaning against the wall, cigar in hand indicating a new life of safety and leisure, reading a book to demonstrate his embrace of education and freedom. The man's visage leaves the impression of satisfaction and dignity.

Courtesy of the Civil War Library and Railroad Museum, Philadelphia

right to raise their own children. A mother bristled when her old master claimed a right to whip her children. She informed him that "he warn't goin' to brush none of her chilluns no more." The freed men and women were too much at risk to act recklessly, but, as one man put it, they were tired of punishment and "sure didn't take no more foolishment off of white folks."

Many black people wanted to minimize contact with whites because, as Reverend Garrison Frazier told General Sherman in January 1865, "There is a prejudice against us . . . that will take years to get over." To avoid contact with overbearing whites who were used to supervising them, blacks abandoned the slave quarters and fanned out to distant corners of the land they worked. "After the war my stepfather come," recalled Annie Young, "and got my mother and we moved out in the piney woods." Others described moving "across the creek" or building a "saplin house . . . back in the woods." Some rural dwellers established small, all-black settlements that still exist along the back roads of the South.

Blacks' Search for Independence

Even once-privileged slaves desired such independence and social separation. One man turned down his master's offer of the overseer's house and moved instead to a shack in "Freetown." He also declined to let the former owner grind his grain for free because it "make him feel like a free man to pay for things just like anyone else."

In addition to a fair employer, what freed men and women most wanted was the ownership of land. Land represented self-sufficiency and a chance to gain compensation for generations of bondage. General Sherman's special Field Order Number 15, issued in February 1865, set aside 400,000 acres of land in the Sea Islands region for the exclusive settlement of freedpeople. Hope swelled among ex-slaves as forty-acre plots, mules, and "possessary titles" were promised to them. But President Johnson ordered them removed in October and the land returned to its original owners under army enforcement. A northern observer noted that slaves freed in the Sea Islands of South Carolina and Georgia made "plain, straight-forward" inquiries as they settled on new land. They wanted to be sure the land "would be theirs after they had improved it." Everywhere, blacks young and old thirsted for homes of their own.

Freedpeople's Desire for Land

But most members of both political parties opposed genuine land redistribution to the freedmen. Even northern reformers who had administered the Sea Islands during the war showed little sympathy for black aspirations. The former Sea Island slaves wanted to establish small, self-sufficient farms. Northern soldiers, officials, and missionaries of both races brought education and aid to the freedmen but also insisted that they grow cotton for competitive market.

"The Yankees preach nothing but cotton, cotton!" complained one Sea Island black. "We wants land," wrote another, but tax officials "make the lots too big, and cut we out." Indeed, the U.S. government eventually sold thousands of acres in the Sea Islands, 90 percent of which went to wealthy investors from the North. At a protest against evictions from a contraband camp in Virginia in 1866, freedman Bayley Wyatt made black desires and claims clear: "We has a right to the land where we are located. For why? I tell you. Our wives, our children, our husbands, has been sold over and over again to purchase the lands we now locates upon; for that reason we have a divine right to the land."

Black Embrace of Education

Ex-slaves everywhere reached out for education. Blacks of all ages hungered for the knowledge in books

Link to Jourdan Anderson's letter to his former master.

that had been permitted only to whites. With freedom, they started schools and filled classrooms both day and night. On log seats and dirt floors, freed men and women studied their letters in old almanacs and in discarded dictionaries. Young children brought infants to school with them, and adults attended at night or after "the crops were laid by." Many a teacher had "to make herself heard over three other classes reciting in concert" in a small room. The desire to escape slavery's ignorance was so great that, despite their poverty, many blacks paid tuition, typically $1 or $1.50 a month. These small amounts constituted major portions of a person's agricultural wages and added up to more than $1 million by 1870.

The federal government and northern reformers of both races assisted this pursuit of education. In its brief life, the Freedmen's Bureau founded over four thousand schools, and idealistic men and women from the North established others funded by private philanthropy. The Yankee schoolmarm—dedicated, selfless, and religious—became an agent of progress in many southern communities. Thus did African Americans seek a break from their past through learning. More than 600,000 were enrolled in elementary school by 1877.

Blacks and their white allies also saw the need for colleges and universities. The American Missionary Association founded seven colleges, including Fisk and Atlanta Universities, between 1866 and 1869. The Freedmen's Bureau helped to establish Howard University in Washington, D.C., and northern religious groups, such as the Methodists, Baptists, and Congregationalists, supported dozens of seminaries and teachers' colleges.

During Reconstruction, African American leaders often were highly educated individuals; many were from the prewar elite of free people of color. Francis Cardozo, who held various offices in South Carolina, had attended universities in Scotland and England. P. B. S. Pinchback, who became lieutenant governor of Louisiana, was the son of a planter who had sent him to school in Cincinnati. Both of the two black senators from Mississippi, Blanche K. Bruce and Hiram Revels, possessed privileged educations. Bruce was the son of a planter who had provided tutoring at home; Revels was the son of free North Carolina blacks who had sent him to Knox College in Illinois. These men and many self-educated former slaves brought to political office not only fervor but education.

Freed from the restrictions and regulations of slavery, blacks could build their own institutions as they saw fit.

Growth of Black Churches

The secret churches of slavery came into the open; in countless communities throughout the South, ex-slaves "started a brush arbor." A brush arbor was merely "a sort of . . . shelter with leaves for a roof," but the freed men and women worshiped in it enthusiastically. "Preachin' and shouting sometimes lasted all day," they

▲ African Americans of all ages eagerly pursued the opportunity to gain an education in freedom. This young woman in Mt. Meigs, Alabama, is helping her mother learn to read.

Smithsonian Institution, photo by Rudolf Eickemeyer

recalled, for the opportunity to worship together freely meant "glorious times."

Within a few years, independent branches of the Methodist and Baptist denominations had attracted the great majority of black Christians in the South. By 1877, in South Carolina alone, the African Methodist Episcopal (A.M.E.) Church had a thousand ministers, forty-four thousand members, and its own school of theology, while the A.M.E. Zion Church had forty-five thousand members. In the rapid growth of churches, some of which became the wealthiest and most autonomous institutions in black life, the freedpeople demonstrated their most secure claim on freedom and created enduring communities.

The desire to gain as much independence as possible also shaped the former slaves' economic arrangements.

Rise of the Sharecropping System

Since most of them lacked money to buy land, they preferred the next best thing: renting the land they worked. But the South had a cash-poor

Aunt Phebe, Uncle Tom, and Others: Character Studies Among the Old Slaves of the South

◀ Churches became a center of African American life, both social and political, during and after Reconstruction. Churches large and small, like this one, Faith Memorial Church in Hagley Landing, South Carolina, became the first black-owned institutions for the postfreedom generation.

economy with few sources of credit, and few whites would consider renting land to blacks. Most blacks had no means to get cash before the harvest, so other alternatives had to be tried.

Black farmers and white landowners therefore turned to sharecropping, a system in which farmers kept part of their crop and gave the rest to the landowner while living on his property. The landlord or a merchant "furnished" food and supplies, such as draft animals and seed, needed before the harvest, and he received payment from the crop. White landowners and black farmers bargained with one another; sharecroppers would hold out, or move and try to switch employers from one year to another. As the system matured during the 1870s and 1880s, most sharecroppers worked "on halves"—half for the owner and half for themselves.

The sharecropping system, which materialized as early as 1868 in parts of the South, originated as a desirable compromise between former slaves and landowners. It eased landowners' problems with cash and credit, and provided them a permanent, dependent labor force; blacks accepted it because it gave them freedom from daily supervision. Instead of working in the hated gangs under a white overseer, as in slavery, they farmed

their own plots of land in family groups. But sharecropping later proved to be a disaster. Owners and merchants developed a monopoly of control over the agricultural economy, as sharecroppers found themselves riveted in ever-increasing debt (see page 557).

The fundamental problem, however, was that southern farmers as a whole still concentrated on cotton. In freedom, black women often chose to stay away from the fields and cotton picking, to concentrate on domestic chores. Given the diminishing incentives of the system, they placed greater value on independent choices about gender roles and family organization than on reaching higher levels of production. The South did recover its prewar share of British cotton purchases, but the rewards diminished. Cotton prices began a long decline, as world demand fell off.

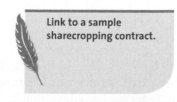

Link to a sample sharecropping contract.

Thus, southern agriculture slipped deeper and deeper into depression. Black sharecroppers struggled under a growing burden of debt which reduced their independence and bound them to landowners and to furnishing

Visualizing THE PAST

Sharecropping: Enslaved to Debt

Sharecropping became an oppressive system in the postwar South. A new labor structure that began as a compromise between freedmen who wanted independence and landowners who wanted a stable work force evolved into a method of working on "halves" and where tenants owed endless debts to the furnishing merchants, who owned plantation stores like this one, photographed in Mississippi in 1868. Merchants recorded in ledger books, like the one at right, the debts that few sharecroppers were able to repay. Why did both former slaves and former slaveowners initially find sharecropping an agreeable, if difficult, new labor arrangement? What were the short- and long-term consequences of the sharecropping system for the freedpeople and for the Southern economy?

This Mississippi plantation store, shown in 1868, is a typical example of the new institution of the furnishing merchant and its power over post-slavery agriculture in the South.

Amistad Center for Art & Culture, Hartford, CT. Simpson Collection/Art Resource, New York

Smithsonian Institution, Division of Community Life

Furnishing merchants kept such ledger books for decades; they became the record of how sharecroppers fell deeper in debt from year to year, and "owed their soul" to the country store.

merchants almost as oppressively as slavery had bound them to their masters. Many white farmers became debtors, too, gradually lost their land, and joined the ranks of sharecroppers. By the end of Reconstruction, over one-third of all southern farms were worked by sharecropping tenants, white and black. This economic transformation took place as the nation struggled to put its political house back in order.

Johnson's Reconstruction Plan

When Reconstruction began under President Andrew Johnson, many expected his policies to be harsh. Throughout his career in Tennessee, he had criticized the wealthy planters and championed the small farmers. When an assassin's bullet thrust Johnson into the presidency, many former slaveowners shared the dismay of a North Carolina woman who wrote, "Think of Andy Johnson [as] the president! What will become of us—'the aristocrats of the South' as we are termed?" Northern Radicals also had reason to believe that Johnson would deal sternly with the South. When one of them suggested the exile or execution of ten or twelve leading rebels to set an example, Johnson replied, "How are you going to pick out so small a number? . . . Treason is a crime; and crime must be punished."

Like his martyred predecessor, Johnson followed a path in antebellum politics from obscurity to power. With

Andrew Johnson of Tennessee

no formal education, he became a tailor's apprentice. But from 1829, while in his early twenties, he held nearly every office in Tennessee politics: alderman, state representative, congressman, two terms as governor, and U.S. senator by 1857. Although elected as a southern Democrat, Johnson was the only senator from a seceded state who refused to follow his state out of the Union. Lincoln appointed him war governor of Tennessee in 1862; hence his symbolic place on the ticket in the president's bid for reelection in 1864.

Although a Unionist, Johnson's political beliefs made him an old Jacksonian Democrat. And as they said in the mountainous region of east Tennessee, where Johnson established a reputation as a stump speaker, "Old Andy never went back on his raisin.'" Johnson was also an ardent states' rightist. Before the war, he had supported tax-funded public schools and homestead legislation, fashioning himself as a champion of the common man. Although he vehemently opposed secession, Johnson advocated limited government. He shared none of the Radicals' expansive conception of federal power. His philosophy toward Reconstruction may be summed up in the slogan he adopted: "The Constitution as it is, and the Union as it was."

Through 1865, Johnson alone controlled Reconstruction policy, for Congress recessed shortly before he

▲ Combative and inflexible, President Andrew Johnson contributed greatly to the failure of his own Reconstruction program.

Library of Congress

became president and did not reconvene until December. In the following eight months, Johnson formed new state governments in the South by using his power to grant pardons. He advanced Lincoln's leniency by extending even easier terms to former Confederates.

Johnson had owned house slaves, although he had never been a planter. He accepted emancipation as a result

Johnson's Racial Views

of the war, but he did not favor black civil and political rights. Johnson believed that black suffrage could never be imposed on a southern state by the federal government, and that set him on a collision course with the Radicals. When it came to race, Johnson was a thoroughgoing white supremacist. He held what one politician called "unconquerable prejudices against the African race." In perhaps the most blatantly racist official statement ever delivered by an American president, Johnson declared in his annual message of 1867 that blacks possessed less "capacity for government than any other race of people. No independent government of any form has ever been successful in their hands; . . . wherever they have been left to their own devices they have shown a constant tendency to relapse into barbarism."

Such racial views had an enduring effect on Johnson's policies. Where whites were concerned, however, Johnson seemed to be pursuing changes in class relations. He proposed rules that would keep the wealthy planter class at least temporarily out of power.

White southerners were required to swear an oath of loyalty as a condition of gaining amnesty or pardon,

Johnson's Pardon Policy

but Johnson barred several categories of people from taking the oath: former federal officials, high-ranking Confederate officers, and political leaders or graduates of West Point or Annapolis who joined the Confederacy. To this list, Johnson added another important group: all ex-Confederates whose taxable property was worth more than $20,000. These individuals had to apply personally to the president for pardon and restoration of their political rights. The president, it seemed, meant to take revenge on the old planter elite and thereby promote a new leadership of deserving yeomen.

Johnson appointed provisional governors, who began the Reconstruction process by calling state constitutional conventions. The delegates chosen for these conventions had to draft new constitutions that eliminated slavery and invalidated secession. After ratification of these constitutions, new governments could be elected, and the states would be restored to the Union with full congressional representation. But only those southerners who had taken the oath of amnesty and had been eligible to vote on the day the state seceded could participate in this process. Thus unpardoned whites and former slaves were not eligible.

If Johnson intended to strip former aristocrats of their power, he did not hold to his plan. The old white

Presidential Reconstruction

leadership proved resilient and influential; prominent Confederates won elections and turned up in various appointive offices. Then Johnson started pardoning planters and leading rebels. He hired additional clerks to prepare the necessary documents and then began to issue pardons to large categories of people. By September 1865, hundreds were issued in a single day. These pardons, plus the rapid return of planters' abandoned lands, restored the old elite to power and quickly gave Johnson an image as the South's champion.

Why did Johnson allow the planters to regain power? Personal vanity may have played a role, as he turned proud planters into pardon seekers. He was also determined to achieve a rapid Reconstruction in order to deny the Radicals any opportunity for the more thorough racial and political changes they desired in the South. And Johnson needed southern support in the 1866 elections; hence, he declared Reconstruction complete only eight months after Appomattox. Thus, in December 1865, many Confederate congressmen traveled to Washington to claim seats in the U.S. Congress. Even Alexander Stephens, vice president of the Confederacy, returned to Capitol Hill as a senator-elect from Georgia.

The election of such prominent rebels troubled many northerners. Some of the state conventions were slow to repudiate secession; others admitted only grudgingly that slavery was dead and wrote new laws to show it.

Furthermore, to define the status of freed men and women and control their labor, some legislatures merely

Black Codes

revised large sections of the slave codes by substituting the word *freedmen* for *slaves*. The new black codes compelled former slaves to carry passes, observe a curfew, live in housing provided by a landowner, and give up hope of entering many desirable occupations. Stiff vagrancy laws and restrictive labor contracts bound freedpeople to plantations, and "anti-enticement" laws punished anyone who tried to lure these workers to other employment. State-supported schools and orphanages excluded blacks entirely.

It seemed to northerners that the South was intent on returning African Americans to servility and that Johnson's Reconstruction policy held no one responsible for the terrible war. But memories of the war—not yet even a year over—were still raw and would dominate political behavior for several elections to come. Thus, the Republican majority in Congress decided to call a halt to the results of Johnson's plan. On reconvening, the House and Senate considered the credentials of the newly elected southern representatives and decided not to admit them. Instead, they bluntly challenged the president's authority and established a joint committee to study and investigate a new direction for Reconstruction.

The Congressional Reconstruction Plan

Northern congressmen were hardly unified, but they did not doubt their right to shape Reconstruction policy. The Constitution mentioned neither secession nor reunion, but it gave Congress the primary role in the admission of states. Moreover, the Constitution declared that the United States shall guarantee to each state a "republican form of government." This provision, legislators believed, gave them the authority to devise policies for Reconstruction.

They soon found that other constitutional questions affected their policies. What, for example, had rebellion done to the relationship between southern states and the Union? Lincoln had always believed secession impossible—the Confederate states had engaged in an "insurrection" within the Union in his view. Congressmen who favored vigorous Reconstruction measures argued that the war had broken the Union and that the South was subject to the victor's will. Moderate congressmen held that the states had forfeited their rights through rebellion and thus had come under congressional supervision.

These theories mirrored the diversity of Congress itself. Northern Democrats, weakened by their opposition to the war in its final year, denounced any idea of racial equality and supported Johnson's policies.

The Radicals

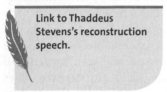

Link to Thaddeus Stevens's reconstruction speech.

Conservative Republicans, despite their party loyalty, favored a limited federal role in Reconstruction. The Radical Republicans, led by Thaddeus Stevens, Charles Sumner, and George Julian, wanted to transform the South. Although a minority in their party, they had the advantage of clearly defined goals. They believed it was essential to democratize the South, establish public education, and ensure the rights of the freedpeople. They favored black suffrage, supported some land confiscation and redistribution, and were willing to exclude the South from the Union for several years if necessary to achieve their goals.

Born of the war and its outcome, the Radicals brought a new civic vision to American life; they wanted to create an activist federal government and the beginnings of racial equality. A large group of moderate Republicans, led by Lyman Trumbull, opposed Johnson's leniency but wanted to restrain the Radicals. Trumbull and the moderates were, however, committed to federalizing the enforcement of civil, if not political, rights for the freedmen.

One overwhelming political reality faced all four groups: the 1866 elections. Ironically, Johnson and the Democrats sabotaged the possibility of a conservative coalition. They refused to cooperate with conservative or moderate Republicans and insisted that Reconstruction was over, that the new state governments were legitimate, and that southern representatives should be admitted to Congress. Among the Republicans, the Radicals' influence grew in proportion to Johnson's intransigence and outright provocation.

Trying to work with Johnson, Republicans believed a compromise had been reached in the spring of 1866.

Congress Versus Johnson

Under its terms, Johnson would agree to two modifications of his program: extension of the Freedmen's Bureau for another year and passage of a civil rights bill to counteract the black codes. This bill would force southern courts to practice equality under the ultimate scrutiny of the federal judiciary. Its provisions applied to public, not private, acts of discrimination. The Civil Rights Bill of 1866 was the first statutory definition of the rights of American citizens and is still on the books today.

Johnson destroyed the compromise, however, by vetoing both bills (they later became law when Congress overrode the president's veto). Denouncing any change in his program, the president condemned Congress's action and revealed his own racism. Because the civil rights bill defined U.S. citizens as native-born persons who were taxed, Johnson claimed it discriminated against "large

Link to the text of President Johnson's veto of the Civil Rights Bill of 1866.

▲ The Memphis race riots during Reconstruction. Unarmed blacks are gunned down by well-armed whites in this scene, reinforced by a Congressional investigation.

Library of Congress

numbers of intelligent, worthy, and patriotic foreigners . . . in favor of the negro." The bill, he said, operated "in favor of the colored and against the white race."

All hope of presidential-congressional cooperation was now dead. In 1866, newspapers reported daily violations of blacks' rights in the South and carried alarming accounts of antiblack violence—notably in Memphis and New Orleans, where police aided brutal mobs in their attacks. In Memphis, forty blacks were killed and twelve schools burned by white mobs, and in New Orleans, the toll was thirty-four African Americans dead and two hundred wounded. Such violence convinced Republicans, and the northern public, that more needed to be done. A new Republican plan took the form of the Fourteenth Amendment to the Constitution.

Of the five sections of the Fourteenth Amendment, the first would have the greatest legal significance in later

Fourteenth Amendment

years. It conferred citizenship on "all persons born or naturalized in the United States" and prohibited states from abridging their constitutional "privileges and immunities" (see the Appendix for the Constitution and all amendments). It also barred any state from taking a person's life, liberty, or property "without due process of law" and from denying "equal protection of the laws." These resounding phrases have become powerful guarantees of African Americans' civil rights—indeed, of the rights of all citizens, except for Indians, who were not granted citizenship rights until 1924.

Nearly universal agreement emerged among Republicans on the amendment's second and third sections. The fourth declared the Confederate debt null and void, and guaranteed the war debt of the United States. Northerners rejected the notion of paying taxes to reimburse those who had financed a rebellion, and business groups agreed on the necessity of upholding the credit of the U.S. government. The second and third sections barred Confederate leaders from holding state and federal office. Only Congress, by a two-thirds vote of each house, could remove the penalty. The amendment thus guaranteed a degree of punishment for the leaders of the Confederacy.

The second section of the amendment also dealt with representation and embodied the compromises that produced the document. Northerners disagreed about whether blacks should have the right to vote. As a citizen of Indiana wrote to a southern relative, "[a]lthough there is a great deal [of] profession among us for the relief of the darkey yet I think much of it is far from being sincere. I guess we want to compel you to do right by them while we are not willing ourselves to do so." Those arched words are indicative not only of how revolutionary Reconstruction had become, but also of how far the public will, North and South, lagged behind the enactments that became new constitutional cornerstones. Many northern states still maintained black disfranchisement laws during Reconstruction.

Emancipation finally ended the three-fifths clause for the purpose of counting blacks, which would increase southern representation. Thus, the postwar South stood to gain power in Congress, and if white southerners did not allow blacks to vote, former secessionists would derive the political benefit from emancipation. That was more irony than most northerners could bear. So Republicans determined that, if a southern state did not grant black men the vote, their representation would be reduced proportionally. If they did enfranchise black men, their representation would be increased proportionally. This compromise avoided a direct enactment of black suffrage but would deliver future black southern voters to the Republican Party.

The Fourteenth Amendment specified for the first time that voters were "male" and ignored female citizens, black and white. For this reason, it provoked a strong reaction from the women's rights movement. Advocates of women's equality had worked with abolitionists for decades, often subordinating their cause to that of the slaves. During the drafting of the Fourteenth Amendment, however, female activists demanded to be heard. Prominent leaders, such as Elizabeth Cady Stanton and Susan B. Anthony, ended their alliance with abolitionists and fought for women, while others remained committed to the idea that it was "the Negro's hour." Thus, the amendment infused new life into the women's rights movement and caused considerable strife among old allies. Many male former abolitionists, white and black, were willing to delay the day of woman suffrage in favor of securing freedmen the right to vote in the South.

In 1866, however, the major question in Reconstruction politics was how the public would

The South's and Johnson's Defiance

respond to the congressional initiative. Johnson did his best to block the Fourteenth Amendment in both North and South. Condemning Congress for its refusal to seat southern representatives, the president urged state legislatures in the South to vote against ratification. Every southern legislature, except Tennessee's, rejected the amendment by a wide margin.

To present his case to northerners, Johnson organized a National Union Convention and took to the stump himself. In an age when active personal campaigning was rare for a president, Johnson boarded a special train for a "swing around the circle" that carried his message into the Northeast, the Midwest, and then back to Washington. In city after city, he criticized the Republicans in a ranting, undignified style. Increasingly, audiences rejected his views, hooting and jeering at him. In this whistle-stop tour, Johnson began to hand out American flags with thirty-six rather than twenty-five stars, declaring the Union already restored. At many towns, he likened himself to a "persecuted" Jesus who might now be martyred "upon the cross" for his magnanimity toward the South.

And, repeatedly, he labeled the Radicals "traitors" for their efforts to take over Reconstruction.

The elections of 1866 were a resounding victory for Republicans in Congress. Radicals and moderates whom Johnson had denounced won reelection by large margins, and the Republican majority grew to two-thirds of both houses of Congress. The North had spoken clearly: Johnson's official policies of states' rights and white supremacy were prematurely giving the advantage to rebels and traitors. Although the Radicals may have been out ahead of public opinion, most northerners feared Johnson's approach more. Thus, Republican congressional leaders won a mandate to pursue their Reconstruction plan.

But Johnson and southern intransigence had brought the plan to an impasse. Nothing could be accomplished as long as the "Johnson governments" existed and the southern electorate remained exclusively white. Republicans resolved to form new state governments in the South and enfranchise the freedmen.

After some embittered debate in which Republicans and the remaining Democrats in Congress argued over the meaning and memory of the Civil War itself, the First Reconstruction Act passed in March 1867. This plan, under which the southern states were actually readmitted to the Union, incorporated only a part of the Radical program. Union generals, commanding small garrisons of troops and charged with supervising elections, assumed control in five military

Reconstruction Acts of 1867–1868

districts in the South (see Map 16.1). Confederate leaders designated in the Fourteenth Amendment were barred from voting until new state constitutions were ratified. The act guaranteed freedmen the right to vote in elections as well as serve in state constitutional conventions and in subsequent elections. In addition, each southern state was required to ratify the Fourteenth Amendment, to ratify its new constitution by majority vote, and to submit it to Congress for approval (see Table 16.1).

Thus, African Americans gained an opportunity to fight for a better life through the political process, and ex-Confederates were given what they interpreted as a bitter pill to swallow in order to return to the Union. The Second, Third, and Fourth Reconstruction Acts, passed between March 1867 and March 1868, provided the details of operation for voter registration boards, the adoption of constitutions, and the administration of "good faith" oaths on the part of white southerners.

In the words of one historian, the Radicals succeeded in "clipping Johnson's wings." But they had hoped Congress could do much more. Thaddeus Stevens, for example, argued that economic opportunity was essential to the freedmen. "If we do not furnish them with homesteads from forfeited and rebel property," Stevens declared, "and hedge them around with protective laws . . . we had better left them in bondage." Stevens therefore drew up a plan for extensive confiscation and redistribution of land, but it was never realized.

Failure of Land Redistribution

Table 16.1 Plans for Reconstruction Compared

	Johnson's Plan	Radicals' Plan	Fourteenth Amendment	Reconstruction Act of 1867
Voting	Whites only; high-ranking Confederate leaders must seek pardons	Give vote to black males	Southern whites may decide but can lose representation if they deny black suffrage	Black men gain vote; whites barred from office by Fourteenth Amendment cannot vote while new state governments are being formed
Officeholding	Many prominent Confederates regain power	Only loyal white and black males eligible	Confederate leaders barred until Congress votes amnesty	Fourteenth Amendment in effect
Time out of Union	Brief	Several years; until South is thoroughly democratized	Brief	3–5 years after war
Other change in southern society	Little; gain of power by yeomen not realized; emancipation grudgingly accepted, but no black civil or political rights	Expand public education; confiscate land and provide farms for freedmen; expansion of activist federal government	Probably slight, depending on enforcement	Considerable, depending on action of new state governments

Map 16.1 The Reconstruction

This map shows the five military districts established when Congress passed the Reconstruction Act of 1867. As the dates within each state indicate, conservative Democratic forces quickly regained control of government in four southern states. So-called Radical Reconstruction was curtailed in most of the others as factions within the weakened Republican Party began to cooperate with conservative Democrats.

Source: Copyright © Cengage Learning

Racial fears among whites and an American obsession with the sanctity of private property made land redistribution unpopular. Northerners were accustomed to a limited role for government, and the business community staunchly opposed any interference with private-property rights, even for former Confederates. Thus, black farmers were forced to seek work in a hostile environment in which landowners opposed their acquisition of land.

Congress's quarrels with Andrew Johnson grew still worse. To restrict Johnson's influence and safeguard its plan, Congress passed a number of controversial laws. First, it limited Johnson's power over the army by requiring the president to issue military orders through the General of the Army, Ulysses S. Grant, who could not be dismissed without the Senate's consent. Then Congress passed the Tenure of Office Act, which gave the Senate power to approve changes in the president's cabinet. Designed to protect Secretary of War Stanton, who sympathized with the Radicals, this law violated the tradition that a president controlled appointments to his own cabinet.

All of these measures, as well as each of the Reconstruction Acts, were passed by a two-thirds over-

Constitutional Crisis

ride of presidential vetoes. The situation led some to believe that the federal government had reached a stage of "congressional tyranny" and others to conclude that Johnson had become an obstacle to the legitimate will of the people in reconstructing the nation on a just and permanent basis.

Johnson took several belligerent steps of his own. He issued orders to military commanders in the South, limiting their powers and increasing the powers of the civil governments he had created in 1865. Then he removed military officers who were conscientiously enforcing Congress's new law, preferring commanders who allowed disqualified Confederates to vote. Finally, he tried to remove Secretary of War Stanton. With that attempt, the confrontation reached its climax.

Impeachment is a political procedure provided for in the Constitution as a remedy for crimes or serious abuses of power by presidents, federal judges, and other high government officials. Those impeached (judged or politically indicted) in the House are then tried in the Senate. Historically, this power has generally not been used as a means to investigate and judge the private lives of presidents, although in recent

Impeachment of President Johnson

times it was used in this manner in the case of President Bill Clinton.

Twice in 1867, the House Judiciary Committee had considered impeachment of Johnson, rejecting the idea once and then recommending it by only a 5-to-4 vote. That recommendation was decisively defeated by the House. After Johnson tried to remove Stanton, however, a third attempt to impeach the president carried easily in early 1868. The indictment concentrated on his violation of the Tenure of Office Act, though many modern scholars regard his efforts to obstruct enforcement of the Reconstruction Act of 1867 as a far more serious offense.

Johnson's trial in the Senate lasted more than three months. The prosecution, led by Radicals, attempted to prove that Johnson was guilty of "high crimes and misdemeanors." But they also argued that the trial was a means to judge Johnson's performance, not a judicial determination of guilt or innocence. The Senate ultimately rejected such reasoning, which could have made removal from office a political weapon against any chief executive who disagreed with Congress. Although a majority of senators voted to convict Johnson, the prosecution fell one vote short of the necessary two-thirds majority. Johnson remained in office, politically weakened and with less than a year left in his term. Some Republicans backed away from impeachment because they had their eyes on the 1868 election and did not want to hurt their prospects of regaining the White House.

In the 1868 presidential election, Ulysses S. Grant, running as a Republican, defeated Horatio Seymour, a New York Democrat. Grant was

Election of 1868

not a Radical, but his platform supported congressional Reconstruction and endorsed black suffrage in the South. (Significantly, Republicans stopped short of endorsing black suffrage in the North.) The Democrats, meanwhile, vigorously denounced Reconstruction and preached white supremacy. Indeed, in the 1868 election, the Democrats conducted the most openly racist campaign to that point in American history. Both sides waved the "bloody shirt," accusing each other as the villains of the war's sacrifices. By associating themselves with rebellion and with Johnson's repudiated program, the Democrats went down to defeat in all but eight states, though the popular vote was fairly close. Participating in their first presidential election ever on a wide scale, blacks decisively voted en masse for General Grant.

In office, Grant acted as an administrator of Reconstruction but not as its enthusiastic advocate. He vacillated in his dealings with the southern states, sometimes defending Republican regimes and sometimes currying favor with Democrats. On occasion, Grant called out federal troops to stop violence or enforce acts of Congress. But he never imposed a true military occupation on the South. Rapid demobilization had reduced a

▲ Thomas Waterman Wood, who had painted portraits of society figures in Nashville before the war, sensed the importance of Congress's decision in 1867 to enfranchise the freedmen. This oil painting, one in a series on suffrage, emphasizes the significance of the ballot for the black voter.

Cheekwood Museum of Art, Nashville, Tennessee

federal army of more than 1 million to 57,000 within a year of the surrender at Appomattox. Thereafter, the number of troops in the South continued to fall, until in 1874 there were only 4,000 in the southern states outside Texas. The later legend of "military rule," so important to southern claims of victimization during Reconstruction, was steeped in myth.

In 1869, the Radicals pushed through the Fifteenth Amendment, the final major measure in the constitutional revolution of Reconstruction.

Fifteenth Amendment

This measure forbade states to deny the right to vote "on account of race, color, or previous condition of servitude." Such wording did not guarantee the right to vote. It deliberately left states free to restrict suffrage on other grounds so that northern states could continue to deny suffrage to women and certain groups of men—Chinese immigrants, illiterates, and those too poor to pay poll taxes.

▲ A Republican Party brass band in action during the 1868 election campaign in Baton Rouge, Louisiana. The Union regimental colors and soldiers' caps demonstrate the strong federal presence in the South at this pivotal moment in radical Reconstruction.

Although several states outside the South refused to ratify, three-fourths of the states approved the measure, and the Fifteenth Amendment became law in 1870. It, too, had been a political compromise, and though African Americans rejoiced all across the land at its enactment, it left open the possibility for states to create countless qualification tests to obstruct voting in the future.

With passage of the Fifteenth Amendment, many Americans, especially supportive northerners, considered Reconstruction essentially completed. "Let us have done with Reconstruction," pleaded the *New York Tribune* in April 1870. "The country is tired and sick of it. . . . Let us have Peace!" But some northerners, like abolitionist Wendell Phillips, worried. "Our day," he warned, "is fast slipping away. Once let public thought float off from the great issue of the war, and it will take . . . more than a generation to bring it back again."

Politics and Reconstruction in the South

From the start, Reconstruction encountered the resistance of white southerners. In the black codes and in private attitudes, many whites stubbornly opposed emancipation, and the former planter class proved especially unbending because of their tremendous financial loss in slaves. In 1866, a Georgia newspaper frankly observed that "most of the white citizens believe that the institution of slavery was right, and . . . they will believe that the condition, which comes nearest to slavery, that can now be established will be the best." And for many poor whites who had never owned slaves and yet had sacrificed enormously in the war, destitution, plummeting agricultural prices, disease, and the uncertainties of a growing urban industrialization drove them off land, toward cities, and into hatred of the very idea of black equality.

Fearing loss of control over their slaves, some planters attempted to postpone freedom by denying or misrepresenting events. Former slaves reported that their owners "didn't tell them it was freedom" or "wouldn't let [them] go." Agents of the Freedmen's Bureau reported that "the old system of slavery [is] working with even more rigor than formerly at a few miles distant from any point where U.S. troops are stationed." To hold onto their workers, some landowners claimed control over black children and used guardianship and apprentice laws to bind black families to the plantation.

White Resistance

Whites also blocked blacks from acquiring land. A few planters divided up plots among their slaves, but most condemned the idea of making blacks landowners. A Georgia woman whose family was known for its support of religious education for slaves was outraged that two property owners planned to "rent their lands to the Negroes!" Such action was, she declared, "injurious to the best interest of the community."

Adamant resistance by whites soon manifested itself in other ways, including violence. In one North Carolina town, a local magistrate clubbed a black man on a public street, and in several states bands of "Regulators" terrorized blacks who displayed any independence. Amid their defeat, many planters believed, as a South Carolinian put it, that blacks "can't be governed except with the whip." And after President Johnson encouraged the South to resist congressional Reconstruction, many white conservatives worked hard to capture the new state governments while others boycotted the polls in an attempt to defeat Congress's plans.

Very few black men stayed away from the polls. Enthusiastically and hopefully, they voted Republican.

Black Voters and the Southern Republican Party

Most agreed with one man who felt he should "stick to the end with the party that freed me." Illiteracy did not prohibit blacks (or uneducated whites) from making intelligent choices. Although Mississippi's William Henry could read only "a little," he testified that he and his friends had no difficulty selecting the Republican ballot. "We stood around and watched," he explained. "We saw D. Sledge vote; he owned half the county. We knowed he voted Democratic so we voted the other ticket so it would be Republican." Women, who could not vote, encouraged their husbands and sons, and preachers exhorted their congregations to use the franchise. Zeal for voting spread through entire black communities.

Thanks to a large black turnout and the restrictions on prominent Confederates, a new southern Republican Party came to power in the constitutional conventions of 1868–1870. Republican delegates consisted of a sizable contingent of blacks (265 out of the total of just over 1,000 delegates throughout the South), some northerners who had moved to the South, and native southern whites who favored change. The new constitutions drafted by this Republican coalition were more democratic than anything previously adopted in the history of the South. They eliminated property qualifications for voting and holding office, and they turned many appointed offices into elective posts. They provided for public schools and institutions to care for the mentally ill, the blind, the deaf, the destitute, and the orphaned.

The conventions broadened women's rights in property holding and divorce. Usually, the goal was not to make women equal with men but to provide relief to

▲ Southern blacks attempting to vote are halted by White Leaguers in this engraving by J. H. Wares. The black man doffing his cap holds a "Republican ticket" but it will not get him to the ballot box, guarded by the election judge with a loaded pistol.

thousands of suffering debtors. In white families left poverty-stricken by the war and weighed down by debt, it was usually the husband who had contracted the debts. Thus, giving women legal control over their own property provided some protection to their families.

Under these new constitutions, the southern states elected Republican-controlled governments. For the first

Triumph of Republican Governments

time, the ranks of state legislators in 1868 included black southerners. It remained to be seen now how much social change these new governments would foster. Contrary to what white southerners would later claim, the Republican state governments did not disfranchise ex-Confederates as a group. James Lynch, a leading black politician from Mississippi, explained why African Americans shunned the "folly" of disfranchising whites. Unlike northerners who "can leave when it becomes too uncomfortable," landless former slaves "must be in friendly relations with the great body of the whites in the state. Otherwise . . . peace can be maintained only by a standing army." Despised and lacking material or social power, southern Republicans strove for acceptance, legitimacy, and safe ways to gain a foothold in a depressed economy.

Far from being vindictive toward the race that had enslaved them, most southern blacks treated leading

rebels with generosity and appealed to white southerners to adopt a spirit of fairness. In this way, the South's Republican Party condemned itself to defeat if white voters would not cooperate. Within a few years, most of the fledgling Republican parties in the southern states would be struggling for survival against violent white hostility. But for a time, some propertied whites accepted congressional Reconstruction as a reality.

Reflecting northern ideals and southern necessity, the Reconstruction governments enthusiastically promoted industry. Accordingly, Reconstruction legislatures encouraged investment with loans, subsidies, and short-term exemptions from taxation. The southern railroad system was rebuilt and expanded, and coal and iron mining made possible Birmingham's steel plants. Between 1860 and 1880, the number of manufacturing establishments in the South nearly doubled.

Industrialization and Mill Towns

This emphasis on big business, however, produced higher state debts and taxes, drew money away from schools and other programs, and multiplied possibilities for corruption in state legislatures. The alliance between business and government took firm hold, often at the expense of the needs of common farmers and laborers. It also locked Republicans into a conservative strategy and doomed them to failure in building support among poorer whites.

Poverty remained the lot of vast numbers of southern whites. On a daily basis during the Reconstruction years, they had to subordinate politics to the struggle for livelihood. The war had caused a massive one-time loss of income-producing wealth, such as livestock, and a steep decline in land values. From 1860 to 1880, the South's share of per capita income fell from nearly equal to only 51 percent of the national average. In many regions, the old planter class still ruled the best land and access to credit or markets.

As many poor whites and blacks found farming less tenable, they moved to cities and new mill towns. Industrialization did not sweep the South as it did the North, but it certainly laid deep roots. Attracting textile mills to southern towns became a competitive crusade. "Next to God," shouted a North Carolina evangelist, "what this town needs is a cotton mill!" In 1860, the South counted some 10,000 mill workers; by 1880, the number grew to 16,741 and by the end of the century, to 97,559. In thousands of human dramas, poor southerners began the multigenerational journey from farmer to mill worker and other forms of low-income urban wage earner.

Policies appealing to African American voters never went beyond equality before the law. In fact, the whites who controlled the southern Republican Party were reluctant to allow blacks a share of offices proportionate to

Republicans and Racial Equality

their electoral strength. Aware of their weakness, black leaders did not push very far for revolutionary economic or social change. In every southern state, they led efforts to establish public schools, although they did not press for integrated facilities. In 1870, South Carolina passed the first comprehensive school law in the South. By 1875, 50 percent of black school-age children in that state were enrolled in school, and approximately one-third of the three thousand teachers were black.

Some African American politicians did fight for civil rights and integration. Many were from cities such as New Orleans or Mobile, where large populations of light-skinned free blacks had existed before the war. Their experience in such communities had made them sensitive to issues of status, and they spoke out for open and equal public accommodations. Laws requiring equal accommodations won passage, but they often went unenforced.

The vexing questions of land reform and enforcement of racial equality, however, all but overwhelmed the Republican governments. Land reform largely failed because in most states whites were in the majority, and former slaveowners controlled the best land and other sources of economic power. Economic progress was uppermost in the minds of most freedpeople. Black southerners needed land, and much land did fall into state hands for nonpayment of taxes. Such land was offered for sale in small lots. But most freedmen had too little cash to bid against investors or speculators. South Carolina established a land commission, but it could help only those with money to buy. Any widespread redistribution of land had to arise from Congress, which never supported such action.

Within a few years, as centrists in both parties met with failure, white hostility to congressional Reconstruction began to dominate. Some conservatives had always wanted to fight Reconstruction through pressure and racist propaganda. They put economic and social pressure on blacks: one black Republican reported that "my neighbors will not employ me, nor sell me a farthing's worth of anything." Charging that the South had been turned over to ignorant blacks, conservatives deplored "black domination," which became a rallying cry for a return to white supremacy.

Myth of "Negro Rule"

Such attacks were inflammatory propaganda and part of the growing myth of "Negro rule," which would serve as a central theme in battles over the memory of Reconstruction. African Americans participated in politics but hardly dominated or controlled events. They were a majority in only two out of ten state constitutional writing conventions (transplanted northerners were a majority in one). In the state legislatures, only in the lower house in South Carolina did blacks ever constitute a majority. Sixteen blacks won seats in Congress before Reconstruction was over, but none was ever elected

Pig Iron, Birmingham, *Harper's Weekly*, March 26, 1887

▲ One notable success in Reconstruction efforts to stimulate industry was Birmingham, Alabama. Here workers cast molten iron into blocks called pigs.

governor. Only eighteen served in a high state office, such as lieutenant governor, treasurer, superintendent of education, or secretary of state.

In all, some four hundred blacks served in political office during the Reconstruction era, a signal achievement by any standard. Although they never dominated the process, they established a rich tradition of government service and civic activism. Elected officials, such as Robert Smalls in South Carolina, labored tirelessly for cheaper land prices, better healthcare, access to schools, and the enforcement of civil rights for black people. For too long, the black politicians of Reconstruction were the forgotten heroes of this seedtime of America's long civil rights movement.

Conservatives also assailed the allies of black Republicans. Their propaganda denounced whites from

Carpetbaggers and Scalawags

the North as "carpetbaggers," greedy crooks planning to pour stolen tax revenues into their sturdy luggage made of carpet material. Immigrants from the North, who held the largest share of Republican offices, were all tarred with this rhetorical brush.

In fact, most northerners who settled in the South had come seeking business opportunities, as schoolteachers, or to find a warmer climate; most never entered politics. Those who did enter politics generally wanted to

democratize the South and to introduce northern ways, such as industry and public education. Carpetbaggers' ideals were tested by hard times and ostracism by white southerners.

Carpetbaggers' real actions never matched the sensational stereotypes, although by the mid-1870s even some northerners who soured on Reconstruction or despaired over southern violence endorsed the images. Thomas Wentworth Higginson, a Union officer and commander of an African-American regiment during the Civil War, suggested that any Yankee politician who remained in the South by 1874 was, more likely than not, a "mean man," a "scoundrel," and "like Shakespeare's Shylock." And that same year, the African-American editors of the *Christian Recorder* distanced themselves from carpetbaggers. The "corrupt political vampires who rob and cheat and prey upon the prejudices of our people" and "feed upon the political carcass of a prostrate state," the paper insisted, were not black folks' allies. The white southern counter-revolutionaries seemed to be winning the propaganda war.

Conservatives also invented the term *scalawag* to discredit any native white southerner who cooperated with the Republicans. A substantial number of southerners did so, including some wealthy and prominent men. Most scalawags, however, were yeoman farmers, men from mountain areas and nonslaveholding districts who had been Unionists under the Confederacy. They saw that

they could benefit from the education and opportunities promoted by Republicans. Sometimes banding together with freedmen, they pursued common class interests and hoped to make headway against the power of long-dominant planters. In the long run, however, the hope of such black-white coalitions floundered in the quicksand of racism.

Taxation was a major problem for the Reconstruction governments. Republicans wanted to repair the war's

Tax Policy and Corruption as Political Wedges

destruction, stimulate industry, and support such new ventures as public schools. But the Civil War had destroyed much of the South's tax base. One category of valuable property—slaves—had disappeared entirely. And hundreds of thousands of citizens had lost much of the rest of their property—money, livestock, fences, and buildings—to the war. Thus, an increase in taxes (sales, excise, and property) was necessary even to maintain traditional services. Inevitably, Republican tax policies aroused strong opposition, especially among the yeomen.

Corruption was another serious charge levied against the Republicans. Unfortunately, it was often true. Many carpetbaggers and black politicians engaged in fraudulent schemes, sold their votes, or padded expenses, taking part in what scholars recognize was a nationwide surge of corruption in an age ruled by "spoilsmen" (see pages 548). Corruption carried no party label, but the Democrats successfully pinned the blame on unqualified blacks and greedy carpetbaggers among southern Republicans.

All these problems hurt the Republicans, whose leaders also allowed factionalism along racial and class lines to

Ku Klux Klan

undermine party unity. But in many southern states, the deathblow came through violence. The Ku Klux Klan (its members altered the Greek word for "circle," *kuklos*), a secret veterans' club that began in Tennessee in 1866, spread through the South, and rapidly evolved into a terrorist organization. Violence against African Americans occurred from the first days of Reconstruction but became far more organized and purposeful after 1867. Klansmen sought to frustrate Reconstruction and keep the freedmen in subjection. Nighttime harassment, whippings, beatings, rapes, and murders became common, as terrorism dominated some counties and regions.

Although the Klan tormented blacks who stood up for their rights as laborers or individuals, its main purpose was political. Lawless nightriders made active Republicans the target of their attacks. Leading white and black Republicans were killed in several states. After freedmen who worked for a South Carolina scalawag started voting, terrorists visited the plantation and, in the words of one victim, "whipped every . . . [black] man they could lay their hands on." Klansmen also attacked

Union League clubs—Republican organizations that mobilized the black vote—and schoolteachers who were aiding the freedmen.

Klan violence was not a spontaneous outburst of racism; very specific social forces shaped and directed it. In North Carolina, for example, Alamance and Caswell Counties were the sites of the worst Klan violence. Slim Republican majorities there rested on cooperation between black voters and white yeomen, particularly those whose Unionism or discontent with the Confederacy had turned them against local Democratic officials. Together, these black and white Republicans had ousted officials long entrenched in power. The wealthy and powerful men in Alamance and Caswell who had lost their accustomed political control were the Klan's county officers and local chieftains. They organized a deliberate campaign of terror, recruiting members and planning atrocities. By intimidation and murder, the Klan weakened the Republican coalition and restored a Democratic majority.

Klan violence injured Republicans across the South. One of every ten black leaders who had been delegates to the 1867–1868 state constitutional conventions was attacked, seven fatally. In one judicial district of North Carolina, the Ku Klux Klan was responsible for twelve murders, over seven hundred beatings, and other acts of violence, including rape and arson. A single attack on Alabama Republicans in the town of Eutaw left four blacks dead and fifty-four wounded. In South Carolina,

The Granger Collection, New York

▲ Cartoon, depicting a freedman, John Campbell, vainly begging for mercy in Moore County, North Carolina, August 10, 1871. The image evokes the power, fear, and mystery of the Klan without actually showing its bloody deeds.

five hundred masked Klansmen lynched eight black prisoners at the Union County jail, and in nearby York County, the Klan committed at least eleven murders and hundreds of whippings. According to historian Eric Foner, the Klan "made it virtually impossible for Republicans to campaign or vote in large parts of Georgia."

Thus, a combination of difficult fiscal problems, Republican mistakes, racial hostility, and terror brought down the Republican regimes. In most southern states, Radical Reconstruction lasted only a few years (see Map 16.1). The most enduring failure of Reconstruction, however, was not political; it was social and economic. Reconstruction failed to alter the South's social structure or its distribution of wealth and power.

Retreat from Reconstruction

During the 1870s, northerners increasingly lost the political will to sustain Reconstruction in the South as a vast economic and social transformation occurred in their own region as well as in the West. Radical Republicans like Albion Tourgée, a former Union soldier who

The Granger Collection, New York

▲ *The Carpetbagger*, American lithograph song sheet music cover, ca. 1869. Emanating from the heyday of anti-carpetbagger propaganda, the figure seems to be part Uncle Sam and part scheming scoundrel with his bag full of Yankee notions, both religious and secular.

moved to North Carolina and was elected a judge, condemned Congress's timidity. Turning the freedman out on his own without protection, said Tourgée, constituted "cheap philanthropy." Indeed, many African Americans believed that, during Reconstruction, the North "threw all the Negroes on the world without any way of getting along." As the North underwent its own transformations and lost interest in the South's dilemmas, Reconstruction collapsed.

In one southern state after another, Democrats regained control, and they threatened to defeat

Political Implications of Klan Terrorism

Republicans in the North as well. Whites in the old Confederacy referred to this decline of Reconstruction as "southern redemption," and during the 1870s, "redeemer" Democrats claimed to be the saviors of the South from alleged "black domination" and "carpetbag rule." And for one of only a few times in American history, violence and terror emerged as a tactic in normal politics.

In 1870 and 1871, the violent campaigns of the Ku Klux Klan forced Congress to pass two Enforcement Acts and an anti-Klan law. These laws made actions by individuals against the civil and political rights of others a federal criminal offense for the first time. They also provided for election supervisors and permitted martial law and suspension of the writ of habeas corpus to combat murders, beatings, and threats by the Klan. Federal prosecutors used the laws rather selectively. In 1872 and 1873, Mississippi and the Carolinas saw many prosecutions; but in other states where violence flourished, the laws were virtually ignored. Southern juries sometimes refused to convict Klansmen; out of a total of 3,310 cases, only 1,143 ended in convictions. Although many Klansmen (roughly 2,000 in South Carolina alone) fled their state to avoid prosecution, and the Klan officially disbanded, the threat of violence did not end. Paramilitary organizations known as Rifle Clubs and Red Shirts often took the Klan's place.

Klan terrorism openly defied Congress, yet even on this issue there were ominous signs that the North's commitment to racial justice was fading. Some conservative but influential Republicans opposed the anti-Klan laws. Rejecting other Republicans' arguments that the Thirteenth, Fourteenth, and Fifteenth Amendments had made the federal government the protector of the rights of citizens, these dissenters echoed an old Democratic charge that Congress was infringing on states' rights. Senator Lyman Trumbull of Illinois declared that the states remained "the depositories of the rights of the individual." If Congress could punish crimes like assault or murder, he asked, "what is the need of the State governments?" For years, Democrats had complained of "centralization and consolidation"; now some Republicans seemed to agree with them. This opposition foreshadowed a more general revolt within Republican ranks in 1872.

Both immigration and industrialization surged in the North. Between 1865 and 1873, 3 million immigrants entered the country, most settling in the industrial cities of the North and West. Within only eight years, postwar industrial production increased by 75 percent. For the first time, nonagricultural workers outnumbered farmers, and wage earners outnumbered independent craftsmen. And by 1873, only Britain's industrial output was greater than that of the United States. Government financial policies did much to bring about this rapid growth. Low taxes on investment and high tariffs on manufactured goods aided the growth of a new class of powerful industrialists, especially railroad entrepreneurs.

Industrial Expansion and Reconstruction in the North

Railroads became the symbol of and the stimulus for the American age of capital. From 1865 to 1873, thirty-five thousand miles of new track were laid, a total exceeding the entire national rail network of 1860. Railroad building fueled the banking industry and made Wall Street the center of American capitalism. Eastern railroad magnates, such as Thomas Scott of the Pennsylvania Railroad, the largest corporation of its time, created economic empires with the assistance of huge government subsidies of cash and land. Railroad corporations also bought up mining operations, granaries, and lumber companies. In Congress and in every state legislature, big business now employed lobbyists to curry favor with government. Corruption ran rampant; some congressmen and legislators were paid annual retainers by major companies.

This soaring capitalist-political alliance led as well to an intensified struggle between labor and capital. As captains of industry amassed unprecedented fortunes in an age with no income tax, gross economic inequality polarized American society. The work force, worried a prominent Massachusetts business leader, was in a "transition state . . . living in boarding houses" and becoming a "permanent factory population." In Cincinnati, three large factories employed as many workers as the city's thousands of small shops. In New York or Philadelphia, workers increasingly lived in dark, unhealthy tenement housing. Thousands would list themselves on the census as "common laborer" or "general jobber." Many of the free labor maxims of the Republican Party were now under great duress. Did the individual work ethic guarantee social mobility in America or erode, under the pressure of profit making, into a world of unsafe factories, child labor, and declining wages? In 1868, the Republicans managed to pass an eight-hour workday bill in Congress that applied to federal workers. The "labor question" (see Chapter 18) now preoccupied northerners far more than the "southern" or the "freedmen" question.

Then, the Panic of 1873 ushered in over five years of economic contraction. Three million people lost their jobs as class attitudes diverged, especially in large cities.

Debtors and the unemployed sought easy-money policies to spur economic expansion (workers and farmers desperately needed cash). Businessmen, disturbed by the widespread strikes and industrial violence that accompanied the panic, fiercely defended property rights and demanded "sound money" policies. The chasm between farmers and workers on the one hand, and wealthy industrialists on the other, grew ever wider.

Disenchanted with Reconstruction, a largely northern group calling itself the Liberal Republicans bolted the party in 1872 and nominated Horace Greeley, the famous editor of the *New York Tribune*, for president. The Liberal Republicans were a varied group, including foes of corruption and advocates of a lower tariff. Normally such disparate elements would not cooperate with one another, but two popular and widespread attitudes united them: distaste for federal intervention in the South and an elitist desire to let market forces and the "best men" determine policy and events.

Liberal Republican Revolt

The Democrats also gave their nomination to Greeley in 1872. The combination was not enough to defeat Grant, who won reelection, but it reinforced Grant's desire to avoid confrontation with white southerners. Greeley's campaign for North-South reunion, for "clasping hands across the bloody chasm," was a bit premature to win at the polls but was a harbinger of the future in American politics. Organized Blue-Gray fraternalism (gatherings of Union and Confederate veterans) began as early as 1874. Grant continued to use military force sparingly and in 1875 refused a desperate request from the governor of Mississippi for troops to quell racial and political terrorism in that state.

Dissatisfaction with Grant's administration grew during his second term. Strong-willed but politically naive, Grant made a series of poor appointments. His secretary of war, his private secretary, and officials in the Treasury and Navy Departments were involved in bribery or tax-cheating scandals. Instead of exposing the corruption, Grant defended the culprits. In 1874, as Grant's popularity and his party's prestige declined, the Democrats recaptured the House of Representatives, signaling the end of the Radical Republican vision of Reconstruction.

The effect of Democratic gains in Congress was to weaken legislative resolve on southern issues. Congress had already lifted the political disabilities of the Fourteenth Amendment from many former Confederates. In 1872, it had adopted a sweeping Amnesty Act, which pardoned most of the remaining rebels and left only five hundred barred from political office holding. In 1875, Congress passed a Civil Rights Act, partly as a tribute to the recently deceased Charles Sumner, purporting to guarantee black people equal accommodations in public

General Amnesty

places, such as inns and theaters, but the bill was watered down and contained no effective provisions for enforcement. (The Supreme Court later struck down this law; see page 555.)

Democrats regained control of four state governments before 1872 and a total of eight by the end of January 1876 (see Map 16.1). In the North, Democrats successfully stressed the failure and scandals of Reconstruction governments. As opinion shifted, many Republicans sensed that their constituents were tiring of southern issues and the legacies of the war. Sectional reconciliation now seemed crucial for commerce. The nation was expanding westward rapidly, and the South was a new frontier for investment.

Nowhere did the new complexity and violence of American race relations play out so vividly as in the West.

The West, Race, and Reconstruction

As the Fourteenth Amendment and other enactments granted to blacks the beginnings of citizenship, other nonwhite peoples faced continued persecution. Across the West, the federal government pursued a policy of containment against Native Americans. In California, where white farmers and ranchers often forced Indians into captive labor, some civilians practiced a more violent form of "Indian hunting." By 1880, thirty years of such violence left an estimated forty-five hundred California Indians dead at the hands of white settlers.

In Texas and the Southwest, the rhetoric of national expansion still deemed Mexicans and other mixed-race Hispanics to be debased, "lazy," and incapable of self-government. And in California and other states of the Far West, thousands of Chinese immigrants became the victims of brutal violence. Few whites had objected to the Chinese who did the dangerous work of building railroads through the Rocky Mountains. But when the Chinese began to compete for urban, industrial jobs, great conflict emerged. Anticoolie clubs appeared in California in the 1870s, seeking laws against Chinese labor, fanning the flames of racism, and organizing vigilante attacks on Chinese workers and the factories that employed them. Western politicians sought white votes by pandering to prejudice, and in 1879 the new California constitution denied the vote to Chinese.

If we view America from coast to coast, and not merely on the North-South axis, the Civil War and Reconstruction years both dismantled racial slavery and fostered a volatile new racial complexity, especially in the West. During the same age when early anthropologists employed elaborate theories of "scientific" racism to determine a hierarchy of racial types, the West was a vast region of racial mixing and conflict. Some African Americans, despite generations of mixture with Native Americans, asserted that they were more like whites than the nomadic, "uncivilized" Indians, while others, like the Creek freedmen of Indian Territory, sought an Indian

Granger Collection

▲ Anti-Chinese cartoon, "Every Dog (No Distinction of Color) Has His Day." The imagery here links Native Americans, African Americans, and Chinese immigrants in the same racist and xenophobic fear.

identity. In Texas, whites, Indians, blacks, and Hispanics had mixed for decades, and by the 1870s forced reconsideration in law and custom of who was white and who was not.

During Reconstruction, America was undergoing what one historian has called a reconstruction of the very idea of race itself. As it did so, tumbling into some of the darkest years of American race relations, the turbulence of the expanding West reinforced the new nationalism and the reconciliation of North and South based on a resurgent white supremacy.

Following the Civil War, pressure for expansion reemerged (see Chapter 22), and in 1867 Secretary of

Foreign Expansion

State William H. Seward arranged a vast addition of territory to the national domain through the purchase of Alaska from Russia. Opponents ridiculed Seward's $7.2 million venture, calling Alaska "Frigidia," "the Polar Bear Garden," and "Walrussia." But Seward convinced important congressmen of Alaska's economic potential, and other lawmakers favored the dawning of friendship with Russia.

Also in 1867, the United States took control of the Midway Islands, a thousand miles northwest of Hawai'i. And in 1870, President Grant tried unsuccessfully to

The "Back to Africa" Movement

In the wake of the Civil War, and especially after the despairing end of Reconstruction, some African Americans sought to leave the South for the American West or North, but also to relocate to Africa. Liberia had been founded in the 1820s by the white-led American Colonization Society (ACS), an organization dedicated to relocating blacks "back" in Africa. Some eleven thousand African Americans had emigrated voluntarily to Liberia by 1860, with largely disastrous results. Many died of disease, and others felt disoriented in the strange new land and ultimately returned to the United States.

Reconstruction reinvigorated the emigration impulse, especially in cotton-growing districts where blacks had achieved political power before 1870 but were crushed by violence and intimidation in the following decade. When blacks felt confident in their future, the idea of leaving America fell quiet; but when threatened or under assault, whole black communities dreamed of a place where they could become an independent "race," a "people," or a "nation" as their appeals often announced. Often that dream, more imagined than realized, lay in West Africa.

Before the Civil War, most blacks had denounced the ACS for its racism and its hostility to their sense of American birthright. But letters of inquiry flooded into the organization's headquarters after 1875. Wherever blacks felt the reversal of the promise of emancipation the keenest, they formed local groups such as the Liberia Exodus Association of Pinesville, Florida; or the Liberian Exodus Arkansas Colony; and many others.

At emigration conventions, and especially in churches, blacks penned letters to the ACS asking for maps or any information about a new African homeland. Some local organizers would announce eighty or a hundred recruits "widawake for Liberia," although such enthusiasm rarely converted into an Atlantic voyage. The impulse was genuine, however. "We wants to be a People," wrote the leader of a Mississippi emigration committee; "we can't be it heare and find that we ar compel to leve this Cuntry." Henry Adams, a former Louisiana slave, Union soldier, and itinerant emigration organizer, advocated Liberia, but also supported "Kansas fever" with both Biblical and natural rights agruments. "God . . . has a place and a land for all his people," he wrote in 1879. "It is not that we think the soil climate or temperature" elsewhere is "more congenial to us—but it is the idea that pervades our breast 'that at last we will be free,' free from oppression, free from tyranny, free from bulldozing, murderous southern whites."

By the 1890s, Henry McNeal Turner, a free-born former Georgia Reconstruction politician, and now Bishop of the African Methodist Episcopal Church, made three trips to Africa and vigorously campaigned through press and pulpit for blacks to "Christianize" and "civilize" Africa. Two shiploads of African Americans sailed to Liberia, although most returned disillusioned or ill. Turner's plan of "Africa for the Africans" was as much a religious vision as an emigration system, but like all such efforts then and since, it reflected the despair of racial conditions in America more than realities in Africa. The numbers do not tell the tale of the depth of the impulse in this link to the world: in 1879–1880, approximately twenty-five thousand southern blacks moved to Kansas, whereas from 1865 to 1900, just under four thousand emigrated to West Africa.

◄ Departure of African American emigrants to Liberia aboard the *Laurada*, Savannah, Georgia, March 1896. The large crowd bidding farewell to the much smaller group aboard the ship may indicate both the fascination and the ambivalence for this issue among blacks in the South. (*Illustrated American Magazine*, March 21, 1896).

© Bettmann/Corbis

annex the Dominican Republic. Seward and his successor, Hamilton Fish, also resolved troubling Civil War grievances against Great Britain. Through diplomacy they arranged a financial settlement of claims on Britain for damage done by the *Alabama* and other cruisers built in England and sold to the Confederacy. They recognized that sectional reconciliation in Reconstruction America would serve new ambitions for world commerce and expansion.

Meanwhile, the Supreme Court played its part in the northern retreat from Reconstruction. During the Civil

Judicial Retreat from Reconstruction

War, the Court had been cautious and inactive. Reaction to the *Dred Scott* decision (1857) had been so vehement, and the Union's wartime emergency so great, that the Court had avoided interference with government actions. The justices breathed a collective sigh of relief, for example, when legal technicalities prevented them from reviewing the case of Clement Vallandigham, a Democratic opponent of Lincoln's war effort who had been convicted by a military tribunal of aiding the enemy. But in 1866, a similar case, *Ex parte Milligan*, reached the Court.

Lambdin P. Milligan of Indiana had plotted to free Confederate prisoners of war and overthrow state governments. For these acts, a military court sentenced Milligan, a civilian, to death. Milligan challenged the authority of the military tribunal, claiming he had a right to a civil trial. Reasserting its authority, the Supreme Court declared that military trials were illegal when civil courts were open and functioning.

In the 1870s, the Court successfully renewed its challenge to Congress's actions when it narrowed the meaning and effectiveness of the Fourteenth Amendment. The *Slaughter-House* cases (1873) began in 1869, when the Louisiana legislature granted one company a monopoly on the slaughtering of livestock in New Orleans. Rival butchers in the city promptly sued. Their attorney, former Supreme Court justice John A. Campbell, argued that Louisiana had violated the rights of some of its citizens in favor of others. The Fourteenth Amendment, Campbell contended, had revolutionized the constitutional system by bringing individual rights under federal protection, safeguarding them from state interference.

But in the *Slaughter-House* decision, the Supreme Court dealt a stunning blow to the scope of the Fourteenth Amendment. The Court declared state citizenship and national citizenship separate. National citizenship involved only matters such as the right to travel freely from state to state, and only such narrow rights, held the Court, were protected by the Fourteenth Amendment.

The Supreme Court also concluded that the butchers who sued had not been deprived of their rights or property in violation of the due-process clause of the amendment. Shrinking from a role as "perpetual censor" for civil rights, the Court's majority declared that the framers of the recent amendments had not intended to "destroy" the federal system, in which the states exercised "powers for domestic and local government, including the regulation of civil rights." Thus, the justices severely limited the amendment's potential for securing and protecting the rights of black citizens—its original intent.

The next day, the Court decided *Bradwell v. Illinois*, a case in which Myra Bradwell, a female attorney, had been denied the right to practice law in Illinois because she was a married woman, and hence not considered a free agent. Pointing to the Fourteenth Amendment, Bradwell's attorneys contended the state had unconstitutionally abridged her "privileges and immunities" as a citizen. The Supreme Court rejected her claim, declaring a woman's "paramount destiny . . . to fulfill the noble and benign offices of wife and mother."

In 1876, the Court weakened the Reconstruction era amendments even further by emasculating the enforcement clause of the Fourteenth Amendment and revealing deficiencies inherent in the Fifteenth Amendment. In *U.S. v. Cruikshank,* the Court overruled the conviction under the 1870 Enforcement Act of Louisiana whites who had attacked a meeting of blacks and conspired to deprive them of their rights. The justices ruled that the Fourteenth Amendment did not give the federal government power to act against these whites who had murdered possibly as many as one hundred blacks. The duty of protecting citizens' equal rights, the Court said, "rests alone with the States." Such judicial conservatism, practiced by justices, all of whom had been appointed by Republican presidents Lincoln and Grant, left a profound imprint down through the next century, blunting the revolutionary potential in the Civil War amendments.

As the 1876 elections approached, most political observers saw that the nation was increasingly focused on

Disputed Election of 1876 and Compromise of 1877

economic issues and that the North was no longer willing to pursue the goals of Reconstruction. The results of a disputed presidential election confirmed this fact. Samuel J. Tilden, the Democratic governor of New York, ran strongly in the South and needed only one more electoral vote to triumph over Rutherford B. Hayes, the Republican nominee. Nineteen electoral votes from Louisiana, South Carolina, and Florida (the only southern states not yet under Democratic rule) were disputed; both Democrats and Republicans claimed to have won in those states despite fraud committed by their opponents (see Map 16.2).

To resolve this unprecedented situation, Congress established a fifteen-member electoral commission. Membership on the commission was to be balanced

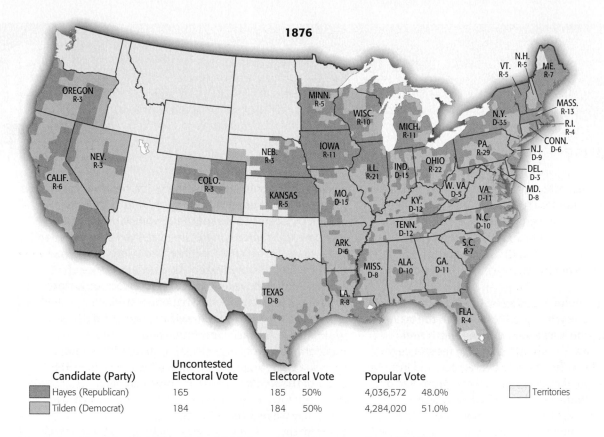

1876

Candidate (Party)	Uncontested Electoral Vote	Electoral Vote		Popular Vote	
Hayes (Republican)	165	185	50%	4,036,572	48.0%
Tilden (Democrat)	184	184	50%	4,284,020	51.0%

Territories

Map 16.2 Presidential Election of 1876 and the Compromise of 1877

In 1876, a combination of solid southern support and Democratic gains in the North gave Samuel Tilden the majority of popular votes, but Rutherford B. Hayes won the disputed election in the electoral college, after a deal satisfied Democratic wishes for an end to Reconstruction.

Source: Copyright © Cengage Learning

between Democrats and Republicans. Because the Republicans held the majority in Congress, they prevailed, 8 to 7, on every attempt to count the returns, with commission members voting along strict party lines. Hayes would become president if Congress accepted the commission's findings.

Congressional acceptance was not certain. Democrats controlled the House and could filibuster to block action on the vote. Many citizens worried that the nation would slip once again into civil war, as some southerners vowed, "Tilden or Fight!" The crisis was resolved when Democrats acquiesced in the election of Hayes based on a "deal" cut in a Washington hotel between Hayes's supporters and southerners who wanted federal aid to railroads, internal improvements, federal patronage, and removal of troops from southern states. Northern and southern Democrats simply decided not to contest the election of a Republican who was not going to continue Reconstruction policies in the South. Thus, Hayes became president, inaugurated privately inside the White

House to avoid any threat of violence. Southerners relished their promises of economic aid, and Reconstruction was unmistakably over.

Southern Democrats rejoiced, but African Americans grieved over the betrayal of their hopes for equality. The Civil War had brought emancipation, and Reconstruction had guaranteed their rights under law. But events and attitudes in larger white America were foreboding. In a Fourth of July speech in Washington, D.C., in 1875, Frederick Douglass anticipated this predicament. He reflected anxiously on the American centennial to be celebrated the following year. The nation, Douglass feared, would "lift to the sky its million voices in one grand Centennial hosanna of peace and good will to all the white race . . . from gulf to lakes and from sea to sea." Douglass looked back on fifteen years of unparalleled change for his people and worried about the hold of white supremacy on America's historical memory: "If war among the whites brought peace and liberty to the blacks, what will peace among the whites bring?" Douglass's

Legacy FOR A PEOPLE AND A NATION

The Lost Cause

All major wars and their aftermath compel a struggle over their memory. Sometimes losers prevail over winners in contests to shape historical memory. After the Civil War, white southerners and their northern allies constructed a "Lost Cause" tradition, a potent and racially exclusive version of the war and Reconstruction that persists in American culture today.

The Lost Cause emerged among ex-Confederates as a mourning ritual and a psychological response to the trauma of defeat. But with time it also took root in selective reinterpretations of the war's causes; in southern resistance to Reconstruction; in doctrines of white supremacy; and in a mythic, nostalgic popular culture enjoyed and promoted by northerners and southerners alike. Lost Cause advocates— from high-ranking officers to common soldiers writing reminiscences to women leading memorial associations—argued that the war had never been about slavery, that the Confederates had only lost to Yankee numbers and resources, and that the nation should reconcile by equally honoring both southern and northern sacrifice. In the industrial, urban, multiethinic America of the emerging twentieth century, an Old South of benevolent masters and faithful slaves, of Robert E. Lee portrayed as America's truest Christian soldier, provided a romantic, sentimentalized road to reunion.

From 1865 to the 1880s, this Confederate legend had been forged by wartime participants determined to vindicate the Confederacy. By the 1890s, however, Lost Cause culture emerged especially with the United Daughters of the Confederacy. Elite southern white women built monuments, lobbied congressmen, delivered lectures, ran essay contests for schoolchildren, and strove to control the content of history textbooks, all in the service of an exalted South. Above all, Lost Causers advocated a story not at all about loss, but about what one historian has called a "victory narrative." This new victory was the nation's triumph over the racial revolution and constitutional transformations of Reconstruction. In his 1881 memoir, Jefferson Davis argued that slavery "was in no wise the cause of the conflict" and that slaves had been "contented with their lot." He also declared the Lost Cause not lost: "Well may we rejoice in the regained possession of self-government.... This is the great victory ... a total non-interference by the Federal government in the domestic affairs of the States." These stories and images reverberated in the very heartbeat of Jim Crow America, and they endure in modern tastes for Civil War memorabilia, such as the epic *Gone with the Wind*, the 2003 film *Gods and Generals*, and uses of the Confederate flag to oppose civil rights and affirmative action. And the Confederate state rights tradition is employed today by some states and advocacy groups to resist federal stimulus money as well as national healthcare reform.

question would echo down through American political culture for decades.

SUMMARY

Reconstruction left a contradictory record. It was an era of tragic aspirations and failures but also of unprecedented legal, political, and social change. The Union victory brought about an increase in federal power, stronger nationalism, sweeping federal intervention in the southern states, and landmark amendments to the Constitution. But northern commitment to make these changes endure had eroded, and the revolution remained unfinished. The mystic sense of promise for new lives and liberties among the freedpeople, demonstrated in that first Decoration Day in Charleston, had eroded if not died.

The North embraced emancipation, black suffrage, and constitutional alterations strengthening the central government. But it did so to defeat the rebellion and secure the peace. As the pressure of these crises declined, Americans, especially in the North, retreated from Reconstruction. The American people and the courts maintained a preference for state authority and a distrust of federal power. The ideology of free labor dictated that property should be respected and that individuals should be self-reliant. Racism endured and transformed into the even more virulent forms of Klan terror and theories of black degeneration. Concern for the human rights of African Americans and other reforms frequently had less appeal than moneymaking in an individualistic, industrializing society.

New challenges began to overwhelm the aims of Reconstruction. How would the country develop its immense resources in an increasingly interconnected national economy? Could farmers, industrial workers, immigrants, and capitalists coexist? Industrialization not only promised prosperity but also wrought increased exploitation of labor. Moreover, industry increased the nation's power and laid the foundation for an enlarged American role in international affairs. The American imagination again turned to the conquest of new frontiers.

In the wake of the Civil War, Americans faced two profound tasks—the achievement of healing and the dispensing of justice. Both had to occur, but they never developed in historical balance. Making sectional reunion compatible with black freedom and equality overwhelmed the imagination in American political culture, and the nation still faced much of this dilemma more than a century later.

SUGGESTIONS FOR FURTHER READING

David W. Blight, *Race and Reunion: The Civil War in American Memory* (2001)

W. E. B. Du Bois, *Black Reconstruction in America* (1935)

Eric Foner, *Reconstruction: America's Unfinished Revolution, 1863–1877* (1988)

William Gillette, *Retreat from Reconstruction, 1869–1879* (1980)

Gerald Jaynes, *Branches Without Roots: The Genesis of the Black Working Class in the American South, 1862–1882* (1986)

Moon-Ho Jung, *Coolies and Cane: Race, Labor, and Sugar in the Age of Emancipation* (2006)

Michael Perman, *The Road to Redemption* (1984)

George Rable, *But There Was No Peace* (1984)

Heather Richardson, *West from Appomattox: The Reconstruction of America after the Civil War* (2007)

Elliot West, "Reconstructing Race," *Western Historical Quarterly* (Spring 2003)

CourseMate

Go to the CourseMate website for primary source links, study tools, and review materials for this chapter. www.cengagebrain.com

Appendix

Declaration of Independence in Congress, July 4, 1776

When, in the course of human events, it becomes necessary for one people to dissolve the political bonds which have connected them with another, and to assume, among the powers of the earth, the separate and equal station to which the laws of nature and of nature's God entitle them, a decent respect to the opinions of mankind requires that they should declare the causes which impel them to the separation.

We hold these truths to be self-evident: That all men are created equal; that they are endowed by their Creator with certain unalienable rights; that among these are life, liberty, and the pursuit of happiness; that, to secure these rights, governments are instituted among men, deriving their just powers from the consent of the governed; that whenever any form of government becomes destructive of these ends, it is the right of the people to alter or to abolish it, and to institute new government, laying its foundation on such principles, and organizing its powers in such form, as to them shall seem most likely to effect their safety and happiness. Prudence, indeed, will dictate that governments long established should not be changed for light and transient causes; and accordingly all experience hath shown that mankind are more disposed to suffer, while evils are sufferable, than to right themselves by abolishing the forms to which they are accustomed. But when a long train of abuses and usurpations, pursuing invariably the same object, evinces a design to reduce them under absolute despotism, it is their right, it is their duty, to throw off such government, and to provide new guards for their future security. Such has been the patient sufferance of these colonies; and such is now the necessity which constrains them to alter their former systems of government. The history of the present King of Great Britain is a history of repeated injuries and usurpations, all having in direct object the establishment of an absolute tyranny over these states. To prove this, let facts be submitted to a candid world.

He has refused his assent to laws, the most wholesome and necessary for the public good.

He has forbidden his governors to pass laws of immediate and pressing importance, unless suspended in their operation till his assent should be obtained; and, when so suspended, he has utterly neglected to attend to them.

He has refused to pass other laws for the accommodation of large districts of people, unless those people would relinquish the right of representation in the legislature, a right inestimable to them, and formidable to tyrants only.

He has called together legislative bodies at places unusual, uncomfortable, and distant from the depository of their public records, for the sole purpose of fatiguing them into compliance with his measures.

He has dissolved representative houses repeatedly, for opposing, with manly firmness, his invasions on the rights of the people.

He has refused for a long time, after such dissolutions, to cause others to be elected; whereby the legislative powers, incapable of annihilation, have returned to the people at large for their exercise; the state remaining, in the mean time, exposed to all the dangers of invasions from without and convulsions within.

He has endeavored to prevent the population of these states; for that purpose obstructing the laws for naturalization of foreigners; refusing to pass others to encourage their migration hither, and raising the conditions of new appropriations of lands.

He has obstructed the administration of justice, by refusing his assent to laws for establishing judiciary powers.

He has made judges dependent on his will alone, for the tenure of their offices, and the amount and payment of their salaries.

He has erected a multitude of new offices, and sent hither swarms of officers to harass our people and eat out their substance.

He has kept among us, in times of peace, standing armies, without the consent of our legislatures.

He has affected to render the military independent of, and superior to, the civil power.

He has combined with others to subject us to a jurisdiction foreign to our constitution, and unacknowledged by our laws, giving his assent to their acts of pretended legislation:

For quartering large bodies of armed troops among us;

For protecting them, by a mock trial, from punishment for any murders which they should commit on the inhabitants of these states;

For cutting off our trade with all parts of the world;

For imposing taxes on us without our consent;

For depriving us, in many cases, of the benefits of trial by jury;

For transporting us beyond seas, to be tried for pretended offenses;

For abolishing the free system of English laws in a neighboring province, establishing therein an arbitrary government, and enlarging its boundaries, so as to render it at once an example and fit instrument for introducing the same absolute rule into these colonies;

For taking away our charters, abolishing our most valuable laws, and altering fundamentally the forms of our governments;

For suspending our own legislatures, and declaring themselves invested with power to legislate for us in all cases whatsoever.

He has abdicated government here, by declaring us out of his protection and waging war against us.

He has plundered our seas, ravaged our coasts, burned our towns, and destroyed the lives of our people.

He is at this time transporting large armies of foreign mercenaries to complete the works of death, desolation, and tyranny already begun with circumstances of cruelty and perfidy scarcely paralleled in the most barbarous ages, and totally unworthy the head of a civilized nation.

He has constrained our fellow-citizens, taken captive on the high seas, to bear arms against their country, to become the executioners of their friends and brethren, or to fall themselves by their hands.

He has excited domestic insurrection among us, and has endeavored to bring on the inhabitants of our frontiers the merciless Indian savages, whose known rule of warfare is an undistinguished destruction of all ages, sexes, and conditions.

In every stage of these oppressions we have petitioned for redress in the most humble terms; our repeated petitions have been answered only by repeated injury. A prince, whose character is thus marked by every act which may define a tyrant, is unfit to be the ruler of a free people.

Nor have we been wanting in our attentions to our British brethren. We have warned them, from time to time, of attempts by their legislature to extend an unwarrantable jurisdiction over us. We have reminded them of the circumstances of our emigration and settlement here. We have appealed to their native justice and magnanimity; and we have conjured them, by the ties of our common kindred, to disavow these usurpations, which would inevitably interrupt our connections and correspondence. They, too, have been deaf to the voice of justice and of consanguinity. We must, therefore, acquiesce in the necessity which denounces our separation, and hold them, as we hold the rest of mankind, enemies in war, in peace friends.

We, therefore, the representatives of the United States of America, in General Congress assembled, appealing to the Supreme Judge of the world for the rectitude of our intentions, do, in the name and by the authority of the good people of these colonies, solemnly publish and declare, that these United Colonies are, and of right ought to be, FREE AND INDEPENDENT STATES; that they are absolved from all allegiance to the British crown, and that all political connection between them and the state of Great Britain is, and ought to be, totally dissolved; and that, as free and independent states, they have full power to levy war, conclude peace, contract alliances, establish commerce, and do all other acts and things which independent states may of right do. And for the support of this declaration, with a firm reliance on the protection of Divine Providence, we mutually pledge to each other our lives, our fortunes, and our sacred honor.

Articles of Confederation

Whereas the Delegates of the United States of America in Congress assembled did on the fifteenth day of November in the Year of our Lord One Thousand Seven Hundred and Seventy seven, and in the Second Year of the Independence of America agree to certain articles of Confederation and perpetual Union between the States of Newhampshire, Massachusetts Bay, Rhode Island and Providence Plantations, Connecticut, New York, New Jersey, Pennsylvania, Delaware, Maryland, Virginia, North Carolina, South Carolina and Georgia in the Words following, viz. "Articles of Confederation and perpetual Union between the states of Newhampshire, Massachusetts Bay, Rhode Island and Providence Plantations, Connecticut, New York, New Jersey, Pennsylvania, Delaware, Maryland, Virginia, North Carolina, South Carolina and Georgia.

Article I The Stile of this confederacy shall be "The United States of America."

Article II Each state retains its sovereignty, freedom and independence, and every Power, Jurisdiction and right, which is not by this confederation expressly delegated to the United States, in Congress assembled.

Article III The said states hereby severally enter into a firm league of friendship with each other, for their common defence, the security of their Liberties, and their mutual and general welfare, binding themselves to assist each other, against all force offered to, or attacks made upon them, or any of them, on account of religion, sovereignty, trade, or any other pretence whatever.

Article IV The better to secure and perpetuate mutual friendship and intercourse among the people of the different states in this union, the free inhabitants of each of these states, paupers, vagabonds and fugitives from Justice excepted, shall be entitled to all privileges and immunities of free citizens in the several states; and the people of each state shall have free ingress and regress to and from any other state, and shall enjoy therein all the privileges of trade and commerce, subject to the same duties, impositions and restrictions as the inhabitants thereof respectively, provided that such restriction shall not extend so far as to prevent the removal of property imported into any state, to any other state of which the Owner is an inhabitant; provided also that no imposition, duties or restriction shall be laid by any state, on the property of the united states, or either of them.

If any Person guilty of, or charged with treason, felony, or other high misdemeanor in any state, shall flee from Justice, and be found in any of the united states, he shall upon demand of the Governor or executive power, of the state from which he fled, be delivered up and removed to the state having jurisdiction of his offence.

Full faith and credit shall be given in each of these states to the records, acts and judicial proceedings of the courts and magistrates of every other state.

Article V For the more convenient management of the general interests of the united states, delegates shall be annually appointed in such manner as the legislature of each state shall direct, to meet in Congress on the first Monday in November, in every year, with a power reserved to each state, to recall its delegates, or any of them, at any time within the year, and to send others in their stead, for the remainder of the Year.

No state shall be represented in Congress by less than two, nor by more than seven Members; and no person shall be capable of being a delegate for more than three years in any term of six years; nor shall any person, being a delegate, be capable of holding any office under the united states, for which he, or another for his benefit receives any salary, fees or emolument of any kind.

Each state shall maintain its own delegates in a meeting of the states, and while they act as members of the committee of the states.

In determining questions in the united states, in Congress assembled, each state shall have one vote.

Freedom of speech and debate in Congress shall not be impeached or questioned in any Court, or place out of Congress, and the members of congress shall be protected in their persons from arrests and imprisonments, during the time of their going to and from, and attendance on congress, except for treason, felony, or breach of the peace.

Article VI No state without the Consent of the united states in congress assembled, shall send any embassy to, or receive any embassy from, or enter into any conference, agreement, or alliance or treaty with any King, prince or state; nor shall any person holding any office of profit or trust under the united states, or any of them, accept of any present, emolument, office or title of any kind whatever from any king, prince or foreign state; nor shall the united states in congress assembled, or any of them, grant any title of nobility.

No two or more states shall enter into any treaty, confederation or alliance whatever between them, without the consent of the united states in congress assembled, specifying accurately the purposes for which the same is to be entered into, and how long it shall continue.

No state shall lay any imposts or duties, which may interfere with any stipulations in treaties, entered into by the united states in congress assembled, with any king, prince or state, in pursuance of any treaties already proposed by congress, to the courts of France and Spain.

No vessels of war shall be kept up in time of peace by any state, except such number only, as shall be deemed necessary by the united states in congress assembled, for the defence of such state, or its trade; nor shall any body of forces be kept up by any state, in time of peace, except such number only, as in the judgment of the united states, in congress assembled, shall be deemed requisite to garrison the forts necessary for the defence of such state; but every state shall always keep up a well regulated and disciplined militia, sufficiently armed and accoutred, and shall provide and constantly have ready for use, in public stores, a due number of field pieces and tents, and a proper quantity of arms, ammunition and camp equipage.

No state shall engage in any war without the consent of the united states in congress assembled, unless such state be actually invaded by enemies, or shall have received certain advice of a resolution being formed by some nation of Indians to invade such state, and the danger is so imminent as not to admit of a delay, till the united states in congress assembled can be consulted: nor shall any state grant commissions to any ships or vessels of war, nor letters of marque or reprisal, except it be after a declaration of war by the united states in congress assembled, and then only against the kingdom or state and the subjects thereof, against which war has been so declared, and under such regulations as shall be established by the united states in congress assembled, unless such state be infested by pirates, in which case vessels of war may be fitted out for that occasion, and kept so long as the danger shall continue, or until the united states in congress assembled shall determine otherwise.

Article VII When land-forces are raised by any state for the common defence, all officers of or under the rank of colonel, shall be appointed by the legislature of each state respectively by whom such forces shall be raised, or in such manner as such state shall direct, and all vacancies shall be filled up by the state which first made the appointment.

Article VIII All charges of war, and all other expences that shall be incurred for the common defence or general welfare, and allowed by the united states in congress assembled, shall be defrayed out of a common treasury, which shall be supplied by the several states, in proportion to the value of all land within each state, granted to or surveyed for any Person, as such land and the buildings and improvements thereon shall be estimated according to such mode as the united states in congress assembled, shall from time to time direct and appoint. The taxes for paying that proportion shall be laid and levied by the authority and direction of the legislatures of the several states within the time agreed upon by the united states in congress assembled.

Article IX The united states in congress assembled, shall have the sole and exclusive right and power of determining on peace and war, except in the cases mentioned in the sixth article—of sending and receiving ambassadors—entering into treaties and alliances, provided that no treaty of commerce shall be made whereby the legislative power of the respective states shall be restrained from imposing such imposts and duties on foreigners, as their own people are subjected to, or from prohibiting the exportation or importation of any species of goods or commodities whatsoever—of establishing rules for deciding in all cases, what captures on land or water shall be legal, and in what manner prizes taken by land or naval forces in the service of the united states shall be divided or appropriated—of granting letters of marque and reprisal in times of peace—appointing courts for the trial of piracies and felonies committed on the high seas and establishing courts for receiving and determining final appeals in all cases of captures, provided that no member of congress shall be appointed a judge of any of the said courts.

The united states in congress assembled shall also be the last resort on appeal in all disputes and differences now subsisting or that hereafter may arise between two or more states concerning boundary, jurisdiction or any other cause whatever; which authority shall always be exercised in the manner following. Whenever the legislative or executive authority or lawful agent of any state in controversy with another shall present a petition to congress, stating the matter in question and praying for a hearing, notice thereof shall be given by order of congress to the legislative or executive authority of the other state in controversy, and a day assigned for the appearance of the parties by their lawful agents, who shall then be directed to appoint by joint consent, commissioners or judges to constitute a court for hearing and determining the matter in question: but if they cannot agree, congress shall name three persons out of each of the united states, and from the list of such persons each party shall alternately strike out one, the petitioners beginning, until the number shall be reduced to thirteen; and from that number not less than seven, nor more than nine names as congress shall direct, shall in the presence of congress be drawn out by lot, and the persons whose names shall be so drawn or any five of them, shall be commissioners or judges, to hear and finally determine the controversy, so always as a major part of the judges who shall hear the cause shall agree in the determination: and if either party shall neglect to attend at the day appointed, without showing reasons, which congress shall judge sufficient, or being present shall refuse to strike, the congress shall proceed to nominate three persons out of each state, and the secretary of congress shall strike in behalf of such party absent or refusing; and the judgment and sentence of the court to be appointed, in the manner before prescribed, shall be final and conclusive; and if any of the parties shall refuse to submit to the authority of such court, or to appear to defend their claim or cause, the court shall nevertheless proceed to pronounce sentence, or judgment, which shall in like manner be final and decisive, the judgment or sentence and other proceedings being in either case transmitted to congress, and lodged among the acts of congress for the security of the parties concerned: provided that every commissioner, before he sits in judgment, shall take an oath to be administered by one of the judges of the supreme or superior court of the state, where the cause shall be tried, "well and truly to hear and determine the matter in question, according to the best of his judgment, without favour, affection or hope of reward:" provided also that no state shall be deprived of territory for the benefit of the united states.

All controversies concerning the private right of soil claimed under different grants of two or more states, whose jurisdictions as they may respect such lands, and the states which passed such grants are adjusted, the said grants or either of them being at the same time claimed to have originated antecedent to such settlement of jurisdiction, shall on the petition of either party to the congress of the united states, be finally determined as near as may be in the same manner as is before prescribed for deciding disputes respecting territorial jurisdiction between different states.

The united states in congress assembled shall also have the sole and exclusive right and power of regulating the alloy and value of coin struck by their own authority, or by that of the respective states—fixing the standard of weights and measures throughout the united states—regulating the trade and managing all affairs with the Indians, not members of any of the states, provided that the legislative right of any state within its own limits be not infringed or violated—establishing and regulating post-offices from one state to another, throughout all the united states, and exacting such postage on the papers passing thro' the same as may be requisite to defray the expences of the said office—appointing all officers of the land forces, in the service of the united states, excepting regimental officers—appointing all the officers of the naval forces, and commissioning all officers whatever in the service of the united states—making rules for the government and regulation of the said land and naval forces, and directing their operations.

The united states in congress assembled shall have authority to appoint a committee, to sit in the recess of congress, to be denominated "A Committee of the States," and to consist of one delegate from each state; and to appoint such other committees and civil officers as may be necessary for managing the general affairs of the united states under their direction—to appoint one of their number to preside, provided that no person be allowed to serve in the office of president more than one year in any term of three years; to ascertain the necessary sums of Money to be raised for the service of the united states, and to appropriate and apply the same for defraying the public expences—to borrow money, or emit bills on the credit of the united states, transmitting every half year to the respective states an account of the sums of money so borrowed or emitted—to build and equip a navy—to agree upon the number of land forces, and to make requisitions from each state for its quota, in proportion to the number of white inhabitants in such state; which requisition shall be binding, and thereupon the legislature of each state shall appoint the regimental officers, raise the men and cloath, arm and equip them in a soldier like manner, at the expence of the united states, and the officers and men so cloathed, armed and equipped shall march to the place appointed, and within the time agreed on by the united states in congress assembled: But if the united states in congress assembled shall, on consideration of circumstances judge proper that any state should not raise men, or should raise a smaller number than its quota, and that any other state should raise a greater number of men than the quota thereof, such extra number shall be raised, officered, cloathed, armed and equipped in the same manner as the quota of such state, unless the legislature of such state shall judge that such extra number cannot be safely spared out of the same, in which case they shall raise, officer, cloath, arm and equip as many of such extra number as they judge can be safely spared. And the officers and men so cloathed, armed and equipped, shall march to the place appointed, and within the time agreed on by the united states in congress assembled.

The united states in congress assembled shall never engage in a war, nor grant letters of marque and reprisal in time of peace, nor enter into any treaties or alliances, nor coin money, nor regulate the value thereof, nor ascertain the sums and expences necessary for the defence and welfare of the united states, or any of them, nor emit bills, nor borrow money on the credit of the united states, nor appropriate money, nor agree upon the number of vessels of war, to be built or purchased, or the number of land or sea forces to be raised, nor appoint a commander in chief of the army or navy, unless nine states assent to the same: nor shall a question on any other point, except for adjourning from day to day be determined, unless by the votes of a majority of the united states in congress assembled.

The congress of the united states shall have power to adjourn to any time within the year, and to any place within the united states, so that no period of adjournment be for a longer duration than the space of six Months, and shall publish the Journal of their proceedings monthly, except such parts thereof relating to treaties, alliances or military operations as in their judgment require secresy; and the yeas and nays of the delegates of each state on any question shall be entered on the Journal, when it is desired by any delegate; and the delegates of a state, or any of them, at his or their request shall be furnished with a transcript of the said Journal, except such parts as are above excepted, to lay before the legislatures of the several states.

Article X The committee of the states, or any nine of them, shall be authorised to execute, in the recess of congress, such of the powers of congress as the united states in congress assembled, by the consent of nine states, shall from time to time think expedient to vest them with; provided that no power be delegated to the said committee, for the exercise of which, by the articles of confederation, the voice of nine states in the congress of the united states assembled is requisite.

Article XI Canada acceding to this confederation, and joining in the measures of the united states, shall be admitted into, and entitled to all the advantages of this union: but no other colony shall be admitted into the same, unless such admission be agreed to by nine states.

Article XII All bills of credit emitted, monies borrowed and debts contracted by, or under the authority of congress, before the assembling of the united states, in pursuance of the present confederation, shall be deemed and considered as a charge against the united states, for payment and satisfaction whereof the said united states, and the public faith are hereby solemnly pledged.

Article XIII Every state shall abide by the determinations of the united states in congress assembled, on all questions which by this confederation are submitted to them. And the Articles of this confederation shall be inviolably observed by every state, and the union shall be perpetual; nor shall any alteration at any time hereafter be made in any of them; unless such alteration be agreed to in a congress of the united states, and be afterwards confirmed by the legislatures of every state.

AND WHEREAS it hath pleased the Great Governor of the World to incline the hearts of the legislatures we respectively represent in congress, to approve of, and to authorize us to ratify the said articles of confederation and perpetual union. Know Ye that we the undersigned delegates, by virtue of the power and authority to us given for that purpose, do by these presents, in the name and in behalf of our respective constituents, fully and entirely ratify and confirm each and every of the said articles of confederation and perpetual union, and all and singular the matters and things therein contained: And we do further solemnly plight and engage the faith of our respective constituents, that they shall abide by the determinations of the united states in congress assembled, on all questions, which by the said confederation are submitted to them. And that the articles thereof shall be inviolably observed by the states we respectively represent, and that the union shall be perpetual. In Witness whereof we have hereunto set our hands in Congress. Done at Philadelphia in the state of Pennsylvania the ninth Day of July in the Year of our Lord one Thousand seven Hundred and Seventy-eight, and in the third year of the independence of America.

Constitution of the United States of America and Amendments*

Preamble

We the people of the United States, in order to form a more perfect union, establish justice, insure domestic tranquillity, provide for the common defense, promote the general welfare, and secure the blessings of liberty to ourselves and our posterity, do ordain and establish this Constitution for the United States of America.

Article I

Section 1 All legislative powers herein granted shall be vested in a Congress of the United States, which shall consist of a Senate and a House of Representatives.

Section 2 The House of Representatives shall be composed of members chosen every second year by the people of the several States, and the electors in each State shall have the qualifications requisite for electors of the most numerous branch of the State Legislature.

No person shall be a Representative who shall not have attained to the age of twenty-five years, and been seven years a citizen of the United States, and who shall not, when elected, be an inhabitant of that State in which he shall be chosen.

Representatives and direct taxes shall be apportioned among the several States which may be included within this Union, according to their respective numbers, *which shall be determined by adding to the whole number of free persons, including those bound to service for a term of years and excluding Indians not taxed, three-fifths of all other persons.* The actual enumeration shall be made within three years after the first meeting of the Congress of the United States, and within every subsequent term of ten years, in such manner as they shall by law direct. The number of Representatives shall not exceed one for every thirty thousand, but each State shall have at least one Representative; *and until such enumeration shall be made, the State of New Hampshire shall be entitled to choose three, Massachusetts eight, Rhode Island and Providence Plantations one, Connecticut five, New York six, New Jersey four, Pennsylvania eight, Delaware one, Maryland six, Virginia ten, North Carolina five, South Carolina five, and Georgia three.*

When vacancies happen in the representation from any State, the Executive authority thereof shall issue writs of election to fill such vacancies.

The House of Representatives shall choose their Speaker and other officers; and shall have the sole power of impeachment.

Section 3 The Senate of the United States shall be composed of two Senators from each State, *chosen by the legislature thereof,* for six years; and each Senator shall have one vote.

Immediately after they shall be assembled in consequence of the first election, they shall be divided as equally as may be into three classes. The seats of the Senators of the first class shall be vacated at the expiration of the second year, of the second class at the expiration of the fourth year, and of the third class at the expiration of the sixth year, so that one-third may be chosen every second year; and if vacancies happen by resignation or otherwise, during the recess of the legislature of any State, the Executive thereof may make temporary appointments until the next meeting of the legislature, which shall then fill such vacancies.

No person shall be a Senator who shall not have attained to the age of thirty years, and been nine years a citizen of the United States, and who shall not, when elected, be an inhabitant of that State for which he shall be chosen.

The Vice-President of the United States shall be President of the Senate, but shall have no vote, unless they be equally divided.

The Senate shall choose their other officers, and also a President *pro tempore,* in the absence of the Vice-President, or when he shall exercise the office of President of the United States.

The Senate shall have the sole power to try all impeachments. When sitting for that purpose, they shall

---

*Passages no longer in effect are printed in italic type.

be on oath or affirmation. When the President of the United States is tried, the Chief Justice shall preside: and no person shall be convicted without the concurrence of two-thirds of the members present.

Judgment in cases of impeachment shall not extend further than to removal from the office, and disqualification to hold and enjoy any office of honor, trust or profit under the United States: but the party convicted shall nevertheless be liable and subject to indictment, trial, judgment and punishment, according to law.

Section 4 The times, places and manner of holding elections for Senators and Representatives shall be prescribed in each State by the legislature thereof; but the Congress may at any time by law make or alter such regulations, except as to the places of choosing Senators.

The Congress shall assemble at least once in every year, and such meeting *shall be on the first Monday in December, unless they shall by law appoint a different day.*

Section 5 Each house shall be the judge of the elections, returns and qualifications of its own members, and a majority of each shall constitute a quorum to do business; but a smaller number may adjourn from day to day, and may be authorized to compel the attendance of absent members, in such manner, and under such penalties, as each house may provide.

Each house may determine the rules of its proceedings, punish its members for disorderly behavior, and with the concurrence of two-thirds, expel a member.

Each house shall keep a journal of its proceedings, and from time to time publish the same, excepting such parts as may in their judgment require secrecy; and the yeas and nays of the members of either house on any question shall, at the desire of one-fifth of those present, be entered on the journal.

Neither house, during the session of Congress, shall, without the consent of the other, adjourn for more than three days, nor to any other place than that in which the two houses shall be sitting.

Section 6 The Senators and Representatives shall receive a compensation for their services, to be ascertained by law and paid out of the treasury of the United States. They shall in all cases except treason, felony and breach of the peace, be privileged from arrest during their attendance at the session of their respective houses, and in going to and returning from the same; and for any speech or debate in either house, they shall not be questioned in any other place.

No Senator or Representative shall, during the time for which he was elected, be appointed to any civil office under the authority of the United States, which shall have been created, or the emoluments whereof shall have been increased, during such time; and no person holding any office under the United States shall be a member of either house during his continuance in office.

Section 7 All bills for raising revenue shall originate in the House of Representatives; but the Senate may propose or concur with amendments as on other bills.

Every bill which shall have passed the House of Representatives and the Senate, shall, before it become a law, be presented to the President of the United States; if he approve he shall sign it, but if not he shall return it with objections to that house in which it originated, who shall enter the objections at large on their journal, and proceed to reconsider it. If after such reconsideration two-thirds of that house shall agree to pass the bill, it shall be sent, together with the objections, to the other house, by which it shall likewise be reconsidered, and, if approved by two-thirds of that house, it shall become a law. But in all such cases the votes of both houses shall be determined by yeas and nays, and the names of the persons voting for and against the bill shall be entered on the journal of each house respectively. If any bill shall not be returned by the President within ten days (Sundays excepted) after it shall have been presented to him, the same shall be a law, in like manner as if he had signed it, unless the Congress by their adjournment prevent its return, in which case it shall not be a law.

Every order, resolution, or vote to which the concurrence of the Senate and House of Representatives may be necessary (except on a question of adjournment) shall be presented to the President of the United States; and before the same shall take effect, shall be approved by him, or being disapproved by him, shall be repassed by two-thirds of the Senate and House of Representatives, according to the rules and limitations prescribed in the case of a bill.

Section 8 The Congress shall have power

To lay and collect taxes, duties, imposts, and excises, to pay the debts and provide for the common defense and general welfare of the United States; but all duties, imposts and excises shall be uniform throughout the United States;

To borrow money on the credit of the United States;

To regulate commerce with foreign nations, and among the several States, and with the Indian tribes;

To establish an uniform rule of naturalization, and uniform laws on the subject of bankruptcies throughout the United States;

To coin money, regulate the value thereof, and of foreign coin, and fix the standard of weights and measures;

To provide for the punishment of counterfeiting the securities and current coin of the United States;

To establish post offices and post roads;

To promote the progress of science and useful arts by securing for limited times to authors and inventors the exclusive right to their respective writings and discoveries;

To constitute tribunals inferior to the Supreme Court;

To define and punish piracies and felonies committed on the high seas and offenses against the law of nations;

To declare war, grant letters of marque and reprisal, and make rules concerning captures on land and water;

To raise and support armies, but no appropriation of money to that use shall be for a longer term than two years;

To provide and maintain a navy;

To make rules for the government and regulation of the land and naval forces;

To provide for calling forth the militia to execute the laws of the Union, suppress insurrections, and repel invasions;

To provide for organizing, arming, and disciplining the militia, and for governing such part of them as may be employed in the service of the United States, reserving to the States respectively the appointment of the officers, and the authority of training the militia according to the discipline prescribed by Congress;

To exercise exclusive legislation in all cases whatsoever, over such district (not exceeding ten miles square) as may, by cession of particular States, and the acceptance of Congress, become the seat of government of the United States, and to exercise like authority over all places purchased by the consent of the legislature of the State, in which the same shall be, for erection of forts, magazines, arsenals, dockyards, and other needful buildings; —and

To make all laws which shall be necessary and proper for carrying into execution the foregoing powers, and all other powers vested by this Constitution in the government of the United States, or in any department or officer thereof.

Section 9 The migration or importation of such persons as any of the States now existing shall think proper to admit shall not be prohibited by the Congress prior to the year 1808; but a tax or duty may be imposed on such importation, not exceeding $10 for each person.

The privilege of the writ of habeas corpus shall not be suspended, unless when in cases of rebellion or invasion the public safety may require it.

No bill of attainder or ex post facto law shall be passed.

No capitation, or other direct, tax shall be laid, unless in proportion to the census or enumeration herein before directed to be taken.

No tax or duty shall be laid on articles exported from any State.

No preference shall be given by any regulation of commerce or revenue to the ports of one State over those of another; nor shall vessels bound to, or from, one State, be obliged to enter, clear, or pay duties in another.

No money shall be drawn from the treasury, but in consequence of appropriations made by law; and a regular statement and account of the receipts and expenditures of all public money shall be published from time to time.

No title of nobility shall be granted by the United States: and no person holding any office of profit or trust under them, shall, without the consent of the Congress, accept of any present, emolument, office, or title, of any kind whatever, from any king, prince, or foreign state.

Section 10 No State shall enter into any treaty, alliance, or confederation; grant letters of marque and reprisal; coin money; emit bills of credit; make anything but gold and silver coin a tender in payment of debts; pass any bill of attainder, ex post facto law, or law impairing the obligation of contracts, or grant any title of nobility.

No State shall, without the consent of Congress, lay any imposts or duties on imports or exports, except what may be absolutely necessary for executing its inspection laws: and the net produce of all duties and imposts, laid by any State on imports or exports, shall be for the use of the treasury of the United States; and all such laws shall be subject to the revision and control of the Congress.

No State shall, without the consent of Congress, lay any duty of tonnage, keep troops or ships of war in time of peace, enter into any agreement or compact with another State, or with a foreign power, or engage in war, unless actually invaded, or in such imminent danger as will not admit of delay.

Article II

Section 1 The executive power shall be vested in a President of the United States of America. He shall hold his office during the term of four years, and, together with the Vice-President, chosen for the same term, be elected as follows:

Each State shall appoint, in such manner as the legislature thereof may direct, a number of electors, equal to the whole number of Senators and Representatives to which the State may be entitled in the Congress; but no Senator or Representative, or person holding an office of trust or profit under the United States, shall be appointed an elector.

The electors shall meet in their respective States, and vote by ballot for two persons, of whom one at least shall not be an inhabitant of the same State with themselves. And they shall make a list of all the persons voted for, and of the number of votes for each; which list they shall sign and certify, and transmit sealed to the seat of government of the United States, directed to the President of the Senate. The President of the Senate shall, in the presence of the Senate and House of Representatives, open all the certificates, and the votes shall then be counted. The person having the greatest number of votes shall be the President, if such number be a majority of the whole number of electors appointed; and if there be more than one who have such majority, and have an equal number of votes, then the House of Representatives shall immediately choose by ballot one of them for President; and if no person have a majority, then from the five highest on the list said house shall in like manner choose the President. But in choosing the President the votes shall be taken by States, the representation from each State having one vote; a quorum for this purpose shall consist of a member or members from two-thirds of the States, and a majority of all the States shall be necessary to a choice. In every case, after the choice of the President, the person having the greatest number of votes of the electors shall be the Vice-President. But if there should remain two or more who have equal votes, the Senate shall choose from them by ballot the Vice-President.

The Congress may determine the time of choosing the electors and the day on which they shall give their votes; which day shall be the same throughout the United States.

No person except a natural-born citizen, *or a citizen of the United States at the time of the adoption of this Constitution,* shall be eligible to the office of President; neither shall any person be eligible to that office who shall not have attained to the age of thirty-five years, and been fourteen years a resident within the United States.

In cases of the removal of the President from office or of his death, resignation, or inability to discharge the powers and duties of the said office, the same shall devolve on the Vice-President, and the Congress may by law provide for the case of removal, death, resignation, or inability, both of the President and Vice-President, declaring what officer shall then act as President, and such officer shall act accordingly, until the disability be removed, or a President shall be elected.

The President shall, at stated times, receive for his services a compensation, which shall neither be increased nor diminished during the period for which he shall have been elected, and he shall not receive within that period any other emolument from the United States, or any of them.

Before he enter on the execution of his office, he shall take the following oath or affirmation:—"I do solemnly swear (or affirm) that I will faithfully execute the office of the President of the United States, and will to the best of my ability preserve, protect and defend the Constitution of the United States."

Section 2 The President shall be commander in chief of the army and navy of the United States, and of the militia of the several States, when called into the actual service of the United States; he may require the opinion, in writing, of the principal officer in each of the executive departments, upon any subject relating to the duties of their respective offices, and he shall have power to grant reprieves and pardons for offenses against the United States, except in cases of impeachment.

He shall have power, by and with the advice and consent of the Senate, to make treaties, provided two-thirds of the Senators present concur; and he shall nominate, and by and with the advice and consent of the Senate, shall appoint ambassadors, other public ministers and consuls, judges of the Supreme Court, and all other officers of the United States, whose appointments are not herein otherwise provided for, and which shall be established by law: but Congress may by law vest the appointment of such inferior officers, as they think proper, in the President alone, in the courts of law, or in the heads of departments.

The President shall have power to fill up all vacancies that may happen during the recess of the Senate, by granting commissions which shall expire at the end of their next session.

Section 3 He shall from time to time give to the Congress information of the state of the Union, and recommend to their consideration such measures as he shall judge necessary and expedient; he may, on extraordinary occasions, convene both houses, or either of them, and in case of disagreement between them, with respect to the time of adjournment, he may adjourn them to such time as he shall think proper; he shall receive ambassadors and other public ministers; he shall take care that the laws be faithfully executed, and shall commission all the officers of the United States.

Section 4 The President, Vice-President and all civil officers of the United States shall be removed from office on impeachment for, and on conviction of, treason, bribery, or other high crimes and misdemeanors.

Article III

Section 1 The judicial power of the United States shall be vested in one Supreme Court, and in such inferior courts as the Congress may from time to time ordain and establish. The judges, both of the Supreme and inferior courts, shall hold their offices during good behavior, and shall, at stated times, receive for their services a compensation which shall not be diminished during their continuance in office.

Section 2 The judicial power shall extend to all cases, in law and equity, arising under this Constitution, the laws of the United States, and treaties made, or which shall be made, under their authority;—to all cases affecting ambassadors, other public ministers and consuls;—to all cases of admiralty and maritime jurisdiction;—to controversies to which the United States shall be a party;—to controversies between two or more States;— *between a State and citizens of another State;*—between citizens of different

States;—between citizens of the same State claiming lands under grants of different States, and between a State, or the citizens thereof, and foreign states, citizens or subjects.

In all cases affecting ambassadors, other public ministers and consuls, and those in which a State shall be party, the Supreme Court shall have original jurisdiction. In all the other cases before mentioned, the Supreme Court shall have appellate jurisdiction, both as to law and fact, with such exceptions, and under such regulations, as the Congress shall make.

The trial of all crimes, except in cases of impeachment, shall be by jury; and such trial shall be held in the State where said crimes shall have been committed; but when not committed within any State, the trial shall be at such place or places as the Congress may by law have directed.

Section 3 Treason against the United States shall consist only in levying war against them, or in adhering to their enemies, giving them aid and comfort. No person shall be convicted of treason unless on the testimony of two witnesses to the same overt act, or on confession in open court.

The Congress shall have power to declare the punishment of treason, but no attainder of treason shall work corruption of blood, or forfeiture except during the life of the person attainted.

Article IV

Section 1 Full faith and credit shall be given in each State to the public acts, records, and judicial proceedings of every other State. And the Congress may by general laws prescribe the manner in which such acts, records, and proceedings shall be proved, and the effect thereof.

Section 2 The citizens of each State shall be entitled to all privileges and immunities of citizens in the several States.

A person charged in any State with treason, felony, or other crime, who shall flee from justice, and be found in another State, shall on demand of the executive authority of the State from which he fled, be delivered up, to be removed to the State having jurisdiction of the crime.

No person held to service or labor in one State, under the laws thereof, escaping into another, shall, in consequence of any law or regulation therein, be discharged from such service or labor, but shall be delivered up on claim of the party to whom such service or labor may be due.

Section 3 New States may be admitted by the Congress into this Union; but no new State shall be formed or erected within the jurisdiction of any other State; nor any State be formed by the junction of two or more States, or parts of States, without the consent of the legislatures of the States concerned as well as of the Congress.

The Congress shall have power to dispose of and make all needful rules and regulations respecting the territory or other property belonging to the United States; and nothing in this Constitution shall be so construed as to prejudice any claims of the United States, or of any particular State.

Section 4 The United States shall guarantee to every State in this Union a republican form of government, and shall protect each of them against invasion; and on application of the legislature, or of the executive (when the legislature cannot be convened), against domestic violence.

Article V

The Congress, whenever two-thirds of both houses shall deem it necessary, shall propose amendments to this Constitution, or, on the application of the legislatures of two-thirds of the several States, shall call a convention for proposing amendments, which, in either case, shall be valid to all intents and purposes, as part of this Constitution, when ratified by the legislatures of three-fourths of the several States, or by conventions in three-fourths thereof, as the one or the other mode of ratification may be proposed by the Congress; provided *that no amendments which may be made prior to the year one thousand eight hundred and eight shall in any manner affect the first and fourth clauses in the ninth section of the first article;* and that no State, without its consent, shall be deprived of its equal suffrage in the Senate.

Article VI

All debts contracted and engagements entered into, before the adoption of this Constitution, shall be as valid against the United States under this Constitution, as under the Confederation.

This Constitution, and the laws of the United States which shall be made in pursuance thereof; and all treaties made, or which shall be made, under the authority of the United States, shall be the supreme law of the land; and the judges in every State shall be bound thereby, anything in the Constitution or laws of any State to the contrary notwithstanding.

The Senators and Representatives before mentioned, and the members of the several State legislatures, and all executive and judicial officers, both of the United States and of the several States, shall be bound by oath or affirmation to support this Constitution; but no religious test shall ever be required as a qualification to any office or public trust under the United States.

Article VII

The ratification of the conventions of nine States shall be sufficient for the establishment of this Constitution between the States so ratifying the same.

Done in Convention by the unanimous consent of the States present, the seventeenth day of September in the year of our Lord one thousand seven hundred and eighty-seven and of the Independence of the United States of America the twelfth. In witness whereof we have hereunto subscribed our names.

Amendments to the Constitution*

Amendment I

Congress shall make no law respecting an establishment of religion, or prohibiting the free exercise thereof; or abridging the freedom of speech, or of the press; or the right of the people peaceably to assemble, and to petition the government for a redress of grievances.

Amendment II

A well-regulated militia being necessary to the security of a free State, the right of the people to keep and bear arms shall not be infringed.

Amendment III

No soldier shall, in time of peace, be quartered in any house without the consent of the owner, nor in time of war, but in a manner to be prescribed by law.

Amendment IV

The right of the people to be secure in their persons, houses, papers, and effects, against unreasonable searches and seizures, shall not be violated, and no warrants shall issue but upon probable cause, supported by oath or affirmation, and particularly describing the place to be searched, and the persons or things to be seized.

Amendment V

No person shall be held to answer for a capital, or otherwise infamous crime, unless on a presentment or indictment of a grand jury, except in cases arising in the land or naval forces, or in the militia, when in actual service in time of war or public danger; nor shall any person be subject for the same offense to be twice put in jeopardy of life or limb; nor shall be compelled in any criminal case to be a witness against himself, nor be deprived of life, liberty, or property, without due process of law; nor shall private property be taken for public use without just compensation.

Amendment VI

In all criminal prosecutions, the accused shall enjoy the right to a speedy and public trial, by an impartial jury of the State and district wherein the crime shall have been committed, which district shall have been previously ascertained by law, and to be informed of the nature and cause of the accusation; to be confronted with the witnesses against him; to have compulsory process for obtaining witnesses in his favor, and to have the assistance of counsel for his defense.

Amendment VII

In suits at common law, where the value in controversy shall exceed twenty dollars, the right of trial by jury shall be preserved, and no fact tried by a jury shall be otherwise reexamined in any court of the United States, than according to the rules of the common law.

Amendment VIII

Excessive bail shall not be required, nor excessive fines imposed, nor cruel and unusual punishments inflicted.

Amendment IX

The enumeration in the Constitution, of certain rights, shall not be construed to deny or disparage others retained by the people.

Amendment X

The powers not delegated to the United States by the Constitution, nor prohibited by it to the States, are reserved to the States respectively, or to the people.

Amendment XI

[Adopted 1798]

The judicial power of the United States shall not be construed to extend to any suit in law or equity, commenced or prosecuted against one of the United States by citizens of another State, or by citizens or subjects of any foreign state.

Amendment XII

[Adopted 1804]

The electors shall meet in their respective States, and vote by ballot for President and Vice-President, one of whom, at least, shall not be an inhabitant of the same State with themselves; they shall name in their ballots the person voted for as President, and in distinct ballots the person voted for as Vice-President, and they shall make distinct lists of all persons voted for as President, and of all persons voted for as Vice-President, and of the number of votes for each, which lists they shall sign and certify, and transmit sealed to the seat of government of the United States, directed to the President of the Senate;— the President of the Senate shall, in the presence of the

---

* The first ten Amendments (the Bill of Rights) were adopted in 1791.

Senate and House of Representatives, open all the certificates and the votes shall then be counted;—the person having the greatest number of votes for President shall be the President, if such number be a majority of the whole number of electors appointed; and if no person have such majority, then from the persons having the highest numbers not exceeding three on the list of those voted for as President, the House of Representatives shall choose immediately, by ballot, the President. But in choosing the President, the votes shall be taken by States, the representation from each State having one vote; a quorum for this purpose shall consist of a member or members from two-thirds of the States, and a majority of all the States shall be necessary to a choice. And if the House of Representatives shall not choose a President whenever the right of choice shall devolve upon them, before *the fourth day of March* next following, then the Vice-President shall act as President, as in the case of the death or other constitutional disability of the President.

The person having the greatest number of votes as Vice-President shall be the Vice-President, if such number be a majority of the whole number of electors appointed; and if no person have a majority, then from the two highest numbers on the list the Senate shall choose the Vice-President; a quorum for the purpose shall consist of two-thirds of the whole number of Senators, and a majority of the whole number shall be necessary to a choice. But no person constitutionally ineligible to the office of President shall be eligible to that of Vice-President of the United States.

Amendment XIII

[Adopted 1865]

Section 1 Neither slavery nor involuntary servitude, except as a punishment for crime whereof the party shall have been duly convicted, shall exist within the United States, or any place subject to their jurisdiction.

Section 2 Congress shall have power to enforce this article by appropriate legislation.

Amendment XIV

[Adopted 1868]

Section 1 All persons born or naturalized in the United States, and subject to the jurisdiction thereof, are citizens of the United States and of the State wherein they reside. No State shall make or enforce any law which shall abridge the privileges or immunities of citizens of the United States; nor shall any State deprive any person of life, liberty, or property, without due process of law; nor deny to any person within its jurisdiction the equal protection of the laws.

Section 2 Representatives shall be apportioned among the several States according to their respective numbers,

counting the whole number of persons in each State, excluding Indians not taxed. But when the right to vote at any election for the choice of Electors for President and Vice-President of the United States, Representatives in Congress, the executive and judicial officers of a State, or the members of the legislature thereof, is denied to any of the male inhabitants of such State, being twenty-one years of age and citizens of the United States, or in any way abridged, except for participation in rebellion, or other crime, the basis of representation therein shall be reduced in the proportion which the number of such male citizens shall bear to the whole number of male citizens twenty-one years of age in such State.

Section 3 No person shall be a Senator or Representative in Congress, or Elector of President and Vice-President, or hold any office, civil or military, under the United States, or under any State, who, having previously taken an oath, as a member of Congress, or as an officer of the United States, or as a member of any State legislature, or as an executive or judicial officer of any State, to support the Constitution of the United States, shall have engaged in insurrection or rebellion against the same, or given aid or comfort to the enemies thereof. Congress may, by a vote of two-thirds of each house, remove such disability.

Section 4 The validity of the public debt of the United States, authorized by law, including debts incurred for payment of pensions and bounties for services in suppressing insurrection or rebellion, shall not be questioned. But neither the United States nor any State shall assume or pay any debt or obligation incurred in aid of insurrection or rebellion against the United States, or any claim for the loss or emancipation of any slave; but all such debts, obligations, and claims shall be held illegal and void.

Section 5 The Congress shall have power to enforce, by appropriate legislation, the provisions of this article.

Amendment XV

[Adopted 1870]

Section 1 The right of citizens of the United States to vote shall not be denied or abridged by the United States or by any State on account of race, color, or previous condition of servitude.

Section 2 The Congress shall have power to enforce this article by appropriate legislation.

Amendment XVI

[Adopted 1913]

The Congress shall have power to lay and collect taxes on incomes, from whatever source derived, without apportionment among the several States, and without regard to any census or enumeration.

Amendment XVII

[Adopted 1913]

Section 1 The Senate of the United States shall be composed of two Senators from each State, elected by the people thereof, for six years; and each Senator shall have one vote. The electors in each State shall have the qualifications requisite for electors of [voters for] the most numerous branch of the State legislatures.

Section 2 When vacancies happen in the representation of any State in the Senate, the executive authority of such State shall issue writs of election to fill such vacancies: Provided, that the Legislature of any State may empower the executive thereof to make temporary appointments until the people fill the vacancies by election as the Legislature may direct.

Section 3 This amendment shall not be so construed as to affect the election or term of any Senator chosen before it becomes valid as part of the Constitution.

Amendment XVIII

[Adopted 1919; Repealed 1933]

Section 1 After one year from the ratification of this article the manufacture, sale, or transportation of intoxicating liquors within, the importation thereof into, or the exportation thereof from the United States and all territory subject to the jurisdiction thereof, for beverage purposes, is hereby prohibited.

Section 2 The Congress and the several States shall have concurrent power to enforce this article by appropriate legislation.

Section 3 This article shall be inoperative unless it shall have been ratified as an amendment to the Constitution by the legislatures of the several States, as provided by the Constitution, within seven years from the date of the submission thereof to the States by the Congress.

Amendment XIX

[Adopted 1920]

Section 1 The right of citizens of the United States to vote shall not be denied or abridged by the United States or by any State on account of sex.

Section 2 The Congress shall have power to enforce this article by appropriate legislation.

Amendment XX

[Adopted 1933]

Section 1 The terms of the President and Vice-President shall end at noon on the 20th day of January, and the terms of Senators and Representatives at noon on the 3rd day of January, of the years in which such terms would have ended if this article had not been ratified; and the terms of their successors shall then begin.

Section 2 The Congress shall assemble at least once in every year, and such meeting shall begin at noon on the 3rd day of January, unless they shall by law appoint a different day.

Section 3 If, at the time fixed for the beginning of the term of the President, the President-elect shall have died, the Vice-President-elect shall become President. If a President shall not have been chosen before the time fixed for the beginning of his term, or if the President-elect shall have failed to qualify, then the Vice-President-elect shall act as President until a President shall have qualified; and the Congress may by law provide for the case wherein neither a President-elect nor a Vice-President-elect shall have qualified, declaring who shall then act as President, or the manner in which one who is to act shall be selected, and such persons shall act accordingly until a President or Vice-President shall have qualified.

Section 4 The Congress may by law provide for the case of the death of any of the persons from whom the House of Representatives may choose a President whenever the right of choice shall have devolved upon them, and for the case of the death of any of the persons from whom the Senate may choose a Vice-President whenever the right of choice shall have devolved upon them.

Section 5 Sections 1 and 2 shall take effect on the 15th day of October following the ratification of this article.

Section 6 This article shall be inoperative unless it shall have been ratified as an amendment to the Constitution by the Legislatures of three-fourths of the several States within seven years from the date of its submission.

Amendment XXI

[Adopted 1933]

Section 1 The eighteenth article of amendment to the Constitution of the United States is hereby repealed.

Section 2 The transportation or importation into any State, Territory, or Possession of the United States for delivery or use therein of intoxicating liquors, in violation of the laws thereof, is hereby prohibited.

Section 3 This article shall be inoperative unless it shall have been ratified as an amendment to the Constitution by conventions in the several States, as provided in the

Constitution, within seven years from the date of submission thereof to the States by the Congress.

Amendment XXII

[Adopted 1951]

Section 1 No person shall be elected to the office of President more than twice, and no person who has held the office of President, or acted as President, for more than two years of a term to which some other person was elected President shall be elected to the office of President more than once. But this article shall not apply to any person holding the office of President when this article was proposed by the Congress, and shall not prevent any person who may be holding the office of President, or acting as President, during the term within which this article becomes operative from holding the office of President or acting as President during the remainder of such term.

Section 2 This article shall be inoperative unless it shall have been ratified as an amendment to the Constitution by the legislatures of three-fourths of the several States within seven years from the date of its submission to the States by the Congress.

Amendment XXIII

[Adopted 1961]

Section 1 The District constituting the seat of Government of the United States shall appoint in such manner as the Congress may direct:

A number of electors of President and Vice-President equal to the whole number of Senators and Representatives in Congress to which the District would be entitled if it were a State, but in no event more than the least populous State; they shall be in addition to those appointed by the States, but they shall be considered for the purposes of the election of President and Vice-President, to be electors appointed by a State; and they shall meet in the District and perform such duties as provided by the twelfth article of amendment.

Section 2 The Congress shall have the power to enforce this article by appropriate legislation.

Amendment XXIV

[Adopted 1964]

Section 1 The right of citizens of the United States to vote in any primary or other election for President or Vice-President, for electors for President or Vice-President, or for Senator or Representative in Congress, shall not be denied or abridged by the United States or any State by reason of failure to pay any poll tax or other tax.

Section 2 The Congress shall have the power to enforce this article by appropriate legislation.

Amendment XXV

[Adopted 1967]

Section 1 In case of the removal of the President from office or of his death or resignation, the Vice-President shall become President.

Section 2 Whenever there is a vacancy in the office of the Vice-President, the President shall nominate a Vice-President who shall take office upon confirmation by a majority vote of both Houses of Congress.

Section 3 Whenever the President transmits to the President pro tempore of the Senate and the Speaker of the House of Representatives his written declaration that he is unable to discharge the powers and duties of his office, and until he transmits to them a written declaration to the contrary, such powers and duties shall be discharged by the Vice-President as Acting President.

Section 4 Whenever the Vice-President and a majority of either the principal officers of the executive departments or of such other body as Congress may by law provide, transmit to the President pro tempore of the Senate and the Speaker of the House of Representatives their written declaration that the President is unable to discharge the powers and duties of his office, the Vice-President shall immediately assume the powers and duties of the office as Acting President.

Thereafter, when the President transmits to the President pro tempore of the Senate and the Speaker of the House of Representatives his written declaration that no inability exists, he shall resume the powers and duties of his office unless the Vice-President and a majority of either the principal officers of the executive department[s] or of such other body as Congress may by law provide, transmit within four days to the President pro tempore of the Senate and the Speaker of the House of Representatives their written declaration that the President is unable to discharge the powers and duties of his office. Thereupon Congress shall decide the issue, assembling within forty-eight hours for that purpose if not in session. If the Congress, within twenty-one days after receipt of the latter written declaration, or, if Congress is not in session, within twenty-one days after Congress is required to assemble, determines by two-thirds vote of both Houses that the President is unable to discharge the powers and duties of his office, the Vice-President shall continue to discharge the same as Acting

President; otherwise, the President shall resume the powers and duties of his office.

Amendment XXVI

[Adopted 1971]

Section 1 The right of citizens of the United States, who are eighteen years of age or older, to vote shall not be denied or abridged by the United States or by any State on account of age.

Section 2 The Congress shall have power to enforce this article by appropriate legislation.

Amendment XXVII

[Adopted 1992]

No law, varying the compensation for the services of the Senators and Representatives, shall take effect, until an election of Representatives shall have intervened.

Presidential Elections

Year	Number of States	Candidates	Parties	Popular Vote	% of Popular Vote	Electoral Vote	% Voter Participation[a]
1789	10	**George Washington**	No party			69	
		John Adams	designations			34	
		Other candidates				35	
1792	15	**George Washington**	No party			132	
		John Adams	designations			77	
		George Clinton				50	
		Other candidates				5	
1796	16	**John Adams**	Federalist			71	
		Thomas Jefferson	Democratic-Republican			68	
		Thomas Pinckney	Federalist			59	
		Aaron Burr	Democratic-Republican			30	
		Other candidates				48	
1800	16	**Thomas Jefferson**	Democratic-Republican			73	
		Aaron Burr	Democratic-Republican			73	
		John Adams	Federalist			65	
		Charles C. Pinckney	Federalist			64	
		John Jay	Federalist			1	
1804	17	**Thomas Jefferson**	Democratic-Republican			162	
		Charles C. Pinckney	Federalist			14	
1808	17	**James Madison**	Democratic-Republican			122	
		Charles C. Pinckney	Federalist			47	
		George Clinton	Democratic-Republican			6	
1812	18	**James Madison**	Democratic-Republican			128	
		DeWitt Clinton	Federalist			89	
1816	19	**James Monroe**	Democratic-Republican			183	
		Rufus King	Federalist			34	
1820	24	**James Monroe**	Democratic-Republican			231	
		John Quincy Adams	Independent Republican			1	

Presidential Elections (continued)

Year	Number of States	Candidates	Parties	Popular Vote	% of Popular Vote	Electoral Vote	% Voter Participation[a]
1824	24	**John Quincy Adams**	Democratic-Republican	108,740	30.5	84	26.9
		Andrew Jackson	Democratic-Republican	153,544	43.1	99	
		Henry Clay	Democratic-Republican	47,136	13.2	37	
		William H. Crawford	Democratic-Republican	46,618	13.1	41	
1828	24	**Andrew Jackson**	Democratic	647,286	56.0	178	57.6
		John Quincy Adams	National Republican	508,064	44.0	83	
1832	24	**Andrew Jackson**	Democratic	701,780	54.2	219	55.4
		Henry Clay	National Republican	484,205	37.4	49	
		Other candidates		107,988	8.0	18	
1836	26	**Martin Van Buren**	Democratic	764,176	50.8	170	57.8
		William H. Harrison	Whig	550,816	36.6	73	
		Hugh L. White	Whig	146,107	9.7	26	
1840	26	**William H. Harrison**	Whig	1,274,624	53.1	234	80.2
		Martin Van Buren	Democratic	1,127,781	46.9	60	
1844	26	**James K. Polk**	Democratic	1,338,464	49.6	170	78.9
		Henry Clay	Whig	1,300,097	48.1	105	
		James G. Birney	Liberty	62,300	2.3		
1848	30	**Zachary Taylor**	Whig	1,360,967	47.4	163	72.7
		Lewis Cass	Democratic	1,222,342	42.5	127	
		Martin Van Buren	Free Soil	291,263	10.1		
1852	31	**Franklin Pierce**	Democratic	1,601,117	50.9	254	69.6
		Winfield Scott	Whig	1,385,453	44.1	42	
		John P. Hale	Free Soil	155,825	5.0		
1856	31	**James Buchanan**	Democratic	1,832,955	45.3	174	78.9
		John C. Frémont	Republican	1,339,932	33.1	114	
		Millard Fillmore	American	871,731	21.6		
1860	33	**Abraham Lincoln**	Republican	1,865,593	39.8	180	81.2
		Stephen A. Douglas	Democratic	1,382,713	29.5	12	
		John C. Breckinridge	Democratic	848,356	18.1	72	
		John Bell	Constitutional Union	592,906	12.6	39	
1864	36	**Abraham Lincoln**	Republican	2,206,938	55.0	212	73.8
		George B. McClellan	Democratic	1,803,787	45.0	21	

Presidential Elections (continued)

Year	Number of States	Candidates	Parties	Popular Vote	% of Popular Vote	Electoral Vote	% Voter Participation[a]
1868	37	**Ulysses S. Grant**	Republican	3,013,421	52.7	214	78.1
		Horatio Seymour	Democratic	2,706,829	47.3	80	
1872	37	**Ulysses S. Grant**	Republican	3,596,745	55.6	286	71.3
		Horace Greeley[b]	Democratic	2,843,446	43.9		
1876	38	**Rutherford B. Hayes**	Republican	4,036,572	48.0	185	81.8
		Samuel J. Tilden	Democratic	4,284,020	51.0	184	
1880	38	**James A. Garfield**	Republican	4,453,295	48.5	214	79.4
		Winfield S. Hancock	Democratic	4,414,082	48.1	155	
		James B. Weaver	Greenback-Labor	308,578	3.4		
1884	38	**Grover Cleveland**	Democratic	4,879,507	48.5	219	77.5
		James G. Blaine	Republican	4,850,293	48.2	182	
		Benjamin F. Butler	Greenback-Labor	175,370	1.8		
		John P. St. John	Prohibition	150,369	1.5		
1888	38	**Benjamin Harrison**	Republican	5,447,129	47.9	233	79.3
		Grover Cleveland	Democratic	5,537,857	48.6	168	
		Clinton B. Fisk	Prohibition	249,506	2.2		
		Anson J. Streeter	Union Labor	146,935	1.3		
1892	44	**Grover Cleveland**	Democratic	5,555,426	46.1	277	74.7
		Benjamin Harrison	Republican	5,182,690	43.0	145	
		James B. Weaver	People's	1,029,846	8.5	22	
		John Bidwell	Prohibition	264,133	2.2		
1896	45	**William McKinley**	Republican	7,102,246	51.1	271	79.3
		William J. Bryan	Democratic	6,492,559	47.7	176	
1900	45	**William McKinley**	Republican	7,218,491	51.7	292	73.2
		William J. Bryan	Democratic; Populist	6,356,734	45.5	155	
		John C. Wooley	Prohibition	208,914	1.5		
1904	45	**Theodore Roosevelt**	Republican	7,628,461	57.4	336	65.2
		Alton B. Parker	Democratic	5,084,223	37.6	140	
		Eugene V. Debs	Socialist	402,283	3.0		
		Silas C. Swallow	Prohibition	258,536	1.9		
1908	46	**William H. Taft**	Republican	7,675,320	51.6	321	65.4
		William J. Bryan	Democratic	6,412,294	43.1	162	
		Eugene V. Debs	Socialist	420,793	2.8		
		Eugene W. Chafin	Prohibition	253,840	1.7		
1912	48	**Woodrow Wilson**	Democratic	6,296,547	41.9	435	58.8
		Theodore Roosevelt	Progressive	4,118,571	27.4	88	
		William H. Taft	Republican	3,486,720	23.2	8	
		Eugene V. Debs	Socialist	900,672	6.0		

Presidential Elections (continued)

Year	Number of States	Candidates	Parties	Popular Vote	% of Popular Vote	Electoral Vote	% Voter Participation[a]
		Eugene W. Chafin	Prohibition	206,275	1.4		
1916	48	**Woodrow Wilson**	Democratic	9,127,695	49.4	277	61.6
		Charles E. Hughes	Republican	8,533,507	46.2	254	
		A. L. Benson	Socialist	585,113	3.2		
		J. Frank Hanly	Prohibition	220,506	1.2		
1920	48	**Warren G. Harding**	Republican	16,143,407	60.4	404	49.2
		James M. Cox	Democratic	9,130,328	34.2	127	
		Eugene V. Debs	Socialist	919,799	3.4		
		P. P. Christensen	Farmer-Labor	265,411	1.0		
1924	48	**Calvin Coolidge**	Republican	15,718,211	54.0	382	48.9
		John W. Davis	Democratic	8,385,283	28.8	136	
		Robert M. La Follette	Progressive	4,831,289	16.6	13	
1928	48	**Herbert C. Hoover**	Republican	21,391,993	58.2	444	56.9
		Alfred E. Smith	Democratic	15,016,169	40.9	87	
1932	48	**Franklin D. Roosevelt**	Democratic	22,821,857	57.4	472	56.9
		Herbert C. Hoover	Republican	15,761,841	39.7	59	
		Norman Thomas	Socialist	884,781	2.2		
1936	48	**Franklin D. Roosevelt**	Democratic	27,752,869	60.8	523	61.0
		Alfred M. Landon	Republican	16,674,665	36.5	8	
		William Lemke	Union	882,479	1.9		
1940	48	**Franklin D. Roosevelt**	Democratic	27,307,819	54.8	449	62.5
		Wendell L. Willkie	Republican	22,321,018	44.8	82	
1944	48	**Franklin D. Roosevelt**	Democratic	25,606,585	53.5	432	55.9
		Thomas E. Dewey	Republican	22,014,745	46.0	99	
1948	48	**Harry S Truman**	Democratic	24,179,345	49.6	303	53.0
		Thomas E. Dewey	Republican	21,991,291	45.1	189	
		J. Strom Thurmond	States' Rights	1,176,125	2.4	39	
		Henry A. Wallace	Progressive	1,157,326	2.4		
1952	48	**Dwight D. Eisenhower**	Republican	33,936,234	55.1	442	63.3
		Adlai E. Stevenson	Democratic	27,314,992	44.4	89	
1956	48	**Dwight D. Eisenhower**	Republican	35,590,472	57.6	457	60.6
		Adlai E. Stevenson	Democratic	26,022,752	42.1	73	
1960	50	**John F. Kennedy**	Democratic	34,226,731	49.7	303	62.8
		Richard M. Nixon	Republican	34,108,157	49.5	219	
1964	50	**Lyndon B. Johnson**	Democratic	43,129,566	61.1	486	61.7
		Barry M. Goldwater	Republican	27,178,188	38.5	52	
1968	50	**Richard M. Nixon**	Republican	33,045,480	43.4	301	60.6
		Hubert H. Humphrey	Democratic	31,850,140	42.7	191	

Presidential Elections (continued)

Year	Number of States	Candidates	Parties	Popular Vote	% of Popular Vote	Electoral Vote	% Voter Participation[a]
		George C. Wallace	American Independent	171,422	13.5	46	
1972	50	**Richard M. Nixon**	Republican	47,169,911	60.7	520	55.2
		George S. McGovern	Democratic	29,170,383	37.5	17	
		John G. Schmitz	American	1,099,482	1.4		
1976	50	**James E. Carter**	Democratic	40,830,763	50.1	297	53.5
		Gerald R. Ford	Republican	39,147,793	48.0	240	
1980	50	**Ronald W. Reagan**	Republican	43,904,153	50.7	489	52.6
		James E. Carter	Democratic	35,483,883	41.0	49	
		John B. Anderson	Independent	5,720,060	6.6		
		Ed Clark	Libertarian	921,299	1.1		
1984	50	**Ronald W. Reagan**	Republican	54,455,075	58.8	525	53.3
		Walter F. Mondale	Democratic	37,577,185	40.6	13	
1988	50	**George H. W. Bush**	Republican	48,886,097	53.4	426	50.1
		Michael S. Dukakis	Democratic	41,809,074	45.6	111[c]	
1992	50	**William J. Clinton**	Democratic	44,909,326	43.0	370	55.2
		George H. W. Bush	Republican	39,103,882	37.4	168	
		H. Ross Perot	Independent	19,741,048	18.9		
1996	50	**William J. Clinton**	Democratic	47,402,357	49.2	379	49.1
		Robert J. Dole	Republican	39,196,755	40.7	159	
		H. Ross Perot	Reform	8,085,402	8.4		
		Ralph Nader	Green	684,902	0.7		
2000	50	**George W. Bush**	Republican	50,456,169	47.9	271	51.2
		Albert Gore	Democratic	50,996,116	48.4	266	
		Ralph Nader	Green	2,783,728	2.7		
2004	50	**George W. Bush**	Republican	62,039,073	50.7	286	55.3
		John F. Kerry	Democratic	59,027,478	48.2	251	
		Ralph Nader	Independent	240,896	0.2		
2008	50	**Barack Obama**	Democratic	69,498,459	53.0	365	61.7
		John McCain	Republican	59,948,283	46.0	173	
		Ralph Nader	Independent	739,165	0.55		

Candidates receiving less than 1 percent of the popular vote have been omitted. Thus the percentage of popular vote given for any election year may not total 100 percent.

Before the passage of the Twelfth Amendment in 1804, the electoral college voted for two presidential candidates; the runner-up became vice president.

Before 1824, most presidential electors were chosen by state legislatures, not by popular vote.

[a]Percent of voting-age population casting ballots.
[b]Greeley died shortly after the election; the electors supporting him then divided their votes among minor candidates.
[c]One elector from West Virginia cast her electoral college presidential ballot for Lloyd Bentsen, the Democratic Party's vice-presidential candidate.

Presidents and Vice Presidents

1. *President* George Washington 1789–1797
   Vice President John Adams 1789–1797

2. *President* John Adams 1797–1801
   Vice President Thomas Jefferson 1797–1801

3. *President* Thomas Jefferson 1801–1809
   Vice President Aaron Burr 1801–1805
   Vice President George Clinton 1805–1809

4. *President* James Madison 1809–1817
   Vice President George Clinton 1809–1813
   Vice President Elbridge Gerry 1813–1817

5. *President* James Monroe 1817–1825
   Vice Priesident Daniel Tompkins 1817–1825

6. *President* John Quincy Adams 1825–1829
   Vice President John C. Calhoun 1825–1829

7. *President* Andrew Jackson 1829–1837
   Vice President John C. Calhoun 1829–1833
   Vice President Martin Van Buren 1833–1837

8. *President* Martin Van Buren 1837–1841
   Vice President Richard M. Johnson 1837–1841

9. *President* William H. Harrison 1841
   Vice President John Tyler 1841

10. *President* John Tyler 1841–1845
    Vice President None

11. *President* James K. Polk 1845–1849
    Vice President George M. Dallas 1845–1849

12. *President* Zachary Taylor 1849–1850
    Vice President Millard Fillmore 1849–1850

13. *President* Millard Fillmore 1850–1853
    Vice President None

14. *President* Franklin Pierce 1853–1857
    Vice President William R. King 1853–1857

15. *President* James Buchanan 1857–1861
    Vice President John C. Breckinridge 1857–1861

16. *President* Abraham Lincoln 1861–1865
    Vice President Hannibal Hamlin 1861–1865
    Vice President Andrew Johnson 1865

17. *President* Andrew Johnson 1865–1869
    Vice President None

18. *President* Ulysses S. Grant 1869–1877
    Vice President Schuyler Colfax 1869–1873
    Vice President Henry Wilson 1873–1877

19. *President* Rutherford B. Hayes 1877–1881
    Vice President William A. Wheeler 1877–1881

20. *President* James A. Garfield 1881
    Vice President Chester A. Arthur 1881

21. *President* Chester A. Arthur 1881–1885
    Vice President None

22. *President* Grover Cleveland 1885–1889
    Vice President Thomas A. Hendricks 1885–1889

23. *President* Benjamin Harrison 1889–1893
    Vice President Levi P. Morton 1889–1893

24. *President* Grover Cleveland 1893–1897
    Vice President Adlai E. Stevenson 1893–1897

25. *President* William McKinley 1897–1901
    Vice President Garret A. Hobart 1897–1901
    Vice President Theodore Roosevelt 1901

26. *President* Theodore Roosevelt 1901–1909
    Vice President Charles Fairbanks 1905–1909

27. *President* William H. Taft 1909–1913
    Vice President James S. Sherman 1909–1913

28. *President* Woodrow Wilson 1913–1921
    Vice President Thomas R. Marshall 1913–1921

29. *President* Warren G. Harding 1921–1923
    Vice President Calvin Coolidge 1921–1923

30. *President* Calvin Coolidge 1923–1929
    Vice President Charles G. Dawes 1925–1929

31. *President* Herbert C. Hoover 1929–1933
    Vice President Charles Curtis 1929–1933

32. *President* Franklin D. Roosevelt 1933–1945
    Vice President John N. Garner 1933–1941
    Vice President Henry A. Wallace 1941–1945
    Vice President Harry S Truman 1945

33. *President* Harry S Truman 1945–1953
    Vice President Alben W. Barkley 1949–1953

34. *President* Dwight D. Eisenhower 1953–1961
    Vice President Richard M. Nixon 1953–1961

35. *President* John F. Kennedy 1961–1963
    Vice President Lyndon B. Johnson 1961–1963

36. *President* Lyndon B. Johnson 1963–1969
    Vice President Hubert H. Humphrey 1965–1969

37. *President* Richard M. Nixon 1969–1974
    Vice President Spiro T. Agnew 1969–1973
    Vice President Gerald R. Ford 1973–1974

38. *President* Gerald R. Ford 1974–1977
    Vice President Nelson A. Rockefeller 1974–1977

39. *President* James E. Carter 1977–1981
Vice President Walter F. Mondale 1977–1981

40. *President* Ronald W. Reagan 1981–1989
Vice President George H. W. Bush 1981–1989

41. *President* George H. W. Bush 1989–1993
Vice President J. Danforth Quayle 1989–1993

42. *President* William J. Clinton 1993–2001
Vice President Albert Gore 1993–2001

43. *President* George W. Bush 2001–2009
Vice President Richard B. Cheney 2001–2009

44. *President* Barack H. Obama 2009–
Vice President Joseph R. Biden 2009–

Justices of the Supreme Court

	Term of Service	Years of Service	Life Span
John Jay	1789–1795	5	1745–1829
John Rutledge	1789–1791	1	1739–1800
William Cushing	1789–1810	20	1732–1810
James Wilson	1789–1798	8	1742–1798
John Blair	1789–1796	6	1732–1800
Robert H. Harrison	1789–1790	—	1745–1790
James Iredell	1790–1799	9	1751–1799
Thomas Johnson	1791–1793	1	1732–1819
William Paterson	1793–1806	13	1745–1806
*John Rutledge**	1795	—	1739–1800
Samuel Chase	1796–1811	15	1741–1811
Oliver Ellsworth	1796–1800	4	1745–1807
Bushrod Washington	1798–1829	31	1762–1829
Alfred Moore	1799–1804	4	1755–1810
John Marshall	1801–1835	34	1755–1835
William Johnson	1804–1834	30	1771–1834
H. Brockholst Livingston	1806–1823	16	1757–1823
Thomas Todd	1807–1826	18	1765–1826
Joseph Story	1811–1845	33	1779–1845
Gabriel Duval	1811–1835	24	1752–1844
Smith Thompson	1823–1843	20	1768–1843
Robert Trimble	1826–1828	2	1777–1828
John McLean	1829–1861	32	1785–1861
Henry Baldwin	1830–1844	14	1780–1844
James M. Wayne	1835–1867	32	1790–1867
Roger B. Taney	1836–1864	28	1777–1864
Philip P. Barbour	1836–1841	4	1783–1841
John Catron	1837–1865	28	1786–1865
John McKinley	1837–1852	15	1780–1852
Peter V. Daniel	1841–1860	19	1784–1860
Samuel Nelson	1845–1872	27	1792–1873
Levi Woodbury	1845–1851	5	1789–1851
Robert C. Grier	1846–1870	23	1794–1870
Benjamin R. Curtis	1851–1857	6	1809–1874
John A. Campbell	1853–1861	8	1811–1889
Nathan Clifford	1858–1881	23	1803–1881
Noah H. Swayne	1862–1881	18	1804–1884
Samuel F. Miller	1862–1890	28	1816–1890

Justices of the Supreme Court (continued)

	Term of Service	Years of Service	Life Span
David Davis	1862–1877	14	1815–1886
Stephen J. Field	1863–1897	34	1816–1899
Salmon P. Chase	1864–1873	8	1808–1873
William Strong	1870–1880	10	1808–1895
Joseph P. Bradley	1870–1892	22	1813–1892
Ward Hunt	1873–1882	9	1810–1886
Morrison R. Waite	1874–1888	14	1816–1888
John M. Harlan	1877–1911	34	1833–1911
William B. Woods	1880–1887	7	1824–1887
Stanley Mathews	1881–1889	7	1824–1889
Horace Gray	1882–1902	20	1828–1902
Samuel Blatchford	1882–1893	11	1820–1893
Lucius Q. C. Lamar	1888–1893	5	1825–1893
Melville W. Fuller	1888–1910	21	1833–1910
David J. Brewer	1890–1910	20	1837–1910
Henry B. Brown	1890–1906	16	1836–1913
George Shiras Jr.	1892–1903	10	1832–1924
Howell E. Jackson	1893–1895	2	1832–1895
Edward D. White	1894–1910	16	1845–1921
Rufus W. Peckham	1895–1909	14	1838–1909
Joseph McKenna	1898–1925	26	1843–1926
Oliver W. Holmes	1902–1932	30	1841–1935
William D. Day	1903–1922	19	1849–1923
William H. Moody	1906–1910	3	1853–1917
Horace H. Lurton	1910–1914	4	1844–1914
Charles E. Hughes	1910–1916	5	1862–1948
Willis Van Devanter	1911–1937	26	1859–1941
Joseph R. Lamar	1911–1916	5	1857–1916
Edward D. White	1910–1921	11	1845–1921
Mahlon Pitney	1912–1922	10	1858–1924
James C. McReynolds	1914–1941	26	1862–1946
Louis D. Brandeis	1916–1939	22	1856–1941
John H. Clarke	1916–1922	6	1857–1945
William H. Taft	1921–1930	8	1857–1930
George Sutherland	1922–1938	15	1862–1942
Pierce Butler	1922–1939	16	1866–1939
Edward T. Sanford	1923–1930	7	1865–1930

Justices of the Supreme Court (continued)

	Term of Service	Years of Service	Life Span
Harlan F. Stone	1925–1941	16	1872–1946
Charles E. Hughes	1930–1941	11	1862–1948
Owen J. Roberts	1930–1945	15	1875–1955
Benjamin N. Cardozo	1932–1938	6	1870–1938
Hugo L. Black	1937–1971	34	1886–1971
Stanley F. Reed	1938–1957	19	1884–1980
Felix Frankfurter	1939–1962	23	1882–1965
William O. Douglas	1939–1975	36	1898–1980
Frank Murphy	1940–1949	9	1890–1949
Harlan F. Stone	1941–1946	5	1872–1946
James F. Byrnes	1941–1942	1	1879–1972
Robert H. Jackson	1941–1954	13	1892–1954
Wiley B. Rutledge	1943–1949	6	1894–1949
Harold H. Burton	1945–1958	13	1888–1964
Fred M. Vinson	1946–1953	7	1890–1953
Tom C. Clark	1949–1967	18	1899–1977
Sherman Minton	1949–1956	7	1890–1965
Earl Warren	1953–1969	16	1891–1974
John Marshall Harlan	1955–1971	16	1899–1971
William J. Brennan Jr.	1956–1990	34	1906–1997
Charles E. Whittaker	1957–1962	5	1901–1973
Potter Stewart	1958–1981	23	1915–1985
Byron R. White	1962–1993	31	1917–
Arthur J. Goldberg	1962–1965	3	1908–1990
Abe Fortas	1965–1969	4	1910–1982
Thurgood Marshall	1967–1991	24	1908–1993
Warren C. Burger	1969–1986	17	1907–1995
Harry A. Blackmun	1970–1994	24	1908–1998
Lewis F. Powell Jr.	1972–1987	15	1907–1998
William H. Rehnquist	1972–2005	33	1924–2005
John P. Stevens III	1975–2010	35	1920–
Sandra Day O'Connor	1981–2006	25	1930–
Antonin Scalia	1986–	—	1936–
Anthony M. Kennedy	1988–	—	1936–
David H. Souter	1990–2009	19	1939–
Clarence Thomas	1991–	—	1948–
Ruth Bader Ginsburg	1993–	—	1933–

Justices of the Supreme Court (continued)

	Term of Service	Years of Service	Life Span
Stephen Breyer	1994–	—	1938–
John G. Roberts	2005–	—	1955–
Samuel A. Alito, Jr.	2006–	—	1950–
Sonia Sotomayor	2009–	—	1954–
Elena Kagan	2010–	—	1960–

Note: Chief justices are in italics.

*Appointed and served one term, but not confirmed by the Senate.

Index